The Joy of Eating

The Joy of Eating

A Guide to Food in Modern Pop Culture

Jane K. Glenn

BLOOMSBURY ACADEMIC
NEW YORK • LONDON • OXFORD • NEW DELHI • SYDNEY

BLOOMSBURY ACADEMIC
Bloomsbury Publishing Inc
1359 Broadway, New York, NY 10018, USA
50 Bedford Square, London, WC1B 3DP, UK
29 Earlsfort Terrace, Dublin 2, Ireland

BLOOMSBURY, BLOOMSBURY ACADEMIC and the Diana logo are trademarks of
Bloomsbury Publishing Plc

First published in the United States of America by ABC-CLIO 2022
Paperback edition published by Bloomsbury Academic 2025

Copyright © Bloomsbury Publishing Inc, 2025

For legal purposes the Acknowledgments on p. xi constitute an extension of this copyright page.

COVER PHOTO: (Azara/Milkmoon Kitchen)

All rights reserved. No part of this publication may be reproduced or transmitted in any form
or by any means, electronic or mechanical, including photocopying, recording, or any
information storage or retrieval system, without prior permission in writing from the publishers.

Bloomsbury Publishing Inc does not have any control over, or responsibility for,
any third-party websites referred to or in this book. All internet addresses given
in this book were correct at the time of going to press. The author and publisher
regret any inconvenience caused if addresses have changed or sites have
ceased to exist, but can accept no responsibility for any such changes.

Library of Congress Cataloging-in-Publication Data
Names: Glenn, Jane K., author.
Title: The joy of eating : a guide to food in modern pop culture / Jane K. Glenn.
Description: Santa Barbara, California : ABC-CLIO, [2022] |
Includes bibliographical references and index.
Identifiers: LCCN 2021023271 (print) | LCCN 2021023272 (ebook) |
ISBN 9781440862090 (print) | ISBN 9781440862106 (ebook)
Subjects: LCSH: Food—United States—History. | Food habits—Social
aspects—United States. | Food in popular culture—United States. |
BISAC: SOCIAL SCIENCE / Agriculture & Food (see also POLITICAL SCIENCE /
Public Policy / Agriculture & Food Policy) | SOCIAL SCIENCE / Popular Culture
Classification: LCC TX360.U6 G56 2022 (print) | LCC TX360.U6 (ebook) |
DDC 641.300973—dc23
LC record available at https://lccn.loc.gov/2021023271
LC ebook record available at https://lccn.loc.gov/2021023272

ISBN: HB: 978-1-4408-6209-0
PB: 979-8-2163-8294-2
ePDF: 978-1-4408-6210-6
eBook: 979-8-2161-0726-2

To find out more about our authors and books visit www.bloomsbury.com
and sign up for our newsletters.

Contents

Preface   ix

Acknowledgments   xi

Introduction   xiii

Chronology   xix

Entries

All-Star Chef Classic   1

America's Test Kitchen   4

Art, Food in (Antiquity through the Renaissance)   7

Art, Food in (Impressionism through Contemporary Art)   10

Asian American Cuisine   15

Aspen Food and Wine Classic   20

Austin Food + Wine Festival   23

Ayden Collard Festival   27

Baby Food   31

Bar Rescue   36

Barbecue   41

Batali, Mario   45

Bayless, Rick   50

Beard, James   56

Best Thing I Ever Ate, The   59

Bizarre Foods with Andrew Zimmern   61

Bourdain, Anthony   66

Brown, Alton   73

Cake and Cupcake Trends   79

California Avocado Festival   83

Celebrities and Food   87

Chang, David   91

Chef's Table   94

Child, Julia   98

Chocolate Events and Destinations   104

Chopped   109

Coffee Culture   113

Cooked   116

Cooks vs. Cons   119

Craft Brewing and Microbreweries   121

Culinary Awards, The Evolution of   124

Deen, Paula   128

Deer River Wild Rice Festival   132

Documentary Films, Food and Beverages in   135

Eating Competitions   140

Farmhouse Rules   145

Fiction, Food in   147

Fictional Television (1950s–1970s), Food and   150

Fictional Television (1980s–), Food and   154

Fieri, Guy   159

Films, Food in   162

Flay, Bobby   167

Florida Strawberry Festival   170

Food and Beverage Museums, International   173

Food and Beverage Museums, U.S.   176

Food Failures   178

Food Trucks   181

Galloping Gourmet, The 185

Garten, Ina 187

Gilroy Garlic Festival 191

Great British Bake Off, The 194

Grilled Cheese Festivals 201

Hazan, Marcella 204

Holidays and Food 208

Ice Cream Trends 216

Imagery Found in Foods 222

International Horseradish Festival 224

Iron Chef 227

Lagasse, Emeril 232

Latin American Cuisine 236

Laurentiis, Giada De 241

Magazines, Food 246

Maine Lobster Festival 248

Maple Syrup Festivals 253

MasterChef 256

Mind of a Chef, The 259

Nonfiction, Food in 262

Novelty Dining Experiences 265

Pépin, Jacques 271

Photography, Food 274

Pioneer Woman, The 278

Politicians' Food Gaffes 283

Politics and Food 286

Puck, Wolfgang 289

Radio and Podcasts, Food-Themed (1920s–1970s) 294

Radio and Podcasts, Food-Themed (1980s–) 297

Ramsay, Gordon 300

Ray, Rachael 304

Roadside Food Attractions   308

Samuelsson, Marcus   313

Sherman, Sean   317

South Beach Wine & Food Festival   320

Spam Jam Festival   322

Stewart, Martha   324

Super Bowl Sunday   329

Super Size Me   332

Taste of Chicago   336

Television, Food Channels on   338

Top Chef   343

Tosi, Christina   346

Trends, Food   351

Twitty, Michael   355

Two Fat Ladies   358

Unusual Food Events, International   362

Unusual Food Events, U.S. (Midwest, West, and Southwest Regions)   370

Unusual Food Events, U.S. (Southeast and Northeast Regions)   372

Unusual Foods   375

Websites, Food   380

What the Fluff?   383

Wine and Spirits   386

Worst Cooks in America   392

Bibliography of Recommended Resources   395

Index   399

Preface

In 1961, Julia Child introduced the American public to an entirely new, joy-infused approach to cooking and eating high-quality food. Fueled by growing culinary changes that had already begun to ripple throughout the nation as a result of World War II, Child helped set in motion a food renaissance that is still in bloom today. *The Joy of Eating* explores this golden age of food in contemporary American popular culture, illustrating our fascination with and affinity for food in the arts, entertainment, mass media, and our own homes. This single-volume work provides depth and academic gravity by tying broader themes and larger contexts into each entry, weaving historical and sociological backgrounds into discussions of contemporary issues. For example, an entry on a food-themed reality television show will discuss the show's popularity in direct relation to contemporary trends, significant economic events, and even as a tool to trace the evolution of various foods in humans' diets.

FEATURES

Designed like a veritable menu, entries are split into various courses to aid with readers' digestion of each topic. Some entries have fewer courses than others, dictated by the subject and scope of each. The "Starters" course summarizes the primary topic, sprinkling in significant dates and high-level background information. The "Entrée" course dives deeper into the subject, drawing out historical and sociological storylines and providing deeper analysis. Notable individuals who support the narrative of the main subject are described in the "Accompanied By" course, when applicable. Throughout this volume, "Small Plates" offer sidebars in the form of recipes, interesting details about the subject at hand, or information about related individuals or cuisines. Sweeter moments are captured in the lighthearted "Dessert" course, which utilizes irreverence and anecdotes to add additional flavor to the subject.

Because this work is organized alphabetically instead of topically, the "Suggested Pairings" section includes related entry titles to give the viewer a valuable road map of which entries would complement the one they have just finished reading. The "Best Enjoyed while Eating" serves as both a veritable nightcap for each entry—a final sip of the content—and also shares suggested dishes and beverages that readers are highly encouraged to try at home as a form of personalizing each subject. "Further Reading" sections list cited and other significant sources, and readers are highly encouraged to use the fascinating topics listed in the "Bibliography of Recommended Resources" to delve deeper into a myriad of subjects that are served in smaller quantities throughout this book.

SUBJECTS

Eating is a form of celebration, and this book serves as a tool to help readers celebrate each and every subject selected. The work comprises 100 entries and a chronological timeline, both of which encompass topics ranging from whimsical food fads to deeper dives into the complex history of American foodways. The primary subjects of the book include:

- Notable individuals including chefs, cooks, and culinary television personalities
- The incorporation of food and cuisine in the arts
- Food festivals, events, and destinations
- Influential food-themed television shows, films, radio shows, and podcasts
- Significant and unusual trends within contemporary food culture

It is intentional that the entries in this work do not provide an exhaustive list of each individual, event, or culinary trend associated with these primary topics. Topics have been selected with care to showcase some of the most prominent and influential trends and individuals within culinary popular culture and to offer a broad lens of foodways and customs that are significant to a number of demographics.

The *central timeline* of this book includes significant food-related fads, events, individuals, entertainment, and media coverage from postwar America through modern day. It's important to note that various entries highlight the history of food culture outside of this timeline—even back to ancient times and informed speculation of the future of fads to come—in order to supply a significant amount of context for contemporary issues and trends. Additionally, the diverse range of individuals highlighted in this work were selected to showcase some of the most popular and influential individuals in their field, all of whom contribute to cuisine deemed "American food." These chefs, cooks, writers, and television hosts represent a wide range of racial and ethnic backgrounds, nationalities, LGBTQIA+ communities, culinary expertise, and more.

Readers are welcomed to this book in the spirit that history can be made even more delicious with an interesting road map. It was designed and written in the hope that after sampling these bite-sized topics, readers will identify broader story arcs that provide them with a greater understanding of, and craving for, America's voracious appetite for food-centric education, entertainment, and media.

Acknowledgments

This book would not have been possible without my editors: Catherine Lafuente and Erin Ryan. Your editing skills, wisdom, boundless enthusiasm for food-themed discussions, and friendship have meant the world to me. Thank you for allowing me to write this book.

I am also immensely grateful to Azara Golston of Milkmoon Kitchen for lending her beautiful photography and cake skills to the cover of this book; to Acquisitions Editor Jessica Gribble for her unwavering encouragement; and to Robin Tutt, Nicole Azze, and Angel Daphnee for turning this smorgasbord of words into a bound volume.

This work would not have been possible without the support I received from my book-loving family: my husband, Tom; our children, Milo and Lucia; and my parents, Dan and Karen, who cursed me with a lifelong obsession of storytelling.

I wish to dedicate this book to Anthony Bourdain, who helped us all feel more connected through food and stories, and to Julia Child, who threw her fist into the air and showed me that if I wasn't ready to fail, I wasn't ready to cook. She was right: about cooking and everything else.

Introduction

Food and joy are fascinating bedfellows. Eating and drinking, like sleeping, seeking shelter from the elements, and breathing, are all easily filed under "things human beings need to survive," yet joy is not something we typically associate with seeking shelter, breathing, or even sleeping, aside from feeling cozy and calm as we settle into a comfortable sleeping spot. And yet, when circumstances allow, we often feel thrilled to be served something aesthetically beautiful or when we bite into something marvelous. Eating creates a complex relationship between our physical body and emotional mind. Food is obviously necessary for our body to grow, heal, and properly function, but it is also closely associated with our need for comfort, our religious and spiritual practices, our formative memories, and our social connections.

Author Marcel Proust is best known for his description of biting into a madeleine, which unexpectedly evokes powerful memories from his childhood. Humans are profoundly affected by the aromas, textures, flavors, and memories associated with our food. As writer and television host Anthony Bourdain taught us over the course of his career, we are primed to learn about unfamiliar cultures, people, and places by way of the soothing and familiar practices of cooking and eating in good company. Many of us ask others, "Where were you when . . . ?" in relation to a significant tragic or celebratory event. In addition to remembering where we were during those events, many of us also preserve notable food memories in long-term storage. These memories might include the specific type of champagne we drank at our wedding or a clear, cherished memory of feeding our child mashed sweet potato as her first food.

OUR PERSONAL HISTORIES WITH FOOD

Nostalgia can be a very influential factor in our joyful associations with food. Before you begin reading the entries in this book, I encourage you to ask yourself, Which foods and drinks are closely tied with your memories of childhood? What food memories come to mind when you think about your history with your family, and what foods and cooking anecdotes do you associate with your ancestors? Outside of your family, what communities are you a part of, and what role has food played for you within those communities? What feelings of joy have you felt recently in relation to eating, and what feelings of happy anticipation do you experience regarding foods and drinks you might have in the future? Your answers to these questions will help you connect with the personal stories and relationships you'll read about other people and the foodways they hold dear.

My own family's joyful relationships with food have piqued my curiosity since childhood. Every morning, my father drinks coffee from a vintage ceramic mug bearing the logo of Steak 'n Shake, the hamburger stand-turned-chain that reminds him of his happy childhood in Indiana and his father's Indianapolis racetrack career. Similarly, my mother never looks as happy as she does when she is reminiscing about her favorite childhood foods in Buffalo, New York: a classic dog from Ted's Hot Dogs, beef on weck, and a chocolate cone from Anderson's Frozen Custard. For my in-laws, any mention of Chicago staples like Chicago dogs or Portillo's Italian beef immediately changes the tenor of the conversation into one that's lighthearted and reminiscent.

In my own life, I can't see cheddar Goldfish crackers without feeling affection for two young children I babysat in my teenage years. Their father, a renowned artist named Scott Fraser, frequently dotted his contemporary realism paintings with Goldfish crackers. Fraser's decision to use their favorite snack as a powerful metaphor in his work took on even more meaning and depth for me as I researched this book, specifically the prominent roles that food has played throughout art history.

My heart also swells with nostalgia when I think of movies and books I enjoy that have memorable food-themed scenes, a topic that is covered in various entries on fiction and nonfiction books and films alike. The familiar tastes of the food we grew up with provide comfort and balance, and for some, even a sense of sanctuary. Readers will find ruminations on nostalgia in entries like Grilled Cheese Festivals, the Florida Strawberry Festival, What the Fluff, and many more.

Many years ago, I read the following quotation by Holocaust survivor Gerda Weissmann Klein at the New England Holocaust Memorial in Boston, Massachusetts: "Ilse, a childhood friend of mine, once found a raspberry in the concentration camp and carried it in her pocket all day to present to me that night on a leaf. Imagine a world in which your entire possession is one raspberry and you give it to your friend." Over the years I have frequently wondered what it would be like to experience biting into a tart, sweet, bright-red raspberry in the midst of such a harrowing nightmare. Klein's words have left me with the firm belief that the joy of eating is far from frivolous—or even simply nostalgic—but rather something deeply human and tremendously sacred.

FROM THE BATTLE OF MIDWAY TO THE BATTLE OF THE SOUS CHEFS

During World War II, many housewives walked out of their traditional roles in the home and began serving their families and communities in different ways—such as filling their husband's shoes in the workforce, volunteering in wartime efforts, and growing victory gardens. When the war ended, many women glanced askance at the kitchen and knew that spending much of their time cooking, or paying a cook to help all day, was no longer a priority in their households. Many in the nation had a new understanding of freedom, and freedom tasted *good*. During this era, the advent of electric appliances and processed "convenience" foods helped women spend less time in the kitchen and more time pursuing their own interests.

After years of war, heartache, and loss, the nation was seeing the reunification of families, a coast-to-coast baby boom, and economic prosperity. In short, the country was primed for joy, and many families had a little extra cash on hand to treat themselves to some fun commodities. In 1948, brothers Richard and Maurice McDonald revamped their "McDonald's Bar-B-Que" stand into an ultraefficient burger joint, and in doing so, ushered in a new landscape of what would become the fast-food industry. In short order, the popular hamburger stand inspired fast-food spin-offs such as Americanized tacos, which also became part of the fabric of our nation's tablecloth.

By the early 1960s, Julia Child's televised cooking show *The French Chef* was drawing more men, women, and children into the kitchen to cook for pleasure instead of viewing the ritual as a chore. The inventions of convenience products, the fast-food industry, and entertaining culinary programming resulted in a convergence of food and popular culture that has seen unrelenting popularity for 60 years and counting. The meteoric rise of culinary television led to the concept of "celebrity chefs," and as a result, many of the entries in this work are devoted to television shows, channels, and personalities that helped fuel this booming industry.

FOOD'S RELATIONSHIP WITH RACE, ETHNICITY, AND NATIONALITY

One of the most valuable story arcs in this volume is the theme of diversity, particularly the rich variety of foodways celebrated by people of all ethnicities, races, and nationalities. Mexican American writer Gustavo Arellano notes that when there are tensions between members of two ethnic groups, the dominant group often mocks or disparages minorities' foods. For example, within mainstream American culture, cruel jokes have often stereotyped people of Asian descent as having eaten cats or dogs, or used the word "beaner" as a slur for people of Mexican descent in reference to the prevalence of beans in Mexican American cuisine. Despite the painful prevalence of these social biases, Arellano notes that acceptance of other cultures' foods is often the first step toward a gradual acceptance of *people* from those cultures. Throughout this work, readers will find histories of America's immigrants, refugees, indigenous communities, and enslaved people in relation to the incredible cuisines they helped shape in spite of, or as a direct result of, the adversity they faced.

Today, Americans are more open to exploring new cuisines than at any other time in the nation's history. Increasingly more people are open to and excited about global cuisines, and the nation is becoming more accepting of the fact that

"American food" is as diverse as the cultural melting pot its people represent. Within the last few decades, international cuisines and lesser-known regional domestic cuisines have come into fashion, accompanied by unprecedented interest in learning more about the cultures, history, and authenticity of these foodways.

In the 1980s, "eating Chinese food" in America typically entailed buying Chinese American fast food in folded-up (American-made) takeout boxes. For today's "foodies," who are just as hungry for food as they are of entertainment and history related to their food, "eating Chinese food" might mean cooking Cantonese cuisine for a date night at home while watching a documentary about the origins of Chinese American food. Korean American chef and *Lucky Peach* magazine cofounder Roy Choi has noted that American food culture is rife with images that can make non-Caucasian Americans feel like outsiders, such as the fictional Caucasian characters featured in the logos for Gerber and Quaker Oats brands. Choi remembers seeing these logos as a child and feeling like his own cultural heritage was not represented in mainstream American foods, which inspired him to define Asian American "fusion" in the dishes and cuisines he's helped develop throughout his career.

In addition to exploring the histories and influences of Asian American and Latin American cuisines in contemporary American society, this work also delves into the complex and fascinating histories of Southern and soul foodways. Entries devoted to topics such as the history of barbecue, the work of culinary historian Michael Twitty, and the career of Ethiopian-Swedish chef Marcus Samuelsson explore how some of America's most beloved cuisines sprang from the ingenuity of enslaved peoples. Additionally, the culinary experiences of—and influences from—Native American and Indigenous people are explored in entries about the Deer River Wild Rice Festival, Oglala Lakota Sioux chef and activist Sean Sherman, and the histories of traditional holiday foods in America.

FOOD-THEMED EVENTS

In contemporary times, there are no shortages of food-themed events, both domestically and abroad. Food festivals and other food- and beverage-related events are often serious in tenor, such as the formal Aspen Food and Wine Classic in Aspen, Colorado, where chefs and high-end restaurants run demonstrations of high-end culinary techniques and share samples of their cutting-edge foods. Within Americans' seemingly bottomless appetite for food-related celebrations, there is also a large niche dedicated to outlandish, silly, and off-the-wall food-related events. A growing trend in food tourism (also known as gastronomic or culinary tourism) around the world has seen Americans and international travelers traveling to areas of their own country and even other countries to witness celebrations of unusual foods or ordinary foods celebrated in unusual ways.

When it comes to food-themed social activism, few things could seem more diametrically opposed to issues of hunger or food insecurity than expensive food festivals that appear to be frivolous. However, many food festivals' origins stem from a desire to raise money for communities in need. Many unusual food events take place in small (even tiny) towns that see exponential tourism upticks for each festival, and more often than not, festival organizers donate proceeds to underserved populations and food banks. Food festivals often seek to elevate foods, cuisines, and historic cultural rituals that organizers fear are being pushed out of vogue due to modern technology, reduced interest in traditional agricultural practices, and changing trends in popular culture. As such, these events blend entertainment with efforts to educate festivalgoers about cultural ties that make the celebrated foods meaningful to the immediate and outlying communities.

MODERN FOOD

Today, there are countless food-centric television shows, websites, podcasts, radio shows, events, and locales that are celebrated within popular culture. Diners in past decades may have had to rely on travel guides or printed restaurant reviews to choose a restaurant. In comparison, today's diners are just as likely to select a restaurant or type of cuisine based on what they saw on a reality television show, and they might write their own review (peppered with selfies) online while they eat. Diners of days past had to rely on small talk or comfortably bored silence while waiting for the check. Today, it's more likely to find someone on their smartphone, indulging in something like a food-themed Buzzfeed quiz called "We Know What You Should Name Your Baby Based On the Sandwich You Make" (author note: Buzzfeed says that my "ham, cucumber, tomato and mayo on a croissant" choice indicates that my baby should have been named "Olivia").

According to food writer Laura Shapiro, "Food talks—but somebody has to hear it." In contemporary American society, as evidenced by the wealth of cooking shows, culinary travelogues, books, films, and podcasts, *many* of us are listening. As seasoned chef and television host Andrew Zimmern has said, "I've been saying it for 20 years: Food is good. Food with a story is better. Food with a story you've never heard of is best of all, and food with a story you've never heard of but that you can relate to is the holy grail." With luck, readers will find numerous unfamiliar and relatable food stories in the pages of this work.

In the immortal words of Julia Child (and all of France): bon appétit!

Chronology

1784
Founding father and former president Thomas Jefferson brings the first-known recipe for ice cream to the United States, a treat that he encountered during the time he spent in France. The recipe, assumed to be penned by his butler Adrien Petit, likely helped kick off a craze in the nation that shows no sign of slowing down well over two centuries later.

1850s
The California gold rush draws Chinese immigrants to the United States by the thousands. The first known Chinese restaurants—primarily Cantonese in style—begin cropping up as a result.

1882
The Chinese Exclusion Act goes into effect, banning almost all immigrants from China from entering the United States. Anti-Chinese sentiment and violence increases for decades. In 1915, the act is modified to allow certain qualified restaurateurs to immigrate to the United States for the purposes of running Chinese eateries.

1890s
Street vendors selling tamales, known as *tamaleros*, spread across the country's cities. Tamaleros experience a meteoric rise in popular culture, becoming the subject of everything from lunchtime darlings to the subject of hit songs.

1904
Ice cream cones are sold by vendors at the World's Fair in St. Louis, Missouri, launching a national trend for the crunchy rolled cones.

1917
America enters World War I, and the country begins rationing numerous foods in order to supply food desperately needed by troops and European allies. Domestically, patriots are encouraged to eliminate food waste and roll up their sleeves to learn skills such as canning.

1920
In January, the 18th Amendment goes into effect timed with the passage of the Volstead Act, banning the sale, transportation, and manufacturing of "intoxicating liquors." This era, dubbed Prohibition, leads to illegal liquor

production and sales, ushering in a rise of organized crime and illicit bars and restaurants.

1924
The Betty Crocker School of the Air radio show premiers, featuring a fictional character named Betty Crocker who offers cooking pointers. The show becomes one of the longest running in the nation, offering a valuable source of cooking ideas for cash-strapped housewives during the Great Depression.

1928
Seeking a new logo, baby food executives at the Gerber company launch a contest asking artists to send in their most adorable baby portraits. The winning work—an unfinished charcoal sketch of a four-month-old girl—goes on to become the advertising poster child of baby food for the rest of the century.

1928
Inventor Otto Rohwedder's first automatic bread-slicing machine kicks into business at the Chillicothe Baking Company in July. Loaves of commercially produced, presliced Wonder Bread gain considerable popularity over the next decade, and inspire future colloquialisms about "the best (invention) since sliced bread."

1929
The stock market crash in October leads to a four-year period known as The Great Depression, in which economic hardship ravages the nation. Americans find themselves seeking new sources for (and types of) food and beverages as the result of significantly reduced budgets and drastic changes in the restaurant and beverage industries.

1931
Irma Rombauer self-publishes *The Joy of Cooking*, a work that she hopes will bring more personable and relatable cooking tips and Depression-era recipes to American tables. Initially selling the work door to door as a means to support herself in the aftermath of her husband's death, Rombauer sees astronomical sales of the work over her lifetime (it went on to sell more than 18 million copies).

1934
Zacatecan immigrant Aurora Guerrero introduces Americans to the first nationally recognized form of the taco at her Los Angeles restaurant. *Taquitos* (small, rolled, deep-fried tortillas stuffed with shredded beef and topped with guacamole sauce) become a fad that is still in full swing nearly 100 years later.

1936
Carl Mayer, nephew of the Oscar Mayer company's founder, premiers the first "Wienermobile," an automobile shaped like a hot dog that serves as a mobile advertisement. The company begins featuring little people as drivers who drive the Weinermobile and attend local events in character as "Little Oscar" to promote hot dog sales.

1939
World War II breaks out, leading to more widespread wartime rationing of food in the United States. Staples like coffee, meat, cheese, sugar, and fruit become relative delicacies, and Americans take to planting "Victory Gardens" and sharing inventive recipes as part of their patriotic food-related efforts.

1950s
"Cooking convenience" becomes a nationwide fad. The rising popularity of convenience foods (processed and/or premade foods) and innovative kitchen appliances like blenders, refrigerators with automatic ice makers, hand-held mixers, and electric ranges create radical changes within households, liberating housewives from some of their previous culinary responsibilities.

1954
In the summer of this year, milkshake-mixing-machine salesman Ray Kroc visits the first McDonald's restaurant, opened by brothers Maurice and Richard McDonald in 1940. Kroc is amazed by the efficient workflow and highly limited menu at the small San Bernadino, California, drive-up restaurant, and becomes inspired to create a fast-food corporation based on the brothers' prototype.

1954
In November, a sales representative for Swanson & Sons foods spares the company from losing money on an excess of frozen Thanksgiving turkeys by repackaging the turkey meat alongside vegetables, stuffing, and potatoes: the first-ever frozen "TV" dinner.

1961
The United States military presence grows in South Vietnam. Four years later, American combat troops enter the Vietnam War, and remain engaged in conflict until a peace agreement is signed in 1973. The combination of American soldiers' exposure to Southeast Asian cuisine and increased immigration between Asia and the United States leads to the inception of the first Vietnamese and Thai restaurants in the nation. Military members' individual rations (*C-rations*) also inspire new food trends, such as adding Tabasco hot sauce to bland canned foods.

1961
After nearly a decade of researching, writing, and editing, authors Julia Child, Simone Beck, and Louisette Bertholle publish the first volume of *Mastering the Art of French Cooking*. Over the next 50 years, the book goes on to sell roughly 1.5 million copies.

1962
In February, Julia Child appears on Boston public television show *I've Been Reading* with her own hot plate, whisk, pan, and chicken eggs in tow for an omelet-making demonstration. Viewers are so delighted with Child's appearance (and the new concept of an exotic French-style omelet) that two years later, WGBH launches her own show, *The French Chef.*

1962
In March, after years of studying local franchise operations and Mexican American cooking techniques, entrepreneur Glen Bell opens the first Taco Bell in Downey, California. In just five years' time, Southern California boasts 100 Taco Bell locations.

1969
The Woodstock Music and Art Fair takes place in upstate New York from August 15 to 18, drawing an estimated 400,000 attendees. In advance of the event, numerous food vendors (including Coney Island vendor Nathan's Hot Dogs) withdraw their interest in selling concessions due to ambiguous and astronomical attendance estimates. Three individuals manage to set up a hamburger stand, but concertgoers set fire to the structure. In response to the food shortages, tens of thousands of food donations are airlifted to the site and local Good Samaritans pass out free food. One of the most popular items is granola, which goes on to become a novel breakfast trend around the country.

1970s
Chef and activist Alice Walters and graphic artist David Lance Goines publish a series of highly stylized and illustrated recipes entitled *Thirty Recipes Suitable for Framing*, and in 1971, Waters opens her iconic restaurant, Chez Panisse. Waters' culinary activism becomes a driving force for various food movements in the 1970s that focus on healthy, organic ingredients sourced from local farms.

1981
In January, Jelly Belly corporation sends 3.5 tons of jelly beans to Washington, D.C., to celebrate the inauguration of Ronald Reagan. The president was a longtime loyal customer of the brand, having eaten the company's jelly beans since 1966 as a way to combat his pipe smoking habit. Over the course of his presidency, Reagan shares Jelly Belly jars decorated with the presidential seal as official White House gifts to heads of state and other dignitaries.

1981
Chocolate M&Ms become the first candy to be launched into space on the Columbia spaceship. Astronauts go on to enjoy the candies on more than 130 subsequent missions, often delighting television viewers by tossing the candies into the zero-gravity environment and floating around to eat them.

1985
Tortillas also make their debut in space, thanks to American astronauts' cravings and NASA's enthusiastic approval (tortillas prove to be far less hazardous than their more crumbly counterpart: bread).

1993
Food Network, d.b.a. Television Food Network, debuts with two cooking shows in November.

1993
Iron Chef premiers in Japan, leading to a significant pop culture phenomenon in Japan and abroad. An American version of the show debuts on Food Network in 2005.

1996

Talk show host Oprah Winfrey states that she never wants to eat another hamburger in an on-air segment about food safety and the dangers of mad cow disease. Her comment draws ire from members of the beef industry who blame Winfrey for a significant drop in the price and popularity of beef shortly thereafter. Winfrey is sued for damages by the Texas cattle industry, but she wins her case at trial.

1998

Archaeologists researching the artifacts left in a Brooklyn, New York, home built around 1719 discover a centuries-old collection of recipes. One lists instructions to make a "Demon Cake" (presumably named for the difficulty of removing the molasses-rich batter from the bowl). Another recipe describes steps to make mincemeat pie, starting with the instruction to "get a cow."

1999

Television host and writer Martha Stewart becomes a media mogul with the launch of Martha Stewart Living Omnimedia. Within a year, she earns the title of America's first female self-made billionaire.

2006

Avocado toast becomes one of the biggest food trends in the United States, gracing brunch tables from California to New York City and drawing rave reviews and scathing criticism (primarily geared toward millennials, the generation among whom the dish is deemed most popular).

2009

Chopped premiers on the Food Network. Its three-round, high-stakes elimination format goes on to become the hottest trend for reality food shows.

2010

Pop music star Lady Gaga (the stage name of singer Stefani Germanotta) makes international pop culture headlines for wearing a dress fashioned out of raw beef to the MTV Video Music Awards.

2013

Pastry chef Dominique Ansel debuts the Cronut—a hybrid croissant-donut pastry filled with cream—at his bakery in New York. A writer from restaurant blog *Grub Street* publishes a review of the new trend, and within days, Ansel's bakery has become the epicenter of one of the nation's newest hot culinary trends.

2017

The #MeToo movement gains momentum across the United States, connecting multiple people who allege that they were the victims of sexual abuse and/or harassment from powerful individuals within prominent industries. A number of high-profile chefs are accused of abusive behavior, calling various "social norms" into question regarding the culture within the restaurant and bar industry.

2018

Food writer and television personality Anthony Bourdain dies by suicide at the age of 61. Bourdain's loss is grieved in countries worldwide, and fans, culinary professionals, and journalists alike publish numerous reflections about his culinary and cultural legacies.

2020

In March of 2020, the global COVID-19 pandemic spreads across the United States. Restaurants and bars are shuttered across the country, many of which permanently close. As restaurateurs struggle to reopen with limited capacities and new mandated safety measures, an Independent Restaurant Coalition forms to lobby Congress for financial relief for the approximately 11 million Americans employed by independent restaurants.

All-Star Chef Classic

STARTERS

The All-Star Chef Classic is a four-day culinary event that takes place at L.A. Live, an entertainment complex in downtown Los Angeles, California. The first Classic was held in 2014 and has taken place in early March nearly every year since then. It was cofounded by prior *Edible LA* magazine editor Lucy Lean and Krissy Lefebvre, a former contestant on the reality show *The Apprentice* and wife of celebrity chef Ludo Lefebvre. The duo launched the festival in partnership with the Anschutz Entertainment Group (AEG).

The All-Star Chef Classic draws top chefs from California and around the globe to do cooking demonstrations, wine pairings, and tastings in a unique stadium-seating venue. The event consists of two main elements: the "Masters Dinner Series," in which the audience watches chefs work while enjoying a seated multicourse meal, and an open marketplace concept called a "Chef's Tasting Arena" that invites guests to amble through various booths, sampling different foods from each station and watching demonstrations up close. In past years, tickets to the event ranged from $65 for a single lunch session to $425 or more for VIP access to a Masters Dinner Series. A portion of the event's ticket sales benefits charitable organizations.

ENTRÉE

In 2014, 25 chefs from Los Angeles and various international cities gathered in what would become an annual springtime culinary event. Crowds were drawn to a concept that resembled a mash-up of an intimate high-end meal served by the restaurant's executive chef and a high-energy dinner theater performance. The venue spaces were custom-designed for the All-Star Chef Classic and included strategically placed lights and cameras, LED television screens, and headset microphones for each chef, giving attendees close-up sights and sounds of the chefs and their creations. The inaugural Classic featured a French-themed Masters Dinner, a "Savor the Season" theme in the Tasting Arena, and a lineup of all-female chefs serving up culinary delights at an All-Star lunch. The event wasn't entirely seamless; as with any inaugural event, there were a number of technical glitches involving the myriad of big screens, elaborate camera setups, and occasional interrupted choreography in which the chefs were unsure of what to do next (Mendoza 2014).

In 2015, the event expanded its offerings with American and British Masters Dinners in addition to the French demonstration. The festival hired Billy Harris, a comic who has hosted a number of high-profile culinary events, as the event's emcee. In an interview with *Haute Living* magazine, cofounders Lean and Lefebvre said that event-goers' primary attraction to the event was the one-on-one interaction audience members were able to have with top chefs in the field and the intimate environment in which they received stories and cooking tips from the pros.

Forty-six chefs joined the 2016 program, which included French, Mexican, Spanish, American, Asian, and Asian-fusion Masters Dinners. The following year, more than 55 chefs gathered to participate in American, Asian, French, and inaugural Italian Master Dinners. The booth-walking event included a new regional theme, featuring tastings from 18 chefs who specialized in Southern cooking. In 2018, the lineup included 40 chefs, with new additions such as a "haute vegetable" themed Master Dinner, an "All-Star Women Masters Dinner," and regional fare from the Middle East represented in the tasting arena.

While the event is largely geared toward sophisticated adult "foodies," the Classic hosts cooking demonstrations and lessons for children as well. In 2014, Waylynn Lucas hosted a pie-making lesson on "Pi Day" (a celebration for the mathematical constant "pi" that takes place every March 14) for over 200 youngsters. In 2016, actress Sarah Michelle Gellar hosted the "Little Masters" cooking class.

The Classic has donated some of the proceeds from ticket sales to charitable causes. In 2014, actress Alison Sweeney and Billy Harris hosted a four-course luncheon prepared by chefs Suzanne Goin and Jenn Louis. The event benefited City of Hope, a cancer research and treatment center in Southern California. In 2015, the same event (dubbed "Cuisine for the Cure") took place, focusing on "superfoods" (typically thought of as whole foods that are packed with vitamins and minerals and minimal to no preservatives or added sugars) to help draw attention to nutritious food's role in health and wellness. Goin and Louis were joined by Food Network personality Aaròn Sánchez and pastry chef Brooks Headley in the preparation of the luncheon.

L.A. Kitchen has also been a recipient of the Classic's donations. The organization, whose mission statement is that "neither food nor people should go to waste," seeks uses for discarded food, trains disadvantaged people to find work, and provides nutritious meals for the hungry.

ACCOMPANIED BY

Some of the California-based chefs who have made recurring appearances at the Classic include Ludo Lefebvre of L.A.'s Trois Mec restaurant and LudoBird, a gourmet food truck that serves up fried chicken; David LeFevre of Southern California's Manhattan Beach Post and Fishing With Dynamite; Nancy Silverton, L.A.-based chef and baker who has been widely credited with the popularization of artisan sourdough bread; and Michael Cimarusti of L.A.'s Providence and Best

Girl restaurants. Other familiar faces include Sang Yoon of L.A.'s Lukshon; Spanish tapas guru José Andrés of L.A.'s Bazaar and D.C.'s Zaytinya and TFG; brothers Michael Voltaggio of L.A.'s ink.well and Bryan Voltaggio, *Top Chef* contestant and owner of Maryland's Volt, Aggio, and Voltaggio Brothers Steak House. Additional returning chefs in 2018 include Nyesha Arrington of Santa Monica's Native and Duff Goldman, owner of L.A.'s Duff's Cakemix and television personality on Food Network's *Ace of Cakes*.

Notable appearances of chefs traveling within the United States and international cities include those of Alain Ducasse of London's Dorchester, Monaco's Le Louis XV, and Paris's Jules Verne restaurants; Jean-Georges Vongerichten, a French-born chef whose renowned restaurants are located all over the globe; Alain Passard of Paris's l'Arpege; Iñaki Aizpitarte of Paris's Le Chateaubriand and Le Dauphin; Naomi Pomeroy of Portland, Oregon's Beast; and Wylie Dufresne, considered the leader of the molecular gastronomy trend and known for his New York City restaurants: Du's Donuts, Alder, and wd~50.

SUGGESTED PAIRINGS

See also: Aspen Food and Wine Classic; Novelty Dining Experiences; South Beach Wine & Food Festival; *Top Chef*.

Entry best enjoyed while eating: Daniel Doherty's "East End Eels" British Masters Dinner of smoked eel, horseradish, *samphire* (a sea vegetable similar to asparagus), *crème fraîche* (a thick custardy cream made popular in French cuisine), and *matcha* (powdered green tea leaves) served alongside Sven Chartier's oysters that are prepared with fermented turnip and pear. Give a nod to the 2018 inclusion of Middle Eastern fare with a salad of Israeli couscous, lemon juice, feta, parsley, Greek yogurt, and olive oil. Finish with a slice of Waylynn Lucas's grapefruit, pistachio, and coconut cake and a cold glass of champagne or Southern-style sweet tea.

Further Reading

All-Star Chef Classic, Los Angeles. 2018. "Meet the Chefs." https://www.allstarchefclassic.com/talent/meet-the-chefs

Hallock, Betty. 2014. "All-Star Chef Classic Debuts in L.A. with 'Restaurant Stadium.'" *L.A. Times*, January 22, 2014.

L.A. Kitchen. 2018. "Mission Statement." http://www.lakitchen.org/mission-vision/

L.A. Live. 2015. "All-Star Chef Classic Live at Restaurant Stadium." https://www.lalive.com/events/la-live/detail/all-star-chef-classic-6

Lean, Lucy. 2015. "Happy Pi Day—Best Rhubarb and Strawberry Pi Day Pie Recipe." https://lucylean.com/celebrating-kitchen-kids-with-pie/

Mendoza, Mariecar. 2014. "All-Star Chefs Classic Feeds Fans Appetite for Celebrity Chefs." *Los Angeles Daily News*, March 24, 2014.

Schreffler, Laura. 2015. "Krissy Lefebvre and Lucy Lean of All-Star Chef Classic Are Dreamers." *Haute Living*, March 5, 2015.

Sproul, Suzanne. 2015. "All-Star Chef Classic in Los Angeles Showcases Top Culinary Figures, New Trends." *Los Angeles Daily News*, March 6, 2015.

Wang, Andy. 2015. "True Brit, French Twist at All-Star Chef Classic." *L.A. Magazine*, March 6, 2015. http://www.lamag.com/digestblog/true-brit-french-twist-star-chef-classic/

America's Test Kitchen

STARTERS

The *America's Test Kitchen* brand encompasses an eponymous television show and radio show—as well as a number of associated magazines, food websites, and cookbooks—which are all known for testing and reviewing a wide array of recipes and cooking gadgets. According to *America's Test Kitchen*'s website, the show is the "most-watched television cooking show on public television—more than 2 million viewers tune in per week." The brand's print products boast a number of best-selling cookbooks and magazines that each feature a specific type of cuisine, kitchen appliance, or diet.

The food-media powerhouse was founded in the form of *Cook's Magazine* in 1980 by then-amateur cook and marketing professional Christopher Kimball. The magazine was transformed into *Cook's Illustrated* in 1993, a "how to" publication that led to the development of the television show and multimedia conglomerate. The show first aired on public television in 2001. As of 2021, the show had run for 21 seasons. The show's 15,000-square-foot Boston-based office and studios are home to "60 test cooks, editors, and cookware specialists." Every recipe is tested exhaustively by Test Kitchen professionals, who also solicit the help of amateur recipe testers. This community of nearly 60,000 at-home cooks are asked to try recipes and supply feedback to the Test Kitchen teams regarding the clarity of instructions and quality of the finished product.

ENTRÉE

Measuring bagels with a ruler, conducting a Tasting Lab on anchovy flavor, and discussing the merits of where to buy pork chops doesn't automatically bring the word *joy* to mind. In fact, the show's format and underlying purpose—the pursuit of testing food and food preparation tools—sounds almost devoid of joy. In a 2012 interview with the *New York Times Magazine*, *America's Test Kitchen* founder Christopher Kimball went as far as to say that he "hates the idea that cooking should be a celebration or a party" and ventured the opinion that cooking is, in essence, a monotonous chore.

Upon closer inspection, the nearly 500 episodes that make up the *America's Test Kitchen* television show illustrate an approachable scientific exploration in the pursuit of creating a great deal of joy. Since 2001, the cooks on *America's Test Kitchen* have gone to great lengths to analyze what makes many of America's favorite dishes delicious, delightful, and accessible. The team has also shown how to prepare, assemble, and enjoy each dish more easily and efficiently. While the concept behind the show could have evolved into episodes characterized by serious clinical trials of ingredients' chemical reactions and dry comparisons of crock pot power wattages, each episode has an undertone of delight due to the questions *behind* the exhaustive analyses. Week after week, in 30-minute episode increments, the show's cooks and viewers have asked and sought answers to questions such as, What makes the fluffiest biscuit? What transforms tuna sandwiches from a dreaded sack lunch item into a delicious lunch? What makes chocolate mousse so inexplicably decadent?

The "test cooks" on the show help viewers explore dishes from every angle. The show begins with an analysis of the best ingredients for the featured dish, followed by instructions on the preparation techniques that would yield the best results. Taste tests are discussed thoroughly, inviting viewers to awaken their own senses at home as they take more time to consider flavors and flavor variations. "Gadget" reviews help home cooks decide whether to splurge on new tools for their kitchen, ranging from traditional kitchen supplies to more newfangled appliances bordering on whimsical. The show's upbeat nature and focus on efficiency appeals to viewers' desires to create a special dining experience in a short period of time. Every week, the test cooks offer dozens of insights and educational tips that come in equally handy in a kitchen or in a conversation at a cocktail party.

America's Test Kitchen applies meticulous focus on a wide array of foods, treating an analysis of a humble baked bean dish with the same reverence as a tutorial on preparing steak au poivre. Shows covering classic American fare such as peanut butter cookies and hamburgers rub shoulders with episodes focusing on global cuisines like Char Siu (Chinese barbecue pork), Tinga de Pollo (chicken tacos), and Dolsot Bibimbap (Korean rice bowls).

ACCOMPANIED BY

The show's founder and primary host, Christopher Kimball, was an integral part of the show in front of and behind cameras. After attending Columbia University, where he majored in primitive art, Kimball worked in sales and marketing before enrolling in cooking classes. His interest in the nitty-gritty details behind recipes led him to launch the magazine that became *Cook's Illustrated*, which is notably bereft of advertisements (and the flashy, color-drenched photography of many contemporary food magazines).

Kimball parted ways with the *America's Test Kitchen* brand when he was let go from the company in 2015, reportedly due to a contract dispute. At the age of 65, Kimball channeled his efforts into Milk Street, another Boston-based venture featuring an instructional-cooking television show, radio show, magazine, and online cooking school. *America's Test Kitchen* filed a lawsuit against Kimball, claiming that he had infringed on their intellectual property and used company resources to help create a business that presented a direct competition. In an interview with the *Washington Post* in 2016, Kimball asserted that Milk Street diverged from his previous, more "meat-centric" cooking, which featured recipes primarily from Northern Europe. He also pointed to a focus on travel as a distinguishing feature.

In his stead, two cooks who had been on the show from its inception hosted the 17th season: Julia Collin Davison and Bridget Lancaster. The show features additional culinary experts from a variety of backgrounds who specialize in tasting, cooking, and analyzing the science behind cooking. Each episode follows the same formulaic segments of introducing and cooking a dish, ingredient taste tests and experiments, gadget demos, and concluding thoughts. For example, an episode on "Pantry Pastas" in Season 17 begins with hosts Lancaster and Collin Davison highlighting various popular pastas. In keeping with the show's theme, the hosts highlight high-quality pasta dishes that can be "pulled from the pantry at a moment's notice." They joke that after tasting "millions" of variations, they've identified the flavor errors in many Pasta e Ceci dishes and that they'll help viewers avoid the same pitfall. As Lancaster and Davison pepper the dish with chickpeas and pancetta (and a side of lighthearted jokes), the recipe comes together in a seemingly effortless manner. Collin Davison receives in-depth pointers from Jack Bishop, *America's Test Kitchen* chief creative officer and "tasting expert," on buying high-quality domestic Parmesan cheese.

The next segment features test cook Dan Souza, who illustrates the science behind the aging process of the cheese. The episode wraps up with another test cook, Elle Simone, walking Lancaster through another recipe (this time, for Penne Arrabbiata—meaning angry pasta). "We won't make it *too* angry," Simone jokes. Other notable cast members include Adam Reid and Lisa McManus, self-described "gadget gurus" who tests kitchen tools for the show's "Equipment Corner" segments. Additional test cooks include Tim Chin, Keith Dresser, Rebecca Hays, and Erin McMurrer.

DESSERT

In the "Ultimate Sticky Bun" episode (Season 17), Collin Davison and Lancaster are overtaken by the deliciousness of their freshly baked sticky buns. The hosts attempt to keep their composure, but they're interrupted by each other's laughter as their analysis becomes less formal and harder to hear as polite bites turn into frenzied eating.

"I would not throw these out of bed," Lannister deadpans as she starts rapidly stuffing sticky bun into her mouth. "That is some weird-shaped pecan on there. I'd better get that," she adds. Collin Davison devolves into giggles, sticky bun bites crowding her own cheeks. As Lannister begins licking her plate clean, video crew members can be heard laughing behind the cameras. Collin Davison manages to deliver the straightforward voiceover recapping the recipe, but Lannister has the final word, flying a sticky bun, airplane style, toward her mouth: "phhhbbbbt."

SUGGESTED PAIRINGS

See also: Child, Julia; *Cooked*; *Mind of a Chef, The*; Television, Food Channels on.

Entry best enjoyed while eating: Pan-seared salmon with cilantro-mint chutney (quick-brined with salt to hold in moisture, cooked in a cold, nonstick pan that's slowly heated); farro salad with asparagus, sugar snap peas, and tomatoes (tossed with a zesty vinaigrette to enhance the flavors); foolproof corn on the cob (cooked for 10 minutes in boiling water that's left to cool); light and fluffy chocolate mousse (made with *three* types of chocolate: semisweet, Dutch-processed cocoa, and white chocolate chips).

Further Reading

America's Test Kitchen. 2021. https:www.americastestkitchen.com

Bittman, Mark. 2013. *How to Cook Everything.* Revised 10th Anniversary Ed. New York: Houghton Mifflin Harcourt.
Ember, Sydney. 2015. "Christopher Kimball, Founder of America's Test Kitchen, to Leave the Company." *New York Times*, November 16, 2015.
Halberstadt, Alex. 2012. "Cooking Isn't Creative, and It Isn't Easy." *New York Times Magazine*, October 11, 2012.
Krystal, Becky. 2016. "Home Cooking's Headed for a Mash-up 'Watershed Moment'." *Washington Post*, October 17, 2016.
Krystal, Becky. 2016. "Six Take-aways from America's Test Kitchen's Lawsuit against Christopher Kimball." *Washington Post*, November 2, 2016.
López-Alt, J. Kenji. 2015. *The Food Lab: Better Home Cooking Through Science.* New York: W.W. Norton & Company.

Art, Food in (Antiquity through the Renaissance)

STARTERS

Art is one of the oldest forms of media that tells us about popular themes and trends in cultures. Food has been a central theme in artworks spanning back to the earliest definitions of art, including Neanderthal cave paintings in Spain that are estimated to be 64,000 years old. Art historians have found fascinating clues about human history, religion, and daily life from food-related works spanning from prehistoric records of animals and vegetation through twentieth-century artworks alike. The artworks themselves served as functional documentation, communication with the afterlife, political statements, and even whimsical forms of entertainment.

Some artists sought to illustrate food or drinks to document themes that had deep cultural significance or to use the ripening and spoilage of fruits and vegetables as metaphors for sexuality, virility, aging, corruption, the passage of time, and the cyclic nature of life. Many artists simply captured people preparing and eating food as key pieces of their subjects' everyday lives. *New York Times* journalist Ligaya Mishan argues that food has cultural freight and helps to define social strata. She notes that throughout time "food has always had a story: It is ephemeral—destined to be consumed or spoiled—and thus, in a subgenre of still lifes called *vanitas*, a reminder of mortality" (2018).

ENTRÉE

Food in art traces back to Paleolithic era cave paintings, which are some of the oldest known forms of art. The symbolism and meaning of these paintings have been a mystery for tens of thousands of years. For example, it's easy to assume that bison were frequently used as subjects simply because they were a valuable and common food source. However, culinary writer Gillian Riley notes that these images rarely depict dead bison, or the preparation of bison of food, and some of the most common animals the Paleolithic are believed to have eaten, like reindeer, are rarely depicted at all. With this in mind, even the most ancient form of art poses fascinating questions. Were these paintings physical manifestations of people's longing for a food source that was difficult to come by? Could these images allude to ancient artists' religious or spiritual beliefs, elevating the animals to something higher than simply a source of food? We may never know the answers to these questions, but in our efforts to study them, we are able to better understand the commonalities between ourselves and our ancestors.

In contrast to Paleolithic art, ancient art (4000 BCE–400 CE) contains significant clues about food's role in the artists' lives. Ancient Egyptians believed that deities and departed souls needed food and beverages in the afterlife, so they lined tombs of the dead with a wide array of things to eat and drink. Uncertain if the gods and deceased souls would be able to use the food in its physical form, the Ancient Egyptians also left functional artistic depictions of foods and beverages in the form of still life carvings and three-dimensional wooden models illustrating scenes like cattle in slaughterhouses or the production of beer.

From antiquity throughout the Renaissance (1400–1600 CE), some of the most popular subjects for artists to paint were still life paintings of fruits and vegetables. Some artists who depicted food in their work, such as Greek painter Peiraikos and sixteenth-century Dutch painter Pieter Aertsen, drew criticism for focusing on the minutiae of daily life (seen as vulgar—far too "common"—by critics who dictated a strict hierarchy of art subjects).

Food and beverage depictions in art have a lengthy history of being veritable Trojan horses—presumably innocent subject matters that secretly carry powerful messages for those willing to engage with them. Paintings dating back to the

---

Small Plates

The Mystery of the Foodless Feasters

In medieval art, the *absence* of food in food-themed scenes has been a source of significant interest to art historians. Manuscript curator Christine Sciacca of the Getty Museum has noted that in illuminated manuscripts, scenes involving feasts and religious meals carefully walk a line between illustrating the importance of meals versus appearing to condone gluttony. Eating anything in excess was considered a sin, so artists attempted to find a middle ground by illustrating plates of food without showing anyone lifting the food to their mouths. Some scenes use gluttony as a cautionary tale, such as *The Feast of Dives* (ca. 1510–1520) by Flemish artist Master of James IV of Scotland. The work depicts an aristocratic man failing to offer any of his feast to a beggar (Lazarus). In an inset image, Lazarus is shown being escorted to heaven by angels.

In stark contrast to the pious modesty of food in these centuries, many artists of the late Renaissance through the Baroque period (1600–1800 CE) used food to boast about their society's abundance of food. The wide spectrum of colors and textures used to paint foods and drinks was also well suited to show off the rich pigments of the artists' modern paints. Across Europe, luxurious imported and exported foods were highly prized. One significant source of pride for the Dutch was the Netherlands' booming dairy business. Johannes Vermeer's work *The Milkmaid* (c. 1660) depicts the simple act of pouring milk using a stunning study of light and color: hallmarks of his artworks, which also helped define the Dutch Golden Age.

medieval period (ca. 300–1400 CE) often used apples to represent the Old Testament's story of the original sin, when Eve fell from grace after biting into an apple in the Garden of Eden. Other fruits frequently nod to classical mythology, such as grapes that signified Dionysis, the ancient Greek god of wine. Similarly, Roman poet Ovid used pomegranates in *Metamorphoses* (ca. 8 CE) to symbolize the goddess Venus's fertility and desire, as well as to explore themes of resurrection (Meagher 2009). Throughout art history, numerous artists have explored Catholic themes of transubstantiation using evocative images of wine and bread.

In the late 1500s, court painter Giuseppe Arcimboldo (1527–1593) brought food to new artistic heights by making the bold choice to paint his subject, Holy Roman Emperor Rudolf II, using composite images of fruits and vegetables. These humorous paintings seemed remarkably ahead of their time, falling from fashion but coming back into vogue in contemporary times. The rare and exotic fruits and vegetables Arcimboldo used weren't simply intended to be comedic. Each of the ingredients denoted regions in the New World that rulers, including Rudolf II, wished to dominate. The imaginative portraits cast the royal subjects in a majestic light, constructing their likeness using the bounty of luxuries available to them (Tucker 2011).

The first known painting of High Renaissance master Leonardo da Vinci (1452–1519) was the result of the food-loving artist's insatiable appetite. At the age of 17, da Vinci was an apprentice under Andrea Verrocchio (1435–1488), who forced the young man to paint an angel in the corner of his work *The Baptism of Christ* (ca. 1475) as a punishment for routinely guzzling sweets. Da Vinci's career began as a line cook and chef, and his notes describe a longing for more creativity and ingenuity in the kitchen. He invented numerous kitchen gadgets, including a giant man-powered whisk twice the size of the cook who would have had to climb inside to use it. To date, one of the most famous paintings in the world is his mural *The Last Supper* (ca. 1490s). This work has inspired countless recreations, such as one sculpted entirely out of rock salt by workers in a Polish salt mine. The work is thought to have been completed around 1280 CE, carved over time and hundreds of feet underground by miners who hoped the artwork would offer them protection and divinity (Legro 2011).

Giuseppe Arcimboldo's oil painting *Summer* (1572) is one in a series of four depicting a man in each season of his life. The composite image of foods like cucumber, wheat, peach, cherries, and grapes speak to both the abundance of fresh summer foods and the prime of this man's life. (Steve Estvanik/Dreamstime.com)

DESSERT

- Caravaggio, whose full name was Michelangelo Merisi da Caravaggio, had a peculiar food-related crime in his (lengthy) police record: assault with artichokes. The artist ordered eight fried artichokes at a restaurant, half-fried in butter and half-fried in oil. Upon the delivery of the dish, the waiter suggested that the artist needed sniff each one to determine which had been cooked in oil versus butter. An enraged Caravaggio, who interpreted the suggestion as an insult, threw the artichokes in the waiter's face and drew his sword.

- Leonardo da Vinci kept a running list of foods he loathed that his servant made him eat anyway, including "jellied goat, hemp bread, white mosquito pudding, inedible turnips, and eel balls" (Legro 2011). Considering the number of inventions da Vinci devised in his lifetime, it's somewhat of a mystery that cheap delivery pizza was not among them.

SUGGESTED PAIRINGS

See also: Art, Food in (Impressionism through Contemporary Art); Trends, Food; Wine and Spirits.

Entry best enjoyed while eating: Take a bite out of the turnips and bread assembled on canvas in *Munich Still Life* (1882) by Irish-American William Harnett, a master of *trump l'oei* (a style designed to "trick the eye" into thinking the subject matter is really there). Following that, have whatever prison meal is offered where you're spending time for biting into a classic work of art.

Further Reading

Legro, Michelle. 2011. "Top Chef, Old Master: Leonardo Da Vinci in the Kitchen." *Lapham's Quarterly*, September 15, 2011.

Mishan, Ligaya. 2018. "These Artists Are Creating Work That's about, and Made from, Food." *The New York Times,* November 29, 2018.

Oppenheim, Odela. 2015. https://www.metmuseum.org/blogs/now-at-the-met/2015/food-and-feasts-in-middle-kingdom-egypt

Riley, Gillian. 2014. *Food in Art: From Prehistory to the Renaissance*

Sciacca, Christine. 2015. "Why Aren't People Eating in Medieval Depictions of Feasts?" The Iris: Behind the Scenes of the Getty. Blog Post, November 23, 2015. https://blogs.getty.edu/iris/why-arent-people-eating-in-medieval-depictions-of-feasts/

Tucker, Abigail. 2011. "Arcimboldo's Feast for the Eyes." *Smithsonian Magazine*, January 2011.

Art, Food in (Impressionism through Contemporary Art)

STARTERS

Food has been a central theme throughout art history. The twentieth and twenty-first centuries have seen artists and audiences alike questioning the boundaries of what art is, whereas many of their predecessors were more beholden to strict rules and hierarchies within art dictated to them by critics. In recent decades, art has been redefined to include less traditional mediums and forms, opening the door for performance artists, installation pieces, multimedia works, and cuisine itself to be considered fine art. Beginning around the Impressionist era and lasting through contemporary art, details once deemed overly common and "vulgar" like half-eaten plates of food are now commonly featured as primary subjects.

Contemporary food-themed artworks frequently evoke age-old metaphors for religious ideology, impermanence, spoilage, and fertility, and food still inspires classical styles of still lifes and portraits of everyday living. Artists in recent decades have also used food as a tool of counterculture to highlight stigmatized themes of sexuality, disease, sustainability, violence, and race and gender inequality. Modern culinary trends have taken a tip from contemporary art, invoking diners' senses of smell, taste, touch, and hearing in addition to the visual aesthetic of the food. Patrons of high-end restaurants might be served sculptural fronds of greens, geometric slabs of fish and wild rice, aromatic scents released from glass cloches, or brightly colored purees painted with brushes on crisp paper to delight their senses. These concepts were foreshadowed in Italian writer Filippo Tommaso Marinetti's *The Futurist Cookbook* (1932), "in which the recipes include instructions for diners to take bites while simultaneously stroking sandpaper and being sprayed with carnation perfume" (Mishan 2018). In this way, the modern age has become a formal intersection between the fine art world and the world of food.

ENTRÉE

From the mid-eighteenth century through the late nineteenth century, art trends swung from lush landscapes and passionate portraits of Romanticism (late 1700s–1850) to the far more focused and literal illustrations of common people and details of everyday life in the Realism period (1840s–1880s). Claude Monet, one of the most influential artists of the Impressionism movement (1860s–1880s), captured foods in a fascinating range of styles. His *Still Life: Quarter of Beef* (ca. 1864)—a blunt oil painting depicting a slab of raw beef and bulb of garlic—is barely recognizable as being made by the same artist as that of *The Galettes* (1882), depicting two pastries in bright colors and a painterly style of thick brush strokes. This style was very similar to Post-Impressionist (1885–1910) works by Vincent Van Gogh, whose dark work *The Potato Eaters* (1885) barely resembles the highly evocative, colorful, and thick brush strokes used in his later still lifes of bright lemons and apples.

In the twentieth and twenty-first centuries, many artists abandoned the practice of making statements about religion and virtues with food imagery, experimenting with the subject as a way to portray a wide spectrum of ideas and emotions. Modern art giant Pablo Picasso was fascinated with food, cooking, and cutlery, and he included these subjects in scores of his paintings, drawings, ceramics, and sculptures. Cafes held profound significance for him; he spent much of his time in Parisian cafes seeking familiar Catalan tastes of home, socializing, and working. In 2018, the Picasso Museum of Barcelona held an exhibit entitled Picasso's

Small Plates

Big Banana: A Sign of the Times

Andy Warhol, a former commercial artist in the 1950s advertising scene, explored concepts of mass production and making art for the masses as opposed to the elite throughout his career. In 1967, his artwork of a single banana graced the cover of the premier collaboration album for artists The Velvet Underground & Nico, for whom he served as a manager during his Exploding Plastic Inevitable multimedia tour. The banana—which peeled back to reveal a sticker on the cover of some albums—became an emblem for nascent music genres like art rock and punk, and it serves as a visual example of the countercultural "sex, drugs, and rock and roll" attitude embodied by much of the arts scene in the 1960s.

Andy Warhol's first solo exhibit featured 32 soup cans, mirroring the way Campbell's 32 available flavors of soup would have appeared on grocery store shelves at the time. Much like the soup itself, which the artist claimed to have eaten at lunch every day for 20 years, the paintings were made using a commercial method of printmaking and symbolized Warhol's view that art should be for the masses, not just the elite. (Laurence Agron/Dreamstime.com)

Kitchen that linked his artworks, photographs, and life history to the gastronomy world. Spanish chef Ferran Adria, the father of molecular gastronomy, provided opening remarks with his provocative question "What is food?" that cast doubt on the blurred line between cuisine and art.

One of the most famous artists of the Surrealist movement (1916–1950), Rene Magritte, chose food as a provocative metaphor in his self-portrait *Son of Man* (1946). The self-portrait shows a man in a bowler hat and jacket, whose face is hidden by a large green apple suspended in space. Apples were one of Magritte's most common motifs, and he used them to create tension between visible and invisible elements in his compositions. In 1962, Andy Warhol painted his now-iconic collection of 32 "Campbell's Soup Cans," which became some of the most iconic images within the Pop art genre (1950s–1960s), challenging critics to articulate the firm boundary between "art" and "reality." This served as a precursor to food becoming more celebrated as art itself in the twenty-first century.

Throughout the remainder of the 1960s and 1970s, food remained a highly popular medium for experimental artworks and art performances. True to his name, bookmaker Dieter Roth, whose surname is pronounced "rot," explored themes of decay and temporarily by mashing foods like chocolate, lard, and cheese into his poetry journals. He also created a self-portrait in the form of a bust covered in birdseed and chocolate "intended to be placed in a garden and pecked into oblivion" (Goldstein 2013). Similarly, sculptor Antony Gormley created a work called "Bed" (1980–1981) using 8,640 slices of bread dipped in paraffin wax to construct a mattress with his own sleeping form indented in the center (Gormley ate his own weight in bread to hollow out the negative spaces). The finished work and processes of creating it symbolized the Catholic practice of equating bread with Christ and represented themes of birth, death, and transformation (Manchester 2000).

The themes of virtue, religion, beauty, and decay in these works resembled artworks tracing back to medieval times, but they also indicated the artists' desires to thumb their noses at elite ideas and practices surrounding the fine arts. Author Kevin West writes, "Using food as an artistic medium opened new doors for the artist, not least because it can become an organic, visceral analogue for the body in ways that bronze or marble never could." He references examples like Joseph Beuys' 1963 sculpture *Chair with Fat*, in which a wedge of fat on a chair symbolizes human laziness, and Felix Gonzalez-Torres' 1991 *Untitled*, in which the artist paid homage to his partner who had died of AIDS by stacking 175 pounds of individually wrapped candies in the corner of a gallery. Those viewing the artwork were asked to each eat one candy to honor (and internalize) his partner's life (West 2017).

Contemporary art (1970s–) frequently uses food in works pertaining to feminism, class, and status. Judy Chicago's installation piece *The Dinner Table* (1974) is "a 48-foot-long triangular dinner table with place settings for 39 culturally notable women, some real and some mythical, from prehistory to the modern women's movement." The triangular shape serves as a way to make the place settings grow larger as the "scale" of the table increases, symbolizing women's increasingly more powerful roles in contemporary society (Butler 2017). Jana Sterbak's artwork "Vanitas: Flesh Dress for an Albino Anorectic"—fifty pounds of flank steaks sewn together in the form of a dress—suggested women's objectification in the male gaze, as well as concepts of biological decay. This imagery has resurfaced in numerous ways in modern popular culture, such as a dress made from raw beef that pop singer and provocateur Lady Gaga (Stefani Germanotta) wore in 2010 to the MTV Music Video Awards show.

Today, food is seen more frequently than ever as a medium and primary subject in artworks, and a source of art itself. Photographers and catering companies alike have fueled a trend of using food as clothing, such as *nyotaimori*, the practice of using nude models as human serving platters for sushi, typically seen at high-end parties. Others use unsettling performance art pieces, a fad largely carried over from the 1970s, to convey issues around sustainability and waste. One example is contemporary married artist duo "Honey and Bunny" (Sonja Stummerer and Martin Hablesreiter), who play out scenes like two diners wrapped like mummies in Saran Wrap who have to cut through countless layers of plastic on their table to access their meal.

DESSERT

That bread really tied the room together, man: Surrealist artists Pablo Picasso and Salvador Dali both used culinary themes in much of their art, even making various plates and cutlery over the course of their careers. In 1933, Picasso attended a show to see Dali's "Retrospective Bust of a Woman," a bust of a woman with corn cobs around her neck and a baguette balancing an ink stand on her head. The piece, which explores gender roles and visual consumption, was enjoyed by none more than Picasso's dog, who enthusiastically made a break for the baguette and ate it on the spot.

SUGGESTED PAIRINGS

See also: Art, Food in (Antiquity through the Renaissance); Imagery Found in Foods; Politics and Food; Radio and Podcasts, Food-Themed (1920s–1970s)

Entry best enjoyed while eating: A Magritte-themed meal designed by artist Elaine Tin Nyo and Chef Lynn Bound in 2013 for New York City's Museum of Modern Art (MOMA). The culinary artists paid homage to "A Young Girl Eating Bird" (1927) with a dark chocolate bird shell filled with rum-soaked raspberries; nodded to "Pink Bells, Tattered Skies" (1930) using rose-hued cheese puffs and a blue Prosecco and pineapple cocktail; and creatively reimagined "Elective Affinities" (1933) as pappardelle pasta served with arugula, grated asiago, and a prominently featured cracked soft-boiled egg.

Further Reading
Bottinelli, Sylvia, and Margherita D'ayala Valava, eds. 2017. *The Taste of Art*. Fayetteville: University of Arkansas Press.
Butler, Sharon. 2017. "A Brief History of Food as Art." *Smithsonian Magazine*, January 13, 2017.
Catalan News. 2018. "Food, Art, and New Gastronomy: A New Exhibit at the Picasso Museum." *Catalan News*, May 23, 2018.
Caws, Mary Ann, Charles Stuckey, and Wyatt Allgeier. 2017. "Art and Food." Interview, *Gagosian Quarterly*. Winter, 2017 issue.
Goldstein, Andrew. 2013. "MoMA Curator Sarah Suzuki on How Dieter Roth Invented the Artist's Book." *Artspace*, June 20, 2013. https://www.artspace.com/magazine/interviews_features/expert_eye/moma_curator_sarah_suzuki_dieter_roth_interview-51366
Manchester, Elizabeth. 2000. "Antony Gormley: Bed." Tate Museum, May 2000. https://www.tate.org.uk/art/artworks/gormley-bed-t06984
Mishan, Ligaya. 2018. "These Artists Are Creating Work That's about, and Made from, Food." *T: The New York Times Style Magazine*. November 29, 2018.

Stanska, Zuzanska. 2018. "The Story of Velvet Underground & Nico Andy Warhol." *Daily Art Magazine*, January 3, 2018.
West, Kevin. 2017. "Will Work with Food." *Surface*, December 8, 2017.

Asian American Cuisine
STARTERS

Asian foods have been part of the American landscape since the mid-nineteenth century, and today, many Asian cuisines rank among Americans' favorite foods. The terms "Asian cuisine" and "Asian American cuisine" have a multitude of definitions within the American lexicon, but flavors and dishes from these countries have become highly prized in contemporary U.S. food culture. For example, there are currently more than 40,000 Chinese restaurants across America, approximately three times more than there are McDonald's fast-food restaurants (CBS News 2016).

Flavors found in the southwest Asian countries of India, Pakistan, Burma, and Sri Lanka often include curries, naan (leavened flatbread), lamb, chicken, mutton, and goat, sauces with a tomato or yogurt base, chilies, ginger, curry powder, turmeric, cinnamon, garlic, hot spices, coconut, and the use of *ghee* (butter oil). Predominant religions (including Buddhism, Hinduism, Islam, and Sikhism) in these regions often prohibit the consumption of foods like beef and pork.

Northeastern Asian foods from China, Korea, and Japan tend to focus on sauces and oils, such as vinegar and soy sauce. Rice and noodles are staple foods and are often served stir-fried with meats and vegetables. Japanese diets often incorporate batter-fried foods called *tempura*, and *sushi* and *sashimi*, which pair raw fish with seaweed, rice, and vegetables. Chinese cuisines often incorporate soybean products like tofu, eggs, a vast array of meats, bean sprouts, dark leafy greens, snow peas, and seasonings like chiles, sesame seeds, garlic, ginger, and coriander. Korean recipes use many of the same seasonings and oils, as well as staples like rice, noodles, and tofu. Korean diets also frequently include fermented foods like *gochujang* (fermented bean paste) and *kimchi* (fermented, pickled cabbage, and/or other vegetables).

The Southeastern Asian countries of Vietnam, Cambodia, Thailand, and Malaysia often incorporate ingredients like coconut milk, noodles, garlic, ginger, citrus, cilantro, mint, and basil. Some common dishes from this area that have gained wide popularity in the United States include spring rolls, tropical fruits, curries, bean sprouts, fish sauces, *pho* (a noodle soup with stock, thin slices of meat, bean sprouts, and spices), *banh mi* (baguettes with pork, pickled vegetables, and chiles), and *pad thai* (a stir-fried noodle and vegetable dish).

ENTRÉE

Chinese food first came to America's shores in the 1850s as a result of immigration during California's Gold Rush. Many of the earliest immigrants were

Cantonese, and Cantonese cuisine remained the dominant style of Chinese food served in the United States for well over a century. However, anti-Chinese prejudice spread throughout the country in the mid- to late-nineteenth century, and in 1882, the Chinese Exclusion Act harshly restricted the number of Chinese immigrants allowed in the country, which further fanned the flames of anti-Chinese sentiment. In 1915, the act was modified to allow specific merchants to apply for visas, which ushered in a new wave of Chinese restaurant owners.

Despite strong Asian immigrant prejudice that still presided across the country, Chinese restaurants gained popularity all across the United States. By the 1930s, Chinese restaurants were generating upward of $154.2 million in New York City alone and surpassed Chinese laundries as the most likely place of employment for these immigrants (Lee 2015). Patrons who supported the Chinese restaurant industry prior to the end of World War II included African Americans, bohemians, and Jewish immigrants, many of whom found the inexpensive price point particularly appealing and related on many levels to the immigrants who ran the businesses (Chen 2017).

The booming restaurant trend proved to be more than a passing fad. After World War II, the number of Asian American immigrants soared, ushering in more Chinese and Japanese American restaurants. Popular Japanese fare included steak, sushi, and noodles, and common Chinese fare included chop suey (a food whose history and nationality are debated) and Mongolian beef (which is not thought to have originated in Mongolia). Many Chinese food dishes in the 1960s used ingredients like tomatoes, onions, and carrots, cloyingly sweet fruits like maraschino cherries, and highly sweetened sauces that reflected Americans' preferences instead of authentic Cantonese fare. Then, throughout the 1960s and 1970s, events like the Vietnam War (1955–1975) and continued immigration from Asian countries led to the early growth of Vietnamese and Thai restaurants in the United States. Over the following decades, a larger presence of Indian, Filipino, Korean, and Asian Pacific restaurants and cuisines emerged in the United States.

By the 1980s, Chinese food had become very popular, particularly in the form of takeout and restaurants that served *dim sum* (stuffed dumplings often featured in table side cart services). Overall, Chinese food had become one of the most popular "ethnic cuisines" and one of the most frequently consumed foods in the United States (The National Restaurant Association 1989). Today, the term "ethnic cuisine" is falling out of vogue. Around the mid-twentieth century, Americans referred to dishes from places like Asia and South or Central America as simply "foreign." By today's standards, terms like "ethnic cuisine" are considered by some to be inaccurate or negative. Globalization has helped normalize the practice of blending various international and domestic cuisines, and the term "ethnic" when describing food can imply a negative connotation regarding non-Anglo Americans' culinary contributions. The term "ethnic cuisine" has also been problematic regarding which cultural cuisines are deemed "ethnic." For example, it's more common for Indian food to receive this label, whereas French or Japanese food typically does not.

In the 1990s and 2000s, the P.F. Chang's and Panda Express franchises grew exponentially, helping to spread the Asian American cuisine craze even more. In

2016, Panda Express saw sales of just under $3 billion in the United States. As of 2017, P.F. Chang's had over 300 locations worldwide, with plans to bring its American spin on Chinese food to a new location in Shanghai (Restaurant Business 2017; Wohl 2018). The popularity of more traditional and authentic restaurants has been on the rise in recent decades as well. Americans' acceptance of and interest in more diverse foods has led to trending sales for foods like green tea and *matcha* (green-tea-leaf powder), Vietnamese pho, Taiwanese *boba* (also called bubble tea, made with tapioca pearls, milk, and flavored tea), ramen, Korean barbecue, Indian curries, and many more.

Asian American cuisine is common in many American kitchens as well. Many Americans own tools that originated in Asia like woks, cleavers, bamboo sushi rolling mats, rice cookers, and chopsticks or ingredients like basil, lemongrass, ginger, wasabi, sriracha (hot chili and garlic sauce), soy sauce, and fish sauce. Asian-themed instructional and reality cooking shows have also achieved notable popularity in the United States, such as the PBS network's *Yan Can Cook* and *Simply Ming* and the Food Network's *Iron Chef*, in addition to countless Asian cuisine segments and featured food on a myriad of other cooking shows.

While the growing cultural acceptance of these cuisines feels like a hopeful move away from the pervasive exclusion and bigotry that many Asian Americans have faced throughout history, there are still concerns about prevailing attitudes toward Asian American cuisine that indicate prejudice and ethnic imbalances in American culture. Krishnendu Ray, chair of nutrition and food studies at New York University, points out that Americans have historically viewed cuisines from places like China and India as less prestigious and valuable than cuisines from Europe or Japan. "(Chinese food is) the cooking of a billion people, over thousands of years of written records and connoisseurship," Ray said in a 2016 *Washington Post* interview, adding that Americans aren't typically willing to pay the same amount of money for Chinese or Indian food as they are for things like Japanese or French food.

A vast majority of the inexpensive Japanese restaurants in the United States are actually run by Chinese Americans. This is the result of Chinese immigrants' frustration that foods like sushi are typically valued at higher price points, whereas Chinese food entrées are typically expected to be very inexpensive. Ray noted that 70 percent of Indian restaurants in Manhattan are run by Pakistani and Bangladeshi restaurateurs as well (Ferdman 2016). Despite the fact that a diverse range of Asian cuisines are becoming more appreciated than ever in the United States, many Asian Americans in the food industry still feel subjected to discrimination and economic inequalities.

ACCOMPANIED BY

The oldest Chinese restaurant in the United States is located (surprisingly, to some) in Butte, Montana. The family-run Pekin Noodle Parlor was founded in 1911 by Hum Yow and Tam Kwong Yee. The pair sold the restaurant to Yow's great-nephew and Yee's great-grandson, Ding Kuen Tam "Danny Wong," in the early 1950s. Wong went on to share ownership of the restaurant with his son, Jerry

Tam, who was named a semifinalist in 2020 for a James Beard Foundation Award in the category of Outstanding Hospitality. Wong, who passed away in 2020, immigrated from China as a teenager and went on to become an iconic member of his community. Remembered by many as a charitable cook and cultural ambassador, Wong entertained a number of celebrities in the Pekin Noodle Parlor over the years, including stunt motorcyclist Evel Knievel. The two became close friends, and in an interesting twist of fate, the men passed away exactly thirteen years apart, down to the same day and nearly the same time.

In the mid-1960s and 1970s, Hiroaki "Rocky" Aoki, a notable trendsetting Asian American restaurateur, opened a Benihana restaurant that featured chefs who prepared Japanese fare on a grill in front of customers using theatrical flare and impressive knife skills to delight customers. Today, Benihana restaurants remain popular in mainstream American culture. In the 1990s, chefs Martin Yan and Ming Tsai became well-known names in the culinary industry as chefs, public television show cooking personalities, and cookbook authors. Tsai is a James Beard Foundation Award winner and Emmy-nominated television host, as is Yan, who has hosted more than 2,000 cooking shows in his career.

Other notable Asian American culinary leaders including Corey Lee, who served as the head chef of the French Laundry and received three Michelin stars for his San Francisco restaurant, Benu. Restaurateur and television personality David Chang founded New York City's trendy Momofuku Noodle Bar, among others. His food has been met with similar popularity as the dishes served by Roy Choi, whose Kogi BBQ food truck helped spark a nationwide food truck (and Asian Latin cuisine fusion) trend. Danny Bowien is the James Beard award-winning founder of Mission Chinese Food and Mission Burger Bar in San Francisco and is also the featured chef on the seventh season of PBS's *The Mind of a Chef* (2017).

The White House has also seen several visiting and full-time Asian American chefs in recent years. Cristeta Comerford is both the first female and first minority to have received the prestigious title of executive chef at the White House. First Lady Laura Bush hired her in for the role in 2005 after Comerford had worked as an assistant chef in the White House for a decade. Eddie Huang gained notoriety for his Taiwanese bun shop in Manhattan, his television appearances on Food Network and Viceland shows, and his 2013 book *Fresh off the Boat*, which was adapted into a primetime sitcom by ABC. *Fresh off the Boat* illustrated Huang's family's experience as immigrants in the United States and the relationship they held with both Taiwanese and American food. *New York Times* reporter Jennifer 8. Lee produced a documentary called *The Search for General Tso* (2014) that explores the origins of the General Tso dish and other Chinese American foods. Lee also authored a book called *The Fortune Cookie Chronicles* that illustrates the history of Chinese immigration via food trends in the United States.

Chef Jenny Dorsey explores her Chinese American identity through a dinner series called *Asian in America*, which offers six courses featuring Asian and Asian American cuisine and also incorporates spoken word and poetry readings. In 2013, Cornell University classmates Dave Rossi and Fung Lam opened a restaurant in Shanghai called Fortune Cookie with the intention of bringing "Americanized" Chinese food to China. American and Chinese patrons alike visited the restaurant to dine on foods deemed unusual in modern Shanghai like General Tso's Chicken, lo mein, and sweet and sour pork, some of which were cooked with imported American condiments such as Heinz ketchup and Skippy peanut butter.

DESSERT

Fortune cookies—those plastic-wrapped, crisp almond cookies folded around a slip of paper with a fortune (which might be more along the lines of an adage or vague general *advice* than predicting one's future)—were long thought to be invented by Chinese or Chinese-Americans. However, various evidence points to the cookie having originated in Japan. Japanese immigrant Suyeichi Okamura reportedly regularly baked them for customers and the Golden Gate Park's Japanese Tea Garden, and various works of Japanese literature and art from the 1800s allude to the treat as well.

The Japanese inspiration for the cookie was larger and more cracker-like than the ones consumed en masse today, and Japanese bakers are thought to have abandoned the practice of tucking the paper inside the treat for fear that people would choke. Today, the humble fortune cookie has become a pop culture phenomenon unto itself, ranging from fortune-cookie-shaped jewelry to gag fortune cookie toilet paper and entire websites devoted to fortune cookie quotations. Though the exact origins may remain somewhat mysterious, our cookies remind us that *"the only certainty is that nothing is certain . . .* [lucky numbers: 17, 23, 6, 25, 42]."

SUGGESTED PAIRINGS

See also: Bourdain, Anthony; Chang, David; *Iron Chef*; Latin American Cuisine; *Mind of a Chef, The*; Trends, Food.

Entry best enjoyed while eating: Crispy Thai spring rolls filled with glass noodles, pork, soy sauce, vegetables, and sweet chili sauce; sweet and sour pork with pineapple from the Pekin Noodle Parlor (served with a sauce that is brown instead of bright red because the restaurant didn't initially have access to the ketchup or red food coloring used elsewhere); an Alaska sushi roll filled with crab, salmon, cucumber, and avocado; and Ming Tsai's East-meets-West ginger cake served with cardamom cream.

Further Reading
Cast, Michael, and Tracy Thornton. 2020. "Butte Icon Danny Wont Leaves a Legacy of Kindness." *Montana Standard*, December 1, 2020.
CBS News. 2016. "Small Wonders of Design: The Chinese Take-Out Box." May 22, 2016, https://www.cbsnews.com/video/small-wonders-chinese-take-out-boxes/
Chandler, Adam. 2014. "Why American Jews Eat Chinese Food on Christmas." *The Atlantic*, December 23, 2014.
Chen, Yong. 2014. *Chop Suey, USA*. New York: Columbia University Press.
Chen, Yong. 2017. "The Rise of Chinese Food in the United States." Oxford Research Encyclopedia of American History, 2017.
Coe, Andrew. 2009. *Chop Suey: A Cultural History of Chinese Food in the United States*. New York: Oxford University Press.
Ferdman, Roberto A. 2016. "How Americans Pretend to Love 'Ethnic Food.'" *The Washington Post*, April 22, 2016.

Greenbaum, Hilary, and Dana Rubinstein. 2012. "The Chinese Takeout Container Is Uniquely American." *New York Times Magazine*, January 13, 2012.

Jung, John. 2009. *Sweet and Sour: Life in Chinese Family Restaurants*. Cypress, CA: Yin & Yang Press.

Le, C.N. 2018. "Asian Cuisine & Foods." Asian-Nation: The Landscape of Asian America. http://www.asian-nation.org/asian-food.shtml

Lee, Heather R. 2015. "The Untold Story of Chinese Restaurants in America." Scholars Strategy Network, May 20, 2015. https://scholars.org/brief/untold-story-chinese-restaurants-america

Lee, Jennifer 8. 2008. *The Fortune Cookie Chronicles*. New York: Hachette Book Group.

"Martin Yan." n.d. Public Broadcasting System. http://www.pbs.org/food/chefs/martin-yan/

"Ming Tsai." n.d. Public Broadcasting System. http://www.pbs.org/food/chefs/ming-tsai

The National Restaurant Association. 1989. *The Market for Ethnic Foods: A Consumer Attitude and Behavior Study*. Washington, DC: National Restaurant Association.

Pentilla, Annie. 2016. "Sharing History: Butte's Pekin Restaurant Featured in NYC Exhibit." *Montana Standard*, November 21, 2016.

Restaurant Business. 2017. "Top 500: Panda Express." https://www.restaurantbusinessonline.com/top-500-chains-2017/panda-express

Wohl, Jessica. 2018. "P.F. Chang's Wants to Be the American Bistro of Shanghai." AdAge, March 27, 2018. https://adage.com/article/cmo-strategy/p-f-chang-s-aims-american-bistro-shanghai/312865/

Aspen Food and Wine Classic

STARTERS

Hailed by the Aspen Chamber of Commerce's website as "one of the nation's most prestigious epicurean events," the Aspen Food and Wine Classic is one of *the* places to be every summer for celebrity chefs, serious players in the restaurant and wine industries, and foodies whose appetites for being "in the know" rival their appetites for cutting-edge culinary delights. Dubbed "the granddaddy" of food festivals by the *New York Time*s and the "crème de la crème of culinary festivals" by *Forbes*, the *Food & Wine* magazine-sponsored event is noted for being a prestigious affair within the culinary world. The Classic takes place in Aspen, Colorado, a city that sits 8,000 feet above sea level and is known for its world-class skiing and classical music offerings, high-end luxury real estate, shopping, and restaurants. The Classic takes place every year over the course of a weekend in June and comprises upward of 100 seminars, dinners, demonstrations, parties, and panel discussions. In 2015, more than 50 renowned sommeliers and 70 celebrity chefs took part in the Classic's presentations.

ENTRÉE

Colorado's ski industry has been attracting tourists for nearly a hundred years, but every spring, the state's high country experiences a small migration of tourists who pack up their skis and head home as the last of the season's powder melts. In

1982, a wine shop owner named Gary Plumley and his friends, Bob and Ruth Kevan of Chez Grand'mere (a restaurant in neighboring Snowmass), hatched a plan to introduce a small-scale wine festival to the area. Their hope was to attract fun-goers to the area in what the industry calls its "shoulder season."

Their idea came to fruition in the summer of 1983, in the form of the Aspen/Snowmass International Wine Classic, which drew 300 guests to sample wines from 50 various wine vendors. The event was small scale in nature—hosted on a tennis court and under a tent erected in a parking lot—but the wine tastings and accompanying desserts amid a gorgeous setting resulted in a resounding success. The festival became an annual tradition, and despite financial troubles, the burgeoning festival still managed to draw crowds each year.

In 1986, *Food & Wine* magazine became the official sponsor of the Classic. The magazine saw an opportunity to blend the event's growing popularity with Americans' budding interest in "celebrity chefs" and high-end wine experts. Tapping into the potential to make the wine-tasting event more of a cultural landmark, *Food & Wine* renamed the event the Aspen/Snowmass Food and Wine Classic, throwing open the door for a food-lover's frenzy in the process.

In 1987, more than 1,000 people flocked to the Food and Wine Classic to experience food and wine tastings and in the hopes of rubbing shoulders with chefs of famous restaurants during that era, including Wolfgang Puck, Gordon Naccarato, Jimmy Schmidt, and Michael Pieton. The festival's marketing and lineup expanded to appeal to business people in the food industry, bringing exhibitors into the fray and trade opportunities. Various cooking talks and demonstrations provided an educational component to the party atmosphere. By 1995, the Classic was well on its way to becoming *the* place for high-end food and wine celebrations. Attended by more than 5,000 people, the event drew returning appearances from food and wine masters such as Julia Child, Jacques Pépin, Marion Cunningham, Victor and Marcella Hazan, and Rory Callahan, just to name a scant few.

Over the years, America's growing interest in ethnic foods was mirrored in the selection of featured guests, cooking demonstrations, and tastings that were offered. The magazine began an awards ceremony for rising stars in the culinary world, piquing interests in which new faces seen at the Classic were on the brink of food celebrity. Over the next 20 years, events such as a 5K race, cooking challenges between celebrity chef contestants, elite invitation-only parties, and food and wine tastings were added to the lineup.

Aspen draws people from all over the world to experience its breathtaking ski runs and high-end hospitality culture, and its stunning mountain views provide the perfect backdrop for wine and food pairings. Today, the festival draws crowds as elite as the town's culture itself. In 2017, consumer passes to the festival cost upward of $2,000, and the tangle of journalists and film crews documenting the event was described by Food Network personality Gordon Elliott as "a media circus" in recent years ("Food & Wine Classic in Aspen: History" 2014). The festival's page on *Food & Wine*'s website describes a dress code as "casual attire," such as polo shirts and sundresses. Promotional photos for the event feature crowds of laughing food aficionados who are basking in the shower of champagne, corks flying, bottles raised in celebration.

ACCOMPANIED BY

The Aspen Food & Wine Classic has helped make chefs into cultural icons. Today, a number of cookbook writers, restaurateurs, and other culinary television personalities are recognized with the same celebrity status as television and film actors, but when the Classic began, there were far fewer celebrities in the food world.

Wolfgang Puck and Emeril Lagasse were among the first celebrity chefs to make appearances at the festival, as well as Julia Child, arguably the most famous "food celebrity" of that time. Other notable master chefs and wine experts throughout the 1980s and 1990s included Jimmy Schmidt; Michael Pieton; Gordon Naccarato; Jacques Pépin; Marion Cunningham; Marcella, Victor, and Giuliano Hazan; and Rory Callahan. In subsequent years, other notable food icons included Barbara Troop, Bobby Flay, Mario Batali, Susan Feniger, Joshua Wesson, Daniel Boulud, Alton Brown, Curtis Stone, Andrew Zimmern, Giada De Laurentiis, Ming Tsai, David Chang, Tom Colicchio, Gail Simmons, and many more. Non-food celebrities also began making notable appearances at the Classic, such as actresses Alexis Bledel and Allison Janney; Jordan's Queen Noor; television personalities such as Jen Scheft, Kathie Lee Gifford, Hoda Kotb, and Mario Lopez, and numerous others.

The popular cooking competition television show *Top Chef* integrated the Classic into numerous episodes, often bringing the final contestants to the event to prepare and serve dishes there in the final episodes of the season. The festival has also been the site of *Top Chef* cast reunions, featuring demonstrations by "cheftestant" favorites such as Stephanie Izard, Kristen Kish, Mei Lin, Richard Blais, Carla Hall, Rick Bayless, Marcus Samuelsson, and many others.

SUGGESTED PAIRINGS

See also: Batali, Mario; Child, Julia; Pépin, Jacques; Television, Food Channels on; *Top Chef*.

Entry best enjoyed while eating: A bite-sized platter of freshly caught pan-fried trout, pork belly sliders, freshly shucked oysters, seared watermelon cubes, charcuterie, sweet-tea-brined fried chicken, a chilled glass of Rosé, and an oft-refilled flute of champagne.

Further Reading

Bosch, Hayley. 2013. "Insider's Guide to Food and Wine Classic in Aspen." *Forbes,* June 12, 2013.

"Food & Wine Classic in Aspen." Aspen Chamber of Commerce, 2017. https://www.aspenchamber.org/event-calendar/food-wine-classic-aspen

"Food & Wine Classic in Aspen: History." *Food & Wine* magazine, 2014. http://www.foodandwine.com/microsites/classic/pdfs/fw_classic_history.pdf

Hayes, Kelly J. 2017. "Planting Roots: How Food & Wine Began." *Aspen Times Food & Wine* magazine, June 15, 2017.

Klara, Robert. 2015. "How the Food & Wine Classic Became America's Hottest Festival." *AdWeek,* June 7, 2015.

Reedy, Allyson. 2017. "6 Things We Took Away from Aspen Food & Wine 2017." *Denver Post, The Know: Dining News,* June 19, 2017.

Sumlin, Callie. 2017. "13 Things We Learned at the 2017 Food & Wine Classic in Aspen." *5280* magazine, June 21, 2017. http://www.5280.com/2017/06/13-things-learned-2017-aspen-food-wine-classic

Austin Food + Wine Festival

STARTERS

The Austin Food + Wine Festival is a two-day event that takes place annually in Austin, Texas. The festival started in 2012 as a collaboration among event-planning business C3 Presents, *Food & Wine* magazine, and several Texas-based restaurateurs. The event draws top chefs, winemakers, and sommeliers, who put on a weekend of food, beer, wine, and cocktail tastings, culinary demonstrations, and more. In recent years, tickets have been sold at $250 for a weekend pass, which grants access to the festival's tastings and professional demonstrations, and at $625 for full access, including additional evening events and hands-on demonstrations with grilling pros.

The festival replaced the Texas Hill Country Wine and Food Festival, self-proclaimed as one of the "premier epicurean celebrations in the Southern United States." The Texas Hill festival transitioned into what is now the Austin Food and Wine Alliance, a nonprofit run by volunteers that organizes grants, educational opportunities, and events to raise "awareness and innovation in the Central Texas culinary community" ("About the Alliance" 2017). Proceeds from the Austin Food + Wine Festival benefit the Alliance in an effort to promote (and encourage innovative practices in) locally made wine and artisanal foods and craft brewed beer, and spirits.

ENTRÉE

Austin, Texas, has gained notoriety for a number of its unique characteristics. Often referred to as "the live music capital of the world" before people also recall that it's the Texas *state* capital, both tourists and locals delight in Austin's culinary and music scene. Austin was listed by the Census Bureau as the fastest-growing U.S. city in 2015, helping to give credence to the saying that "everything is bigger in Texas."

As such, the funky urban hub provides an ideal background for the two-day celebration of smoked meats, scorched peppers, and much more, which—with the exception of the event's cancellation in 2016 due to heavy rain—has drawn large crowds each year. The Austin Food + Wine Festival presents a gourmet take on what are often classified as non-gourmet foods, such as tacos, biscuits, pulled pork sandwiches, and cold pints of beer. The event takes place in April, held at the Auditorium Shores and Fair Market park, right along the banks of the Colorado River. The park is just a stone throw's away from the Ann W. Richards Congress Avenue Bridge, a structure that is home to upward of 1.5 million Mexican free-tailed bats. Large crowds often gather in the evenings to watch the bats emerge at dusk to eat, before the onlookers dive into heaping plates of burgers, brisket, and ribs themselves.

Festivalgoers are treated to a busy schedule of tastings, demonstrations, presentations, and book signings from celebrated chefs, sommeliers, and vitners (winemakers). The mornings and early afternoons are akin to an upscale block party or brunch. Crowds mill through tasting pavilions to sample artisan-made foods and libations; sample dishes showcasing notable dishes from various Texas-based top chefs; pop into events like Vegan-themed beach tailgate parties; learn how to make margaritas, frittatas, and Bloody Marys; and hobnob with culinary icons. A roaring fire pit sets the stage for hot-off-the grill barbecued and smoked meats, which attendees gobble up as fast as the chefs serve them up. In a report published by *Eater*, vendors in 2015 were encouraged to prepare enough food for 1,000 samples per day, but many grand tasting chefs ran out of "bites" to pass out by 2:00 p.m. the first day.

Before the festival's main attractions begin, ticket holders can attend Feast Under the Stars: a five-course meal that consists of local cuisine, wines, and cocktails, hosted by award-winning Texas chefs. During the main festival, the pavilions host "Lone Star Nights" (formerly "Taste of Texas"), a recreation of a global night market, in which chefs turn out foreign twists on their local culinary creations. Another wildly popular attraction is the "Rock Your Taco" event, a competition challenging chefs to put original spins on classic taco fare, samples of which festival crowds get to enjoy. The definition of "taco" gets stretched a bit, but within the confines of creativity, meats, fruits, and peppers generally mingle atop some type of shell or corn base in the final creations.

There are no shortages of grilling demonstrations in this barbecue celebration event. One of the most notable ones is hosted by Chef Tim Love. Cited by *Austin Monthly* magazine as "the world's largest hands-on grilling demo," the lighthearted demonstration entails Love explaining his way through the process of prepping his grill before grilling up meats, fish, and sides from a stage in front of a huge audience. Each person in attendance gets a table space and personal grill to practice on, and both Love and the crowd swill wine and tequila and trade laughs while they practice the art of heating coals, skewering kebabs, and flipping tongs together.

ACCOMPANIED BY

The Founders

The festival's founding members include Tim Love, whose cuisine is described as urban Western style. He started his culinary career in Fort Worth, Texas, before expanding his restaurant empire across the country. In addition to appearances at numerous food and wine festivals, Love is also a television personality, a former Iron Chef champion, and host of CNBC's *Restaurant Startup*.

Tyson Cole, another founding member, is a renowned Texas-based sushi chef whose culinary roots started in college, when he took a job as a dishwasher at a local sushi restaurant to help pay for school. The dishwashing job led to a lifelong passion for the art of fine sushi. Cole's Austin-based restaurants Uchi and Uchiko have earned the chef a James Beard Foundation Award. The third founder, Jesse

Small Plates

"Rock Your Taco" Contenders

The Austin Food + Wine Festival's annual taco competition draws a wide variety of chefs, who each put their own spin on the classic taco fare to delight and surprise the crowd and judges alike. Although their creations often drift from what could arguably be defined as a "real taco," the results can be wildly creative and fun. In recent years, taco creations have included the following combinations:

- Pastrami taco with pickled cabbage, herbs, and mango labneh (a thick Middle-Eastern style of strained yogurt)—*Chef Alon Shaya*
- Sugar-smoked masu (sea trout) taco with Asian pears, pickled ramps (wild onions), and yuzo kosho, a Japanese paste made from chile, salt, and citrus zest—*Chef Tyson Cole*
- A fried duck-fat taco shell housing goat heart, chicken liver mousse, parsley salad, and lemon crema (similar to crème fraîche, but tangier and thinner in consistency)—*Chef David Bull*
- Za'atar (Middle-Eastern spice blend) tostada with cucumber salad, harissa oil (made from Tunisian chile), and hummus—*Chef Amanda Freitag*
- Bay scallop, avocado crème fraîche, preserved lemon, and crispy banana taco with cilantro—*Chef Matt Bolus*
- Crispy potato "taco" shell with chili-flavored carpaccio Wagyu beef, arugula, and a fermented lime vinaigrette dressing—*Chef Tim Love*
- Charred octopus taco with feta, diced olive salsa, tarator (tahini, ground walnuts, and garlic), and harissa—*Chef Hugh Acheson*
- Asian-inspired "taco" of minced duck meat and pineapple salsa, served atop crispy pita chips—*Chef Ming Tsai*
- Cumin picadillo (picadillo is a traditional Cuban beef stew) sourced from Texas beef producer 44 Farms, served with cucumber and poblano salsa, queso blanco, black beans, and avocado—*Chef Jason Dady*
- Chorizo shell, shrimp, pickled ramps, watermelon radishes, cilantro, garlic, yogurt, and salsa verde—*Chef Jimmy Bannos*

Dessert Tacos:

- Corn cake, hazelnuts, Texas-grown strawberries, strawberry flavored whipped cream, and freeze-dried kernels of corn—*Chef Christina Tosi*
- Tostada with cinnamon, passion fruit, pineapple, and lime—*Chef Jodi Elliott*

Herman, is an East Coast restaurateur who founded another James Beard Foundation nominated restaurant, La Condesa, in Austin, before collaborating on the festival to help celebrate the city's unique culinary strengths.

Local and National Top Chefs

A wide array of Texas-based chefs (and other grill master chefs beloved of Texans) have graced the festival's scene over the last five years. Local culinary masters have included Barley Swine and Odd Duck chef Bryce Gilmore; advanced sommelier Vilma Mazaite, Franklin Barbecue chef Aaron Franklin; *Top Chef* competitor and judge Hugh Acheson; and owner and pastry chef of Play Dough, Janina O'Leary, just to name a few.

In addition to the famed Texan chefs, vitners, and sommeliers, more national and internationally based talent appearances have included people such as Iron Chef Masaharu Morimoto, Travel Channel "Bizarre Foods" host Andrew Zimmern (who joined Elliot in 2015 for a lighthearted demo involving the pair donning luchador and Hulk Hogan outfits), international restaurateur Marcus Samuelsson, pastry chefs and judges on Fox's *MasterChef* and *MasterChef, Jr.* Graham Elliot and Christina Tosi, and James Beard Foundation winner and *Simply Ming* star Ming Tsai, among many others.

In keeping with the lighthearted atmosphere, the festival has enlisted the entertainment of Josh Beckerman, a blogger, mentalist, and comedian known as the "Foodie Magician" who roams the crowd performing tricks. One of Beckerman's most popular acts is to have a subject think about a restaurant, which he then manages to guess correctly.

SUGGESTED PAIRINGS

See also: Aspen Food and Wine Classic; Barbecue; *MasterChef*; South Beach Wine & Food Festival; *Top Chef*.

Entry best enjoyed while eating: A barbacoa, wild oryx, goat meat, brisket, carnitas, and shrimp taco sampler, served on piping hot corn tortillas and topped with an assortment of cilantro, beans, avocado, and salsas. Find room in your stomach afterward to enjoy a marshmallow that's been roasted over an open fire pit and a *fideua* inspired by Chef Shawn Cirkiel: a flaky biscuit topped with locally sourced strawberry preserves, pistachios, and whipped cream.

Further Reading

"About the Alliance." 2017. Austin Food & Wine Alliance. http://austinfoodwinealliance.org/about/

Carbon, Nicole. 2012. "The Inaugural Austin Food & Wine Festival." *Austin Woman Magazine*, March 2012.

"Chef Tim Love: About." 2017. http://cheftimlove.com

"Congress Avenue Bridge: A Little History." Bat Conservation International, 2017. http://www.batcon.org/our-work/regions/usa-canada/protect-mega-populations/cab-intro

Gordiner, Jeff. 2011. "Sleight of Hand with Your Dinner." *New York Times*, September 27, 2011.

McCarron, Meghan. 2015. "Hangover Observations from the 2015 Austin Food & Wine Festival." April 27, 2015. https://austin.eater.com/2015/4/27/8505749/hangover-observations-from-the-2015-austin-food-wine-festival#15

Odam, Matthew. 2017. "10 Tasty Takeaways from the 2017 Austin Food & Wine Festival." *Austin 360: Dining Blog*, May 1, 2017. http://dining.blog.austin360.com/2017/05/01/10-tasty-takeaways-from-the-2017-austin-food-wine-festival/

Rubin, Cynthia. 2016. "Austin Food + Wine Festival 2016 Hands-On Grilling with Tim Love." *Austin Monthly*, March 28, 2016. http://www.austinmonthly.com/Austin-Food-Wine-Festival-2016-Hands-on-Grilling-with-Tim-Love

Wood, Virginia B. 2014. "Seduced by Austin." *The Austin Chronicle*, April 25, 2014. https://www.austinchronicle.com/food/2014-04-25/seduced-by-austin/

Ayden Collard Festival

STARTERS

For more than 40 years, the small town of Ayden, North Carolina, has hosted the Ayden Collard Festival, an event that pays homage to collard greens. In recent years, the festival has attracted upward of 6,000 visitors—an impressive feat for a town of just over 5,000 people. Festivities include a parade through the town, the collard queen "Miss Ayden" beauty pageant, a collard greens eating competition, a collard cooking competition, live music, carnival rides, a talent show, and an art show.

ENTRÉE

Every September since 1976, the small, relatively quiet town of Ayden, North Carolina, has dusted off the carnival equipment, shone the tiaras, "one-two, one-two, check?" tested the sound equipment, and rolled out the red carpet for one seriously unsuspecting guest of honor: the humble collard green.

Collards are emblematic of both the South and soul food cooking. They are a staple in many Southern kitchens, prominently featured at the dinner table next to dishes like ham, black-eyed peas, cornbread, and okra. Packed with iron, vitamins A and C, beta carotene, calcium, and more, collards are a member of the cabbage family and are similar to kale, spinach, and mustard greens. They have an earthy, somewhat bitter flavor and are typically cooked until tender, served plain or

---

Small Plates

Collards in the News

Collards, along with other Southern-style and traditional soul food dishes, are beginning to see more popularity nationwide. Restaurants, farmers markets, and home kitchens have seen rising demand for a variety of greens, and the collard crop does well outside of the South due to its tolerance for frost. Its growing popularity has been met with controversy at times, such as a promotional Whole Foods tweet in January of 2016 that encouraged shoppers to try a "collard green and roasted peanut" recipe, which was criticized by some for cultural appropriation. CNN's Cara Reedy wrote about the chilly reception this tweet received from many readers, and stated that she was "tired of people 'discovering' things that have been a part of black culture for hundreds of years."

Making matters worse for the politics of the humble collard, high-end department store Neiman Marcus made a baffling decision to offer a luxury version of collard greens in 2016. Collards rounded out the store's offerings of other high-end holiday food "gifts," and Neiman Marcus promoted a cooked, then frozen version of the side dish for a staggering $66, plus $15 for shipping. A few weeks prior to Thanksgiving, NPR ran a story on the luxury collards in relation to a trending topic on Twitter, #GentrifiedGreens. Paired with Neiman Marcus's similar offerings, such as a complete Thanksgiving dinner priced at $495, an argument for a gentrified meal could certainly be made.

seasoned with onions or hot sauce. Former First Lady Michelle Obama describes them in her cookbook *American Grown* as "quick-growing, taking as little as sixty days from planting to harvest . . . to achieve the best taste, collards need to be cooked for longer periods than other greens."

The origin of collards is thought to go back as far as the prehistoric era, and the vegetable has been eaten for centuries. Collards are thought to have initially grown wild in Asia Minor, before a mild-tasting variant of collards was grown by ancient Romans in addition to kale. The Romans (and/or Celts) were likely to have introduced the produce to the British Isles as early as 400 BC.

African Americans are widely credited with popularizing collards in the United States, starting as far back as the slavery era. Enslaved people had to utilize careful cooking techniques to make the most of the meager rations of meat and produce they were given by their owners. Greens such as collards were often cooked using slow cooking processes that Africans used to soften the produce and distill the cooking liquid into a type of healthy gravy. The undesirable cuts of meat that enslaved people were offered, such as pig's feet, also had to be creatively cooked in order to make a meal that could feed a whole family.

Although Ayden touts itself as the "collard capital of the world," North Carolina's official state vegetable is the sweet potato. South Carolina nabbed the collard green as its own official state vegetable in 2011 at the urging of nine-year-old Mary Grace Wingard. (Whoever said children are averse to vegetables had obviously never met young Mary Grace, or the fourth graders in Wilson, North Carolina, who lobbied hard to make the sweet potato an official state emblem in the mid-1990s.)

ACCOMPANIED BY

Ayden itself has an interesting history. Originally called "Ottertown" in the early 1800s, the region was known for its association with Otter Dennis, a rumored criminal and ne'er-do-well who lived there. According to the Collard Festival website, more criminals convened in the area, earning the town the name "Aden" (. . . as in, *of sin*) in the 1870s. The spelling changed, "to help dignify the name," but the colorful history remained.

Much like Otter Dennis, the collard also became famous in the area for less-than beloved reasons. The vegetable provoked the ire of the woman who could be credited with the festival's origin story. According to a letter from Willis E. Manning Jr., the former president of the local chamber of commerce, resident Lois Theuring wrote to the *Ayden-NewsLeader* in 1975 to express what she did and didn't like about life in her small town, ending every paragraph with the sentiment "but I hate collards!"

Manning and a colleague were hopeful that introducing a festival to Ayden could draw tourists to the town. They asked Theuring to poll the town on what type of festival would be most popular, and jokingly suggested that she could head up a collard green festival. Readers suggested a number of ideas: a Cucumber Festival, the "Garden of Ayden-Almost Paradise," a Harvest Festival, "Progressive Ayden Day," and a September Fun Festival. Perhaps inspired by Theuring's opinionated stance, or perhaps just out of fondness for the humble green, residents ultimately chose to honor their town with a collard festival, and the rest is history.

The collard festival is closely tied with Bum's restaurant, a barbecue joint in town run by the Dennis family (who are relatives of the infamous Otter Dennis). In an oral history interview conducted by Southern Foodways Alliance, owner Latham "Bum" Dennis and his son, Larry Dennis, describe what makes their collards so notable. Latham says the family grows "what we call a cabbage collard. They're not as green as most collards you see. We like to think that it's the soil in Pitt County that makes our collards a little different" (Fertel 2011).

One notable collard eating champion is Mort Hurst, a North Carolinian professional eating competitor. As reported by the Raleigh *News and Observer* in 2015, Hurst was named Ayden's collard-eating champion in 1984, eating a total of 7.5 pounds of collards (topped with ketchup) in 30 minutes, before additionally wolfing down three pounds of shrimp. According to WNCT-TV, East Carolina's CBS affiliate, Hurst came out of pro-eating retirement in 2017 to see if he could beat the ghost of his prior self. Another competitor at the event said Hurst "sat down and told (them) to eat harder and faster" (Gibbs 2017). Competitor Larry Maxey offered optimism in the face of going collard to collard with a pro: "Keep eating, 'cause if the leader pukes, you're in the running again."

DESSERT

According to a 2016 article in North Carolina's *The Daily Reflector*, the 1976 Collard Festival featured the following amazing human talents:

- The second runner up of the eating contest ate three pounds of collards in under 20 minutes. (The *Reflector* does not report how he felt immediately afterwards).
- In total, contestants ate 35 pounds of collard greens during the competition.
- The winner of the collard cooking contest won the hearts of the judges using "pork and sidemeat to give her collards their award-winning flavor." (Side meat is salted pork that has been brined and fried; almost identical to bacon. It's fair to guess that if one wants to win the collard cooking contest, try serving your dish with pork, squared.)
- In addition to collard-themed events, a notably non-collard (perhaps *collered*?) competition was held for Ayden's finest pets. Among the categories were "Most Colorful Cat," "Most talented cat," "largest dog," and "most talented dog." The category of "most unusual animal" went to an alligator.

(*Daily Reflector* Archives, 2016)

SUGGESTED PAIRINGS

See also: California Avocado Festival; Deer River Wild Rice Festival; Eating Competitions; Trends, Food; What the Fluff?

Entry best enjoyed while eating: Collard greens, boiled and mixed with ham gravy, Bum's restaurant style. Serve alongside barbecue pork, black-eyed peas, cornbread, a hefty serving of warm banana pudding and a cold glass of sweet tea.

Further Reading

Daily Reflector Archives. 2016. "Back in the Day: Ayden Promotes Appetite for Collards." *Daily Reflector*, September 3, 2016.

Fertel, Rien T. 2011. Oral history interview, Latham "Bum" Dennis and Larry Dennis. Bum's Restaurant, Ayden, N.C. December 11, 2011. Southern Foodways Alliance. Project: Southern BBQ Train—North Carolina. http://www.southernfoodways.org/assets/NorthCarolinaBBQ_Bums.pdf

Gibbs, Emily. 2017. "Mort Hurst Named Winner of Ayden Collard Festival Eating Competition." WCNT-TV, September 9, 2017. http://wnct.com/2017/09/09/mort-hurst-named-winner-of-ayden-collard-festival-eating-competition/

"History of the Ayden Collard Festival." n.d. Ayden Collard Festival. www.aydencollardfestival.com/history

Kennedy, Merrit. 2016. "Neiman Marcus Is Selling Frozen Collard Greens for $66 Plus Shipping." *Must Reads*, November 2, 2016. http://www.npr.org/sections/thetwo-way/2016/11/02/500374724/neiman-marcus-is-selling-frozen-collard-greens-for-66-plus-shipping

Obama, Michelle. 2012. *American Grown: The Story of the White House Kitchen Garden and Gardens Across America.* New York: Crown Publishing Group.

Reedy, Cara. 2016. "Whole Foods Gets in Hot Water With Black Twitter." *CNN Money, U.S.,* January 14, 2016. http://money.cnn.com/2016/01/14/news/companies/whole-foods-collard-greens-black-twitter/

B

Baby Food

STARTERS

The concept of "baby food" dates back roughly to the mid-1800s, when newly emerging manufacturing and canning technologies seized on the opportunity to incorporate products geared toward infants, as well as the elderly and infirm. Since then, it has become a booming industry, defined as products geared toward infants and toddlers that are easy to eat, often in the form of cereals, purees, and beverages. According to a 2015 Nielsen report, 87 percent of baby food and 66 percent of formula sales worldwide come from North America and Europe, estimating that global sales would reach $35 billion that year. In fact, baby food sales reached over $53 billion that year, and a Zion Market Research estimated that those sales would head north of $76.4 billion by 2021 ("Baby Food Market Share, 2015–2021: Global Industry Trends Will Reach USD 76.48 Billion" 2017).

This booming business has flourished in light of dramatic cultural shifts in thinking about breastfeeding, formula, and "table foods" and how, when, and how much of each type parents should feed to babies during their first year of life. Strong competition between baby food companies and intense emotional reactions from parents regarding the process of feeding and nurturing their young have led to a dizzying number of baby food products on the market. Today's products are largely marketed to be vibrant, playful, and filled with "pure" ingredients, intent on fostering entertainment and satisfaction among their customers.

ENTRÉE

Up until the mid-nineteenth century, babies were typically exclusively breastfed for the majority of their first year, at which point they were likely to start receiving soft, ground, easy-to-eat foods made at home. A shift in American culture led women to start feeding cow's milk to their children to supplement, or replace, breastmilk—a trend that historians note caught on rapidly and dramatically. Infant mortality rates began to climb; as of 1897, nearly one in five babies in Chicago died before their first birthday, reportedly at the rate of 15 "hand fed" (non-breastfed) babies to every 1 breastfed baby. Many physicians and public health campaigns began advocating for longer periods of exclusive breastfeeding. They also advocated for safer and cleaner cow's milk production standards, such as pasteurization followed by storing the milk on ice. In a study of breastfeeding rates and public health in the twentieth and twenty-first centuries, researcher Jacqueline Wolf identified numerous reasons for these cultural shifts away from breastfeeding. Some women were struggling with breastfeeding and lactation issues, and others preferred feeding their babies cow's milk for logistical reasons and physical and emotional issues (Wolf 2003).

From the late 1800s through the 1920s, these significant cultural shifts in attitudes toward breastfeeding were additionally influenced by the rise of mass-produced consumer foods. Companies began selling infant formula, and fruits and vegetables were introduced into infant diets as well. Food historian Ann Bentley, author of the book *Inventing Baby Food*, explained in an interview with *The Atlantic* magazine that the success of early baby food companies, such as Gerber, was due to numerous factors. One was the fact that mothers were relieved to have more flexibility. This era was also marked by the cultural notions that breastfeeding was "primitive and uncivilized" compared to the more contemporary, chic, and "scientific" alternative of processed baby food. A third strong contributing factor was the role women typically filled as the family's primary caretakers of infants, as well as the family's primary consumer. Manufacturing companies took note of this and ran early baby food advertising campaigns targeted toward mothers. Nestle advertised a sweetened condensed milk mixture as "better than milk"—a powerful message to young mothers who were eager to give their children the best start.

Over the next nearly 100 years, public attitudes toward manufactured baby food continued to wax and wane. The numbers have been dramatic; 90 percent of American babies were given mass-produced baby food after World War II

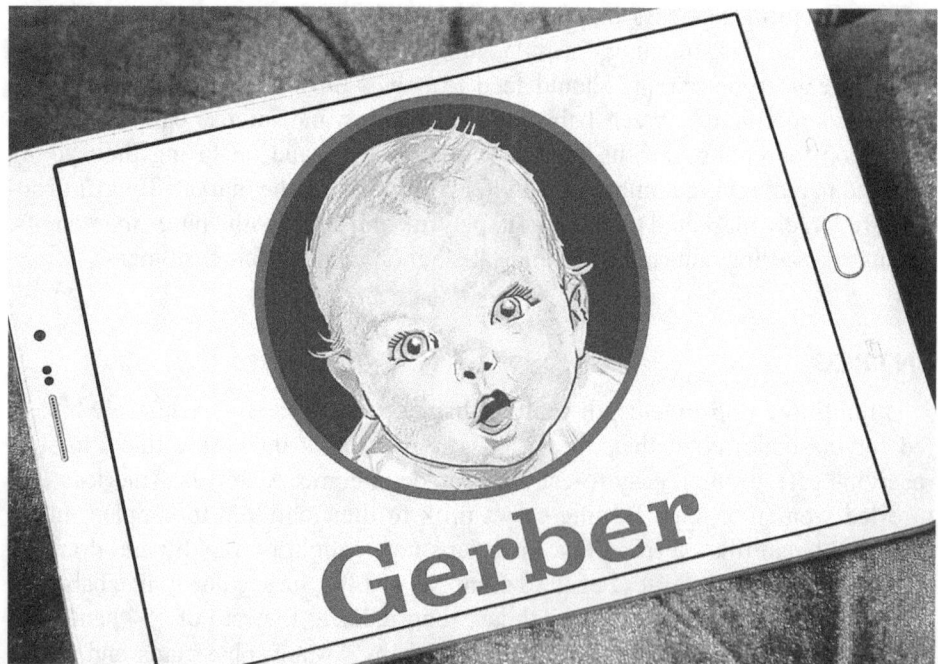

The Gerber Corporation began in 1927 when Daniel and Dorothy Gerber utilized Daniel's family's canning company to produce strained vegetable purees for their daughter, Sally, who was unable to eat solid foods. Today, Gerber is one of the largest and most easily recognized brands in the baby food industry worldwide. (Mohamed Ahmed Soliman/Dreamstime.com)

(Bentley 2014). Breastfeeding rates have been strongly influenced by a wide array of factors, including changes in medical research, the economy, women's careers outside of (and inside) the home, adoption, cultural stigmas, and advertising efforts for commercially made baby foods. In the 1970s and 1980s, Nestlé faced global boycotts due to the company's aggressive marketing techniques of infant formula in developing countries. Formula is still heavily promoted, but the companies that sell it are now under greater pressure to modify their marketing operations and advertise the benefits and current recommendations for breastfeeding. Discussions between parents and nutrition experts can still often be characterized as polarizing and contentious regarding breastfeeding, formula feeding, and exposure to purees and/or solid "table foods."

Mass-produced baby foods have come a long way from the sugar, fat, and preservative-laden varieties of the 1920s. Modern American consumers largely want baby foods with simple, organic, and aesthetically pleasing ingredients. Companies like Nestlé, which started in the late 1860s, and Gerber, which started in the 1920s (and merged with Nestlé in 2007), have had to continually adapt to dramatic shifts in national and international preferences, as well as research and regulations.

The Modern Baby Food Industry

Baby food today is often a far cry from the various wheat rusk, barley mixtures, and malted milk concoctions of the past. Many companies strive to meet modern consumer demands for reduced quantities of sugar, salt, preservatives, and other fillers in their baby's foods, with a focus on "whole" and organic foods. Families are turning back toward the age-old tradition of making baby food at home to supplement breastmilk and/or formula at age-appropriate times. Current medical guidelines suggest introducing various table foods around six months of age ("Infant Food and Feeding" 2017). Start-ups and mega corporations alike are competing with products that feed into the do-it-yourself (DIY) trend, creating packaging and advertisements that are eye-catching and brightly colored and tout minimal, all-natural ingredients. A 2014 *New York Times* article noted a rise in ingredients that are perceived as in vogue with modern parents, such as ancient grains, pomegranate, kale, squash, quinoa, as well as other "exotic" flavors. Baby food companies also have to stay abreast of relevant medical statistics, such as birth rates, which are prone to declining during events such as the 2008 recession.

Overall, the economy, birth rate, and consumer interest in the United States have led to strong baby food sales. In 2017, top-selling brands included Gerber, Plum Organics, Beechnut, Happy Baby, and Stonyfield, raking in between $34 and $235 million each ("Dollar Sales of the Leading Baby Food and Snack Brands 2017" 2017). In other fields, DIY trends have been healthy for sales of kitchen appliances like immersion blenders, vegetable steamers, and food-safe freezer containers. And in keeping with the national trend of merging food with entertainment, the market is filled with children's mealtime novelties, such as toddler utensils shaped like construction vehicles, silicone placemats in whimsical shapes, and animal-themed cups in every color of the rainbow. One of the most notable baby food products in recent years has been purees and strained foods packaged

> **Small Plates**
>
> **The Story behind the Gerber Baby**
>
> Few infant icons, if any, have garnered more familiarity than that of "The Gerber Baby." In 1928, the Gerber company launched a contest, seeking a baby portrait for their advertising campaigns. Among the fancy oil paintings and other submissions they received was a partially unfinished charcoal sketch of one Ann Turner Cook, the four-month-old neighbor of the sketch artist, Boston resident Dorothy Hope Smith. The committee was taken with the baby, whose bright sparkling eyes, wafting strands of baby-fine hair, and delighted expression channeled the image of a baby who looked happy, healthy, and nurtured—a perfect advertisement to help promote baby food.
>
> The artist didn't even have the chance to complete the sketch before Gerber began using it as their official trademark in 1931. For the next 40 years, speculation about the baby's identity spread, including rumors that it was a baby portrait of actor Humphrey Bogart, senator Bob Dole, or actresses Elizabeth Taylor, Jane Seymour, or Brooke Shields. (The candidates were humorously unlikely, considering the fact that when the image was created, Taylor and Shields hadn't been born yet, and Bogart was 29.) In November of 2017, the *real* Gerber baby celebrated her 91st birthday. Ann Taylor Cook, who helped inspire one of the most internationally recognized brands to date, used her Gerber fame in her adult years to help draw attention to her passion later in life: writing murder mysteries. Did Cook's taste for fame at a young age help inspire her to become a writer? It's hard to say, but the proof might be found in the Gerber pudding.

in pouches. Pouches, which also meet consumers' interest in convenience foods, were "by far the biggest driver of the increased dollar amount of baby food sales in the last few years," according to a *New York Times* interview with Hain Celestial children's division manager Robyn Mermelstein.

Additionally, various companies specializing in door-to-door deliveries have also started catering to baby food consumers. Targeted toward middle- to upper-class families, websites promote eye-catching, sophisticated-looking products. Photographs feature products like chic open glass jars filled with parfait-style layers of ingredients like pureed kabocha squash, flax, wheat germ oil, amaranth, and spirulina. Artfully drafted diagrams point out elements like Omega-3 and beta-carotene-packed ingredients in each meal. Celebrity appearances help boost sales for some companies, such as endorsements from actresses Molly Sims and Jennifer Garner. Baby food company Yummy Spoonfuls' website copy shares bite-sized company philosophies, denouncing sugar additives and promoting foods that are "vibrant," "nourishing," and intended to "make us better with every bite."

Unusual Uses for Baby Food

Leave it to Americans to use baby food for other reasons than . . . feeding babies. According to food historian Bentley, baby food companies cleverly sent recipe ideas that incorporated their products to numerous publications in the mid-twentieth century. In 2016, *Bon Appétit* writer Callie Wright wrote about her experience in adding Prosecco with baby food peaches, carrot food cake with pureed carrots, and an approximate recreation of White Castle burgers using jars of strained beef, inspired by a 1985 *Chicago Tribune* recipe. The results? "Baby food is probably best left to the babies," she says, aside from the tasty peach-infused bellini.

In the 2010s, tabloids splashed headlines about various actresses losing weight on the "baby food diet," consisting of 1 healthy typical meal and 14 servings of baby food purees per day. (The fad purportedly dates back to the 1980s but has seen resurgences in popular culture.) Cooking Light's Jamie Vespa criticized the diet in the magazine's nutrition column, citing baby food's inadequate amounts of healthy fats, protein, and fiber and calling it gimmicky and unsustainable (Holland 2017). In more cheery uses, tasting baby food has seen great popularity as a game at baby showers and as a challenge in viral videos on YouTube and other social media channels. Most notably, fans of baby food have flocked to the National Baby Food Festival in Freemont, Michigan, since 1990. The celebration lasts five days, and includes events such as a bib decorating contest, baby food eating competition, a baby crawling contest, and bubble gum blowing competitions (Bissell 2017).

DESSERT

The National Baby Food Festival is held in Freemont, Michigan, a city dubbed the Baby Food Capital of the World (and, not coincidentally, is home to the Gerber Company). Upward of 50,000 people attend the event each year, according to the festival's website. Lifestyle publication *Booth Features* described the adult baby food-eating contest as a humorously "sloppy affair," requiring blindfolded subjects to try feeding baby food to bib-sporting partners as quickly as possible in the allotted time.

SUGGESTED PAIRINGS

See also: Celebrities and Food; Eating Competitions; Trends, Food; Unusual Foods.

Entry best enjoyed while eating: Homemade macaroni and cheese with diced carrots, green peas, and pureed butternut squash hidden in the cheese sauce. Serve with a side dish of organic strawberry applesauce and a cold glass of chocolate skim milk (preferable served in a cup shaped like a monkey, presentation optional).

Further Reading

"About Us." 2018. https://yummyspoonfuls.com/about/

"Baby Food Market Share, 2015–2021: Global Industry Trends Will Reach USD 76.48 Billion." Nasdaq Globe Newswire, October 12, 2017. https://globenewswire.com/news-release/2017/10/12/1144986/0/en/Baby-Food-Market-Share-2015-2021-Global-Industry-Trends-Will-Reach-USD-76-48-Billion.html

Becky, Julie. 2014. "How Canned Baby Food Became King." *The Atlantic*, November 24, 2014.

Bentley, Amy. 2014. *Inventing Baby Food: Taste, Health, and the Industrialization of the American Diet*. California Studies in Food and Culture, Book 51. Oakland: University of California Press.

Bissell, Joel. 2017. "Unique Michigan Festival Focuses on Babies and the Food They Eat." *Muskegon News*, July 23, 2017.

"Dollar Sales of the Leading Baby Food and Snack Brands 2017." Statista, 2017. https://www.statista.com/statistics/186146/top-baby-food-and-snack-brands-in-the-us/

Holland, Kimberly. 2017. "Why Adults Shouldn't Eat Baby Food." *Cooking Light*, February 7, 2017.

"Infant Food and Feeding." American Academy of Pediatrics, 2017. https://www.aap.org/en-us/advocacy-and-policy/aap-health-initiatives/HALF-Implementation-Guide/Age-Specific-Content/pages/infant-food-and-feeding.aspx

Krasny, Jill. 2012. "Every Parent Should Know the Scandalous History of Infant Formula." Business Insider, June 25, 2012.

Muse, Katie. 2017. "Original Gerber Baby, Ann Turner Cook, Turns 91." *Fox 9 News*, November 21, 2017.

Olver, Lynne, ed. 2015. "Food Timelines FAQs: Baby Food." http://www.foodtimeline.org/foodbaby.html

Strom, Stephanie. 2014. "As Parents Make Their Own Baby Food, Industry Tries to Adapt." *New York Times,* April 25, 2014.

2017 National Baby Food Festival. 2018. http://babyfoodfestival.com/

Veltman, Dawn A. 2011. "National Baby Food Festival Events Include Baby Food Eating Contest, Cook-Off, Bed Race, and More." *Booth Features*. July 17, 2011. http://www.mlive.com/entertainment/muskegon/index.ssf/2011/07/national_baby_food_festival_ev.html

"Who Is the Gerber Baby?" 2018. https://www.gerber.com/why-gerber/meet-the-gerber-baby

Wolf, Jacqueline H. 2003. "Low Breastfeeding Rates and Public Health in the United States." *American Journal of Public Health* 93, no. 12 (December): 2000–2010.

Wright, Callie. 2016. "Oh, the Things You Can Cook with . . . Baby Food?" *Bon Appétit*, July 12, 2016. https://www.bonappetit.com/entertaining-style/trends-news/article/cooking-with-baby-food

Bar Rescue

STARTERS

Bar Rescue is a reality television show that premiered in July of 2011 on the cable network SpikeTV and has run for five seasons, generating 144 episodes. In 2018, SpikeTV was rebranded as the Paramount network, which kept *Bar Rescue* in its lineup. The program's host and executive producer is Jon Taffer, owner and chairman of Taffer Dynamics, a consulting and development advising firm.

Bar Rescue blends the human drama of reality television with a business makeover component. In each episode, Taffer meets with bar owners whose businesses are failing due to issues such as poor financial management, catastrophic public relations issues, marketing missteps, mismanagement, and personnel problems. After monitoring the businesses and discussing the financial and management issues with the owners, Taffer and his crew make changes to the bar and, if necessary, its management. These changes are part of an effort to turn profits around and educate the owners about their previous business pitfalls. The show has been met with continuous popularity; according to Nielsen ratings, the first season had an average of 1 million viewers per episode, increasing to 1.8 million viewers per episode by the third season.

ENTRÉE

In the media, Jon Taffer is often referred to as "the Gordon Ramsay of the bar industry." *Bar Rescue* is largely known for Taffer's rough, loud approach with clients that entails shouting, using profanity, and sometimes escalating conflicts into physical confrontations. The clients are bar owners who have appealed to *Bar Rescue* to help pull their business out of dire financial straits. *Bar Rescue* episodes begin with an overview of the episode's featured bar and its purveyors, an overview of the city where the bar is located, stats about how many other bars are in the area per square mile, and an overview of the bar's setup and offerings. The show's crew sets up hidden cameras around the bar, and Taffer enlists additional cast members such as customers, food critics, and mixologists to weigh in on their impression of the drinks, food, and staff. Taffer and his crew watch the scenes unfold from video monitors in an SUV while discussing issues they see with the quality of the service and the bar's operations.

When the "reconnaissance" phase is done, Taffer often bursts on to the scene and confronts the bar's managers over infractions he's witnessed, ranging from raw chicken that's being handled unhygienically to illicit gambling operations that are taking place. After he closes the bar until further notice, he says the show's signature phrase: "shut it down!" Over the next four days, the bar's staff and the show's crew work together to revamp the establishment, put staff and management through training, assess the demographics of bar-goers in the area to determine new marketing approaches, and make changes to the bar's libation and food menu and pricing structure. Taffer's team puts the bar through a "stress test," bringing a large group of patrons in to test the staff's skills and the bar's new offerings in a fast-paced setting.

Bar Rescue's website describes the show as follows: "bad drinks, wild staffs, and wasted owners conspire against (Taffer) and his experts as they give failing businesses one last shot at success." The host's professional website describes his role as "revamping and rescuing bars on the brink" and touts the fact that he and his experts "understand the science behind a bar's success and spare no details in their rescues, tackling everything from the perfect pour to the height of the bar stools" (Taffer 2018). As of 2018, the website listed 147 bars that have been on the show—95 of which are still open, 48 of which are closed, and 4 of which have sold or moved.

Topical Appeal

When the *Bar Rescue* aired in 2011, it joined the ranks of several similar shows that had gained popularity shortly before, during, and after the Great Recession in the United States (2007–2009). Two examples include Gordon Ramsay's *Kitchen Nightmares* (2007) on Fox network, which followed chef Ramsay as he delivered "tough love" to failing restaurants, and *Tabatha Takes Over* (2008) on the Bravo network, in which stylist expert Tabatha Coffey took on disastrous hair salon businesses with a flinty approach.

In the years following, a number of shows followed suit that focused on industry professionals giving transformative makeovers to properties, businesses, and people alike. SpikeTV produced numerous (shorter-lived) shows that blended reality show drama with recession-themed business angles. *Bar Rescue*'s longer-lasting appeal may have likely been due to its focus on salvaging struggling mom and pop businesses, a sector of the economy for which many American viewers wanted to see more happy endings.

According to the Bureau of Labor Statistics, food service and drinking establishments saw 10 consecutive months of significant job losses during the Great Recession (2007–2009). This was a devastating blow, considering the fact that between 1990 and 2007, that sector had only seen a single, stint of job losses over the course of three consecutive months. The sector lost 18,000 jobs between September and December of 2008, and the recession saw a decrease of 28 percent of jobs in the leisure and hospitality industry between 2007 and 2009 (Davila 2011). The ripple effects from these severe changes in the industry lasted for years afterward, making the struggles of *Bar Rescue's* bar owners relatable to many viewers on a personal level.

During *Bar Rescue*'s first season, the show received 150 applications from bar owners who hoped that Taffer would help turn their business around. Of those applications, only 10 bars received revamps (Gelt 2011). Over the course of the show's run, the question of whether being featured on the show truly helps the bars it features has been a matter of debate. Taffer and his team do make some significant changes, such as changing the establishments' names, menu items, sanitation measures, management practices, and other critical operations that have helped many bars stay open and turn a profit. However, critics have pointed to the breakneck pace that Taffer and his crew take to overhaul the business within five days. The show has received scorn for issues such as implementing dramatic changes without securing the necessary permissions and permits or for casting the bar owners in a light that some proprietors have taken offense to (Gelt 2011).

Controversies

Reality television is typically known for staging, encouraging, "loosely scripting," and otherwise egging-on drama, but some of what the show has framed as dramatic entertainment has landed the team in trouble. In 2014, one of the prior subjects of the show filed a lawsuit against Taffer and his wife Nicole, and *Bar Rescue* production company Bongo LLC. Paul Wilkes, a physician and owner of a Las Vegas bar named the Sand Dollar, pressed charges for assault, battery, and intentional infliction of emotional distress, among other offenses. Wilkes and his lawyers claimed that he was pressured by *Bar Rescue*'s host and story writers to act outrageous, lewd, inappropriate, and misogynistic on camera, specifically toward Nicole . The lawsuit alleges that Taffer responded by smashing a plastic cup filled with alcohol in Wilkes' face, punching him, and tearing his shirt.

Another *Bar Rescue* controversy that caught media attention was an episode filmed at the Pit and Barrel bar—formerly named "BoondoxXx BBq" before Taffer and his crew renamed it—in Nashville, Tennessee. The show portrayed the bar's owner, Chris Ferrell, as being quick to lose his temper at his staff. The end of the show implied that Ferrell had fewer anger management issues after the show and was less prone to angry outbursts at his bar. However, a day before the episode was set to air, news outlets reported that Ferrell had allegedly shot and killed a friend of his, country singer Wayne Mills, after hours in the bar while the two men were engaged in a dispute. SpikeTV pulled the episode from its regularly scheduled spot in light of the incident, but failed to cancel a late-night repeat showing. Some viewers were upset, claiming that in light of allegations against Ferrell, the episode had inaccurately painted him as a man whose tendency to lash out was corrected with the help of the show. Ferrell went on to receive a 20-year sentence for second-degree murder.

In a far cry from lawsuits and murderous bar fights, Taffer also caught the ire of bar industry professionals after a seemingly innocuous interview he did in 2016 with the *Huffington Post* about proper etiquette in bar settings and his favorite drinks. Thousands of professional bartenders took to social media and the press, decrying an error he made in the interview as saying that tequila is made from mescaline, a psychotropic, hallucinogen-causing drug (very different from what tequila is—*mezcal*, a type of agave-based spirit). Many in the industry also took umbrage with other statements Taffer made in the interview, calling into question the claim in *Bar Rescue*'s introduction that "no one knows more about bar science than Jon Taffer." His interview also received negative press for statements such as listing the "Old Fashioned" as the most "underrated cocktail" (the same year, *Drinks International magazine* listed the cocktail as the number-one best-selling cocktail in "100 of the world's best bars").

ACCOMPANIED BY

Jon Taffer

As a young man, Taffer studied political science and cultural anthropology at the University of Denver and had political aspirations of running for Congress. As a student, he worked part-time as a bartender. He left school after two years and moved to Los Angeles, where he played drums and worked for a well-known bar in West Hollywood called the Troubadour (White 2015). Taffer became the manager of the Troubadour, which launched him into a career that entailed numerous management positions in the hospitality industry. In 1983, he and a cocreator opened a Glenn Mills, Pennsylvania nightclub called Pulsations Nightclub.

The television host is the author of a number of books about management and business operation advice and teaches online courses, offering his "success formula" for improving businesses. Early in his career, he lost $600,000 in a failed business venture trying to launch a startup, an experience he told *Business Insider* he didn't regret due to the lessons he learned. Taffer told the *New York Times* in 2016 that earlier in his career, he owned a bar that ran a competition called *Thanks for the Mammaries*, in which one winning woman received a breast augmentation. In return, she had to provide bras to the bar, which they bronzed and hung in the men's room. Citing how politics and cultural sensitivities have changed since that time (the early 1980s), Taffer said "I mean, I did midget-tossing in Long Beach . . .

this was a different time. I would *never* suggest doing anything like that today" (Cox 2016).

DESSERT

You don't see that every day: In an episode titled "Yo Ho-Ho and a Bottle of Dumb," Taffer tries overhauling a pirate-themed bar by changing the theme and name of the establishment to "Corporate." Summarizing the episode, Thrillist writer Andy Kryza joked that "tears are shed by pirates using weird fake English accents." After the show filmed, the bar's staff members revolted against their new branding, burning the Corporate sign in effigy. Kryza notes that they once again converted the space into a pirate-themed bar . . . which promptly went under, this time permanently (2016).

SUGGESTED PAIRINGS

See also: Craft Brewing and Microbreweries; Documentary Films, Food and Beverages in; Ramsay, Gordon.

Entry best enjoyed while eating: A basket of piping hot buffalo chicken wings served with bleu cheese dressing, celery, and carrot sticks (don't be tempted to snack on the bowls of mixed nuts available on the bar beforehand, which Taffer refers to as—let's just say, *unhygienic*). Enjoy alongside a Bloody Mary served with lime, bacon, horseradish, and a bacon-salt rim.

Further Reading

Bar Rescue Updates. 2018. http://www.barrescueupdates.com/p/all-bar-rescue-updates.html

Cox, Ana Marie. 2016. "Jon Taffer Sees Shakespeare in Reality TV." *New York Times*, February 17, 2016.

Davila, Eliot. 2011. "The 2007–09 Recession: Leisure and Hospitality." Bureau of Labor Statistics, Monthly Labor Review, April, 2011. https://www.bls.gov/opub/mlr/2011/04/art9full.pdf

DeJesus, Erin. 2013. "Spike TV Apologizes for Bar Rescue Episode Aired the Day Owner Allegedly Shot Patron." *Eater*, November 25, 2013. https://www.eater.com/2013/11/25/6323683/spike-tv-apologizes-for-bar-rescue-episode-aired-the-day-owner

Feloni, Richard. 2015. "'Bar Rescue' Host Jon Fatter Explains the Valuable Lesson He Learned from Losing $600,000 Early in His Career." *Business Insider*, April 30, 2015.

Gelt, Jessica. 2011. "Jon Taffer Bails Out Joints on 'Bar Rescue.'" *L.A. Times*, August 30, 2011.

Internet Movie Database. n.d. "Bar Rescue." http://www.imdb.com/title/tt1863526/?ref_=ttep_ep_tt

Kryza, Andy. 2016. "The Worst 'Bar Rescue' Makeovers Ever." Thrillist, December 30, 2016.

O'Neil, Luke. 2016. "Why the Bartending World Is Pissed at Jon Taffer of Bar Rescue." *Vice*, March 23, 2016. https://munchies.vice.com/en_us/article/xympd4/why-the-bartending-world-is-pissed-at-jon-taffer-of-bar-rescue

Piscione, Gabriel. 2016. "Why You Should Never Take Shots with the Bartender, Plus Other Drinking Tips from Jon Taffer." *Huffington Post*, March 29, 2016.

Smith, Hamish. 2016. "The World's 50 Best Selling Classic Cocktails 2016." *Drinks International*, January 28, 2016. http://drinksint.com/news/fullstory.php/aid/5869/The_World_s_50_Best_Selling_Classic_Cocktails_2016.html

Taffer, Jon. 2018. "Jon Taffer: Bar Rescue." jontaffer.com/bar-rescue/

White, Ronald D. 2015. "Consultant Raises the Bar on 'Reaction Management.'" *LA Times*, June 20, 2015.

Barbecue

STARTERS

Barbecue is a cornerstone of American cuisine and culture. Its definition and the relative superiority of various regional styles is hotly debated across the country. However, it is generally accepted that barbecue is defined as both a specific type of food and for describing social gatherings in which grilled food is made and enjoyed. Barbecue is largely defined as meat that has been cooked over indirect heat for a long period of time. Traditionally using a wood fire, this "low and slow" method smokes the meat, creating a rich flavor and tender texture. Purists loyal to various regional specialties will argue that the meat used must be pork, beef, sausage, poultry, and/or mutton (sheep), but a wide array of proteins are used with various sauces and/or dry rubs (herbs and spices) to create mouthwatering dishes.

Barbecue's history is complex and deeply entwined with American history itself. Traced back to Native American origins that were adopted by European explorers, barbecue has played a significant social role in American society since before the country's founding. The earliest form of barbecue was defined broadly as "smoked meat . . . cooked outside, intended for large groups" (Wei 2015). Its popularity waned toward the end of the twentieth century, as electric and gas was used for heat and bottled sauce took the place of that made from scratch. However, over the last two decades, barbecue's popularity and pop culture presence has surged. Today, many are drawn to the craft of barbecue as a time-honored labor of love and source of pride. Each year, barbecue is the focus of festivals all across the nation, as well as cook-offs, high-stakes competitions, reality shows, books, songs, and even a number of tattoos. Entire websites are devoted to barbecue, featuring everything from how to win competitions to more unusual angles, such as the BBQ Jew (whose motto is "What happens when the 'chosen people' choose pork") Countless articles and features are written and filmed on the subject, and entire columns and journalists are devoted to the subject. Despite the vast array of interpretations and divisive controversies within the topic, barbecue (both as a noun and a verb) is widely considered to be a unifying element of American identity.

ENTRÉE

In 2010, journalist Jon Fasman wrote a primer for American barbecue in an article for *The Economist*. "It IS a noun, not a verb," his lede began. Preempting

Celebrations featuring barbecue trace back throughout American history. Here, a man prepares barbecued meat to serve to festival goers at the 1939 Gonzales County Fair in Gonzales, Texas. (Library of Congress)

angry feedback, he added, "American barbecue falls into four broad geographic categories—and understand, letter-to-the-editor writers, that this is a crude sketch, not holy writ." Those four broad categories of barbecue in the United States include Memphis, Kansas City, Texas, and North Carolina, each of which have distinct styles. Popular international varieties include Korean *gogigui* barbecue, Argentinian *asado*, Indian *tandoor*, and many others.

Despite the wealth of flavors and styles around the world, some Americans dismiss international fusions seen in many modern barbecue styles, deeming the variations "inauthentic." However, even traditional American barbecue dishes represent a diverse array of cultural and national influences. For example, the Memphis dry rub is infused with oregano and thyme, thanks to its inventor, Greek-American restaurateur Charlie Vergos, and in areas of Texas, traditional barbecue styles are infused with Mexican flavors (Solares; Carman 2016). Celebrity chef Rick Bayless, whose culinary start was at his parents' barbecue restaurant, believes that all cuisines need to evolve. "The BBQ world is just like the mole world in Mexico—it can change by town, and it doesn't mean any one is worse than the other," he told First We Feast (Bolois 2015).

Today, the media is occasionally criticized for not featuring women and people of color as leaders in the barbecue field often, often only featuring the "pop" in mom and pop restaurants. African Americans played a significant role in barbecue's history. According to historian Robert Moss, barbecues were significant on plantations as celebrations and functional gatherings. African American enslaved people often served as the chefs and pitmasters, refining the technique of smoking the meat over time. Although their motives were not necessarily benevolent, slave owners sometimes allowed slaves to have their own barbecues, which were rare recreational opportunities. In the years following the Civil War and Emancipation, whites drifted away from Fourth of July celebrations, but African Americans continued to celebrate the event with barbecue celebrations.

Today, barbecues are very different from the gatherings that could draw hundreds of thousands in nineteenth-century America, but their community focus prevails. The nation's appetite for the topic spans countless festivals, such as the Jack Daniels World Championship Invitational, American Royal World Series, and International Bar-B-Q Festival, which draw tens of thousands of spectators and BBQ teams. Reality television shows and docuseries like TLC's *BBQ Pitmasters* (2009), Destination America's *BBQ Pit Wars* (2014), Food Network's *Eat, Sleep, BBQ* (2017), and PBS's *Barbecue University* (2003) air nationwide. In 2017, the documentary *Barbecue* explored international themes of barbecue cultures.

This photograph, taken in the 1930s as part of the Federal Writers' Project, shows a counter of bread serving as boundary segregating white and Black barbecue attendees at an annual celebration held on the Alabama plantation of F. M. Gay. (Library of Congress)

ACCOMPANIED BY

Aaron Franklin

Arguably the most famous pitmaster in the world, Aaron Franklin (1977–) is often credited with craft barbecue's immense popularity in recent years. Despite having worked in his parents' barbecue restaurant as a youth, Franklin had to turn to the early search engine Ask Jeeves in his early twenties to learn how to smoke brisket (Boskovitch 2018). In 2009, Franklin and his wife Stacy opened a roadside barbecue trailer, and in 2011, they opened Franklin Barbecue in Austin, Texas. Six days a week, people line up to feast on Franklin's brisket, ribs, pulled pork, sausage, turkey, barbecue sides, and pies.

The restaurant's line is legendary. It can be three to five hours long and has included celebrities such as Jimmy Kimmel and Anthony Bourdain, who reviewed it as "the finest brisket I've ever had" (Furlong 2012). Rapper Kanye West once tried cutting the line, but was turned back by the general manager. In 2014, President Obama used his executive power to be the first person to cut the line, starting an uproar on Twitter. In 2015, Franklin won a James Beard Award for the Best Chef, Southwest, the first time a pitmaster and barbecue had ever been so highly honored.

DESSERT

- **New York *City*?** Although barbecue is most associated with the "barbecue belt" throughout the South, New York City is making a (controversial, of course!) name for itself on the BBQ scene.
- **McBaby back ribs:** From the 1930s through the 1950s, barbecue evolved into the first fast food. It was the original fare on the McDonald's menu.
- **A month of "mmm":** In the United States, the month of May is designated as "National Barbecue Month."
- **Hallowed halls:** In 2012, *Washington Post* "Smoke Signals" columnist Jim Shahin proposed a Barbecue Museum in the four "barbecue capitals and a permanent exhibit in the Smithsonian National Museum of American History.
- **Do as we don't eat:** Kentucky is best known for its mutton barbecue, although only 10 percent of the state's bbq joints regularly serve it (Carman 2016).

SUGGESTED PAIRINGS

See also: Ayden Collard Festival; Bayless, Rick; *Chef's Table*.

Entry best enjoyed while eating: A little taste of the BBQ from each major region. A Memphis pulled-pork sandwich in a tomato-based sauce; Kansas City burnt ends (double-smoked brisket pieces) in a sweet red sauce; East Texas hot links (all-beef sausages); and chopped whole-hog pork with a pepper vinegar sauce. Save room for a bite of macaroni and cheese, collard greens, hush puppies, watermelon, cornbread, and chess pie.

Further Reading

BBQ Jew. n.d. "About." https://bbqjew.com/

Bolois, Justin. 2015. "The Future of BBQ, According to Rick Bayless." *First We Feast*, October 22, 2015. https://firstwefeast.com/eat/2015/10/the-future-of-bbq-according-to-rick-bayless

Boskovitch, Ben. 2018. "Aaron Franklin Built the Best BBQ Joint in America by Giving a Damn." *Esquire*, April 9, 2018.

Carman, Tim. 2016. "The Most Influential BBQ in America." *First We Feast*. Panel discussion with various field experts. https://firstwefeast.com/features/the-most-influential-bbq-in-america/

Fasman, Jon. 2010. "Fire in the Hole: Barbecue Navigates the Twin Perils of Mass Appeal and Nostalgia." *The Economist*, December 16, 2010.

Furlong, Maggie. 2012. "Anthony Bourdain Talks 'No Reservations,' 'Hunger Games' and the Death of Angry Bobby Flay." *Huffington Post*, May 15, 2012. https://www.huffpost.com/entry/anthony-bourdain-no-reservations_n_1412384

Geiling, Natasha. 2013. "The Evolution of American Barbecue." *Smithsonian Magazine*, July 18, 2013.

Moss, Robert. 2010. *Barbecue: The History of an American Institution*. Tuscaloosa: The University of Alabama Press.

Shahin, Jim. 2012. "A Modest Proposal for a Real BBQ Museum." *The Washington Post*, October 16, 2012.

Solares, Nick. 2015. "The American Barbecue Regional Style Guide." Eater, June 16, 2016. https://www.eater.com/2016/6/16/11889444/where-to-eat-barbecue-styles

Wei, Clarissa. 2015. "An Illustrated History of Barbecue in America." *First We Feast*, June 9, 2015. https://firstwefeast.com/eat/2015/06/illustrated-history-of-barbecue-in-america

Batali, Mario (1960–)

STARTERS

There are few fields in the cuisine world in which Mario Batali isn't known. Considered to be one of the best-known contemporary chefs working in America, Batali is a television personality, owner of more than 20 restaurants and food and wine markets worldwide, cookbook author, philanthropist, and social activist. Born on September 19, 1960, Batali—one of three children—was raised in Seattle, Washington by his parents, Armandino and Marilyn Batali. After attending Rutgers University, he began his formal culinary training in London, but dropped out after several months. Instead of pursuing formal education further, he joined British celebrity chef Marco Pierre White as an apprentice. Following in the Batali family's Italian footsteps, he then lived in Bologna for three years, where he worked at a trattoria in Borgo Capanne, a tiny village in Northern Italy.

Batali returned to the United States with the goal of bringing his passion for Italian food to New York. He cofound two popular restaurants in Manhattan before starring in his first show on the Food Network in 1997. Over the next two decades, he went on to open nearly 20 more restaurants, food markets, and wine shops in numerous major cities; to star and guest star in a number of culinary television shows; and to write 11 cookbooks. His restaurants join the ranks of some of the most successful and sought after in New York City. In addition to achieving the food industry's renowned D'artagnan Cervena "Who's Who of Food & Beverage" award in 2001, he has been honored with the James Beard Foundation's "Best Chef: New York City" award and *GQ* Magazine's "Man of the Year" chef award, and he was named the James Beard Foundation's "Outstanding Chef of the Year" in 2005.

ENTRÉE

Mario Batali has a great deal of culinary expertise, in addition to having a bevy of serious accolades to his name. But the persona presented by Batali is anything but somber. The chef stands out in most crowds, instantly recognizable for his red hair, typically pulled back in a ponytail, and the signature bright orange Crocs—foam clogs that resemble rainbow-hued boating shoes. For most of his career, Batali was known for wearing Crocs with everything from chef coats to formal suits, even donning the orange shoes and matching bright orange socks (with shorts) when cooking for the Obama family at the White House.

Batali came of age in an era that was going through an interesting food evolution. Television personalities and chefs like Julia Child were helping to steer Americans away from the heavily processed food of the 1950s and the rationed and short-supplied meals of the 1930s and 1940s, which had been ravaged by World War II, the crash of the stock market, and the depletion of much of America's fertile farmlands. Americans were becoming increasingly aware of foreign cuisines, beginning to experiment with things like French cooking in their own homes, and utilizing flavor profiles that were outside of the steak, potatoes, and corn staples of the American diet. Batali was raised in an era of "food awakening" in the United States, an exciting time for an impressionable young mind who would later go on to hone authentic, creative Italian cuisine for American palates. The cuisine world was also beginning to take itself less seriously in some areas. Batali was born a mere three days before "Yikes . . . Stripes! . . ." Fruit Stripe gum was introduced to the American public, a product that resembles the irreverent approach he would take to his career.

Mario's father, Armandino, was employed as an engineer with Boeing, and he moved to Spain in the late 1970s for work, where the family was exposed to a community mentality of growing and sharing food together as a socially shared experience. Inspired by what would later be branded by Americans in the 2000s as a "farm to table" way of approaching food, the Batali family returned to the United States. with the goal of sharing Mediterranean-inspired foods in a neighborly way with their community. His family followed the trend set by Mario's great-great-grandfather, who had immigrated from Italy to Montana in 1899 as a coal miner before heading further west to settle in the Pacific Northwest. He and Mario's great-great-grandmother had operated an Italian foods market in 1903, which inspired Mario's parents to open their own cured meat shop, Salumi, in 1999 after Armandino retired from a career as an engineer for Boeing.

Mario's education was marked by going to high school in Spain before returning to the States and attending Rutgers College in New Jersey. Traditional education didn't hold the focus of the young world traveler with an enormous appetite for life—he dropped out of Le Cordon Bleu after only a few months in post-college study in London, choosing to act as an apprentice for chef Marco Pierre White instead (later, he would tell *The Atlantic* journalist Corby Kummer at the magazine's Food Summit that he was "foolish" to leave, and expressed remorse for his impatience). In a video interview produced by culinary website *Serious Eats*, Batali recounted a heated exchange between him and White during their collaboration, in which White insisted that Batali remake a risotto dish that Batali had just completed for the restaurant's dinner crowd. Batali pushed back, insisting that the risotto was of high quality, and in response, he alleges that White threw the hot pot of the rice dish, hitting Batali in the chest. That night, Batali left. With no intention of returning to the British celebrity chef's empire, he surreptitiously poured salt in all of White's sauces that had been prepared for the evening to provoke face-scrunching, negative reviews from that night's diners.

Perhaps embodying a modification of the saying "if you can't handle the hot risotto pan, get out of the . . . country," Batali sought out an immersive experience back in the soils of the Mediterranean, this time working in a trattoria in Northern Italian village. He learned the ins and outs of authentic Italian cuisine there and, as he writes on his website, returned with the cooking philosophy to "use the best local ingredients as simply as possible, and serve them with flourish and joy." Batali followed through of his goal of bringing Italian cooking to America, starting with the Hudson Valley and spreading to Manhattan, where he worked at Italian restaurant Rocco and cofounded Pó restaurant. Pó went on to enjoy great success before closing its doors in 2017, due to what owner Stephen Crane described as "a 120 percent increase in (an already) $10,000 a month rent" for the hot-spot West Village business (Tuder 2017).

Pairing up with restaurateur Joe Bastianich, Batali also opened Babbo Ristorante e Enoteca in 1998, located in Manhattan's hip Greenwich Village. A 2017 *New York Times* review describes Babbo as "(the Batali) empire's spiritual home, where the original formula of adventure and pleasure and curious-minded indulgence is still intact" (the same review went on to describe the feeling of early dinner service at Babbo as "roll(ing) along like a skateboard on new concrete," but criticized the plodding pace of later dinner service).

As his Italian restaurant ventures became wildly popular, Batali was also offered his first starring role in a television show on the Food Network—*Molto Mario* ("molto" meaning "more" in Italian). He would go on to star, compete, and guest star in a number of other shows, including Food Network's *Ciao America*, *Mediterranean Mario*, and *Iron Chef America* and fellow celebrity chef shows like *The Rachael Ray Show*, *Martha*, and *No Reservations*. Batali and the Food Network severed their professional working relationship after 11 years, allegedly due to Batali's insistence that the network renew the shows he hosted if they wanted him to continue competing on *Iron Chef* (Ad Week Staff 2007). In 2011, Batali was one of the cohosts behind the ABC daytime food-themed talk show *The Chew*.

Batali's restaurant offerings have grown significantly over the last two decades—the chef owns 22 restaurants scattered across New York, California, Las Vegas, and Singapore, such as Del Posto, Osteria Mozza, and Otto Enoteca Pizzeria. In addition to traditional restaurants, he also owns numerous marketplaces that offer high-end Italian food and wine, such as Eataly New York. Many of his ventures have been met with prestigious accolades, such as BABBO earning a Michelin one star and Del Posto being initiated into *Relais & Chateaux Guidebook*.

As a splash of color in the midst of an otherwise serious affair, Batali's bright orange footwear was seen dashing around the White House lawn in September of 2016 in preparation for President Obama's final state dinner. First Lady Michelle Obama had requested that Batali host the dinner, which was in honor of Italy's Prime Minister, Matteo Renzi (and involved feeding hundreds of White House guests, in addition to the president and prime ministers themselves). According to an interview about the event with the *New York Times* in 2016, Batali summed up his feelings on the event: "These are some of my favorite people on the whole planet, and they're asking me to cook for the final state dinner of the presidency, and, oh, by the way, it's the Italians who are coming? It doesn't get better."

Typically seen as a gregarious party animal, the celebrity chef's positive public persona was dramatically challenged when four women alleged that Batali had engaged in sexual misconduct toward them in prior years. Batali issued an apology via the popular website *Eater*, in which he admitted that he had behaved inappropriately toward various women during his career. The apology itself went on to garner controversy. Batali printed the apology in his email newsletter, with an unusual postscript: "in case you're searching for a holiday-inspired breakfast, these Pizza Dough Cinnamon Rolls are a fan favorite," he wrote, including a link to the recipe on his website. The tone of his postscript and the inclusion of a self-promotional recipe in an apology about sexual misconduct struck many as insensitive and inauthentic, sparking a number of sarcastic and critical comments on Twitter and other social media platforms (Ducharme 2017).

After allegations surfaced, Batali stepped away from the positions he held at his restaurants and on "The Chew." The allegations against Batali came on the heels of numerous other 2017 allegations against men in high-profile positions, such as film mogul Harvey Weinstein, television hosts Matt Lauer and Charlie Rose, comedian Louis C.K., and actor Kevin Spacey, among many others. In the restaurateur and food celebrity world, additional accusations of misconduct were made about chef Johnny Iuzzini, Charlie Hallowell, and Ken Friedman, sparking a wider debate about whether the restaurant industry has prevailing issues of misogyny and disrespect toward women and what improvements can and should be made on a wide scale to make the food industry more welcoming and safe for everyone (Hauser, Moskin, and Serverson 2017).

ACCOMPANIED BY

Batali is married to Susi Cahn, whose family ran the iconic Coach handbag empire before turning their attention to a bucolic venture in upstate New York called Coach Dairy Goat Farm. The couple have two sons together, Leo and

Benno. After Batali and Joe Bastianich's highly successful debut of Babbo Ristorante e Enoteca in 1998, Batali went on to join Joe and his mother, fellow celebrity chef Lidia Bastianich, in a business venture called Batali & Bastianich Hospitality Group. Presently, the partners cohost more than 30 renowned restaurants worldwide. In the wake of Batali's departure from his business ventures, Batali & Bastianich Hospitality Group informed their employees that the company was being rebranded, including a new (forthcoming) name and a stronger commitment to ensuring a respectful workplace (Plagianos 2018).

There are numerous celebrities, of both foodie and non-foodie fame, Batali is known for rubbing shoulders with—some of whom were featured in a black-and-white show made for Hulu called *The High Road*, in which Batali pals around with other celebrities such as George Stephanopoulos, Julianna Margulies, Isabella Rossellini, and Anthony Bourdain, just to name a few. The show gives the sense that Batali has many friends and professional colleagues who love to play tourist in Manhattan with him, as they are followed joking around and talking together in museums, double-decker buses, and iconic sites like The Empire State Building.

SUGGESTED PAIRINGS

See also: Bourdain, Anthony; *Iron Chef*; Ray, Rachael.

Entry best enjoyed while eating: Baked manicotti baresi al forno, filled with veal, lamb, prosciutto cotto, Italian herbs, and egg, topped with cheese and tomato sauce. (*Batali tip:* it is "*importantissimo* to undercook the pasta" when boiling it so that it isn't overdone after baking in the oven.) Serve with blistered shishito peppers in a sherry vinaigrette dressing and a cold tumbler of brown sugar old-fashioneds.

Further Reading

Ad Week Staff. 2007. "Mario Batali Fired From Food Network." September 5, 2007. http://www.adweek.com/digital/mario-batali-fired-from-food-network/

Batali, Mario. 2014. *Farm to Table: Simple, Delicious Recipes Celebrating Local Farmers*. New York: Grand Central Life & Style.

Batali, Mario. 2017. http://wwwmariobatali.com/about

Brand, Madeline. 2006. "Taking the Heat in Mario Batali's Kitchen." NPR's *Day to Day*. Podcast audio, June 5, 2006.

Conlin, Jennifer. 2007. "For Mario Batali, It's Molto Michigan." *The New York Times*, August 17, 2007.

Ducharme, Jamie. 2017. "Mario Batali's Sexual Misconduct Apology Came with a Cinnamon Roll Recipe." *Time*, December 16, 2017. http://time.com/5067633/mario-batali-cinnamon-rolls-apology/

Faircloth, Kelly. 2013. "Mario Batali Loves His Orange Crocs So Much, He Just Ordered 200 Pairs." *Jezebel*, November 25, 2013.

Hauser, Christine, Julie Moskin, and Kim Serverson. 2017. "Mario Batali Steps Away from Restaurants Amid Sexual Misconduct Allegations." *New York Times*, December 11, 2017.

Hirshfeld Davis, Julie. 2016. "Mario Batali (Yes, in His Orange Crocs) to Prepare Obamas' Last State Dinner." *New York Times*, October 16, 2016.

Kumer, Corby. 2012. "Mario Batali on 'Sadistic' TV and Martha Stewart on Raising Chickens." *The Atlantic*, May 25, 2012.

Plagianos, Irene. 2018. "Mario Batali's Restaurant Empire Plans Name Change After Misconduct Allegations." *Eater*, January 9, 2018. https://ny.eater.com/2018/1/9/16867930/mario-batali-company-name-change

Plagianos, Irene, and Kitty Greenwald. 2017. "Mario Batali Steps Away from Restaurant Empire Following Sexual Misconduct Allegations." *Eater*, December 11, 2017. https://ny.eater.com/2017/12/11/16759540/mario-batali-sexual-misconduct-allegations

Tuder, Stefanie. 2017. "After 24 Years, Pó Closes in the West Village." *Eater, New York*. https://ny.eater.com/2017/4/27/15442026/po-closed-west-village-nyc

Bayless, Rick (1953–)

STARTERS

Rick Bayless is an American celebrity chef and television personality who is considered by many to be the leading expert on authentic Mexican cuisine in the country. Known for his PBS cooking show *Mexico: One Plate at a Time*, which premiered in 2003, Bayless also garnered a significant amount of national fame when he won the competition reality show *Top Chef Masters* in 2009. In addition to his work in television, he has written a number of cookbooks; runs nine highly acclaimed restaurants in the Chicago area; and is a teacher, humanitarian, and performance artist.

The first of his restaurants, Frontera Grill, opened in 1987. Bayless opened a sister restaurant, Topolobampo, next door to Frontera in 1989 before expanding to seven additional Mexican restaurants around the city. During his career, he has been nominated for and received a wide array of awards. He has received seven James Beard Awards in categories that include Outstanding Chef, Outstanding Restaurant, and best cookbook and podcast. In 2007, he received the International Association of Culinary Professionals' (IACP) Humanitarian of the Year Award and was named to the Order of the Aztec Eagle by the Mexican government in 2012, the highest distinction the Mexican government bestows upon foreigners. In 2016, Bayless was honored by the Julia Child Foundation for Gastronomy and the Culinary Arts with a Julia Child award.

ENTRÉE

Bayless was raised in a family of restaurateurs in Oklahoma City, Oklahoma. His family ran a barbecue restaurant called the Hickory House, which closed in 1986 after more than 30 years of service. Bayless grew up working in the family's restaurant, and he graduated from Northwest Classen High School his junior year while simultaneously running the restaurant's catering business. In his first year out of high school, Bayless attended Oklahoma City University, the only school willing to accept a student as young as he was (Cathley 2016). In an interview with *First We Feast* magazine, Bayless said that getting his culinary start in a barbecue restaurant that had an indoor brick pit helped him gain a deeper appreciation for the "primal instinct" of eating food prepared over an open fire. "Live-fire cooking . . . is who I am. The soul is all about live-fire cooking," he told reporter Justin Bolois (2017).

Learning the craft of barbecued meats also primed him for the painstaking preparation of many of the Mexican foods he went on to master later in his career. "When I hear big chefs are going to 'barbecue,' I roll my eyes," he told the magazine, "It only counts when you've also done all the apprenticeship." In a discussion about dishes that helped shape his young career, Bayless recounted memories of making peach cobbler with his grandmother when he was young, noting the long process of processing Oklahoma-grown, sun-kissed peaches that filled her kitchen. He also noted how important the sense of smell is to a chef and how adept he became at paying attention to the aroma of food while learning to make barbecue ribs in his parents' restaurant (Bolois 2015, 2017).

Originally drawn to a potential career as a theater actor, a family trip to Mexico in his teenage years proved to be a pivotal experience that would change the course of his professional and personal pursuits. Bayless completed his undergraduate education at the University of Oklahoma, where he studied Spanish literature, language, and cultural studies. He followed his nascent love of these cultural studies to the University of Michigan, where he began a PhD program in anthropological linguistics. He didn't complete the doctorate, however, due to his increasing fascination with the cuisines and culinary techniques of Mexico and pre-Columbian civilizations.

Mexico

From 1980 to 1986, Bayless and his wife Deann lived in Mexico, where he penned his first cookbook: *Authentic Mexican: Regional Cooking from the Heart of Mexico*. Bayless spent his years there traveling through each of the country's states, learning the history, culture, and geography of the country in addition to learning how to master cooking various regional cuisines. He visited countless Mexican kitchens, recording the methods of preparation and every ingredient list he encountered by memory, not wanting to run the risk of people thinking he was a police officer writing them up while they cooked (Rayner 2010).

Spending the mid-1980s traveling through Mexico gave Bayless an American insider's view into a world of Mexican cooking that wasn't well known in the states—a view that he wanted to share with other Americans. His first cookbook is an ode to fresh, savory, authentic Mexican food and incorporates ingredients such as fish, tomatillos, chipotle chiles, picante, cilantro, poblanos, guacamole, lime, and corn masa. In the book's preface, Bayless wrote about his desire to expand Mexican American cuisine beyond its limited fare at the time. Recipes for things like Yucatecan marinated shrimp tacos, fish steamed in banana leaves, and fresh green tomatillo salsa entice readers who might be more familiar with ground beef tacos and sopapillas to try new flavors and preparation techniques.

While observing Mexican cooks at work, one of the foods he was most taken with was *mole* (pronounced "molay"), a rich sauce with a chocolatey undertone.

Mole has been featured throughout his television show and cookbook recipes, in addition to his restaurant dishes. He told *Guardian* reporter Rayner "black mole requires controlled burning of the chiles, the seeds, the onions ... it's the hardest thing in the world" (2010). To prepare the sauce properly, one must cook the chiles until just before they begin to burn, removing them moments before the flavor would otherwise become bitter. The process is so difficult to master that Bayless told *First We Feast* that it took him 10 years of working on the recipe before he put it on the menu at his own restaurants. Even after its introduction to his restaurants, Bayless has only entrusted the task of preparing black mole to one employee, who has worked with Bayless for over 20 years (Rayner 2010).

Career

Bayless's first cookbook, published by William Morrow in 1987, was met with significant success. A blurb on the book jacket from renowned *New York Times* food editor Craig Claiborne hails Bayless as "one of the greatest contributors to the Mexican table imaginable." Bayless and Deann opened their first restaurant, Frontera Grill, in Chicago the same year. The restaurant would go on to national and international acclaim, and it was met with so much popularity initially that the couple opened Topolobampo just two years later (the restaurants are nestled next to each other on a busy downtown Chicago street and share a doorway). Noted as one of the few fine-dining Mexican restaurants in the nation, Topolobampo has achieved honors including a James Beard Outstanding Restaurant award and a Michelin four-star rating.

The next three decades were met with similar success stories as Bayless continued to expand his Mexican food empire. He opened fast-casual Xoco, Xoco Bistro (later named Fonda Frontera), Tortas Frontera (at O'Hare International Airport), Lena Brava, Cerveceria Cruz Blanca, Frontera Fresco, and Frontera Cochina. The restaurants attract diners from all walks of life. Topolobampo has seen the likes of President Barack Obama and his wife, First Lady Michelle Obama, who have dined on dishes like scallop and lobster with tomatillo-corn sauce and sweet corn tamales on the date nights since the president's years in the Senate (Kindelsperger 2010). Nearby, diners at Xoco—which was designed with uncomfortable chairs in order to discourage lengthy lounging—fill up on items such as breakfast chilaquiles, short rib tacos, Mexican hot chocolates, and fried churros dipped in melted chocolate.

In 1996, Bayless premiered his product line Frontera Foods, which includes items such as chips, salsas, and grilling spice blends. In 2003, his PBS television show *Mexico: One Plate at a Time* premiered, a popular instructional cooking show that has aired for 11 seasons. In 2009, Bayless won the Top Chef Master on the first season of Bravo channel's eponymous show, a competition reality program that pits world-renowned chefs against each other in a number of culinary challenges.

Bayless has adhered to a seemingly inexhaustible schedule over the years. In addition to running his restaurants, starring in and directing *Mexico, One Plate at a Time*, and taking annual research trips to Mexico with staff, he also writes cookbooks, collaborates with chefs from all over the world, and judges food competitions. He participates in cultural dialogues about the present state and future of Mexican American cuisine via avenues such as his podcast *The Feed* and events like ModMex, a conference he organized to help facilitate collaboration between contemporary Mexican and American chefs. In addition to teaching culinary skills through his books and PBS show, he teaches classes and workshops, both in person and online with educational video company Craftsy.

In recent years, some critics have accused Bayless of cultural appropriation, a concept that is generally defined as when an individual uses something from another culture inappropriately. Numerous chefs have been faced with similar accusations when they cook cuisines other than the ones primarily used in their culture of origin. Bayless's critics have accused him of profiting from a culture that is not his own and have questioned whether he has more freedom as a white chef to experiment in others' cuisines than minorities might. Some hold the opinion that Bayless has profited off recipes and cuisines that he learned from Mexican chefs and authors who never received recognition for their work. In a 2016 interview with Dan Pashman of the *Sporkful* podcast, Bayless responded to these accusations with a statement that generated its own controversy: "Because I'm white, I can't do anything with Mexican food . . . is that plain racism, then?" He also stated he has done everything possible to make the cuisine his own. Both critics and defenders of his adoption of authentic Mexican cuisine have been part of a wider cultural dialogue in recent years about authentic and intentionally nonauthentic interpretations of cuisines from around the world.

Philanthropy

In 2003, Bayless and his staff established a charitable organization called Frontera Farmer Foundation, which supports small farms in the Midwest through grants. To date, the Foundation has awarded more than $1.3 million in more than 128 grants to Midwestern family farms. Four years later, he established a scholarship program that offers a full-ride scholarship to Kendall College's culinary arts program to students of Mexican American heritage who attend Chicago's public schools. Bayless occasionally holds fundraising events for his charitable causes, such as an elaborate house party in which Wilco drummer Glenn Kotche performed while Bayless and his team created an atmosphere that "sought to explore the relationship between art and food," piping the sound of the percussion and aromatic fragrances of the meal's preparation to the party's guests, creating a somewhat hallucinogenic ambiance (McKeever 2014).

ACCOMPANIED BY

Bayless and his wife Deann have shared a professional partnership since their marriage in 1979. Deann Bayless has contributed to all of Rick's cookbooks, in addition to being a producer for *Mexico: One Plate at a Time* and a part of the couple's Frontera Foundation team. She was a founding partner in the Bayless's flagship restaurant, Fronterra, as well as their subsequent restaurants and product line. Deann has also helped mentor numerous restaurateurs and professional women in the culinary field (Daley 2013). The couple have a daughter, Lanie, with whom Rick wrote a cookbook, *Rick & Lanie's Excellent Kitchen Adventures*, in collaboration with his (then) teenage daughter to offer family-focused meals to readers.

Rick's parents, Levita and John Bayless, ran the Hickory House restaurant in Oklahoma City from the early 1950s through the late 1980s. The couple raised three children (Rick's brother Skip Bayless is known to many as well, as a sports commentator on television and sports writer). Bayless's great-uncles owned a chain of Jones Brothers grocery stores in Oklahoma City, and his grandfather ran a drive-in that served fare such as hamburgers and milkshakes. Additionally, Bayless has cited his grandmother's carefully prepared dinners for extended families in various interviews about profound culinary memories (Froelke Coburn 2012).

DESSERT

Bayless has been noted for his unusual blend of skills as both a chef and an anthropological expert in a culture that wasn't widely known before in the United States. The list below represents just a few unusual projects and passions Bayless has pursued.

- **On display:** Bayless donated several items from his early career to the Smithsonian's National Museum of American History, including things like a typewriter and notes from his field work in the 1980s (this nod to his Mexican culinary career is similar to the Julia Child exhibit at the same museum, which has a recreation of her kitchen on display to honor the work she did to introduce Americans to French cuisine).
- **On the stage:** Bayless acted throughout high school and college. He attributes a lot of his interest in television work as a combination of culinary and theater work. In 2012, he starred in a theatrical production about a chef called *Cascabel*, which premiered in Chicago.
- **Presidential standing:** Rumors flew shortly after Barack Obama's presidential election that Bayless might be tapped to be the family's White House chef. In addition to the Obamas' visits to Bayless's restaurants during president's senate years, President Obama once made a reservation under a fake name during his presidency, causing a media frenzy when he arrived at Topolobampo in a fleet of Secret Service vehicles. Bayless denied the claim that he had been asked to be the White House's head chef, but he went on to be a guest chef for a state dinner honoring Mexico, including President Felipe Calderon as one of the guests. On the menu? Mole, of course.
- **Odd jobs:** In an interview with *Chicago Magazine*, Bayless said that at the White House state dinner, he and his staff were instructed that all 400 guests

needed to be served in a span of four minutes. A similar challenge is posed at the end of a state dinner, which is signaled by the president putting down his or her fork, at which point all guests' plates are whisked away regardless of whether they had finished the rest of their meal.

- **Where's the chef?** Bayless is known to dash across the street from Frontera Grill during a busy work day to spend his break taking dance lessons and also does challenging yoga techniques as a daily practice.
- **Raking in the dough:** According to an article by Chicago's *Eater,* Bayless's garden at his urban Wicker Park home yields $30,000 worth of produce every year. This doesn't account for the additional produce harvested from the rooftop garden at Frontera Grill, which his chefs use to create their daily salsas.

SUGGESTED PAIRINGS

See also: *Bizarre Foods with Andrew Zimmern*; Child, Julia; Latin American Cuisine; *Top Chef.*

Entry best enjoyed while eating: Tortilla chips and fresh tomatillo-avocado salsa; red chile seafood soup with *epazote* (a pungent herb); chicken tinga tacos seasoned with onion, tomato, and chipotle salsa; and a sweet flan de cafe (flan made from condensed milk, goat's milk caramel sauce, cloves, and cinnamon). Serve alongside a cold Mundet's apple soda or a margarita served on the rocks with blanco tequila, orange liqueur, and a salted rim.

Further Reading

Bayless, Rick. 2007. *Authentic Mexican: Regional Cooking from the Heart of Mexico.* 20th Anniversary Ed. New York: Harper Collins.

Bolois, Justin. 2015. "The Future of BBQ, According to Rick Bayless." *First We Feast*, October 22, 2015. https://firstwefeast.com/eat/2015/10/the-future-of-bbq-according-to-rick-bayless

Bolois, Justin. 2017. "The 10 Dishes That Made My Career: Rick Bayless." *First We Feast*, February 27, 2017. https://firstwefeast.com/features/rick-bayless-career-changing-dishes/

Cathey, David. 2016. *Classic Restaurants of Oklahoma City.* Charleston, SC: The History Press.

Chicago Chef Rick Bayless Accepts Julia Child Award at Smithsonian Food History Gala. 2016. Press Release, The National Museum of American History. October 24, 2016.

Daley, Bill. 2013. "Deann Groen Bayless, Restaurateur." *Chicago Tribune*, November 3, 2013. *The Feed* podcast. http://www.thefeedpodcast.com

Forbes, Paula. 2012. "Rick Bayless Named to Mexico's Order of the Aztec Eagle." *Eater*, June 7, 2012. https://www.eater.com/2012/6/7/6579701/rick-bayless-named-to-mexicos-order-of-the-aztec-eagle

Froelke Coburn, Marcia. 2012. "12 Things You Didn't Know About Rick Bayless." *Chicago Magazine*, February 21, 2012. http://www.chicagomag.com/Chicago-Magazine/March-2012/12-Things-You-Didnt-Know-About-Rick-Bayless/

Godoy, Maria, and Kat Chow. 2016. "When Chefs Become Famous Cooking Other Cultures' Food." *NPR*'s The Salt, March 22, 2016. https://www.npr.org/sections/the

salt/2016/03/22/471309991/when-chefs-become-famous-cooking-other-cul tures-food

Kindelsperger, Nick. 2010. "Obama Makes Surprise Visit at Topolobampo." *Grub Street*, November 1, 2010. http://www.grubstreet.com/2010/11/obama_makes_surprise_visit_at.html

McKeever, Amy. 2014. "Is Rick Bayless the Most Interesting Man in the World?" *Eater*, September 25, 2014. https://www.eater.com/2014/9/25/6843585/rick-bayless-the-most-interesting-man-in-the-world

Noyes Saini, Anne. 2016. "Other People's Food, Part One: White Chef, Mexican Food." *Sporkful* podcast, March 21, 2016. http://www.sporkful.com/other-peoples-food-part-1-rick-bayless-white-chef-mexican-food/

NPR Staff. 2010. "Rick Bayless Serves Street Food at the White House." *NPR's Weekend Edition*, May 15, 2010.

Rayner, Jay. 2010. "Rick Bayless: The Obamas' Favourite Chef." March 13, 2010. https://www.theguardian.com/lifeandstyle/2010/mar/14/rick-bayless-obama-favourite-chef

Beard, James (1903–1985)

STARTERS

James Beard was an American cook, television personality, culinary teacher, restaurateur, and restaurant consultant. He wrote a syndicated column, published countless cooking articles, and authored more than two dozen cookbooks. Beard helped cultivate passion for cooking, particularly American food, and was at the forefront of food-themed television and teaching. He published his first cookbook *Hors d'Oeuvre and Canapés* in 1940, and many of the cookbooks that followed were award-winning and best-selling works. His television premiere was on *I Love to Eat* (1946–1947), a recurring live segment he hosted on NBC in the earliest days of food television.

Beard established the James Beard Cooking School in 1955, starting out of his home in New York City, New York, and eventually opened a second branch in Seaside, Oregon. His work inspired the launch of the James Beard Foundation, a nonprofit organization known for scholarships, leadership initiatives, and awards that encourage culinary excellence. Beard is widely hailed by critics, writers, and chefs as a significantly influential figure in American culinary history and culture.

ENTRÉE

"In the beginning, there was James Beard," food critic Gael Greene wrote in a 1985 *New York Magazine* tribute. She described him as "a man whose life was about savoring every deliciousness, living each moment, and sharing the abundance." This cheerful, confident nature and unapologetic adoration of food is what many appreciated about Beard. He infused his cooking instruction with contagious enthusiasm, and his jovial personality was the perfect match for numerous product endorsements. In many ways, Beard seemed ahead of his time, such as the way he embraced America's growing media and technology landscape in the second half of the century. A natural storyteller, he threw himself into countless writing endeavors for books, newspapers, and magazines and taught cooking demonstrations in front of both televised and live audiences alike. For a man born in 1903, Beard would have fit in almost seamlessly with the Bobby Flays and Alton Browns of today.

Julia Child, a fellow celebrity cook and friend of Beard's, described him as the quintessential American cook, "an endearing and always lively teacher (who) loved work, loved people, loved his work, loved gossip, loved to eat, loved a good time" (Beard 1999). In many ways, Beard helped pave the way for food as a source of joy in contemporary American culture and media, blending international and domestic cuisines into recipe collections that people of all cooking abilities could find approachable and enjoyable. In 1954, the *New York Times* dubbed Beard "the dean of American cookery," a label that followed him (sometimes rephrased "the father of American cooking") throughout the rest of his life. Others have called him a pioneer of the farm-to-table movement.

Many have also called Beard the first "foodie," meaning someone who is passionate about food and current food trends. Writer Betty Fussell notes that the serious accolades he received clashed with his big personality and large stature. Fussell described Beard, a man who was 6'4" tall and roughly 300 pounds, as a broad, bald, "laughing Buddha" with a warm smile, small mustache, and a bow tie (Fussell 2016). Despite his "foodie" status and recognizable role in the culinary scene, Beard balked at any snobbish association with his career and deemed the term "gourmet chef" and other popular jargon at the time "particular abominations" (Krebs 1985).

James Beard was born in Portland, Oregon, in 1903, and he attended Reed college in 1923. Some debate exists as to why he abruptly left school, but numerous journalists and biographer Robert Clark ascertain that Beard was expelled for having relationships with other men. As a young man, Beard dreamed of being an actor and singer. After his year at Reed, he joined a traveling theater troupe in which he performed and studied abroad before returning to the United States in 1927. Seeking means to supplement his struggles as an actor, Beard opened a catering business and food store called Hors d'Oeuvre Inc. in 1935. He compiled some of his favorite catering recipes for his first cookbook, which many have cited as the first time "cocktail food" received serious critique and substantial attention.

His ensuing cookbooks covered topics like outdoor grilling, bread, pasta, casseroles, fish, and other "simple foods." Titles such as *How to Eat Better for Less Money* (1954) and *How to Eat (and Drink) Your Way through a French (or Italian) Menu* (1971) denote his interest in making healthy, sophisticated food more affordable and accessible to the average home cook. Nearly 60 years before it would become chic in popular culture, he was also an outspoken advocate for cooking with farm-raised, natural, whole foods.

> **Small Plates**
>
> **The Gay Architects of Modern American Food**
>
> Near the end of his life, James Beard chose to make his sexual orientation public. "By the time I was 7, I knew that I was gay. I think it's time to talk about that now," Beard wrote while drafting his memoir. Although many of Beard's friends knew that he was gay, *The New York Times* writer Frank Brini wrote that due to powerful social stigmas during that era, Beard and his LGBTQ peers likely had to suppress a core part of their true selves in an effort to hide part of their identity from the general public. *Lucky Peach* writer John Birdsall referred to Beard as one of three gay "architects of modern food"—also naming writer Richard Olney and *Times* critic Craig Claiborne—who helped revolutionize American cuisine. Birdsall wrote, "Food that takes pleasure seriously, as an end in itself, an assertion of politics or a human birthright, the product of culture—this is the legacy of gay food writers who shaped modern American food." Fittingly, Birdsall's article went on to win a James Beard Award (Bruni 2017; Birdsall 2014).

At the age of 81, Beard passed away from cardiac arrest. A *New York Times* obituary published in the midst of the diet-fad-obsessed 1980s cruelly focused on how overweight the chef was, noting that he'd been on a diet for the last decade of his life. Beard's lasting legacy would be his passions for seeking joy through cooking food from scratch, sharing communal meals, and the simple pleasure of delicious flavors. As he wrote in the foreword to *The James Beard Cookbook* (1959), "Good food has a magic appeal. You may grow old, even ugly, but if you are a good cook, people will always find a path to your door."

ACCOMPANIED BY

James Beard attributed much of his love of cooking to his mother, Elizabeth Beard, an English woman who ran a residential hotel. She was one of 12 children in her family and was raised by her aunt and uncle due to her parents' inability to care for all of their children. James's father, John Beard, was one of 16 children and worked in Portland's customs house. Elizabeth was 42 years old when she delivered James, who was reportedly a 14-pound baby. Throughout his youth, James's parents showed him how to cook meals with food like berries they had picked and fish they had caught themselves (Jones 1990).

Beard shared numerous traits with his friend Julia Child, who was another dominating force in the food writing world during that era. Like Child, Beard achieved culinary fame later in life; he was in his late thirties when he published his first cookbook. He worked closely with editor Judith Jones, who was significantly influential in Julia's career as well. Jones and her husband went on to write a biography about Beard's life. Similarly to Child, Beard also served abroad during World War II, doing cryptography (translating languages into secret codes) and serving with the United Seaman's Service. After his death, Child urged a group of his friends to formally designate his house as an epicenter of culinary education, which inspired the creation of the James Beard Foundation in 1986.

DESSERT

Describing his earliest memory of food, Beard wrote that he remembered crawling up to a giant onion and eating it "skin and all." He also wrote about contracting malaria at the age of three, recalling that he was so ill that he could only eat chicken jelly made by his family's Chinese cook (1964 [2001]).

In 1985, *New York Times* obituary writer Alin Krebs quoted Beard as saying "I believe that if ever I had to practice cannibalism, I might manage if there were enough tarragon around" in an essay about "the worst things that could happen to mankind gastronomically" (1985).

SUGGESTED PAIRINGS

See also: Child, Julia; Culinary Awards, The Evolution of; *Farmhouse Rules*; Fiction, Food in; Hazan, Marcella.

Entry best enjoyed while eating: Beard's brandade de morue (a spread made of salt cod and olive oil served on toast triangles); cellophane noodle Beard's brandade de morue salad; tart tatin (upside-down apple tart); and French Seventy-Fives, a champagne cocktail.

Further Reading

Beard, James. 1959. *The James Beard Cookbook*. New York: Dell.

Beard, James. 1999. *James Beard's Theory and Practice of Good Cooking*. Foreword by Julia Child. New York: Running Press.

Beard, James. (1964) 2001. *James Beard's Delights and Prejudices*. Philadelphia: Running Press.

Birdsall, John. 2013. "America, Your Food Is So Gay." *Lucky Peach*, Gender Issue, September 17, 2013.

Bruni, Frank. 2017. "Food, Sex and Silence." *New York Times*, Opinion, April 22, 2017.

Fussell, Betty. 2016. *Eat, Live, Love, Die: Selected Essays*. "James Beard, American Icon." Berkeley: Counterpoint.

Greene, Gael. 1985. "The Father of Us All." *New York*, June 3, 1985.

James Beard Foundation. 2020. "About Us." https://www.jamesbeard.org/about

Jones, Evan. 1990. *Epicurean Delight: Life and Times of James Beard*. New York: Knopf.

Krebs, Albin. 1985. "James Beard, Authority on Food, Dies." *New York Times*, January 4, 1985.

Best Thing I Ever Ate, The (2009–)

STARTERS

The Best Thing I Ever Ate is a reality show that features the favorite dishes of various celebrity chefs, food television personalities, and other people in the public eye who want to wax rhapsodic about their favorite foods. The show started on the Food Network and was transferred to the Cooking Channel, a spin-off of the network (Cain 2018). *The Best Thing I Ever Ate* accumulated eight seasons between 2009 and 2017. Episodes are 30 minutes long and feature vignettes of guests discussing their favorite foods in various categories as well as interviews with chefs and restaurateurs. The tone of the show is upbeat and lighthearted, with fast-paced editing and an energetic score. A spin-off program followed suit, called *Best Thing I Ever Made* (2011), in which celebrities detail recipes they love making at home and in their restaurants. *The Best Thing I Ever Ate* was nominated for a James Beard Foundation award for "Television Program On Location" in 2010 and was also nominated for a Daytime Emmy for directing in 2011.

ENTRÉE

Describing the first two episodes of *The Best Thing I Ever Ate*, a staff writer for food website Eat Me Daily wrote, "It's a celebration of American food, little love letters to food celebs' favorite restaurants, and you get the sense that they actually mean it" (2009). Due to the fact that the show features restaurants of all price points from all around the country, it offers ideas of where a wide range of audiences could feasibly go to enjoy the same foods. *The Best Thing I Ever Ate* also pulls the curtain back on a personal part of celebrities' lives, which has been a topic of public fascination that goes back through the ages. Audiences learn about each celebrity guest's past, personal things that they love to eat, nostalgic memories, "guilty pleasure" secrets, and surprising interests through stories about food. Guests explain what they love about each dish and detail the ingredients and preparation of it as footage filmed in the restaurant illustrates what they're describing. Each episode presents a different theme, such as desserts, barbecue, or foods specific to a certain region or state.

The variety of featured foods spans all types of cuisines and meals. Food Network personality and chef Adam Gertler recalls his favorite banana cream pie from Bandera, a Los Angeles restaurant he once worked at; *Good Eats* host Alton Brown delights in Korean Bibim-bop at Hankook Taqueria in Atlanta; and *Ace of Cakes* pastry chef Duff Goldman expresses exaltations over the beef ribs at the Salt Lick BBQ in Driftwood, Texas. Celebrity chef Giada De Laurentiis describes the joys of made-to-order donuts at Seattle's Lola; *Iron Chef*'s Cat Cora introduces audiences to Spicy Broccoli from the W Hotel in New York City; and Emeril Lagasse fawns over the Kale Soup at St. John's Club in Fall River, Massachusetts. Chefs like Ina Garten make everything from meatloaf to shrimp-and-swordfish curry seem like experiences unto themselves, dishes worth traveling to places like East Hampton and Sagaponack, New York.

Getting personal recommendations from highly acclaimed chefs is a treat for food fanatics and is akin to learning top secrets from industry professionals. In recent years, chefs have frequently been asked by the media to spill the beans on their favorite and least favorite meals. Audiences resonate with the personal stories of what other people eat, and why they eat it, whether the discussion is about foods as simple as "rice" or as exotic as "crying tiger pork."

DESSERT

Comedian Mo Rocca, describing the "Gateway of India" pizza at Houston's Bombay Pizza: "If there's not an adjective for cilantro, there needs to be one now because this pizza is very *cilantran*."

SUGGESTED PAIRINGS

See also: Brown, Alton; Celebrities and Food; Larentiis, Giada De; Television, Food Channels on.

Entry best enjoyed while eating: Inspired by some of the favorites on the show—a Middle Eastern veggie burger with roasted tomato, arugula, tahini, and charred onions from Shouk in Washington, D.C.; A handcrafted India Lime Fizz cocktail from the Velvet Tango Room in Ohio; and Denver-based Colt & Gray's sticky toffee pudding and bourbon ice cream.

Further Reading

"The Best Thing I Ever Ate." n.d. Food Network Staff. https://www.foodnetwork.com /shows/the-best-thing-i-ever-ate

Cain, Brooke. 2018. "Raleigh Native Fanny Slater Takes Cooking Channel to Wilmington for 'Best Thing I Ever Ate.'" *The News & Observer*, January 5, 2018.

"Food Network's The Best Thing I Ever Ate." 2009. Eat Me Daily staff. June 22, 2009.

Bizarre Foods with Andrew Zimmern

STARTERS

Bizarre Foods with Andrew Zimmern is a television show on the Travel Channel that explores unusual foods across the globe, as well as the reason each type of food is eaten, how it's prepared, and how it ties into the local history, ecology, and cultural practices. The show, which was developed and is hosted by chef, writer, and educator Andrew Zimmern (1961–), premiered in 2006 and has run for 12 seasons. Numerous spin-off shows have followed suit, including *Bizarre Foods Delicious Destinations* (2010), *Bizarre Foods America* (2012), *Andrew Zimmern's Driven by Food* (2014), and *Zimmern's List* (2018), as well as *Bizarre World* (2009), which expanded beyond the focus on unusual foods to include features on unique cultures around the world.

Bizarre Foods received two CableFax awards in 2009, and Zimmern's role in the *Bizarre* franchise has garnered several James Beard Awards, including "Outstanding Personality/Host" and best "Television Program on Location." Zimmern has written three books related to the series, including *The Bizarre Truth* (2010), *Andrew Zimmern's Bizarre World of Food* (2011), and *Andrew Zimmern's Field Guide to Exceptionally Weird, Wild, Wonderful Foods* (2012).

ENTRÉE

While reading the TV guide information for an episode of *Bizarre Foods*, it would be easy to develop the suspicion that this show was produced from the perspective of judgment or condescension toward other cultures. The word "bizarre" is largely defined as "unusual," but often carries a negative connotation. Even the title of the show suggests that the foods featured will all be compared to "normal food" (presumably American fare found at a typical American brewpub or fast-food restaurant). Upon closer investigation, however, the show's intention is to introduce viewers to a wide array of cultural practices, as well as the environmental, economic, and sociological issues associated with food consumption and food waste.

Dressed in a cheeky luchador wrestling costume, Andrew Zimmern draws laughter from the crowd as he competes in a "mystery basket" competition with Texan chef Tim Love at the 2015 Austin Food + Wine Festival. (Jill Meyer/Dreamstime.com)

Bizarre Foods' fare is not for the faint of heart, though host Andrew Zimmern tries to transform viewers with queasy stomachs into curious onlookers who are willing to become more open minded. In 2006, the show began with a pilot following Zimmern sampling street foods in a number of Asian cities. In the years following, there are few places Zimmern hasn't visited and few foods he hasn't eaten on the show. His travels have taken him to more than 170 countries, sampling the likes of rice-and-raisin-stuffed pancreas, cow spleen, raw pig testicles, fruit bats, sea cucumber intestines, flame-grilled pack rat, and winged ants, just to name a scant few.

Zimmern and his crew fly all over the world to film him snacking on a wide variety of foods that are iconic in certain cities, towns, and regions. The spinoff show *Delicious Destinations* has been met with confusion and criticism from some viewers due to the fact that Zimmern records his narration in front of a green screen in a domestic studio instead of traveling to every location featured.

After 12 years of production, *Bizarre Foods*' focus has shifted to include a deeper look at history in the United States. In February of 2017, a Travel Channel press release reported that the show's eleventh season premier attracted more than a million viewers, a significant uptick from earlier seasons' premieres. The premiere episode featured a culinary trip along the Lewis and Clark trail in the Pacific Northwest that entailed sampling meals such as salt-dried Pacific lamprey and edible barnacles.

Themes in *Bizarre Foods*

Zimmern offers a few simple rules for trying foods that are outside of one's comfort zone: always try something twice and never insult someone by disparaging their food. He readily admits that he doesn't like everything he eats, but he says he doesn't criticize foods that he doesn't like. Instead, he indicates his preference on camera with reactions ranging from enthusiastic reviews to saying things like "how interesting" or commenting on the food's texture or spice level. The foods aren't always extreme in nature; viewers also watch Zimmern sample treats such as pistachio candy in Aleppo, Navajo frybread in Arizona, and escargot (snails) with porcini mushrooms in San Francisco. But it's dishes along the likes of kombucha bacteria pancakes in Brooklyn, rotten ketchup and confederate biscuits in Missouri, pig uterus soup in Vietnam, and deep-fried shark in Trinidad & Tobago that catch the most attention among critics and fans.

The essence of the show could be distilled into two words: *adventure* and *advocacy*. In any given episode, Zimmern is found engaging in activities such as biting into tarantulas, pulling out a crustacean's innards, and dunking horse mane (the fat at the base of the horse's hair) into soy sauce with people from all walks of life. In addition to the jet setting and bizarre food elements, Zimmern has said that he wants to be known best for his advocacy in areas like social justice and environmental protection. In an interview with *Esquire* magazine in 2017, the chef discussed issues such as food insecurity and human-made environmental crises. He stated the assertion that fellow celebrity chefs should do more to raise awareness of issues such as food waste and hunger, and he discussed his frustration about the amount of food that is wasted or untapped in the name of it not being part of one's own culture.

Zimmern has also been vocal about how divided the United States has become in recent years, notably in the wake of the 2016 presidential campaign. His position on politics is an underlying message in the show, and he encourages people not to "practice contempt prior to investigation when it comes to people" (Rense 2017). Zimmern has also been outspoken about the pitfalls of fast foods and highly processed foods. He touts the benefits of sustainable and farm-to-table approaches to food as not only being healthier but also socially engaging, which helps to disarm people in light of political and other ideological differences.

Food Taboos

Bizzare Foods' blend of comparative cultural studies, anthropology, gastronomy, and social advocacy taps into a fascinating global history of food taboos. A food that is "taboo" is prohibited altogether, or restricted in type or quantity. Throughout history, virtually every culture has had food taboos. Many of these are grounded in a scientifically sound basis, such as the avoidance of eating animal waste products and other foods that are poisonous or rotten. Other taboos often spring from emotional and ethical roots, such as the avoidance of eating animals that are considered to be highly intelligent or compassionate. Many religious texts and laws prohibit specific foods, such as kosher dietary laws in the

Jewish faith, which strictly prohibit foods like a number of animals and their by-products. In some cultures, foods are seen as embodying harmful or helpful spirits or properties and may be denied or restricted for certain members, such as women who are pregnant or menstruating.

In a publication by the *Journal of Ethnobiology and Ethnomedicine*, researcher Victor Benno Meyer-Rochow discusses these and other explanations for food taboos, such as ego (for example, chiefs who forbid people below their status from eating preferred foods), environmental impact, and mythology as motivating factors. He provides examples from his field work, such as Nigerian groups who won't allow children to eat eggs or meat out of fear the foods will make children inclined to steal things. Certain Nigerian tribes also encourage pregnant women to eat leftover food that has been consumed by a rat due to their shared belief that the leftovers will lead to an easier childbirth. Regarding the benefits of food taboos, Meyer-Rochow writes that, in some cases, food taboo "aids in the cohesion of this group, helps that particular group maintain its identity in the face of others, and therefore creates a feeling of 'belonging'" (2009).

In America, a vast segment of the population has food taboos about eating horse or dog meat, insects, or parts of any animal's bodies like sex organs, digestive organs, and parts of the animal's face and head. However, in many other cultures these foods are considered delicacies. In an interview with the *University of Texas News*, anthropology professor Brian Stross notes that various cultures have even eaten human flesh in some form. He references a practice among some indigenous Venezuelan groups in which members "drink a plantain soup mixed with bones and ashes of dead family members" to honor the dead (Smith 2009). Papua New Guinean indigenous groups were discovered in recent decades to have a similar practice, and as recently as the last couple of hundred years, mummies were sometimes stolen from tombs and sold to Europeans, who consumed the remains for medicinal purposes.

ACCOMPANIED BY

Andrew Zimmern

The creator and host of the show has been interested in food since he was a youth, and he attributes his open-mindedness about global cuisines to traveling with his family when he was young. Like many other celebrity chefs, Zimmern had an interesting road to culinary fame. As a young man, he cooked in various restaurants in Long Island and attended Vassar College, where he studied art history. After college, he struggled with an increasingly destructive alcohol and drug addiction. He attributes some of the suffering that fueled his addiction to a traumatizing accident his mother had when he was a teenager. His addiction issues set him on a path that resulted in him being homeless in New York City. Squatting in an abandoned building, he stole to support his drug habit. With the help of some friends, Zimmern eventually made his way to a Minnesota-based treatment center, which opened the door to a sober and stable future (Spence 2018). After treatment, Zimmern got a job at washing dishes at a fine-dining Minnesota restaurant called Café Un Deux Trois, where he was promoted to the role of executive chef in a matter of weeks.

His culinary work at Un Deux Trois was met with enthusiasm and wide acclaim. He cofounded two production companies: Foodworks in 1997 and Intuitive Content in 2014. In addition to his success in high-end restaurants, television and web shows, and books, Zimmern also has a foothold in nearly every other culinary field imaginable. He created a culinary podcast called "Go Fork Yourself," launched a restaurant called Andrew Zimmern's Canteen in Kansas City and Minneapolis football stadiums, writes for *Food & Wine* magazine and Delta's *Sky* magazine, and has been named one of "America's 50 Most Powerful People in Food" by *The Daily Meal*, among other distinctions. He teaches about entrepreneurship and food issues at Babson College and funds a scholarship to help disadvantaged youth follow a culinary path. In 2020, the television personality premiered a new show, *What's Eating America*, and helped form a trade group called the Independent Restaurant Coalition (IRC) with other high-profile restaurateurs such as Tom Colicchio, Camilla Marcus, José Andrés, and Marcus Samuelsson. The members of the IRC lobbied for a relief plan to benefit independent restaurant owners who were financially devastated by the international coronavirus pandemic. Zimmern lives in Minnesota and shares a teenage son, Noah, with his ex-wife Rishia Haas.

DESSERT

Zimmern has confessed in various interviews that in spite of his *Bizarre Foods* reputation for eating foods like dinosaur and 3,000-year-old butter, some of his favorite foods include the more humble likes of gas station fried chicken, coffee ice cream, mini hot dogs in barbecue sauce, and his grandmother's roast chicken.

The food star's personal food aversions include hot oatmeal, walnuts, and raw cookie dough. But you won't hear the chef turn up his nose in disgust, even at these. "If I'm served them somewhere else I always eat them because I'd rather be a good dinner guest," Zimmern told *Travel & Leisure* magazine in 2018.

SUGGESTED PAIRINGS

See also: Asian American Cuisine; Aspen Food and Wine Classic; Bourdain, Anthony; Latin American Cuisine; Unusual Foods.

Entry best enjoyed while eating: Hawaiian-style octopus with sea salt, lemongrass, ginger, chiles, and taro leaves; a hot cup of Chinese donkey-rib soup over rice; Rocky Mountain oysters (deep-fried calf testicles) served with lemon and ketchup; and two "chocolate-chirp cookies," baked with chocolate chips and dry-roasted crickets.

Further Reading

Berman, John, and Mary Flynn. 2010. "Stomach Soup, Anyone? Confessions of 'Bizarre Foods' Eater." *Nightline,* ABC News, July 27, 2010. http://abcnews.go.com/Nightline/bizarre-foods-eater-andrew-zimmern/story?id=11251833

Berman, Joshua. 2009. "Interview with Andrew Zimmern: Travels in a 'Bizarre World.'" September 15, 2009. http://www.worldhum.com/features/travel-interviews/interview-with-andrew-zimmern-travels-in-a-bizarre-world-20090909/

Leasca, Stacey. 2018. "This Is the One 'Bizarre Food' Andrew Zimmern Says All Travelers Need to Try." *Travel and Leisure*, January 23, 2018.

Meyer-Rochow, Victor Benno. 2009. "Food Taboos: Their Origins and Purposes." *Journal of Ethnobiology and Ethnomedicine* 5 (June): 18. https://doi.org/10.1186/1746-4269-5-18

Rense, Sarah. 2017. "Somehow, It's Still Possible to Surprise Andrew Zimmern." *Esquire*, January 30, 2017.

Simoons, F. J. 1994. *Eat not This Flesh: Food Avoidances from Prehistory to the Present*. Madison: University of Wisconsin Press.

Smith, Marjorie. 2009. "Food Taboos and Oddities: Q&A with Brian Stross." December 6, 2009. https://news.utexas.edu/2009/12/06/food-taboos-and-oddities-qa-with-brian-stross

Spence, Shay. 2018. "Andrew Zimmern Reveals the 'Traumatic' Event that Led him Down the Path of Addiction at Age 13." *People*, January 17, 2018.

Travel Channel Press Release. 2017. "Bizarre Foods with Andrew Zimmern Delivers Its Highest-Rated Premiere Episode Since April 2015." February 3, 2017.

Travel Channel Staff. 2018a. "Meet Andrew Zimmern." http://www.travelchannel.com/shows/bizarre-foods/articles/meet-andrew-zimmern

Travel Channel Staff. 2018b. "10 Things You Didn't Know About Me." *Bizarre Foods, Travel Channel*. http://www.travelchannel.com/shows/bizarre-foods/articles/10-things-you-dont-know-about-me

Zimmern, Andrew. 2009. *The Bizarre Truth: How I Walked Out the Door Mouth First . . . and Came Back Shaking My Head*. New York: Broadway Books.

Zimmern, Andrew. 2012. *Andrew Zimmern's Field Guide to Exceptionally Weird, Wild, Wonderful Foods: An Intrepid Eater's Digest*. New York: Feiwel & Friends.

Bourdain, Anthony (1956–2018)

STARTERS

Anthony Bourdain was a writer, chef, producer, and television host who was often referred to as one of the most influential and best-known chefs in the industry. Bourdain achieved celebrity status almost overnight as a result of his book *Kitchen Confidential* (2000), a mega-bestselling tell-all memoir about the restaurant industry. The book was an extension of an essay he'd published in *The New Yorker* magazine the prior year. His writing career included the publication of cookbooks, graphic novels, crime fiction, and numerous essays.

Following the success of his early written work, Bourdain became a household name on television, including his travelogue food shows *Anthony Bourdain: Parts Unknown* (2013–) and *Anthony Bourdain: No Reservations* (2005–2012), among others. He was the executive producer of the hit show *The Mind of a Chef* (2012–) and *The Taste* (2013–2015) and a producer, writer, and actor in a number of film projects. Additionally, he was a frequent guest star and judge on popular reality food shows such as *Top Chef*. In recent years, he aspired to develop a large-scale food market in Manhattan. Inspired by Singapore's open-air food courts, Bourdain intended to bring street food vendors from around the world to work there.

Over the course of his career, Bourdain was the recipient of numerous renowned awards. In 2001, *Bon Appétit* dubbed him Food Writer of the Year, and in 2008, he received the honor of the James Beard Foundation's "Who's Who of Food and Beverage in America." In 2012, he received an honorary CLIO award. *No Reservations* won a Creative Arts Emmy in 2009 and 2010, followed by a Critics Choice award in 2013. *Parts Unknown* was nominated for 25 Emmy awards in total, winning 5 between 2013 and 2016, as well as a Peabody award in 2014.

ENTRÉE

"At the base of my right forefinger is an inch-and-a-half diagonal callus, yellowish brown in color, where the heels of all the knives I've ever owned have rested," Bourdain wrote in his best-selling memoir *Kitchen Confidential*. "I'm proud of this one. It distinguishes me as a cook

Anthony Bourdain in Los Angeles, California, at the 2014 Creative Arts Emmy Awards ceremony. Bourdain continued to win media awards after his untimely death in 2018, including two posthumous Creative Emmy awards in 2019 for his CNN travel show "Parts Unknown." (Starstock/Dreamstime.com)

... you can feel it when you shake my hand, just as I feel it on others of my profession" (296). The publication of *Kitchen Confidential* transformed Bourdain into a celebrity almost instantaneously. To many readers who worked in the restaurant industry, the descriptions in his book felt like a secret handshake between people who had been in the trenches together in kitchens all across the country.

The memoir served as a "tell all," exposing the general culture of restaurant kitchens as bawdy and dramatic. His book describes roaring stovetop flames, interpersonal drama, drug addiction issues, and frequent injuries—a far cry from the tinkling classical music and restrained conversation murmurs taking place in the adjacent white-tablecloth-adorned dining rooms. Readers were fascinated to learn secrets of this unfamiliar world, and many professional food industry workers recognized themselves—and their own callused and scarred hands—in Bourdain's poetic, gritty descriptions of kitchen life.

Bourdain exuded an interesting mix of pride and self-deprecation about his skills as a professional chef. He noted the irony in the fact that he was eventually embraced by a number of high-profile, world-class chefs in his career—not because of his skills in the kitchen, which he had worked hard to hone, but because of his skills telling stories about kitchen life. Bourdain's life story seemed to have been peppered with the same grit and sentimentality as his writings. Tony, as he was called by friends and family, was born in 1956 and grew up in New Jersey with his parents and a younger brother. At the age of nine, Bourdain traveled to France with his family, a trip in which his intense relationship with food and fine cuisine largely began.

Kitchen Confidential describes his time in France as an experience that exposed him to rebellious joys, such as underage drinking, smoking, and exploring World-War-II-era tunnels on the beach with his brother and other boys. He also discovered more sophisticated pleasures: the complex tastes and textures of rich soft cheese and baguettes, the forbidden lure of foods like sweetbreads and horsemeat, and—in what he describes as a poignant rite of passage—cutting open and devouring his first raw oyster, straight from the Mediterranean Sea. The adventure of travel, connections with others, rebellion, thoughtful literary observations, and the taste and experience of authentic local cuisines he described from this trip would go on to become the hallmarks of his career.

As a young man, Bourdain attended Vassar College for two years before dropping out. He has described himself during these years as sometimes wearing nunchucks on campus and writing papers for classmates in exchange for drugs. His restaurant career started as a dishwasher at the Flagship, a restaurant in the Cape Cod town of Provincetown, Massachusetts, which drew large tourist populations each summer. Bourdain attended the renowned Culinary Institute of America in Hyde Park, New York, and continued to work his way up the restaurant career rungs in Provincetown.

After graduating from culinary school, he married his high school girlfriend, Nancy Putkoski, and secured a job at the renowned Rainbow Room in New York City's Rockefeller Center. Over the next two decades, Bourdain worked at a wide variety of restaurants before becoming the executive chef at a Manhattan brasserie called Les Halles. Inspired from some of his prior employers, Bourdain's management style was shrewd, highly detail oriented, and extremely focused on the importance of punctuality and demonstrating consistent excellence in the workplace.

Writing

Bourdain wrote the restaurant industry exposé essay "Don't Eat Before Reading This" during his time at Les Halles. He originally submitted the essay to a small weekly New York publication and was met with rejection. Following his mother's suggestion, he submitted it to *The New Yorker*, where it was accepted. Within a couple of days of the essay's publication, Bourdain was offered a book deal to write *Kitchen Confidential*. Although he had previously studied creative writing under the guidance of Gordon Lish in a writing workshop, Bourdain has described the writing process of his mega-bestseller as unfussy and fast paced, writing at 5:00 a.m. before leaving for work every day. Over the next two decades,

Bourdain continued to be a prolific writer. His work encompassed a broad range of culinary subjects and genres, from *Typhoid Mary* (2001), a biographical sketch of a cook who was accused of bringing an outbreak of typhoid fever to Long Island, to graphic novels *Get Jiro* (2012) and *Get Jiro: Blood and Sushi* (2015).

Bourdain's essays have been published in the *New York Times*, *Food Arts* magazine, *Bon Appétit*, *Vanity Fair*, *Lucky Peach*, *The Times of London*, *Gourmet*, and the *Independent*, just to name a few. His 2006 publication *The Nasty Bits* compiled fiction with a number of his essays, and in 2010, he came out with *Medium Raw*, a new collection of essays in the style of *Kitchen Confidential*. Cookbooks included *Les Halles Cookbook* (2004), which offered insight into his French cuisine expertise, and *Appetites* (2016), cowritten by Laurie Woolever, geared toward home cooking and family meals. He also published print companions for his television shows, including *A Cook's Tour* (2002) and *No Reservations* (2007). In 2013, Bourdain became the owner of his own publishing line, Anthony Bourdain Books, under an imprint of HarperCollins publishers called Ecco Books.

Television Work

Throughout his career, Bourdain was exhaustively referred to as America's "bad boy chef," inspired by scathing comments he made about people and trends in the food industry, his prior involvement with drugs, and his rock star aesthetic of clothing and tattoos. Although the clichéd "bad boy" label hounded him into his sixties, he was also often discussed with reverence for his poetic sensibilities, affable nature, and ability to connect television audiences in a personal way to the people, places, and food he encountered on his travels.

The four television shows Bourdain starred in spanned across three major networks over the course of 16 years, but essentially portrayed the same theme. The chef and his crews wandered all corners of the globe in search of delicious, interesting, and authentic regional food, forging connections with people and places in the process. In 2002, the Food Network signed Bourdain on for two seasons of *A Cook's Tour*, in which he traveled the world looking for the "perfect meal." The show lasted for two seasons and 35 episodes before ending in 2003, giving Bourdain exposure to foreign cultures and foods that were new to him—a significant career change for someone who was in his mid-forties at the time.

Over the next 16 years, the focus of Bourdain's various shows shifted slightly to reflect their networks. *A Cook's Tour* was a travel show mostly centered around food, with a focus on some foods that were perceived as "dangerous" and exotic. The show gained more travel focus on *No Reservations* (2005–2012), a food-themed travel memoir that ran for 142 episodes on the Travel Channel. When Bourdain left the Travel Channel in 2011, the next iteration of his show began—CNN's *Parts Unknown*—which took on a decidedly more political focus. *Parts Unknown* filmed 11 seasons between 2013 and 2018. Bourdain's insistence on maintaining creative control was a driving force of his switch between networks.

The hundreds of episodes Bourdain starred in took viewers to parts of the world and featured foods that many Americans have never seen before. In Vietnam,

Bourdain ate a beating cobra's heart that had been removed seconds earlier from a still-living snake; in Iceland, he ate putrid-smelling fermented shark. He swigged a shot of Vodka in St. Petersburg before diving into a frozen river, and he feasted on pounded yam in Laos. Conflict zones weren't off limits either; Bourdain and his crew traveled through Libya (where he received instruction on operating an automatic firearm should his crew come under fire), Iran, Gaza, and even explored the Congo River by boat, a journey inspired by Joseph Conrad's novel *Heart of Darkness*. Episodes set in the United States also took a critical approach to exploring local cuisine. In one *Parts Unknown* episode, Bourdain discovered that people from cheesesteak-famous Philadelphia drove to New Jersey to try the Garden State's cheesesteak variations. In another episode, he focused on multicultural foods in Houston, Texas, highlighting the city's immigrants from places such as Vietnam and Ecuador.

In 2017, the *Washington Post* reported that Bourdain had been banned from Azerbaijan because *Parts Unknown* had filmed a segment in Nagorno-Karabakh, a region controlled by Armenia (the Azerbaijani government considers travel to the occupied region without permission a criminal offense). Numerous episodes of his shows also captured startling events, such as when the *No Reservations* crew unexpectedly found themselves in a warzone when Hezbollah forces in Beirut came under retaliatory missile attack from Israel. In Borneo, Bourdain killed a pig with a spear on camera for *No Reservations* and repeated the event a decade later when revisiting the area for *Parts Unknown*. The act of killing the first pig deeply affected Bourdain and his crew, and the incidents were criticized by some animal rights activists. Bourdain defended the event as part of honoring the request of his hosts and their culture.

Considering the similarity between his first two shows, Bourdain's move to CNN took some by surprise, since CNN was often considered a news journalism channel, and Bourdain was not considered a traditional journalist. In a 2017 profile on Bourdain in the *New Yorker*, film director Darren Aronofsky called Bourdain's style "personal journalism" in regard to his way of disarming his subjects with informal discussion and personable company over a shared meal, resulting in strong interviews and memorable stories. Bourdain maintained that the bias he infused into his show and writing did not qualify him as a journalist, saying, "I want you to feel the way I feel when I see things" (Kahn 2018). The unconventional show's placement on the network was met with success, averaging 820,000 viewers an episode as of 2015 (Yahr 2016).

On June 8, 2018, many were shocked worldwide when news outlets reported that Bourdain had died in a French hotel room as a result of suicide. A reporter for the *New York Times* wrote, "Anthony Bourdain understood that eating was simply a way of taking the world inside you ... His globe-trotting, globe-eating series were full of wonder, humor and lusty eating pleasure. But above all, they were about people, for whom food is the most intimate form of expression" (Poniewozik 2018).

ACCOMPANIED BY

In a 2012 essay in *Bon Appétit* magazine, Bourdain wrote that he attributed much of his joy of food—and approach to cooking and traveling—to his father,

> ### Small Plates
>
> **Street Food Chic**
>
> Street food is defined as ready-to-eat food that's served in open public places. The practice of selling food on the street dates back to ancient Mesopotamia, evolving over time from food sold from baskets to fare served out of wheelbarrows, trailers affixed to bicycles, carts parked along curbs, and trays attached to straps worn around the neck. Today, an estimated 2.5 billion individuals regularly consume street food, accounting for roughly a third of the earth's population.
>
> In many places, street food's popularity is due to its affordability and ease of procuring for many low-income individuals. Street food booths and vendors are also a significant part of the culture in cities such as Bangkok, Thailand; Ho Chi Minh City, Vietnam; Marrakech, Morocco; and Singapore. In the United States, street food culture has been particularly prominent in urban areas like Los Angeles, California; New York City, New York; Austin, Texas; and Portland, Oregon.
>
> Anthony Bourdain was credited as being an "evangelist for street food," bringing a media spotlight to fare that is often overlooked (Keefe 2017). Although street food has such a long history and is a staple in many cities across the globe, it is a rising star in terms of attention and appeal in pop culture, sophistication, and clout. Notably, Singaporean chef Chan Hon Meng received the first ever coveted Michelin star to be awarded to street food vendors. The chef received the award in 2016 for his Hong Kong-style soy sauce chicken, rice, and noodle food stall.
>
> Bourdain's proposed large-scale market in Manhattan sought to capitalize on the open market food stalls like Chan's that he experienced across the world. Bourdain didn't want to simply emulate the experiences he'd seen in places like Bangkok, Singapore, and Ho Chi Minh City; he wanted to bring the vendors and flavors of those places straight to Manhattan, issuing visas and arranging accommodations for the street food vendors in the process.
>
> Many share Bourdain's affinity for street food, and view the act of eating it as an emotional experience. Buying roasted chestnuts from cart vendors at Christmas; slathering ketchup, mustard, and onions on hot dogs purchased from carts in New York City; savoring market-bought crêpes while strolling the streets of Paris; sampling bahn mi sandwiches from street food stalls in Saigon; or enjoying a breakfast of Chilaquiles purchased from a food vendor Mexico are the type of details many cherish from travel memories. As it turns out, some of the most memorable meals don't require a reservation.

Pierre Bourdain (1930–1987). His father was born in Manhattan and worked in the classical music recording industry. Bourdain's mother, Gladys, worked for the *New York Times* as a copy editor, and his paternal grandparents were from France, which played a significant role in his discovery of international cuisines. Bourdain's parents exposed him to a wide array of cuisines, exploring new restaurants and unusual foods in Manhattan as a family.

Bourdain was married twice—first to Nancy Putkoski in 1985, a high school girlfriend he had followed to Vassar. The two divorced in 2005 after a 20-year marriage. In 2007, Bourdain married Ottavia Busia, a mixed martial-arts fighter. The pair was introduced by chef Éric Ripert when Busia worked as a hostess at Le Bernadin, one of Ripert's world-famous restaurants. Busia and Bourdain decided to try to have a child together after he returned from his harrowing experience filming *No Reservations* in Beirut. Their daughter Ariane was born in 2007, and the couple wed less than two weeks later (Kahn 2018). Bourdain was quoted in the press about the toll that his intense travel schedule took on his family at times, citing a mere 20 weeks spent in New York in all of 2016 and average of 250 days a year spent on the road. His marriage to Busia ended in 2016. Later that year, reports surfaced that he was in a serious relationship with Italian film actress Asia Argento, a vocal member of the #MeToo movement. During their time together, Bourdain broadcast his support of the movement and Argento's role in it.

DESSERT

- **Who would play you?** *Kitchen Confidential* was made into a television show that enjoyed a short run; Bradley Cooper played the character based on Bourdain.
- **Filed under "F" for "full":** In a profile on Bourdain, journalist Oliver Strand of *Vogue* described the chef as "consuming such a staggering variety of food that he's something like the Library of Congress of eating."
- **Instagram worthy:** "Excuse me, I'm going to have to take a picture of this. I want to make other people feel bad about what they're eating"—Bourdain, while eating grilled beluga caviar in Basque Country (Fuhrmeister 2017).
- **Taste of NOLA:** Bourdain was hired to write various restaurant scenes for the HBO drama series *Treme* by the show's creator David Simon.
- **Travel tip:** Bourdain offered this advice to *Esquire* on how to find a good place to eat in a new city: "provoke nerd fury online." He suggested finding online food forums and posting (a fictitious story) about something great you ate at a specific restaurant. "All these annoying foodies will bombard you with angry replies," he said, and they will likely offer better suggestions in the process.

SUGGESTED PAIRINGS

See also: Asian American Cuisine; *Bizarre Foods with Andrew Zimmern*; Documentary Films, Food and Beverages in; Food Trucks; Latin American Cuisine; *Mind of a Chef, The*; Television, Food Channels on.

Entry best enjoyed while eating: Cape-Cod-inspired oysters grilled with butter, tabasco and lime; Malaysian *Kuching laksa*, a spicy noodle soup with a stock and coconut milk base; Vietnamese *do chua* salad, pickled carrots, and daikon radish with scallions, bean sprouts, eggs, and herbs; and Les Halles' chocolate mousse, made with orange liqueur.

Further Reading

Bourdain, Anthony. 2000. *Kitchen Confidential: Adventures in the Culinary Underbelly*, updated edition, 2007. New York: HarperCollins Publishers.

Bourdain, Anthony. 2011. "A Beginning. An End." Tumblr post, July 29, 2011. http://anthonybourdain.tumblr.com/post/8216534507/a-beginning-an-end

Bourdain, Anthony. 2012. "Ever Wonder How Anthony Bourdain Came to Be Anthony Bourdain? (All the Credit Goes to Dad)." *Bon Appétit*, May 31, 2012.

Davies, Dave. 2017. "Anthony Bourdain on 'Appetites,' Washing Dishes and the Food He Still Won't Eat." National Public Radio, aired on *Fresh Air*, October 17, 2017.

Erikson, Amanda. 2017. "Anthony Bourdain Just Got Banned from Azerbaijan." *The Washington Post*, "World Views." October 27, 2017.

The Food People. 2012. "Street Food Revolution." Infographic. https://thefoodpeople.co.uk/infographics/street-food

Fuhrmeister, Chris. 2017. "Anthony Bourdain Parts Unknown in San Sebastián: Just the One-Liners." *Eater*, May 7, 2017. https://www.eater.com/2017/5/7/15547682/anthony-bourdain-parts-unknown-san-sebastian

Hunt, Kristin. 2015. "A Brief History of Anthony Bourdain Insulting Other Food Celebrities." *Thrillist,* July 14, 2017. https://www.thrillist.com/eat/nation/anthony-bourdain-celebrity-chef-feuds

Kahn, Howie. 2018. "Anthony Bourdain's Globalist Mission." *The Wall Street Journal*, March 28, 2018.

Keefe, Patrick Radden. 2017. "Anthony Bourdain's Moveable Feast." *The New Yorker*, February 13 & 20, 2017 Issue.

Poniewozik, James. 2018. "The Man Who Ate the World: Anthony Bourdain." *The New York Times*, June 8, 2018.

Ratledge, Ingela. 2011. "Anthony Bourdain's Celebrity Chef Smackdown." *TV Guide*, August 18, 2011. http://www.tvguide.com/news/anthony-bourdains-celebrity-1036482/

Strand, Oliver. 2016. "Anthony Bourdain on Authenticity, Expectations, and Opening the Country's Most Ambitious Food Hall." *Vogue*, October 21, 2016.

Yahr, Emily. 2016. "How Anthony Bourdain Went from CNN's Biggest Risk to Its Most Unexpected Star." *The Washington Post*, September 20, 2016.

Brown, Alton (1962–)

STARTERS

Alton Brown is an American television show host, writer, and producer who is best known as the host of Food Network's *Good Eats* and the emcee on *Iron Chef America*. Brown has served as a judge, host, and guest star on a large number of television shows, including *Iron Chef* spin-offs, culinary travel shows *Feasting on Asphalt* and *Feasting on Waves*, and reality competitions *Cutthroat Kitchen* and *Food Network Star*. In addition to authoring a number of cookbooks, Brown also performs in a food-themed theatrical variety show and hosts a culinary podcast. Brown has been nominated several times for various James Beard awards, winning for his cookbook *I'm Just Here for the Food* in 2003, and as "Best TV Food Personality" for *Good Eats* in 2011. *Good Eats* won a Peabody Award in 2006, a rare honor for an educational cooking show. Brown received a Shorty Award, which honors achievements in social media, and was the host of the James Beard Award ceremony in 2015.

ENTRÉE

Brown, a lover of bow ties, cast iron skillets, bourbon, and wristwatches, has been honing his culinary storytelling skills for nearly two decades. Born in Los

Angeles, Brown's family moved to Georgia when he was in elementary school. In high school, he discovered a passion for jazz. He played saxophone and loved listening to jazz legends like Miles Davis. He graduated at the age of 16, and after a short period of feeling adrift while trying to find a direction in life, he studied theater and film at LaGrange College and the University of Georgia. His career began in filmmaking, in which he made a living as a director of photography, editor, and director, primarily on television commercials.

Whereas many television culinary celebrities began their career in the culinary world and moved into television, Brown's path took the opposite route. In the 1990s, Brown became interested in the rise of cooking show popularity, but he was uninspired by the style in which they were filmed. In a 2016 interview with *Bitter Southerner* magazine, Brown recalled his reaction to the way cooking was traditionally taught on television: "God these are boring, I'm not really learning anything . . . To learn means to really understand. You never got those out to those shows." He recalled jotting a note down one day that was an idea to create a show that could serve as a combination of Julia Child, Mr. Wizard, and Monty Python—a colorful, comedic spin on culinary television. "It's very difficult to teach people. You got to engage brains," Brown said, citing his inspiration to create a show that delved into the science of cooking, while entertaining viewers as they learned to cook alongside him (Reece 2016).

Television Work

Brown followed his passion for educating the masses about cooking via television, but there was a hitch along the way: he wasn't a professional cook. With the support of his then-wife, DeAnna Brown, he attended the New England Culinary Institute in Vermont. After graduating from culinary school, Brown's first foray into television was the show *Good Eats*, which he wrote, produced, and starred in. The show premiered on the Food Network channel on July 7, 1999. The half-hour program enjoyed a run of 19 seasons and over 250 episodes, ending in 2012 (though staying alive through reruns on Netflix and the Cooking Channel and recently getting slated for an internet-based sequel).

Good Eats stuck to Brown's initial vision for an instructional television show peppered with humor and educational elements beyond simply showing how to cook specific dishes. It was described by the *New York Times* as a "smart mix of history, science and cooking, shot with homemade props and a cinematographer's sensibility" and being "more sophisticated than anything the network had ever shown" (Severson 2016). Hosted by Brown, the show uses funny props, fictitious scenarios, and other whimsical means of explaining the science behind various cooking and baking techniques. It also delves into the history and pop culture appeal of the foods he's preparing.

Each episode features a specific type of food or cuisine, ranging from arguably mundane dishes like oatmeal or dinner rolls to international dishes like Japanese Katsuobushi (dried tuna flakes, a popular ingredient) and squid-stuffed squid. A frequent theme of the show is to demonstrate ways to use cooking equipment in conventional and unconventional ways. Brown does this both to inspire ingenuity in the kitchen and to encourage home cooks to find multiple uses for each kitchen gadget. In an interview with *Food Network Magazine*, Brown said that he wanted *Good Eats* to educate viewers about "common but little-understood foods and food science" (Cohen 2009). As such, many of the recipes he presents in his shows and cookbooks are for foods that are commonly only eaten as pre-packaged snacks. His recipe for barbecue potato chips in *EveryDayCook* requires the equivalent of a free afternoon and an outdoor butane cooker (or the instruction to at least remove the batteries from the indoor smoke detectors). In the twelfth season of *Good Eats*, an entire episode called "Flat Is Beautiful" is devoted to cooking homemade crackers.

In 2005, Brown was cast as the host of *Iron Chef America*, the spinoff of the original *Iron Chef*, which premiered in Japan. The production entailed a grueling schedule of filming two episodes a day in New York City. Commenting on the unusual and varied ingredients he was tasked with commenting on during the shows, Brown joked that he was out of his league, having not had "16 different types of kelp" to choose from while grocery shopping at Kroger before (Reece 2016).

In 2012, Brown joined the cast of the show *Food Network Star*, alongside celebrity chefs such as Giada De Laurentiis and Bobby Flay. The show featured chefs who were vying to prove that they had the culinary skills and strong personalities to be featured in their own show. The following year, Brown joined the cast of Food Network's *Cutthroat Kitchen*, a cooking competition that introduced an element of comedy by allowing chefs to sabotage each other. At the beginning of each show, chefs were allotted a specific amount of money, which they were allowed to spend in order to hinder other chefs' progress. For the unfortunate sabotaged chefs, Brown ordered humorous handicaps of his own devising, such as having to use miniature cooking equipment, cooking an entrée while rolling around in a tube, or cooking crepes in a pan that had been folded into half. The show racked up an impressive 15 seasons in four years.

From 2006 through 2008, Brown hosted a culinary travelogue documentary series on the Food Network called *Feasting on Asphalt* and its complement, *Feasting on Waves*. Episodes followed Brown's motorcycle trip along the Mississippi River, from the Gulf of Mexico up through Minnesota, sampling local foods along the way. He published a companion book, *Feasting on Asphalt: The River Run* about the adventure in 2008, complete with recipes for regional fare such as Louisiana-style grilled alligator tail and vegetable borscht. The third season, dubbed *Feasting on Waves*, features Brown's travels in the Caribbean, in which he documents Caribbean history alongside sampling traditional local foods. A European season called *Feasting on Rails* was considered, and Brown—an avid pilot who flies a twin-engine plane—also wanted to do *Feasting in Air and Space*.

Variety Shows

In addition to a seemingly exhausting lineup of television shows and appearances, books, podcast recordings, and numerous other responsibilities, Brown's

> **Small Plates**
>
> **Cupcakegate**
>
> In 2012, the Transportation Security Administration (TSA) faced criticism for confiscating a traveler's cupcake before she boarded the plane. "Cupcakegate," as the story was referred to in a TSA blog post that month, stemmed from the organization's discomfort with the cupcake's unusual storage container—a glass jar—as well as the cupcake's thick layer of frosting. The TSA stood behind their decision, citing the thick layer of icing as a gel, one of the substances that TSA strictly limits on flights.
>
> When asked by *Condé Nast's Traveler* if TSA was in the wrong to have confiscated the offending confection, Brown flexed his dictionary-level memory for food: "Icing is *not* a gel (. . .) we get that word from *gelatin*, which implies coagulated proteins," he told the magazine. "Technically frosting is a condensed syrup, so I would argue with TSA that they were out of (their) mind" (Cohen 2012).
>
> Moral of the story? If you want to bring a curious container of dessert on board with sky-high levels of icing, your best bet is to see if you can bring it aboard Alton Brown's personal jet.

drive to create creative culinary entertainment inspired a live variety show. In 2013, his theatrical show "Inevitable Edible Tour" sold more than 150,000 tickets to sold-out shows in more than 100 cities. Brown's performance blended a number of his passions: he played the guitar and sang songs about food, performed comedy routines with puppets, and presented off-the-wall cooking demonstrations that required audience members in the first few rows to don ponchos. In 2017, a second variety show of the same nature, "Eat Your Science Tour," hit the road for a 40-city tour—with new causes for ponchos, new puppets, and new science-fueled cooking wizardry.

ACCOMPANIED BY

Family

Brown's parents hailed from Cornelia, Georgia. They returned to Georgia in Alton's youth to afford his father, Alton Brown Sr., the opportunity to open a radio station. When Brown was in sixth grade, his father passed away in a reported suicide that Alton has questioned as a possible murder. At the time of his death, Brown Sr. was wearing a high-quality wristwatch, which Brown was given in his youth. In college, the watch was stolen during a break-in of Brown's apartment. Incredibly, twenty years after the robbery, Brown found his father's watch for sale on eBay and was able to verify the authenticity of the Omega Chronostop due to notes his father had kept about the timepiece when he was alive. Brown restored the watch and still wears it today. His mother, who he told the *New York Times* "didn't have a lot of respect for me until I was famous," was an editor for Brown Sr.'s radio show and married four more times after her late husband's death (Severson 2016). Brown's grandmother, Mae Parsons Skelton, helped impart a love of cooking to him at a young age, and even went on to cook biscuits with him in an episode of *Good Eats*.

Brown had a short-lived marriage shortly after college, and he later went on to marry DeAnna (née Collins), a video producer who went on to produce episodes for, and eventually run, Alton's production company. DeAnna helped Brown develop and pitch *Good Eats* to various networks, even coming up with the show's name. In 1999, the couple had a daughter, Zoey, who has appeared on a number of episodes of the show. In recent years, Brown has had some significant changes in his life. His marriage to DeAnna ended in 2015, and his views on his religious faith shifted around this time as well. He resigned from the Baptist church he and his family attended and made significant changes to his diet and exercise regime. Brown has described changing his habits to have one alcoholic or sweet indulgence to look forward to each week.

DESSERT

- **Fun fact:** In his pre-culinary television profession, Alton Brown was the director of photography for the band R.E.M.'s music video "The One I Love" in 1987.
- **That's so analog:** Brown has been credited for inventing "Analog Tweets." In response to queries he receives on Twitter, Brown doodles whimsical drawings on Post-Its, which he then tweets photos of.
- **Biggest misconception?** "That I'm a chef," Brown told *Bon Appétit* in 2016, "which I do not purport to be in any way, shape, or form."
- **Using a gadget for many tasks:** The food photography in *EveryDayCook* was all shot on an iPhone camera. The photos were taken by his brand manager, Sarah De Heer, a colleague who is credited with transforming his social media into having an enormous following. De Heer also helped to develop #ABRoadEats, a popular program in which fans tweet suggestions of where Brown and his crew should eat while on the road.
- **On being primarily recognized as a "science guy":** Brown finds his celebrity status in the science field amusing, considering the fact that he failed his science courses as a student and had to take a number of them again.

SUGGESTED PAIRINGS

See also: Best Thing I Ever Ate, The; Iron Chef; Laurentiis, Giada De; Roadside Food Attractions; Television, Food Channels on.

Entry best enjoyed while eating: Perfect scrambled eggs (the dish Alton says everyone should know how to make), cooked with a dollop of mayo and harissa; hot cocoa with a pinch of cayenne pepper and homemade miniature marshmallows; and a short stack of nitrous-oxide pancakes, made exactly as the pioneers would have—with eggs, flour, sugar, buttermilk, a whipped cream siphon, and an N_2O charger.

Further Reading
"Alton Brown's 'Eat Your Science Tour'." 2017. Press release, October 25, 2017.

Bilow, Rochelle, 2016. "Alton Brown on What the 'Cutthroat Kitchen Cameras Never Saw.'" *Bon Appétit,* April 7, 2016.

Brown, Alton. 2008. *Feasting on Asphalt: River Run.* New York: Stewart, Tabori, and Chang.

Brown, Alton. 2016. *EveryDayCook.* New York: Ballantine Books.

Burns, Bob. 2012. "Cupcakegate." Transportation Security Administration blog, January 9, 2012. https://www.tsa.gov/blog/2012/01/09/cupcakegate

Clymer, Benjamin. 2017. "Talking Watches with Alton Brown." Hodinkee, July 17, 2017. https://www.hodinkee.com/articles/talking-watches-with-alton-brown

Cohen, Arianne. 2009. "Good Eats: Behind the Scenes." *Food Network Magazine.* https://www.foodnetwork.com/recipes/articles/good-eats-behind-the-scenes

Cohen, Billie. 2012. "Alton Brown on Flying, Airplane Food, and Why Frosting Is Definitely Not a Gel." *Conde Nast Traveler,* July 16, 2012.

Reece, Chuck. 2016. "Alton Brown: The Bitter Southerner Interview." *Bitter Southerner.* http://bittersoutherner.com/alton-brown

Severson, Kim. 2016. "Alton Brown, Showman of Food TV, Pulls Back the Curtain." *New York Times*, September 26, 2016.

Cake and Cupcake Trends

STARTERS

Although its definition can be difficult to distinguish from various sweetened breads and other spongy desserts, cake is one of the most ubiquitous and enduring sweets used to commemorate celebrations around the world. Cake trends can be traced back to ancient times, and continue to evolve in contemporary times in countless variations. Some of the most popular contemporary trends entail highly elaborate cake decorations, as well as mini-cakes in the form of cupcakes and cake pops (cake crumbs that are rolled into balls, coated in icing, and served on lollipop sticks). Cakes are typically made with four basic ingredients—a source of fat (like butter or oil), sugar, flour, and eggs. They range from light, airy concoctions served plain or with fruit to multitiered creations filled with different-flavored layers and covered in thick frosting. Cake has been highly visible in popular culture in recent decades and is featured in a number of reality television shows, books, decorating and baking classes, websites, and articles. The dessert is celebrated in a wide variety of forms, ranging from pop art to community festivals, expos and trade shows, jewelry, fashion, and even mascots and Halloween costumes.

ENTRÉE

"Cake is more than foodstuff: it is the stuff of happy memories and comfort," author Alyssa Levene wrote in *Cake: A Slice of History* (2016, 5). Cake's definition, she explains, is difficult to articulate because of the wide variety of styles and varying ingredients it has adopted over the centuries. Sources ranging from lawyers to the judges on *The Great British Bake-Off* have included cake's "role in celebrations" as one of the dessert's key defining factors. Cake has been present in social celebrations dating back to ancient history, and bakers have a centuries-old history of delighting crowds with their lavish, over-the-top cake shapes and designs.

High-end cakes have enjoyed a resurgence in popularity in recent years. Fueled in part by social media sites such as Pinterest, trending cake designs are coveted and requested at weddings, birthdays, anniversaries, quinceaneras, and other celebrations. Many home cooks are returning to the tradition of creating labor-intensive birthday cakes for their children, as opposed to the boxed mix variety. Cake mixes, which first appeared around the 1920s, weren't initially popular due to customers' concern that they weren't making a "real" cake. Using a tip from

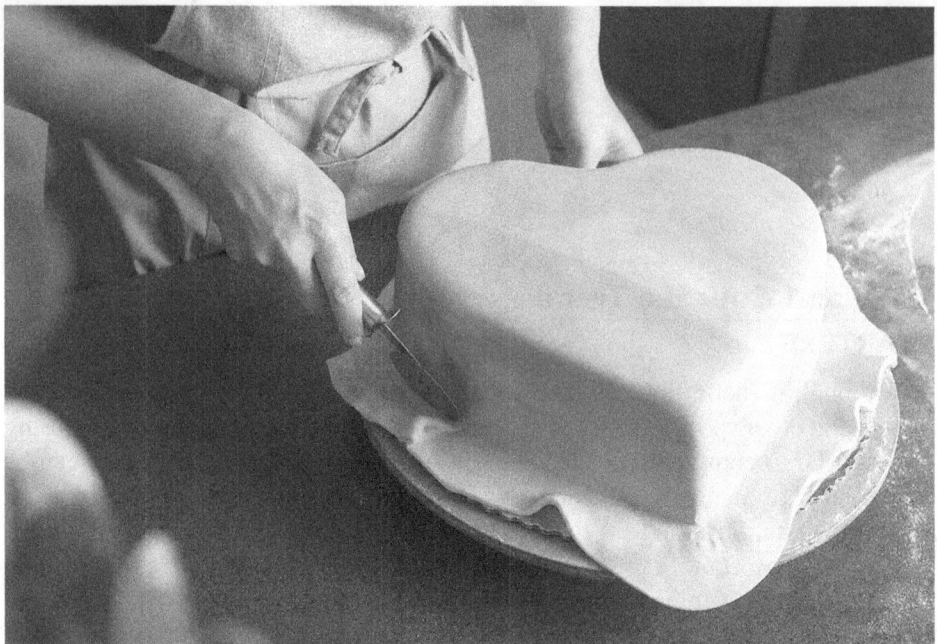

Contemporary cake designs often entail the use of fondant, a type of pliable, edible icing with the consistency of dough. Fondant is often used to create whimsical cake toppers and to help sculpt cakes into the likeness of other objects. (Andreaobzerova/Dreamstime.com)

psychologists, the Duff baking company replaced powdered eggs in the recipe with fresh eggs that customers needed to supply. Requiring home cooks to crack an egg did the trick in providing customers with the sense that they were "really" cooking, and as a result, boxed cake mix sales soared.

In recent years, popular design trends have included edible gold and other shimmering metallics; cakes designed to look like geodes (rocks with crystals inside); cakes designed to look like purses, women's shoes, and pets; cakes in ombre colors that cascade from light to dark; cakes in the shape of realistic hand-crafted sugar flowers and bold geometric patterns; gravity-defying sculptural cakes that appear to balance various segments in thin air; cakes designed to look like giant raindrops; and "shabby chic" cakes designed to look both rustic and elegant.

Cake in the Media

As with other trending food passions, there are no shortage of cake- and cupcake-themed television shows. Bakers and nonbakers alike tune in for competition shows like Food Network's *Cupcake Wars* (2009–) and its spinoff *Cake Wars* (2015), in which pastry chefs compete over the course of several rounds to incorporate unusual flavors and match their cake or cupcake to the episode's designated celebration themes. TLC's *Cake Boss* (2009) follows the stresses, challenges, and successes of family-run Carlo's Cake Shop in Hoboken, New Jersey, which specializes in artistic cakes depicting whimsical scenes, places, and things. The show spurred the spinoff *The Next Great Baker* (2010). Food Network also saw success with *Ace of Cakes* (2006), a reality show about Duff Goldman's Charm City Cakes shop in Baltimore, Maryland. Episodes followed Goldman's crew as they raced to create and deliver cakes, like one shaped like the Tower of London for Tom Clancy's birthday. Viewers also enjoyed cake shows like WE TV's *Amazing Wedding Cakes* (2008), TLC's *Ultimate Cake-Off* (2009), Netflix's *Nailed It!* (2018), and more.

The internet is another platform that's helped fuel cake's popularity, such as the popular humor website Cake Wrecks, which profiles professional cakes that have gone "horribly, hilariously wrong." The website debuted in 2008, the same year that a nationwide craze was set off for cake pops after blogger Angie Dudley shared a recipe for them on her blog Bakerella. Eight years previously, people around the nation went wild for cupcakes after an episode of the HBO show *Sex and the City* featured a brief scene of the lead characters enjoying a cupcake at New York City's Magnolia bakery. New cupcake shops popped up around the world, such as Sprinkles, which originated in Beverly Hills. Sprinkles' owner, *Cupcake Wars* judge Candace Nelson, also introduced "cupcake ATMs," which dispensed the baked treat 24-7 from select locations. In 2017, Netflix's comedic drama *Master of None* gently poked fun of the pop culture cupcake craze with a plotline involving the lead character, played by comedian Aziz Ansari, grappling with the futility of his career while hosting a fictitious show called *Clash of The Cupcakes*.

History of Cake

The origin of cake goes back roughly 4,000 years to the use of unleavened cakes created with barley and spelt, referred to as griddle cakes. Ancient Egyptians, credited as the first to honor birthdays as celebrations for pharaohs, played a key role in developing sophisticated celebratory cakes. This tradition was adopted by the Greeks and Romans, who also incorporated cakes in important rituals, and even had early forms of professional bakeries. The Greeks made moon-shaped cakes to honor the goddess of the moon, Artemis, and adorned the cakes with candles to emulate the moon's radiant light. Paintings and pottery also depicted the use of cakes in first-century CE China, and cake-baking tools were found in excavations of Pompeii (Levene 2016; Nowak n.d.). As legend has it, in 878 CE, Alfred the Great was scolded for his negligence over letting cakes burn due to his distraction over a Viking invasion of his territory.

Although the history of cakes goes back through the ages, the affordability and ease of baking them is a relatively new invention. Cakes of the past, such as gingerbreads dating back to the mid-fourteenth century, consisted of expensive ingredients that weren't easy to come by, making them a special delicacy. Dried fruits; nuts; and spices such as cloves, cinnamon, and ginger were prized and rare ingredients. It wasn't until after the Industrial Revolution that the prevalence of processed flour, refined sugar, and tools like the whisk and enclosed ovens led to the invention of the lighter and spongier cakes that are often seen today (Levene 2016).

America has contributed a lot to the cake world, as well, such as the layer cake, which *NPR* writer Nina Martyris referred to as "the perfect metaphor for a nation built on waves of immigrants." America's melting pot of nations, cultures, and people is well reflected in its cake history. Anne Byrn, author of *American Cake*, noted that African American cooks of the antebellum South were some of the best bakers in our history. Their advancements of cake recipes and artful incorporation of ingredients like coconut provided a lasting legacy. Similarly, the German roots of the Pennsylvania Dutch are to be thanked for treats like coffee cake, Angel Food cake, and applesauce cake. In times of shortages, such as during and after significant wars, cake bakers used their creativity to substitute key sources of sugar, eggs, flour, and fats, which are still used today for health conscious and vegan recipes.

DESSERT

- **Wait for it:** Birthday parties are thought to stem from the German *kinderfest*, a tradition in the 1700s in which a child would be awakened on his or her birthday with a cake lit with candles . . . and then had to wait until after *dinner* to blow out the (replaced-throughout-the-day) candles and dig in.
- **The Emperor-Cake's new clothes:** At an English wedding in 1942, a nine-year-old bridesmaid was reduced to tears when, at cake-cutting time, the large, frosted cake on display was revealed to be a cardboard facade hiding a small, plain fruit cake. The ruse was due to rationing during World War II. "I was never so disappointed in all my life," the bridesmaid reported in her adult years (Levene 2016).
- **But I saw it on the internet!** One of the most famously quoted lines in history is "let them eat cake," attributed to Marie Antoinette. Ironically, there is no historical record that the French queen ever said those words, and historians argue that she is unlikely to have said it at all.
- **Kingdom of Ding Dongs:** In the 1970s, the Hostess corporation advertised their snack cakes in a series of commercials featuring characters such as Twinkie the Kid, a cowboy riff on the cream-filled Twinkie sponge cake; King Ding Dong, representing the brand's cream-filled chocolate cakes; and Captain Cupcake, who took command on the dessert-seas of the S.S. Hostess.
- **Literal interpretations:** Writer Jen Yates is best known for her blog, Cake Wrecks, which features photos and comedic descriptions of "professional cakes gone horribly wrong." Many of the fan-favorite cakes are grocery store creations adorned with text describing the customer's *order request* itself. Much to their surprise, many customers have picked up cakes from their local bakeries with wobbly frosting letters exclaiming (often misspelled) phrases like "I Want Sprinkles," "Thanks for a Great Year in Purple," and, "Literally Just Write 'Wedding Cake.'"

SUGGESTED PAIRINGS

See also: Child, Julia; *Great British Bakeoff, The*; Ice Cream Trends; Tosi, Christina.

Entry best enjoyed while eating: In honor of Prince Harry and Meghan Markle's royal wedding cake in 2018, a slice of lemon and elderflower cake with buttercream, decorated with fresh flowers.

Further Reading

Byrn, Anne. 2016. *American Cake*. New York: Rodale Books.

Cake Wrecks. n.d. "The Cake Wrecks Team." http://cakewrecks.com/about

Levene, Alysa. 2016. *Cake: A Slice of History*. New York: Pegasus Books Ltd.

Martyris, Nina. 2016. "Make America Bake Again: A History of Cake in the U.S." NPR's *The Salt*, November 7, 2016.

Nowak, Claire. n.d. "Here's Why You Should Thank the Ancient Greeks for Your Birthday Cake." *Reader's Digest*. https://www.rd.com/culture/origin-of-birthday-cake/

"Royal Wedding Cake." n.d. Queen Victoria. http://www.queenvictoria.victoriana.com/RoyalWeddings/Royal_Wedding_Cake.html

California Avocado Festival

STARTERS

The California Avocado Festival is an annual community festival held in downtown Carpinteria, California, located in southeastern Santa Barbara County. The festival pays homage to all things avocado, including foods that incorporate avocado (traditionally and creatively), contests, live music, and arts and crafts. Notably, the festival boasts that it creates the world's "largest vat of guacamole." The event has taken place for 32 years and is held annually in October over the course of three days. Touted as one of the largest free festivals in the country, and one of the largest festivals held annually in California, it is a significant event for the community of Carpinteria. The festival is joined by a number of similar avocado celebrations each year in the state.

ENTRÉE

California produces about 90 percent of the nation's avocado crops, which accounts for the variety of avocado-themed festivals held there throughout the year (California Avocado Commission). For more than three decades, visitors have turned out in hundreds of thousands to celebrate avocados throughout the state. The California Avocado Festival was founded in 1986 by a group of community leaders searching for a fundraising opportunity for the community's nonprofit organizations, as well as to draw tourism to the city. Thirty-two years later, the festival is still going strong, drawing more than 100,000 visitors to the event each fall. The event has also grown to include seven volunteer board members, a paid administrator staff member, and hundreds of event volunteers. The City of Carpinteria and local chamber of commerce also provide support for the event, helping to recruit volunteers and plan for public safety measures (California Avocado Festival Inc 2018).

The event has entailed virtually everything related to the humble avocado. The contest for "best guacamole" considers the presentation, taste, and originality of contestants' guacamole (a dip traditionally made from mashed ripe avocados, tomatoes, onions, lime juice, salt, and cilantro). A similar contest is held for the largest avocado, which the California Tourism Board claims has awarded blue ribbons to avocados that exceed four pounds. This is especially impressive considering the fact the average Hass avocado weighs six ounces (Szalay 2014). The festival also holds a contest for the "best dressed avocado," in which children create costumes for their avocados, "strong man/woman" contests that entail competing to see who can hold the bags of the fruit for the longest time, an arts and crafts contest, and "best booth" prizes.

The food at the festival incorporates avocados into a wide variety of traditional and nontraditional dishes. Festivalgoers feast on heaping mounds of guacamole served with salty tortilla chips, scoops of avocado-flavored ice cream and gelato, deep-fried avocado, avocado chocolate truffles, avocado garlic chimichurri fries, tri-tip steak with guacamole, and avocado brownies. Local breweries get in on the fun, too; Carpinteria's Island Brewery serves up pints of AVO IPA and Avocado Honey Ale. To keep visitors entertained, the AvoFest (as it's sometimes called) features 75 bands on four stages over the three-day event (California Avocado Festival Inc 2018).

Other Avocado Celebrations

Another large festival in the state is the Fallbrook Avocado Festival. Fallbrook, an unincorporated county located just shy of 60 miles north of San Diego, boasts the title "Avocado Capital of the World." The festival takes place in the spring and—like Carpinteria's—was founded around 1986. An estimated 70,000 visitors turn out to enjoy the festivities, which include carnival rides, avocado cooking demonstrations, a children's car race and "Little Miss and Mister Avocado" contest, a "largest avocado" and guacamole contest, and Art of the Avocado art show (SeeCalifornia 2018a).

La Habra Heights, the home of the "mother tree" that bore the original Hass Avocados, also has an annual festival that honors avocados, as does Morro Bay, which adds margaritas in the festival's spotlight (SeeCalifornia 2018b). Not to be left out of the California avocado frenzy, San Francisco has "Avocado Con," a food truck festival located in the city's Mission Bay neighborhood. The food offerings are as diverse as they come, ranging from Vietnamese avocado-topped banh mi sandwiches to raspberry-avocado cream puffs, albacore tuna stuffed with avocado, and avocado boba milkshakes.

History and Popular Use of the Avocado

Amazingly, the complex and much-beloved avocado, or *Persea americana* by its Latin name, goes back to the Cenozoic Era, during which time ancient mammals such as giant sloths and mammoths ate the fruits whole and dispersed their seeds via their excrement (Handwerk 2017). Avocados originated in North America sometime between 7000 and 5000 BCE, flourishing in Mexico, the West Indies, and Central America. Avocado seeds found with the remains of Inca mummies suggest domestication of the plant may have taken place sometime around 500 BCE. The Aztecs bred avocados, which they called *ahuacatl* (named for a male part of the anatomy the fruit resembles), later renamed by the Spanish conquistadors to *aguacate*, a word that was easier for them to pronounce. Avocados have also been referred to as "alligator pears," and—by some in South America—"the apple of the winter."

Between 1914 and the mid-1970s, the leading variety of avocado was *Fuerte* (meaning strong), which had a smooth green skin and lacked the bumpy exterior many avocados are known for now. In 1926, Rudolph Hass tried growing avocados from a new variety of Guatemalan seeds, but was put off by the dark bumpy skin, since fruit that's black often indicates rotten produce. Hass's sons convinced him that despite the exterior's arguably unpleasant appearance, the taste of the new avocado was delicious. The Hass avocado had a humble start for many years before its popularity boomed in the 1970s. By the 1990s, Fuerte avocados comprised a tiny percentage of California's avocado production, and Hass avocados accounted for 95 percent of California's avocados (Shepherd and Bender 2013).

By the year 2015, avocados had become so popular that Americans were consuming an average of seven pounds of them a year (Fereira and Perez 2017). Some European countries and China have also had higher avocado consumption rates in recent years, putting a strain on the California avocado supply. Avocado sales soared to record highs, due in part to the continuing popularity of the fruit and the fact that avocado supplies alternate between larger and smaller crops, and 2017 was a "smaller crop" year. For small restaurants and restaurant chain giants alike, those that serve avocados have faced steep prices to keep their customers happy in recent years (Judkis 2017).

ACCOMPANIED BY

Carpinteria Resident Remembered

In 2017, the AvoFest honored the memory of Denise Cohen, a Carpinteria resident. Cohen, who was 58, and her boyfriend, Boy Taylor, were killed during a mass shooting that took place at the Route 91 Festival, an outdoor country music festival in Las Vegas, Nevada. Cohen had been planning to volunteer at the Avocado Festival for the second year in a row before her passing. To honor her memory, a local band called Dusty Jugz dedicated an hour-long set of country music to Cohen during the avocado festival.

DESSERT

Fun facts about the humble avocado:

- In addition to the famous Hass, and once-famous Fuerte avocados, other varieties include Bacon, Gwen, Lamb Hass, Pinkerton, Reed, and Zutano.

- In 1935, Rudolph Hass patented his avocado tree, one of the earliest fruit trees to receive a patent.
- The "mother" tree, from which all future Hass avocados originated from, grew in a La Habra Heights backyard for 76 years. The wood from the dead tree is kept in storage and is occasionally used to make specialty items such as plaques for the California Avocado Society (Shepherd and Bender 2013).
- As of 2018, we live in a time in which one can purchase a box of avocados whose exteriors have been decorated with custom logos, a service offered by San Francisco based CustomAvocados.com. The motto of the parent company, Branded Fruit, is simply "we print logos on produce!"

SUGGESTED PAIRINGS

See also: Gilroy Garlic Festival; Super Bowl Sunday; Trends, Food.

Entry best enjoyed while eating: Inspired by the recipe for AvoFest's 2012 guacamole blue-ribbon winner, awarded to Cherisse Kirkendall: Guacamole made from seven Hass avocados, four seeded and diced Roma tomatoes, one cup finely diced red onion, two tablespoons Lawry's garlic salt, and a dash of pepper. Pro tip: use a potato masher to mash the avocados and stop while the texture is still chunky.

Further Reading
California Avocado Commission. n.d. "Avocado Fun Facts." https://www.californiaavocado.com/the-california-difference/fun-avocado-facts
California Avocado Festival, Inc. 2018. https://avofest.com/
Ferreira, Gustavo, and Agnes Perez. 2017. "Fruit and Tree Nuts Outlook." Economic Research Service, USDA. April 3, 2017.
FunCheap SF. 2018. "2018 'Avocado Con' Food Truck Festival | SF." April 18, 2018. http://sf.funcheap.com/avocado-food-festival-slicing-dicing-scooping-sf/
Handwerk, Brian. 2017. "Holy Guacamole: How the Hass Avocado Conquered the World." *Smithsonian Magazine*, July 28, 2017.
Judkis, Maura. 2017. "Avocado Prices Are at Record High—Just in Time for Cinco de Mayo." *The Washington Post*, May 2, 2017.
Nguyen, Vicky. 2017. "Las Vegas Shooting Victim Remembered at California Avocado Festival." Fox KKFX 11, October 6, 2017.
Rylah, Juliet Bennett. 2017. "How San Diego Became the Avocado Capital of the U.S." *Culture Trip*, July 9, 2017.
SeeCalifornia. 2018a. "California Avocado Festivals." http://www.seecalifornia.com/festivals/california-avocado-festivals.html
SeeCalifornia. 2018b. "Fallbrook, CA Travel, Photos Information and News." http://www.seecalifornia.com/california-cities/fallbrook.html
Shepherd, John, and Gary Bender. 2013. "A History of the Avocado Industry in California." In *Avocado 205 Production in California*, edited by G. S. Bender, Vol. 2, pp. 1–18. The University of California 206 Cooperative Extension, San Diego County and The California Avocado Society, California 207 US. http://ucanr.edu/sites/alternativefruits/files/166369.pdf

Szalay, Jessie. 2014. "Avocados: Health Benefits, Risks and Nutrition Facts." *Live Science*, October 23, 2014. https://www.livescience.com/45209-avocado-nutrition-facts.html

Visit California. 2018. "California Avocado Festival." http://www.visitcalifornia.com/event/california-avocado-festival

Celebrities and Food

STARTERS

Foods and beverages that are associated with people in the public eye often take on a public life of their own. Many are fascinated with celebrity lifestyles and often emulate the types of foods, types of diets, and ways of preparing food associated with celebrities. Restaurants that attract star power often see significant traffic upticks in the number of customers they serve, who often want to catch a glimpse of someone famous during their meal. The advertising industry has harnessed the public's fascination with celebrity diets by signing actors, singers, and other notable figures for high-paying promotional deals to sell their products. Magazine and television interviews with celebrities frequently focus on what the celebrities eat most days and what foods they "cheat" with, drawing attention to how thin celebrities maintain their physiques. Many celebrities also turn the earnings from their films, book deals, album sales, and other projects into seed money for restaurants, vineyards, ice cream shops and more, propelling their love of food and beverages into high-profile passion projects and business ventures.

ENTRÉE

Sometimes food that would otherwise be disregarded as unremarkable or unsavory is launched to great heights in popular culture due to the popularity of the person associated with eating it. Perhaps the best-known example is one of Elvis Presley's favorite foods: a fried peanut butter and banana sandwich. The musician known as the King was also known for a Wonder Bread sandwich with peanut butter and cheese and a sandwich dubbed "Fool's Gold Loaf," purportedly consisting of a peanut butter and jelly sandwich topped with a pound of bacon, served on an entire loaf of Italian bread and deep fried. Despite the fact that Elvis was a musician, not a chef or public figure in the food industry, the public's fascination runs so deep with what he ate that there are a dozen or more cookbooks inspired by his meals, such as *I Love Elvis Cookbook* (1998) and *Fit for a King: The Elvis Presley Cookbook*. The books contain recipes associated with his cook, Alvena Roy, dishes he ordered at various restaurants, and fare featured from Elvis and Priscilla Presley's wedding reception.

Celebrity Leftovers

The influence of celebrities and food can perhaps best be seen in the exorbitant lengths people will go to in order to obtain the same piece of food or eat at the same establishment that a public figure has been associated with. The Museum of Celebrity Leftovers in Cornwall, England, is a testament to this fact: the tiny museum houses tiny remnants of things celebrities ate, ranging from fragments of eggshell used to make an egg sandwich for comedian Hugh Dennis to the remnants of a slice of bread pudding once snacked on by Prince Charles.

Auctions draw high bidders for celebrity foods, such as a piece of gum previously chewed by pop singer Britney Spears that went for $14,000 on the online auction website eBay in 2004. The seller leveraged the situation by bidding against himself to inflate the price significantly. Other sales followed suit, with unsubstantiated claims that sellers also had pieces of gum previously chewed by the singer (Silverman 2004). Similarly, in the year 2000 a radio DJ auctioned off a leftover breakfast that pop singer Justin Timberlake had nibbled on at the station during an interview. The remnant of Timberlake's French toast sold on eBay for $1,025 (Takahashi 2000). In 2012, a slice of toast with Vegemite spread that was half-eaten by One Direction band member Niall Horan went for just shy of $100,000 after Horan tasted a bite of it on an Australian morning show (Maloney 2012).

Celebrity Restaurants, Alcohol Products, Vineyards

Actors, comedians, writers, and musicians often pursue a passion (or strict business interest) in food and beverages. HGTV renovation darlings Chip and Joanna Gaines have been credited with tripling the number of tourists who visit Waco, Texas on an annual basis. Visitors were first drawn to the city due to the popularity of the Gaines' reality home makeover show *Fixer Upper*, and the tourist boom continued to increase when the couple opened a restaurant, bakery, and

---

Small Plates

One Man's Crust Is Another Man's Treasure

Raise the topic of a celebrity's food waste going at auction for tens of thousands of dollars, and the inevitable response will be: "*why?*" Researchers George E. Newman and Paul Bloom published an article on their findings of this very subject after studying high-profile celebrity items that sold at auction. Newman and Bloom analyzed buyers' motivations, summarizing their findings that many people ascribe to something they call *magical contagion* "a form of magical thinking in which people believe that a person's immaterial qualities or essence can be transferred to an object through physical contact." The researchers noted that the amount of physical contact a celebrity had with the item influences the sale of that item. Auction pieces from celebrities who were deemed "liked individuals," such as President John F. Kennedy, sold at higher prices if they were considered to have not been sanitized or otherwise cleaned after the individual last touched the item.

Conversely, items from "disliked" individuals (such as Bernard Madoff, who was sentenced in a high-profile Ponzi scheme) sold at higher prices if they *had* been sanitized. The researchers determined that individuals who put a lot of financial value on celebrities' former items, such as partially consumed food, had a conscious or subconscious belief that some "essence" of that person would be carried home with them within the gum, French toast, or bit of crumbled eggshell they had just spent top dollar for.

coffee shop (Magnolia Table, Silos Baking Company, and Magnolia Press, respectively) starting in 2018 (Skinner 2018). Similarly, blogger and Food Network star Ree Drummond's Mercantile store and restaurant has drawn between 6,000 and 15,000 visitors a week to the town of Pawhuska, Oklahoma, which has a population of only 3,500 (Calderone 2017).

A number of actors and actresses have added restaurateur to their resume over the course of their career, including Channing Tatum (Saints & Sinners, New Orleans), Jessica Biel (Au Fudge, Los Angeles), Sandra Bullock (Walton's Fancy and Staple, Austin), Gloria and Emilio Estefan (Estefan Kitchen, Miami), Robert de Niro (Nobu, Malibu), Michael Jordan (1000 North, Jupiter, Florida), Jay-Z (The 40/40 Club, New York City), and many others. The beverage industry is also a popular one, favored by stars such as singer Maynard James Keenan of the bands Tool and A Perfect Circle, who owns vineyards called Caduceus Cellars and Merkin Vineyards in Jerome, Arizona. Actor George Clooney enjoyed a highly successful side business, as well; his tequila company Casamigos sold for a whopping $1 billion in 2017. Known best for his role in *Ghostbusters*, actor Dan Akroyd found a new calling in the spirits industry by founding Crystal Head Vodka company, which sells the filtered liquor in glass skulls. The number of additional celebrities who are investors in and owners of restaurants, breweries, and other companies in the industry is too high to list in its entirety. The clientele of each establishment can be partially attributed to the interest and worth customers place on the fact that a celebrity has endorsed the food and beverages there and might be serving the food him or herself, if the customer is particularly lucky.

Diets and Celebrity Endorsements

The advertising industry has long relied on star power to help sell its wares. In recent decades, formal and informal celebrity endorsements of various foods and drinks have helped sway customers to the tune of thousands, and even millions of dollars. Talk show host and media mogul Oprah Winfrey is a spokesperson for weight loss company Weight Watchers, in which she owns about 5 million shares, or 8 percent of the company (LaVito 2019). Winfrey has also launched a line of prepared foods called "O! That's Good" in joint partnership with Kraft Heinz and partnered with the Starbucks corporation to sell a Teavana Oprah Chai beverage. In 1996, Winfrey became one of the most influential food figures in U.S. history when she aired an episode that highlighted controversial practices in the beef industry. Cattle ranchers in Texas filed a $10.3 million defamation lawsuit against her when she stated that the information on the show would make her stop eating hamburgers forever. The ranchers lost the lawsuit, and beef sales plummeted to the lowest point in 10 years as a result of the show (Stephey 2011).

Many more public figures have helped create enormous diet trends, such as actress Gwyneth Paltrow, whose brand "Goop" has become synonymous with fads such as cleanses, detoxes, and "clean eating." Paltrow and her brand have been the subject of numerous controversies for promoting ideas like eating a specific diet and exercising with the goal of living at one's "leanest livable weight," or participating in a "food stamp challenge," for which critics took aim at Paltrow for incorporating ingredients that seemed extraneous for a stretched-thin budget. Another celebrity who received a chilly reception for a food endorsement was racing driver Emerson Fittipaldi, who eschewed the Indianapolis 500 tradition of taking a sip from a bottle of milk to celebrate his win, taking a swig instead from a bottle of orange juice to promote his Brazilian orange juice farms (much to the ire of the American Dairy Society).

DESSERT

As a promotional stunt for a then-unnamed film project, actor Jeff Goldblum created a small craze in 2017 when he handed out free food to onlookers in Sydney, Australia, from a food truck dubbed "Chef Goldblum." The actor chatted with every customer in line, posing for photos and cheerfully handing out "fancy hot dogs," noting cryptically that he was doing a project that was somehow related to the food stunt.

SUGGESTED PAIRINGS

See also: Food and Beverage Museums, International; Pioneer Woman, The; Politicians' Food Gaffes; Politics and Food.

Entry best enjoyed while eating: Quinoa stir fry with green beans, a macrobiotic entrée inspired by singer Madonna; fruit with sour cream and cottage cheese, once touted by actress Elizabeth Taylor; water with lemon and cayenne, a "cleanse" fad attributed in part to singer Beyoncé; and a gin and tonic made with actor Ryan Reynolds' Aviator Gin.

Further Reading
Calderone, Ana. 2017. "Ree Drummond's Oklahoma Restaurant Gets 6,000 Visitors Per Day—in a Town of Only 3,500." *People*, February 24, 2017.
Kennedy, Emma. 2012. "Emma's Eccentric Britain: the Museum of Celebrity Leftovers, Cornwall." *The Guardian*, May 18, 2012.
LaVito, Angelica. 2019. "Oprah Winfrey's Stake in Weight Watches Falls by 48 Million in Minutes after Shares Crater 30 Percent." CNBC, February 26, 2019. https://www.cnbc.com/2019/02/26/oprah-winfreys-stake-in-weight-watchers-falls-by-48-million-in-minutes.html
Maloney, Devon. 2012. "People Will Pay $100,000 for One Direction's Discarded Toast." Spin, April 12, 2012. https://www.spin.com/2012/04/people-will-pay-100000-one-directions-discarded-toast/
Newman, George E., and Paul Bloom. 2014. "Physical Contact Has Effects on Celebrity Auctions." *Proceedings of the National Academy of Sciences*, 111, no. 10: 3705–3708.
Rack, Jessie. 2015. "Dining Like Darwin: When Scientists Swallow Their Subjects." *NPR*, The Salt, August 12, 2015.
Silverman, Stephen M. 2004. "Britney's Used Chewing Gum Sold on eBay." *People*, September 3, 2004.
Skinner, Paige. 2018. "Biggest 'Fixer Upper' Success? It's Waco." *The New York Times*, December 12, 2018.
Stephey, M. J. 2011. "Top Ten Oprah Controversies." *Time*, May 25, 2011.
Takahashi, Corey. 2000. "Justin Timberlake's French Toast Is Sold on eBay." *Entertainment Weekly*, March 24, 2000.

Williams, A.R. 2015. "Packing Food for the Hereafter in Ancient Egypt." *National Geographic* The Plate, April 5, 2015. https://www.nationalgeographic.com/people-and-culture/food/the-plate/2015/04/05/packing-food-for-the-hereafter-in-ancient-egypt/

Chang, David (1977–)

STARTERS

David Chang is an American chef, television personality, writer, and the owner and founder of the Momofuku restaurant group. He is also the creator of the food magazine *Lucky Peach* (2011–2017). Chang opened his first restaurant, Momofuku Noodle Bar, in New York City in 2004. He opened restaurants Momofuku Ssäm Ba, Momofuku Ko, and Milk Bar in 2008. As the restaurant group gained popularity, Chang's cookbook *Momofuku* came out in 2009, which shared recipes and techniques from his kitchens. In 2010, Chang opened Ma Peche in New York and broadened his brand to Australia, opening Momofuku Seiobu in Sydney. Two years later, he continued expanding his international brand with Momofuku Toronto. Chang was also a featured chef on the PBS show *The Mind of a Chef* (2012), executive-produced and narrated by Anthony Bourdain.

In recent years, Chang has also opened a fast-food fried chicken chain called Fuku, followed by a "digital" delivery-only restaurant. He developed a condiment line, supported by employees who test ingredient combinations at his Momofuku development lab. In 2018, he opened his first West coast restaurant, Majordomo, started a media platform of the same name, and released a food podcast called "The David Chang Show." The same year, the first season of the docuseries *Ugly Delicious* premiered on Netflix, hosted and executive-produced by Chang. Across his various business endeavors, he was honored with eight James Beard Foundation awards between 2006 and 2014 and received the S. Pellegrino "50 Best Restaurants" award five times between 2011 and 2014. Momofuku Ko has been awarded two Michelin stars, and *Time* named him one of the "100 most influential people" of 2010. Chang has also been designated as the best chef of the year by *Food & Wine*, *Bon Appetit*, and *GQ* magazines, and he has been dubbed one of the "most influential people in the 21st century" by *Esquire* magazine.

ENTRÉE

In the "Noodles" episode of *The Mind of a Chef*, David Chang stands in a kitchen, smiling as he bites into a brick of uncooked, commercially mass-produced ramen noodles. As he chews, he tears open a small packet of seasoning, sprinkles the salt-and-MSG powder on top of the noodle brick, and takes another crunchy bite. Next to him is a pot of "real" ramen, the kind he learned to make after years of studying culinary arts and shadowing cooks in Japan. This moment sums up Chang's personality well. Chang rebels against the idea of good food having to be "high-end," hates snobbery, and touts the virtues of foods ranging from authentic Italian pizzas to Domino's takeout. He hates the concept of celebrity chefs, despite the fact that he *is* one.

David Chang received an award for Best Food Podcast at the iHeartRadio Podcast awards in January 2020. "The Dave Chang Show" invites culinary guests to discuss topics ranging from racial equity in the industry to which snacks reduce stress during a global pandemic. (Hutchinsphoto/Dreamstime.com)

Chang grew up in Virginia and attended Trinity College in Connecticut, where he majored in religious studies. He was drawn especially to Thoreau, on whom he wrote his thesis, and was fascinated by the social reformer's approach to putting great care and thought into repetitive chores (a philosophy he later brought into his cooking work ethic). Chang ate large quantities of instant ramen during his school years, and he was fascinated by the noodle-making processes he was exposed to in ramen shops. He received formal training in New York at the French Culinary Institute (later renamed the International Culinary Center) and began working at the Mercer Kitchen, a sophisticated restaurant in New York's SoHo district. He was so intent on getting his next job at Craft (the up-and-coming restaurant of chef and *Top Chef* judge Tom Colicchio) that Chang worked there answering phones until he earned his way into the kitchen.

Driven by his curiosity to learn more about the art of noodles, Chang moved to Japan for a period of time, where he studied ramen-making methods in the kitchens he worked in and ate at. In 2004, Chang took the leap to open his own restaurant. Momofuku is Japanese for "lucky peach," and it is also an homage to the inventor of instant ramen, Momofuku Ando. The restaurant's initial staple entrées were ramen and pork buns, cooked to Chang's precise standards. However, the precision and demands he required of his cooks has taken its toll; Chang is infamous for angry outbursts he's had toward his staff in the past, which he has described as rages in which he turned into "a complete maniac" (MacFarquhar 2008). Chang's subsequent restaurants have reflected his varied culinary and philosophical interests, ranging from the high-end Ko (meaning "son of") to Milk Bar, a bakery expansion of his Momofuku brand. At the helm of the bakery is pastry chef Christina Tosi, who develops deceptively simple (but elaborately developed and widely sought-after) desserts.

In 2011, Chang partnered with writer Peter Meehan to publish *Lucky Peach* magazine, which presented an artistic, eclectic, urban take on food. The magazine was similar to his 2018 Netflix docuseries, *Ugly Delicious*, which is a multifaceted exploration and discussion about food and cooking. Chang partnered with Oscar-winning documentary filmmaker Morgan Neville (*20 Feet from Stardom*) to do the show, which focuses on foods that aren't regarded as glamorous. Like *Lucky Peach*'s format, each episode focuses on a single subject, such as pizza, barbecue, and fried rice. *Ugly Delicious* dissects traditional and nontraditional approaches to foods, explores cultural influences and fusions, delves into the history of various foods, and engages in discussion with a wide range of experts and food enthusiasts alike. In a 2018 interview with *Vanity Fair*, Chang said the show approaches broader issues like authenticity, tradition, and immigration, sometimes using the show's focus on food as "a Trojan horse to talk about something else."

ACCOMPANIED BY

Family

Chang's father, Joe, was born in North Korea, and his mother, Sherri, was born in South Korea. Joe moved to New York City in 1963 and spent his first few nights there sleeping in a movie theater, with nowhere else to go. Joe worked his way up in his career, starting as restaurant dishwasher and eventually going on to own a golf equipment business and restaurants of his own. Joe hoped David might become a champion golfer instead of a restaurateur because he didn't want the same life for his son as he'd had. David, the youngest of four children in the family, did become a champion junior golfer, but found his true passion in the art of ramen making. Although his father worried about his son's pursuit of a culinary career, he helped fund Momofuku's beginnings with a $130,000 loan (Richman 2007; Finn 2007).

Friends and Colleagues

Chang has collaborated frequently with Anthony Bourdain, both of whom have sometimes been noted for their similar penchant for profane language and strongly worded, opinionated statements. In addition to casting Chang as the subject for the first season of *The Mind of a Chef*, Bourdain was one of many A-list chefs who wrote for *Lucky Peach*. The first season of *Ugly Delicious* features a number of Chang's friends and culinary colleagues, including comedian and actor Aziz Ansari (*Master of None*), actor Steven Yeun (*The Walking Dead*), late night talk show personality Jimmy Kimmel, restaurant critic Ruth Reichl, writer/producer David Simon (*The Wire*), journalist Jennifer 8. Lee, and chef Daniel Boulud, just to name a few.

DESSERT

- One of Chang's philosophies that has been embraced by some of his staff in the kitchen: "You can always add, but you can't take it out" (Roberts 2012).

- Chang had a recurring acting role in David Simon's HBO show *Treme*, playing a chef who works for a Manhattan restaurant called "Lucky Peach." Joining him on the show were fellow chefs Jonathan Waxman, Eric Ripert, Wylie Dufresne, Tom Colicchio, and Alfred Portale (Anthony Bourdain also wrote a number of restaurant scenes).
- The terrorist attacks on September 11, 2001, helped Chang decide to open his first restaurant. He told *Fortune* in 2012 that losing friends in the attack changed his mentality about potential career failures.
- When a customer threatened to sue over Momofuku's lack of vegetarian broth, Chang and co-chef Joaquin Baca rebelled by combing through their menu and identifying vegetarian offerings they could add pork to (Patronite and Raisfeld 2007).
- In 2018, Chang served as NBC's "food and culture expert" during the 2018 Winter Olympics in Pyeongchang, South Korea.

SUGGESTED PAIRINGS

See also: Asian American Cuisine; Magazines, Food; Television, Food Channels on; Trends, Food; *Mind of a Chef, The*; *Top Chef*; Tosi, Christina.

Entry best enjoyed while eating: Momofuku's ramen with pork belly, pork shoulder, and poached egg; a steamed pork bun with scallions, quick-cured cucumbers, and hoisin sauce (Sriracha optional); and a hibiscus iced tea.

Further Reading

Cavendish, Steve. 2011. "A First Look at Lucky Peach from David Chang and McSweeny's." *Chicago Tribune*, June 22, 2011.
Chang, David, and Peter Meehan. 2009. *Momofuku*. New York: Clarkson Potter Publishers.
Finn, Robin. 2007. "Rising Star Knows What, Not Who, Is Cooking." *New York Times*, May 18, 2007.
MacFarquhar, Larissa. 2008. "Chef on the Edge." *The New Yorker*, March 24, 2008.
Patronite, Rob, and Robin Raisfeld. 2007. "The I Chang," *New York*, June 12, 2007.
Richman, Alan. 2007. "Chef David Chang." *GQ*, November 11, 2007.
Roberts, Daniel. 2012. "David Chang Grows Up." *Fortune*, October 11, 2012.
Roberts, Daniel. 2013. "David Chang Broke All the Rules." *Time*, September 26, 2013.
Zuckerman, Esther. 2018. "David Chang Calls His New Food Show a Tasty but Filling 'Trojan Horse.'" *Vanity Fair*, February 2, 2018.

Chef's Table

STARTERS

Chef's Table is a Netflix docuseries that follows the personal and professional lives of renowned chefs around the world. The show premiered in 2015 and has four seasons, as well as a miniseries spinoff called *Chef's Table: France* (2016) that consists of four episodes devoted entirely to French chefs. The show's creator and executive producer, who also directed several episodes, is David Gelb, director of the feature-length documentary *Jiro Dreams of Sushi* (2011). *Chef's Table* episodes are 50 minutes long and focus exclusively on one chef per episode.

The show is highly stylized and cinematic. Episodes are shot in HDTV and use dramatic lighting and backdrops, creative camera angles, and editing set to classical music. The plot lines blend documentary style with staged scenes to create a profile of each chef, detailing their restaurant and approach to cooking; their philosophies about food and life; and the relationships they hold with customers, friends, and family. *Chef's Table* has been nominated for seven Emmy awards since 2015 and won an International Documentary Association Award for "Best Episodic Series" in 2015.

ENTRÉE

Slovenian chef Ana Roš's face fills the screen, smiling as she gazes at an exquisitely plated dish on the table in front of her. Classical music swells as she raises her fork, brings the first bite to her mouth, and closes her eyes. The next scenes show us what the flavors evoke in her mind: catching marble trout in a cold river stream; a delicate chanterelle mushroom peeking through the grass, rising in the sun; heavy wheels of mountain sheep's cheese bobbing in a basin of liquid. This moment from Season 2 of *Chef's Table* summarizes much of the show itself—an artistic feast for the eyes and emotional segment that seeks to bring viewers into the passion, evocative memories, and manual labor that visionary chefs put into their life's work.

"It's really a show about people," Gelb told *Eater* in 2016. "We don't give explanations on how to cook things. It's psychological, character-driven filmmaking." The show uses an artistic medium to depict cooks elevating food to an artform. The foods featured on the show range from surprisingly minimal and simple, like the brook trout Francis Mallman caught and cooked over coals, to astoundingly unusual, like Grant Achatz's dishes that are painted onto a table like it's a canvas. Each episode is flooded with classical music, including the show's theme: Vivaldi's "Winter" from *The Four Seasons*, reimagined by composer Max Richter.

Inspired by a scene in *Jiro Dreams of Sushi* in which tasting courses are described as a concerto, each *Chef's Table* episode features "food symphonies"—shots of plated food set to classical music. The production quality is the result of top-of-the-line digital cameras; scenes lit with soft, natural daylight; time-lapse shots; optical diopters, which increase the magnification of a camera lens for close-up shots; and footage captured from drones and helicopters. The crew also quickly learned the pace and function of each featured member of the various kitchen staffs in order to work in concert as they filmed them (Smith 2016).

ACCOMPANIED BY

The following are just a selection of the master chefs profiled on the show.

Season One

The premiere begins with Italian chef Massimo Bottura of Osteria Francescana restaurant in Modena, Italy. Bottura helps heroically save troves of Parmigiano Reggiano parmesan cheese that had been harmed in a massive earthquake. Viewers also meet Francis Mallman (Patagonia Sur in Buenos Aires), an unconventional Argentinian chef who lives on a remote island and touts the virtues of cooking over an open fire. Next, it explores the work of Niki Nakayama (N/Naka in Los Angeles), who specializes in a Japanese meal called *kaiseki,* which embraces seasonal ingredients and asks the diner to reflect in gratitude for nature's bounty.

Season Two

In a similar story arc to numerous other chefs' profiles on the show, Enrique Olvera (Pujol, Mexico City, Mexico) had a philosophical shift in his culinary career. He began moving away from the European style of food he'd learned in school and began to feature Mexican cuisine in a contemporary and chic manner. Dominique Crenn (Atelier Crenn, San Francisco) is also featured, the first female chef in the United States to receive two Michelin stars (notably, receiving the first in the first year of opening her restaurant). Speaking with *Variety* in 2016, Crenn said of her episode, "It's a platform for me to express that you can do whatever you dream to do, you just have to go for it. It's not about perfection, it's about evolution. Maybe it can help young women—I hope it can inspire a lot of them."

Chef's Table: France

The four episodes that make up the miniseries explore the gastronomy innovations happening in France, the country that many consider the heart of fine cuisine. Alain Passard (L'Arpege, Paris) is a three-star Michelin chef who made the decision to serve only vegetarian dishes, making waves in French culture as a result. His contemporary culinary artforms are balanced with stories about the importance his grandmother's cooking played in his life.

Season Three

Jeong Kwan is a Buddhist nun who cooks world-class vegan cuisine at the Baekyangsa Temple in South Korea. Her connection to food is demonstrated as spiritual, emotional, and peaceful. The episode depicts her as lacking any ego, despite being revered by other talented chefs such as Buddhist Eric Ripert. American Ivan Orkin (Ivan Ramen) braved cultural divides by opening ramen restaurants in New York and Tokyo. In the show, he shares the grief he and his wife experienced when her pregnancy with the couple's second child ended in a miscarriage. Reacting to Orkin's description of grieving the loss with his then two-year-old son, *Eater* wrote "perhaps the moment wherein the series reaches out from its genre of chef hagiography to touch your heart" (Stein 2017).

Another episode profiles Vladimir Mukhin (White Rabbit, Moscow) who pores over Russian history books seeking traditional foods that he can modernize while preserving the flavors of the past. One notable sequence shares his discovery of moose lip *shchi* (cabbage soup) in his research. Inspired, he creates moose lip dumplings in his kitchen, much to the quiet shock of his staff. Mukhin notes that moose lip dishes have caught on in other Russian restaurants.

Season Four

The last season is devoted to the art of pastry. Episode one leads with Christina Tosi (Milk Bar, New York), an American pastry chef whose joy for life and confections is palpable. Tosi shares insights into the art of unfussy, seemingly simple desserts such as birthday cakes left unfrosted on the sides and cereal-milk flavored soft serve. In the media, *Chef's Table* was criticized by some for featuring Tosi as the only woman out of four featured pastry chefs, particularly since females vastly outnumber males in the pastry profession.

DESSERT

- **Not your average video shoot:** For Francis Mallman's episode, the crew had to take several flights to get from Los Angeles to the coast of Patagonia. The flights were followed by a six-hour drive on a barely distinguishable mud road and a 90-minute boat ride to a remote island, La Isla. Once there, they had to rely entirely on natural light and use a generator for the camera and microphone batteries (Smith 2016).
- **I'll have the, er, "road less traveled" with a side of ketchup?** At Atelier Crenn, the menu is served in poem form, evoking feelings and images about the foods instead of listing the actual names of the foods.
- **Tart Tears:** Season three's Nancy Silverton once made Julia Child cry while the duo taped an episode of *Baking With Julia*. Upon realizing that the chef had teared up, Silverton feared that Child had burned her mouth on Silverton's freshly baked tart, until Child proclaimed, "This is the most delicious dessert I've ever had!" (Parsons 2015).

SUGGESTED PAIRINGS

See also: Documentary Films, Food and Beverages in; *MasterChef*; *Mind of a Chef, The*.

Entry best enjoyed while eating: A gourd filled with smoking baby corn (husks attached), Chicatana ant, coffee, and chile costeño mayonnaise (Olvera); Roe buck, fermented cottage cheese, little red fruits (Roš); Moose lip dumplings (Mukhin); layered confetti birthday cake with frosting and sprinkles on top (Tosi).

Further Reading
Del Barco, Mandalit, and Maria Godoy. 2016. "Chef Niki Nakayama Is a Modern Master of An Ancient Japanese Meal." *NPR* All Things Considered, November 23, 2016.

Fetters, Ashley. 2016. "How to Take a Next-Level Food Photo, According to the Visionary Behind 'Chef's Table.'" *GQ,* May 27, 2016.
Galarza, Daniela. 2016. "Netflix's 'Chef's Table' Returns for Second, Third, and Fourth Seasons." *Eater,* March 8, 2016.
Gilbert, Sophie. 2018. "*Chef's Table: Pastry* Isn't about Pastry." *The Atlantic,* April 15, 2018.
Orkin, Ivan. 2013. *Ivan Ramen: Love, Obsession, and Recipes from Tokyo's Most Unlikely Noodle Joint.* Berkeley: Ten Speed Press.
Parsons, Russ. 2015. "Then There's the Time Nancy Silverton Made Julia Child Cry." *Los Angeles Times,* July 7, 2015.
Saperstein, Pat. 2016. "Dominique Crenn on 'Chef's Table': 'It's Not about Me Cooking." *Variety,* June 13, 2016.
Smith, J. Travis. 2016. "'Chef's Table' Cinematographers Reveal the Secrets of the Show.'" *Gear Patrol,* Behind the Lens, May 23, 2016.
Stein, Joshua David. 2017. "Review: Two Hits and One Misfire from 'Chef's Table' Season 3.'" *Eater,* March 15, 2015. https://www.eater.com/2017/3/15/14937284/chefs-table-season-three-episode-review-virgilio-martinez-ivan-orkin-tim-raue
Tosi, Christina. 2015. *Milk Bar Life: Recipes and Stories.* New York: Clarkson Potter.

Child, Julia (1912–2004)

STARTERS

Julia Child was a television personality, culinary teacher, and chef who is widely credited with popularizing French cuisine and French cooking techniques in the United States. She was also an early pioneer of instructional television, and her early shows marked the beginning of highly popular food television programming in the country. Child's cookbooks include *The Art of French Cooking* (coauthored with Simone Beck and Louisette Bertholle), published in 1961, and its companion publication, *The Art of French Cooking, Volume Two,* published in 1970. She went on to write 14 more cookbooks between 1968 and 2000 and coauthored a memoir called *My Life in France* with her nephew, Alex Prud'homme, in 2000.

The success of her first cookbook provided the impetus for her first television show, *The French Chef,* which ran from 1962 to 1966 (reruns aired until 1970), and a color version of the show ran from 1970 to 1973. Between 1978 and 1983, she starred in several year-long programs, and in 1993, she cohosted a special called *Cooking in Concert* with Jacques Pépin and Graham Kerr, followed by *More Cooking in Concert* in 1995. She hosted five additional cooking shows between 1993 and 2000, in addition to many guest appearances on other cooking and lifestyle programs, late-night shows, history programs, and children's shows.

Child received many honors in her lifetime, including a Peabody Award in 1964 and an Emmy Award in 1966 for her work on *The French Chef.* She was the first educational television professional to win an Emmy. Child received Daytime Emmy Awards in 1996 and 2001 for *In Julia's Kitchen with Master Chefs* and *Julia & Jacques Cooking at Home,* and she was also the recipient of numerous notable book awards during her career. In 1966, she was featured on the cover of

Time magazine. She received more than 10 honorary doctorates from colleges and universities and was awarded the National Order of Merit from the French government in 1976, which honors distinguished civil and military achievements. In 1993, Child was the first woman to be inducted into the esteemed Culinary Art Institute's Hall of Fame. In 1999, First Lady Hillary Clinton honored Child with a Sara Lee Frontrunner Award, which recognizes women who helped shape the country's past and future, and in 2000, the French government awarded the chef with the Legion of Honor. In 2003, President George W. Bush presented Child with the Presidential Medal of Freedom, the highest civilian honor.

In 1995, the decorated chef established the Julia Child Foundation for Gastronomy and Culinary Arts. The foundation provides grants, scholarships, and internships for culinary historians, food writers, and other food and beverage professionals. In 2015, the foundation and the Smithsonian's National Museum of American History cofounded the Julia Child Award to honor individuals who profoundly influence how Americans eat and prepare food. In 2001, just a few years before her death, Child donated the contents of her kitchen to the Smithsonian's National Museum of American History. The museum houses an exhibit that is an exact reproduction of her kitchen, including her furniture, her many cookbooks, and the strategic placement she used to store her utensils and cookware.

A permanent exhibit at the Smithsonian Museum depicts Julia Child's kitchen from her home in Cambridge, Massachusetts. Child donated the items, which represent her tools, dishes, and other cooking equipment she used from the 1940s until 2001. (Gavril Margittai/Dreamstime.com)

ENTRÉE

Julia Child is considered to be a legend in American food culture for her contributions to the advancement of Americans' passion for French cuisine, and home cooking in general. As a chef, she researched food and cooking techniques exhaustively in her quest to provide the most efficient and high-quality recipes and tutorials possible. This obsessive attention to detail was softened by a warm, witty on-screen persona. Standing at six feet two inches tall, Child's physical appearance and bold personality were unusual for a female television host of her era. Child encouraged amateur and professional cooks alike to experiment, fail, and succeed with gusto, promoting a confident, creative attitude in the kitchen. To offset the frustration that often accompanies ambitious culinary pursuits, Child treated cooking disasters with a *c'est la vie* ("that's life") attitude and made a career out of translating esoteric recipes and techniques into ones that home cooks could understand and recreate.

Child, neé Julia Carolyn McWilliams, was born in Pasadena, California, in 1912. The oldest of three children, Julia was spirited and curious in her youth. Biographer Bob Spitz described her as being uninterested by cuisine and cooking techniques growing up, but typically having an immense appetite (Spitz 2012). Child attended Smith College, where she played basketball, performed in drama productions, and majored in history. She graduated in 1934 and found herself adrift as she tried finding meaningful work and friendships. Child moved to New York City in hopes of becoming a novelist, and she was hired as a copywriter for a home furnishing retailer.

Service during the War

When the United States entered World War II, Child wanted to assist in the war efforts. She applied for a number of volunteer efforts, but was turned away by organizations like Women Accepted for Volunteer Service (WAVES) and Women's Army Corps (WACS) due to their concern that she was too tall (Child and Prud'homme 2006, 79). She was eventually hired as a typist for the U.S. Information Agency in Washington, D.C., which proved to be an unhappy endeavor because of the highly menial nature of the work. Child used her network to land a job at the newly founded Office of Strategic Services (OSS), an intelligence-gathering organization that was the precursor to the Central Intelligence Agency.

Child worked directly for OSS director William J. Donovan, and she climbed the ranks from junior research assistant to researcher. She was responsible for assessing classified materials like reports, photographs, and transcripts, flagging details and identifying code names for military experts to review (Spitz2012, 102). She worked a grueling schedule and was promoted to the Emergency Rescue Equipment Section (ERES), which specialized in identifying lifesaving measures for pilots downed at sea. Julia helped the ERES develop rescue kits and a cutting-edge shark repellant, which went on to become standard-issue supplies for pilots and sailors and was even used by Apollo astronauts through the 1970s (Arena 2018).

Unsatisfied with clerical work, Child pursued espionage work and assignments in foreign locales. She applied for reassignment in the OSS's new bases in

Southeast Asia, and in 1944, her application was approved. As one of 4,500 women who served in the OSS, she was one of only three women aboard her train from D.C. to attend boot camp in California and one of only nine women on her dangerous boat voyage across the Pacific. Nine prior ships carrying troops had been destroyed by Japanese submarines along the same route (CIA 2007; Spitz 2012, 105). Child's division was briefly stationed in India before being transferred to Ceylon (present-day Sri Lanka). There she served as a senior civilian intelligence officer, identifying classified information and working directly with spies. Despite the serious and dangerous nature of the work, Child's playful side remained intact; she was known for playing pranks on colleagues throughout her military career (Spitz 2012, 111).

In May of 1944, Child met her future husband. Paul Child was also stationed in the OSS's South East Asia Command, and the two became close friends. They were separated in the fall when Paul was sent to Chongqing, China, and Julia—who still wanted to be a spy—was reassigned to Kunming, China. Despite being denied an official espionage role, Child worked closely with spies in Kunming. One of her responsibilities was to pay them with quantities of opium. In 1945, Paul was also stationed in Kunming, and the two kindled a romantic relationship. One of the primary passions they shared was for food, and they bonded over the local Chinese delicacies that were unlike anything they'd had at home.

Culinary Career

When the war ended, Paul and Julia returned home and traveled across the United States together. They married in September of 1946, despite having been in a serious car accident en route to their rehearsal dinner the day before. Julia was thrown through the windshield and out of the car, resulting in serious lacerations and other injuries. At the wedding, Paul walked with a cane and Julia walked down the aisle sporting bandages and stitches, but the couple still celebrated with joy. In 1948, Paul was hired as a diplomat for the United States Information Service and was stationed in Paris. On November 3, the couple enjoyed a fateful lunch in the city of Rouen. The simultaneous simplicity and complexity of the fare—which consisted of fish in a butter and wine sauce, oysters, wine, salad, and cheese—ignited a new joy of eating for Julia.

Over the course of the six years she lived in France, Julia learned French, frequented local markets and food shops, and enrolled at the elite Le Cordon Bleu cooking academy. The director pressured her to stick to a six-week course for housewives, but Child enrolled in a year-long cooking course alongside former GIs and other aspiring chefs. Despite failing her final exam on the first try (reportedly because the director created an overly difficult test for the American who had irked her), Child received her diploma in 1951. The following year, she teamed up with French cooks Simone Beck and Louisette Bertholle, who wanted to bring their passion for French recipes to American audiences. They opened their own cooking school, L'Ecole des Trois Gourmandes, and began writing a cookbook that evolved into an enormous nine-year project of arduous scientific testing, exhausting writing and editing schedules, and intense daily cooking sessions. In

1961, after problems with publishers and countless revisions, *Mastering the Art of French Cooking* was finally published. The book featured 524 French recipes with step-by-step techniques and expert advice for home cooks.

Just before the book's publication, the Childs returned to the United States, settling in Cambridge. Tracking the success of her cookbook, public television station WGBH brought Julia on for a promotional spot that led to her own television show, *The French Chef*, in which she demonstrated numerous recipes from the cookbook. The show premiered in 1962 and began airing nationwide a year later. Julia was skilled in fearless and engaging on-air performances, which gave her an advantage over numerous other chefs who were dynamic in the kitchen but seemed self-conscious and detached on camera.

Julia's cookbook and television show were so successful that people began recognizing her in public, and her book signings and in-store demonstrations started to draw enormous crowds. While this phenomenon is relatively common today, the concept of a chef being as easily recognized as a Hollywood actor was practically unheard of in that era (today, Child is widely considered to have been the first "celebrity chef"). Some grocery stores carried copies of her book so customers could refer to the recipes they'd come in to shop for. Similarly, the ingredients featured in each episode of *The French Chef* were known to fly off the shelves in grocery stores around the country.

Over the next 40 years, Child's professional ambition never seemed to wane. She worked tirelessly on her television shows and wrote cookbooks simultaneously. She became the first educational television star in the early 1960s, and family members watched her show together in many households regardless of their interest in cooking. When color television entered the market, Child insisted on joining the color revolution. She told WGBH that she would leave the station if they didn't tape her shows using this radically new technology. 1,000 tons of equipment were brought to perform a test taping of *The French Chef* in color, transforming unappealing gray images of food into vibrant, colorful scenes that helped make each meal look significantly more appetizing (Spitz 2012, 366).

Child was a pioneer in television in many ways, notably for her scrupulous attention to detail and quality, her unconventional choice of career for a woman in the 1960s, and her humorous way of improvising on camera. If a tool or ingredient didn't work properly, she tossed it over her shoulder. If food fell on the floor or stove, she scooped it back in the pan, reassuring her viewers that dinner guests would never find out what had happened. Child also recommended and sipped on wine, champagne, and beer during her show. This bordered on scandalous for the era, but she defended alcohol's inclusion in her program as a critical element of French cuisine. She eschewed corporate sponsorships, turning down multiple fortunes in the process. At various points in her career, Child was criticized for prioritizing business matters over requests made by friends. Some critiqued the chef for using profane, risqué, and homophobic language at times. She was also widely praised for generously sharing profits with stations and colleagues, and was beloved by many people who considered her to be a close personal friend.

Toward the end of her life, Child suffered from kidney failure. The medications she took for her condition caused her to lose her sense of taste, and she quietly stopped taking the medication in order to enjoy food again as her quality of life diminished. When her doctors urged her to undergo urgent treatment for kidney sepsis, she chose not to, saying that she would rather not live at all if she couldn't control her quality of life (Spitz 2012). In memorials, many recalled her signature catch phrase—*bon appetit!*—which was delivered joyfully each episode, leaving viewers with an urge to raise their glasses over a shared meal with Julia and each other.

ACCOMPANIED BY

Child's immediate family included her parents, John McWilliams II (1880–1962) and Julia Carolyn McWilliams (1877–1937), neé Weston, who went by Caro. The family came from money; John's father had come to California as a gold prospector and became a banker, grooming John to work in banking and financing with him. John was reportedly very conservative and judgmental and hated anything foreign, particularly (and ironically, as it would turn out) intellectuals and French culture (Spitz 2012, 42). Caro's family owned a well-known paper company. The McWilliamses raised their children—Julia, her brother John III (1914–2002), and her sister Dorothy (1917–2006)—in an upper-class home in Pasadena.

Paul Child (1902–1994) began his career an artist and teacher. He joined the OSS's Visual Presentation Division, using his artistic skills to design war rooms and other military assignments. Paul and his twin brother Charlie shared a lifelong passion for art, and Paul pursued painting and photography for most of his life. He retired from government services in 1961 and became Julia's business partner, helping her do everything from scripting shows to preparing props, even frantically washing dishes off-camera during live segments. Paul was a devoted supporter of Julia's talents and career throughout their relationship. He designed her kitchen in Cambridge, raised the countertops to accommodate her height, and diagrammed a space for every kitchen tool. In 1974, Paul suffered from a series of strokes, and he passed away in 1994 after many years of illness.

During her time in Paris, Julia teamed up with cooking teacher and author Simone "Simca" Beck (1904–1991), who became a lifelong friend and helped the Childs build a home on her property in France. Simca and Julia teamed up to teach cooking courses and write *Mastering the Art* with Louisette Bertholle (1905–1999), whose contributions to the cookbook were eventually outpaced by Child's exhaustive researching, testing, and writing process.

DESSERT

- **Celebrity salad during Prohibition:** Julia's parents took her to Tijuana when she was a child to eat at chef Caesar Cardini's restaurant. The chef's recently invented "Caesar's salad" drew patrons from far and wide, and the margaritas provided a verboten pleasure for the adults.
- **Voice of an era:** Many commented on the warbly sound of Child's voice, which she often took offense to (she saw nothing unusual about it). Biographer Bob Spitz attributed her "hooting," as he described it, to unusually long vocal chords.

- **Mastering the art of publishing:** Julia, Simone, and Louisette's smash success publication of *Mastering the Art of French Cooking* has seen more than 1.6 million copies printed to date.
- **In due time:** Julia didn't develop strong cooking skills until she was well into her thirties. Before marrying, she often cooked frozen meals, and early in her marriage, she "exploded a duck and set the oven on fire" trying to woo Paul by cooking for him (Reichl 2012).
- **Bon mots:** Some of Julia's most famous quotations include: "A party without cake is just a meeting," "With enough butter, everything is good," and "I was 32 when I started cooking. Until then, I just ate" (Young n.d.).

SUGGESTED PAIRINGS

See also: Asian American Cuisine; Films, Food in; *Galloping Gourmet, The*; Nonfiction, Food in; Pépin, Jacques; Television, Food Channels on.

Entry best enjoyed while eating: A chicken liver mousse hors d'oeurve; a bowl of *Boeuf Bourguignon* stew; a slice of warm, homemade French bread with butter; crêpes Suzette served with liquor flambé; and a glass of red Burgundy wine.

Further Reading

Arena, Jenny. 2018. "Spaceflight and Surviving Shark Attacks." Smithsonian Air and Space Museum. https://airandspace.si.edu/stories/editorial/spaceflight-and-surviving-shark-attacks

Central Intelligence Agency (CIA). 2007. "A Look Back . . . Julia Child: Life Before French Cuisine." December 13, 2007. www.cia.gov/news-information/featured-story-archive/2007-featured-story-archive/julia-child.html

Child, Julia, Simone Beck, and Louisette Bertholle. 2009. *Mastering the Art of French Cooking* (Two-Volume Boxed Set). New York: Alfred A. Knopf.

Child, Julia, and Alex Prud'homme. 2006. *My Life in France*. New York: Alfred A. Knopf.

The Julia Child Foundation for Gastronomy and the Culinary Arts. 2012. https://juliachildfoundation.org

Reichl, Ruth. 2012. "Julia Child's Recipe for a Thorough Modern Marriage." *Smithsonian Magazine*, June 2012.

The Smithsonian National Museum of American History. n.d. "Julia Child's Kitchen." http://americanhistory.si.edu/food/julia-childs-kitchen

Spitz, Bob. 2012. *Dearie: The Remarkable Life of Julia Child*. New York: Alfred A. Knopf.

Young, Erica. n.d. "The Ten Best Things Julia Ever Said." *Taste of Home*, https://www.tasteofhome.com/article/julia-child-quotes/

Chocolate Events and Destinations

STARTERS

Chocolate is often described as one of the most popular treats in the world. The history of chocolate consumption is thought to go back as much as 3,000 years. It has been met with increasing popularity in the twentieth century due to its mass production and a cultural shift over centuries from being a food that only the elite could enjoy to something that all social classes have access to. Today, chocolate can be found in everything from inexpensive candy to high-end desserts. In the twentieth century, the definition of chocolate was broadened to include products in which some (or much) of the cacao and cocoa butter content had been replaced with additives such as corn syrup and palm oil. Despite what many see as a widespread reduction in quality, chocolate remains so beloved that an enormous number of festivals and tourist attractions pay homage to it around the world every year. The treat is often the theme of fundraising events due to its wide appeal and enormous popularity.

Chocolate is seen in countless regional variations and is consumed and revered in different ways across cultures. Chocolate consumption in the United States is estimated at 9.5 pounds per person annually, trailing Switzerland at 20 pounds, Germany at 17.4 pounds, and Ireland and the United Kingdom, at 16.5 pounds per person (McCarthy 2015). According to the World Cocoa Foundation, the vast majority of cocoa comes from 5 million family-owned farms, which produce four and a half million tons of cocoa beans annually.

Cocoa trees flourish in tropical environments that are within 15–20 degrees of the equator. Africa accounts for a majority of global cocoa production, followed by areas of Asia, Oceania, and Latin America. Chocolate has become a major economic asset, currently the 110th most traded product, with exports and imports in the billion dollar ranges ("Chocolate" 2018). In the United States, chocolate sales are expected to exceed $20 billion by 2025. Although market fluctuations can occur from cocoa farms' environmental challenges and cultural pressures for higher-quality and organic products, the world's love for chocolate remains exceptionally stable. Today, "chocolate tourism" brings local, national, and international visitors to festivals, plantation tours, factories, chocolate-centric theme parks, museums, and other attractions around the world ("Cocoa Value Chain: From Farmer to Consumer" n.d.; Thompson 2018).

ENTRÉE

Attractions in the United States

New York City hosts The Big Chocolate Show each year, a three-day event in which chocolatiers, chocolate experts, pastry chefs, and other industry professionals converge to host tasting classes, demonstrations, and panel discussions. Touted as New York's largest chocolate show, the October event includes chocolate celebrities from across the world, such as chocolatier Jacques Torres. Classes entail subjects like how to pair chocolate with wine and coffee, how to make chocolates with a 3D printer, and professional tips for cooking with cacao. The event falls during Chocolate Week NYC, an autumn celebration of the city's chocolate industry at large. Since 2014, the city has also enjoyed an annual Valrhona Hot Chocolate Festival in January, in which artisanal hot chocolate recipes are sold in various bakeries to benefit underserved high school students who are seeking culinary careers.

Burlington, Wisconsin, holds an annual ChocolateFest that draws more than 35,000 visitors ("Chocolatefest" 2018). The festival started in 1985 as a collaboration between city officials and the Nestle corporation, which had a large factory in the city at the time. Burlington named itself "Chocolate City, U.S.A.," a nickname that was responded to with an (unsuccessful) lawsuit by longtime Nestle rival, Hershey Foods (Miller 1990). Held over Memorial Day Weekend, the ChocolateFest features contests for chocolate sculpting, designing fashion out of chocolate wrappers, and chocolate-eating contests.

In Alabama, all proceeds from the Mobile Chocolate Festival benefit victims of domestic violence. In its tenth year, the annual event includes chocolate fashion design contests, bake-offs, and fare from local vendors. Similarly, the money raised from the Ghiradelli Chocolate Festival in San Francisco benefits a nonprofit that provides meals to senior citizens and people with debilitating illnesses. The festival is located at Ghiradelli Square, a famous chocolate tourism destination due to the chocolate factory that took root there around the turn of the century. The festival's events include chocolate-making lessons, gourmet chocolate tastings, and a contest challenging competitors to eat an enormous "chocolate earthquake" ice cream sundae without using their hands.

On the island of Hawaii, the Big Island Chocolate Festival raises money for the island's cacao farmers in addition to a number of local nonprofits on the island. The two-day festival includes a cacao bean "taste off" judged by professionals and a contest for the island's young chefs. Starting in 2009, the Southwest Chocolate & Coffee Festival in Albuquerque, New Mexico, attracts more than 18,000

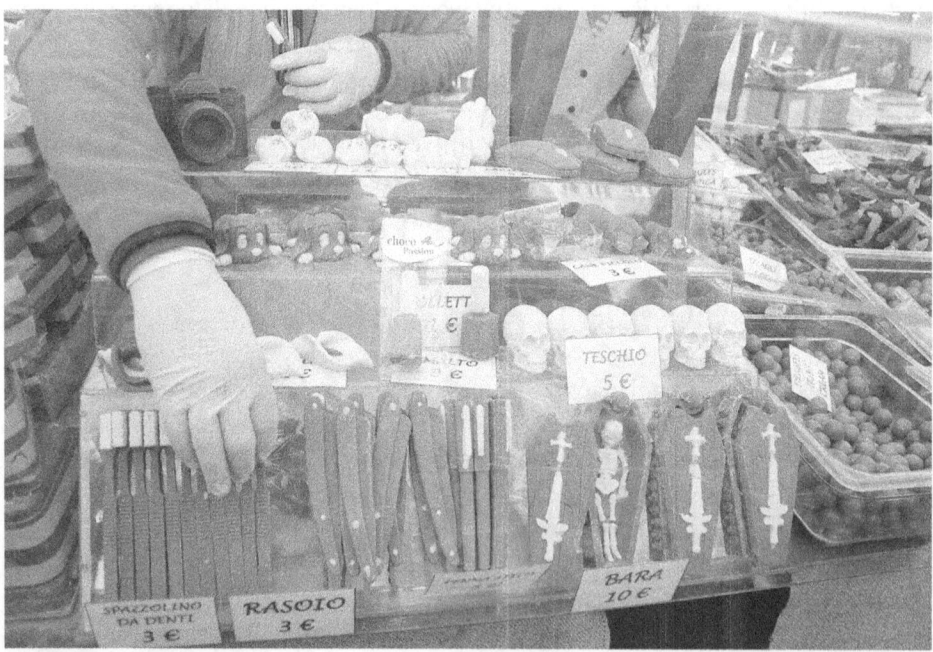

A vendor at ChocoMoments, an annual chocolate festival in the Italian province of Pavia, arranges a whimsical assortment of chocolates shaped like toothbrushes, skulls, coffins, straight razors, and more. (Hua3000/Dreamstime.com)

attendees every spring. The festival's mission includes supporting small culinary businesses and educating visitors about the production of chocolate and coffee. In addition to these events, there are *many* more festivals, factories, tours, and celebrations throughout the United States, signifying the broad and whimsical appeal that chocolate holds in American culture.

Attractions Abroad

One of the most noted international chocolate festivals is Eurochocolate in Perugia, the capital city of Italy's Umbria region. Here, the famed factory known as the "Perugina Chocolate House" draws visitors year-round to sample *baci* chocolates (the Italian word for "kiss"). The festival draws 1 million visitors over the course of its 10-day run, serving up chocolate treats from vendors all over Europe (Vora 2018). In the fall, London hosts The Chocolate Show, touted as the largest chocolate event in the United Kingdom. The week-long homage to chocolate is linked to Salon du Chocolat, a wide-scale chocolate and cocoa trade fair event that started in 1995. The Salon holds 20 events a year that draw an estimated million visitors (Salon du Chocolat 2018).

When it comes to chocolate tourism, other hot spots include Switzerland, one of the most famous chocolate-making countries in the world, where nineteenth-century-style cars of the Chocolate Train takes guests on a day-long trip through towns like medieval Gruyeres and Broc. Stops include tours of a cheese factory and the Maison Cailler-Nestle chocolate factory, in which visitors are treated to history lessons and tastings of the classic Swiss treats. Tourist destinations certainly don't end in Europe, however; there are a wide array of large-scale events across the globe. Just to name a few: Peru draws visitors to sample the "world's rarest chocolate," called Pure Nacional. Popular attractions include plantation and factory tours, as well as the Choco Museo, a museum devoted to chocolate with locations in several countries. Adventure seekers are also drawn to Costa Rica's attractions, such as the Rainforest Chocolate Tour, in which guests participate in each phase of the chocolate production process (Kiniry 2015).

History of Chocolate

In popular culture, chocolate is featured prominently in scores of contemporary books, films, and songs. Chocolate also plays a significant role in several American holidays, particularly Valentine's Day, Christmas, Easter, and birthday celebrations. However, for much of chocolate's history, only the most elite members of society were allowed to savor the treat. Chocolate is thought to possibly go back as far as 1400 BCE, due to the discovery in recent years of cacao residue on Honduran pottery from that era. (A quick note on terminology: *cacao* refers to the bean from which the *chocolate* product is made, and similarly spelled *cocoa* refers to chocolate in its powdered form.) All chocolate comes from *Theobroma cacao*—"food of the gods"—the Latin name for the cacao tree. Chocolate is thought to have originated in Mesoamerica. Cacao beans were significant in Aztec and

Mayan civilizations. Ancient documentation shows that they were used as currency and were considered sacred in both cultures (Fiegl 2008; Coe and Coe 2013). For most of its history, chocolate was consumed in liquid form, often poured from high above or stirred with a type of swizzle stick to create a thick froth on top. When the Spanish conquered the Aztecs, they brought chocolate back to Europe with them, preferring to drink it sweetened with sugar or honey due to its otherwise bitter flavor.

ACCOMPANIED BY

The process of transforming chocolate into an edible and delicious treat is a highly complex process that goes back centuries or more. Chocolate would be very different today had Conrad van Houten not invented the laborious process of separating cacao butter—the fat content—of chocolate in 1828. He applied considerable scientific processes to "pulverize what remained and (treated) the mixture with alkaline salts to cut the bitter taste" (Fiegl 2008). His invention led to the solid form of chocolate that has since been through countless iterations.

Other famous names in chocolate history include Rodolphe Lindt, a Swiss inventor who helped refine chocolate, and Jean Tobler, whose company went on to become Toblerone. In England, the Fry family's business determined how to make a solid form of chocolate in 1847, and the Cadbury company hit huge success in 1868 when they introduced chocolate candies in small, beautiful boxes. Noticing chocolate's commercial success, German-born Henri Nestle (who was becoming famous for milk-based baby food) and Swiss chocolatier Daniel Peter (who invented milk chocolate) founded the Nestlé company. The United States joined the fray when Milton S. Hershey founded the Hershey Chocolate Company in 1893. Others followed suit, such as Frank Mars, whose 1925 candy manufacturing business would go on to become a mega corporation.

DESSERT

- In the United States, more than 40,000 brands of chocolate bars and candies have been manufactured since the early 1900s (Smith 2006).
- In recent years, unusual chocolate trends have included chocolate hummus, ginger-turmeric chocolate bars, and espresso in a chocolate-coated ice cream cone.
- When melted, chocolate can recrystallize in six different configurations, which has been compared to the structure and various phases of carbon. Chocolatiers also have to temper the sweet, similar to the process of improving steel (Handwerk 2015).
- Chocolate is frequently requested as a treat by astronauts and has been sent into orbit in the form of chocolate sauce in a tube, cocoa, and more. The most famous chocolate treat in space is M&Ms, which astronauts have fun eating in zero-G.

- Chocolate's health benefits have long been argued, but research does indicate that regularly consumed, small portions of high quality dark chocolate can be beneficial for heart and brain health.

SUGGESTED PAIRINGS

See also: Cake and Cupcake Trends; Fiction, Food in; Food and Beverage Museums, International; Food and Beverage Museums, U.S.; Ice Cream Trends.

Entry best enjoyed while eating: A pain au chocolat fresh from Jacques Torres' oven; a mug of hot chocolate made with fresh vanilla beans, cinnamon, and homemade marshmallow cubes; and, if you must eat an entree after dessert, a chicken and cheese enchilada topped with Mexican chocolate mole sauce.

Further Reading

"Chocolate." 2018. The Economic Complexity Observatory (OEC). https://atlas.media.mit.edu/en/profile/hs92/1806/

"Chocolatefest." 2018. Travel Wisconsin. https://www.travelwisconsin.com/events/fairs-festivals/chocolatefest-38778

"Cocoa Value Chain: From Farmer to Consumer." n.d. World Cocoa Foundation Staff. http://www.worldcocoafoundation.org/about-cocoa/cocoa-value-chain/

Coe, Sophie D., and Michael D. Coe. 2013. *The True History of Chocolate*. New York: Thames & Hudson.

Fiegl, Amanda. 2008. "A Brief History of Chocolate." *Smithsonian*, March 1, 2008.

Handwerk, Brian. 2015. "What Physics Tells Us about Making the Perfect Chocolate." *Smithsonian Magazine*, February 13, 2015.

Kiniry, Laura. 2015. "Chocolate Destinations Around the World to Drool Over." *Smithsonian Magazine*, February 11, 2015.

McCarthy, Niall. 2015. "The World's Biggest Chocolate Consumers." *Forbes*, July 22, 2015. https://www.forbes.com/sites/niallmccarthy/2015/07/22/the-worlds-biggest-chocolate-consumers-infographic/?sh=75026d6e4484

Miller, Bryan. 1990. "Burlington, WI: The Chocolate War." *Chicago Reader*, September 6, 1990.

Salon du Chocolat. 2018. https://www.salon-du-chocolat.com/presentation/?lang=en

Smith, Andrew F. 2006. *Encyclopedia of Junk Food and Fast Food*. Santa Barbara: Greenwood.

Thompson, Alyse. 2018. "Report: U.S. Chocolate Market to Surpass $20 Billion by 2025." *Candy Industry*, March 21, 2018. https://www.candyindustry.com/articles/88102-report-us-chocolate-market-to-surpass-20-billion-by-2025

Vora, Shivani. 2018. "From Peppers to Pork Pies, The Most Interesting Food Festivals of the Year." *The New York Times*, February 21, 2018.

Chopped

STARTERS

Chopped is a reality show on Food Network that follows four chefs competing for a cash prize, usually $10,000. Chefs are tasked with creating a three-course meal using key ingredients that they were not privy to before the show began filming. Before each course, the ingredients are revealed from a "mystery basket." The ingredients range from mundane to unusual, and they require a great deal of creativity to incorporate in a single dish. The show premiered in 2009 and has racked up 35 seasons and 495 episodes, which includes specials such as *Chopped Champions*, *Chopped: Impossible*, and *Chopped All-Stars*.

A spin-off show, *Chopped Junior*, aired in 2007 and has run for 7 seasons, featuring contestants between the ages of 9 and 14 (IMDB; Jazynka 2017). The longevity of *Chopped* also inspired two international variations, *Chopped, Canada* (2014), and *Chopped, South Africa* (2014). *Chopped* received two James Beard awards in 2012 for "Best Television Program in a Studio or Fixed Location" and "Best Media Personality/Host." In 2012, the show was also inducted into the Culinary Hall of Fame.

ENTRÉE

Imagine that you have been tasked with making an appetizer for three highly acclaimed culinary judges, and you have no idea what ingredients it will comprise. A basket is opened, revealing a jar of pickled pigs' feet, jicama, culantro (similar to the herb *cilantro*), and an entire frosted tres leches cake. Almost instantly, you are expected to start assembling these ingredients (and whatever else is stocked in the studio's refrigerator and pantry) into an extraordinary cohesive dish. The set is filled with cameras and crew members, the clock is set for 30 minutes, and if you fail, or cut yourself, the world will see.

This is the world of competitive cooking on television, specifically in the realm of *Chopped*. Host Ted Allen conceived the idea for the show with the program's executive producer Linda Lea. The duo filmed a pilot for *Chopped* at the Culinary School at the Art Institute of New York, envisioning a mansion as the setting for the competition. The host of the show was a butler who held a Chihuahua, and at the end of each round, the losing dish was to be eaten by the dog. Although Allen admits the concept was a little "trippy" for the likes of Food Network, executives liked the crux of the show, which Allen has described as, "Can you cook something beautiful out of these four incongruous ingredients, or not?" (Sytsma 2012).

Today's high-stakes cooking competitions feel almost too numerous to count, but in 2009, *Chopped* was one of the few of its kind. It was preceded by reality competition shows *Iron Chef* (which aired in the United States in 1999) and *The Next Food Network Star* (2005). However, the format of *Chopped* struck a chord with viewers and network executives. It became the basic formula for many of the reality shows that followed: competitors face off in various fast-paced rounds, and one contestant is eliminated each round, leaving two to face off for the grand prize. A 2014 *Atlantic* article wrote that *Chopped* is largely to blame (or to thank, depending on your appetite for culinary entertainment) for today's common culinary show themes: "a larger-than-life host, a specifically defined challenge, bombastic music, a set time limit, a panel of judges, and a cast of contestants whose back-story and biographical detail serves to heighten the stakes and fan the [program's] already heated dramatic flame" (Kohli and Quartz staff 2014).

This style is a far cry from the instructional cooking shows that had dominated the airwaves in prior decades, which prioritized education over entertainment. The show's appeal has reached audiences who aren't necessarily interested in cuisine or cooking, but are drawn to the sport-like pace and energy of the competition. As Food Network's senior vice president Bob Tuschman told *The Atlantic*, audiences enjoy watching "how (chefs) use their culinary expertise to cook their way out of the corner they find themselves boxed into" (2014).

The "dramatic flame" of *Chopped* and its related army of spinoff and specials is fanned on set with the help of 14 cameras recording the action, which producers watch from a booth while logging key moments that they want highlighted in the finished cut. Filming takes 12 or more hours, followed by a 37-day editing process to capture all of the sautéing, grilling, ice cream churning, dashing, nail-biting, panicking, and tasting that takes place over the course of an hour-long episode (Rosner and Morabito 2016). At the end of the third round, judges determine which of the two remaining chefs created the most delicious, ingenious, and pleasing meal, weighing whether infractions such as forgetting or intentionally eliminating an ingredient warrant dismissal. A metal cloche is dramatically removed from a plate to reveal the dish created by the losing chef, signifying that he or she has been *chopped*.

The decision to include unrelated ingredients was made mostly to create a game-like challenge, but over the course of the show, a deeper message has emerged from it: the importance of cutting down on food waste. In 2017, the *Washington Post* reported that Americans throw away roughly 27 million tons of food annually, a $144 billion hit to the economy. In a study of food waste in Nashville, Denver, and New York, researchers determined that the average American consumer is wasting 3.5 pounds of food per week, two-thirds of which is in the form of food that is still considered edible (Dewey 2017). *Chopped* has shared the message throughout several shows (including several episodes specifically focused on leftover ingredients) that applying creativity to ingredients and embracing leftover food is environmentally and economically valuable.

ACCOMPANIED BY

Host

Ted Allen (1965–) is an American television personality, writer, and passionate amateur chef. He holds a bachelor's degree in psychology from Purdue University and a master's degree in journalism from New York University. Earlier in his career, Allen was a senior editor and restaurant critic for *Chicago* magazine. He has written for various publications such as *Esquire* and *Bon Appetit* magazines and has published two cookbooks. Allen was cast as the food and wine expert in Bravo's *Queer Eye for the Straight Guy* (2003), the first all-gay cast on American television (Rosner and Morabito 2016). The show received an Emmy in 2004 for "Outstanding Reality Program." In the years following, Allen was a host on the first four seasons of Bravo's *Top Chef* (2004–) and Food Network's *Chopped*, *Best Ever*, and *All-Star Academy*, a competition for amateur chefs. Allen lives in Brooklyn with his husband, interior decorator Barry Rice.

Judges

The long-term judges on *Chopped* include Amanda Freitag (competitor, *The Next Iron Chef: Redemption*), Alex Guarnaschelli (Butter, New York; competitor, *Iron Chef America*), Aarón Sanchez (New Orleans, Johnny Sanchez), Geoffrey Zakarian (The National and The Lamb Club, New York), Marc Murphy (Benchmarc Restaurants by Marc Murphy brand), Scott Conant (Scarpetta, New York), and Chris Santos (The Stanton Social, New York). Visiting celebrity judges include Alton Brown (*Good Eats*), television culinary mogul Martha Stewart, Marcus Samuelsson (Red Rooster, New York), Rocco DiSpirito (Union Pacific, New York), Christina Tosi (Milk Bar, New York), and Nancy Silverton (Osteria Mozza, La Brea Bakery, Los Angeles), just to name a scant few.

DESSERT

A Food Network blog shared the most common cooking mistakes that *Chopped* chefs make. The list includes: Under- or overcooking as a result of poor planning, cross-contamination mistakes, overcrowding deep fryers, opening the oven too often to peek inside, using a pan that's too cold, and under-seasoning.

SUGGESTED PAIRINGS

See also: *MasterChef*; Television, Food Channels on; *Top Chef*.

Entry best enjoyed while eating: Tackle your own *Chopped* challenge! Create an entrée from the ingredients *Chopped Junior* chefs received in the spinoff's premier: venison tenderloin, baby eggplant, a chocolate milkshake, and couscous.

Further Reading

"All the Things You Didn't Know About Ted Allen." n.d. Food Network. https://www.foodnetwork.com/profiles/talent/ted-allen/all-the-things-you-didnt-know-about-chopped-host-ted-allen

Allen, Ted. n.d. "About." Tedallen.net.

"Chopped." n.d. IMDB. https://www.imdb.com/title/tt1353281/

"Chopped, Jr." n.d. IMDB. https://www.imdb.com/title/tt5226884/

Curtis, Cameron. 2012. "Congratulations to Ted Allen and Chopped on James Beard Journalism Awards." https://www.foodnetwork.com/fn-dish/events/2012/05/congratulations-to-ted-allen-and-chopped-on-james-beard-journalism-awards

Dewey, Caitlin. 2017. "Why Americans Have Stopped Eating Leftovers." *The Washington Post*, October 31, 207.

Jazynka, Kitson. 2017. "Boy Who Loves to Cook Risks Being 'Chopped.'" *The Washington Post,* January 3, 2017.

Kohli, Sonali, and Quartz staff. 2014. "When Cooking Became Competition." *The Atlantic*, October 2, 2014.

Rosner, Helen, and Rob Morabito, 2016. "Ted Allen Explains the Hoax That Is His Career." *Eater*, interview with Ted Allen. August 22, 2016.

Sytsma, Allen. 2012. "Ted Allen on His New Book, Crushing Chefs' Dreams, and Chopped's Lost Chihuahua." Grub Street, May 22, 2012. http://www.grubstreet.com/2012/05/ted-allen-in-my-kitchen-interview-book-tour-dates.html

Coffee Culture

STARTERS

Coffee has been enjoyed for centuries, but the culturally embraced idea of a routine coffee break and the notion of a coffee shop as someplace to have a first date, job interview, or lengthy study session are largely unique to the United States as of the twentieth and twenty-first centuries. The word "coffee" is no longer limited to a cup of the strong-brewed beverage, served black or with a splash of cream and sugar. Patrons frequently stay in coffee shops for hours, enjoying everything from traditional cups of coffee to fruit smoothies; hot chocolate; and frozen blends of coffee, sugar, and syrups. Starbucks chairman Howard Schultz calls coffee

Caffe Reggio, one of the oldest coffee shops in the United States, was opened in 1927 by Italian-American Domenico Parisi in New York City's Greenwich Village neighborhood. Parisi reportedly saved his earnings working as a barber for 40 years to import this $1,000 espresso machine from Italy. The machines, which were powered by steam and coal in the early twentieth century, would go on to help fuel an espresso craze across United States starting in the 1980s. (Library of Congress)

shops a "third place," a space for work and recreation outside of the home and office. Espresso is at the heart of many Americans' recreation time and work days, serving as a frequent treat and booming element of the economy. Coffee is widely reported as the most popular caffeinated drink in the United States.

Coffee retail giant Starbucks employs 175,000 employees at 8,000 stores across the country (Kisby 2018). Other large corporations like Dazbog, Caribou Coffee, Dunkin Donuts, and McDonalds add significantly to the number of retail coffee offerings nationwide. Combined with the number of small, privately owned coffee houses, many Americans are within easy access of the beverage almost 24-7 and have a dizzying array of coffee styles and price points to choose from.

ENTRÉE

Discussions about coffee houses often expose an interesting intersection of cultural issues. Newspapers and magazines often point to coffee shops as linked with gentrification, although researchers hotly debate whether the coffee houses tend to be the first sign of gentrification or if their arrival is more a symptom of prior gentrification shifts in the area. The term "gentrification" was coined by British sociologist Ruth Glass when she wrote about urban developments in London in 1964. She noted that as areas of the city became more modern and wealthy, working-class families were pushed out by incoming lower and upper echelons of the middle class (Staley 2018).

Coffee culture is often described as primarily benefiting the "leisure class," those who have enough free time and disposable income to be able to indulge in expensive coffee drinks and significant amounts of time to spend in coffee shops. In 2015, the Specialty Coffee Association of America reported that the retail value of the coffee market is roughly $48 billion in the United States and that 35 percent of polled individuals between the ages of 18 and 24 reported drinking "specialty coffee" every day. This has developed into a polarizing topic in contemporary culture wars; older generations sometimes use the price and daily habit of purchasing specialty coffee to criticize the spending habits of younger individuals, primarily millennials (individuals born between 1981 and 1996).

Specialty coffee is defined by the quality of the beans, which require careful cultivation, processing, storage, and roasting. Quality is everything in a modern movement often referred to as the "third wave," in which the quality of the beans, roasting methods, complexity, and sustainability of the coffee's origins are scrutinized. Coffee—once ubiquitously consumed in the United States via an instant, powdered form—is now frequently sampled the way wine is tasted, in events referred to as "cuppings." These tastings are especially popular at independent coffee shops that tout fine coffees (Wallace 2008).

Coffee's History

"Second only to oil, coffee is the most valuable legally traded commodity in the world," food historian Tori Avey wrote in 2013. Coffee's origin story is that of an

Ethiopian goat herder who noticed that his goats were highly energized after consuming the fruit of coffee plants. Much like the journey chocolate takes from plant to plate, the production process of harvesting, processing, drying, roasting, and brewing coffee is complex and has evolved over a long period of time. Roasting is thought to have started in the thirteenth century, and the modern form of coffee is traced to Arabia around the same time. Muslims celebrated the caffeination of the beverage, in particular. The coffee trade flourished through parts of the Middle East, Europe, and beyond, inciting a significant coffee trend in Britain, in particular. Between 1652 and 1700, an estimated 2,000 coffee houses opened in London, serving as important places in which to hold intellectual dialogues (Avey 2013; Koehler 2017).

Coffee also reached the shores of the New World in the early eighteenth century. In 1773, the Boston Tea Party was a pivotal historic event for coffee, which became the new drink of choice after the political uprising. Coffee played a large role in the daily lives of many American soldiers, such as Civil War soldiers, whose rifles were equipped to store and even grind coffee beans. World War I soldiers were so dependent on relatively recent invention of instant coffee that in 1918, the army ordered upward of 37,000 pounds of it a day (a staggering amount compared to the national production of 6,000 pounds per day). Today, in its various forms, an estimated 2.25 billion cups of coffee are consumed around the world per day (Koehler 2017; Pendergrast 2010, 137).

DESSERT

- **Take a break:** The workday coffee break is thought to have originated during a social reform movement in the early 1900s. Workplaces began to designate lunch rooms as places where workers could get away from the "drudgery" of their work, and employers and employees alike began setting up communal coffee resources. The term "coffee break" flourished in the 1950s with the help of employees who were eager for a recreational break, as well as companies who didn't mind the perceived productivity boosts from their caffeinated employees.
- **Trading one stimulant for another:** Stoughton, Wisconsin holds an annual Coffee Break Festival. According to local lore, coffee breaks originated in Stoughton thanks to the local Norwegian immigrants who worked at tobacco warehouses. Many of those employees were women who could walk home during their work breaks to tend to their children and savor a cup of coffee before returning to the warehouse. The festival entails a coffee brew-off, helicopter rides, and a "java jog," among other caffeinated events.
- **The percolator of youth:** The health benefits of coffee are hotly debated. In 2018, *National Geographic* highlighted new research that indicates those who drink two or three cups of (caffeinated or decaf) coffee a day have relatively healthier livers and circulatory systems and may have a lower chance of dying prematurely from any cause compared to their peers.

SUGGESTED PAIRINGS

See also: Chocolate Events and Destinations; Craft Brewing and Microbreweries; Wine and Spirits.

Entry best enjoyed while eating: A hot slice of hot cinnamon coffee cake, a BLT sandwich with coffee-marinated bacon, and a glass of iced Vietnamese coffee with condensed milk.

Further Reading

Avey, Tori. 2013. "History of Coffee." *PBS* The History Kitchen, April 8, 2013. http://www.pbs.org/food/the-history-kitchen/history-coffee/

Hemler, Allison. 2009. "Coffee's History in America, A Short Primer." Serious Eats. https://newyork.seriouseats.com/2009/11/coffee-chronicles-coffee-in-america-new-amsterdam-market-starbucks.html

Kisby, Roger. 2018. "Starbucks, at the Intersection of Race and Class in America." *The New York Times,* May 29, 2018.

Koehler, Jeff. 2017. "In WWI Trenches, Instant Coffee Gave Troops a Much-Needed Boost." NPR, April 6, 2017.

Pendergrast, Mark. 2010. *Uncommon Grouns: The History of Coffee and How It Transformed our World.* New York: Basic Books.

Specialty Coffee Association Sustainability Council. 2015. "U.S. Specialty Coffee Facts & Figures." http://www.scaa.org/?page=resources&d=facts-and-figures

Staley, Willy. 2018. "When 'Gentrification' Isn't about Housing." *The New York Times*, January 23, 2018.

Stamberg, Susan. 2002. "The Coffee Break." *Morning Edition*, NPR. December 2, 2002.

Valencia, Ana. 2017. "Coffee Professionals Discuss: What Is Specialty Coffee?" Perfect Daily Grind. July 10, 2017. https://www.perfectdailygrind.com/2017/07/coffee-professionals-discuss-specialty-coffee-mean/

Wallace, Hannah. 2008. "Do I Detect a Hint of . . . Joe?" *The New York Times*, May 29, 2008.

Zuckerman, Catherine. 2018. "Coffee Is Good for You." *National Geographic* magazine, March 2018.

Cooked

STARTERS

Cooked is a Netflix documentary series that debuted in 2016. The one-season, four-episode series is based on the eponymous 2013 book written by food historian, author, and anthropologist Michael Pollan. *Cooked*, which stars Pollan, explores the ancient elements of cooking and how they have transformed food and culture. Each episode follows one of these elements, which include fire, water, air, and earth. The series seeks to explain how cooking with flame, incorporating water and air into food preparation, and utilizing microbes (bacteria and other tiny organisms) transforms food, bodies, and cultures. The show was produced by Jigsaw Productions and Netflix and was shot and produced by Oscar-award winning filmmaker Alex Gibney (*Taxi to the Dark Side*, 2007; *Enron, The Smartest Guys in the Room* 2005). *Cooked* was nominated for an International Documentary Award in 2016.

ENTRÉE

"Cooking is all about connection, I've learned, between us and other species, other times, other cultures (human and microbial both), but, most important, other people. Cooking is one of the more beautiful forms that human generosity takes," Pollan wrote in his *New York Times* best-selling book *Cooked* (2013, p. 415). Both the book and the ensuing documentary series explore these themes in context, looking in depth at how ancient methods of cooking and baking have helped shape the world. Pollan theorizes that many Americans' departure from cooking with age-old traditions—or cooking much at all—is leading to health and cultural issues that he argues should be analyzed more closely and rectified.

The documentary follows various masters of their culinary crafts, blending high-quality cinematography with lyrical music and editing techniques to help tell the story of what cooking means to people all over the world. The "Fire" episode features fire-roasting techniques of the Martu, an Aboriginal tribe in Western Australia that balances modern living with traditional hunting and cooking techniques in the outback. Fire is presented as a primeval means of cooking, one that also awakens our senses and deeply enriches the flavor and complexity of food. In "Water," Pollan illustrates cooking with pots in India to illustrate this relatively recent invention in human history, one that dramatically influenced the way we prepare a wide variety of foods. Before the invention of durable cookware, he points out, our means of cooking were highly limited.

"Air" provides an in-depth look at how something as seemingly innocuous as an air bubble in bread signifies a transcendent invention in human history: the transformation of wheat into flour. Pollan points out that flour doesn't provide much nutrition on its own, but when incorporated with water, yeast, and air, it is a food that has become one of biggest diet staples across the globe. In the episode, Moroccan bakers demonstrate bread-baking techniques with choreography almost reminiscent of a dance piece. Many of the bakers have been perfecting these techniques since childhood. The critical importance of grain as a food and a commodity used to trade and barter is illustrated with the example of a Moroccan milner who uses an ancient granary to grind wheat brought in by locals.

The "Earth" episode investigates the process of fermentation, focusing on the microbes found in fermented foods like kimchi, kombucha, cheese, beer, and sauerkraut. The episode features a nun who makes cheese using wooden barrels. It also follows a group of Peruvian women who chew and spit out pieces of yucca root, collecting their saliva to produce enzymes that will "cook" the root. Many of Pollan's writings explore the importance of microbes in our diets and in our guts, with a focus on bacteria's role in our health, physical wellness, and even emotions. In an interview with the Yale School of Forestry and Environmental Studies, Pollan said that he "was amazed to learn that first, we are only 10 percent human, if you're counting cells, and 90 percent bacterial," noting that the enormous presence of microbes in the human body makes him see the relationship between humans' bodies and the environment differently (Hitt 2013). Throughout both the book and documentary series, international portraits of cooks and bakers are interspersed with scenes of Pollan cooking in his own kitchen, reinforcing his point that Americans should spend more time in their kitchens, cooking healthy meals for themselves and their families.

ACCOMPANIED BY

Born in 1955, Pollan grew up in Long Island, New York. He attended Bennington College, Oxford University, and Columbia University, and he lives in the Bay Area of California with his wife Judith Belzer, an artist, and his son Isaac. Pollan developed a deep passion for cooking and cultural relationships between food and nature, of which he has written about extensively for more than 30 years. An author, activist, and professor of journalism, he is widely associated with trends such as the farm-to-table movement, as well as other organic and sustainable food practices. Pollan made an appearance in the Oscar-nominated documentary *Food, Inc* in 2009 and penned five *New York Times* best-selling novels, including *Cooked: A Natural History of Transformation* (2013), *The Omnivore's Dilemma: A Natural History of Four Meals* (2006), *and The Botany of Desire: A Plant's Eye View of the World* (2001). In 2009, he was labeled one of the top 10 new "thought leaders" by *Newsweek*, and in 2010, he was named by *Time* as one of the world's 100 most influential people.

DESSERT

In a 2009 *New York Times Magazine* article titled "Out of the Kitchen, Onto the Couch," Pollan credits Julia Child's television show *The French Chef* with improving "the quality of life around our house." Pollan wrote that when he was young, part of the allure of watching the show was waiting for Child to drop something on the floor, but he notes that her approach to cooking helped his family (and families across the nation) embrace quality cooking in a new way.

SUGGESTED PAIRINGS

See also: *Chef's Table*; Documentary Films, Food and Beverages in; Nonfiction, Food in.

Entry best enjoyed while eating: A loaf of freshly baked sourdough bread ("air"); brined roast chicken with roasted root vegetables ("fire"); sauerkraut seasoned with sea salt, juniper berries, and caraway seeds ("earth"); a simple chickpea soup ("water"); and, inspired by Pollan's favorite dessert at Chez Panisse, a simple locally sourced bowl of fruit.

Further Reading
"About Michael Pollan." n.d. https://michaelpollan.com/about
Hitt, Jack. 2013. "Michael Pollan on the Links Between Biodiversity and Health." *Yale Environment 360*. May 28, 2013. https://e360.yale.edu/features/michael_pollan_on_the_links_between_biodiversity_and_health
Pollan, Michael. 2009. "Out of the Kitchen and Onto the Couch." *New York Times Magazine*, July 29, 2009.
Pollan, Michael. 2013. *Cooked: A Natural History of Transformation*. New York: The Penguin Press.

Spangler, Todd. 2016. "Netflix to Launch Food Docu-Series from Michael Pollan, Alex Gibney." *Variety*, January 15, 2016. https://variety.com/2016/digital/news/netflix-cooked-docu-series-michael-pollan-alex-gibney-1201680981/

Cooks vs. Cons

STARTERS

Cooks vs. Cons is a reality television show that pits professional and amateur chefs against each other in a cooking competition. The show first aired on the Food Network in 2016 and has run for 57 episodes over the course of five seasons. Produced by Cakehouse Media and distributed by Food Network, the show stars chef and television personality Geoffrey Zakarian and a panel of guest judges. Frequent judges include cookbook author and co-host of *The Chew* Daphne Oz and chef and *Chopped* judge Alex Guarnaschelli.

ENTRÉE

Cooks vs. Cons invites amateur cooks to ask themselves questions like, "Could my lasagna recipe give Emeril Lagasse's lasagna a run for its money?" The hour-long reality cooking competition invites judges and home audiences alike to guess which competitors are amateurs and which are professionals as they vie for the title of last chef standing. At the end of the competition, the winner receives a sizeable check; $10,000 for professional chefs or $15,000 for amateurs (Stevens 2016). The show includes other quirks made famous by programs like *Chopped* and *Iron Chef*, such as making contestants use unusual foods in their creations, adhering to a strict time restriction of 30 minutes to create their dishes, and not knowing what the challenge will be before it's announced.

In one episode, chefs begin the competition with the direction to create their own take on a Sloppy Joe sandwich. The twist? One of the key ingredients in their sandwich must be sourced from a select group of pies on the set. Although a Sloppy Joe is typically thought of as a loose-meat sandwich slathered in tomato and Worcestershire sauce and served on a bun, the contestants' creations range from fruit-filled concoctions to dishes more similar to a Shepherd's Pie. Other episodes follow a similar structure, with challenges such as using cookies as an ingredient in a meat-and-potatoes entrée, incorporating canned soup into a plate of nachos, and using lemon as a new twist in breakfast sandwiches.

Throughout the show, judges analyze the chefs' techniques, skills, agility in the kitchen, creativity, and the quality of their dishes. In the first round, contestants must all use the same type of required ingredient to make the same general category of food. In the second round, they can use a special ingredient in any dish of their choosing. Over the course of the episode, chefs are eliminated based on the judges' favorite dishes from each round. Before the final winning dish is revealed, the contestants deliver the show's catchphrase to reveal their identities, saying "I . . . am . . . a . . ." before exclaiming "cook!" or "con!" Zakarian and the judges delight in amazement or celebrate their correct guesses as the cooks describe their specialty and restaurant and cons describe their actual professions, which range from window washers to scientists to yoga instructors.

Cooks vs. Cons highlights the professional and amateur chefs' aspirational desires, an angle that many production companies are hungry to feature. Aspirational content often fares well in this industry, as seen by the double-digit increases the show enjoyed in the second season of viewers between ages 25 and 54 and between the ages of 25 and 34 (Steinberg 2016). Fans of *Cooks vs. Cons* range from skilled chefs to individuals who consider themselves utterly devoid of culinary skills. One of the common ties that bind this audience together is the fun they share in fantasizing about being recognized as a talented chef. The show also offers the widely beloved storyline in which an underdog can beat a professional, highly acclaimed master of his or her trade.

ACCOMPANIED BY

The show's host is restaurateur, chef, and television personality Geoffrey Zakarian, known for his acclaimed restaurants Town and Country in New York City, among others. Zakarian is featured in a number of Food Network shows and has authored a number of cookbooks. In 2011, *The New York Times* reported that the celebrity chef was filing bankruptcy after prior Country employees filed a class action lawsuit against him for allegedly not paying them what they were owed. Frequent judges include Daphne Oz and Alex Guarnaschelli, as well as less-frequent appearances by fellow chefs, television personalities, and restaurateurs Graham Elliot, Kardea Brown, Sunny Anderson, Curtis Stown, Ted Allen, Marcus Samuelsson, and Richard Blais, just to name a few.

SUGGESTED PAIRINGS

See also: *Chopped*; *Iron Chef*; Television, Food Channels on.

Entry best enjoyed while eating: University of Virginia writer Renee Spillane suggests the following recipes, inspired by the unusual twists seen on *Cooks vs. Cons*: Bacon-fried rice balls flavored with Sriracha, caramelized eggplant topped with a paprika yogurt sauce, and a beer-battered waffle served with carne asada (marinated steak).

Further Reading

"Cooks vs. Cons." n.d. IMDB. https://www.imdb.com/title/tt5569062/

Fox, Nick. 2011. "Star Chef, Facing a Suit, Files for Bankruptcy." *The New York Times*, April 27, 2011.

Spillane, Renee. 2017. "13 *Cooks vs. Cons* Inspired Recipes." *Spoon University*, June 25, 2017. https://spoonuniversity.com/lifestyle/recipes-inspired-by-cooks-vs-cons

Steinberg, Brian. 2016. "Food Network's *Cooks vs. Cons* Will Return for Second Season." *Variety*, April 15, 2016. https://variety.com/2016/tv/news/cooks-vs-cons-second-season-food-network-1201754568/

Stevens, Ashlie D. 2016. "The 'Cooks vs. Cons' Dream: How the Food Network Got Back in Touch with Its Aspirational Roots." *Salon*, July 17, 2006. https://www.salon

.com/2016/07/17/the_cooks_vs_cons_dream_how_the_food_network_got_back_in_touch_with_its_aspirational_roots/

Craft Brewing and Microbreweries

STARTERS

Craft brewing in America is largely defined as the efforts of small-scale, independent, and traditional brewers who primarily use traditional, artisanal methods to brew beer. Craft brewers tend to primarily focus on creating high-quality beers with big flavors, blending traditional staple ingredients like malted barley with ingredients that are region-specific. Many often add interesting or unusual ingredients. In industry terms, a *craft brewery* produces fewer than 6 million barrels per year, has less than 25 percent of their brewery controlled by a member of a non-craft-beer alcohol industry, and uses traditional methods for a majority of its production (Brewers Association 2018c). Similarly, a *microbrewery* is defined as producing fewer than 15,000 barrels a year, and 75 percent of its sales must take place off-site (Brewers Association 2018b).

Craft brewing has been met with immense popularity across the United States in recent decades. Craft beers and microbreweries, which produce small amounts of beer compared to their corporate mega-competitors, gained significant popularity in the late 1980s and 1990s. Interest in craft beer was fueled by Americans' opinions that these beverages provided a refreshing change from the ubiquitous light, lager-style beer that had dominated the industry for decades, produced by mega-corporations such as Anheuser-Busch and MillerCoors. As craft brewing became more popular among homebrewers and brewery owners, unique American styles began to emerge. These styles, such as India Pale Ales (IPAs), ambers, fruit beers, and farmhouse ales, deviated from typical European styles like lagers, porters, and stouts. As of 2010, large beer corporations have seen declining sales as craft brewing has seen extraordinary growth, and homebrewing continues to flourish as a hobby and an entrepreneurial quest.

ENTRÉE

Craft brewing is often referred to as a cultural revolution, a comparison that isn't wildly hyperbolic considering its history. The history of beer reportedly traces as far back as Mesopotamia. Early American varieties consisted primarily of corn-based lagers (Goldfarb 2017). Prior to the twentieth century, beer drinkers in the United States typically imbibed lighter beers sourced from corn or rice or the malt-based lagers shared by European immigrants. German and English beers competed for popularity, in particular. In the late 1800s and early 1900s, breweries and saloons flourished, although independent brewers began to lose ground to early corporations like Miller Brewing Company and Anheuser-Busch.

Prohibition dramatically changed America's brewing industry. President Woodrow Wilson ordered a prohibition in 1917 that was intended to temporarily preserve the domestic use of grain for food, but Congress passed the Eighteenth Amendment shortly thereafter. This forbid the manufacturing, sale, or transportation of "intoxicating liquor." When alcohol was legalized again under President Franklin Roosevelt's administration in the 1930s, Americans found their options mostly limited to lighter lager styles sourced from corn and rice products. Laws prohibiting home brewing of alcohol higher than 0.5 percent remained in effect until a new bill was passed in 1979 that eased federal restrictions on home brewing.

During the 1970s, with the help of enormous marketing campaigns from the still-reigning corporate giants, light lagers accounted for a vast majority of Americans' beers. Simultaneously, a number of individuals around the country took advantage of the new alcohol production laws. These beer enthusiasts sought to preserve traditional brewing styles, and a small wave of homebrewing enthusiasts began to grow. In the 1980s, many craft brewers began successfully selling their "full-flavored beer," and the trend gained momentum. By the mid-1990s, demand for alternatives to the beer sold by large corporations was strong, and independent breweries began flourishing on a wider scale. The trend became so popular that many financial investors hopped on board in hopes of profiting from the trend, but many lacked experience in or a passion for the craft. As a result, the craft beer industry experienced many failed and shuttered businesses, but a string of passionate crafters pushed through, welcoming a second giant wave of craft beer enthusiasm.

Today, craft beer is considered to be a surprising success story by many beer enthusiasts and economics enthusiasts alike. Mass-produced beer consumption declined in the 2000s thanks in part to the increasing popularity of wine and cocktails in the United States, but craft-brewed beers—which are typically more expensive than domestic beer—saw extraordinary sales. According to a business analysis in *The Atlantic*, between the years 2008 and 2016 "the number of brewery establishments expanded by a factor of six, and the number of brewery workers grew by 120 percent (. . .) a 200-year-old industry has sextupled its establishments and more than doubled its workforce in less than a decade" (Thompson 2018). The reporter, Derek Thompson, attributes much of the "craft boom" both to consumer demand in the wake of decades of "lite" beer and to dramatic changes in the country's alcohol regulatory history. In light of these changes, large alcohol companies have been met with significant restrictions that allow smaller businesses to compete for store shelves and bar taps alike.

As of 2013, there were an estimated 2,360 craft breweries in the United States, a far cry from the mere 89 breweries (of any type) running in the United States in 1978 (Fromson 2013; Goldfarb 2017). The earliest craft breweries that made it big were largely in California and New England, including The Boston Beer Company, Sierra Nevada, New Albion Brewing, and Anchor Brewing. Today, craft brewing can be found nationwide, notably concentrated in Oregon, Colorado, and the Mid-Atlantic region (Fromson 2013). The Brewers Association reported a slowdown in barrel production during 2016, but noted that this "cooling" reflected the fact that the extreme annual growth seen in recent years is unsustainable long term and that the industry was still booming. In an attempt to stay abreast of America's changing preferences, the nation's four largest beer corporations have adopted the strategy of acquiring and selling craft beers, as well (Kell 2017).

ACCOMPANIED BY

In 1965, Frederick "Fritz" Maytag III (1937–) purchased Anchor Brewing Company in San Francisco, California. He is credited with inventing Liberty Ale, considered to be the first modern IPA, as well as pioneering the effort to focus on quality and unique varieties of beer in the United States (Goldfarb 2017). Jim Koch (1949–) established Boston Beer Company, ranked as the second largest craft brewery producer in 2017 (Brewers Association 2018a). Koch is best known for his family's recipe, called Sam Adams Boston Lager. The beer's popularity helped transform him into a billionaire, and he is frequently referred to as the person who started the craft beer revolution in America. A few other notable craft brewing pioneers include Brewers Association founder Charlie Papazian; Jack McAuliffe, founder of New Albion Brewing in Sonoma, California (1976); Kim Jordan and Jeff Lebesch, founders of New Belgium Brewery in Fort Collins, Colorado (1991); and Sierra Nevada founder Ken Grossman in Chico, California (1979), among many others.

DESSERT

Many craft brewers infuse their business practices with tongue-in-cheek fun, such as beer names that celebrate pop culture. A few examples include O'Dell Brewing Company's "Fee Fi Fo Fum IPA," Brewery Ommegang's "Take the Black Stout" and "Fire and Blood Red Ale" (homages to the book and television series *Game of Thrones*), *Star Wars* themes like Sierra Nevada's "Empire Strikes Back Imperial Stout," and Verboten Brewery's "Where's Carl?" IPA, which pokes fun at a youngster in the television show *The Walking Dead*, whose parents often failed to keep a close eye on him during a zombie apocalypse.

SUGGESTED PAIRINGS

See also: *Bar Rescue*; Super Bowl Sunday; Wine and Spirits.

Entry best enjoyed while drinking: A mixed sampler of local craft brews, including an American Pale Ale, New England IPA, Raspberry Sour Ale, American Amber Lager, Pumpkin Stout, and an American Imperial Porter.

Further Reading

Akkam, Alia. 2016. "Fourteen Beer Pioneers You Need to Know." *Zagat*, March 22, 2016. https://www.zagat.com/b/14-beer-pioneers-you-need-to-know

Brewers Association. 2018a. "Brewers Association Releases 2017 Top 50 Brewing Companies by Sales Volume." https://www.brewersassociation.org/press-releases/brewers-association-releases-2017-top-50-brewing-companies-by-sales-volume/

Brewers Association. 2018b. "Craft Beer Industry Market Segments." https://www.brewersassociation.org/statistics/market-segments/

Brewers Association. 2018c. "History of Craft Brewing." https://www.brewersassociation.org/brewers-association/history/history-of-craft-brewing/

Eng, Dinah. 2013. "Jim Koch: Samuel Adams's Beer Revolutionary." *Fortune*, March 21, 2013.

Fromson, Daniel. 2013. "Idea of the Week: Mapping the Rise of Craft Beer." *The New Yorker*, June 6, 2013.

Goldfarb, Aaron. 2017. "An Illustrated History of Craft Beer in America." *First We Feast*, March 6, 2017.

"Jim Koch." n.d. "Billionaires 2015." *Forbes*. https://www.forbes.com/profile/jim-koch/#609c5d9a23d9

Johnson, Bryan. 2016. "The History of Beer in America." Great Fermentations, June 27, 2016. http://www.greatfermentations.com/the-history-of-beer-in-america/

Kell, John. 2017. "How Craft Beer's Popularity Is Hurting Craft Beer." *Fortune*, March 28, 2017.

Thompson, Derek. 2018. "Craft Beer Is the Strangest, Happiest Economic Story in America." *The Atlantic*, January 19, 2018.

Culinary Awards, The Evolution of

STARTERS

Of the countless culinary awards in existence today, some of the most highly regarded in the United States and around the world include the James Beard Foundation Award, the World's 50 Best Restaurants List, and the Michelin Guide. The oldest is the Michelin Guide, which was founded in 1900 by brothers Andre and Edouard Michelin, who owned the Michelin tire company in Clermont-Ferrand, France. The pair initially published the guide as a way to encourage people to take recreational drives in the early years of the automotive industry (and, by no coincidence, to buy more tires while doing so). The guide listed notable restaurants in various regions, rating them between one and three stars to indicate "very good," "excellent, worth a detour," and "exceptional, worth a special journey." Today, the Michelin Guide is widely considered one of the highest honors in the industry. Starred restaurants are limited to those in cities in which the guide is published, including 4 cities in North America, 2 in South America, 22 in Europe, and 7 in Asia (Michelin Guide 2018).

The James Beard Foundation Awards began in 1990 as part of the eponymous culinary nonprofit that promotes the culinary arts and offers scholarships to culinary students. Often referred to as "the Oscars of food," these awards honor individuals and businesses specializing in American food and beverages. Categories include top restaurants, chefs, pastry chefs, food writers, wine and spirits innovators, and many more. The World's 50 Best Restaurants list was first published in 2002 by William Reed Media, a marketing business that originated in 1862 as a grocery industry marketing service. The list highlights 50 restaurants from all corners of the globe.

ENTRÉE

Receiving a Michelin star, James Beard Award, or "50 Best" nomination can undoubtedly change a culinary professional's life. But as esteemed as these awards are, their role in the culinary world is evolving along with food's ever-changing role in popular culture. Former heavyweight names in the "culinary recognition" arena included the Zagat guidebook and the "Who's Who of Food and Beverage in America" award. The highly esteemed "Who's Who" award was introduced by *Cook's Magazine* in 1984 and was later acquired by the James Beard Foundation.

Zagat was first published in 1979 by Tim and Nina Zagat due to the lack of restaurant guides available at the time. The once heavily consulted guidebook, which used surveys to gauge which restaurants diners enjoyed the most, was acquired by Google in 2011 and restaurant-recommendation website The Infatuation in 2018. This shift offers a look at how the internet has helped change the dining landscape. Zagat was first published when crowdsourcing was more challenging, but the internet dramatically changed the way people read about and rated restaurants. Today, people search the esteemed restaurant review archives of the *New York Times* and free sites like Yelp, which allow people to post and read restaurant reviews with ease. Despite the plethora of reviews available for virtually any restaurant, many diners still revere esteemed culinary awards as a way to separate the opinions of culinary experts from the masses.

Although elite awards continue to be highly sought after by many in the industry, some culinary professionals are becoming disillusioned with or disinterested in the honor. One reason for this is the intense pressure that many chefs and restaurateurs feel they are under to earn (and continue earning) the honors. In recent years, heavy speculation circulated that the suicides of two high-profile French chefs—Benoit Violier of Restaurant de l'Hotel de Ville and Bernard Loiseau of La C'ote d'Or—were linked to the pressure they felt to maintain their three-Michelin-star status (Steinberger 2016). Michael Ellis, the international director of the Michelin Guide, maintains that the stars are not given to chefs; they are bestowed upon restaurants (Kashner 2015). However, many chefs feel virtually inseparable from their establishments' accolades.

ACCOMPANIED BY

Michael Ellis has argued that Michelin stars are an intangible thing that cannot be rejected. However, an increasing number of chefs have attempted to give their stars back in recent years. In 2013, Spanish chef Julio Biosca rejected the star his restaurant Casa Julio received because he feared it would limit his ability to be innovative in his kitchen. Many other chefs have echoed this concern about top awards, citing fears that they'd be unable to veer from the menu and presentation of what earned them the honors in the first place and not be able to experiment without fear of being "punished" by future reviewers.

For chefs like Karen Keyngaert, one key factor in rejecting the Michelin star was economic pressure. She has noted that many of the diners who flock to restaurants based on their elite status expect "elite fare," with specific expectations for prices, ambiance, and types of food served. These expectations can be limiting and economically unsustainable for restaurants. Belgian chef Frederick Dhooge also rejected his star, citing the pressure of not being able to cook foods like fried chicken due to their perceived simplicity or lower-class status. Many cuisines,

Small Plates

A Tale of Two Bouches

In 2017, the Michelin Guide awarded a star to Le Bouche à Oreill ("word of mouth"), a small restaurant located in Bourges, France, on a street named route de la Chapelle. When the restaurant's owner, Veronique Jacquet, heard the news by way of a local radio announcement, she was nothing short of shocked. As it happens, Jacquet's restaurant is a small, working-class brasserie that only serves lunch, and offers fare like wine by the jug, lasagna, breads, and cheeses served on tables with plastic tablecloths. Jacquet was confused about receiving the award, since the restaurants typically selected by Michelin are associated with white starched linens and menu items such as foie gras and caviar.

Her reaction was founded; Michelin had intended to award the star to an identically named Bouche à Oreill restaurant located on a nearly identically named street (*rue* de la Chapelle), roughly 100 miles away in the city of Boutervilliers. This restaurant, known better for dishes like Breton lobster and fricassee of asparagus, is owned by Aymeric Dreux. When Dreux learned about the unfortunate mix-up, he invited Jacquet and her cafe's cook, Penelope Salmon, to dine at his restaurant.

Michelin's mistake remained in print, and diners inundated Jacquet's previously quiet establishment in Bourges, excited to see what was so spectacular about the tiny roadside restaurant. Armed with only four waiters and a limited number of small tables, Jacquet and her team were quickly overwhelmed. Jacquet's restaurant may not be elite, but as *le bouche à oreill* has it, it is still endearing. Diners who have reviewed the establishment on Google have shared comments such as "Michelin should think about giving a second star for the price," "legendary establishment, reinstate the Michelin star!" and simply, "good stuff."

such as American barbecue and pizza, are not recognized by Michelin and others, which many criticize as an increasingly antiquated worldview that European and Asian fare are superior to other cuisines. Many critics of these awards also point to the relatively low number of women awarded by top organizations, compared to the vast number of men and male-run restaurants that receive honors (Sutton 2018).

When Michelin makes its annual announcement of winners, chefs are shocked if they don't receive the same number or more stars than they were previously awarded. When Daniel Boulud's Manhattan restaurant Daniel lost one of its three stars in 2014, Boulud's staff mourned for 24 hours. Gordon Ramsay was reportedly devastated over the loss of two stars from his New-York-based restaurant The London in 2013 (Kashner 2015; Sutton 2018). Maintaining a certain rank on the "50 Best" list can also be highly stressful, as can simply hoping to be nominated for a James Beard award. The trends in recent years indicate that cultural worship of elite awards seems to be experiencing some changes, as diners and chefs alike have begun to embrace restaurants and cuisines that are not ranked among the world's most elite. Will the pressure-cooker genre of elite culinary awards stay the same or wane as culinary trends evolve? Only time will tell.

SUGGESTED PAIRINGS

See also: Barbecue; Bourdain, Anthony; Novelty Dining Experiences.

Entry best enjoyed while eating: Dishes from 2018 award-winners: Rabbit two ways, with jambalaya okra and sweet corn puree (Highlands Bar & Grill, AL; James Beard "Outstanding Restaurant"); "a singular interpretation" of beef fillet alla Rossini with foie gras and caviar (Osteria Francescana, Italy; Best Restaurant in the World, "50 Best"); and cucumber lollipop with peanuts (Ultraviolet, China; Michelin three stars).

Further Reading

James Beard Foundation. n.d. "History." https://www.jamesbeard.org/about/history

Kashner, Sam. 2015. "The Fault in Their Stars." *Vanity Fair*, November 2015.

Michelin Guide. 2018. https://guide.michelin.com

Mount, Ian. 2014. "The Curse of the Michelin-Star Restaurant Rating." *Fortune,* December 11, 2014. http://fortune.com/2014/12/11/michelin-star-restaurants-down-side/

Staelens, Stefanie. 2017. "Why the Chef of an All-Female Kitchen Rejected Her Michelin Star." *Vice*, January 8, 2017. https://munchies.vice.com/en_us/article/vvqmp3/why-the-chef-of-an-all-female-kitchen-rejected-her-michelin-star

Steinberger, Michael. 2016. "Michelin and the Deaths of Two French Chefs." *The New Yorker*, February 5, 2016.

Sutton, Ryan. 2018. "A Handy Guide to Understanding Restaurant Awards." *Eater*, June 15, 2018. https://www.eater.com/2017/5/1/15462142/james-beard-awards-michelin-stars-worlds-50-best

Zagat. n.d. "Our History." https://www.zagat.com/about-us/our-history

Deen, Paula (1947–)

STARTERS

Paula Deen is an American chef and television personality who specializes in Southern cuisine. The author of 17 cookbooks, Deen owns and operate The Lady & Sons restaurant in Savannah, Georgia. The restaurant's website touts being named "International Meal of the Year" in 1999 by *USA Today*'s food critics. Deen operates additional restaurants in Tennessee, Georgia, Texas, and South Carolina. Over the course of 14 years, Deen starred in several shows on the Food Network, including *Paula's Home Cooking* (2002), which received a Daytime Emmy award in 2007; *Paula's Party* (2006); and *Paula's Best Dishes* (2008). In 2013, Deen was dropped from the Food Network and a number of high-profile endorsement deals in the wake of a lawsuit over issues at her former restaurant, Uncle Bubba's Seafood and Oyster House.

In recent years, Deen has debuted two new television shows. *Positively Paula* (2016) premiered on Rural Media Group's RFD-TV channel, and *Sweet Home Savannah* (2016) premiered on the home shopping network EVINE, in which she cooks and promotes various products from her own merchandise lines. Additional ventures in recent years include the release of a cooking-themed radio show and podcast and the publication of new cookbooks and other recipe tutorials that promote healthier versions of the butter- and sugar-heavy fare she was known for earlier in her career.

ENTRÉE

In the world of food television, Paula Deen is known best for her big Southern personality and unapologetically unhealthy fare stocked with butter, sugar, and grease. Peppering her presentations with "y'alls" and bawdy humor, Deen enjoyed a successful run on her Food Network shows, which primarily featured Southern comfort foods like chocolate pecan pie, old-fashioned biscuits, and pulled-pork sandwiches. Born in Albany, Georgia in 1947, Deen married Jimmy Deen shortly after graduating from high school. The couple had two sons together, James and Robert. Deen's parents both passed away when she was in her twenties, and in the wake of their loss, she suffered from agoraphobia, an anxiety condition that often renders people homebound due to their fear of being unsafe in situations outside of their homes. In 1989, Deen's marriage ended in divorce, and she was faced with tight financial circumstances as a single parent.

Deen's interest in Southern cooking and challenges with agoraphobia inspired her to launch an in-home catering business called The Bag Lady, which specialized in boxed lunches, as a means to pull her family out of poverty. Her teenage sons helped the venture by delivering the lunches to customers. In 1991, the business evolved into a restaurant called The Lady at The Best Western in Savannah, Georgia. Deen and her sons opened The Lady & Sons in downtown Savannah five years later. The restaurant was met with success, aided in part by Deen's first cookbook, *The Lady & Sons* (1998), and various regionally and nationally acclaimed reviews.

Deen began expanding her career horizons to television, starting with an appearance on the home shopping network QVC. Her ensuing television shows on the Food Network helped introduce her to an even larger base of home television viewers, and for more than a decade, she was a familiar face on the network's lineup. Deen also signed a number of endorsements and other partnerships with high-profile companies such as Philadelphia Cream Cheese, Walmart, Smithfield pork, Walmart, J.C. Penny, Target, Sears, and more. Her merchandise has spanned from kitchen appliances to food, clothing, and even dog food. Deen's cookbooks have sold over 8 million copies, and her magazine *Cooking with Paula* reached a circulation of over 1 million readers (Black 2012).

Paula Deen appears at the Creative Arts Daytime Emmy award celebration held in June 2007. Deen took home two awards for her Food Network show *Paula Deen's Home Cooking* in the lifestyle program and host categories. (Carrienelson1/Dreamstime.com)

Controversies

In 2013, a lawsuit was filed against Paula Deen, alleging that she and her brother, Earl Hiers, had engaged in instances of racial discrimination, acts of racism, and sexual harassment. The suit was filed by Lisa T. Jackson, a former general manager of Uncle Bubba's Seafood and Oyster House, which Deen and Hiers owned at the time. Another former employee, Dora Charles, also came forward to air grievances about inappropriate workplace behaviors at the restaurant. Between the lawsuit and Charles's statements, Deen was accused of allegations ranging from using the

N-word, asking a cook to dress up as Aunt Jemima (a black character dating back to minstrel shows) in front of customers, to paying Charles less than her white peers, among others. Hiers was accused of showing pornography to employees at work. Deen denied some of the allegations, such as proposing an Aunt Jemima costume, but apologized for other behaviors, such as using the racial epithet in the past and discussing a plantation-themed wedding for her brother that included black waiters dressed as servants in period costumes (Severson 2013; John 2013).

When asked during her deposition if she had ever used the racial slur, Deen answered "of course," but said it had probably been a "very long time" since she had done so. Noting that things have "changed since the '60s in the South," she added that she and her family objected to the use of hurtful racist language (Duke 2013). Hiers admitted to frequently viewing pornography using the restaurant's computers and struggling with drug and alcohol abuse. The lawsuit was dismissed, and both parties reached a settlement agreement. Adding to the controversy was the fact that the plaintiff was white. The judge ruled that Jackson could not claim to be a victim of racial discrimination that targeted African American employees. Jackson issued a statement after the hearings in which she recanted her allegations, saying that Deen "will never tolerate discrimination or racism of any kind toward anyone" (Lynch 2013). Despite the lawsuit's dismissal, the event caused Deen to lose her endorsements as national corporate sponsorships cut ties with her, and the Food Network announced they would not renew her contracts. In 2014, the *Savannah Morning News* reported that she had abruptly closed Uncle Bubba's Seafood and Oyster House, which came as a shock to employees who arrived for work only to receive severance checks in the parking lot. The closing was communicated on the restaurant's website (Landers and Dickstein 2014).

The lawsuit was not Deen's sole public controversy. In 2012, she spoke at a *New York Times* Talk and mentioned the hardship her great-grandfather faced when he lost his slaves at the end of the Civil War. She faced some criticism for doing so and for using terms like "workers" in lieu of "slaves." The same year, she announced that she had Type 2 diabetes as it was revealed that she and her sons had signed a highly lucrative endorsement to promote Victoza, a diabetes medication made by the company Novo Nordisk. As part of the promotional campaign, the trio promoted healthy diet changes like portion control and lighter recipes. Critics were angered to learn that Deen had known about her health condition for years before revealing it, while still promoting foods laden in fat, salt, and sugar. Many called Deen's motives into question and wondered if her admission was solely driven by profit. Ensuing media coverage ranged from accusations that Deen was helping to further America's obesity epidemic to those arguing that she was being unfairly maligned in an industry that was often associated with butter-filled dishes (Black 2012; Moskin 2012).

In 2015, Deen fired her social media manager after a photo was posted to Twitter that showed Deen dressed as Lucy and her son Bobby dressed as Cuban American character Ricky Ricardo from the show *I Love Lucy*. Bobby sported dark makeup as part of his costume, which was reminiscent of blackface stage makeup previously used in minstrel shows by white actors who mimicked African Americans. Despite this and the other controversies she's faced, Deen and her sons have been re-emerging in the pop culture spotlight in recent years. Deen came out with a podcast and radio show in 2015, as well as a new cookbook called *Paula Deen Cuts the Fat: 250 Favorite Recipes All Lightened Up*. She also appeared on ABC's *Dancing with the Stars*, in which celebrities compete in a series of physically challenging dance routines. Her show *Positively Paula* also presented a healthier angle than her previous shows had, introducing some vegan recipes.

ACCOMPANIED BY

In 2004, Deen married Michael Groover (1956–), a Savannah-based tugboat pilot. Groover occasionally appeared on Deen's television shows and published a memoir called *My Delicious Life with Paula Deen* in 2009. In 2018, after vying for the honor nine previous times, Groover won the Ernest Hemingway look-alike contest that's held annually in Key West, Florida. Groover beat 150 other entrants, some of whom had traveled from all over the world to compete in the contest (Associated Press 2018).

Deen's sons have been constant partners in her career. Robert "Bobby" Deen was born in 1970 and has worked at The Lady & Sons alongside his brother and mother since its inception. In 2006, Bobby was listed as one of *People* magazine's "hottest bachelors" of the year, and in 2014, he traded in his bachelor fame, marrying Venezuelan-born health coach Claudia Lovera. James "Jamie" Deen was born in 1967. He is married to Brooke Deen, and the couple have two children, Jack and Matthew. Jamie and Bobby have appeared on many of Paula's shows and starred in a number of their own. Bobby has appeared on several Cooking Channel and Food Network programs, and the brothers hosted a Food Network show together called *Road Tasted* (2006). Jamie and Bobby continue to co-manage The Lady & Sons and have also published several cookbooks.

DESSERT

One of Deen's more sugar-laden controversies involved her connection to the "donut burger," which she claims to have invented during a 2008 episode of *Paula's Home Cooking*. The burger consists of a cheeseburger topped with bacon and a fried egg, bookended by Krispy Kreme glazed donuts in lieu of buns. Deen's sons later said that she was doing a "spoof" on a dish served at the ballpark for the Gateway Grizzlies, a Frontier League baseball team in Illinois (Chou 2013). Others have traced the donut burger's origins to a pub named Mulligan's in Decatur, Georgia, internet blogs, and more. Whatever the origin—and perhaps the concoction was invented by more than one party at different times—the donut-encased cheeseburger has made a significant name for itself in pop culture as a quintessentially *"only in America . . ."* dish.

SUGGESTED PAIRINGS

See also: Ayden Collard Festival; Barbecue; Television, Food Channels on.

Entry best enjoyed while eating: Deep-fried turkey with gravy; broccoli salad with bacon, onions, raisins, cheese, and mayonnaise; peach cobbler with whipped cream; and a glass of Paula's watermelon cooler with a sprig of mint.

Further Reading

Associated Press. 2018. "Paula Deen's Husband Wins Hemingway Look-Alike Contest on Ninth Try." *USA Today*, July 22, 2018.

Black, Jane. 2012. "What Paula Deen Didn't Bring to the Table." *The Washington Post*, January 20, 2012.

Chou, Jessica. 2013. "The Deen Brothers on Mama Paula Deen, That Donut Burger, and Sibling Rivalry." The Daily Meal, March 15, 2013. https://www.thedailymeal.com/deen-brothers-mama-paula-deen-donut-burger-and-sibling-rivalry

Duke, Alan. 2013. "Celeb Chef Admits Using 'N-Word.'" CNN, July 3, 2013. https://www.cnn.com/2013/06/19/showbiz/paula-deen-racial-slur

"The History of the Lady and Sons." n.d. http://www.ladyandsons.com/beginnings/

John, Arit. 2013. "Sorry, Paula Deen, Aunt Jemima Costumes Are Still Pretty Racist." *The Atlantic*, July 25, 2013.

Landers, Mary and Cory Dickstein. 2014. "Uncle Bubba's, Co-Owned by Paula Deen and Her Brother, Closes After 10 Years." *Savannah Morning News*, April 3, 2013.

Lynch, Renee. 2013. "Paula Deen Goes Viral Amid 'N-Word' Controversy." *Los Angeles Times*, June 19, 2013.

Moskin, Julia. 2012. "Chef Has Diabetes, and Some Say 'I Told You So.'" *The New York Times*, January 17, 2012.

"Paula's Life So Far." 2006. https://web.archive.org/web/20120421103328/http://www.cookingwithpauladeen.com/articles.php?id=34

Severson, Kim. 2013. "At Georgia Restaurant, Critics Jump to Defend a Chef from Her Critics." *The New York Times*, June 23, 2013.

Deer River Wild Rice Festival

STARTERS

Amid a national food festival circuit that's rife with slow-cooked meats, melted cheeses, deep-fried potatoes, and finely tempered chocolates, the citizens of Deer River, Minnesota, pay homage annually to a more humble food: wild rice. Every year, an estimated 7,000–10,000 festivalgoers flock to Deer River, a small town whose population tipped the scale at 930 people as of the year 2010, according to the U.S. Census Bureau. The first Wild Rice Festival started in 1948 and has continued every July since. Although there are several other wild rice festivals in the Great Lakes region, Deer River prides itself for having earned the title "World's Largest Wild Rice Festival."

The Wild Rice Festival is sponsored by the local Lions Club, which uses some profits from the event as a fundraising opportunity for the community. Some of the money is used to fund a free swimming program for local youth. The festival is family-friendly and is free to attend, making the event affordable and appealing to a wide range of people.

According to the festival's website, the annual gathering started nearly seven decades ago to "bring the community together to celebrate the abundance of one of the area's natural staples, wild rice." Modern-day festivities include a parade, fireworks, bingo, a Pow Wow featuring the live music of Leech Lake Band of Ojibwe, and a "turtle feed" (consisting of sampling snapping turtle stew). In keeping with Minnesota potluck traditions, there are also numerous wild rice hot dishes, and dinner is hosted by the local United Methodist church.

ENTRÉE

Deer River is located in Itasca County, Minnesota. This small city—located in the space of just 1.29 square miles—is located just outside of the Chippewa National Forest and the Leech Lake Band of Ojibwe tribal reservation. Minnesota boasts 11,842 lakes, 6,564 natural rivers and streams, and 10.6 million acres of wetlands (down from 18.6 million in the year 1850) within the state's borders, making it an ideal location for the production of wild rice. The grain that festival participants turn out year after year to celebrate is steeped in a fascinating history. American Indian tribes have harvested the grain for generations, but modern-day industrialization poses numerous challenges to the communities that have been harvesting the rice by hand for hundreds of years.

Wild rice is very significant within the cultural history and diet of the Ojibwe people (sometimes spelled *Ojibway* or *Ojibwa*). Harvesting the grain by hand is no easy task, but the Ojibwe are experts at the craft. Wild rice grows in shallow

A vast majority of the world's supply of wild rice (called "manoomin" in the Ojibwe language) has come from Minnesota. Unrelated to common rice, this aquatic grass plant has served as a staple in Minnesota's Ojibwe culture and diet for hundreds of years. (Mona Makela/Dreamstime.com)

flooded areas, including the borders of lakes and streams, wetlands, ponds, and inland and coastal fresh marshes. Although the rice is plentiful—Minnesota has 1,200 basins and streams in which wild rice grows—it can be a challenging grain to harvest.

Rice harvesters, who are called ricers, venture into the aquatic grasses by canoe, using a forked push-pole to minimize damaging the plants. The pole actually helps keep the rice beds healthy due to the fact that it stirs up nutrients that have settled in the sediment under the water. Ricers knock the rice (located at the top of the grasses) into the canoe using wooden paddles, called knockers. Even this step requires expertise on how and where to bat at the seeds to dislodge them from the plants.

In a 2015 interview with the *Saint Cloud Times*, harvester and wetland management leader Ray Norrgard says that when he first began his career, he was netting "30 pounds (of rice) on a good day." Five years later, after learning how to identify rice when it's ripe, keep a watchful eye on the season for dangers like strong winds and water level changes, and use expert collection methods, Norrgard could collect upward of 150 pounds of rice in a day (Wessel 2015).

Another harvester, Simon Zornes of White Earth, MN, spoke with the *Park Rapids Enterprise* in 2017 about the complexities of working with wild rice. Harvesting is only legal from mid-August through the end of September, and separating the grain from its protective husk is a tedious process. Zornes told the *Enterprise* that although many experienced ricers bring in 200–400 pounds of rice a day at the most, he can "put 500 pounds of wild rice in (his) boat in one day." After several days on the water, he can take home thousands of pounds of rice (Geisen).

Much of the rice these lifelong harvesters collect will be consumed by their family members instead of being sold. Deer River and the other festivals that celebrate wild rice give people the opportunity to learn more about the vendors of wild rice and what an amazing history this harvest has in America's history. Festival-goers are likely to find a new appreciation for the grain's history and relationship to the people who harvest it, as well as a new interest in wild rice, itself. Much as a wine's flavor is affected by the specific conditions in which the grapes were grown (a term the French call *terroir*), the flavor of wild rice varies based on the specific lake or pond in which it grows. The flavor can be described as distinctive, strong, and nutty. In addition to being delicious, wild rice is praised for its health benefits as a high-fiber, low-fat, and high-protein food.

ACCOMPANIED BY

According to lore from the Ojibwe tribe, the Anishinaabe-Ojibwe people were led to Minnesota by a series of prophecies that began in the year 900 BCE. Ojibwe history describes seven prophecies that warned of the coming of the white race and drove a westward migration over the next 500 years. The Anishinaabe-Ojibwe traveled from their origin along the Saint Lawrence River in Canada through northern areas of modern-day Maine, Vermont, Niagara Falls, and into the Great Lakes region.

According to one of the seven prophecies, the Ojibwe learned they would find prosperity in a land where "food grows on water"—in this case, wild rice, a grain that is found on aquatic grasses that thrive on the lakes, streams, and marshes of the Great Lakes region. Accounts of European explorers in the first half of the seventeenth century describe encounters with Ojibwe tribespeople in the Great Lakes region, marking the beginning of 200 years of battles between the Native Americans and white explorers over territory in the region ("Ojibwe Waasa-Inaabidaa: History Timeline" 2017).

SUGGESTED PAIRINGS

See also: Ayden Collard Festival; Florida Strawberry Festival; Food Trucks; Gilroy Garlic Festival; Maine Lobster Festival; Unusual Food Events, U.S. (Midwest, West, and Southwest Regions).

Entry best enjoyed while eating: A wild rice burger, was made popular (in part) by Minnesota's Duluth Grill. To make a homemade version, form a patty using a mixture of wild rice, mushrooms, eggs, mayonnaise, and seasonings and grill. Add cheddar cheese and serve on whole grain buns, with a side of steak fries, a tossed green salad, and a glass of cold horchata (a traditional Mexican beverage made from pureed rice, cinnamon, and sugar).

Further Reading

Child, Brenda J. 2013. *Holding Our World Together: Ojibwe Women and the Survival of Community.* New York: Penguin Books.

Geisen, Shannon. 2017. "Anishinaabe Wild Rice Harvester Shares Heritage." *Park Rapids Enterprise,* October 21, 2017. http://www.parkrapidsenterprise.com/news/local/4347132-anishinaabe-wild-rice-harvester-shares-heritage.

Lakes, Rivers, and Wetlands Facts. 2017. "Minnesota Department of Natural Resources." http://www.dnr.state.mn.us/faq/mnfacts/water.html

"Ojibwe Waasa-Inaabidaa: History Timeline." 2017. http://www.ojibwe.org/home/about_anish_timeline.html

Schultz, Thomas. 2015. "World's Largest Rice Festival." Interview with Brad Box, Rice Festival representative. Resorts and Lodges, https://www.resortsandlodges.com/travelblog/b/worlds-largest-wild-rice-festival/

Wessel, Ann. 2015. "Finding Wild Rice Is Just The Start of Harvest Process." *St. Cloud Times,* August 13, 2015. http://www.sctimes.com/story/news/local/2015/08/13/finding-wild-rice-just-start-harvest-process/31660913/

"Wild Rice Establishment." 2001. Conservation sheet 644b, National Resources Conservation Services, April. USDA. http://ucanr.edu/sites/WildRice/files/256324.pdf

Vennum, Thomas. 1988. *Wild Rice and the Ojibway People.* St. Paul: Minnesota Historical Society Press.

Documentary Films, Food and Beverages in
STARTERS

Documentary films are largely defined as films that explore contemporary or historical nonfiction subjects. Ranging in style from objective (although the question of pure objectivity in any kind of filmmaking is always debated) to highly subjective, documentary films have become increasingly popular in recent decades. Despite accounting for a small percentage of theatrical box office sales, documentary films have slowly gained more mainstream appeal, as both theatrical and made-for-television or streaming releases. Amateur and aspiring professional filmmakers are gaining more access to high-quality video and editing equipment than ever before, which has helped boost the number of productions made each year. Historically, documentaries have often been independent ventures, separate from major film companies, but streaming video services have helped increase the popularity of these smaller films. In addition to the cable networks that have funded documentary programming in recent decades, internet-on-demand powerhouses like Netflix, Hulu, and Amazon have recently started investing in original documentary programming to appeal to consumers' growing appetites for nonfiction films.

Documentaries rarely used to feature culinary storylines or main subjects, but food and beverages have seen a significant uptick in coverage and popularity in recent years. Many films about the food and beverage industry have focused on social issues such as sustainability; ethical questions about agricultural practices and animal slaughter; corporate powers in the food industry; and broad cultural issues of nutrition, health, and emotional connections to food. Others tell engaging stories about individuals who work in the food industry, ranging from profiles of sommeliers obsessing over their certifying exams about all conceivable varietals of wine to the story of a Korean child's efforts to raise a single pig. In many different surveys about the best and most influential documentaries of all time, food-themed documentaries such as *Jiro Dreams of Sushi* (2011), *Food, Inc.* (2008), and *Super Size Me* (2004) are often included in the top 100 titles.

ENTRÉE

Documentaries often follow social justice issues, politics, and other current events, and food and beverage documentaries are no exception. Major themes in these films often include the use of genetically modified organisms (GMOs), farm-to-table and organic food trends, nutrition concerns and the fast-food industry, and the claimed health benefits of a wide range of diets. One of the earliest food-centric documentary films to gain widespread appeal was *Super Size Me*. The film follows filmmaker Morgan Spurlock as he tests his negative perception of the McDonald's fast-food chain firsthand. A similar film in the United Kingdom, *McLibel*, was completed in 1997 and re-released a year after *Super Size Me*, in 2005. Directed by Frannie Armstrong and Ken Loach, the film followed the longest-running libel trial in English legal history. The legal struggle involved Helen Steel and Dave Morris (referred to by the media as the McLibel Two), who were sued by McDonald's for circulating a Greenpeace leaflet that accused the fast-food chain of a wide array of grievances, including contributing to obesity rates, animal cruelty, and environmental harm (Spanner Films n.d.; BBC News 2000). *Super Size Me* and *McLibel* came out in an era when McDonald's was facing some additional legal troubles in the United States, and the films helped to galvanize widespread public criticism against the fast-food industry.

In 2008, the documentary *Food, Inc.* also took aim at corporations in the U.S. food industry. Filmmaker Robert Kenner highlighted topics such as corporate interests that compete with consumer health and how drastically food production practices have changed in the United States over time, often with negative consequences. *Food, Inc.* also explores how science and technology have led to radical modifications of food, compares food costs to health benefits, and blames the food industry for various national health concerns, such as increased rates of diabetes and obesity. The film received an Academy Award nomination in 2010, and the PBS program P.O.V. received an Emmy for its premiere.

Similar films include *Forks Over Knives* (2011), directed by Lee Fulkerson, which promotes plant-based diets and illustrates health problems linked to the consumption of meat and highly processed foods. A number of documentaries feature health concerns about sugar such as *Fed Up!* (2014), which draws comparisons between sugar addiction and drug addiction. In *King Corn* (2007), the filmmakers join the corn industry themselves, analyzing agricultural subsidies and national controversies over high-fructose corn syrup in the process. Actor Leonardo DiCaprio has been the executive producer for several food documentaries, such as *Cowspiracy: The Sustainability Secret* (2014), which portrays the animal agricultural industry as a significant factor behind global issues such as climate change, deforestation, and hazardous changes to the oceans.

What the Health (2017) alleges that various food and health industry organizations are involved in covering up food-related health problems. The director, Kip Andersen, has been accused of mischaracterizing food science research studies to support outrageous and controversial claims about the consumption of animal products. Other films prefer to take more personal, limited approaches to food and health issues, such as *Soul Food Junkies* (2012) by filmmaker Byron Hurt. *Soul Food Junkies* looks at African Americans' relationship with soul food and how the high levels of fat, sugar, and salt in many of the Hurt family's favorite dishes likely led to his father's pancreatic cancer, a disease that disproportionately affects African Americans (Hurt 2013).

Food documentaries about social justice issues and diets tend to have polarizing receptions. These films are often credited with helping people to become better educated and more proactive about personal health and well-being, as well as responsible environmental practices. However, some films are widely criticized for promoting unsubstantiated claims, pseudoscientific findings, and even gimmicks, drawing viewers in with entertainment value and/or "scare tactics" to help sway viewers' opinions about various subjects. Reviewers have criticized a number of food documentaries for oversimplifying complex problems, proposing poor solutions to complex problems, and even lending undue credibility to various conspiracy theories.

Not all food documentaries are designed to promote or shame various facets of the food industry. Many focus more on using artistic, thoughtful, or entertaining ways of telling stories about people, trends, and locations in the food world. *Jiro Dreams of Sushi* (2013), by filmmaker David Gelb, is one of the most popular of these documentaries. Gelb documented the life of Jiro Ono, who is widely professed to be the greatest living sushi chef. Ono's Michelin-starred restaurant, called Sukiyabashi Jiro, is a tiny enclave within a subway station in Tokyo, Japan. Sukiyabashi Jiro is typically filled to capacity with diners, many of whom may have gone to great lengths to secure reservations and may have traveled internationally to eat there. The film paints an intimate portrait of 85-year-old Ono, who slaves over the perfection of his craft.

Spinning Plates (2013) peers into the lives of the people behind three significantly different restaurants: Alinea, a three-star Michelin and "World's 50 Best" restaurant in Chicago, Illinois; Breitbach's Country Dining, a 150-year old restaurant in Balltown, Iowa; and La Cocina de Gabby, a family-run Mexican restaurant in Tucson, Arizona. The film weaves stories together about the trials and tribulations each of the chefs face, drawing parallels between their experiences. Grant Achatz struggles to advance his career while battling cancer, Breitbach's community rallies around the restaurant after a catastrophic fire, and La Cocina de Gabby's looming foreclosure challenges the owners' determined attempts to be profitable.

Though not as common as food-based documentaries, beverage industry films are also beginning to gain broader appeal. *Somm* (2012) follows the efforts of four sommeliers who are trying to pass the Master Sommelier exam, an honor of high prestige and seemingly impossible requirements. *Sour Grapes* (2016) offers a different flavor: a crime story that follows the exploits of a wine savant who made his fortune selling fraudulent wines to high-powered investors and auction houses. 2013's *Crafting a Nation* explores the rise of the American craft brewing scene through profiles of a wide range of breweries, and Ken Burns' *Prohibition* (2011) offers a five-and-a-half-hour exploration of the profound effect the prohibition of alcohol had on the American economy, as well as Americans' views of morality.

SUGGESTED PAIRINGS

See also: *Chef's Table*; *Cooked*; Craft Brewing and Microbreweries; Nonfiction, Food in; *Super Size Me*; Wine and Spirits.

Entry best enjoyed while eating: Succotash with (responsibly sourced, Fair Trade) poached scallops; a vegan fig and green pea salad; shrimp nigiri with yellowfin tuna and octopus sashimi; a pint of American India Pale Ale; and a '92 Screaming Eagle Cabernet Sauvignon, estimated at $12,500 a glass.

Further Reading

Associated Press. 2004. "McDonald's Phasing Out Supersize Fries, Drinks." NBC News, March 3, 2004.

BBC News. 2000. "McLibel Pair Get Police Payout." July 5, 2000. http://news.bbc.co.uk/2/hi/uk_news/820786.stm

Hurt, Byron. 2013. "Soul Food Junkies." Independent Lens. http://www.pbs.org/independentlens/films/soul-food-junkies/

Jones, Ellen E. 2011. "Reel to Real: Can Documentaries Change the World?" *The Guardian*, October 6, 2011.

Rapold, Joseph. 2013. "Troubles in the Kitchen: Spinning Plates Looks at Life in 3 Restaurants." *The New York Time*, October 24, 2013.

Spanner Films. n.d. "McLibel: The Postman and Gardner Who Took on McDonald's and Won." https://www.spannerfilms.net/films/mclibel

Willett, Megan. 2014. "How to Get a Seat at the Legendary 'Jiro Dreams of Sushi' Restaurant." *Business Insider*, July 8, 2014. https://www.businessinsider.com/get-reservations-at-sukiyabashi-jiro-2014-6

E

Eating Competitions

STARTERS

Eating competitions date back centuries, and history is rife with legendary individuals who were famous for their "bottomless appetites" and tales about royalty that held extraordinary feasts. In times when food was scarce for many, such as the Renaissance era, body fat was seen as a symbol of beauty and worth. Those who had the most access to food were typically very wealthy, and elite members of society would eat excessively to flaunt their privilege. In the mid-1800s, improvements in food storage, preservation, and production led to larger quantities of food being made available to a broader segment of the population, which helped the gluttonous trend flourish. Around this time, eating contests became a trending theme at local fairs around the United States, primarily to entertain crowds, but also as a way to highlight and celebrate local fare ranging from corn on the cob to watermelons.

A crowd watches a pie eating contest in 1939 at a 4-H Club fair in Cimarron, Kansas. Eating contests have long been a popular form of entertainment at celebrations such as county fairs, even during times of food scarcity such as the Great Depression. (Library of Congress)

Pies became a favorite dish for eating competitions, and rules such as competitors having to eat with their hands behind their backs led to iconic images of competitors diving nose-first into dishes, their faces covered in food.

Eating contests also began to crop up in locations such as military bases during World War I. Contests that employed gimmicks began to catch on, including the promotional efforts of Nathan Handwerker, owner of Nathan's Hot Dogs in Coney Island, New York. His hot dog eating contest became an annual Fourth of July tradition, and with the help of professional publicists, it eventually became a significant national event. The success of Nathan's hot dog contests led to the founding of the Major Eating League (MLE) in the mid-1990s, which established the concept of competitive eating. MLE's events are timed and require strict adherence to safety rules, which differs from many amateur contests. With the help of televised events and corporate sponsorships, throngs of competitive eaters now train year-round for events, seeking fame, championship titles, and monetary winnings.

ENTRÉE

The earliest known recorded eating contest comes from Norse mythology. The thirteenth-century text *Prose Edda* tells of the Norse gods Thor and Loki trying to beat each other at a series of challenges set out by a giant king named Utgarda-Loki (in old Norse, these characters were frequently called "giants" or "devourers"). Utgarda pits Loki against a man named Logi by placing them at opposite ends of a table and challenging them to eat an enormous spread of food, including a trough of meat in the center. They reach the center simultaneously, but Loki is

---

Small Plates

Yankee *Homo sapiens* versus Hungry *Struthio camelus*

Nathan Handwerker's inaugural hot-dog eating contest was not the only promotional ploy that was used to generate sales during the Progressive Era. Eating contests were gaining popularity in other regions of the United States, sometimes drawing upon strange or exciting-sounding premises to attract viewers. In 1919, one such food-themed gimmick was a spaghetti-eating contest between Yankees baseball player Ping Bodie (1887–1961) and an ostrich named Percy in Jacksonville, Florida. Prior to the contest, Percy had been dubbed "the world's greatest eater" by the Jacksonville Chamber of Commerce on account of his voracious appetite.

Aided by the cheers of fans, Ping and Percy faced off, matching each other plate for plate for numerous rounds. Percy ate every serving that was placed in front of him (as well as a nearby watch and chain that an official had been using to time the event), but the bird started experiencing fatigue by the seventh round. Ping continued to polish off plates and Percy tried to keep up, but the bird began showing signs of distress—a sagging beak, bloodshot eyes, and swollen sides—and a number of onlookers who felt sorry for his plight began to leave. Eventually the bird dropped to his knees and, as ostriches are wont to do, buried his head in a plate of spaghetti, thus securing Ping's fate as the winner (Harper 1999).

Hot dog eating contests are among the most famous, and competitive, in the world. (Russ Ensley/Dreamstime.com)

dismayed to find that Logi has eaten everything in front of him down to the wooden trough itself, thus winning the contest. Loki later learns that "Logi," Norse for "fire," is not just a man but the human embodiment of fire.

Much has been written about royalty's penchants for gorging on feasts over the centuries. These feasts were largely viewed as a status symbol and sign of wealth, as food was relatively scarce for the lower classes. Various lore also exists about individuals who were renowned for their gluttony, such as Nicholas Wood, "The Great Eater of Kent" in the seventeenth century. Wood's skills were recorded by English poet John Taylor, who documented the Great Eater's visit to places like fairs, where he amazed audiences by eating enormous meals. Wood was reportedly forced into unexpected retirement when he lost all of his teeth while eating a mutton shoulder, including the bone.

In the United States, eating contests emerged around 1916. Some believe modern competitive eating traditions stemmed from a 1916 contest at Coney Island's famous Nathan's Hot Dog stand, in which four immigrants competed to see who could eat the most hot dogs as a way to prove who was "most patriotic." An Irish man was declared the winner for consuming 13 frankfurters. In 1972, public relations agents Morty Matz and Max Rosen attempted to create a nationwide spectacle out of Nathan's contest and put their young employee George Shea on the project. In the mid-1990s, George and his brother Richard Shea were able to draw hundreds of thousands of spectators at the event, which led the pair to develop the International Federation of Competitive Eating, later renamed MLE (Suddath 2008). Since 2004, network ESPN has done a live broadcast of the event on the Fourth of July, and the MLE sponsors an additional 80–100 competitive eating contests a year.

Hot dogs aren't the only item on the menu; each year, amateur and professionals compete to eat a dizzying quantity of an enormous variety of foods. MLE's contests include moon pies, tacos, poutine, Buffalo wings, salt potatoes, cheese curds, pizzas, hamburgers, ice cream, gyoza, jalapenos, corned beef, and pickles, just to name a few. The contests aren't always just fun and games; in addition to the ongoing stress and pressure many top competitors endure, there are also health risks. Competitors risk injury to their hands (including biting their fingers or cutting themselves with utensils), jaws, throats, and a significant amount of stress on their digestive systems.

A 2007 University of Pennsylvania study found that trained competitive eaters' stomachs stretch significantly into their abdomens during binges, which could cause permanent damage over time. Drinking too much liquid, especially alcohol, also come with significant risks, as does perforation of the stomach and the possibility of morbid obesity. A significant number of people have died in eating contests from choking, which is of particular risk to amateurs who are unused to gorging on large amounts of food quickly or who are intoxicated during the event. Some contests have entrants sign waivers, but in many cases, businesses are not protected from liability simply because an entrant acknowledged risk (Galarza 2017).

ACCOMPANIED BY

Competitive eating would have never been invented without Nathan Handwerker (1892–1974), who originally worked for a Coney Island salesman named Charles Feltman. Feltman is rumored to be the first in the United States who sold a frankfurter atop a bun. Handwerker opened his own stand in 1916, selling the fare for a fraction of Feltman's price. Using his wife's family recipe, which notably included garlic, Handwerker's hot dogs went on to be called the world's most famous hot dogs. Today, one of the most famous competitive eaters is Takeru Kobayashi (1978–). The Japanese professional stunned the crowd at Nathan's 2001 contest when he ate 50 hot dogs in 10 minutes, doubling the previous record.

Kobayashi has incited some controversy, such as working in the United States on a visa that typically is only granted to athletes with "extraordinary ability" (competitive eating's status as a sport is a controversial topic in itself). He was banned from the MLE due to a dispute over the contract's endorsement and exclusivity restrictions, and he was arrested in 2010 when he attempted to force his way into a hot dog contest despite the ban. One of his top rivals is Joey Chestnut (1983–), an American who has won Nathan's contest 11 times, including setting a world record in 2018 for eating 74 hot dogs in 10 minutes. Miki Sudo (1985–) won the women's competition that year, finishing 37 hot dogs in the same amount of time.

DESSERT

Competitive eating has its fair share of inventive strategies. When Kobayashi smashed Nathan's hot dog eating record in 2001, his technique entailed breaking his hot dogs into half, eating both halves at once, and then soaking the buns in water before consuming them (this technique has since become standard practice among many competitive eaters). He also is known for wiggling while he swallows to help the food go down. Other professionals' strategies include training their stomachs to expand over time, breathing rhythmically while eating (similarly to how they would breathe while swimming laps), and keeping their cheeks completely stuffed while they eat.

SUGGESTED PAIRINGS

See also: Novelty Dining Experiences; *Super Size Me*; Trends, Food.

Entry best enjoyed while eating (*if one has properly trained to do so*): 83 slices of pizza in 10 minutes (Geoffrey Esper, 2018); 12 pounds of deep-fried asparagus in 10 minutes (Joey Chestnut, 2014); 8.4 pounds of baked beans in 2 minutes (Sonya Thomas, 2004); and 72 cupcakes in 6 minutes (Patrick Bertoletti, 2012).

Further Reading

"About Us." n.d. Nathan's Famous Hot Dogs. https://nathansfamous.com/about-us/

Berger, Ralph. n.d. "Ping Bodie." Society for American Baseball Research. https://sabr.org/bioproj/person/712236b9

Blitz, Matt. 2014. "The Origin of Competitive Eating Contests." Today I Found Out, June 11, 2014. http://www.todayifoundout.com/index.php/2014/06/origin-competitive-eating-contests/

Galarza, Daniela. 2017. "The Dangers of Eating Contests." *Eater*, April 7, 2017. https://www.eater.com/2017/4/7/15187338/food-eating-contests-danger-liability-lawsuit

Harper, William. 1999. *How You Played the Game: The Life of Grantland Rice*. Columbia: University of Missouri Press.

McCoy, Daniel. n.d. "The Tale of Utgarda-Loki." Norse Mythology for Smart People. https://norse-mythology.org/tale-utgarda-loki/

Nerz, Ryan. 2006. *Eat This Book: A Year of Gorging and Glory on the Competitive Eating Circuit*. New York: St. Martin's Press.

Suddath, Claire. 2008. "A Brief History of Competitive Eating." *Time*, July 3, 2008.

Tepfenhart, Ossiana. 2016. "Competitive Eating: A History." *Feast*, History/Humanity. https://feast.media/competitive-eating-a-history

F

Farmhouse Rules

STARTERS

Farmhouse Rules (2013–) is a Food Network television series hosted by dairy farmer Nancy Fuller on location at her farm in the Hudson Valley region of New York. The cooking show has run for 7 seasons and 82 episodes and consists of 30-minute episodes. Produced by Follow Productions, the series features Fuller preparing and explaining various recipes that have a farm-to-table focus. The dishes and ingredients are primarily sourced from Fuller's land and the surrounding Hudson Valley farming community. On the show, Fuller is sometimes joined by her husband David, with whom she runs the farm and Ginsberg's Foods, a multimillion-dollar foodservice distributor in the Hudson Valley (Potter 2013; Ginsberg's n.d.). Featured recipes are typically rustic and hearty and promote the role of farmers in their communities as well as the value of bringing family members together over shared meals.

ENTRÉE

In a pop culture culinary landscape often marked by elaborate cuisines and cooking techniques, *Farmhouse Rules* offers a more simple and rustic approach to food and cooking. Nancy Fuller brings her farm- and family-based values to the Food Network, teaching viewers how to make dishes like rustic tarts, stovetop macaroni and cheese, garden salads teeming with just-picked vegetables, hunks of crusty bread, and spaghetti topped with lamb meatballs and homemade tomato sauce. Fuller's show features cooking advice and values alike, such as her philosophy that people have become disconnected from what's in their food and where it comes from. She touts the importance of knowing where ingredients like potatoes are sourced and how to incorporate them meaningfully into dishes. Fuller also brings a sense of efficiency and simplicity to the cooking she does, summarizing it as "chop, chop, in the pot" as opposed to fussier, more precise, and labor-intensive cooking techniques. Fuller's love of family and hearty farmhouse fare is complemented by the show's setting, which is filmed on the Ginsberg's seventeenth-century farm in a Dutch stone home that sits on 150 acres of land.

Farmhouse Rules accompanies several other farm-focused Food Network programs, many of which follow home cooks who got their start in blogging. *Girl Meets Farm* (2018–) follows food blogger Molly Yeh, a New Yorker and classical musician who promotes farming and home cooking from her sugar beet farm along the border of North Dakota and Minnesota. *The Pioneer Woman* (2011–) stars blogger Ree Drummond, who prepares hearty meals for her family on a large cattle ranch in Oklahoma, and *Homestead Table* (2018) features blogger Shaye Elliott and her homesteading family in Malega, Washington. These programs reflect Americans' growing interest in locally sourced foods, homesteading practices, organic and fair-trade foods, and the farm-to-table movement. The millennial generation is particularly interested and involved in farm-to-table practices. This movement has been gaining significant traction since the early 2000s, as seen in trends such as increased demand for organic and fair-trade foods and the rising numbers of families who practice sustainable living and agricultural practices like composting, raising chickens and bees, and planting vegetable gardens.

In a 2013 interview with journalist Christy Potter, Fuller recounted a story in which someone told her that they thought chocolate milk was naturally produced by brown cows. Fuller went on to share her concern that many Americans aren't aware of how food is cultivated, produced, and distributed. The farm-to-table movement and urban and suburban families' growing interest in farming is a rebuttal to this consumer disconnect, and it focuses on reconnecting with local farmers, such as participating in farmshare programs and buying food at farmers markets. According to the United States Department of Agriculture, the number of farmers markets in the United States has increased from 2000 in the year 1994 to more than 8,700 today, which also signifies the growing popularity of farm-fresh food across the country.

ACCOMPANIED BY

Nancy Fuller (1949–), also known as Nancy Fuller Ginsberg, was raised on a dairy farm in rural Copake, New York. She inherited her family's farm and pursued her passion for agriculture, antiques, and cooking starting from a young age. Fuller has been married 4 times, has 6 children, and is a grandmother to 13 grandchildren. She has a background as a caterer and currently co-owns Ginsberg's with her husband. Fuller got her start on the Food Network after a videographer she knew was filming on her property and noted her ease in front of the camera. Fuller submitted a demo to the Food Network, which led to her show and an accompanying cookbook, *Farmhouse Rules* (2015). Nancy's husband, David Ginsberg, serves as the CEO and president of Ginsberg's, having initially joined his father's business in the 1970s. He studied cinema at USC, graduating in 1977 before becoming a business and entertainment lawyer, which he practiced in California and New York.

DESSERT

Nancy and David's magazine-worthy farmhouse estate is envied by many, but the couple didn't always see eye-to-eye on its appeal. Fuller was introduced to the property in 2004 and was so enchanted by it that she made an offer on the spot. Her husband was opposed to the idea (the couple already lived on a 400-acre farm) so that when he learned of her offer he called the realtor to cancel the deal. The couple eventually compromised by purchasing the property and renovating an adjacent carriage shed to provide high ceilings and doorways and adding modern conveniences for Ginsberg's liking. The main house reflects Fuller's preferred vintage feel and antique treasures, such as a Mason's mallet that was used as a gavel in meetings. The mallet has since been repurposed into a garlic masher (Kaufman 2015).

SUGGESTED PAIRINGS

See also: Coffee Culture; *Cooked*; Pioneer Woman, The; Trends, Food.

Entry best enjoyed while eating: A cup of corn chowder; roasted beet salad with locally sourced goat cheese and walnuts; pork pot roast with roasted root vegetables simmered in stock and bourbon; chocolate ganache butterscotch pudding made with farm-fresh eggs; and a mug of homemade apple cider.

Further Reading

FarmersMarket.net. 2018. "Why Farmer's Markets Are Becoming More Popular." http://www.farmersmarket.net/article/why-farmers-markets-are-becoming-popular/

Food Network. n.d. "Nancy Fuller Bio." https://www.foodnetwork.com/profiles/talent/nancy-fuller/bio

Fuller, Nancy. 2015. *Farmhouse Rules: Simple, Seasonal Meals for the Whole Family.* New York: Grand Central Life & Style.

Ginsberg's. n.d. "About Us." https://ginsbergs.com/about-us/

Kaufman, Joanne. 2015. "Nancy Fuller, 'Farmhouse Rules' Chef, at Home." *The New York Times*, October 31, 2015.

Potter, Christy. 2013. "Nancy Fuller Keeps It Real on Food Network's Newest Show, 'Farmhouse Rules.'" November 18, 2013. http://christythewriter.com/nancy-fuller-keeps-it-real-on-farmhouse-rules/

United States Department of Agriculture. 2018. "Local Food Directories: National Farmers Market Directory." https://www.ams.usda.gov/local-food-directories/farmers markets

Fiction, Food in

STARTERS

Food's inclusion in works of literature goes back to the most ancient texts and continues to be used in genres of all types today. Much more than simply a documentation of what people ate, food and beverages are often included in literary works as profound metaphors, adding depth to character development, leaving subtle clues behind for readers, and making commentaries on cultural and historical uses of food and drinks. Ranging from ancient staples like bread and ale to contemporary fictional creations like Harry Potter's "Bertie Botts Every-Flavored Beans," food helps bring color, nuance, intrigue, poetry, and literary flavor to all types of fiction.

ENTRÉE

Food's role in ancient texts is not minor by any account. One of the oldest known texts, the Sumerian/Babylonian tale *Epic of Gilgamesh* (c. 2150 BCE) has been compared to other ancient texts in terms of how it presents the temptations of food and intimacy. Gilgamesh is tempted by a "Woman of the Vine" named Siduri, who tries convincing him to give up his quest for immortality and take pleasure in family, wine, and food. This has been compared to the Hebrew Bible's story of Adam and Eve, in which Eve eats a forbidden apple and convinces Adam to do the same, ushering in themes of violence, sin, and shame for the future of humankind. This is echoed in Homer's *Odyssey*, in which Odysseus and his crew are lured into the home of a goddess named Circe, who tempts them with foods like wine and honey before turning Odysseus's men into swine.

Religious texts like the Bible, Talmud, and Quran abound with food, such as grains, bread, wine, grapes, dates, legumes, fish, and meats that were central to cultural diets and beliefs at the time. In transubstantiation, bread and wine are thought to become the actual blood and body of Jesus. Food also plays a key role in the decisions various biblical characters made, such as Esau, who agreed to give up his firstborn child to his brother Jacob for a bowl of red lentil soup and a piece of bread. Egypt's ancient *Pyramid Texts* (2613–2181 BCE) also mention food and beverages as part of the incantations intended for the souls of departed gods, such as cakes, loaves, "joints of meat," and beer. References and parables about food are also found in Confucian, Taoist, Hindu, Avesta, Buddhist, and virtually most other religious texts.

Scholars have found many food-related avenues to study in Shakespeare's works, both as historical insight into important foods in the Elizabethan era and ways in which the Bard used food references as poetic details. In *Coriolanus* (ca. 1605), citizens violently protest the fact that city leaders are hoarding grain away from them, a reality for many audience members during an era in which no fewer than 40 riots over food took place in England between 1586 and 1631. Other scholars have pored over lines such as Hamlet's disdain for "funeral baked meats" served at his mother's second wedding, referring to meats cooked in functional pastries referred to as "coffins." Shakespeare also added foods into his plays' dialogue that audience members would have been eating as they watched. One example is oysters, of which archaeologists found ample evidence while excavating The Globe and The Rose theaters in the late 1980s, concluding that audiences frequently consumed them during performances.

Food has played key roles in Gothic literature, as well. Edgar Allan Poe's *The Cask of Amantillado* (1847) is a macabre tale of revenge in which a man lures a nobleman into the catacombs to murder him, under the guise of seeking a taste of rare sherry wine. Bram Stoker's *Dracula* (1897) drew on Western readers' fear of (and aversion to) consuming blood as Count Dracula preyed on his innocent female visitor. Stoker purportedly said that his idea for *Dracula* stemmed from a nightmare he had about the rise of a vampire king, a dream he attributed to having eaten too much crab at dinner that night (Davison 1997).

Much like Shakespeare's work, literature in the Victorian era was also rife with passages relating to hunger and food scarcity. Writers like Charles Dickens used food as metaphors in many works. Miss Havisham's moldy, decaying wedding cake filled with spiders represented her own physical and emotional decay in the years after she was jilted at the altar in *Great Expectations* (1860). Many readers are quick to associate *Oliver Twist* (1837) with the orphan's meager portions of gruel, which Dickens used to illustrate Oliver's plight and insert his personal commentary on London's Poor Law at the time.

Modernist literature offered a radical change in how authors wrote books and what readers were expected to glean from the texts. Food was a pivotal element in Marcel Proust's *In Search of Lost Time* (1913), in which the narrator describes how the taste of his tea and a madeleine (French cookie) created a profound rush of memories that served as a portal to his past. Food was also an unusual focal point in novels like James Joyce's *Ulysses* (1918), which follows protagonist Leopold Bloom through a day in his life. Steeped in literary metaphors, the stream-of-consciousness descriptions of food often paint his meals in unsavory terms, keeping with Bloom's preoccupation with subjects like death, birth, defecation, urine, earth, and reincarnation. Many authors to follow also used powerful imagery of food to make uncomfortable associations, such as Vladimir Nabokov's *Lolita* (1955), in which a grown man lusts after a child, comparing her lips to lollipops and her skin to apricots. In Nabokov's *Ada: or Ardor* (1969), half-siblings who have an incestuous relationship share a strange meal of roasted bear cub and palm weevil larvae.

French author Marcel Proust famously wrote about an involuntary childhood memory that was triggered by biting into Madeleine cookies dipped in "lime-flower tea." Penguin Books publishers noted that Proust originally wrote this scene about toast with jam and that his editor suggested the now-famous Madeleine sponge cakes as a replacement. (VinceZen/Dreamstime.com)

Children's literature and Young Adult literature often feature food in fascinating ways, as well. Author Roald Dahl used food frequently as a character development tool and plot device. Sweets like giant chocolate cakes, candy bars, and chewing gum serve as metaphors for priggishness, hedonism, and gluttony in books like *Matilda* (1988) and *Charlie and the Chocolate Factory* (1964). Characters set out for an adventure in a giant fruit in *James and the Giant Peach* (1961), and pea soup, hard cider, blueberries, and raisins serve as tools for suspense, coercion, and rebellion in *The Witches* (1983), *The Fantastic Mr. Fox* (1970), and *Danny, Champion of the World* (1975). Young Adult realism like Gary Paulsen's *Hatchet* (1987) explores individuals' all-consuming obsession with food when they are forced to learn how to survive. The young protagonist Brian Robeson fantasizes about cheeseburgers and milkshakes while struggling to forage and hunt for foods like wild berries, turtle eggs, and bird meat after becoming stranded in the Canadian wilderness.

DESSERT

Children's author Dr. Seuss (the pen name of Theodore Geisel) wrote the children's classic *Green Eggs and Ham* (1960) after his editor, Bennett Cerf, bet the author that he couldn't write a book using 50 words or fewer. The work uses 50 words exactly, most famously "green eggs and ham" and "Sam I am."

SUGGESTED PAIRINGS

See also: Cake and Cupcake Trends; Craft Brewing and Microbreweries; Nonfiction, Food in.

Entry best enjoyed while eating: Boeuf en daube stew (*To the Lighthouse*, Virginia Woolf); pimiento-cheese grits with shrimp (*Where the Crawdads Sing*, Delia Owens); ham, turnip greens, and cornbread (*To Kill a Mockingbird*, Harper Lee); tiny cakes marked "eat me" (Lewis Carroll's *Alice in Wonderland*); and Elvin *miruvor* cordial (*The Lord of the Rings*, J. R. R. Tolkein).

Further Reading

Bramley, Anne. 2016a. "Cooking with the Bard: We Suss Out Shakespeare's Forgotten Foods." NPR's The Salt, April 20, 2016. https://www.npr.org/sections/the salt/2016/04/20/475000625/cooking-with-the-bard-we-suss-out-shake speares-forgotten-foods

Bramley, Anne. 2016b. "In Shakespeare's Day, Hunger Tore Through England. His Plays Tell the Tale." NPR's The Salt, April 23, 2016. https://www.npr.org/saections/the salt/2016/04/23/475291416/in-shakespeares-day-hunger-tore-through -england-his-plays-tell-the-tale

Bramley, Anne. 2016c. "Snacking in Shakespeare's Time: What Theatregoers Ate at the Bard's Plays." NPR's The Salt, April 21, 2016. https://www.npr.org/sections/the salt/2016/04/21/475128109/snacking-in-shakespeares-time-what-theatre goers-ate-at-the-bards-plays

Davison, Carol Margaret. 1997. *Bram Stoker's Dracula: Sucking Through the Century, 1897–1997*. Toronto, ON: Dundurn.

Fictional Television (1950s–1970s), Food and

STARTERS

Television shows from the second half of the twentieth century help us understand what types of foods and beverages were in vogue during that era. The evolving portrayals of meals and various foods on television during the postwar era also mirror changes that took place in America during that time. Families went through a cultural shift as women began to reject the role of "housewife," often preferring to be a "hostess" instead, and many women began focusing their efforts on pursuing careers and significant hobbies of their own. Paired with the invention and booming popularity of processed "convenience" foods, the landscape of American dinner tables began dramatically evolving after the war. Television commercials for foods, kitchen appliances, and cooking tools were advertised with the angle of how they could help simplify housewives' lives, and women were welcoming of these time-saving devices.

The invention of television and its explosive popularity changed Americans' lives in the 1950s, and with the television boom came a landslide of food- and drink-related content, advertisements, and product placements. Throughout the 1960s and 1970s, television shows held up a mirror to Americans' changing relationship with and preferences for food. One thing remained consistent: food continued to be portrayed as having a significant cultural gravitational pull. Food brought people together at formal dining room tables, kitchen tables, community bar stools, restaurant booths, and more, in comedic and dramatic scenes alike.

ENTRÉE

Food in the early era of television was often depicted in a manner that could be described as wholesome, idyllic, and virtue-laden, and many of the plots fit that description, as well. For many, 1950s television shows conjure up images of nuclear families, with mothers clad in pearl necklaces, sensible high heels, and starched aprons. The mother's role was in the home kitchen in many of these shows because many American women were responsible for keeping up with housework; caring for children; and providing breakfast, lunch, dinner, and snacks for the family while their husbands worked outside of the home. Shows like *Leave It To Beaver* (1957–1963), *The Donna Reed Show* (1958–1966), and *Father Knows Best* (1954–1960) often depicted happy housewives making substantial meals for their families in gleaming kitchens.

Television shows and families in this era are sometimes referred to as "white bread," characterizing many of the family depictions and plots as having the wholesome nature of Wonderbread, which was also popular in the era. The term is also a nod to the overall lack of racial diversity in this era of programming, which predominantly featured white protagonists.

The 1950s were considered a Golden Era of advertising, particularly for television ads. Brand names jumped to pin down sponsorships with leading programs such as *Lassie* (1954–1971), which helped sell millions of cans of Campbell's soup, and *The Lone Ranger*, which was sponsored by Cheerios and Tootsie Rolls. Blue Bonnet helped persuade mothers to buy their product by adding cutout paper dolls of *Howdy Doody* (1947–1960) characters on the inside of the margarine boxes for children.

Food commercials sometimes became a plotline themselves, such as "Lucy Does a Commercial," a wildly popular episode of the sitcom *I Love Lucy* (1951–1957). The 1952 episode showed Lucy (Lucille Ball) defying her husband Ricky's wishes by starring in a commercial for a fictitious health tonic called Vitameatavegamin. The tonic's main ingredient turned out to be alcohol, and as Lucy did more takes, she became increasingly intoxicated to highly comedic effect. In another food-themed episode of the iconic show the same year, "Job Switching," Lucy and her friend Ethel (Vivian Vance) switched roles with their husbands, Ricky and Fred (Desi Arnaz and William Frawley), for the day. The men suffered through their attempts at homemaking, including blasting chickens from a pressure cooker into the ceiling, while the women struggled to wrap chocolate candies on a conveyor line, resorting to cramming candies into their mouths and dresses in the process.

Similarly, in a 1955 episode of *The Honeymooners* (1955–1956) entitled "Better Living Through Television," the lead characters (Jackie Gleason and Art Carney) filmed a live television commercial in character as chefs. Their commercial featured a gadget intended to replace an assortment of housewives' cooking tools—another sign of an era in which women were seeking reprieve from their laborious cooking duties. Gleason and Carney's commercial began with stiff acting and goofy foibles and devolved into slapstick, such as Gleason's attempt to core an apple while he was suffering from extreme stage fright. While filming the segment live, one of the blades unintentionally became dislodged while Gleason was fidgeting with it, and the blade unexpectedly flew toward the studio's cameras, causing even more hilarity for the cast, crew, and audience.

In 2009, the United States Postal Service printed a stamp commemorating the iconic "I Love Lucy" scene in which actresses Lucille Ball and Vivian Vance had to resort to hiding chocolate in their mouths and clothes on a factory line. (Olga Popova/Dreamstime.com)

> **Small Plates**
>
> **The Reign of the TV Dinner**
>
> As sales of mass-produced televisions boomed across the United States, so did sales of a complementary product: repackaged frozen meals that simply needed to be heated before eating, saving home cooks time in the kitchen. The convenience and informality of so-called "TV dinners" began to lure families away from their dining room tables, and people began eating on tray tables while watching television instead of sitting at the table together and talking.
>
> The origin story of TV dinners is, like many successful products, the result of an accident that proved to be valuable. Swanson & Sons foods, just known as Swanson today, sold fare like frozen chicken in the early 1950s. In 1953, the company overestimated how many frozen turkeys to order for Thanksgiving and found themselves with an excess of 260 tons of meat. One of the company's sales reps, Gerry Thomas, had a "making lemons-into-lemonade" moment of inspiration and suggested that Swanson & Sons package the meal next to sides in aluminum trays reminiscent of food trays he'd seen on airlines. The company agreed, and "TV dinners" were born: little trays of turkey, cornbread stuffing, sweet potatoes, and peas. The company was skeptical that the idea would pay off, but Thomas's instincts proved right, to the tune of 10 million TV dinner sales that year alone (Edwards 2004).

1960s–1970s

The next two decades of television continued to reflect changing trends in society. Episodes of *The Twilight Zone* (1959–1964) tapped into pop culture trends like space exploration, science fiction, apocalypse, and atomic fallouts. In a 1962 episode entitled "To Serve Man," aliens descend on earth, announcing they want to help end famine and war. All seems well until a cryptographer realizes that the aliens' book in his possession entitled "To Serve Man" is a cookbook, and humans are on the menu for their invaders.

Television's dinner scenes and gender stereotypes were also changing in tenor. Programs like *The Mary Tyler Moore Show* (1970–1977) showed women's relationships with food in a new light. The protagonist (Mary Tyler Moore) was far removed from the image of a traditional coiffed housewife. Bucking traditional homemaker stereotypes, Mary was a single, career-focused woman who hosted a number of humorously disastrous dinner parties in her small apartment and suffered through terrible dinner dates in various restaurants. Her peers also offered a more feminist view of cooking, such as on-air "Happy Homemaker" host Sue Ann Nivens (Betty White), who brought a biting humor to her fictional televised cooking segments, and Rhoda (Valerie Harper), who offered advice like "cottage cheese solves nothing; chocolate can do it all," eschewing the notion that women should always be dieting (IMDB 2019).

Another popular show with food and feminist story elements was *Laverne & Shirley* (1976–1983) starring Penny Marshall and Cindy Williams. Laverne and Shirley were friends and roommates who worked together on a bottle cap assembly line at Shotz, a fictional brewery. Penny Marshall's own favorite treat became a staple on the show—her character enjoyed drinking a combination of Pepsi and milk. Despite being set in the late 1950s and 1960s, the show also tapped into the growing popularity of mass-produced beer in the United States in the 1970s. *Laverne & Shirley* was a spinoff of another highly successful show, *Happy Days* (1974–1984). One of two primary locations on *Happy Days* was Arnold's Drive-In, a diner where the teen characters socialized. The locale painted a stereotypical setting for teens in the 1950s and 1960s, rife with hamburgers, milkshakes, and songs playing on jukeboxes.

SUGGESTED PAIRINGS

See also: Child, Julia; Craft Brewing and Microbreweries; Fictional Television (1980s–), Food and.

Entry best enjoyed while eating: Coffee, beans, and trout cooked over an open campfire (inspired by popular Western television shows), and a hearty helping of meatloaf, peas, mashed potatoes, and an old-fashioned served with a maraschino cherry, inspired by the fare featured on many sitcoms and real kitchen tables during this era.

Further Reading

Edwards, Owen. 2004. "How 260 Tons of Thanksgiving Leftovers Gave Birth to an Industry." *Smithsonian Magazine*, December 2004.

Internet Movie Database (IMDB). 2019. "Quotes: *The Mary Tyler Moore Show*, 'Put on a Happy Face' (1973)." https://www.imdb.com/title/tt0642879/characters/nm0001546

Maurer, Elizabeth. 2017. "How Highly Processed Foods Liberated 1950s Housewives." National Women's History Museum, May 11, 2017. https://www.womenshistory.org/articles/how-highly-processed-foods-liberated-1950s-housewives

MeTv Staff. 2017. "Thirteen Things You Might Not Know about Laverne and Shirley." https://www.metv.com/lists/13-things-you-might-not-know-about-laverne-shirley

Murray, Noel. 2010. "*The Honeymooners,* 'Better Living Through Television.'" AV/TV Club, March 11, 2010. https://tv.avclub.com/the-honeymooners-better-living-through-television-1798219335

Fictional Television (1980s–), Food and

STARTERS

Television shows help serve as time capsules that document the types of foods that are popular and widely used during the era in which they are filmed. As such, the evolution of food's role in fictional television shows has mirrored changes within American society. Television programs in the 1950s and 1960s were rife with images of nuclear families sitting down to a hearty meal prepared by mothers, but in the 1980s, food scenes in television were just as likely (if not more likely) to involve informal meals, and often lacked depictions of family gatherings. Many of the shows in this era illustrated the eating habits of demographics like single and childless adults, groups of elderly or young professional friends, or beleaguered working parents. In recent decades, food has increasingly served as a plot device, an illustration of character development, and a tool for delivering humorous punchlines and foreboding suspense. The public's interest in food-themed media continues to grow, sparking more academic and amateur interest alike in how food and beverages are portrayed on television. Advertisers have taken note, as well, and product placement and commercial spots for foods and beverages have become prevalent in the contemporary fictional television landscape.

ENTRÉE

1980s and 1990s

Starting around the 1980s, fictional television characters began gathering for very different meals than television audiences had grown accustomed to seeing on television in the postwar era. Some characters sat on couches watching television as they ate, mirroring many audience members who were doing the same at home. Families in shows like *Family Ties* (1982–1989), *The Cosby Show* (1984–1992), and *Roseanne* (1988–2018) often had high-energy meals filled with jokes, impassioned arguments, and cooking exploits gone wrong. These scenes posed a stark contrast to shows like *Father Knows Best* (1954–1960) in which the family prayed together over their Thanksgiving meal or when "the Beav" learned life lessons while trying Brussels sprouts for the first time in *Leave It to Beaver* (1957–1963).

Meals themselves were changing, too—instead of pot roasts and meatloaf cooked by housewives, characters frequently brought takeout home after a long day of work. Pizza became a frequent staple on television and was practically a character in itself in the animated children's show *Teenage Mutant Ninja Turtles* (1987–1996). Chinese takeout became incredibly popular in the United States in the 1980s, and this trend was reflected on the small screen, such as when teenaged Kevin (Fred Savage) took a job delivering Chinese food in the show *The Wonder Years* (1988–1993).

Television shows also began featuring nontraditional families, such as the adopted children and multiracial family in *Diff'rent Strokes*; foster child Punky and her older, single foster father in *Punky Brewster* (1984–1988); and a widower raising three daughters with the help of two live-in uncles in *Full House* (1987–1995). Traditional sit-down dinners began to feel like scenes from the past as characters ate at informal gatherings. In *The Golden Girls* (1985–1992), four elderly female friends who lived together (played by Beatrice Arthur, Estelle Getty, Rue McClanahan, and Betty White) often discussed life over fare like coffee or dessert. The comedy was often punctuated with food-related jokes, like White's Scandinavian concoction "Spearhoeven Krispies," a dessert that they had to pinch their noses shut to eat. The characters snacked on cheesecake together more than 100 times together throughout the show's seven seasons. The show even inspired a *Golden Girls* cookbook published in 2020, featuring cheesecake and recipes submitted by the actresses themselves (Cooper 2018).

Nontraditional meals were also a large plotline of *M*A*S*H*, which followed the lives of fictional members of the 4077th Mobile Army Surgical Hospital serving in the Korean War. Throughout the show, characters gathered in the army mess tent and traded jokes about the meals served by Private Igor Straminsky (Jeff Maxwell). Food also served as a character development tool, such as

Corporal Radar's (Gary Burghoff) teddy bear and grape Nehi soda accessories or Corporal Klinger's (Jamie Farr) homesick musings for the Hungarian hot dogs at his hometown restaurant. Inspired by the show's fare, Maxwell published a cookbook called *The Secrets of the M*A*S*H Mess* in 1997, with recipes like "Incoming Eggs" and "Bread Bullets."

Other popular shows included *Cheers* (1982–1993), in which adults sought companionship at a bar in Boston, Massachusetts. Like some of the themes explored over cheesecake in *The Golden Girls*, the cast of *Cheers* discussed many contemporary social issues and deepened their relationships over beers. *The Simpsons* (1989–present) also created many memorable moments in food pop culture in its impressive 30-season run. Homer, the endearingly doofy father, never strays far from his beloved donuts and fictional Duff beer. His social activist daughter, Lisa, grapples with the ethical aspects of various foods, like an episode in which she becomes a vegetarian after befriending a lamb. Food was also a frequent comedic device in *Friends* (1994–2004), such as when Joey (Matt LeBlanc) got his head stuck in an uncooked turkey or when Phoebe (Lisa Kudrow) ate a bowl of cereal that was precariously balanced on her pregnant belly.

Seinfeld (1989–1998) was renowned for its observational comedy, which elevates mundane aspects of daily life into relatable jokes. Many of its episodes made food and beverages virtual comic foils, and various brands and individuals associated with food highlighted in various episodes saw upticks in sales after the shows aired. In an episode called "The Soup Nazi" (1995), protagonist Jerry Seinfeld went to great lengths trying to buy soup from a highly temperamental vendor, modeled after a real man named Al Yeganeh whose stern soup-selling practices in New York City became legendary. "The Junior Mint," which aired in 1993, featured Seinfeld and his friend Kramer (Michael Richards) watching a splenectomy surgery. During the procedure, Kramer accidentally drops a Junior Mint into the patient's abdominal cavity. This episode is considered to be one of the most successful product placement examples in television history (Bukszpan 2015; Conradt 2008).

HBO's *Sex and the City* also had a strong influence on various food and beverage sales (1998–2004). It featured four female friends in New York City whose love of cosmopolitans (a pink vodka-based cocktail) spurred a national upsurge in the drink's popularity, followed by many bartenders' reluctance to promote or serve the drink (Odell 2017; Mannheimer 2017). In one episode, the characters ate cupcakes from a Manhattan bakery called Magnolia. As a result, the relatively unknown bakery became a tourist attraction, and its annual sales rose into the millions.

2000s and 2010s

One show that frequently used food in humorous and foreboding ways alike is *The Sopranos* (1999–2007), which chronicles the life of a New Jersey Italian American mobster family. Italian cuisine plays a significant role in many episodes. Tough mobster characters like Paulie "Walnuts" Gualtieri (Tony Sirico) and Christopher Moltisanti (Michael Imperioli) are emasculated in episodes like "The Pine Barrens," in which the pair commit a crime and get stranded in the woods during winter. Hungry and inappropriately dressed for the weather, they gobble down a few relish packets that they find and later fight over Tic Tac mints with slapstick desperation. The character Paulie "Walnuts" received his food-themed nickname from an incident in which he attempted to steal entertainment equipment from a large truck, only to find that it was filled with walnuts instead. In "The Telltale Moozadell" (slang for "mozzarella"), the mob boss's less-than-intelligent son A.J. (Robert Iler) vandalizes his high school gymnasium's pool. He leaves a pizza he had ordered with customized toppings at the pool, which police later use to identify him as the culprit.

Similarly, stickup man Omar Little (Michael K. Williams) on *The Wire* (2002–2008) scares everyone from children to hardened drug dealers on the streets of Baltimore. Omar's penchant for Honey Nut Cheerios cereal is a frequent and endearing detail throughout the show that helps to soften and humanize his character. Food is also linked with freedom, oppression, and power in the show *Orange is the New Black* (2013–2019), which follows the trials and tribulations of the women incarcerated in a minimum-security prison. Characters who are on the outs with the prison's kitchen staff are frequently offered food that has been defiled, and staff changes in the kitchen pose significant moments in the prison's culture. Many characters are shown using food as comfort, escape, and small ways to find peace or joy. In an episode called "Where My Dreidel At?" many Litchfield Penitentiary women pretend they are Jewish in an attempt to qualify for kosher meals, which are tastier than the standard prison fare.

Power and humor are both central food themes in *The Gilmore Girls* (2000–2007), which follows the story of single mother Lorelai (Lauren Graham) and her daughter Rory (Alexis Bledel). The pair find themselves in a commitment to eat dinner every Friday with Lorelai's wealthy, estranged parents. Differences between the characters' class, socioeconomic status, and personalities are punctuated in various foods associated with each character. The grandparents are seen eating foods like salmon puffs and fine wines, while Lorelai's snack choices like PopTarts, ice cream, and candy are a subtle nod to the premature end of her childhood. Rory's best friend Lane favors contraband pizza at the Gilmore's house over fare made by her stern, value-centric mother, like "eggless egg salad," and Rory and Lorelai are never without bottomless cups of coffee, which fuel their busy lives and whip-fast conversations. In the show's revival, Lorelai critically dismisses a number of celebrity chefs who want to work in her inn, including Alice Waters, Anthony Bourdain, April Bloomfield, and David Chang. Actual celebrity appearances on the show by Rachael Ray and Roy Choi helped to perpetuate the joke.

ACCOMPANIED BY

YouTube personality Andrew Rea has amassed a large following from viewers who are interested in food's role in film and television and who want to recreate television's culinary concoctions in their own homes. Rea's channel Binging with Babish attracts "millions of burgeoning chefs and foodies around the world," offering recipes for fare inspired by shows and movies. Recipes range from "M&Ms and Peeps Chili" inspired by *The Good Place* to a dessert in homage to

The Office called "the Michael Scott Pretzel" that is teeming with cinnamon, sugar, caramel, hot fudge, peanut butter, and candy.

DESSERT

- **"I'm going to get ice cream or commit a felony; I'll decide in the car"**: *The Golden Girls* inspired the creation of a cafe devoted to the show, which is open to the public in New York City's Washington Heights neighborhood. Named for actress Rue McLanahan, the Rue La Rue Cafe is decorated to match the set's decor and features the actresses' own recipes and fare inspired by various episodes

- **"So if you love me, stir my eggs, ok?"**: One recurring theory on fan forums of *The Sopranos* was that the show's Easter eggs (clues buried for audiences) involved *actual* eggs, which were frequently discussed, being prepared, or being eaten in scenes preceding various characters' deaths.

- **"Save the liver!"**: Sketch comedy show *Saturday Night Live* has produced a number of food-related spoofs, including a classic bit in which actor Dan Akroyd did an impersonation of Julia Child's *The French Chef*. Dressed in an apron and pearls, Akroyd feigned getting cut while boning a chicken. He continued the cooking tutorial as fake blood gushed from the wound until he lost consciousness from blood loss.

- **Does "D'oh" translate?:** In 2005, an Arabic version of *The Simpsons* was released under the name *Al Shamshoon*. The show underwent significant changes for the Arabic market, such as replacing Homer's beer with juice, swapping out bacon sandwiches for beef hot dogs, and replacing donuts with bread rings called *ka'ak*. Losing many of its American pop culture references in translation, the show ended up being a flop.

- **"Medium rare, a lotta horseradish"**: In *The Wire*, drug dealer character Wee-Bey is interrogated regarding his involvement in various murders. When asked to take the blame for more murders than he'd already admitted to, Wee-Bey says, "For another pit sandwich and some potato salad, I'll go a few more," despite not being responsible for having committed the other crimes. He receives another Baltimore-famous roast beef sandwich, and a prison sentence, but no potato salad . . . the restaurant had run out.

- **"F is for food"**: *Sesame Street* incorporates food in a number of ways, such as modeling healthy eating on Cookie Monster and Gonger's food truck segments. In Season 48, the children's show spoofed the reality show *Top Chef* with culinary judge Padma Lakshmi, who was tasked with judging the muppets' various silly creations.

SUGGESTED PAIRINGS

See also: Cake and Cupcake Trends; Fictional Television (1950s–1970s), Food and; Super Bowl Sunday.

Entry best enjoyed while eating: Waffles with whipped cream served alongside a T-bone steak (*Parks and Recreation*); Chinese takeout eaten while doing detective work (*Law and Order*); and a slice of cherry pie and a cup of diner coffee served "black as midnight on a moonless night" (*Twin Peaks*).

Further Reading

Bukszpan, Daniel. 2015. "*Seinfeld* Is Good for Business." *Fortune,* June 27, 2015. http://fortune.com/2015/06/27/seinfeld-products/

Conradt, Stacy. 2008. "The Stories Behind Ten Famous Product Placements." Mental Floss, April 6, 2008. http://mentalfloss.com/article/18383/stories-behind-10-famous-product-placements

Cooper, Gael Fashingbauer. 2018. "*Golden Girls'* Cookbook Was Inspired by the 1980s Sitcom." The Daily Meal, August 13, 2018. https://www.thedailymeal.com/golden-girls-cookbook-coming-in-2020

Mannheimer, Emma. 2017. "How *Sex and the City* Ruined the Cosmo." *Vice,* Munchies. https://www.vice.com/en_us/article/mb9q58/how-sex-and-the-city-ruined-the-cosmo

Maxwell, Jeff. 1997. *The Secrets of the M*A*S*H Mess: The Lost Recipes of Private Igor.* Nashville: Cumberland House Publishing.

Norwick, Hannah. 2013. "The 25 Best Food Moments in *The Wire*." First We Feast, February 14, 2013. https://firstwefeast.com/eat/2013/02/the-25-best-food-moments-in-the-wire/i-dont-like-the-orange-ones

Odell, Kat. 2017. "Is the Cosmopolitan Making a Comeback?" *Vogue,* April 24, 2017.

Rea, Andrew. 2017. "Binging with Babish: About." https://www.bingingwithbabish.com/about

Fieri, Guy (1968–)

STARTERS

Guy Fieri is an American television show personality, restaurateur, and author. Fieri made his national television debut on the second season of the Food Network's competition show *The Next Food Network Star* in 2005. His win secured the opportunity to host his own Food Network show, *Guy's Big Bite*, which ran 2006 through 2016. He went on to host *Diners, Drive-Ins and Dives* (2007–), *Ultimate Recipe Showdown* (2009–2010), *Tailgate Warriors* (2009–2011), *Guy's Grocery Games* (2013–2018), *Guy's Ranch Kitchen* (2017–2018), *Guy's Family Road Trip* (2018), and a number of others. Fieri made a number of appearances as a guest judge on shows like *Food Network Star* and co-hosted *Rachael vs. Guy: Celebrity Cook-Off* (2012–2014) and *Rachael vs. Guy: Kids Cook-Off* (2013–2013) with celebrity chef Rachael Ray. He made guest appearances on a number of daytime talk shows, late-night network shows, and cable shows such as *The Best Thing I Ever Ate*, and he was the host of the game show *Minute to Win It* between 2010 and 2013 ("Guy Fieri" 2018).

Fieri opened his first restaurant in 1996, Johnny Garlic's, and has since gone on to open 62 more restaurants worldwide ("Guyography" n.d.). His first book was published in 2008, *Diners, Drive-Ins and Dives: An All-American Road Trip . . . with Recipes!* The sequel, *More Diners, Drive-Ins and Dives*, followed in 2009.

Both made the number-one spot on *The New York Times* Best-Seller List. Between 2011 and 2016, Fieri published three cookbooks. In 2009, Fieri went cross-country on a tour called Guy Fieri's Road Show that combined cooking demonstrations with rock concerts, followed by a second tour in 2011. Fieri won a Daytime Emmy Award in 2013 for his show *Guy Fieri's Family Reunion*, which won "Outstanding Special." He received two additional nominations for Daytime Emmys and four Primetime Emmy nominations.

ENTRÉE

Known for his signature spiky bleached-blond hair, two-tone goatee, tattoos, bowling shirts, sunglasses, and chain-link necklaces, Fieri brings a rock-star attitude to eating and food. The restaurateur, whose catchphrase is "welcome to Flavortown!", has a passion for traditional American fare like burgers, chicken wings, sandwiches, barbecue, and nachos. Fieri's love of food started at the age of 10, when he developed a love of soft pretzels during a ski trip. He and his father set up a bicycle cart so he could sell pretzels at local events in his hometown of Ferndale, California. At the age of 15, using money he'd saved from pretzel sales and dishwashing, Fieri studied abroad in Chantilly, France. He developed a passion for the new foods and food markets he was exposed to there and became inspired to open a restaurant of his own. When he returned home, he bussed tables in a hotel restaurant and climbed the ranks to become a flambé chef. He enrolled at the University of Nevada, Las Vegas, and graduated with a Hospital Management degree (Morabito 2018).

In 1996, Fieri teamed up with his new business partner, Steve Gruber, to open Johnny Garlic's in Santa Rosa, California. They dubbed the restaurant's style as a "California pasta grill." The duo was successful in their first venture, and Fieri opened a variety of restaurants over the next few years. In 1999, he opened Tex Wasabi's, a sushi-barbecue fusion restaurant that the website jokingly calls "sushi-barbecue confusion." As his culinary career blossomed, Fieri auditioned for the second season of *Next Food Network Star*. He was cast on the show, won the show's competition, and was under contract for a show of his own by 2006. Fieri became a frequent host and guest on a number of Food Network shows. One of his most successful shows is *Diners, Drive Ins and Dives*, which has run for 28 seasons. On the show, Fieri tours different states in his red 1968 Camaro convertible. Along the way, he visits numerous restaurants, most of which are small and locally owned. Fieri joins members of the staff in the kitchens to watch and sample what's being prepared and interviews customers.

Aside from his television profession, Fieri's international restaurant business could be described as a small empire. His restaurants range from a barbecue restaurant in Atlantic City, New Jersey, to hamburger joints on Carnival Cruise lines and a Mexican restaurant in Las Vegas. His Kitchen + Bar chain can be found across the United States and as far away as Dubai, featuring specialties such as "trash can nachos" and burgers with donkey sauce (one of Fieri's creations: a mayonnaise- and mustard-based aioli). In 2012, Fieri opened an American Kitchen +

Bar in Times Square, New York City, a notoriously competitive location for restaurateurs due to its large number of tourists.

The restaurant was given a blistering review by *New York Times* food critic Pete Wells, who rated the restaurant zero stars. Wells questioned "which part of the donkey we are supposed to think about" when served donkey sauce, described a toasted marshmallow dish as tasting like fish, and referred to an unnamed blue drink as glowing like "nuclear waste" (Wells 2012). Wells's harsh words, which *Forbes* magazine restaurant writer Larry Olmsted described as the most scathing review he'd read in the *Times* in 30 years, led to additional mocking commentary from culinary writers nationwide. Despite the business's apparent success, earning more than $16 million annually, Fieri closed the location at the end of 2017 (Olmstead 2012; Carman 2017). In 2013, Fieri opened Hunt & Ryde Winery in Sonoma Valley, California, named for his two sons.

ACCOMPANIED BY

Guy Fieri married Lori Fieri in 1995, and the pair have two sons together, Hunter and Ryder. Fieri's parents are Penelope and James Ferry, who owned a saddlery store in Ferndale, California, where they raised Guy and his sister Morgan. Fieri's parents were health-food devotees, and cooking was a big part of their family life. When the Fieris married, Guy changed the spelling of his last name (Ferry) to honor the traditional spelling of his Italian relatives. In 2011, Morgan passed away at the age of 38 from melanoma. Before her passing, she cofounded a charity for youth with Guy called "The Guy Fieri Foundation for Inspiration and Imagination." Guy also started a foundation called Cooking With Kids that mentors children in cooking techniques.

DESSERT

Diners, Drive-Ins and Dives is so popular that various websites exist to help fans plan road trips that feature restaurants from the show. Restaurateurs can expect upward of a 200 percent increase in business after being featured on the show, thanks in part to how often reruns are aired profiling the show's droolworthy locales (Fulton 2016).

SUGGESTED PAIRINGS

See also: *Best Thing I Ever Ate, The*; Laurentiis, Giada De; Ray, Rachael; Television, Food Channels On.

Entry best enjoyed while eating: A cheeseburger with bacon, Creole spices, blue cheese, and donkey sauce; French fries tossed in buffalo and "blue-sabi" sauce; deep-fried spicy mac and cheese bites; and Guy's "Cheesecake Challenge": a giant serving of cheesecake topped with hot fudge, pretzels, and potato chips.

Further Reading
Carman, Tim. 2017. "Guy Fieri Is Pulling the Plug on Perhaps the Most Mocked Restaurant in America." *The Washington Post*, December 29, 2017.

"Diners, Drive-Ins, and Dives." 2018. Internet Movie Database (IMDb). https://www.imdb.com/title/tt1020913/fullcredits/?ref_=tt_ov_st_sm

Fulton, Wil. 2016. "Here's What Happens After Guy Fieri Visits a Restaurant." Thrillist, November 30, 2016. https://www.thrillist.com/eat/nation/guy-fieri-diners-drive-ins-dives-behind-scenes

"Guy Fieri." 2018. Internet Movie Database (IMDb). https://www.imdb.com/name/nm2225974/

"Guyography" n.d. Guy Fieri. http://www.guyfieri.com/about.

Morabito, Greg. 2018. "The 12 Days of Guy Fieri: A Look Back at the Pretzel Cart That Started It All." *Eater*, December 6, 2018. https://www.eater.com/2018/12/6/18127978/guy-fieri-pretzel-cart

Olmsted, Larry, 2012. "Is Guy Fieri's Restaurant Really That Bad?" *Forbes*, November 23, 2012.

Wells, Pete. 2012. "As Not Seen on TV: Guy's American Kitchen & Bar." *The New York Times*, November 12, 2012.

Films, Food in

STARTERS

A wide variety of foods, cuisines, beverages, and restaurants have been used on the big screen since the inception of film, ranging from meaningful or comedic props to playing significant and even central roles in the films' plots. Today, there are even various food-themed film festivals that screen food-themed documentaries, dramas, and comedies. One example is the Flatirons Food Festival in Boulder, Colorado, which features culinary-themed cinema ranging from documentaries to films like *Babette's Feast* (1987), a Danish drama about a Parisian refugee who woos a small Danish town with her French cooking. A large number of domestic and foreign films alike have explored the important, whimsical, somber, and irreverent ways in which food and eating play a significant role in people's lives and within each community.

ENTRÉE

Cinema's treatment of food can reveal fascinating insights into pop culture, sociology, and gastronomy trends throughout each decade. Interestingly, some of the earliest images ever committed to film portrayed food. In 1895, the Lumiere Brothers invented the art of filmmaking with short introductory films that included footage of men being served wine in the afternoon and a married couple feeding their baby as they ate breakfast. Food was a significant source of comedy in Charlie Chaplin's 1925 silent film *The Gold Rush*, such as scenes in which Chaplin—a starving prospector—ate his boot with panache during a hard winter and amused dinner party guests by plunging forks into two dinner rolls and making them dance as if they were large feet.

Food has been used symbolically in various war films, such as *The Best Years of Our Lives* (1946), which follows three members of the armed services as they

This still from a 1908 Edison Manufacturing Company film titled *The Lost New Year's Dinner* depicts a couple eating a meal together in a prison cell. Food has been a significant theme in film history dating back to the earliest moving pictures. (Library of Congress)

return home from the war and struggle to readjust to civilian and family life. Food themes symbolize stark differences in the characters' pre- and postwar lives, such as when a former infantryman named Al Stevenson is surprised to discover that his family no longer has a hired cook, and meals are now prepared by his daughter Peggy, who has been studying contemporary food science lessons. Food also symbolizes class and status, such as a story line that follows Fred Derry, a decorated air force bombardier, returning to his old job as a soda jerk due to a widespread scarcity of jobs. One memorable scene features a man named Homer Parrish, a returning navy veteran who lost his hands during his service, eating a chocolate sundae with his prosthetic hooks. The scene offers an unflinching look at the way he must adapt to life with a disability from the war and highlights the amazing ability of both his prosthetics and his perseverance in adapting to his injuries. Alcohol is also a significant plot point: a local bar serves as a sanctuary for community and connection, but some of the veterans abuse alcohol in an attempt to numb pain from their traumas.

In the 1950s, Disney's animated feature *Lady and the Tramp* (1955) delighted audiences with a scene that went on to become a classic, in which the two dogs enjoy a romantic date sharing a plate of spaghetti while the chef and restaurant's owner serenade them. Former studio archivist Steven Vagnini later reported that the famous scene was initially cut from the storyboards by Walt Disney, who thought the idea of two dogs dining on human food would be clumsy and odd (Zakarin 2015). Alfred Hitchcock's thriller *Rear Window* (1954) features a photographer (Jimmy Stewart) who is homebound in a wheelchair after an accident and spends a sweltering summer watching his neighbors through binoculars. Food is often symbolic in the film, such as comfort foods prepared by his nurse (Ruth Gordon), upscale dishes of broiled lobster and rose wine delivered from his chic love interest (Grace Kelly), and a scene in which a character dubbed "Mrs. Lonelyheart" makes dinner for herself and an imaginary date in her apartment before attempting suicide due to loneliness.

The iconic spaghetti and meatballs scene in the Disney film *Lady and the Tramp* is so beloved that it was commemorated on a stamp by the United States Postal Service in 2006. (Sergei Nezhinskii/Dreamstime.com)

Various films have staged entire plot points around meals, such as *Guess Who's Coming to Dinner* (1967). The plot revolves around a biracial couple (Katharine Houghton and Sidney Poitier) gathering their parents (Katharine Hepburn, Spencer Tracy, Bea Richards, and Roy E. Glenn, Sr.) for a dinner to have everyone meet and confront the news that they are engaged to be married. The intimacy of a shared dinner party is contrasted with the tension created by various family members' spoken and unspoken dissenting opinions about biracial relationships. The shared meal at the conclusion of the film represents unity as the characters finally embrace the situation. *My Dinner With Andre* (1981) revolves around a conversation between a theater director (Andre Gregory) and his playwright friend (Wallace Shawn) over a meal shared at an upscale New York City restaurant. The unusual film invites viewers to indulge a plot devoid of action, twists, and the variety of scenes and locale changes most films rely on to keep the audience's attention and interest.

Product placement in films, in which corporations and film studios strike deals to cross-promote their products, became particularly prominent by the 1980s. One example was *E.T.* (1982), in which an extra-terrestrial eats Reese's Pieces candies. The Hershey Corporation went on to see skyrocketing sales of Reese's Pieces as a result of the exposure in the film, an opportunity they paid $1 million for (Mikkelson 2011). Coca-Cola soda has been heavily featured in a number of films, including *Dr. Strangelove* (1964) and *Superman 2* (1978). As part of their marketing strategy, the Coca-Cola company even acquired Columbia Pictures in 1982, to which Pepsi's parent company responded by securing heavy advertising in the film *Back to the Future* (1985).

A number of classic food scenes in film took place in the 1980s, such as *A Christmas Story* (1983), a comedy set in Indiana during the early 1940s. One of the main characters, a beleaguered mother of two and housewife, cooks up American comfort food like meatloaf, red cabbage, peas, toast, and scrambled eggs throughout the film, convincing her youngest son to eat by having him go snout-first into his mashed potatoes like a pig. In 1985, a Japanese comedy called *Tampopo* featured the fictional happenings at a roadside noodle shop and was given the informal title of the first "ramen Western" (similar to the film subgenre called Spaghetti Western, but with an Asian cultural twist). In 1986, the film *Stand By Me* featured a scene about a boy enacting revenge on the town's bullies by vomiting a surreal volume of blueberry pie on them during a pie eating contest. The scene reportedly caused a large number of audience members to get sick during theater showings, as well (McGovern 2016).

In 1989, the film *When Harry Met Sally* used a number of food scenes to illustrate quirky aspects of romantic relationships. A long-running joke in the film is the disdain Harry (Billy Crystal) has for the way Sally (Meg Ryan) orders her food—including specific directions about what she wants, how it should be served, and what off-menu items she wants to substitute various ingredients for. On a car trip, Harry punctuates an argument by trying to spit a mouthful of grape seeds out

Due in large part to its exposure in numerous television shows and films (perhaps most famously in 1989's *When Harry Met Sally*) Katz's Deli is widely considered to be the most famous deli in the United States. (Ryan Deberardinis/Dreamstime.com)

a closed window that he thought was rolled down. The film's most iconic scene is set in New York's famous Katz's Deli, where Sally casually eats a sandwich while performing a theatrical impression of a woman faking pleasure in the bedroom to win an argument with Harry. When she finishes, another diner patron (played by director Rob Reiner's mother, Estelle) utters a line that became wildly popular in popular culture: "I'll have what she's having."

In 1996, the film *Big Night* illustrated cultural trends in the food industry with its portrayal of two brothers (Tony Shalhoub and Stanley Tucci) struggling to keep their Italian restaurant alive in New York City. Set in the 1950s, the film explores the struggle many restaurants encounter to maintain authenticity. The brothers wrestle with customers' requests for entrées like spaghetti and meatballs in lieu of more authentic Italian fare. Some have credited the film with helping to create a cultural revolution that—paired with the celebrity chefs who emerged on television in the 1990s and early 2000s—inspired many Americans to seek more authenticity in their dining experiences.

Food itself continued to play increasingly larger roles in various 2000s films. *Chocolat* (2000), a romantic comedy starring Juliette Binoche and Johnny Depp, is about an eccentric single mother who opens a chocolaterie in a small French town. Her chocolate symbolizes things that are alluring, exciting, forbidden, comforting, and nostalgic for the townspeople. In 2007, Pixar released *Ratatouille*, which follows the trials and tribulations of a rat named Remy who aspires to be a chef in a high-end Parisian restaurant. In a climactic scene of the film, Remy's food causes a hardened restaurant reviewer to flash back in a Proustian memory of ratatouille his mother had made for him as a child. In 2013, the Indian film *The Lunchbox* used food as a key plot device. Set in Mumbai, a young wife attempts to reconnect through her husband with the lunches she prepares and sends via *dabbawalas*, delivery people who bring lunches packed in pails called *tiffins* to people in the workforce. In a twist of fate, the young woman's tiffin is delivered to the wrong man, and the two begin corresponding through letters sent via the lunch boxes. The film presents the preparation, smell, enjoyment, and shared experience of food as a love language in itself; uses food to illuminate differences between social classes; and explores how food can create connections and fosters relationships.

DESSERT

- **An acquired taste:** In *The Gold Rush*, the boot Charlie Chaplin boiled and ate was made out of black licorice. Chaplin was diabetic and had to chew on the candy prop for more than 60 takes, which sent him into insulin shock and required hospitalization.
- **Bye, bye, three-day-old pie:** In the 1965 auto race film *The Great Race*, nearly 2,500 pies were used for what director Blake Edwards envisioned as the biggest pie fight in history. The scene took three days to film, and upon its completion, the crew was allowed to dig into 300 pies that had been spared from battle.

- **Dabba-ling in lunch:** In Mumbai, approximately 50,000 *dabbawalas* deliver 80 million lunches (*dabbas*) a year. According to the Mumbai Tiffinmen's Association, an error only occurs once in every 6 million deliveries, the equivalent of one lost tiffin per month. According to the *Independent*, the system works so well that it has been studied by Harvard Business School "and is reportedly the envy of FedEx" (Henderson 2017).
- **The candy that wasn't:** Mars, Inc. was initially offered the opportunity to feature M&Ms candies in the film *E.T.*, but the corporation passed on the offer. Reece's Pieces went on to gain fame and fortune in one of the most successful product placement campaigns in film history.

SUGGESTED PAIRINGS

See also: Asian American Cuisine; Documentary Films, Food and Beverages in; Fiction, Food in; Nonfiction, Food in; Websites, Food.

Entry best enjoyed while eating: A Katz Deli turkey sandwich with Russian dressing and coleslaw, with half of the turkey removed ("what she was having" in *When Harry Met Sally*); a White Russian with vodka, coffee liqueur, and ice (the iconic drink from *The Big Lebowski*); and a quivering spoonful of green Jell-O (used to illustrate child actress Ariana Richards' terror upon seeing a velociraptor in *Jurassic Park*).

Further Reading

AMC. n.d. "Classic Movies with Memorable Food Scenes." https://www.amc.com/extras/classic-movies-with-memorable-food-scenes#/6

Best Years of Our Lives. 1946. "And For What?" YouTube video clip, 04:36, uploaded November 22, 2016. https://www.youtube.com/watch?v=D4EjRzzRQLI

Carlson, Jen. 2014. "Have What She's Having: Sally's Turkey from Katz's." Gothamist, July 31, 2014. http://gothamist.com/2014/07/31/have_what_shes_having_sallys_turkey.php

Gross, Matt. 2016. "How Stanley Tucci's Big Night Helped Kick off an American Dining Revolution." *The Guardian*, January 24, 2016.

Henderson, Emma. 2017. "How Dabbawalas Became the World's Best Food Delivery System." *Independent*, August 4, 2017.

McGovern, Joe. 2016. "'Stand by Me' Turns 30: The Blueberry Pie Scene Gets an Oral History." Entertainment Weekly, May 12, 2016. https://ew.com/article/2016/05/12/stand-by-me-blueberry-pie/

Mikkelson, Barbara. 2011. "M&Ms and E.T." Snopes Fact-Check, Business. https://www.snopes.com/fact-check/taking-it-et/

Zakarin, Jordan. 2015. "Why the Iconic 'Lady and the Tramp' Spaghetti Kiss Scene Almost Never Happened." *Yahoo! Entertainment,* June 9, 2015. https://www.yahoo.com/entertainment/lady-and-the-tramp-spaghetti-scene-121119404577.html

Flay, Bobby (1964–)

STARTERS

Bobby Flay is an American chef, television personality, restaurateur, and author. Flay has owned a number of high-profile restaurants in the United States, including Mesa Grill in New York City and Las Vegas; BOLO, Bar Americain, and Gato in New York City; Bobby Flay Steak in Atlantic City; and Bobby's Burger Palace in a number of states. Flay started a long television career with the Food Network as the host of shows like *Grillin' & Chillin* (1996–), *The Main Ingredient* (1996), *Hot Off the Grill* (1998), *Boy Meets Grill* (2002), *BBQ with Bobby Flay* (2004–2006), *Iron Chef America* (2004–2014), *Throwdown with Bobby Flay* (2006–2011), *Bobby Flay's Barbecue Addiction* (2011–2013), and *Beat Bobby Flay* (2015–2018). Between 1994 and 2013, the chef authored 12 cookbooks. His culinary honors include winning four Daytime Emmy awards, receiving three James Beard Foundation Awards, being inducted into the Culinary Hall of Fame in 2013, and becoming the first chef to win a star on the Hollywood Walk of Fame in 2015.

ENTRÉE

Bobby Flay is the kind of chef who marches to the beat of his own drum. Born and raised in New York City, Flay was interested in cooking from a very young age. At the age of eight, he asked his parents for an Easy-Bake Oven despite his father's concern that G.I. Joe would be a more fitting toy. By the age of 18, Flay had dropped out of high school and was developing an interest in cooking. At the firm insistence of his father, Flay started working as a prep cook and busboy at a restaurant in New York City's theater district called Joe Allen. The partners went on to convince Flay to attend the renowned French Culinary Institute. After six months of culinary training, Flay worked as a sous chef at an up-and-coming Manhattan restaurant called Brighton Grill. On his first day there, the restaurant's chef showed up too inebriated to work, and Flay was promoted to the chef's role on the spot.

He went on to apprentice under chef Jonathan Waxman, whose specialty is California cuisine, and gained a passion for southwestern cuisine. At the age of 26, Flay teamed up with restaurateur Jerome Kretchmer to run Mesa Grill in New York City, which was deemed "Best Restaurant" in 1992 by *New York Magazine* reviewer Gael Greene and had a successful 22-year run. Flay opened another Mesa Grill at Caesar's Palace in Las Vegas in 2004, which showcased his signature Southwestern fare like tamales, ancho-chile sauces, and bold spice rubs. In 1993, Kretchmer's son Laurence opened a restaurant with Flay in Manhattan's Flatiron district called Bolo, which earned a rare three-star review in the *New York Times* (Flay 2014; Lagorio-Chafkin 2015).

As Flay's culinary career was blossoming, he ventured into a new territory that many chefs were decrying: television. Flay has described the Food Network's early days as being so funding-limited (and relatively unknown to viewers) that they hired Manhattan-based chefs who could come to the studios inexpensively, via cab or subway. Whereas many of Flay's peers were turned off by the idea of being on television, Bobby saw an opportunity to promote his restaurants. He guest-starred on the network in 1994, and within two years, he was hired as the host of *Grillin' & Chillin'*. The chef began pitching his own ideas for shows and found his sweet spot appealing primarily to male audiences, sharing tips for grilling foods like hamburgers and steak. In 2000, Flay was selected to compete against chef Masaharu Morimoto on the Japanese show *Iron Chef*. The episode became the most viewed program in Food Network's history at that time, attracting 960,000 viewers (Marin 2001). Morimoto won by a narrow margin shortly after Flay sparked controversy by jumping on his table to amp up the crowd, standing on his cutting board in the process. Morimoto was appalled by this act and said that Japanese chefs consider cutting boards to be sacred. Flay claims that this television scene was "the moment that brought Food Network into pop culture" (Littleton 2013). His television spots consisted of hosting and judging a number of cooking and competition shows, such as *Throwdown*, in which he competes against cooks all over the United States to try to outdo their most famous dishes.

Flay's television career has spanned more than 25 years, but he has always managed to run a restaurant empire concurrently. In 2005, Flay and Laurence opened a brasserie called Bar Americain, which featured regional American foods inspired by Flay's travels throughout the United States. In an interview with *Inc.* magazine, Flay noted that "when chefs go out to dinner . . . we're looking for a good bourbon and a great burger" (Lagorio-Chafkin 2015). Pursuing his passion for grilling and meat, Flay opened a steakhouse in 2006 called Bobby Flay Steak in Atlantic City. Two years later, he opened Bobby's Burger Palace on Long Island, the first of many in the United States. In 2014, the chef turned his focus to Mediterranean cuisine with Gato, which is considered by some as the most sought-after for reservations in New York City.

ACCOMPANIED BY

Bobby Flay's father, restaurant manager and former lawyer Bill Flay, helped launch the chef's career by telling his son to fill in for a busboy who didn't report for work one day at Joe Allen's. Concerned about the fact that Flay had dropped out of high school with no career path, he told Bobby that he wouldn't receive special treatment at the restaurant and urged him to work hard. Bobby's mother, Dorothy Flay, was a trademark specialist for much of her career and was a single mother to Bobby after she and Bill divorced when their son was young. She passed away in 2018 at the age of 86.

In 1991, Flay married fellow chef Debra Ponzak, who was one of the most prominent chefs in New York at that time. In 1992, both chefs were nominated for the James Beard "Rising Star Chef" award; Ponzak won and presented Flay with the same award the following year. The pair divorced after two years of marriage. In 1995, Flay married Kate Connelly, the cohost of a Food Network show called *Robin Leach Talking Food*. She and Flay had a daughter together, Sophie, in 1996. Connelly and Flay divorced in 1998. In 2005, Flay wed for a third time, this time to actress Stephanie March, and the pair divorced in 2015.

DESSERT

In addition to his culinary passions, Flay is also an avid fan of horse racing. He owns and breeds thoroughbreds and serves on the board of directors for Breeders'

Cup. In 2014, he paid more than $2.1 million for a horse named White Hot Ire, deemed the most expensive filly in the Western Hemisphere that year (Marquardt n.d.).

SUGGESTED PAIRINGS

See also: Bayless, Rick; *Iron Chef*; Television, Food Channels on.

Entry best enjoyed while eating: Tamale with tiger shrimp, roasted garlic, and corn; sweet potato fries with honey mustard and horseradish sauce; and a vanilla bean bourbon milkshake.

Further Reading

"About Bobby." n.d. http://bobbyflay.com/bobby/

"Bobby Flay." n.d. Food Network. https://www.foodnetwork.com/profiles/talent/bobby-flay/bio

"Dorothy B. Flay Obituary." 2018. *Asbury Park Press*. April 25–27, 2018.

Flay, Bobby. 2014. "Bobby Flay: His Winding Path to Success." *Guideposts*, December 5, 2014. https://www.guideposts.org/better-living/positive-living/bobby-flay-his-winding-path-to-success

Krigbaum, Megah. 2015. "Interview with Chef Bobby Flay." *Food & Wine*, March 31, 2015. https://www.foodnetwork.com/profiles/talent/bobby-flay/bio

Lagorio-Chafkin, Christine. 2015. "How Bobby Flay Built a Sizzling Empire." *Inc.* April, 2015.

Littleton, Cynthia. 2013. "Food Network: If You Can't Stand the Heat . . ." https://variety.com/2013/biz/news/food-network-if-you-cant-stand-the-heat-1200796261/

Marin, Rick. 2001. "Lobsters at Five Paces and Egos Bared." *The New York Times*, June 6, 2001.

Marquardt, Lucas. N.d. "The Education of Bobby Flay." *Thoroughbred Daily News*. https://www.thoroughbreddailynews.com/longform/bobby-flay/

Puente, Marla. 2003. "Easy-Bake Oven Gets Its Own Cookbook." USA Today, The Spokesman-Review, May 28, 2003. https://news.google.com/newspapers?nid=1314&dat=20030528&id=aWZWAAAAIBAJ&sjid=uPIDAAAAIBAJ&pg=6718,5926990

"Weddings/Celebrations: Stephanie March, Bobby Flay." 2005. *The New York Times*, February 20, 2005.

Florida Strawberry Festival

STARTERS

The Florida Strawberry Festival is an annual event in Plant City, Florida, that stages a large-scale celebration of Florida's strawberry crop each spring. The 11-day event incorporates strawberry-themed foods, concerts, eating competitions, a beauty pageant, livestock shows, agricultural exhibits, rides, and more. The festival was founded by the Plant City Lions Club in 1930 to celebrate the area's strawberry harvest. The event was restarted in 1948 after a hiatus during World War II and has been operated every year since then by Lions Clubs and various additional civic organizations. Today, the festival is governed by a local board of community directors and draws a large number of attendees each year. For a city with a population just shy of 39,000 people, the Strawberry Festival attracted 560,487 attendees in 2016. As many as 50,000 people attend per day (Hull 2008). The festival, which ranks in the Top 40 Fairs in North America, runs from 10 a.m. until 10 p.m. and offsets its costs by charging for admission (Florida Strawberry Festival 2018).

ENTRÉE

Located in Northeastern Hillsborough County, Florida, Plant City is a modest city of roughly 28 square miles. This unassuming locale boasts the title of the "Winter Strawberry Capital of the World" and is considered to be the headquarters of Florida's nearly $1 billion strawberry industry (Figueroa IV 2018). Hillsborough County area is home to more than 10,000 acres of strawberry crops, and 2,800 farms in the county are valued at over $360 million for their fruit and vegetable crops (Florida Strawberry Festival 2018; Nicholson 2016). Named for Henry B. Plant, a railroad magnate who helped transform Florida's tourism industry, the city welcomes visitors from around the world each spring, multiplying their population by more than 12 times for the event. The Strawberry Festival pays homage to one of America's favorite crops, listed in 2012 by *Produce News* as America's fifth favorite fresh fruit and first most valued berry. Although California supplies roughly 90 percent of domestic strawberries, and the United States imports just shy of 395 million pounds of fresh and frozen strawberries from Mexico each year, Plant City plays a critical role in providing the nation with fresh berries between November and March (Dimartino 2012; Bareuther 2016).

The Florida Strawberry Festival celebrates the nation's love of strawberries and the fruit's importance in the economy of the Sunshine State, which is home to nearly 11,000 acres of strawberry crops (Bareuther 2016). At the event, strawberry-themed gifts and food vendors stretch as far as the eye can see, and a mascot named Mr. Berry greets visitors. Festivalgoers dine on strawberry shortcakes topped with whipped cream (the festival claims its shortcakes are world famous), strawberry milkshakes, chocolate-covered strawberries, and bowls of fresh berries and purchase large flats of strawberries to take home.

Unusual treats are also found in copious quantities, like strawberry peanut brittle; strawberry lasagna; fried strawberry Twinkies; chicken and strawberry tacos; strawberry-basil hand pies; strawberry dessert pizzas; deep-fried strawberries stuffed with cream cheese; hamburgers topped with strawberry cookie crumbles and served on French toast "buns"; meatballs with strawberry jam glaze; and enormous Amish donuts topped with strawberries, whipped cream, and hot fudge. One of the only things missing from the festival's fare is alcohol, which is banned due to the festival's evangelical heritage and commitment to family values (Shopes 2013). A 2018 piece in the *Tampa Bay Times* noted that festival visitors are banned from bringing things like bottled water or pets to the event, but are technically allowed to bring in legal firearms as per the state's concealed carry permit (Cridlin 2018).

Events include races like adult and youth strawberry stemming contests, in which winners take home a trophy and assortment of chocolate-covered strawberries. In the agricultural division, crowds also enjoy events like lamb jumping contests (in which lambs are guided through an obstacle course of low jumps) and lamb costume contests. The festival also hosts a number of eating competitions in which contestants vie for the fastest times to guzzle down fare like strawberry soda, spaghetti topped with strawberries, garlic mashed potatoes topped with strawberry glaze, Amish donuts, and corn dogs. Competitors also race to polish off four-pound strawberry shortcakes to win the championship title and a trophy topped with a pig.

The festival is preceded by a grand parade and an accompanying youth parade through town, and throughout the festival's run, visitors attend afternoon and evening concerts. Past acts have included Alabama, Willie Nelson, Steven Tyler and the Loving Mary Band, Styx, Blake Shelton, Jerry Lee Lewis, Gary Allan, Reba McEntire, Vanilla Ice, Salt-n-Pepa, Brad Paisley, Englebert Humperdink, and Rascal Flatts, just to name a few. The festival also co-sponsors the Florida Strawberry Queen's Scholarship Pageant, in which local girls between the ages of 16 and 20 vie for college scholarships and the title of Strawberry Queen. Throughout their reign, queens wear an enormous crown that weighs nearly a pound, heavy enough to leave a mark in their foreheads that the pageant girls refer to as the "queen's dent" (Hull 2008).

The Strawberry Queen pageant goes back to 1930, and the rules for "Strawberry girls" still reflect traditional values from the past. According to the official rules, Hillsborough County's applicants must have been "born a female" (a phrase many believe is insensitive toward transgender individuals), must be single, and may never have been married or pregnant. No members of the court can get married or pregnant during their year's reign, or their title will be revoked, and they are not allowed to have visible tattoos or body piercings (other than pierced ears). Applicants are studied for moral character and any prior "dishonest, immoral, or indecent" behavior. The appearance and personality of the crowned queen "will be observed for desirable traits," and during her reign, she is expected to speak articulately on matters of the festival, Plant City, and the strawberry industry at large (Florida Strawberry Queens Pageant 2018).

In the last few decades, Plant City's strawberry industry has been met with agricultural challenges that are seen elsewhere in the nation, such as steeply rising production costs, residential development competing with agricultural zones for land, and reduced numbers of agricultural laborers from Mexico due to increased border security and other immigration measures. Despite the steep challenges facing strawberry farmers, the Strawberry Festival remains a large-scale ode to the much-loved berry and the people who devote their lives to it.

DESSERT

Wild strawberries have been eaten since ancient days, but the fruits weren't eaten in significant quantities, in part because they were small and tough. Varietals that were cultivated in later years evolved to be larger and more flavorful, helping the berry become more popular by the early 1800s. Today, a staggering 3 billion pounds of strawberries are grown each year in the United States (Grubinger 2012).

SUGGESTED PAIRINGS

See also: Ayden Collard Festival; California Avocado Festival; Grilled Cheese Festivals.

Entry best enjoyed while eating: A spinach salad with strawberries, walnuts, and feta cheese; spaghetti with strawberry-tomato sauce; strawberry-ginger lemonade; and a slice of warm strawberry-rhubarb pie topped with vanilla bean ice cream.

Further Reading

Bareuther, Carol M. 2016. "Despite Challenges, Florida Strawberry Business Is Growing." Produce Business, December 1, 2016. https://www.producebusiness.com/florida-strawberry-report

Cridlin, Jay. 2018. "Guns Are Allowed at the Florida Strawberry Festival. Beer, Bottled Water and Pets Are Not." *Tampa Bay Times*, February 28, 2018.

Dimartino, Christina. 2012. "In the Know: U.S. Berry Demand and Imports." *The Produce News*, September 17, 2012. http://theproducenews.com/markets-and-trends/8784-in-the-know-u-s-berry-demand-and-imports

Figureoa IV, Daniel. 2018. "Where Have All the Farmers Gone?" *Plant City Observer*, February 9, 2018. https://www.plantcityobserver.com/article/where-have-all-the-farmers-gone

Florida Strawberry Festival. 2018. http://flstrawberryfestival.com/information/

Florida Strawberry Queens Pageant. 2018. "Rules and Regulations." http://flstrawberryfestivalqueenspageant.org/wp-content/uploads/2018/10/2019-queen-rules.pdf

Grubinger, Vern. 2012. "History of the Strawberry." University of Vermont's Fruit and Vegetable Extension. https://www.uvm.edu/vtvegandberry/factsheets/strawberryhistory.html

Hull, Anne. 2008. "The Strawberry Girls." *The New Yorker Magazine*, August 11, 2008.

Nicholson, David. 2016. "Florida Strawberry Festival Attendance Was Highest in Years." *Tampa Bay Times*, March 15, 2016.

Shopes, Rich. 2013. "Strawberry Festival Fueled by Tradition, not Trends." *Tampa Bay Times*, February 27, 2013.

Food and Beverage Museums, International

STARTERS

Food and beverage museums range from broadly themed institutions that explore food heritage and culture in general to those devoted to a single specific food or drink. Brick-and-mortar and digital museums alike exist worldwide that invite viewers to learn more about the foodways, culinary practices, political issues, and food celebrations of countless cultures. International museums range from whimsical to political in nature, each telling a different story of how various food and beverages came to be in their culture and what those foods have meant to their communities.

ENTRÉE

Europe

Those who visit the Denmark Potato Museum might be amused to learn that the potato originated in South America and entered Danish culture in the eighteenth century, known at the time to the Danish people as "German lumps" (Danish Potato Museum 2019). There are many similar museums devoted to the humble potato, stretching from Prince Edward Island's Canadian Potato Museum to Belgium's Frietmuseum, honoring potatoes and Belgian's fries. Other single-food-specific institutions around the world include Germany's European Asparagus Museum, which celebrates Germany's significant asparagus season (and houses an Andy Warhol painting of the vegetable). A pint-sized Carrot Museum draws crowds to a tiny window-front display in an old electrical tower that houses a revolving display of carrot-themed memorabilia and tchotchkes (McBride Jacobson n.d.).

In Ireland, the Cork Butter Museum walks viewers through the history of what the museum deems the country's most important food export. Its exhibits highlight butter-making equipment and vintage butter wrappers in addition to historical overviews of Ireland's dairy industry at large. Another regional specialty is honored at Poland's Rogalowe Muzeum Poznania (Poznan Croissant Museum): the traditional Polish pastry called St. Martin's croissant. Folded 81 times, filled with poppyseed-almond filling, and topped with icing and nuts, these croissants have been deemed a Protected Global Indicator by the European Union (McBride Jacobson n.d.).

Italy, which has long been a popular country for culinary tourism, also hosts a number of food-themed museums. Southern Italy's Museo del Peperoncino (Peperoncino Museum) is located in the country's Calabria region. Since the early 1990s, the region has hosted an annual event called the Festival del Peperoncino (Chili Pepper Festival), which celebrates the country's spicy peppers with music, masked parades, chili pepper eating contests, and attempts at breaking the world record for the longest chili pepper garland.

Asia

Japan hosts no fewer than three museums dedicated to ramen, a dish that consists of noodles, broth, and often an assortment of meats and vegetables. Yokohama, Japan is home to two museums. One is the Shin-Yokohama Ramen Museum, which doubles as a historical museum documenting the history of the beloved noodles and a noodle-themed amusement park. It also houses a 1950s-themed food court with various ramen restaurants. The second is called The CupNoodle Museum, which pays homage to the instant version of ramen noodles sold cheaply in Styrofoam cups. Visitors can make their own ramen to take home and enjoy a virtual tour through a simulated ramen factory. Osaka, Japan, also celebrates instant ramen noodles with the Momofuku Ando Instant Ramen Museum, which features an interactive theater shaped like a noodle cup and a tunnel designed from 800 ramen packages.

In Korea, Seoul's Museum Kimchikan documents kimchi's 1,500-year run as one of Korea's staple foods. The museum houses ancient texts devoted to the spicy fermented cabbage, and it has helped spread the appeal of the dish internationally during the 1988 Seoul Olympics (McBride Jacobson n.d.). The popular Chinese snack of fish balls—boiled or fried cakes made with fish paste and spices—is featured in Taiwan's Tengfeng Fish Ball Museum, where visitors can roll their own fish balls by hand and learn about environmental impacts created by demand for the treats.

Latin America

It is altogether fitting that Brazil is the locale of the Museu do Café (Coffee Museum), as the country is one of the largest coffee exporters on earth, and the industry generates millions of jobs for Brazilians. Located in the city of Santos's former Coffee Stock Exchange building, the museum documents coffee's history and tracks its cultural importance through the ages. Argentina's El Museo del Vino y la Vendimia (Wine and Harvest Museum) illustrates wine's integral role in the country's history. Exhibits include 4,500 artifacts that were used in Argentina's early winemaking days by immigrants from Europe. In Mexico, the Museo del Tequila and Mezcal hosts exhibitions on the country's staple alcoholic beverages of tequila and mezcal (made from agave), as well as Mariachi music.

DESSERT

The Disgusting Food Museum in Malmö, Sweden, boasts "80 of the world's most disgusting foods," including Peruvian roasted guinea pigs, Icelandic aged shark, Guamanian fruit bat soup, and cheese with maggots from Sardinia. The website offers the tongue-in-cheek note that the museum is just across a bridge from Copenhagen, "and yes, Danes are also welcome."

SUGGESTED PAIRINGS

See also: Baby Food; Chocolate Events and Destinations; Food and Beverage Museums, U.S.

Entry best enjoyed while eating: Penne alla vodka, inspired by Russia's Museum of Russia's Vodka; mixed greens topped with mustard dressing, as a nod to Colman's Mustard Shop and Museum in Norwich, UK; and a slice of German banana cake after visiting Germany's Bananenmuseum.

Further Reading

The Danish Museum, Otterup. 2019. Visit Denmark. https://www.visitdenmark.com/denmark/danish-potato-museum-otterup-gdk623931

The Disgusting Food Museum. n.d. https://disgustingfoodmuseum.com/

Langan, Sheila. 2019. "IC Health Month: Kerrygold Butter in Your Morning Coffee Is Our Favorite Health Craze." *Irish Central*, January 9, 2019.

McBride Jacobson, Molly. n.d. "Thirty-Eight Museums Devoted Entirely to Food, From the Delicious to the Disgusting." Atlas Obscura. https://www.atlasobscura.com/lists/38-museums-devoted-to-a-single-food

Rojas, Diana. 2018. "These Are the Five Latin American Food and Drink Museums You Need to Know." *Latin American Post*, June 25, 2018. https://latinamericanpost.com/21788-these-are-the-five-latin-american-food-and-drink-museums-that-you-have-to-know

Food and Beverage Museums, U.S.

STARTERS

Food museums in the U.S. catalog and extol the virtues of foods and beverages. These museums range from small organizations highlighting single ingredients to large-scale, elaborate exhibits documenting the history of a type of cuisine. Drawing on American history, sociology, anthropology, and popular culture, American food museums highlight the fascinating role that food has played in the country's past and present and speculates how food and society's preference for foods will evolve in the future.

ENTRÉE

One of the testaments to food's rising role in popular culture is New York City's Museum of Food and Drink (MOFAD), which began in 2013 as a high-energy, entertaining traveling exhibit that demonstrated a machine called a "puffer gun" that dramatically produced puffed cereal in the 1930s. In 2015, the museum received a permanent space in Brooklyn. Exhibits encourage visitors to make use of all of their senses and promote topics such as culinary history and preservation of endangered culinary arts. New York is also home to the Jell-O Gallery Museum, run by the Historical Society of the town of Le Roy, which pays homage to the fruit-flavored gelatin dessert that became popular thanks in large part to a marketing campaign launched in 1902 promoting Jell-O as America's "most famous" dessert.

Up the coast, the Maine Coast Sardine History Museum documents the important role that sardines and the sardine canneries played in the early twentieth century. More modern-day items are highlighted in Northampton Massachusetts' Beer Can Museum, which hosts a display of 4,000 beer cans (and also serves as a working bar and pool hall).

Pennsylvania is home to a number of food museums. The Hershey Story museum on Chocolate Avenue in Hershey, Pennsylvania, is part of multiple visitor centers that make up Hershey's Chocolate World, operated by Hershey Foods. Visitors to Chocolate World can take a chocolate-making tour, invent their own candy bar at a factory, watch a theatrical history of Hershey's chocolate, and learn about founder Milton Hershey during a trolley tour. The museum offers more information about Hershey's life, including exhibits documenting his innovations in the mass production of milk chocolate and his wide-scale marketing efforts. A smaller chocolate collection can be found at the Candy Americana Museum located in Lititz, Pennsylvania's Wilbur Chocolate Store. The museum houses a collection assembled by Penny Buzzard, wife of the Wilbur Chocolate company's former president. Penny's chocolate memorabilia includes historic porcelain chocolate pots from Europe and Asia, early forms of candy-making machinery, and over a thousand types of chocolate tins and other boxes.

For those seeking a savory accompaniment to their chocolate fix, the Big Mac Museum in Irwin, Pennsylvania, documents the history of McDonald's iconic double cheeseburger. Greeted by a 14-foot-tall Big Mac statue, visitors can order food from the working restaurant section and admire displays of items like a Big Mac Sauce gun and a display of the evolution of Big Mac packaging (Roadside America). Not to be outdone by McDonald's, the chain Wendy's displays memorabilia at the Wendy's headquarters in Dublin, Ohio, including a $105,000 Waterford Crystal reproduction of a Wendy's hamburger and a life-size bronze sculpture of founder Dave Thomas.

Condiments are not left out of American museums, such as the International Vinegar Museum in Roslyn, South Dakota. The museum hosts an annual Vinegar Festival and parade in the town. The National Mustard Museum in Middleton, Wisconsin, boasts a collection of 6,090 mustards from all over the world. The museum was founded by Barry Levenson, a former Assistant Attorney General for the state. In his early years of juggling legal work with opening the museum, Levenson once argued a case before the U.S. Supreme court with a small jar of mustard in his pocket that he'd snagged from his hotel, intent on adding it to his collection. Wisconsin is also home to the National Dairy Shrine, a museum in Ft. Atkinson that blends local history with the story of dairy production in the United States.

The story of flour production is also a significant one in American history, and the Mill City Museum in Minneapolis, Minnesota, documents the history, preservation, and architecture of wheat flour milling, housed in the ruins of what was once a flagship mill in the region. Another regional fixture is the Southern Food and Beverage Museum (SoFAB) in New Orleans, Louisiana, which documents all things related to the unique and multifaceted aspects of Southern cuisine. SoFAB also houses the Museum of the American Cocktail, which showcases exhibits pertaining to a 200-year history of cocktail beverages in the country. Waco, Texas, is home to an institution that focuses on a singular drink: the Dr Pepper Museum. Considered the oldest major soft drink in the nation, the museum documents stories like the soda's introduction to the greater public at the 1904 World's Fair, an exposition that also saw the first mass implementation of ice cream cones and hot dog and hamburger buns.

Further west, the Museum of Ice Cream in Los Angeles and San Francisco, California, invites visitors to celebrate ice cream in whimsical fashion through a series of interactive displays, including a swimming pool of plastic rainbow sprinkles. Initially founded in New York City, the interactive art exhibit was founded by Maryellis Bunn, named in *Forbes*' "30 Under 30" list in 2018, with the intention of creating an interactive space that spoke to millennial audiences. Los Angeles is also the future home of LA Plaza Cocina, a museum in the works that will highlight the important role that Mexican food has played in the city's history. An extension of museum and cultural center LA Plaza de cultura y Artes, Cocina will include lectures, workshops, and classes on Mexican food. Other emerging American food institutions include various pizza museums. Two opened in Chicago and pizza-rival-city New York in 2018, each featuring histories of the regional styles of pizza found in both locations. In 2012, *Washington Post* writer Jim Shahin proposed a National Barbecue Museum in his monthly grilling column. Shahin suggested that the museum could be a facet of Washington D.C.'s Smithsonian

National Museum of American History, with regional outposts in key barbecue cities in the South that drill more deeply into each city's barbecue specialty and history.

DESSERT

Founded in Arlington, Massachusetts, the Burnt Food Museum is an ode to food that has burned to a crisp while the cook became distracted with other matters. Museum curator Deborah Henson-Conant cheekily describes the museum's artifacts as the "greatest original carbonized culinary artwork in the world" and invites people to submit burnt food to be recognized by the museum, but display it in their kitchens at home.

SUGGESTED PAIRINGS

See also: Barbecue; Chocolate Events and Destinations; Food and Beverage Museums, International; Latin American Cuisine.

Entry best enjoyed while eating: SPAM-fried rice, inspired by Austin, Minnesota's SPAM Museum (which pays tribute to a canned pork product that became popular in World War II); salt-and-pepper shrimp as an ode to the Salt and Pepper Shaker Museum in Gatlinburg, Tennessee; and a slice of fruitcake left out to age several days, inspired by a 109-year-old fruitcake tier featured at the Hurricane Valley Pioneer Heritage Museum in Hurricane, Utah.

Further Reading
"Big Mac Museum Restaurant." n.d. Roadside America. https://www.roadsideamerica.com/story/16517
Finney, Teresa. 2019. "Mexican Food Museum and Educational Kitchen to Open in Los Angeles." *Forbes*, January 28, 2019.
"History of Dr. Pepper." n.d. Dr Pepper Museum. https://drpeppermuseum.com/history/
"The History of Jello." n.d. Jello Gallery. http://www.jellogallery.org/history.html
McBride Jacobson, Molly. n.d. "38 Museums Devoted Entirely to Food, From the Delicious to the Disgusting." Atlas Obscura. https://www.atlasobscura.com/lists/38-museums-devoted-to-a-single-food
Shahin, Jim. 2012. "A Modest Proposal for a Real BBQ Museum." *The Washington Post*, October 16, 2012.
Thornton, Denise. 2010. "Spreading the Love." *On Wisconsin*, University of Wisconsin-Madison. Summer, 2010.
Wilbur Chocolate Store History. n.d. http://www.wilburbuds.com/Our-Candy-Store

Food Failures

STARTERS

In recent years, failed attempts at recreating high-end food have become a growing entertainment trend. Culinary television hosts have historically worked hard to avoid and hide mistakes, and home cooks are typically more likely to quietly slide meals gone wrong into the trash than to show their disasters to company. However, food failures have become a source of entertainment to many in recent years, as seen in articles, websites, and even television shows devoted entirely to these culinary mishaps. The concept of "food fails" also extends to snafus committed by high-profile culinary professionals, harsh or sarcastic negative reviews by food critics, and food made by amateurs and professionals alike that look or taste particularly unappetizing or poorly made.

ENTRÉE

"(There's) something deeper to the current fascination with bad food, whether it's unhealthy, inelegant, unpopular, or just plain ugly," Irina Dumitrescu wrote in a 2016 *Atlantic* essay about pop culture's current interest in food that bucks common conventions. One of the earliest viral successes of this trend was in 1999, when writer James Lileks began posting images from a humorous commentary about stomach-turning recipes he found in cookbooks from the 1940s, 1950s, and 1960s. The popularity of his website, which he refers to as "an individually curated pop-culture museum," spurred a related book publication in 2001. Lileks employs a pithy, sarcastic wit alongside photos of often unrecognizable or bizarrely staged foods, such as his captions: "This is cold curried chicken-paste arranged in the shape of a crown. May I never write that sentence again." A website called Cake-Wrecks also garnered significant internet popularity starting in 2008. Founded by blogger Jen Yates, the website features photos sent in by readers of cakes that are unintentionally funny. Many of the cakes show overly literal or misheard directions between customers and the bakery staff, such as a cake from a grocery store with piped letters reading:
Best Wishes Suzanne
Under Neat That
We Will Miss You

In the age of humorous internet images called memes, one popular gag included the hashtag #NailedIt, often documenting a food failure. In 2018, Netflix released an eponymous reality competition show inspired by the meme. In *Nailed It!*, which is in its third season, amateur bakers with poor culinary skills attempt recreating high-end cakes and other confections, to humorous and often disastrous effects. The show highlights how challenging it can be to recreate chic-looking recipes, particularly those highlighted on social media sites like Pinterest, which had an estimated 250 million monthly viewers and an annual revenue of roughly $700 million in 2018 (Lunden 2019). In recent years, many have criticized social media for fueling users' perfectionist tendencies and harming users' confidence and self-esteem. In an era of food perfectionism, the number of emerging television shows, websites, and articles devoted to food failures indicates the humor (and relief) many find in imperfect and anything-but-chic kitchen exploits.

Negative restaurant reviews often have a pop culture following of their own, as well. In 2012, *New York Times* food columnist Pete Wells wrote a scathing review of Guy Fieri's Manhattan restaurant, Guy's American Kitchen & Bar. The review was formulated as a series of rhetorical questions for the chef, in which Wells mocked the establishment and menu. Despite its publication toward the end of the year, the column became the fifth most emailed *Times* article of 2012 and received more than a thousand comments. Similar restaurant reviews have also gone viral, such as restaurant critic Jay Rayner's review in *The Guardian* of London restaurant The Beast, referring to it as both "unintentionally silly" and "ruinously pricey" (Parker 2016; Rayner 2014).

Even well-intentioned press about food has been ushered into food failure culture, such as many critical responses Martha Stewart received about photos she posted on Twitter of various restaurant meals. The photos featured things like soup with splattered broth all over the rim of the bowl and out-of-focus, vomitous-looking "pasta handkerchiefs." Her Tweets garnered attention such as Buzzfeed's articles "Someone Needs to tell Martha Stewart her Food Tweets are Gross," followed by a redemptive "Martha Stewart Finally Stopped Taking Gross Photos" in 2014. The improvement of her photography suggested that even a woman deemed a "lifestyle and media mogul" by the press felt the pressure to make her food look more pristine on social media.

DESSERT

One recurring blooper on the CakeWrecks website includes cakes adorned with images of USB drives, instead of what the customer wanted: a photo that was digitally saved on a USB drive that they gave to the bakery's staff. In one such mishap, a baker photocopied the thumb drive containing the customer's desired photo, printed out an edible picture of the thumb drive itself, and carefully applied the picture to the top of a cake.

SUGGESTED PAIRINGS

See also: Fieri, Guy; Food and Beverage Museums, International; Food and Beverage Museums, U.S.; Television, Food Channels on.

Entry best enjoyed while eating: Eggs Benedict served with a broken Hollandaise sauce; Steak Diane, in which the brandy does not ignite, but the wall next to the stove does; a baguette that's hard enough to be used for softball practice; and a cupcake decorated with a design that's supposed to be a penguin but actually just looks like a melting joystick riddled with tumors.

Further Reading

Dumitrescu, Irina. 2016. "The Curious Appeal of 'Bad' Food." *The Atlantic*, August 5, 2016.

Lileks, James. 2019. The Gallery of Regrettable Food. http://www.lileks.com/institute/gallery/index.html

Lunden, Ingrid. 2019. "Pinterest Sets IPO Range at $15–17, Valuing It at $10.6B vs Previous Valuation of $12.3B." Tech Crunch, April 8, 2019. https://techcrunch.com/2019/04/08/pinterest-ipo-range/

Parker, Ian. 2016. "Pete Wells Has His Knives Out." *The New Yorker*, September 5, 2016.

Rayner, Jay. 2014. "Knives Out: Why We Love Reading Cruel Restaurant Reviews." *The Guardian*, October 30, 2014.

Wells, Pete. 2012. "Restaurant Review: Guy's American Kitchen & Bar in Times Square." *The New York Times*. November 13, 2012.

Yates, Jen. 2019. https://www.cakewrecks.com

Food Trucks

STARTERS

Food trucks, which are broadly defined as any large vehicle from which food is sold, have a long history in the United States. Many food trucks in the United States offer one specific type of fare, such as Hawaiian shave ice, grilled cheese, or donuts. Others offer a wide range of appetizers, tapas, entrées, beverages, and/or desserts, and virtually every type of diet and cuisine can be found in mobile form. Their history traces back to the chuck wagons that fed cowboys during the Reconstruction era (1865–1877). In recent decades, food trucks used to be sparse in numbers and most commonly found near construction sites and amusement parks, but their popularity exploded in the early twenty-first century.

Food trucks' rising star in popular culture is considered to be from a confluence of the nation's growing appetite for international cuisine, as well as economic and social changes that took place during the Great Recession in the late 2000s. In 2017, food truck revenue was valued at $2.7 billion, nearly four times more than the same industry's revenue of $650 million in 2012 (White 2017). Food trucks' role in popular culture has expanded into the entertainment industry, as well, including television shows like *The Great Food Truck Race* (2010–) and *Food Truck Nation* (2018–).

ENTRÉE

In the United States, food trucks have evolved from small, locally owned businesses that specialized in specific types of fare to a fast-growing arm of the food industry. Some food trucks are family owned and locally operated, whereas others are run as franchises or operate as a promotional or catering extension of nationwide chain restaurants like Taco Bell and Applebee's. According to a 2017 market research report by Food Truck Empire, 35 percent of food trucks are owned by individuals, 55 percent are owned by franchises and restaurants, and 10 percent are run by organizations like charities and schools. Fifty percent of food truck investors are over the age of 46, and a whopping 80 percent of food truck owners are men.

Despite the rapid growth within the industry, only 5 percent of owners expand their business to more than one mobile unit. Many food truck proprietors use the venture as a test or starting point to launch their own restaurant or catering business. The average food truck rakes in $750–$1,000 an hour at peak times, typically split between two and four employees, and can bring in upward of $400,000

Food trucks line the street for Food Truck Thursday, a weekly event in midtown Atlanta, Georgia, 2014. The diverse array of options, convenience, and price point of food truck offerings have helped catapult this form of street food into a notable craze worldwide. (Russ Ensley/Dreamstime.com)

a year. New trucks cost between $150,000 and $200,000 on average, roughly a fifth of the cost of operating a restaurant (Food Truck Empire 2017; Caminiti 2017).

The first recognized form of the food truck was the chuck wagon. On the open range, cooks used chuck wagons to store and prepare meals for cowboys on cattle drives in the American West. Undesirable cuts of beef were often referred to as "chuck" in this era, and the term became synonymous with "food" for men on the prairie. The wagons were pulled by mules or oxen and typically stored staples like biscuits, cornbread, black-eyed peas, corn, bison and beef steaks, coffee, water, skillets, and utensils. An ambitious cattleman on the Texas frontier named Charles Goodnight (1836–1929) is credited with inventing the first chuck wagon. Goodnight served as both a Texas Ranger and a Confederate soldier in the Civil War and spearheaded the American cattle ranching industry. In 1866, he designed a chuck wagon using an army surplus Studebaker wagon that was modified to house a hinged cook's table.

A second horse-powered food trend called the "lunch wagon" caught on the following decade. This mobile eatery was devised by a man named Walter Scott in 1872 as a way to feed throngs of hungry workers leaving factory jobs late at night. Scott served homemade meals out of a freight wagon, inspiring many others to begin nighttime lunch wagon business ventures, as well. These lunch wagons are considered by some scholars to have paved the way for diners, which serve patrons

24 hours a day across the country (Nemick 2016). In the late 1800s, sausage carts referred to as "dog wagons" popped up on a number of Ivy League campuses when hungry university students proved to be excellent customers. A famous hot dog wagon appeared in 1936—the Oscar Meyer Weiner Mobile, which has since been transformed into a hot dog-shaped vehicle that travels the country.

Another precursor to the food truck appeared in 1917: mobile canteens that fed hungry soldiers in the army. In the 1950s, ice cream trucks became a cultural fixture in the United States, followed by trucks serving tacos and other small entrées that catered to areas like construction sites where hungry laborers could grab quick, inexpensive meals. The first "real" food truck has been credited by some to a man named Raul Martinez who fashioned an ice cream truck into a taco truck in 1974. In the 1990s and 2000s, food trucks that had once been referred to pejoratively as "roach coaches" were rebranded as sources for "gourmet" food, a term that became abundant in food truck culture. In 1993, a truck called Giovanni's inspired a cult following for the sautéed garlic shrimp and rice it served on the North Shore of O'ahu, Hawaii.

In 2008, a food truck called Kogi in Los Angeles, California, sparked what has widely been hailed as a food truck revolution. Its head chef, Roy Choi, helped develop a Mexican-Korean fusion menu with highlights like short-rib tacos and chicken-kimchi burritos. Kogi's playful and unusual menu consisted of gourmet ingredient pairings at concession stand price, a welcome offering to patrons during the financial hit of the Great Recession (2007–2009). In 2010, *Food & Wine* awarded Choi with their prestigious "Best New Chef" title: a first for a food truck chef. Soon, others began emulating Choi's hip vibe and creative twist on the food truck, particularly Kogi's marketing strategy of notifying patrons about the truck's schedule via social media.

In the decade that followed, food trucks saw explosive growth in popularity, and their locations expanded beyond construction sites to breweries, music events, festivals, parades, clubs, and other cultural gatherings. Today, many cities have embraced food-truck-centric events, such as Denver, Colorado, which hosts upward of 70 gourmet food trucks in one park three days a week for six months each year. Food trucks have been so endearing to Americans that they have found their way to the small and large screen, alike. *The Great Food Truck Race* (2010–), which has run for 10 seasons on Food Network, features a competition between several food truck owners to see who can sell the most meals on the road in a cross-country race.

Cooking Channel's *Food Truck Nation* (2018–) follows chef Brad Miller as he interviews innovative food truck chefs about their notable cuisines In New Zealand, *The Food Truck* (2011–2013) explores ways that food truck culture can offer alternatives to eating junk food. A 2014 film called *Chef* starring Jon Favreau, Dustin Hoffman, and Sofia Vergara follows the story of a high-end chef who leaves the restaurant business to rekindle his passion for food behind the wheel of a food truck. Food trucks are often seen as a launching point for chefs who aspire to run their own restaurants, as well as a landing place for chefs leaving the restaurant industry, motivated by a desire to reclaim more control and a more direct connection between their food and their customers.

SUGGESTED PAIRINGS

See also: Asian American Cuisine; Films, Food in; Grilled Cheese Festivals; Latin American Cuisine.

Entry best enjoyed while eating: A vegan chipotle seitan breakfast burrito with kale (Cinnamon Snail; New York, New York), macaroni and cheese served in a grilled cheese sandwich (Mac Mart; Philadelphia, Pennsylvania), red lentils and lamb stew (Saba's Ethiopian Food; Denver, Colorado), and dark chocolate crème brulee infused with sea salt and raspberry (Torched Goodness; Eudora, Kansas).

Further Reading

Caminiti, Susan. 2017. "The Ten Most Popular Food Trucks in America." CNBC, April 7, 2017. https://www.cnbc.com/2017/04/07/10-most-popular-food-trucks-in-america-.html

Craig, Bruce, and Colleen Taylor Sen. 2013. *Street Food Around the World.* Santa Barbara: ABC-CLIO.

Food Truck Empire. 2017. https://foodtruckempire.com/news/most-food-trucks/

Geller, Matt. 2016. "How Did Food Trucks Become So Popular in Los Angeles?" National Food Truck Association. http://www.nationalfoodtrucks.org/2016/12/21/how-did-food-trucks-become-so-popular-in-los-angeles/

LaFuente, Cat. 2018. "The Untold Truth of Food Trucks." Mashed. https://www.mashed.com/56721/untold-truth-food-trucks/

Nemick, Cassidy. 2016. "The Evolution of the American Diner." http://scalar.usc.edu/works/the-evolution-of-the-american-diner/the-original-lunch-wagons

White, John. 2017. "Why Food Truck Businesses Are Revving Up." https://www.inc.com/john-white/why-food-truck-businesses-are-revving-up.html

Galloping Gourmet, The (1968–1971)

STARTERS

The Galloping Gourmet was a television cooking show starring British host Graham Kerr (1934–). Running from 1969 through 1971, the half-hour show was filmed in Canada and broadcast in the United States and various British commonwealth countries. Kerr mixed cooking instruction with humor as he promoted cuisines from all over the world. The show ended prematurely when Kerr and his wife sustained injuries in a vehicle accident, but reruns of the program continued for decades afterward.

ENTRÉE

The Galloping Gourmet has been described as irreverent, entertaining, decadent, and even a pop cultural phenomenon by various reviewers. Food writer Kathleen Collins described Kerr's show as "the first cooking show to aggressively capitalize on the entertainment potential of the medium" (2009, 106). Kerr's large persona and comedy routines provided a stark contrast to the cooking tutorials demonstrated by and for housewives that were common in that era. The show always began with Kerr running through the audience, hopping up on stage, and jumping over a chair, all while holding a glass of wine (which didn't spill, thanks to a sneaky square of plastic wrap tucked over the top).

The Galloping Gourmet was part of a cultural trend that helped encourage Americans to expand their dietary horizons. Kerr highlighted international cuisines on his show, traveling to foreign locales and starting his shows with pretaped segments highlighting foods and cultural notes from various states and foreign countries. On any given episode, Kerr would prepare dishes such as crab meat baked in phyllo pastry from Australia, rabbit in wine sauce from Italy, or pan-fried red snapper in a tomato-herb sauce from Mexico. Kerr's program has drawn many comparisons over the years to his predecessor, Julia Child, and her show *The French Chef* (1962–1966).

Much like Child, Kerr brought a relaxed approach to cooking in which perfect etiquette was eschewed. He presented cooking as an experiment in which mistakes would happen and could be cured if the cook maintained a cheerful outlook and a few generous sips of wine (Child and Kerr's open consumption of alcohol on television bordered on being seen as scandalous in this era). Where Child was known for dousing her food in butter, Kerr was also renowned for cooking sinfully fatty cuts of meat with generous helpings of things like cream. One notable difference between the appeal of *The French Chef* and *The Galloping Gourmet* was Kerr's sex appeal. Throughout his show, he elicited peals of laughter from the live audience, and he would end the program by bringing a member of the audience on stage to sit at a candlelit table and share a taste of the dish he'd just made. Later, Kerr publicly admitted to having several extramarital affairs over the course of his career (Neman 2014).

New York Times journalist Kirk Johnson attributes the show's significant success to the positive and relaxed message it conveyed amid immense upheaval from civil rights protests and the Vietnam War during this era. Food writer Kathleen Collins argued that the appeal of the show went beyond "hedonism, more just like joy," noting that the crux of the show was in the positive atmosphere viewers associated with his cooking adventures (Johnson 2017). As such, the mid-1960s and early 1970s seem to be the period in American history in which food television made a significant pivot toward entertainment, acceptance, and the enthusiasm to broaden American's cuisine beyond the national borders.

ACCOMPANIED BY

Graham Kerr was born in London in 1934 and was raised as an only child by parents who became hotel managers after World War II. Living on-site where his parents worked, Kerr described being "left to his own devices" much of the time and often found himself in the hotel's kitchens helping out (*Kolbe Times* Staff 2017). He served as a catering officer in the British Armed Forces and the Royal New Zealand Air Force before forging a guest role on a television show led him to host his own cooking show.

Kerr met his future wife, Treena Kerr (1934–2015), in school at the age of 11. The pair married in 1955 and stepped into the hotel restaurant and management business with the help of his parents. Despite not having any formal experience in television, Treena went on to become a producer for *The Galloping Gourmet*. Among her many comedic contributions was the idea of the infamous opening gag to have Graham lope through the audience and leap over chairs. The show's run was cut short in 1971 after the couple suffered severe injuries in a car accident (*Washington Post* journalist Rebekah Denn noted the ironic detail that the Kerrs' RV was rear-ended by a truck hauling vegetables.) In the years that followed, Treena suffered numerous health issues, and the couple adopted a zealous loyalty to health foods and the Christian faith. Treena passed away shortly before the couple's sixtieth wedding anniversary.

DESSERT

After viewing Kerr's cooking program (dubbed "Eggs with Flight Attendant Kerr") in New Zealand, his wife Treena told him that he was "the most unutterably boring man in the whole world." As a seasoned actress, her advice was to "make 'em laugh by any means, and you will have earned the right to inform;" a formula that resonated strongly with not only Kerr's audience but also future cooking audiences to come (Neman 2014).

SUGGESTED PAIRINGS

See also: Beard, James; Bourdain, Anthony; Child, Julia; Wine and Spirits.

Entry best enjoyed while eating: Grapefruit stuffed with crab meat and peppers; deep-fried crepes filled with melted cheese; a pineapple filled with bananas, lime and pineapple gelatin, and cream; and a glass of '69 Chablis.

Further Reading

Collins, Kathleen. 2009. *Watching What We Eat: The Evolution of Television Cooking Shows*. London: Bloomsbury.

Denn, Rebekah. 2018. "The Galloping Gourmet Made Cooking Fun Long Before Food Network. Now He's Back." *Washington Post*, May 11, 2018.

Johnson, Kirk. 2017. "A Slower Pace for the 'Galloping Gourmet.'" *The New York Times*, January 11, 2017.

Kolbe Times Staff. 2017. "A Conversation with Graham Kerr, the Galloping Gourmet." June 3, 2017. https://www.kolbetimes.com/graham-kerr/

Neman, Daniel. 2014. "The Galloping Gourmet Is Still Galloping Along." *The Saint Louis Dispatch*, January 22, 2014.

Garten, Ina (1948–)

STARTERS

Ina Garten is an American celebrity cook and author, best known for her *Food Network* television show, cookbooks, and food emporium in Long Island, New York. Garten's work in the food industry began with her purchase of the Barefoot Contessa food store in the late 1970s, which inspired her to master a variety of cooking, entertaining, and food presentation techniques. She has written and published 10 cookbooks since 1999 and contributes to a variety of magazine columns about cooking and entertaining. Her television show *The Barefoot Contessa* launched in 2002 and has run for 23 consecutive seasons. She has made a number of additional television appearances on shows such as *The Chew*, *The Today Show*, and a variety of *Food Network* shows in addition to her own. Garten's brand has also grown to include a line of baking and cooking products in partnership with gourmet food company Stonewall Kitchen.

ENTRÉE

Ina Garten, née Rosenberg, was born in Brooklyn, NY, in 1948. In a 2015 interview with *CBS Sunday Morning*, Garten joked that she became a cook as an adult because she was never allowed in the kitchen as a child. In the 1950s, mothers were traditionally the ones who prepared meals, and Ina's job, she was told, "was to study" (Altshuctz, 2015). Garten met her future husband Jeffrey at

Celebrity cook and television personality Ina Garten appears with her husband, Jeffrey Garten, at the premiere of the film *Mary Poppins Returns* in Los Angeles, California. The cook devoted an episode of her show *Barefoot Contessa* to hosting a reunion for members of the film's cast and crew, with British-themed treats such as meringue clouds for dessert. (Hutchinsphoto/Dreamstime.com)

the young age of 15, and the couple married in 1968.

In a rough parallel to Julia Child's life, the early years of Garten's career and marriage weren't spent pursuing a profession as a chef. Instead, she started out as a nuclear budget and policy analyst (or as she described it in an Epicurious interview, "a nuclear energy policy wonk") in the White House's Office of Management and Budget. Just as Julia Child was daydreaming about food while working in the espionage field of the Office of Strategic Services, so, too, was Garten while she analyzed nuclear decisions under the Ford and Carter administrations.

Life changed for Ina when she discovered a food store for sale in East Hampton, NY, called The Barefoot Contessa, the title of a 1954 Ava Gardner and Humphrey Bogart film. Garten was feeling restless in her career and impulsively made an offer on the store. The move would propel her toward becoming a household name, just as the film *Barefoot Contessa* followed the story of Ava Gardner's character being propelled to stardom after her film debut. Up to that point, Garten had been a self-taught cook. In 1971, Garten began following the recipes in Julia Child's cookbooks, practicing the art of French cooking with Child's advice as her guide (and with White House dinner guests to test her new skills for). The store presented her with the opportunity to learn a new trade: the ins and outs of buying, preparing, displaying, and marketing foods and recipes.

In a 1981 *New York Times* story called "Exchanging Standard Careers for Dreams," Garten (then still relatively unknown in the food world) was featured as a daughter who'd horrified her parents by giving up a "prestigious White House job" to "open a grocery store." Garten was quoted as saying "My job in Washington was intellectually stimulating, but it wasn't me (. . .) I don't know what it's going to be after this, but I can't stand still." The food shop became immensely popular for both its food and its design and styling. True to her desire to not "stand still," Garten sold the shop to her employees and began to write her first cookbook, honing in on her desire to test and share recipes with a wider audience.

The cookbook flew off shelves, much to Garten (and her publisher's) surprise, and within a few years, she was reluctantly persuaded to bring her craft to television. Not one for dramatic or show-stopping entertainment, Garten's approach to cooking on her *Food Network* show was very different from many of her pan-blazing, sous-chef-scolding competitors. In contrast, *The Barefoot Contessa* is filmed in a custom-built barn-style home next door to the Garten's house in the Hamptons. The space was designed for the production to maximize getting beautiful shots of Garten's dishes, which included things like prosciutto-roasted sea bass, provincial apple tarts, roasted root vegetables, and green salads tossed with large, roasted chicken pieces and drippings straight from the roasting pan.

Her preferred recipes are those that are typically familiar and homey—often simple in nature, but elegant in presentation and in taste. "How easy is that?" is both her best-known catchphrase and the atmosphere of the show. In 2007, upward of 5.9 million viewers were tuning in to see her weekly show on the Food Network, drawn in by her recipes, entertaining tips, or simply the enjoyment of watching Garten's cheerful approach to cooking. In a 2017 interview with *Time* magazine, Garten shared the story of a time she was walking along Madison Avenue in New York City and was stopped by a woman in a fur coat as well as a truck driver in short order to commend her show and cookbooks. "That's the world of food," she told the magazine. "It's everybody."

In keeping with her all-inclusive nature, Garten tests her recipes numerous times until they meet her approval and then gives the instructions to her assistant—a nonprofessional—to test. Garten notes the mistakes or questions her assistant has and modifies the instructions in her recipes accordingly to prevent readers from encountering the same problems. This concern toward the end user is in polar opposition to an element used in many cooking competition shows, such as *The Great British Bake-Off*'s technical challenge, in which bakers receive recipes that intentionally omit instructions that could prevent disasters with their dishes.

Described by PBS journalist Hari Sreenivasan as "one of the most successful, prolific women in America," Garten has created a world in her cookbooks and shows that resonates strongly with viewers who want to find happiness and simplicity in their kitchens and beautiful presentations and warm camaraderie at their dinner tables. In a remarkable career arc from having no formal training at all to teaching herself the skills necessary to train mass numbers of fans to perfect hordes of recipes, Garten's life story almost seems like a fantasy. In turn, many of her fans look to her shows and books in the hopes of transforming the chore of grocery shopping and food preparation into a dinner (and home) that looks as if it, too, is out of a fantasy.

ACCOMPANIED BY

Jeffrey Garten

Ina and Jeffrey met when she visited her brother at Dartmouth College, where Jeffrey was a student. After their wedding in 1968, Jeffrey served for four years in the Vietnam War, during which time Ina took flying lessons and earned her pilot's license. Upon returning to civilian life, Jeffrey earned his MA and PhD at Johns Hopkins, worked on Wall Street, and held senior positions in the administrations of Presidents Nixon, Ford, Carter, and Clinton. Additionally, he became vice president and managing director at Lehman Brothers and entered academia as the dean emeritus and professor of international trade and finance at Yale University's School of Management. Jeffrey's high-powered career takes a quiet back seat in the *Barefoot Contessa*; many of the recipes and meals Ina creates are for Jeffrey, and he is often featured as a guest star on the show. Ina's tenth cookbook is an ode to her husband, *Cooking for Jeffrey*.

Assistants

Despite the impressive number of writing assignments, television shows, and products Garten might be working on at any one time, her team typically consists of two assistants, Barbara Libath and Lidey Heuck. The two help her test recipes and identify areas that could use more fool proofing—tips for success, more explanation, or defining cooking terms. Libath is somewhat close in age to Garten, and the pair have worked together for years. Heuck graduated from Bowdoin College in 2013, helping to lend the perspective of Garten's somewhat younger viewers. In an interview with *Eater* magazine, Garten described an edit she had recently made to a recipe for fig jam based on Heuck's reaction: "she (. . .) put all the stuff in the pot and she thought 'how is this going to happen?' (. . .) So I just wrote in the recipe, 'Don't worry! It's going to work!'" (Sicha 2015).

DESSERT

In a *Vanity Fair* interview following the Proust Questionnaire (an interview parlor game coined by postmodern author Marcel Proust), Garten cites:

- "Cilantro and passive-aggressive people" as the things she most dislikes
- Her personal motto: "most of life's problems can be solved with a good cookie"
- Her most marked characteristic as having superb "parking-space karma"
- Much to the delight of her fans, her husband Jeffrey as the greatest love of her life and her greatest regret as "not marrying Jeffrey sooner."

SUGGESTED PAIRINGS

See also: Child, Julia; Deen, Paula; Laurentiis, Giada De; Ray, Rachael; Television, Food Channels on.

Entry best enjoyed while eating: Ina's Sunday rib roast and mustard horseradish sauce (*Garten's tip:* before preheating the oven to 500 degrees, make sure the oven has been well cleaned). Serve with roasted broccolini and parmesan chive smashed potatoes, saving room for a dish of pumpkin flan in a maple-caramel sauce.

Further Reading

Arnold-Ratliff, Katie. 2012. "What I Learned from Cooking with Ina Garten for a Day," *O Magazine*, September 2012.

Barefoot Contessa. 2017. "About Ina." https://barefootcontessa.com/about

"How the Barefoot Contessa Became One of America's Best Loved Cooks." 2017. *PBS Newshour*, July 21, 2017. Transcript found at https://www.pbs.org/newshour/show/barefoot-contessa-became-one-americas-best-loved-cooks

"Ina Garten Answers the Proust Questionnaire." 2016. *Vanity Fair,* October 2016.

"Ina Garten Was Born to Cook," 2015. Interview with Serena Altschul, *CBS Sunday Morning.* January 25, 2015.

Jeffrey E. Garten. 2017. Yale School of Management, Faculty Research & Centers webpage. http://som.yale.edu/jeffrey-e-garten

Liberman, Sherri, ed. 2011. *American Food by the Decades.* Santa Barbara: Greenwood.

Maynard, Micheline. 2007. "The Barefoot Impresario." *The New York Times*: Your Money, March 18, 2007.

Nemy, Enid. 1981. "Exchanging Standard Careers for Dreams." *The New York Times.* August 7, 1981.

Rienzi, Greg. 2016. "Jeffrey Garten Is a Financier, Academic, and Author—and Yes, He's Married to the Barefoot Contessa." *John Hopkins Magazine,* Spring issue, 2016.

Salkeld, Lauren. n.d. "A Conversation with Ina Garten." Accessed January 2018, https://www.epicurious.com/archive/chefsexperts/celebrity-chefs/inagarteninterviewrecipes

Sicha, Choire. 2015. "Ina Garten Does It Herself." *Eater*, September 30, 2015.

Gilroy Garlic Festival

STARTERS

The Gilroy Garlic Festival is a 40-year-old event that commemorates the bountiful garlic business in Gilroy, California. The city, whose population is just shy of 50,000 citizens, has welcomed more than 3 million visitors over the festival's history. People travel across the nation and even internationally for the event, garnering an official certification from the Guinness Book of World Records as the largest garlic festival in the world. Attendance rates can soar as high as 100,000 visitors or more each year. The focal point of the three-day event is "Gourmet Alley," an outdoor kitchen where garlic is added to a multitude of dishes.

Celebrity chefs perform cooking demonstrations, and a multitude of cooking competitions are held. In "Garlic Showdown," chefs engage in an *Iron Chef* style contest for a $2500 prize. "Garlic Chef Jr.," a play on *MasterChef Jr.*, features youth between the ages of 9 and 18 who compete to see who can use six or more cloves of garlic most innovatively in a dish. Christopher Ranch, the top garlic grower in the state, provides demonstrations of garlic topping (shearing the garlic heads) and braiding garlic stalks. Additionally, the festival hosts music shows, a pageant, fine art vendors, and family-friendly attractions such as a children's entertainment area. Over the course of its history, the festival has donated nearly $12 million to local schools and nonprofit organizations.

ENTRÉE

Gilroy is so devoted to garlic that on the local Chamber of Commerce website even the "i" in the word Gilroy is dotted with an illustration of a head of garlic. Interestingly, it was the festival that made the city's garlic famous, and not vice versa. Located about 30 miles southeast of San Jose, the star crop of Gilroy used to be its ample prune production. In 1978, the spotlight was stolen from prunes when a college president teamed up with local farmers and businessmen in the community to bring notoriety to the city with a celebration of garlic. Today, Gilroy is considered the epicenter for garlic production in the state of California, which produces 90 percent of the garlic sold commercially in the United States. The scent of garlic is so pungent, it can even be detected driving along Highway 101, which cuts through town.

The inaugural garlic festival was held in 1979 with the help of 50 local volunteers, and it served a mission of giving back to the community with charitable donations. The organizing founders were astonished by the attendance that first year—a reported 15,000 people. Vendors and organizers improvised by cooking extra food in nearby home kitchens and calling the festival's supplier to ask them to replace a delivery of kegs with beer trucks. In an interview with *Curbed* magazine, cultural anthropologist Polly Adema noted that when the festival debuted in the late 1970s, Americans weren't widely fond of spicy or odiferous foods. The festival's success was likely aided by its proximity to the Bay Area,

Nearly 85,000 people attended the 19th annual Gilroy Garlic Festival on July 27, 2019. Each summer, Gilroy hosts one of the largest food festivals in the United States. (Sheila Fitzgerald/Dreamstime.com)

where alternative foods and flavors were beginning to gain popularity in this decade.

After the festival's successful first year, members of Gilroy formed a nonprofit organization called the Gilroy Garlic Festival Association. Over the years, the association has continued adding new events to the festival's offerings, such as the Miss Gilroy Garlic Festival Queen pageant, in which contestants between the ages of 18 and 24 are judged on talent, on-stage question, interview, and speech about garlic. In July of 2019, the festival was the site of a shocking tragedy when an armed assailant opened fire on the crowd before killing himself. The gunman wounded 20 and killed 3 people, including 2 children. In the aftermath of the shooting, the festival committee stated that its members didn't want the senseless tragedy to end the festival's prominent history in Northern California. The festival that had been planned for 2020 was postponed due to the international coronavirus pandemic, but festival organizers used the opportunity to reimagine the 2021 festival with creative drive-through and virtual garlic celebrations.

ACCOMPANIED BY

Kiyoshi "Jimmy" Hirasaki (1900–1963) is widely considered to have been the first person to grow and harvest garlic commercially in Gilroy. Hirasaki was born on Kyushu, an island located in southern Japan, and immigrated to California in 1914. He purchased 500 acres of land and tried his hand at growing garlic, which was flourishing in the area at the time. During the Great Depression, Hirasaki was credited with employing numerous members of the community on his farm. He was imprisoned in a North Dakota internment camp during World War II, but reunited with his family and returned to his garlic business in Gilroy after the war ended (Gilroy Dispatch Staff 2005).

The festival was the brainchild of Rudy Melone, the president of Gilroy's Gavilan College. Melone hatched the idea in 1978 after reading about a festival in a small French town that claimed to be the world's garlic capital. Taking umbrage with this claim, Melone worked with the owner of Christopher Ranch to start the first garlic festival. This decision would lead Gilroy residents to take pride in a previously un-celebrated crop referred to by many as "the stinking rose."

DESSERT

- **I want to drink your blood, but your bulb is in the way:** Many subscribe to the belief that garlic can ward off vampires. Bran Stoker's use of garlic in his novel *Dracula* may have been inspired by garlic's historic medicinal merits and use to fend off mosquitoes. In areas of Europe where superstition about vampires ran high, garlic was eaten, rubbed on window sills, carried, and even stuffed in the mouths of the dead in an effort to prevent vampires from attacking the living or rising from the dead.

- **Thanks a ton!** Each year, Christopher Ranch supplies more than two tons of garlic for the food vendors of Gourmet Alley
- **The right amount of mint:** There have been no shortage of bad-breath jokes in press coverage of Gilroy's festival. In 1989, representatives of the Certs company seized the marketing opportunity to pass out breath mints to festivalgoers.
- **Rub your tummy and pat your garlic head:** According to an old wives' tale, the powerful odor that lingers on your hands after mincing garlic can be removed by washing your hands in cold water and then touching stainless steel.

SUGGESTED PAIRINGS

See also: Ayden Collard Festival; Deer River Wild Rice Festival; International Horseradish Festival.

Entry best enjoyed while eating (inspired by fare found at the festival): Pineapple upside-down waffle topped with caramel and garlic, garlic scampi in butter and wine sauce, a scoop of garlic ice cream served in a slice of fresh cantaloupe, and a pint of Golden State Brewery's garlic pale ale.

Further Reading

Gilroy Dispatch Staff. 2005. "The Original Garlic King." https://gilroydispatch.com/2005/07/29/the-original-garlic-king/

Gilroy Garlic Festival. 2019. https://gilroygarlicfestival.com

Judkis, Maura. 2019. "What Is the Gilroy Garlic Festival?" *Washington Post*, July 29, 2019.

Swann, Jennifer. 2018. "The Giant of Santa Clarita County." *Curbed*, October 24, 2018. https://www.curbed.com/a/texas-california/gilroy-california-garlic-festival-chinese-tariffs

Great British Bake Off, The

STARTERS

Britain's enormously popular show *The Great British Bake Off* is an unscripted competition-style television program that premiered in 2010 on Britain's BBC Two channel. Due to its success, the show was rebroadcast in the United States in 2014 under a different name: *The Great British Baking Show.* The name change was reportedly due to the fact that Pillsbury, a U.S. baking company, owns the trademark for the phrase "Bake-Off." *The Great British Baking Show* was introduced to American households as a weekly show on PBS before the station additionally licensed the programming rights to streaming service Netflix.

In a somewhat confusing order of business, *The Great British Baking Show* was shown out of chronological order. The first three seasons of *Bake Off* were not aired in the United States. Instead, the first season in the United States is actually the fifth televised season of *Bake Off*; the second U.S. season is the U.K.'s *fourth* season; and the third and fourth seasons aired in the United States are the *Bake Off*'s sixth and seventh seasons. Among the show's various iterations, one thing has remained consistent: the show has garnered enormous audiences around the globe.

The Great British Bake Off has won a number of National Television Awards and British Academy of Film and Television Arts (BAFTA) awards in the United Kingdom. In addition to the original *Bake Off* and its U.S. *Baking Show* version, the show has had dozens of international adaptations, such as *The Great Australian Bake Off*, *The Great Canadian Baking Show*, *Bake Off Brasil*, *All of Norway Bakes*, *Bake Off Romania*, *The Great American Baking Show*, and *The Great South African Bake Off*, just to name a few. The team behind *Bake Off* has also produced a number of specials, as well as similar spin-offs, such as *The Great British Sewing Bee*, *The Great Pottery Throw Down*, a children's version of the baking competition called *Junior Bake Off*, and a series called *An Extra Slice* that recapped *Bake Off* episodes shortly after they aired.

After a successful seven-season run, Love Productions announced that the show was leaving the BBC to air the eighth season on Channel 4. This move drew the ire of many fans due to their allegiance to and affection for the show's home on the BBC, which is a publicly funded broadcast network. Channel 4 is a rival for-profit channel, and their programming includes commercials.

ENTRÉE

The Great British Bake Off (GBBO) was founded by Richard McKerrow and Anna Beattie of U.K.-based Love Productions. The duo unsuccessfully pitched the idea of the show to the BBC over the course of several years before it was eventually picked up. At its inception, the show didn't seem likely to become a smash success. Set in a pastoral white tent in a British garden, the show follows a low-key, formulaic structure. Twelve amateur bakers compete against each other to be named "star baker" in the hopes of continuing on to win the final title of "*Great British Bake Off* champion." Two expert bakers serve as the show's judges. In the first seven of the GBBO's eight seasons, U.K. baking celebrities Mary Berry and Paul Hollywood filled these roles. Two additional cast mates, Sue Perkins and Mel Giedroyc, served as comic relief akin to a Greek chorus. Mel and Sue, as they're often referred to, provided an ongoing stream of jokes to introduce new challenges. The duo engaged in witty banter with contestants during challenges and shared in the bakers' joys and agonies along the way.

In the GBBO's first season, the cast and crew traveled around England, pitching the tent in various locations to film competitions while onlookers watched. Castmates interviewed various baking experts about the history of baking in-between competition clips, adding an educational element to the show beyond the unscripted competition factor. In later seasons, the show changed the model of a moveable baking feast by pounding the tent stakes into the ground of its new permanent residence: a sprawling English garden at a gorgeous private home in the countryside called Welford Park.

Episode Structure

Each episode is devoted to a specific theme, such as cakes, biscuits, cookies, breads, chocolate, or pastries, and contestants square off in three separate baking challenges per show. In the Signature Challenge, contestants bake one of their own recipes that falls under the required theme. The Technical Challenge is more of a nail-biter: each contestant receives an identical recipe and list of ingredients, and they race to make the most technically perfect version possible of that recipe under a time limit. To make matters more difficult, recipes are typically incomplete and written very sparsely. The instructions fail to include noteworthy tips, such as whether the cake they're baking will sink catastrophically if the baker cracks open the oven door to peek at it during the baking process.

Even an unassuming-sounding technical challenge such as "baguettes" can be very difficult. The recipes include directions that can be a little difficult to envision during a time crunch, such as: "Divide the dough into four pieces. Shape each piece into an oblong by flattening the dough out slightly and folding the sides into the middle. Then roll each up into a sausage—the top should be smooth with the join running along the length of the base" ("Paul Hollywood's Baguette Recipe" 2017). When contestants present their finished product to the judges—for example, freshly baked baguettes—their baking prowess is judged on things like the color, smell, crackle and crunch of the crust, density and texture of the bread, uniformity, taste, and comparison to what the judges have presented as an example of a "perfect baguette." For an amateur baker, going into a challenge blindly and trying to finish with a perfectly baked version of a recipe can be adrenaline-producing.

The final round in each episode is the Showstopper Challenge. This gives the contestants freedom to put their own spin on a recipe in the hopes of wowing the judges with the dish's creative presentation, in addition to its flavor and technical prowess. Showstoppers, as the name suggests, typically involve elaborate presentations, as well as unusual or sophisticated combinations of flavors and baking techniques. During "Bread Week" of season six, baker Paul Jagger sculpted an elaborate lion's face using different types of rolls, loaves, and almonds, adding sprigs of rosemary for whiskers. During a dessert challenge, fellow contestant Nadiya Hussain made a three-tiered display of cream soda, lemonade, and ginger-beer flavored cheesecakes topped with meringue and a soda can that appeared to magically hover above them.

Audience Interest

In 2014, 13.5 million viewers tuned in to watch the show's finale, far surpassing the 12.1 million viewers who tuned in to watch Europe's wildly popular World Cup Final that same year. Two years later, more than 10 million viewers tuned in to watch the beginning of the show's newest season, which *The Atlantic* noted represented roughly half of all television-owning homes in the United Kingdom. Many of the recipes presented on the show were published online, inviting amateur bakers to join the fun at home. Recipes for things like the Technical Challenges also satiated the curiosity of fans, who were curious to see how something like a basic recipe for biscuits could yield results they'd seen on the show, such as a pan filled with one merged doughy blob.

A number of the show's fans enjoyed creating items like "plaited loaves" and "Victorian tennis cakes" in their own kitchens, often posting the results in social media avenues like Twitter, Instagram, and their personal blogs. Buzzfeed writer and editor Scott Bryan put his love of GBBO to the test by attempting all of the technical challenges in Season 6. He posted his results online, with descriptive summaries of his travails such as "Victorian Tennis Cake (aka The Nightmare that Never Bloody Ended)" and "Gluten-Free Pita Breads (aka Yes I Know That These Look Like Potatoes)." One modern benefit to food-television fandom is the possibility of connecting to the cast of the show. For example, in response to posting a photo of his humorously catastrophic fondant tennis cake on Twitter, Bryan received a tweet in response from Season 6 contestant Tamal Ray, simply saying: "totes amazeballs."

In a reality show landscape that often draws contestants with the promise of wealth as a grand prize, GBBO bakers compete for a much more humble prize: a bouquet of flowers and a glass cake stand. Although contestants enter the show as unknown amateur bakers and leave with a certain level of guaranteed fame, considering how many viewers the show has, there is a prevailing sense that the bakers are in the show for the joy of baking and the pursuit of improving their skills more than a grab at celebrity status and wealth. One of the most noted aspects of the show is the lack of mean-spirited competition or judgment that many reality shows (and upscale restaurant kitchens) have gained a reputation for. Some of the critical acclaim the show has been met with credits a good deal of the show's success with its good natured and uncomplicated qualities, especially in an era during which the United Kingdom and the United States alike experienced a notable level of turmoil in politics.

As *The Atlantic* journalist Sophie Gilbert wrote in 2016, one of the most fundamental aspects of the show's appeal was its "understated celebration of the essence of British identity—of afternoon tea, self-deprecation, and scones—but one that makes a deliberate effort to be inclusive of all of Britain's 64 million residents, regardless of their gender, race, religion, or sexuality." Viewers resonated with not only the enjoyment of watching confectionary competitions coming to life in an English tea garden but also of the kindness the contestants employed with each other, supporting each other's baking conquests in ways that can be atypical in a shared work environment.

ACCOMPANIED BY

Trained at the renowned Le Cordon Bleu cooking school in Paris as a teenager, Mary Berry went on to be a highly regarded cookbook writer and television personality in Britain. Berry grew up in World War II-era England and remembers sugar as a treat in baked goods due to rationing in her youth. She endured a number of challenges in her lifetime, including contracting polio as a teenager, which left her with a spine deformity and a weak left arm, as well as the tragic loss of one of her three children, William, when he was a teenager. Rising to international fame on GBBO, Berry once told *The Telegraph* in a 2013 interview that she attributed much of the show's success to being educational, whereas other popular television shows are typically "violent, cruel and noisy." In discussion about celebrity chef Gordon Ramsay's expletive-filled cooking reality show, she expressed strong distaste for his style.

Paul Hollywood, the show's equally notorious judge, was the son of a baker who persuaded him to follow in his footsteps. Originally inspired to become a sculptor, Hollywood instead followed a career as the head baker at a number of exclusive hotels in the United Kingdom. He started his career in television in 2002, in addition to writing a number of cookbooks and contributing to food magazines and newspaper columns. Hosts Mel Giedroyc and Sue Perkins met at the University of Cambridge in 1988, where they began performing comedy sketches together in venues such as the Edinburgh Fringe Festival. They landed a television show called *Light Lunch*, in which they schmoozed and ate with celebrity chefs who prepared lunch. Over the next decade, the duo worked together on a number

---

Small Plates

Nadiya Hussain (1984–)

One of the fans' favorite contestants was Nadiya Hussain, winner of *The Great British Bake Off*'s sixth season. Hussain reacted to the emotionally charged highs and lows of the competition with humorous, exaggerated facial expressions, good-natured witticisms, and heartfelt discussions that many fans and critics found endearing and relatable. Hussain was born and raised in Luton, England, to a British Bangladeshi family. She appeared on *The Great British Bake Off* shortly before the controversial "Brexit" vote took place in 2016, in which Britain made the historic decision to leave the European Union. One of the most contentiously debated issues in Brexit was the immigration of Muslim individuals. In the midst of this cultural dissonance, it's notable that millions of viewers were unified by their delight in the success of a British Muslim woman on the United Kingdom's most popular television show.

After appearing on *The Great British Bake Off*, Hussain disclosed in various press interviews that she suffered from panic attacks due to being the victim of a racist attack as a child. Noting the overwhelmingly positive reactions she had received after appearing on the show, she also expressed dismay about the Islamophobic encounters she continued to experience. In 2017, she told *Radio Times* magazine that she struggled with the question of whether she had been pigeonholed by the public as a "token Muslim" on *The Great British Bake Off*. That same year, she vented frustration on Twitter after being criticized about her identity: "Too brown to be English. Too Muslim to be British. Too Bengali to eat fish fingers! There is no end!"

Following her success on *The Great British Bake Off*, the star baker was asked to bake Queen Elizabeth II's birthday cake in 2016. Hussain also became a cookbook author and columnist in light of her success, and starred in shows such as *Junior Bake Off*, *The Chronicles of Nadiya*, *Nadiya's British Food Adventure*, and *The Big Family Cooking Showdown*. In recognition of her entertainment industry success, Hussain was listed in Debrett's style and etiquette guide "500 Most Influential People in the U.K." in 2016.

of television shows and live comedy appearances before joining *The Great British Bakeoff*. After leaving the show in 2017, they were signed for various other television hosting roles in the United Kingdom, including *The Gift*, *Let's Sing and Dance for Comic Relief*, and *The Generation Game*.

After the show's production company moved GBBO from its home at the BBC to for-profit Channel 4 in the United Kingdom, only Paul Hollywood stayed on with the production. Mary Berry, Sue Perkins, and Mel Giedroyc left the show, citing their allegiance to the BBC, or as the duo put it in a joint statement, "We're not going with the dough" (Ellis-Petersen 2016). The changes in the show brought on new judge Prue Leith, a chef and writer who, like Berry, also attended the Cordon Bleu before becoming a cookbook writer, food columnist, restaurant and catering business owner, and many high-profile culinary positions. Two new comedians joined the show to replace Mel and Sue: *The Mighty Boosh* sitcom actor Noel Fielding and television presenter and host Sandi Toksvig.

DESSERT

Two hallmark characteristics of *The Great British Bake Off* are its gentle sense of humor and innuendo. The following quotations from various castmates serve as good examples:

Small Plates

Bingate

The Great British Bake Off had its fair share of baking disasters, but unlike the show's American reality television counterparts, its castmates have had very few on-camera emotional meltdowns. One notably dramatic moment in the show's history drew a great deal of attention from fans and the press alike. In an uncharacteristically "Un-British" moment of British television, contestant Iain Watters had a bad moment that was broadcast on television for millions of viewers.

In the midst of a Baked Alaska challenge, the bakers were racing against the clock on a very hot day to make homemade ice cream for their confections. Diana Beard removed Watters' ice cream from the freezer for about a minute while she rearranged the freezer's contents to make room for her own ice cream. There is wide debate about how long his ice cream was left out, and if Beard's actions were largely to blame, but Watters' ice cream was quickly reduced to a melted disaster.

In a moment of frustration and disappointment, Watters shocked the crew by swiftly dumping his dessert into the trash bin and walking off camera. Later, he returned to the tent and sheepishly held out the trash bin to judges Mary Berry and Paul Hollywood in a feeble attempt to present his baking efforts. The scene's drama and ensuing fan arguments on social media went down in GBBO history as "Bingate," as the Internet went wild with memes and trending Twitter hashtags such as #JusticeForIain and #BakedAlaskaGate. Demonstrating good sportsmanship, Watters took to Twitter himself, reassuring viewers that Diane was a good person and making fun of himself with the groan-worthy hashtag #MELTDOWN.

- Tamal Ray, describing his polenta cake recipe: "It's 50% grapefruit juice, 50% blood orange juice and then some honey as well. So it's not 50% of the others. Ah, maths" (Hogan 2015).
- Sandy Docherty, sitting in front of her oven while waiting for her bake: "I'm sat here like David Attenborough. If we just sit here very quietly, we'll soon see the brûlées coming out" (Hogan 2015).
- Nadiya, describing a mound of eclairs she was trying to make into the shape of a nun: "This is my eighth nun. I've had some nun disasters, some nun landslides, some nun explosions" (Elgot 2015).
- Ian, as he adds alcohol to a cream horn pastry's filling: "Going to add a little bit of kirsch in there." (Tasting the filling.) "No, I can only taste fear in my mouth right now. Just a bit *more* kirsch" (Hogan 2015).
- Howard Middleton, bragging about his Japanese Pagoda Tea Tower: "When I've done this previously, people were *quite* impressed. That was my mum and dad, though" (Dellner 2013).

SUGGESTED PAIRINGS

See also: Cake and Cupcake Trends; Food Failures; Ice Cream Trends; *Two Fat Ladies*.

Entry best enjoyed while eating: Flaky *kouign amann* (Breton pastries; somewhat like a muffin-shaped, sweet version of a croissant) and a hot mug of café au lait. GBBO tip: only add the sugar to the top layer of your kouign amman to avoid making the pastry too heavy.

Further Reading:
Berry, Mary. 2010. *Mary Berry's Baking Bible*. London: BBC Books.
Campion, Freddie. 2015. "The Great British Bake Off Explained." *GQ*, October 7, 2015.
Dellner, Alexia. 2013. "The Great British Bake Off: Best One-Liners." *Woman and Home*, September 24, 2013. https://www.womanandhome.com/us/life/the-great-british-bake-off-best-one-liners-107037/
Elgot, Jessica. 2015. "How Nadiya Hussain Became a Great British Bake Off Favourite." *The Guardian*, October 7, 2015. https://www.theguardian.com/tv-and-radio/2015/oct/07/nadiya-jamir-hussain-great-british-bake-off-favourite
Ellis-Petersen, Hannah. 2016. "Sue Perkins and Mel Giedroyc to Leave Great British Bakeoff." *The Guardian*, September 13, 2016.
Gilbert, Sophie. 2016. "Why Is the Most Popular U.K. Television Show in Decades Falling Apart?" *The Atlantic*, September 13, 2016.
Goldhill, Olivia. 2013. "Mary Berry: I Hate Gordon Ramsay's Programmes." *The Telegraph*, August 13, 2013.
Hogan, Michael. 2015. "The Great British Bake Off 2015: The Best Quotes, One Liners, and Innuendos." *The Telegraph*, October 7, 2015.
Hollywood, Paul. 2013. *How to Bake*. London: A&C Black.
Hussain, Nadiya Jamir (@BegumNadiya). 2017. "I Get Abuse for Merely Existing." Twitter, October 30, 2017.
"Nadiya Hussain Feared She Was Bake Off's 'Token Muslim.'" BBC News, July 11, 2017. http://www.bbc.com/news/entertainment-arts-40565226

"Paul Hollywood's Baguette Recipe." PBS, Technical challenge recipes courtesy of *The Great British Baking Show*, 2017. http://www.pbs.org/food/recipes/paul-hollywoods-baguettes

Stack, Liam. 2017. "The Great British Bake Off as We Know It Is Over. What Comes Next?" *The New York Times*, August 11.

Grilled Cheese Festivals

STARTERS

Grilled cheese festivals pay homage to an unassuming sandwich that experienced a significant boost in popular culture between the 2000s and 2010s. Today, numerous grilled cheese festivals raise funds for charitable causes, promote competitions to cook unique styles of grilled cheese sandwiches, and promote specific industries or products. The celebrations range from free corporate-sponsored events to festivals that charge upward of $100 for VIP tickets that grant perks to attendees such as early access, commemorative drinkware for beer tastings, and large sample sizes of sandwiches from many different vendors. Crowds can range from modest community gatherings to thousands of people vying for bites of melted cheese on bread. As the nation's number of festivals in this category have grown so have the number of restaurants and food trucks that specialize in (and often solely serve) the beloved sandwich.

ENTRÉE

Grilled cheese sandwiches are synonymous with comfort food in many American homes. Their popularity is notable; in 2017, foot marketing research firm Datassential reported that 51 percent of polled consumers in the United States ranked grilled cheese as their favorite sandwich. Traditionally, grilled cheese is made by melting American, cheddar, or other mild cheeses in between two buttered slices of bread on a hot skillet. Food historians have traced the practice of eating melted cheese on bread as far back as ancient times. For nearly 70 years, the dish has been commonly served alongside a bowl of hot tomato soup (a pairing invented after World War II in an effort to boost schoolchildren's daily allotment of Vitamin C). The sandwich has many international counterparts, such as the open-faced *Welsh rarebit*, Swiss *Raclette*, and French *croque monsieur* with ham; Latin American corn cake *arepas*; and Mexican *quesadillas* (which translates to "little cheesy thing").

The contemporary version of grilled cheese sandwiches first rose to popularity in the United States around the late 1920s thanks to the advent of processed cheese and sliced white bread. The dish saw longevity as Americans continued to rely on these inexpensive ingredients throughout the Great Depression, when food budgets were stretched impossibly thin. There is no shortage of irony that nearly 100 years later the food that once symbolized a humble meal scraped together on meager earnings has become a gourmet commodity. Once synonymous with school cafeterias, grilled cheese now inspires thousands of adults with disposable incomes to spend $100 or more on VIP tickets to try small samples of the fare. Today, the sandwich can frequently be found on menus with upscale ingredients like artisan bread, stone-ground mustard, chutney, and aged cheeses.

One of the best-known and earliest grilled cheese festivals in the United States was the Grilled Cheese Invitational, in which professional and amateur chefs competed for championships across multiple categories. The event ran from 2003 to 2014 and was held annually on April 12, National Grilled Cheese Day. It started as a large gathering of acquaintances, and in its final year, it had become so popular that even the number competitors alone had to be capped at 200 participants. The festival embodied a cheeky spirit, promoting itself as "an almost scary pursuit of perfection in a Grilled Cheese Sammich." Many participants dressed in silly costumes, recited a "pledge to cheese," and were entertained by musical acts and performances of cheese-themed poetry. Entrants' sandwiches were judged on presentation, taste, and festival-specific terms "Wessonality" (style) and "Spaz" (weirdness factor). Numerous categories ranged from traditional takes on the sandwich ("white bread, butter, and orange cheese") to sweet and savory categories in which interior ingredients could widely vary, but had to consist of 60 percent cheese ingredients. The event was sponsored by Kraft singles.

Other notable festivals include the Sacramento Grilled Cheese Festival, an event that is split between an adult-only day consisting of beer and wine tastings and a family-friendly day with live music and entertainment. Although these events are often lighthearted in theme, some have drawn considerable ire, such as Toronto's Grilled Cheese Festival, whose organizers oversold its 2014 event by 700 tickets. Many in attendance that year took to social media to complain about very long lines, inadequate safety measures, and sample sizes ranging from tiny to nonexistent. One festivalgoer tweeted a photo of an empty ketchup bottle with the caption "People lined up for ketchup. And sadness" (Barker 2014). Other food-loving regions such as the Bay Area have also hopped on the grilled cheese bandwagon. The SF Grilled Cheese Festival touts bottomless craft beer, unusual sandwich ingredients like dungeness crab, and free admission for "Baby Swiss" (guests under the age of 10). And from a state that would be remiss to miss out on any cheese-related event, the Wisconsin Grilled Cheese Championship is sponsored by the state's dairy industry, challenging amateur and professional chefs to make the most delicious classic, savory, and dessert grilled cheeses possible.

ACCOMPANIED BY

The Grilled Cheese Invitational (GCI) started in 2003 when its founder, Tim Walker, drew 100 friends to his loft in Los Angeles to partake in a grilled cheese competition. Inspired in part by Burning Man, a cultural performance arts event held in the Nevada desert each year, the festival became so popular that Walker estimated 30,000–40,000 sandwiches were consumed at its 2012 event. He infused the festival with whimsy and humor, kicking off the 2009 GCI by saying, "We are here today to separate the curds from the whey" and dubbing the winner of that day's competition "the next step in human evolution" (Bramen 2009).

Fans of the classic grilled cheese can thank Industrial Revolution icons Otto Frederick Rohwedder (1880–1960) and James L. Kraft (1874–1953) for inventing the bread slicer and processed cheese, respectively. Kraft's ventures started with cheese sales from a horse-drawn wagon, and his customers' wariness with cheese spoilage led to his invention of processed cheese, which he patented in 1916.

DESSERT

Wired magazine notes that the U.S. military helped contribute to the nation's bottomless appetite for grilled cheese. "The army placed its first order for processed cheese—which, at the beginning, came in only one flavor: white—during World War I, buying twenty-five million quarter-pound tins from Kraft," reporter Lew Robertson wrote. Robertson believes this step led the military to become a "raving cheesaholic" by World War II. Over the following decades, the U.S. military and dairy industry partnered up to test and create various forms of dehydrated, powdered, and additional forms of processed cheese to help provide troops with dairy products (2015).

SUGGESTED PAIRINGS

See also: Craft Brewing and Microbreweries; Food Trucks; Trends, Food.

Entry best enjoyed while eating: Restaurant Grilled Cheese Spot's "Government Issued" (American cheese melted on two buttered slices of white bread and cut into triangles); Meltkraft's "Melter Skelter" (aged raclette, barbecue potato chips, jalapeños, pickled green tomatoes, watercress); food truck Sarap Shop's Filipino grilled cheese (loaded with spaghetti and banana ketchup); and Tom and Chee's "Strawberry Lemonade" (mascarpone, mozzarella, strawberry, and candied lemon dessert served between two glazed donuts).

Further Reading
Barker, Sarah. 2014. "Twitter/ @sarahbarker: People Lined up for Ketchup. And Sadness." February 28, 2014. https://twitter.com/sarahbarker/status/439598136118374400
BlogTo Staff. 2014. "Toronto Grilled Cheese Festival Wasn't So Gouda.'" March 1, 2014. https://www.blogto.com/eat_drink/2014/03/toronto_grilled_cheese_festival_wasnt_so_gouda/
Bramen, Lisa. 2009. "Grilled Cheese Invitational." *Smithsonian*, April 28 2009. https://www.smithsonianmag.com/arts-culture/grilled-cheese-invitational-57564428/
Datassential. 2017. "FoodBytes: 2017 Sandwiches Keynote Report." June 2017, Issue 42. https://c.datassential.com/em1/TrendSpotting/Datassential%20-%20FoodBytes%20-%20June%202017.pdf
The Grilled Cheese Invitational. 2019. http://grilledcheeseinvitational.com/
Robertson, Lew. 2015. "How the US Military Helped Invent Cheetos." *Wired*, August 7, 2015.

H

Hazan, Marcella (1924–2013)

STARTERS

Marcella Hazan was an Italian American cookbook writer, self-taught chef, and cooking teacher. Hazan has been credited by many for popularizing authentic Italian food in the United States and Great Britain. She was a culinary mentor for her son, Guiliano Hazan (1958–), who adopted her passion for cooking and teaching; he followed in her footsteps to become a well-known Italian American cooking teacher and writer as well. Some of Marcella's best-known cookbooks include *The Classic Italian Cook Book: The Art of Italian Cooking and the Italian Art of Eating* (1973), *More Classic Italian Cooking* (1978), *Essentials of Classic Italian Cooking* (1992), and her autobiography, *Amarcord: Marcella Remembers* (2008). Hazan received a number of formal honors in her career, including the James Beard Foundation's "Who's Who" award in 1986, "Best Mediterranean Cookbook" award in 1986, and Lifetime Achievement award in 2000. She was the recipient of a Julia Child "Best International Cookbook Award" in 1986 and a Knight of the Order of the Star of Italy in 2003 to honor the cultural bridge she provided between Italian and American cuisines and cultures.

ENTRÉE

Reviews about Marcella (pronounced mar-CHEL-a) Hazan's books often contained nearly as many colorful adjectives and details about her personality as notes about her food. *New Yorker* writer and cartoonist David Sipress described her as "a tough biscotti with a raspy voice who didn't suffer fools gladly and had a surprising preference for Jack Daniels over a glass of wine" (2013). Book critic Craig Seligman reviewed her autobiography with adjectives like "witheringly stern" and "a little eccentric," noting her "scorn for lazy and philistine cooks." Seligman's review ended with an affectionate note crediting her as someone who "probably brought more pleasure into my life than anyone I've never met" (2008). These reviews echo the tone of many others who have written about Hazan's life, describing her short stature, stern teaching methods, and fierce habit of chain smoking in step with gushing praise for her delicious recipes, shrewd teaching skill, and notably bold personality.

Hazan (neé Polini) was born near the Adriatic coast in the Emilia-Romagna region of Italy in 1924. At the age of seven, she suffered an accident running on the beach in Egypt, where her family lived at the time. Ensuing surgeries and a bout of gangrene left her with a permanently undersized arm and hand that bent inward. As a young woman, Hazan's interests lay not in food, but in the sciences. She received her doctorate in biology and natural sciences at the University of Ferrara. In 1955, her marriage to Italian American Victor Hazan—a man with an insatiable love of food—persuaded Marcella to learn how to cook, which she reluctantly agreed to. The couple moved to Queens, New York, to allow Victor to work in his family's business. As she adapted to her new country, Marcella learned English in large part by following Brooklyn Dodgers' games and watching American television.

Marcella funneled much of her homesickness into cooking classic Italian dishes that reminded her of her homeland. As she began to cook more, she enrolled in a Chinese cooking course to expand her skillset. Her classmates asked her to teach them the art of Italian cooking, which set her future career in motion. Starting in 1969, Hazan taught lessons from her home, helping students to capture flavors and traditional methods used in various regions of Italy. Craig Claiborne, food critic for the *New York Times* and a giant in the industry, wrote a piece about the Hazan family in 1970. Claiborne quoted Marcella as having never cooked a day in her life until she married. He noted that Hazan's 12-year-old son preferred his mother's veal to school lunches and speculated that he might grow up to be a *fin bec* (connoisseur) like his father.

Marcella's career arc had notable parallels to another doyenne of the same era: Julia Child (1912–2004). Like Marcella, Julia wasn't born with an innate passion for cooking, but married a man who was obsessed with food as an art form. Chinese cuisine played a significant role in both couples' love stories. Early in their marriages, both women conquered the art of cooking as housewives. Much like Julia's husband, Paul Child, Victor Hazan played a large role in Marcella's career by encouraging her to publish her first cookbook and supporting her efforts to do so. Both the Hazans and Childs paid extreme attention to recipe details and methodically tested their instructions, which helped launch both cooks to fame.

Julia introduced Americans to the concept of embracing French food, inspiring a cultural shift to make sophisticated meals from scratch at home, cook with full fats like butter and cream, and serve alcohol at the dinner table. Meanwhile, Marcella elevated Americans' definitions of Italian food by introducing authentic flavors and recipes from regions all across Italy. Before that point, many only associated Italian food with plates of spaghetti and meatballs served with Chianti and ambiance consisting of red checkered tablecloths and drippy candles. Much like Julia, Hazan sought to simplify recipes and studied ways to bring out the flavors in her food through rigorous trial and error instead of utilizing fancy kitchen gadgets and highly complicated cooking methods. Both women notoriously tested each recipe in their cookbooks numerous times to ensure the accuracy and quality of the instructions they were publishing.

In 2013, Hazan passed away at the age of 89 in her home in Longboat Key, Florida. She and Victor continued their relationship-long tradition of eating lunch together every day up until the day before her death. Regarding Hazan's legacy, television host and fellow Italian cook Lidia Bastianich was quoted in a *New York*

> **Small Plates**
>
> **Marcella Hazan's Famous Tomato, Butter, and Onion Sauce**
>
> Adapted from Marcella Hazan's publications, as printed in *Saveur* magazine, the following recipe is deceptively simple but beloved by many. As son Giuliano wrote, the sauce "unfailingly elicits feelings of comfort and well-being. Its ability to wash away fatigue and anxiety is almost miraculous, and its preparation borders on alchemy" (Coleman 2012).
>
> *Ingredients*
>
> - 1/4 tsp. sugar
> - 8 tbsp. unsalted butter, cut into cubes
> - 1 can (28 oz) whole, peeled imported Italian tomatoes in juice, crushed after opening *or* two pounds of fresh tomatoes that have been blanched, peeled, and coarsely chopped
> - 1 medium yellow onion
> - Kosher salt
> - Freshly ground black pepper
>
> *Instructions*
>
> Peel the onion and cut it into quarters lengthwise. In a 4-quart saucepan, cook butter, sugar, tomatoes and onion together over medium-high heat. Once the mixture is boiling, reduce heat to medium low.
>
> Stir occasionally for roughly 45 minutes until the sauce has reduced slightly and the ingredients' flavors have melded together nicely. Remove the onion pieces, season with salt and pepper to taste before serving. Add while warm to pasta of your choosing, or freeze for future meals. Recipe yields roughly 3 cups.

Times obituary as saying, "She was the first mother of Italian cooking in America." For many, Hazan is still an enduring force of Italian food education and camaraderie through the pages of her cookbooks.

ACCOMPANIED BY

Marcella married Victor Hazan (1928–) in 1955. Victor is a Sephardic Jew who was born in Italy and had a lifelong passion for fine cuisine. His family immigrated to New York in 1939 to run a fur business in the United States. In addition to his love of food, Victor is also a passionate wine connoisseur and has taught classes and published a book about Italian wines. In 1959, he and Marcella welcomed the arrival of their son Giuliano, who learned the art of Italian cooking in his mother's hometown of Cesenatico after college. Much like his parents, Giuliano was raised in both the United States and Italy. As a youth, he worked in the school his mother ran in Bologna, Italy, and went on to run his own cooking school in Verona, Italy. In 2007, Giuliano won the International Association of Culinary Professionals' (IACP) award for Cooking Teacher of the Year. Giuliano is married to a nutrition educator named Lael, and the couple have two daughters, Gabriella and Michela.

DESSERT

- Marcella was initially hesitant to publish cookbooks, primarily due to the fact that she was still learning English when she moved to the United States. Throughout her lifetime, she penned recipes in Italian, and Victor served as her translator on her books.
- When Victor and Marcella moved to New York, they tasked their realtor with finding an apartment in close proximity to Victor's work so he could have Marcella's home-cooked lunch at home every day.
- Julia Child introduced the Hazans to editor Judith Jones, who had helped launch her career, but over the course of their working relationship, Jones and the Hazans developed a highly antagonistic relationship. Both parties went on to write about each other in their memoirs.
- Marcella had never seen a supermarket until she came to the United States. She once described packaged chickens as chickens that seemed to be "lying in coffins."
- In 1976, Marcella started teaching cooking courses in Bologna, Italy. The city cited her classes as the sole reason that Bologna's tourism rate rose an astonishing 25 percent in 1978 (Oulton 2005; Severson 2013).

SUGGESTED PAIRINGS

See also: Batali, Mario; Child, Julia; Laurentiis, Giada De.

Entry best enjoyed while eating: Marcella's "engagement chicken," a roasted bird simply prepared with salt and pepper seasoning and two lemons in the cavity; fresh pasta with nutmeg-seasoned Bolognese sauce that has simmered for four hours; risotto with butter and Parmigiano-Reggiano; and a chilled glass of Prosecco.

Further Reading
Claiborne, Craig. 1970. "There Was a Time She Couldn't Cook . . ." *The New York Times*, October 15, 1970. https://s3.amazonaws.com/s3.documentcloud.org/documents/354971/marcella.pdf
Coleman, Todd. 2012. "Tomato Sauce with Onion and Butter." *Saveur* Issue No 150, "150 Classic Recipes." October 16, 2012.
Hazan, Giuliano. 2012. *Hazan Family Favorites: Beloved Italian Recipes from the Hazan Family*. New York: Stewart, Tabori & Chang.
Hazan, Marcella. 2008. *Amacord: Marcella Remembers*. New York: Gotham Books.
NPR Staff. 2010. "Long View: Marcella Hazan Brings Italy to America." National Public Radio, Morning Edition. December 28, 2010.
Oulton, Randal. 2005. "Marcella Hazan." Cooks Info, September 8, 2005. https://www.cooksinfo.com/marcella-hazan
Seligman, Craig. 2008. "Classic Italian." *The New York Times*, October 3, 2008.
Severson, Kim. 2013. "Marcella Hazan, Author Who Changed the Way Americans Cook Italian Food, Dies at 89." *New York Times*, September 29, 2013.
Sipress, David. 2013. "Marcella Hazan Changed My Life." *The New Yorker*, September 30, 2013.

Holidays and Food

ENTRÉE

Food and holiday celebrations are inseparably linked, and the dishes, drinks, and sweets American families enjoy on major holidays often reflect major trends happening within popular culture. To the delight of many children, Halloween has been linked with copious quantities of candy since roughly World War II. In 2019, the National Retail Federation (NRF) group estimated that Americans spent $2.6 billion on Halloween candy. Trick or treat stems from an ancient Celtic practice of dressing up as evil spirits during the Samhain festival, which observed summer's shift into winter. The Celts believed that the worlds of the living and the dead overlapped one day each year, and dressing up as a demon on that day would improve their odds of not being harmed by a real ghost, demon, or other ghoul.

Another Halloween ritual, carving Jack O' Lantern pumpkins, derives from an Irish legend in which a man named Jack was denied entrance to heaven, and he roamed the earth wearing a turnip he'd carved into a face and lit with a candle. The tradition of trick-or-treating for candy gained traction in the 1920s, save for when sugar was rationed during World War II, and has been a significant American cultural tradition ever since. The early era of American trick-or-treating involved lots of pranks and nighttime mischief. Up through the 1950s, trinkets such as small toys or coins were given out as often as sweets, but candymakers helped convince the public that candy was the superior option. By the 1970s,

Traditional treats like homemade goods and coins waned in favor in the 1970s as individually wrapped, commercially produced candy gained favor. By 2020, sales of Halloween candy in the United States were $4 billion on average. (Leerobin/Dreamstime.com)

manufactured Halloween candy became even more popular as the public questioned whether unwrapped, homemade treats could be tampered with.

One of the most famous Halloween candies, Tootsie Rolls, was so popular in the United States during the early 1900s that the company had to take ads out in local papers "cautioning their customers against accepting inferior imitation" (Kawash 2010a, 2010b). Today, a majority of Americans celebrate by carving pumpkins, throwing parties, and eating candy. Many serve hot apple cider, a drink that was traditionally consumed as a fermented beverage. Cider's history traces back to Julius Caesar's account of Romans in 55 BCE. In France, cider was so prized in the early eleventh century that it could be traded in exchange for rent.

Thanksgiving

Food is at the heart of Thanksgiving, and a typical American meal on this holiday features an oven-roasted turkey served with sides like sweet potatoes, green beans, cranberry sauce, stuffing, rolls, mashed potatoes and gravy, and pumpkin pie, just to name a few. The tradition of serving turkey and stuffing symbolizes the first Thanksgiving, which took place in 1621. The Pilgrims and Wampanoag American Indian tribe reportedly shared a meal at Plymouth Colony, and they are thought to have likely dined on a wild bird stuffed with herbs and onions. Foods like corn, game (such as deer), root vegetables, and beans may have been served as well. In contemporary times, shared seafood dishes like shrimp, scallops, oysters,

Barack Obama pardons Abe, a Thanksgiving turkey, in 2015. The tradition of granting a presidential pardon to a turkey began with President George H. W. Bush. (National Archives)

or salmon are often described as "unorthodox" trends, but the first Thanksgiving likely featured a variety of seafood like mussels and eels (Gambino 2011).

Starting in the 1870s, a poultry dealer began sending unsolicited turkeys to the White House every year as a way to gin up free press for his poultry. By 1914, sending turkeys to the president became a popular trend. The White House fielded a large number of live turkeys, some of which arrived dressed in costumes or packaged in elaborately decorated crates. Beginning in 1947, the poultry industry started presenting each president with the gift of a live turkey in a formal White House ceremony. Many presidents have spared their turkey's life—a tradition that likely began with President Abraham Lincoln, whose son Tad protested the killing of their Christmas turkey in 1863. In 1989, President George H.W. Bush spared his turkey with an official presidential pardon, an act that became tradition for the presidents who followed. According to the National Turkey Federation, nearly 90 percent of Americans eat turkey on Thanksgiving. In 2017, Americans served roughly 44 million turkeys at Thanksgiving, 22 million at Christmas, and 19 million at Easter (NTF 2019).

In the 2000s and 2010s, Thanksgiving recipes for trendy vegetables like cauliflower (a popular gluten-free alternative to bread), Brussels sprouts, and kale graced the pages of many magazines and websites. Since the 1960s, Americans' growing love of soul food has been reflected on Thanksgiving tables with the addition of staples like sweet potato pie, corn bread, and baked macaroni and cheese. Cajun inventions like turducken (a turkey stuffed with a chicken and a duck) and deep-fried turkey surfaced in the 1980s. By the late-1990s, deep-fried turkey had become so popular in mainstream culture that it graced the cover of *Martha Stewart Living* magazine, and turkey frying cooking tools were sold in grocery stores. Another

---

Small Plates

A Rather Unusual Thanksgiving Offering

Like other presidents of the early 1900s, President Calvin Coolidge received a number of turkeys for Thanksgiving. But in 1926, the president often dubbed "Silent Cal" received another animal intended to reach his Thanksgiving table: a live female raccoon. The idea of dining on raccoon meat wasn't necessarily unusual in that era; raccoon meat recipes have been traced back to the days of slavery, and have been published in multiple editions of cookbooks like *The Joy of Cooking*. Coolidge, however, wasn't keen on serving the gift to his family. He not only spared the raccoon's life but also welcomed her into the White House as a personal pet.

The Coolidge family named the raccoon Rebecca and brought her along on a number of presidential functions. Rebecca attended a children's Easter egg hunt in 1927 and joined the family on a trip to South Dakota the same year, joined by numerous dogs and five canaries. Rebecca enjoyed playing with bars of soap in the bathtub and was highly skilled at escaping from confinement. She was known for taking the Secret Service on wild goose chases around the property while she scaled trees and telephone poles. Had the Coolidge family not been such avid animal lovers, perhaps raccoon stew would have found its way onto Americans' traditional Thanksgiving tables.

beloved (and polarizing) trend is canned cranberry sauce, of which Americans are thought to consume 5,062,500 gallons over the holidays. Writer K. Annabelle Smith calculated that this equates to 4 million pounds of cranberries, not counting the additional quantity of *homemade* cranberry sauce some families cook (Smith 2013).

In the 1930s, the wife of a sales executive for the Karo corn syrup brand invented what is widely considered to be the first pecan pie recipe, which was printed on Karo products' packaging. During World War II, the U.S. Department of Agriculture promoted nuts as a preferable alternative to meat, and recipes for dishes like "pecan loaf" proliferated. Pecan pie's popularity increased over the winter holidays due in part to an excess of pecan production during this era, as well as the nuts' fall harvest schedule. Contemporary variations include pecan pie-cheesecake hybrids, chocolate pecan pies, and pecan pie with chia seeds, a hot ingredient in the health food sphere.

First Lady Grace Coolidge (1879–1957) holds Rebecca, a raccoon adopted by the First Family after being sent to the White House as a suggested Thanksgiving entrée. (Library of Congress)

Pumpkin pie is another nod to a food that's native to North America. The first known American recipe for pumpkin pie (custard seasoned with ingredients like ginger and nutmeg and baked in a crust) dates back to 1796. Commercial canning made pumpkin widely available in the 1950s, and convenience cooking trends drove up sales of frozen pumpkin pies in the early 1960s. Spices used to make pumpkin pies in the colonial era like cinnamon, allspice, nutmeg, mace, and ginger still comprise the pie's signature flavor (Terrell 2017).

Hanukkah and Christmas

Traditional Hanukkah and Christmas foods are often steeped in rich history, and their modern counterparts often reflect contemporary food and diet fads. Traditional Hanukkah meals are kosher and often include challah bread, beef brisket, and foods fried in oil to symbolize the miracle of the Menorah, such as latkes (shredded potatoes fried into small pancakes) and sufganiyot (fried donuts). Today, many Hanukkah treats nod to modern fads, like over-the-top donuts filled with custards and topped with candy, and vegan, kale, or prepackaged latkes.

Since the late 1800s, many Jewish Americans have frequented Chinese food restaurants at Christmas. At the turn of the century, many Jewish and Chinese Americans found a shared sense of community within the walls of "chop suey" restaurants while other establishments were closed. Rabbi Joshua Eli Plaut, author of the book *A Kosher Christmas* (2012), told *Vox* that over the last four decades "Chinese restaurants on Christmas have really become this sort of temporary community where Jews in the United States can gather to be with friends and family. It's a secular way to celebrate Christmas, but it's also a time to shut out Christmas and announce your Jewish identity in a safe environment" (Kieles 2018).

Those who celebrate Christmas also indulge in a large number of holiday foods that illustrate cultural shifts over the last century. Across the United States, many Christmas feasts include traditional European-born foods like ham, prime rib, and gingerbread cookies or Latin-American holiday fare like tamales, pozole, and flans. Similarly to pumpkin pie's deep American roots, many Christmas staples like hot chocolate and fruit cake (the latter of which has fallen from popularity and is often given as a gag gift) have histories that date back to colonial holiday traditions. The origins of various Christmas foods have fallen victim to heated debates. One example is candy canes: some believe that candy is "J" shaped for "Jesus" and its red and white stripes represent the blood of Christ. Many food historians disagree, pointing to the candy's origin back to Germany in the 1600s. Legend holds that a candy maker molded the peppermints into canes to mimic those used by shepherds.

Small Plates

You Can't Catch Me, I'm the . . . Gingerbread-Inebriated Bees?

In 2013, the city of Bryan, Texas, took the "everything is bigger in Texas" trope to new heights by creating the largest gingerbread house in history, as verified by Guinness World Records. The house was 21 feet high and spanned 2,520 square feet—the size of many four-bedroom homes and just shy of the length of a tennis court.

In order to construct the staggering confectionary feat, builders had to secure a building permit and baked more than 4,000 "bricks" made out of gingerbread. The panels of the house were secured by candy and frosting, and the recipe used as little baking soda and butter as possible in order to make the structure more sturdy. The finished product used a staggering 7,200 pounds of flour, the same number of eggs, just shy of 3,000 pounds of brown sugar, and 1,800 pounds of butter.

Bill Horton, manager of the Traditions Club where the house was erected, told CBS News, "One problem we did not anticipate was bees on warm days (. . .) they have been coming over, getting so much sugar and stumbling around like they are drunk. But no one has gotten stung" (Reuters 2013).

Major Spring and Summer Holidays

Americans' love of candy extends beyond Halloween to **Valentine's Day** and Easter, both of which inspire enormous candy sales each year. Easter candy sales reached nearly $2.5 billion in 2019, alone. One recent notable intersection of food trends was pastry chef Dominque Ansel's *huevocato* in 2018, a chocolate recreation of an avocado filled with white chocolate egg truffles. The novelty dessert, which was priced at $22, nodded to Americans' love of chocolate at Easter and their ravenous adoration of avocados in the 2010s. The National Confectioners Association has reported that two-thirds of Americans make Easter baskets, more than 90 percent of which include chocolate or candy (Amick 2019). Easter candies represent ancient symbols of pagan festivals and Christianity, such as chocolate rabbits, marshmallow Peeps, and candy eggs. Chocolate Easter bunnies' origins are thought to go back as far as seventeenth-century Germany, and the candy was popularized in the United States by populations like the Pennsylvania Dutch in the 1700s. Confectioners' budget cuts during the Great Depression are thought to be the reason modern-day chocolate bunnies are hollow inside.

In 2018, the NRF estimated that Americans spent $1.8 billion on Valentine's Day candy. The most popular Valentine's candy, Necco-brand Sweethearts, made national headlines in 2018 when its factory was shuttered, causing shortages of the candy. The popular candy hearts, which are stamped with nostalgic sentiments like "be mine" originated in the late 1800s. By the 2000s, 8 billion of the candy hearts—nearly 19 million pounds' worth—were produced annually to keep up with demand. Over the years, Sweethearts candy retired various sayings that had fallen out of date, such as "Fax Me" and "Hep Cat."

On March 17, many Americans celebrate Irish heritage for Saint Patrick's Day. A 2017 U.S. Census Bureau survey revealed that 32.6 million Americans claim Irish heritage (10.1 percent of the population). Traditional Saint Paddy's Day menus in the United States include corned beef, potatoes, cabbage, Irish soda bread, beer, and food dyed green, reminiscent of the country dubbed "Emerald Isle." While many Americans consider these foods to be authentically Irish, they're unlikely to be found in Ireland on Saint Patrick's Day. Beef and potatoes weren't commonly consumed in Ireland until the country fell under English rule. Many Irish immigrants embraced corned beef meals from Jewish-American delis; the beef was a kosher cut of brisket, and cabbage was added due to its affordability. Much as Jewish Americans and Chinese Americans bonded in Chinese restaurants at Christmastime, Irish Americans and Jewish Americans also sought harbor from cultural discrimination together over deli counters.

Another distinctly American Saint Patrick's trend is the cult following for McDonald's Shamrock Shake. Invented in 1970, the Shamrock Shake's flavor has been debated (and likely changed) from lime to dyed-green vanilla, and vanilla with a touch of mint. The seasonal shake is so popular that various websites and apps have developed features to locate the shakes at various participating McDonald's restaurants. Other confectionery novelties that fall far from the authentic Irish tree include special-edition "St. Paddy's Day Lucky Charms" (cereal with marshmallow pieces) and Smartmouth Brewing Company's Lucky Charms flavored beer.

In the summer, food plays a central role in Fourth of July celebrations, which pay tribute to America's independence from England. Grilling is a deeply rooted tradition across the nation, and many grill hot dogs and hamburgers. Others cook traditional barbecue: slow-roasted meat cooking techniques that date back to America's slave-owning plantations. In 2016, the National Hot Dog and Sausage Council reported that 150 million hot dogs were consumed on the Fourth of July. Many families serve red, white, and blue desserts like frosted cakes with blueberries and strawberries arranged to look like the American flag. Budweiser beer has also been a frequent trend on the Fourth of July since the brand's golden years sparked a huge mass-produced pilsner beer trend in the 1970s. More modern fads in the alcohol industry have cemented the inclusion of craft beers and alcoholic drinks like fruit-flavored coolers, canned wines, and hard seltzers. The Fourth of July is also closely associated with ice cream, which Americans enjoy in every form imaginable on hot summer evenings as they wait for the fireworks displays. The frozen dessert is more patriotic than many realize. The first known recipe for ice cream recorded by an American was none other than founding father Thomas Jefferson, who learned how to make it while living in France.

DESSERT

- **Got candy?** The California Milk Processor Board has calculated that the average Jack-O-Lantern bucket can hold about 250 pieces of candy. According to the company's metrics, that could equate to three pounds of sugar and 9,000 calories.
- **Pigeon English:** It's possible that wild turkey was served at the first Thanksgiving in 1621, but foodways historian Kathleen Wall says the fowl shared between parties could just as easily have been duck, goose, swan, or passenger pigeon instead.
- **Cranberry fields forever:** If you took every can of cranberry sauce consumed each year in the United States and placed them together from end to end, the line would stretch for 3,385 miles, the length of 67,500 football fields (Smith 2013).
- **"That sandwich was the only good thing going on in my life!"** Every fall, New Yorkers go nuts for the Thanksgiving croissant: a 2011 brainchild of Momofuku Milk Bar's pastry chef Christina Tosi. The stuffing-flavored dough filled with turkey, cranberry sauce, and gravy typically flies off the bakery's shelves each day.

Business Insider posted a photo of a chalkboard in front of the bakery reading:

We have no more croissants
Like None
Really

SUGGESTED PAIRINGS

See also: Barbecue; Chocolate Events and Destinations; Latin American Cuisine; Stewart, Martha; Super Bowl Sunday; Tosi, Christina; Trends, Food.

Entry best enjoyed while eating: Roast turkey with a side of horseradish and cheddar mashed potatoes; sweet potato and carrot latkes with whipped goat cheese; Martha Stewart's Deep-Dish Pumpkin Meringue Pie; and a scoop of vanilla ice cream made from Thomas Jefferson's recipe (an *easy* little recipe requiring hours of labor and the use of fire, ice, various molds, two "bottles of good cream," six egg yolks, and half a pound of sugar) and topped with crushed chocolate Halloween candy chunks.

Further Reading

Amick, Brian. 2019. "National Confectioners Association Provides Easter Candy Insights." *Bake*, April 1, 2019. https://www.bakemag.com/articles/11921-national-confectioners-association-provides-easter-candy-insights

California Milk Processor Board. 2010. "How Much Is too Much Candy?" October 12, 2012. https://www.prnewswire.com/news-releases/how-much-is-too-much-candy-104781529.html

Eveleth, Rose. 2012. "The History of Trick or Treating Is Weirder Than You Thought. *Smithsonian Magazine*, October 18, 2012.

Gambino, Megan. 2011. "What Was on the Menu at the First Thanksgiving?" *Smithsonian Magazine*, November 21, 2011.

Kawash, Samira. 2010a. "How Halloween and Candy Became Best Friends." *The Atlantic*, October 21, 2010.

Kawash, Samira. 2010b. "Tootsie Roll Tragedy: The Real Leo Hirschfeld Story." Candy Professor, January 4, 2014. https://candyprofessor.com/2014/01/04/tootsie-roll-tragedy-the-real-leo-hirschfeld-story/

Kieles, Jamie Lauren. 2018. "The History of Jews, Chinese Food, and Christmas, Explained by a Rabbi." *Vox*, December 21, 2018. https://www.vox.com/the-goods/2018/12/21/18151903/history-jews-chinese-food-christmas-kosher-american

Maslowski, Susan. 2019. "WV Culinary Team: Pecans Are Nutrition in a Nutshell." *Charleston Gazette-Mail*, November 30, 2019.

National Retail Foundation. 2019. "Retail Holiday and Seasonal Trends: Halloween." https://nrf.com/insights/holiday-and-seasonal-trends/halloween

National Turkey Federation (NTF). 2019. "Turkey History & Trivia." https://www.eatturkey.org/history-and-trivia/

Reuters. 2013. "Twenty-One-Foot-High Gingerbread House in Texas Sets World Record." *CBS News*, December 7, 2013.

Smith, K. Annabelle. 2013. "This Man Made the First Canned Cranberry Sauce." *Smithsonian Magazine*, November 27, 2013.

Terrell, Ellen. 2017. "A Brief History of Pumpkin Pie in America." Library of Congress. https://blogs.loc.gov/inside_adams/2017/11/a-brief-history-of-pumpkin-pie-in-america/

I

Ice Cream Trends

STARTERS

Ice cream has been a treasured dessert in numerous cultures dating back to ancient times. Ice cream's true origins are disputed, but records of its existence have been traced back to the year 200 BCE in China. American-style ice cream is primarily defined as a frozen dessert made with milk or another butterfat, sweetener, and some combination of fruits and/or spices. The mixture is typically churned into a creamy, mostly frozen consistency. Arabic-based *sherbet* (not "sherbert," as many mispronounce it) and non-milk ice desserts such as Italian *sorbet* and *granita*, Hawaiian *shave ice*, and *Italian ice* are sometimes included under a broad definition. Since its inception, people have continued to experiment with new and surprising ways of preparing, serving, and eating ice cream. The treat inspires playfulness and creativity more than many other foods.

Its long history in America and the constant reinventions of its form have led to nearly countless ice cream trends, fads, and crazes.

Ice cream, a dessert that dates back to ancient times, has been a beloved staple of American food since the 1700s. (Tiffany Dahle/Dreamstime.com)

ENTRÉE

Ice cream first made its way onto American soil in the eighteenth century and has been a culturally prized food ever since. As with many fads, ice cream used to be enjoyed almost exclusively by the elite classes due to the lack of refrigeration (and ice), types of ingredients used, and the difficult process of making it. President Thomas Jefferson is credited with bringing a vanilla ice cream recipe to the colonies from France, and President George Washington and First Ladies Abigail Adams and

Dolly Madison reportedly had strong affinities for ice cream as well. In the mid-nineteenth century, soda fountains began to grow in popularity, and ice cream sodas (also called ice cream floats) sprang up shortly thereafter. The formal invention of ice cream sodas (and nearly every other invention related to ice cream crazes) has been debated, but the leading origin story is traced back to a business owner who exasperatedly plopped a spoonful of ice cream in the glass of a customer who complained that his soda was too warm.

In the late 1800s, soda fountain owners found success selling ice cream with hot chocolate syrup ladled on top. Unfounded but widely circulated theories circulate that the treat's name was spelled hot fudge sundae (a variation of its early names *sondi*, *sundi*, and possibly *Sunday*) due to its invention as a loophole to evade strict Blue Laws. The law forbade the consumption of specific foods on the Sabbath, including alcohol and ice cream sodas, so legend holds that the sundae was concocted as a treat that wasn't (yet) prohibited. The wide variety of ice cream scoop shapes that were invented in the early 1900s illustrates ice cream fads of the day: triangular shapes for pie ala mode, conical and oval shapes for sundae scoops, and rectangular shapes for ice cream sandwiches. In an era rife with ice cream inventions and inventors, one that has seen nostalgic longevity is the banana split, consisting of a sliced banana topped with three different ice cream flavors.

The popular (and debated) origin story of ice cream cones is that the edible treats were invented out of necessity by an ice cream vendor at the 1904 World's

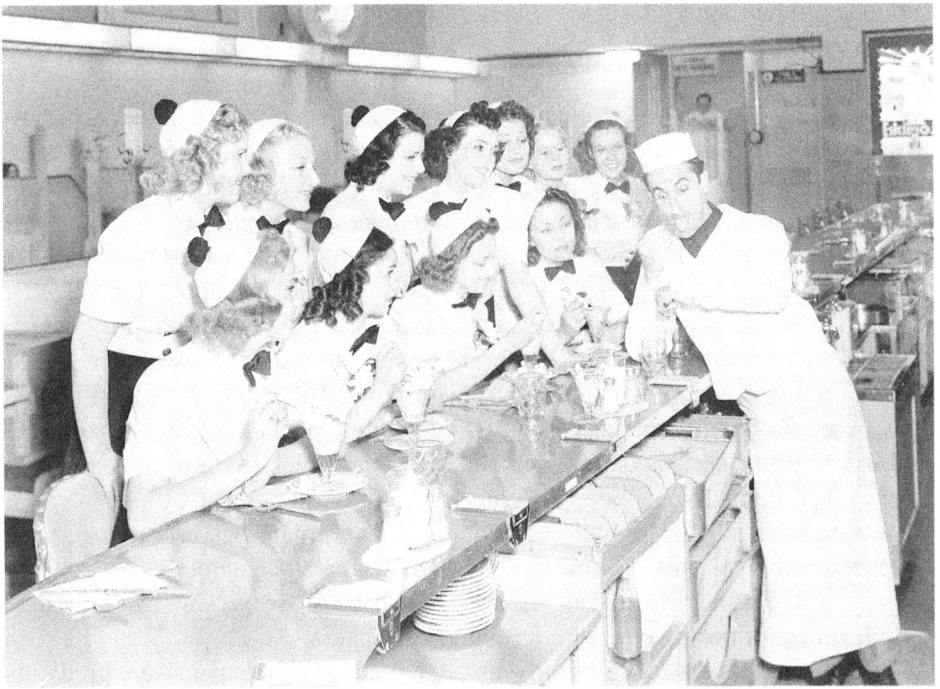

Ice cream sundaes, malts, milkshakes, and banana splits were enormously popular trends at soda fountains and diners across the country in the first half of the twentieth century. Soda shops, ice-cream parlors, and diners are still regarded as nostalgic symbols of American entertainment. (Everett Collection Inc./Dreamstime.com)

Fair in St. Louis, Missouri. As legend has it, the concessionaire ran out of cups, so he started rolling up waffle wafer-cookies from a neighboring vendor's stand and sold scoops in the spontaneously invented edible container. Some argue this seems to be a myth because ample evidence exists that the waffle cones were pre-planned by one or more vendors (likely a measure to get around strict vendor licenses). Additionally, many individuals claimed to have spontaneously invented the cones at the fair; none of whom have valid evidence to show for it (Moss 2019). While various iterations of edible wafer- and biscuit-like containers existed before the World's Fair, ice cream cones' popularity is thought to have largely started at that event, and shortly thereafter, cones saw a meteoric rise that has yet to fall.

The 1920s saw the rise of ice cream novelties such as Eskimo Pies, blocks of ice cream coated in a chocolate candy shell. Other wildly popular products included Dixie Cups (small portable cups of plain ice cream) and flavor combinations, introducing new ingredients like nuts, marshmallows, and chocolate pieces. In the 1930s, ice cream continued to evolve as vendors modified its forms and delivery needs to meet the needs of millions of Americans affected by the Great Depression. Inventions like a warmed ice cream scoop rolled the ice cream instead of packing it down, a cost-effective measure that sold deceptively full-looking bowls to customers. The invention and proliferation of refrigerated ice cream trucks in this era helped deliver inexpensive treats to people far and wide, fueling the craze for the treats even more.

Frozen custard (which incorporates cream and eggs) and soft serve (often airier and lower in fat than traditional ice cream) rose to significant popularity, aided in large part by vendors in Coney Island who helped invent "American" frozen custard and chains like Tastee-Freeze and Dairy Queen that sold soft serve as early as the 1940s. By the 1950s, the automobile craze was becoming a defining part of American culture, and the intersection of the car and ice cream fads proved to be a perfect match. Booming roadside attractions helped fuel the growth of roadstand and mobile ice cream businesses, and Americans' affinity for fast-food restaurants proliferated. For businesses like the fledgling McDonald's franchise, ice cream menu items proved to be a huge crowd pleaser. The invention of the blender in 1911 fueled the popularity of milkshakes (ice cream blended with milk), which became synonymous with burger restaurants and diners. Milkshakes were served with malted or plain milk, often mixed with flavors like chocolate, vanilla, and strawberry. Regional variations sprung up, including concretes (thick frozen custard-based milkshakes) and New England's similarly thick frappes and velvets. In 1955, Aaron Lapin's invention of Reddi-Whip, the first aerosol whipped cream, helped fuel the popularity and convenience of ice cream desserts topped with whipped cream and a maraschino cherry. As drugstore soda fountains began to go the way of the dodo, grocery stores constructed large freezers to accommodate significant quantities of ice cream for hungry shoppers.

Throughout the 1950s, ice cream was often made with inexpensive ingredients and filler. Cartons were often filled with excess air, and artificial flavorings were added to cut down on cost. Consumer pushback in the 1960s led to the rise of higher quality products, and throughout the 1960s and 1970s, premium ice cream made from more natural ingredients was in vogue. The 1970s also saw the rise of frozen yogurt, a lower-fat ice cream and yogurt blend with the consistency of soft serve. Initially called frogurt, the frozen yogurt trend skyrocketed in the 1980s and 1990s, fueled by franchises like TCBY and mall outlets. The treat fell out of vogue in the early 2000s, but various franchises have helped extend the trend to present day.

Ice cream cakes and candy pieces in ice cream were also celebrated trends in these decades, such as a "gourmet" ice cream cake sold in grocery stores called Viennetta. In 1985, Dairy Queen introduced their Blizzard product, a thick milkshake with candy and cookie mix-ins, which was so popular that within two years the chain had sold nearly 175 million of them. The late 1980s and 1990s also saw the rise of a novelty called Dippin' Dots, small pearls of ice cream that are flash-frozen in liquid nitrogen. Marketed as "ice cream of the future," Dippin' Dots likely helped inspire other liquid nitrogen ice cream businesses in the 2000s.

Chilling ice cream well below zero degrees and serving it in unusual ways is a significant contemporary trend, such as Thai rolled ice cream, which is served in rolled ribbons arranged in a cup. As international cuisines have gained popularity, so have their ice cream desserts, like gelato (Italian ice cream), mochi (ice cream nested inside Japanese rice dumplings), and black sesame ice cream (a Japanese dessert made with black sesame seed paste). Unusual flavors like Earl gray tea, garlic, sweet corn, maple bacon, caramel popcorn, beet goat cheese, and lavender have been hugely popular in the 2010s, as well as alcoholic spins like bourbon ice cream and margarita sorbet. The 2000s have also seen

---

Small Plates

Invention of the Cronut

What does a French pastry chef whip up when he wants a donut? Why, a *cronut*, of course. At least, that's what renowned Chef Dominique Ansel's imagination whipped up in 2013 when someone suggested that he add a donut to his eponymous bakery's lineup. Rarely one to follow tradition, Ansel spent months in his kitchen working on the invention of a croissant-donut hybrid. The result was a dessert that combined the thin, flaky, buttery layers of a croissant with the cream-filled, sugar-speckled, glazed sweetness of a donut. Could this be heaven? Dessert-seekers in New York City certainly thought so.

As happenstance would have it, a writer for the Manhattan food restaurant blog *Grub Street* visited Ansel's bakery the same day that Ansel was debuting his newest dessert. *Grub Street*'s web traffic saw an immediate, significant increase after the cronut blog was published. Buzz grew, and curiosity about the new dessert sent New Yorkers flocking in droves to try one for themselves. "We have 100–250 people outside the door every morning," Ansel told the *Village Voice* in 2013, which prompted the bakery to cap cronut sales to two per person, maximum.

The months of tinkering he put into his invention paid off. The cronut became a viral sensation nationally and even internationally. *Time Magazine* listed the cronut as one of "The 25 Best Inventions of the Year (2013)." Other *Time* inventions commended that year included inventions like alcoholic coffee; a swimming pool designed to float on top of the East River while simultaneously filtering the river water below; and an artificial pancreas.

fads along the lines of oversized sundaes and unusual cone and ice cream sandwich interpretations like cookies, brownies, donuts, Hong Kong-inspired bubble waffles, Japanese bean-paste cones shaped like fish, and French American cronuts.

ACCOMPANIED BY

Some of the early ice cream pioneers include Nancy Johnson (1795–1890), who invented the hand-cranked ice cream freezer, which made ice cream more accessible and affordable to be made nationwide. Jacob Fussell (1819–1912) was the first ice cream wholesale salesperson, whose factories churned out millions of gallons of ice cream that was loaded onto trains and shipped all over the East Coast. Though the detailed histories of African American inventors in the 1800s and early 1900s are often sorely lacking, common lore holds that a freed enslaved person named "Aunt" Sallie Shadd (dates unknown) invented the first American ice cream while running a catering business in Wilmington, Delaware. African American Augustus Jackson (1808–1852) served in the White House as a cook under President James Madison and helped popularize the confection in ice-cream-crazed Philadelphia.

Harry Burt (1875–1926) of Youngstown, Ohio, invented Good Humor Bars (chocolate-coated vanilla ice cream on a stick), a product he took from his parlor to the road when he invented the ice cream truck in the 1920s. In the mid-1950s, brothers James Conway (1927–2006) and William Conway (1922–2004) outfitted a fleet of Mr. Softee ice cream trucks with speakers that broadcast music and soft-serve machines. The soft-serve franchise went on to be one of the largest and most successful in the nation. Some of the largest and longest-running ice cream brands include Bryers, a brand started by William Bryer (1828–1882) in 1866, and similarly named Dreyer's, founded in 1928 by Joseph Edy and William Dreyer. Long-running chains include Baskin-Robbins, founded by Burt Baskin (1913–1967) and Irv Robbins (2017–2008) in 1945; Häagen-Dazs, founded by Reuben Mattus (1912–1994) and Rose Mattus (2016–2006) in 1961; and Vermont-based Ben & Jerry's, founded by Ben Cohen (1951–) and Jerry Greenfield (1951–) in 1978.

DESSERT

- **Grape snow cone, my liege?** Snow mixed with sweets like honey or fruit was one of the earliest forms of ice cream, enjoyed by elites such as Alexander the Great (326–353 BCE) and Roman Emperor Nero (37–68 CE).
- **Chocolate chip cookie-nose:** Ben & Jerry's cofounder Ben Cohen has anosmia, meaning he lacks the ability to smell. As a result, the ice cream styles he favored as a taste tester had strong flavors and textures like large chunks. This "over-the-top" ice cream style went on to become the brand's signature style.

- **Game of cones:** Dairy Queen is so protective of its brand that it has trademarked the curl that forms on top of its soft serve since 1948. The fast-food chain is so secretive about their ice cream recipe that it is kept in a safe deposit box, and only a few keys in existence can unlock it.
- **Can we make this a bank holiday?** In 1984, President Ronald Reagan named July National Ice Cream Month, citing the third Sunday of the month National Ice Cream Day. "Ice cream is a nutritious and wholesome food, enjoyed by over ninety percent of people in the United States," his proclamation began. "It enjoys a reputation of being the perfect dessert and snack food."
- *O Captain! My Captain! Our fearful dish is strawberry*: In 1864, a Confederate cavalry seized a large quantity of ice cream from factory workers who were loading it onto a train in Owings Mills, Maryland. The famished soldiers ate it from any container they could find, including their hats. For some (like this author's children), the temperature was too cold for their liking, and they melted it in canteens before eating it.
- **Song of my ice cream:** Poet Walt Whitman wrote about ice cream during the Civil War in a letter home to his mother, describing a ghastly hospital scene. "O I must tell you I gave the boys in Carver hospital a great treat of ice cream a couple of days ago," he wrote in 1864. "(I bought some ten gallons, very nice) [. . .]several of them I saw cannot probably live, yet they quite enjoyed it, I gave everybody some—quite a number western country boys had never tasted ice cream before" (Colleary 2013).

SUGGESTED PAIRINGS

See also: Food Trucks; Holidays and Food; Tosi, Christina; Unusual Foods.

Entry best enjoyed while eating: Cereal milk-flavored soft serve from Milk Bar in New York City; black raspberry frozen custard from Anderson's in Buffalo, New York; and a heaping scoop of Rum Raisin ice cream from Bassett's in Philadelphia, Pennsylvania, considered the oldest operating ice cream shop in the United States.

Further Reading

Colleary, Eric. 2013. "Civil War: Walt Whitman's 'Great Treat of Ice Cream' (1864)." American Table, July 23. http://www.americantable.org/2013/07/civil-war-walt-whitmans-great-treat-of-ice-cream/

Funderberg, Anne Cooper. 2001. *Sundae Best: History of Soda Fountains*. Madison: Popular Press.

International Dairy Foods Association. n.d. "July Is National Ice Cream Month." https://www.idfa.org/news-views/media-kits/ice-cream/july-is-national-ice-cream-month

Moss, Robert. 2019. "How Ice Cream Got Its Cone." Serious Eats, June 26, 2019. https://www.seriouseats.com/2019/06/ice-cream-cone-history.html

Smead, Susan A., and Marc C. Wagner. 2001. "Evolution of the Ice Cream Stand." *What's for Lunch? Food in American Life*. U.S. Department of the Interior, Vol. 24 (4). https://home1.nps.gov/CRMJournal/CRM/v24n4.pdf

What's Cooking America. n.d. "Ice Cream History." https://whatscookingamerica.net/History/IceCream/IceCreamHistory.htm

Imagery Found in Foods

STARTERS

Neuroscientists use a term called "pareidolia" to describe the phenomenon of seeing a human face in objects. This tendency to link two unrelated things with a meaningful connection is referred to as "apophenia," a phenomenon that has captured the interest of psychologists and relative delight of Americans alike. Researchers aren't exactly sure why humans are so prone to seeing faces in inanimate objects. One popular theory is that human brains are "hard wired" to distinguish the features of a human face because it's an evolutionary advantage to quickly spot a face of someone hiding nearby and because discerning others' positive and negative emotions is so critical to our well-being. Others have theorized that people's talent at finding face-like pictures in things like potato chips and pizza slices stems from a deep subconscious desire to ascribe human qualities to everything we observe.

Foods that seem to bear a likeness of religious imagery often accrue a devoted cult following, as well as widespread news coverage. These optical illusions are seen as ironic or entertaining by many, although some find deep meaning in the objects' similarity to other things. Foods bearing a resemblance to religious figures and other celebrities are often enshrined and/or sold for significant sums. In some cases, foods that resemble any type of face whatsoever have adopted a relative level of celebrity of their own.

ENTRÉE

In the twenty-first century, pop culture articles and scholarly journals alike have examined people's interest in seeing things that aren't there. Coverage of this topic is often whimsical in tone, but for some individuals, pareidolia seen in food is a very serious subject. Foods bearing a likeness (a term that can be highly subjective) to American presidents, rock stars, and Christian religious icons have proven particularly lucrative in the United States. One example is a grilled cheese sandwich made by a Florida resident named Diane Duyser, in which the toasted bread resembles (to some observers' eyes) a likeness of the Virgin Mary. The sandwich, minus a bite Duyser took before noticing the image, sold for $28,0000 on auction website eBay to GoldenPalace.com, an online casino. The casino claimed interest in using the sandwich's significant pop cultural interest to "raise money for charity" and "help spread the word" about its mystical powers (BBC Staff 2014).

In contemporary times, there have been no shortages of religious edible iconography, such as a pierogi resembling the face of Jesus, which GoldenPalace.com also bought (the casino is known for lucrative publicity stunts, including the $25,000 purchase of a kidney stone once passed by actor William Shatner). Reports have also been published about people identifying Jesus's image in foods like a pancake, a fish stick, and even a banana peel. There have been numerous stories about Christ imagery in tortillas, such as a *Texas Monthly* article about 80-year-old Ernesto Garza, who considered his bacon-and-egg breakfast taco's resemblance to Jesus to be a miracle. Similarly, numerous workers at a chocolate factory were deeply moved by a two-inch-tall column of chocolate resembling the Virgin Mary that one of the employees had found under a vat.

In 2009, United Press International reported about a couple that regarded a Christlike Cheeto shape with less gravitas. "The couple said the messianic snack, which they named "Cheesus," is missing a right arm, but it features a body, hair, a tiny face and appears to be wearing a robe," the article reported, noting that the couple planned to eat the Cheeto if no one wanted to buy it for a significant sum. Other unusual "food-face" eBay sales have included a potato chip that looked like a drawing of a basic smiley face; a pork rind that loosely resembled a small alien; and slices of toast that several people claimed "proved the innocence" of singer Michael Jackson because, according to the sellers, images of his likeness appeared on the toast during and shortly before his trial for child abuse charges.

Stories about these foods have proliferated in recent years, generating headlines like Buzzfeed's "Twenty-Two People Who Found Jesus in their Food" and "Seven Peppers that Look Like Politicians," National Public Radio's "Man Spots Kate Middleton's Face on a Jelly Bean," and the *New York Post*'s "George Washington Chicken McNugget sells on eBay for $8,100." CNBC's story "Harambe-shaped Cheeto sold for almost $100,000" was one of many about a lumpy Flamin' Hot Cheeto, whose seller insisted it resembled a silverback gorilla that had been shot and killed in an Ohio zoo. Similarly, scholarly studies with titles like "Face-n-Food: Gender Differences in Tuning to Faces" (*PLoS One*, 2015) and "The Potato Chip Really Does Look Like Elvis! Neural Hallmarks of Conceptual Processing Associated with Finding Novel Shapes Subjectively Meaningful" (*Cerebral Cortex*, 2012) indicate cultural interests in understanding the science behind these phenomena.

Aside from scholarly research and religious fervor, the topic of food pareidolia is also frequently accompanied by humor. In 1991, a *Baltimore Sun* reporter interviewed local eggplant farmers who were perplexed by a spate of eggplants with abnormal shapes resembling facial features (specifically resembling President Richard Nixon, actors Bob Hope and Jimmy Durante. and former House Speaker Thomas P. "Tip" O'Neill). A Tennessee coffee shop's cinnamon roll resembling Mother Theresa made international headlines in 2006 as "the nun bun," as well as "the immaculate confection."

In 2005, Australian journalist Karen Stollznow put a Pop Tart selected at random up for sale on eBay, referring to it as a "Pope Tart" and joking about the potential to receive His Holiness through breakfast transubstantiation. Stollznow wrote about the stunt in *Skeptical Inquiry* magazine as a hoax designed to highlight believers' *confirmation bias*, or tendency to interpret something through the lens of their preexisting beliefs as opposed to pure objectivity. The auction received responses ranging from genuine interest to outrage and even landed in the Library of Congress's research collections. Stollznow sold the Pope Tart for $46, noting, "This was measly in comparison to the six-figure sum of the Virgin [Grilled Cheese] Sandwich, but extravagant compared to a $4 pack of Pop Tarts" (2008, 51).

DESSERT

Chocolatier Michele Ferrero reportedly crafted his famous Ferrero Rocher chocolates as an homage to the French rock grotto where 14-year-old Marie-Bernarde Soubirous claimed to have seen apparitions of the Virgin Mary in 1858. Some believe the chocolates' shapes were also designed to mimic the craggy *rochers* where the miracle is said to have occurred.

SUGGESTED PAIRINGS

See also: Art, Food in (Antiquity through the Renaissance); Celebrities and Food; Latin American Cuisine; Trends, Food; Unusual Foods.

Entry best enjoyed while eating: Absolutely nothing! *Ye who finds food with a face, 'tis best to store it in a frozen place.*

Further Reading

BBC Staff. 2004. "'Virgin Mary' Toast Fetches $28,000." BBC News, November 23, 2004.

Driscoll, Michael R., and Arthur Hirsch. "Eggplants Get Their Fifteen Minutes of Fame." *Baltimore Sun*, July 25, 1991.

O'Keeffe, Kevin. 2013. "Beeville Man Sees Jesus in Breakfast Taco." *TexasMonthly*, January 21, 2013.

Poole, Buzz. 2007. *Madonna of the Toast*. New York: Mark Batty Publishing.

Robson, David. 2014. "Neuroscience: Why Do We See Faces in Everyday Objects?" BBC Future, July 29, 2014. https://www.bbc.com/future/article/20140730-why-do-we-see-faces-in-objects

Stollznow, Karen. 2008. "Merchandising God: The Pope Tart." *Skeptical Inquirer*, May/June 2008, 45–51.

UPI Staff. 2009. "Couple Found 'Cheesus' in Cheetos Bag." May 19, 2009. https://www.upi.com/Odd_News/2009/05/19/Couple-found-Cheesus-in-Cheetos-bag/49961242769431/?ur3=1

International Horseradish Festival

STARTERS

The International Horseradish Festival is an annual celebration held in Collinsville, Illinois. The festival was founded in 1987 and has continued every year since then as a celebration of the region's most prized agriculture. Collinsville is the self-proclaimed "Horseradish Capital of the World," and the city and its surrounding area claim to produce between 60 and 80 percent of the nation and world's horseradish supply. Collinsville, whose population is roughly 25,500 citizens, has hosted an estimated 185,000 visitors to the festival over its 33-year run. Festivalgoers can participate in a number of contests and games, enjoy live music, sample a wide variety of horseradish-flavored foods, and see horseradish preparation demonstrations. Additionally, the two-day-long festival hosts a 5k race, a classic car show, carnival games, a youth pageant, and craft vendors. Some proceeds from the event go toward community organizations and projects that help local youth.

ENTRÉE

The history of horseradish is an ancient one. Pliny the Elder (23–79 CE) wrote about its virtues, and the food was used in ancient and medieval times medicinally for numerous ailments. The white root vegetable, a member of the mustard family that can be described as bitter and spicy when grated, is commonly mixed into a sauce with ingredients like vinegar or mayonnaise and served as a condiment. In the United States, horseradish is often paired with prime rib, slathered on artisan sandwiches, or mixed into a Bloody Mary (a spicy tomato-based cocktail). Just east of Saint Louis, Missouri, the floodplains of the Mississippi river along southeast Illinois formed loam-rich soils in an area referred to as the "American Bottom" by archaeologists. Its sandy banks are rich in an element called potash, an element that helps horseradish plants flourish. As such, the town of Collinsville and its surrounding areas have been the site of horseradish farming for generations that date back to German American farmers who settled in the region in the late 1800s.

In 1987, a group of Collins's horseradish growers founded the festival, which initially took place in a small park nestled in an alley. Over the next three-plus decades, the event grew to draw significant crowds. Event participants represent the area's history, such as local vendors who have farmed horseradish for five or more generations (Beck 2018). Festival participants compete for honors and cash prizes in contests to throw horseradish roots and make the best Bloody Mary (a drink favored by brunch crowds comprising tomato juice, vodka, horseradish, and numerous other add-ins).

Youth are invited to participate in events like a root derby contest, in which horseradish roots are carved into cars and raced around a track, and a Little Miss (or Mister) Horseradish Pageant, whose participants range between 4 and 18 years old. Pageant contestants must reside in the Horseradish Capital of the World and compete in categories such as personality, question-answering, and talent. Festival attendees feast on regional and festival fare like pork tenderloin sandwiches in horseradish sauce, corn on the cob, fried pickles, and horseradish chicken wings. Notably, horseradish growers in the area produce a special, extra-hot version of the condiment just for the festival.

Collinsville is experiencing a slowly declining population, as has the entire state of Illinois since 2013. Horseradish growers in the region must contend with dueling challenges of tough years for horseradish—when unseasonably cold, wet, or dry conditions threaten crop productions—as well as diminishing numbers of growers in an already arguably niche agricultural industry. Growers in Eau Claire, Wisconsin—a Collinsville competitor city that often claims to be the major horseradish supplier—have predicted a horseradish shortage in 2020. Whether Collinsville's community will see plentiful crops or a shortage, one thing is guaranteed: the town will still be prepared to celebrate the spicy, humble root that symbolizes the region's history.

ACCOMPANIED BY

Even small towns have their local legends. For the International Horseradish Festival, records were set by individuals like Joey Grzywacz, a local resident who set a festival record in 2010 for hucking a horseradish root a whopping 165 feet and 10 inches (Englert 2011). In the Bloody Mary contest, St. Louis resident Dan Carpenter made a name for himself winning or otherwise placing almost every year for a decade in the early 2000s. His winning recipes typically involved a blend of beef broth, tomato juice, horseradish, citrus juices, homemade pickles, and garlic-stuffed olives (Englert 2011; Keaggy 2011).

DESSERT

Horseradish by the numbers:

- **99:** The estimated percentage of *wasabi* (a spicy green condiment traditionally served with Japanese foods like sushi) in the United States that is actually *horseradish* instead of real wasabi. Most "wasabi" in the nation (and even in Japan) contains 1 percent or less of real wasabi (a finicky plant to grow and harvest) and consists of horseradish powder, green food coloring, and hot mustard.
- **40:** Roughly the size, in feet, of a massive horseradish-shaped balloon that has floated over the festival.
- **1:** The number of world-record winning "largest catsup bottles" that reside in Collinsville, Illinois. (This city must love condiments.)
- **16,000:** The number of fans following Collinsville's "World's Largest Catsup Bottle" Facebook page (catsup is synonymous with the more contemporary spelling, *ketchup*).
- **30:** The number of seconds it took 2010's root-sacking contest winner to fill a sack with 50 pounds of horseradish roots.

SUGGESTED PAIRINGS

See also: Ayden Collard Festival; Gilroy Garlic Festival; Roadside Food Attractions.

Entry best enjoyed while eating: A roast beef sandwich from fast-food franchise Arby's slathered in Horsey Sauce (a sauce made from horseradish and mayonnaise or Miracle Whip introduced by the chain in the 1970s); shrimp with cocktail sauce; and, inspired by past years' festival fare, a slice of horseradish apple pie topped with a scoop of horseradish ice cream.

Further Reading

Beck, Madelyn. 2018. "If It Ain't Got That Zing: A Weekend at the International Horseradish Festival." Harvest Public Media, June 13, 2018. https://will.illinois.edu/news/story/if-it-aint-got-that-zing-a-weekend-at-the-international-horseradish-festiva

Englert, Stuart. 2011. "Horseradish Capital of the World." American Profile, May 10, 2011. https://americanprofile.com/articles/horseradish-capital-of-the-world/

International Horseradish Festival. 2018. https://www.internationalhorseradishfestival.com/index.php/en/

Keaggy, Diane Toroian. 2011. "Horseradish Festival Brings Out Competitive Spirit." *Saint Louis Dispatch*, June 3, 2011.

Nelson, Thomas. 2006. *American Profile Hometown Cookbook: A Celebration of America's Table*. Nashville: Rutledge Hill Press.

Iron Chef

STARTERS

Iron Chef is a Japanese television cooking competition show that met with mass appeal in both Japan and the United States. The show blends reality television with fictional elements, pitting chefs against each other in an intense competition to be named the winning Iron Chef. Originally titled *Ryôri no tetsujin* ("Ironmen of Cooking"), the program premiered on Japan's Fuji Television in 1993 and ran through 1999, at which point Food Network began airing it for U.S. audiences. Fuji Television ran a shorter-lived revival of the program from 2012 through 2013. Altogether, *Iron Chef* ran for 309 episodes and inspired numerous spin-offs and specials, such as *Iron Chef America* (2005–), *Iron Chef USA* (2001), *The Next Iron Chef* (2007– 2012), *Iron Chef Gauntlet* (2017–2018), and *Iron Chef Showdown* (2017). International versions sprung up in Thailand, Great Britain, Israel,

Students compete in a Junior Iron Chef contest in Thailand, 2015. Since the inception of the Japanese show in 1993, television spin-offs and in-person events inspired by the show have proliferated worldwide. (Thiranun/Dreamstime.com)

Australia, Vietnam, Indonesia, and Canada, some of which used catchphrases or themes from the original as their title, like *Knife Fight* or *Allez Cuisine*.

Most shows are an hour long and feature a cook-off battle between an Iron Chef, who has won the competition previously, and a challenging chef, who chooses which Iron Chef to compete against. At the beginning of each show, a secret ingredient is revealed that must be featured by both chefs in multiple courses that they cook within an hour. At the end of the allotted time, judges taste the dishes and award points based on criteria including innovation, how well the main ingredient is featured, taste, and presentation.

ENTRÉE

Just as Helen of Troy was "the face that launched a thousand ships," *Iron Chef* may have been the "reality-drama sports-like cooking show that launched a thousand cooking show imitations." For decades, audiences have been drawn to its over-the-top production, contagious competitive nature, and creative approaches to cooking and cuisine. The original form of the show follows a fictitious premise in which the show's host, Takeshi Kaga, builds a venue called the Kitchen Stadium to fulfill his vision of gladiator-style cooking battles taking place between his reigning Iron Chefs and challenging chefs. They all race against the clock, as they have only one hour to determine what they will make, select their ingredients from the food provided on set, cook multiple dishes, and plate them for the judges.

Various guest judges assess the food in each episode, ranging from renowned food critics to fellow chefs. Throughout the episode, additional suspense and insight is provided by commentators and floor reporters who field information about what techniques, ingredients, and dishes the chefs are all using. Paired with the flamboyant Chairman Kaga character, the commentators and even the busy motion of the cameras provide a high-energy Greek chorus to the culinary battles taking place in the stadium. One notable result of this high-pressure, fast-paced environment is that it attracted viewers regardless of cooking experience or interest. *Iron Chef* was one of the first shows to use cooking as sheer entertainment and to make a game show out of the cutthroat competition already found within the culinary trade. In the late 1990s, cooking instruction was Food Network's biggest focus, but *Iron Chef*'s viewership exceeded that of the popular *Emeril Live* within its first year, at 372,000 viewers an episode compared to *Emeril*'s 350,000. *Iron Chef* helped increase Food Network's competition shows from 2 in 2005 to 16 in 2014, and it was a driving force in the network's brand shift to a model that focused more on entertainment than culinary tutorials (Kohli and Quartz 2014).

One of the most fun elements of *Iron Chef* and its spin-offs is the inventive inclusion of each episode's mystery ingredient. Chefs often walk a fine line between creating an inventive masterpiece or slapping together a culinary disaster. The ingredients range from basic fare like milk, mushroom, garlic, carrot, and sweet potato to exotic and regional-specific items like Horse mackerel, Chinese 100-year-old egg, snapping turtle, and offal (entrails).

> **Small Plates**
>
> **Secrets from the Stadium**
>
> As with most reality shows, *Iron Chef* doesn't always reflect reality. While the chefs really do face grueling cooking challenges and high levels of competition, what viewers see is often far from the truth. For example, the secret ingredients aren't a total surprise to the chefs, as viewers are led to believe. In 2008, ABC's *Nightline* filmed a "behind the scenes" special on *Iron Chef America* and reported that producers asked the chefs to supply grocery lists for three ingredients with the understanding that one ingredient would be chosen as that week's theme. This gave chefs a chance to think about what they'd cook for each potential "secret" ingredient and ensured that their pantries would be stocked with specific ingredients that they needed to make each dish. Before the filming of each episode, chefs merely needed to peek at their pantry to see which of their requested items had been stocked in order to deduce which ingredient they'd be using that week.
>
> Another untruthful element of the show is the implication that challenging chefs decide on the spot which Iron Chef they want to face off against. In reality, the challenger chooses his or her Iron Chef in advance. The show is filmed so that three Iron Chefs are dramatically introduced to the challenger, but only one of whom is a real Iron Chef (the individual who will compete in that episode), and the other two are stand-ins who somewhat physically resemble their Iron Chef counterparts. The crew uses dramatic lighting to mask the fact that the two absent Iron Chefs were presumably working at their day jobs that day or sleeping in.
>
> The fast pace of the show can be a ruse, also. While chefs only have an hour to prepare their five dishes, the action stops for crews to film their final dishes long enough for hot meals to go cold, and the final creations are often too small to provide samples for each of the judges. After the crew films "hero shots" of each dish, the action stops for sous chefs (and even the occasional television producer) to create multiple plates of each dish for the judges to taste. As far as the show's core authenticity goes, producers might cast body doubles for Bobby Flay and occasionally julienne vegetables, but only a real Iron Chef could come up with something as weird as . . . trout ice cream.

ACCOMPANIED BY

Many Iron Chefs on the original cast were so popular on the show that they amassed significant fan bases and received mainstream media coverage. Iron Chef Japanese Rokusaburo Michiba (1931–) wowed audiences with his penchant for making more than the required number of dishes in his allotted time and using his calligraphy skills to pen beautiful menus while viewers nervously watched his time ticking down. Iron Chef Chinese Chen Kenichi (1956–) participated in a record-winning 95 battles, and Iron Chef French Yutaka Ishinabe (1948–) assisted the show's quirky nature by wearing a green chef's coat and holding a bell pepper during his dramatic introductions.

Fellow Iron Chef French Hiroyuki Sakai (1942–) served as the longest-running Iron Chef, racking up a staggering 70 wins over the course of the show. Iron Chef Masaharu Morimoto (1955–) rose to chef stardom after initially pursuing a career as a baseball player. Morimoto starred on both the Japanese show and the *Iron Chef America* spin-off and competed against Iron Chef Bobby Flay (1964–) in a notably tense episode. Flay was responsible for many of the show's controversial moments, such as an episode in 2017 in which he removed his chef's coat during a battle to reveal a T-shirt emblazoned with the words: "This Is My Last Iron Chef Battle Ever." Flay had been associated with *Iron Chef* over the course of 17 years, making his shirt a shocking statement for audience members and the network alike. Flay and Morimoto are joined in the top five American Top Chefs by Michael Symon (1969–); the first female Iron Chef, Cat Cora (1967–); and Mario Batali (1969–). The Japanese cast's commentator was mirrored in the American version of the show by host Alton Brown (1962–), and actor Marc Dacascos (1964–) fills the role as Chairman, playing the fictional nephew of the original Chairman Kaga. The filming schedule was so intense that the network would film two episodes a day. Brown said he had to study upward of 600 pages of research a week in order to accurately comment on technical maneuvers and high-end cooking techniques (Bennett 2017).

DESSERT

- **I'm a snack:** The show was inspired by the words of French lawyer and author Jean Anthelme Brillat-Savarin, who famously quipped "tell me what you eat and I shall tell you what you are."
- **The things we do for work:** Chairman Kaga consumed an estimated 2,389,995 calories from tasting every dish over the course of the show. On *Iron Chef America*, ABC's *Nightline* wrote that *Iron Chef America*'s production entailed 127 crew members, a 10-camera studio, 160 moving lights, and pantries "stocked with 800 pounds of food for each episode, everything from the basics to the bizarre" (Alfonsi and Rosenberg 2008).
- **Lobster not mad; lobster upset:** The first American to beat an Iron Chef was Ron Siegel of San Francisco, California, who bested Hiroyuki Sakai in a lobster battle. Siegel says that appearing on the show led to some interesting moments in his career in the years that followed, such as being featured as a taste tester on Discovery's *Mythbusters* show to see if steak tasted better after it had been exploded.
- **Is something burning?** *Iron Chef's* soundtrack comes from composer Hans Zimmer, who wrote the piece for the firefighter-centric film *Backdraft*.
- **Lost in translation:** Many assume the show's signature phrase uttered by Chairman Kaga, "*allez cuisine!*" is "start cooking" However, it seems to be bungled French, translating directly to the clipped directive of "go kitchen."
- **Everything but the chicken sink:** Kaga made a humorous slip of the tongue in the last episode of Season One, in which he accidentally revealed that week's secret ingredient—chicken—in his opening speech instead of saying the word he intended, *kitchen*.

SUGGESTED PAIRINGS

See also: Batali, Mario; Brown, Alton; Flay, Bobby; *MasterChef*; Television, Food Channels on.

Entry best enjoyed while eating (inspired by the dishes Chairman Kaga deemed the best five over the show's history): Foie gras and scallops with cabbage, canapé-style prawns cooked in chili sauce, foie gras and flatfish served with citrus sauce, scallop salad with vinaigrette sauce, and sea eel with truffle sauce.

Further Reading

Alfonsi, Sharyn, and Sarah Rosenberg. 2008. "*Iron Chef* Secrets Revealed." ABC News, August 1, 2008.

Bennett, Bailey. 2017. "Decades Later, 'Iron Chef' Is Still Defining the Food TV Landscape." Tasting Table, April 20, 2017. https://www.tastingtable.com/culture/national/iron-chef-america-gauntlet-alton-brown

Fuji Television. 2001. *Iron Chef: The Official Book*. Translated by Kaoru Hoketsu. New York: Berkeley Publishing Group.

Jung, Carolyn. 2008. "Take Five with Chef Ron Siegel, on the Tenth Anniversary of His Historic 'Iron Chef' Triumph." Food Gal, August 20, 2008. https://www.foodgal.com/2008/08/take-five-with-chef-ron-siegel-on-the-10th-anniversary-of-his-historic-iron-chef-triumph/

Kohli, Sonali, and Quartz. 2014. "When Cooking Became a Competition." *The Atlantic*, October 2, 2014.

Pogogi Staff. 2017. "A Quick History of Iron Chef Japan." December 17, 2018. https://pogogi.com/quick-history-iron-chef-japan

Vigliotti, Jake. 2017. "The Untold Truth of Iron Chef." Mashed, January 26, 2017. https://www.mashed.com/38874/untold-truth-iron-chef/

L

Lagasse, Emeril (1959–)

STARTERS

Emeril Lagasse is an American chef, restaurateur, television personality, writer, actor, and philanthropist. His cooking style is often called "New New Orleans," referring to his reinvention of numerous classic Creole and Cajun dishes. Lagesse's television career began on a series that was popular throughout the 1980s and 1990s called *Great Chefs*, as well as a PBS series called *Cooking with Master Chefs* (1993) with Julia Child. He gained broader national familiarity as a star on Food Network in the 1990s, hosting *How to Boil Water* (1993–1995) *Essence of Emeril* (1994–2007), and *Emeril Live* (1997–2010).

Over the last 30 years, Lagasse has had recurring guest-starring roles on cooking shows like *Rachael Ray* (2006–) and *Martha* (2005–2012); acted as the food correspondent for lifestyle show *Good Morning America* (1975–); and weighed in as a judge on reality shows like *Top Chef* (2006–). Lagasse hosted *Emeril Green* (2008–2012) on Discovery, *Emeril's Table* (2011) on Hallmark, talk show *The Emeril Lagasse Show* (2010) on Ion Television, and Amazon's *Eat the World with Emeril Lagasse* (2016–), and he starred in a short-lived NBC sitcom called *Emeril* (2001). Lagasse has received a number of notable awards, including a James Beard Foundation Award for "Best Southeast Regional Chef" in 1991, and magazine recognition in 1998 as *GQ*'s "Chef of the Year" and one of *People*'s "Most Intriguing People of the Year." Other honors include Lifetime Achievement Awards from Food Network in 2009, the Taste Awards in 2014, and a James Beard Foundation Award in 2017 for "Humanitarian of the Year." The same year, Lagasse received a Daytime Emmy Award in the Outstanding Culinary Program category for *Eat the World with Emeril Lagasse*.

ENTRÉE

Lagesse's signature phrase—"Bam!"—perfectly symbolizes the era in which Lagasse's career and Food Network saw meteoric rises in popularity. Food television in the 1990s saw a dramatic departure from the ubiquitous staid "cook to the camera" shows of prior years that typically offered straightforward cooking tutorials to television audiences. Lagesse's energetic presence paralleled some of the more notably upbeat personalities of the 1960s and 1970s like Julia Child and Graham Kerr of the *Galloping Gourmet*. Although his shows followed conventional instructional cooking formats, his high energy and exclamations like "Let's kick it up a notch!" infused his shows with an addictive momentum that appealed to viewers for its instruction as much as its entertainment. During these years, Food Network was filming as many shows as they could as inexpensively as possible, so the chef would travel to the studios from New Orleans and film eight episodes a day over the course a few days. *Bam!* was not just a victory cry from an adored television star rising to celebrity chefdom; it was Lagesse's way of startling exhausted camera operators when he noticed them starting to glaze over or risk dozing off during filming.

Lagasse's love of food traces back to his childhood in Fall River, Massachusetts. At the age of 10, he started working in a Portuguese bakery as a dishwasher. Within two years he was promoted to a baker, and he worked night shifts before putting in a full day of school. Lagesse's energetic passion for food inspired him to take a night course on cake decorating and enroll in a vocational high school for culinary arts at the age of 14. A talented drummer as a youth, he was awarded a full ride scholarship to the New England Conservatory of Music, but he turned down the scholarship and attended Johnson and Wales University instead. In 1978, he received an associate's degree in culinary arts, and the university later awarded him with an honorary doctorate for his professional culinary success (Turner 2004).

Lagasse took his culinary studies to France, where he broadened his culinary and cultural horizons. He experienced discrimination in French kitchens in reaction to his Portuguese heritage, but he made the best of his demoted kitchen status and learned as much from his assigned menial tasks as he could. Lagasse returned to the States and took a chef position at the Commander's Palace restaurant in New Orleans, Louisiana. Lagasse opened his first restaurants, Emeril's (1990) and NOLA (1992), in the city where he'd developed his signature "New New Orleans" cuisine. He went on to expand his empire by opening New Orleans–style fish and steakhouses in Las Vegas, Nevada; Universal Studios in Orlando, Florida; and Bethlehem, Pennsylvania. Today he is the proprietor of 11 restaurants nationwide.

While most chefs would be pushed to their limits just running a number of local restaurants, Lagasse pursued the wide-scale expansion of his restaurants while simultaneously putting in long, challenging hours on television. As one of the first 10 people hired at Food Network, Lagasse is often described as a founding member and a cornerstone of the channel's success (Whitaker 2016). Journalist Allen Salkin notes that in the early 1990s through 2010, many viewers considered Food Network "The Emeril Network." Lagesse starred on their primetime 8:00 p.m. lineup five nights a week, and Food Network publicly boasted that they'd signed a seven-figure deal with the chef (to be paid over the course of three years). The chef's television studio sets were top of the line, his appearances on the road were enthusiastically received by excited crowds, and he was quickly becoming a household name.

Despite Lagesse's enormous success with his restaurants and Food Network shows, by the year 2007, Food Network's nascent reality and competition shows like *Iron Chef*, *Iron Chef America*, and *Good Eats* started to attract large viewerships of their own, including younger viewers than the network's prized *Emeril*

Chef Emeril Lagasse (center) poses with Chef Rudi Sodamin (right) and Food Network personality and restaurateur Guy Fieri in 2019. (Hutchinsphoto/Dreamstime.com)

Live, which primarily appealed to older demographics. Food Network knew that competitor networks' shows like *Top Chef* were threatening to eclipse Lagasse's enormous popularity, and executives were keenly aware of the lower production costs for reality-style programs. *Emeril Live*'s in-studio band, live audience, and party style of cooking were losing traction compared to travel shows and gladiator-style chef challenges.

Despite Lagasse's significant role as both a host and programming consultant at the network, consultants pointed to data favoring reality programming as they nudged Food Network to change their programming. Lagasse was offered the chance to join the cast of shows like *Iron Chef* within their lineup, but the network couldn't convince Lagasse to hop on the reality cooking show bandwagon. Lagasse wanted to stay true to his roots as a restaurateur and continue entertaining within the confines of a working studio kitchen as opposed to engaging in cutthroat culinary battles. Food Network canceled his shows despite the 15 years he'd spent fueling the brand's popularity, a move that left the chef reeling (Salkin 2013).

Lagasse's setbacks in television occurred as the Great Recession was taking place, posing a challenging time to wrangle a culinary empire. In a move that surprised some, Lagasse sold everything but his restaurants (the rights to his shows and syndications, licensed products, website, and cookbooks) to another culinary media darling: Martha Stewart. Stewart and Lagasse's companies inked a $50 million merger, the largest at that time for the Martha Stewart Living Omnimedia company. Off camera, Lagasse kept pursuing his passion and creative knack for food. He opened burger restaurants in addition to his more traditional fish and chophouse offerings and continued to develop the charitable organization that he founded in 2002.

Lagasse also returned to television on a smaller scale—this time outside of the studio kitchen setting. He made dozens of appearances as a judge on *Top Chef* (he says he did so after coming to the conclusion that the show had substantial culinary merit) and teamed up with Cooking Channel and Amazon for two travel-related food shows. In 2012, he also appeared in an episode of the HBO drama *Treme*, which follows numerous New Orleans–based characters as they rebuild their lives and community in the wake of Hurricane Katrina. Lagasse's scene was written by celebrity food journalist Anthony Bourdain, who said that he'd wanted to portray the chef as he is off camera: burdened by his responsibility to care for hundreds of employees, weathered by challenging experiences, but unfailingly generous to his loved ones. Today, Lagasse's life and career still serve New Orleans, a city whose Cajun and Creole fare represent a multicultural melting pot. The chef says he credits his career's success not to his years on Food Network but to his "restaurant on Tchoup," his flagship restaurant on Tchoupitoulas street in NOLA's Warehouse District.

ACCOMPANIED BY

Lagasse credits his mother, Hilda Lagasse, with inspiring his early love of cooking. Hilda, who was of Portuguese descent, cooked with him at a young age and helped him understand how happy food can make others. She passed away in 2016. His father, Emeril John Lagasse, wed Hilda in 1949, and the couple raised three children. At the age of 19, Lagasse married Elizabeth Kief, who worked at the same restaurant that he did. The couple divorced in 1986. His second marriage was from 1989 to 1996 to fashion designer Tari Hohn, who helped him launch his first restaurant. In 2000, Emeril married real estate broker Alden Lovelace. The couple cofounded the Emeril Lagasse Foundation, a nonprofit that has raised over $10 million for children's charities to support culinary and nutrition education. Lagasse has four children: Emeril, Jillian, Jessica, and Meril.

DESSERT

- **Pow!** Lagesse's catchphrases include "It ain't rocket science," as well as "Kick it up a notch" and "Aw yeah, babe!" when adding spice or garlic to his dishes. As for his signature "bam!" the chef told *Bon Appetit* in 2015, "I wouldn't change it. I've tried it, believe me. I've tried 'pow.' I've tried all kinds of things. Bam is just kinda me."
- **Chef tested, monkey approved:** Cooking Channel reported that Lagesse's signature banana cream pies each contain 10 bananas, amounting to a whopping 52,000 bananas served per year at Emeril's Restaurant.
- **Spice: the final frontier:** In 2006, Lagesse's recipes were served to the crew of the International Space Station in an effort on NASA's part to supply crew members on long flights with more flavorful, appetizing food. The menu included jambalaya, bacon mashed potatoes, garlic green beans, rice pudding, and mixed fruit.

SUGGESTED PAIRINGS

See also: Batali, Mario; Ray, Rachael; Stewart, Martha; Television, Food Channels on; *Top Chef*.

Entry best enjoyed while eating: New Orleans Barbecue Shrimp (made with stock created from shrimp tails); hot buttermilk rosemary biscuits slathered in butter; a bowl of Hilda Lagasse's Portuguese *caldo verde* (kale soup); quail served with port wine sauce, andouille sausage, and mushrooms (a dish Lagasse once made to convince a local quail-loving councilman to help the chef secure necessary permits); and a slice of his famous banana cream pie with whipped cream and caramel.

Further Reading

Bilow, Rochelle. 2015. "Bam! How Emeril Lagasse Really Feels about His Signature Catchphrase." *Bon Appetit*, April 30, 2015.

Chef Emeril Lagasse Biography. n.d. https://www.emerils.com/about-emeril

Rosenberg, Howard. 2001. "NBC Sitcom 'Emeril' Missing Some Essential Ingredients." *Los Angeles Times*, September 25, 2001.

Salken, Allen. 2013. *From Scratch: Inside the Food Network*. New York: G.P. Putnam's Sons.

"Station Crew 'Kicks It Up a Notch' with Chef Emeril Lagasse." NASA, August 10, 2006. https://www.nasa.gov/mission_pages/station/behindscenes/emeril_ISS_food.html

Turner, Marcia Layton. 2004. *Emeril!: Inside the Amazing Success of Today's Most Popular Chef*. Hoboken: John Wiley & Sons.

Whitaker, Lang. 2016. "A Conversation with the God Emeril Lagasse." *GQ*, August 11, 2016.

Latin American Cuisine

STARTERS

The popularity of Latin cuisines has been growing exponentially in the United States since the late nineteenth century. Immigrants from all areas of Central and South America brought a wealth of foods and foodways with them that have become inextricably linked with American food and food production. Latin cuisine represents a large sector of the Western hemisphere, encompassing traditional foods from all of the countries south of the United States that speak Spanish, French, and/or Portuguese. The traditional foods of Mexico, Central America, South America, and the Caribbean are all represented in the United States. The authenticity and adherence to traditional preparation of these foods varies from region to region. Florida, New York, and Los Angeles are hot spots for dishes and flavors found in Cuba; Mexican-inspired foods are most readily found in the West and Southwest states; and Brazilian fare has become popular in a number of urban areas such as New York, Miami, Dallas, and Chicago.

Some of the most popular Latin fare in America includes tacos, burritos, guacamole, margaritas, *pupusas* (thick corn tortillas stuffed with savory fillings), *empanadas* (Latin American turnovers), churrasco (grilled meat), and mole and chimichurri sauces, among many others. Many cultures have significantly influenced Latin American cuisine over time, including Mesoamericans, Spanish, Portuguese, British, and various British commonwealths, seen in, for example, Jamaican dishes that incorporate spices from India. Today, the American Hispanic food and beverage industry grosses nearly $18 billion a year. Within the United

States, Hispanics account for nearly 20 percent of the population, are the second largest racial or ethnic group in the country, and are the second-fastest growing population in the country. Salsa notably surpassed ketchup in 1992 as America's most popular condiment, and in recent years, tortillas and tortilla chip sales have outpaced the sales of hot dog buns, hamburger buns, and potato chips (Packaged Facts 2016; Flores 2017).

Compared to the fast-food hamburger industry's plateauing and dropping sales, Mexican fast food has been growing considerably over the past 10 years (Seitz-Wald 2013; Mosbaugh 2013). According to recent reports, Latin food has become so popular that it ranks third in popularity after American and Italian fare (such as sandwiches and pizza) and is included in the top two menu items across the country. Though the term "ethnic cuisine" is falling out of style and the meaning of the term is hotly debated, Mexican food is considered one of the three most significant "ethnic" foods in the United States alongside Japanese and Chinese cuisines. In 2017, there were more than 59,800 Mexican restaurants across the country, representing 9 percent of all restaurants in the United States (Olivera 2017; CHD Expert 2017).

ENTRÉE

The term "Mexican food" can have a range of definitions across the United States and in Mexico itself. In California, for example, many Mexican foods incorporate ingredients like seafood and fruit, which are used in traditional foods found throughout various coastal regions of Mexico. From New Mexico up through the San Luis Valley into Colorado, Mexican food has maintained a stronger Spanish influence, with heavy influences from Native American foodways as well. In the American Southwest, staples like green and red chile, potatoes, and even fry bread are common.

One of the earliest Mexican foods to gain wide appeal in the United States was the *tamale* (the singular form in Spanish is *tamal*). The tamale consists of *masa*, a corn-based dough often mixed with lard that is a key component of tortillas and other traditional Latin American foods. Tamales come with various fillings, such as chicken, pork, beef, and cheese, that are mixed together and steamed in a corn husk or banana leaf. The tamale hails from Mesoamerica, where its popularity caught on across most of Central and South America and was highly prized by Spanish explorers. The Spanish sent tamales and other foods they had become enchanted with back to Europe throughout their travels. Many of these foods began to travel the globe and proved to be revolutionary for international cuisines. A number of these have become dietary staples across the world today, including chile peppers, corn, tomatoes, vanilla, and chocolate (Arellano 2012).

One of the other earliest Latin food crazes in the United States was chili, which originated as a spicy, savory stew known as *chile con carne* (pepper with meat). The stew was sold by women dubbed "chili queens" during the late nineteenth century in San Antonio. Food historian Gustavo Arelleno refers to the chili queens as the earliest superstars of Mexican American food and notes that tourists flocked to San Antonio for both the Alamo and the food, describing it as "(not just)

Mexican food on sale, but rather the romance of a vanquished people" (Arellano 2012, 32). In the 1890s, vendors who came to be called "tamale men" (*tamaleros*) started to proliferate, and tamales' popularity spread across the nation through the 1940s, particularly in cities like Chicago and New York. *Tamaleros* ranged from Mexican vendors to those of European and African American descent, and tamales and the vendors who sold them became very well known in popular culture.

In the 1920s, tacos made a significant foray into American culture. Traditionally, tacos are served in the form of soft corn or flour tortillas (the authenticity and arguable superiority of which have long been debated in Latin America and the United States) that are filled with diced, strongly seasoned meats and various vegetables. Anglo-Americans developed a taste for taco shells made from deep-fried tortillas, and with the help of entrepreneurs like Taco Bell founder Glen Bell, traditional Mexican fillings were soon replaced with ingredients like ground beef, shredded cheese, iceberg lettuce, and a chili-based sauce.

Today, items like taco shells made from Doritos chips and burritos stuffed with tater tots signify the extreme derivation American tacos have taken from their original inspiration. More authentic Mexican tacos are still ubiquitous in a myriad of restaurants, carts, and food trucks across the nation and are frequently referred to as "street tacos" by many Anglo-Americans. Tortillas alone have become a staple food in many diets in America and across the globe. They have even become

---

Small Plates

The Rise of Latin Fusion

Latin American food is no stranger to being influenced by and braided with other cultures' cuisines. Within the realm of Latin American cuisine, questions of authenticity and possible cultural appropriation often arise, such as Wyoming-based chain Taco John's coveting the trademark for the phrase "Taco Tuesday" and Good Humor-Bryers reaping long-term sales from a dessert called the Choco Taco. However, fusion, inspiration, and blending of cultures are often celebrated as well, such as fads like the Korean Mexican food fusion trend that began in the mid-1990s in Los Angeles. In 2008, Korean-born Los Angeles chef Roy Choi joined up with a small team of other foodies to create a food truck called Kogi BBQ. The fare includes hybrid inventions like kimchi quesadillas, Korean barbecue burritos, and calamari tacos marinated in ginger, soy, and citrus. Kogi's food created such a sensation that Korean Mexican trends and other hybridizations caught on elsewhere and helped elevate Choi to honors such as being named *Food & Wine*'s "Best New Chef" in 2010 (Arellano, 2014).

The success of Kogi also helped spawn a new fad across the country: the explosive popularity of hip, inventive cuisine sold from food trucks. Today, Latin Asian fusion can be found coast to coast in the United States and around the world. Food trucks and restaurants alike have scrambled to invent various takes on Vietnamese Mexican, Chinese Mexican, Brazilian Japanese, Mexican Indian, Cuban Mexican, Peruvian Chinese, and many other culinary fusions. These inventions have led to cultural mash-ups like pho burritos with rice noodles, hoisin and sriracha sauces, thin-sliced beef, broth, basil, onions, and jalapenos; chicken tikka masala tacos served on naan with chutney, onion, and cilantro; Brazilian beef rib sliders marinated in Xingu beer, served on brioche bread with provolone and onions; and carnitas with spicy wok noodles.

a significant food source in outer space. Since 1985, astronauts have enjoyed tortillas for their flavor, versatility, and shelf life. NASA invested heavily in tortillas upon learning how safe they are compared to foods like bread that crumble easily, posing a risk of clogging air vents.

Americans' love of Latin American food encompasses far more than just Mexican foods. The popularity of Cuban foods has been on the rise nationwide, including a variety of stews, rice and bean dishes, fried empanadas, sweet plantains, and roasted pork. Regional battles play out with dishes like *Cubano* sandwiches, which cities like Miami and Tampa, Florida, disagree on (the former's *Cubano* consists of ham, pork, Swiss cheese, pickles, and mustard on Cuban bread; the latter insists that the sandwich should also include salami and an optional addition of mayonnaise). American menus are seeing more influences from flavors like the *sofrito* bases consisting of pepper, spices, onions, and garlic that are commonly used in Cuban, Portuguese, and Puerto Rican fare.

South American food is seen in many varieties and regions across the United States as well, particularly staples like *queso fresco* (unripened cow's milk cheese), yuca, *aji* peppers, empanadas, *ceviche* (raw seafood cooked in citrus juice), tropical fruits, and *churrasco* (barbecued meat cooked on skewers). Some popular Caribbean fare includes spicy jerk chicken, *roti* flatbread, oxtail stews and curries, and plantains. Central American foods are also on the rise thanks to communities like New Orleans, which is home to the largest Honduran community in the country. Food vendors there have helped Americans develop a new taste for dishes like *baleadas* (thick tortillas filled with ingredients like mashed red beans and Honduran sour cream) and Salvadoran pupusas (Kaplan-Levenson 2014).

ACCOMPANIED BY

Mexican food historian Gustavo Arellano credits Los Angeles restaurant Cielito Lindo as the place where the Mexican food craze likely began in the United States. Aurora Guerrero traveled to America in the 1920s seeking her husband, who was a *bracero* (Mexican laborer). She received permission to open a business under the requirement that she sell something other than tamales, the latest fad in the city. Guerrero developed a recipe for taquitos (rolled tacos) with guacamole that helped kick off what would become a national obsession with tacos. In 1950, a Oaxacan immigrant named Juvencio Maldonado helped further energize the craze with his invention of a machine that could deep-fry multiple taco shells at a time, helping restaurateurs keep up with Anglo-Americans' love of fried tacos without burning themselves or cooking too slowly.

One of the Anglo-Americans who took a keen interest in this fad was California entrepreneur Glen Bell. Bell was inspired to pursue a career in walk-up hamburger stands after eating at the first McDonald's restaurant, but he quickly found that tacos were a more popular menu item. He studied the tacos at various restaurants and stands in the area, asking to see cooking techniques used in various kitchens to emulate the recipe himself. Adapting traditional Mexican tacos to include things like the chili sauce he'd used for hot dogs and ground beef from his burger enterprise, Bell opened a chain called Taco Tia in 1954.

The success of Bell's early restaurants led to the creation of Taco Bell in 1962, which is now the largest taco and burrito chain in the world. With global sales of over $10 billion, the franchise operates in 20 countries and territories (Franchise Times). A similar success story is that of Steve Ells, the founder of fast-casual chain Chipotle. Ells was inspired by burrito vendors in Denver, Colorado, and the large foil-wrapped burritos in San Francisco's Mission neighborhood. Bringing the Mission's assembly-line organization and burrito style to Denver, Ells opened the first Chipotle restaurant in 1993 and quickly added multiple locations as the chain was met with wild success. As of 2017, Chipotle had roughly 2,300 restaurants (Thomas 2017).

DESSERT

- **Presidential approval:** Mexican American food has been beloved by a number of U.S. presidents. President Lyndon B. Johnson reportedly always traveled with a batch of the Texas-style "Pedernales River Chili" that he and his wife, Claudia "Lady Bird" Johnson, loved. President Clinton had a particular fondness for chili con queso and chicken enchiladas; President George W. Bush loved huevos rancheros, and President Obama found turkey chili homey and comforting.
- **Election fail:** Legend has it that Gerald Ford lost the 1976 election against Jimmy Carter due to a culinary gaffe on the campaign trail. When offered a tamale in San Antonio, Texas, Ford bit into it without removing the corn husk first. CBS correspondent Bob Schieffer described the event by saying that Ford almost choked as he tried getting the tamale down. "Carter won Texas and Carter won the presidency, and it may have been a tamale that did it," Mike Huckabee said in an episode of the podcast "The Sporkful" (Saini 2016).
- **I canned believe it:** The revolution of processed and canned foods led to a long history of America's obsession with putting all kinds of foods into cans. Unfortunately, Latin American cuisine was no exception to this. Americans have purchased beef tamales, menudo, *mole* (a complex stew that is often studied by chefs with PhD-research-level intensity), and even tortillas all packed into small cans. Just open the lid, plop on a plate, and . . . *vamonos* (let's move on)!

SUGGESTED PAIRINGS

See also: Asian American Cuisine; Bayless, Rick; Chocolate Events and Destinations; Politics and Food.

Entry best enjoyed while eating: Barbacoa (seasoned beef) taquitos; chiles en nogada (roasted poblano peppers stuffed with meat, pomegranate seeds, a nut-based cream sauce, and herbs); picadillo (a Cuban hash with ground beef, tomatoes, and a number of ingredients that vary by region like olives and raisins); a bottle of Mexican Coca-Cola; and a Chilean leche asada (baked custard with caramel sauce) for a sweet dessert.

Further Reading

Arellano, Gustavo. 2012. *Taco USA: How Mexican Food Conquered America.* New York: Scribner.

Arellano, Gustavo. 2013. "5 Mexican Foods That Should've Never Been Sold in a Can... but Were (or Are)." *OC Weekly*, October 9, 2013.

CHD Expert. 2017. "Press Release: CHD Expert Evaluates the Mexican Restaurant Industry, the Second Most Popular Menu Type in the USA." April 24, 2017. https://www.chd-expert.com/blog/press_release/chd-expert-evaluates-mexican-restaurant-industry-second-popular-menu-type-usa/

Flores, Antonio. 2017. "How the U.S. Hispanic Population Is Changing." Pew Research Center, September 18, 2017. http://www.pewresearch.org/fact-tank/2017/09/18/how-the-u-s-hispanic-population-is-changing/

Franchise Times. n.d. "Taco Bell." http://www.franchisetimes.com/Top-200/Taco-Bell.

Kaplan-Levenson, Laine. 2014. "In the Big Easy, Food Vendors Create a Little Honduras." NPR, The Salt, October 20, 2014.

Morse, Parker. 2018. "Why the U.S. Hispanic Grocery Market Is One to Watch." The Marketing Insider, April 24, 2018. https://www.mediapost.com/publications/article/318111/why-the-us-hispanic-grocery-market-is-one-to-wat.html

Mosbaugh, Erin. 2013. "Tortillas Now Outsell Burger and Hot Dog Buns in the U.S." First We Feast. https://firstwefeast.com/eat/2013/10/the-popularity-of-mexican-food-in-the-u-s-is-on-the-rise

Olivera, Kimberly. 2017. "The Rise of Latino Food Culture in the U.S." *Abasto*, October 10, 2017.

Packaged Facts. 2016. "Hispanic Foods and Beverages in the U.S., 6th Edition." https://www.packagedfacts.com/Hispanic-Foods-Beverages-10335332/

Saini, Anne Noyes. 2016. "When a Tamale Determines the Presidency." The Sporkful, podcast. July 11, 2016. http://www.sporkful.com/when-a-tamale-determines-the-presidency/

Seitz-Wald, Alex. 2013. "Actually, Salsa Dethroned Ketchup 20 Years Ago." *The Atlantic*, October 17, 2003.

Thomas, Lauren. 2017. "Chipotle Begins Search for New CEO." CNBC, November 29, 2017. https://www.cnbc.com/2017/11/29/chipotle-mexican-grill-begins-search-for-new-ceo.html

Laurentiis, Giada De (1970–)

STARTERS

Giada De Laurentiis is an Italian American chef, television host, cookbook author, and restaurateur. She has starred in a number of Food Network shows, including *Everyday Italian* (2003), *Giada's Weekend Getaways* (2007), *Giada in Paradise* (2007), *Giada at Home* (2008), *Giada Entertains* (2016), *Giada's Holiday Handbook* (2015), and *Giada in Italy* (2015). She has been featured as a guest, competitor, and mentor on a wide variety of food-related television shows, including *Food Network Star*, *Beat Bobby Flay*, *Iron Chef*, *The Today Show*, *The Best Thing I Ever Ate*, and many more.

De Laurentiis has written nine cookbooks, most of which have been listed on the *New York Times* best-seller list, and eight children's books about young people's culinary themed adventures in international cities. In 2008, she won a Daytime Emmy Award as the host of *Everyday Italian*, and she has received eight additional Emmy nominations for various programs. In 2012, she won a Gracie Award for "Outstanding Host" and was inducted into the Culinary Hall of Fame.

ENTRÉE

Like many chefs, Giada's love of food began at the family dinner table. Born in Rome, Italy, in 1970, her introduction to food was interwoven with the experience of being raised in a large Italian family. She frequently found herself in her family's kitchen and DDL Foodshow, an Italian specialty foods store run by her grandfather with locations in Los Angeles and New York City. De Laurentiis's parents moved to the United States and divorced when she was young, and her mother raised the children in southern California. The aspiring chef was interested in culinary school from a young age, but her parents discouraged her, worried that she was too young to know what she wanted yet. Instead, De Laurentiis attended the University of California Los Angeles (UCLA). Paying her own way through school, she graduated with a major in anthropology, an impressive feat as the first person in her family to go to college (Moore 2018; Fecteau 2018).

Chef Giada De Laurentiis appears at an Italian food festival in San Diego, California, 2011. (Outline205/Dreamstime.com)

DeLaurentiis still had dreams of pursuing a culinary career, particularly as a pastry chef. She enrolled in a culinary and pastry arts program at the prestigious Le Cordon Bleu school in Paris, France, where many other famous alumni such as Julia Child, Mario Batali, Mary Berry, and Ming Tsai have studied. "I didn't speak French, the classes were in French . . . I don't know what I was thinking," De Laurentiis later said of the experience (Fecteau 2018). Taking the intimidating leap paid off, however, as it helped her find work as a professional chef at both Wolfgang Puck's restaurant Spago and the Ritz-Carlton in Beverly Hills. She also opened her own catering business, called GDL Foods.

In 2002, a Food Network executive read an article about the De Laurentiis family in a *Food & Wine* magazine article. Impressed by Giada's food styling skills and recipes, the executive contacted her to do a demo for television. "I wasn't looking to get into TV," De Laurentiis later said in an interview. "My family was in the movie business, so I was never interested in that world" (Murphy 2011). However, fate intervened, and the former chef-turned-food-stylist eventually found herself on the set of *Everyday Italian*, ginning up the courage to face the cameras.

Despite De Laurentiis's fears of whether or not she had the personality to star as a solo television host, the trial proved to be a highly successful fit. The young chef set her show apart from other cooking shows by filming episodes from inside a home kitchen, instead of a studio designed to look like a kitchen. She told personal stories in a cheerful manner, weaving Italian culture into recipe tutorials to help give the show a personal angle. Viewers responded favorably to the cozy and upbeat vibe. By 2005, De Laurentiis's appearances were attracting significant crowds, such as a 500-person line for one of her book signings outside a Williams-Sonoma store in Washington, D.C. She told the *Washington Post* that her cooking show had changed from biweekly airings to two airings a day in the last year, which caused her viewership to grow exponentially (Sagon 2005).

In the years following, additional Food Network shows such as *Giada at Home* and *Giada Entertains* continued to feature cozy, in-home settings and upbeat atmospheres. De Laurentiis also ventured outside to share her love of travel and culture in a series of travel-themed food shows. *Giada's Weekend Getaways* featured profiles of local restaurants and fun things to do in various cities, such as an episode set in Santa Fe, New Mexico, that featured the restaurant where breakfast burritos were invented, a chocolatier that creates Day of the Dead–themed truffles, other regional fare like roasted chile rellenos, and notable local hikes and sculptures. *Giada in Italy* took viewers to De Laurentiis's home country, where the chef cooked traditional Italian dishes in the company of her family members, and visited a number of eateries, markets, and scenic tourist destinations to share the sources of her culinary inspirations with viewers.

In 2014, De Laurentiis opened her first restaurant, Giada, located in the Cromwell hotel on the Las Vegas Strip. The restaurant specializes in Giada's signature California-infused Italian fare, and it was reported by *Elle* magazine as being the first female-run branded restaurant on the strip. The restaurant's opening faced scathing criticism from *New York Times* food critic Pete Wells, who described the fare in harsh terms such as "flaccid bucatini," "[food that] might have come from the children's menu of any restaurant in America except an Italian one," and "dry chicken pieces that seemed to have no relationship to the original bird" (Wells 2014).

In a 2018 interview with *People* magazine, De Laurentiis said that she had been stung by the reviewer's words but acknowledged that chefs open themselves up to criticism with their cooking and restaurants, and she defended the quality of her service and dishes. In 2018, the chef opened a second restaurant in Las Vegas, called Pronto, a fast-casual eatery located in hotel and casino Caesars Palace. She opened a third restaurant the same year, called GDL Italian by Giada, at the Horseshoe Casino in Baltimore, Maryland. In addition to her television shows, restaurants, and line of cookbooks, De Laurentiis has also expanded to licensed merchandise such as Italian food products, kitchen appliances and tools, and apparel. Various lines are sold by retailers like Target and Williams-Sonoma. Additionally, she owns her own production company, called Linguine Pictures.

ACCOMPANIED BY

The entertainment business runs deep in Giada's family tree. Her mother, Veronica De Laurentiis, is an actress and author. She was born in Rome in 1950 and married producer and actor Alex De Benedetti, Giada's father. Veronica's parents, Silvana Mangano and Dino De Laurentiis, were also an actress and film producer, respectively. In a 2018 interview with *The Cut*, Giada shared that Dino was concerned about the potential harm her entertainment career could do to the family's name, considering how well known he'd become in the industry. As a result, she says that she has always been careful to prioritize her family when making decisions and asks herself if they would be proud of the choices she's considering (Bateman 2018).

Giada grew up with three siblings: Eloisa, Igor, and Dino. In 2003, Dino passed away from melanoma at the age of 29. In his honor, Giada partnered with the organizations Stand Up 2 Cancer and the Melanoma Research Alliance to help promote melanoma detection and prevention measures. Giada married Todd Thompson, a fashion designer for retail brand Anthropologie. The couple welcomed daughter Jade in 2008, likely named after her mother, as Giada (pronounced "Jah-duh") means "jade" in Italian. De Laurentiis and Thompson divorced in 2014 after 11 years of marriage.

DESSERT

In De Laurentiis's early catering days, her first assignment was to cook Thanksgiving dinner for a client's family. After preparing the holiday meal, De Laurentiis began to carry the turkey to the table on a platter, only to trip over the family's large dog. The dog beat the chef to the pile of turkey meat, rendering the main course a lost cause. "There was no longer a turkey for Thanksgiving, but lots of sides," De Laurentiis said in an interview with *The Feast*, "so I whipped up some pasta really fast . . . I was pretty horrified." Not the best moment for a new caterer, but undoubtedly a treasured Thanksgiving memory for the family's dog.

SUGGESTED PAIRINGS

See also: Batali, Mario; Child, Julia; Ray, Rachael; Television, Food Channels on.

Entry best enjoyed while eating: Parmigiano polenta served with pesto; lemon spaghetti (be sure to save some pasta water to use in the sauce, a Giada requirement!); swordfish kebabs grilled with lemon and rosemary; a salted caramel and berry panna cotta; and a double espresso sweetened with a touch of agave.

Further Reading
"About V." n.d. http://veronicadelaurentiis.com/about-v/

Bateman, Kristen. 2018. "How I Get It Done: Giada De Laurentiis." *The Cut*, May 22, 2018. https://www.thecut.com/2018/05/giada-de-laurentiis-how-i-get-it-done.html

Collins, Michelle. 2014. "The Interview Where Giada De Laurentiis Stops Being Polite, and Starts Getting Real." *Elle*, July 2, 2014.

Fecteau, Jessica. 2018. "Giada De Laurentiis on New York Times Restaurant Review: 'I Spent Two Days Bawling My Eyes Out.'" *People*. https://people.com/food/giada-de-laurentiis-restaurant-review-reaction/

"Giada De Laurentiis." n.d. Food Network. https://www.foodnetwork.com/profiles/talent/giada-de-laurentiis/bio

Moore, Brett. 2018. "Celebrity Chef Giada De Laurentiis Bio." Updated August 21, 2018. https://www.thespruceeats.com/giada-de-laurentiis-1665010

Murphy, Jen. 2011. "Interview with TV Chef Giada De Laurentiis." *Food & Wine*, October 17, 2011.

Sagon, Candy. 2005. "The Food Network's Latest 'It' Girl." *The Washington Post*, April 20, 2005.

Wells, Pete. 2014. "You Don't Need to Tell Them Giada Sent You." *The New York Times*, August 12, 2014.

Magazines, Food

STARTERS

Food and beverage magazines have been in circulation in the United States since 1941. Over the last eight decades, food and beverage magazines have tackled a broad range of subjects and embodied a multitude of styles and mediums. Contemporary food magazines range from formal print publications with glossy photos to digital magazines teeming with videos, online reader engagement, and irreverent or otherwise informal commentary. Readers seek these publications out due to their interest in everything from traditional recipes and cooking techniques to food journalism, photography, niche culinary subjects, and thematic works that blend journalism with art.

The consumer magazine industry has struggled with sales and advertising issues in recent years. According to a 2014 Pew Research Center report, overall magazine print circulation (including single-copy sales, subscriptions, and digital versions) had been lagging since 2008, and print ad numbers has been in decline since 2005 (Matsa 2014). However, digital magazine readership has seen significant increases, and food magazines are among the most popular type of magazine in the United States. In 2017, Time Inc. sold itself to Meredith Corporation with backing by the Koch brothers, a business deal that brought 22 major food magazines under the Meredith brand. Today, many food magazine staffs are seeking ways to monetize millennial readers' interests in food, such as sustainability and ethical food production and interesting features stories about food (Nielsen 2016). Magazine staffs are faced with the challenge of determining how much content to offer in print and/or online and how to develop a social media presence that will engage viewers and attract ad revenue.

ENTRÉE

The first significant U.S. culinary magazine was *Gourmet*, which was founded in 1941 and ended in 2009. Condé Nast, the magazine's parent company, ended *Gourmet*'s run in favor of *Bon Appetit* magazine, which showed stronger sales and ad revenue (Severson 2009). *Bon Appetit* has been in circulation since 1956 and covers topics ranging from recipes to food and wine recommendations. The magazine has added digital content, including a large social media presence, YouTube channel, and streaming-video television shows to its repertoire.

Cooking magazines have traditionally been marketed toward women and included other categories like home decor, party planning, and etiquette. Despite significant gender role shifts that have taken place in American society since the inception of cooking magazines, a number of periodicals in circulation today still echo the format and content of older publications. *Woman's Day* started as a grocery store handout in 1931 and continues to offer similar content almost 90 years later, including recipes; party menu ideas; and articles on health, relationships, and ideas for the home. *Martha Stewart Living* took off in 1990 as a quarterly magazine intended to complement the eponymous television program, hosted by media mogul Martha Stewart. The magazine, which is now monthly and available in print and digital form, offers recipes, craft tutorials, columns, and entertaining tips. Fellow culinary and television personality Rachael Ray launched *Every Day with Rachael Ray* in 2005. The magazine offers recipes, kitchen tool recommendations, videos, and lighthearted content on subjects like pet care and gift guides.

Other food magazines limit their content much more to cooking techniques and recipes. These range in readership from amateur home cooks to aspiring or practicing professional chefs. Gourmet offerings include *Food & Wine* magazine, founded in 1978, which offers recipes for higher-end fare and content about travel and wine. *Saveur* launched in 1994, with many stories that blend food, wine, and travel, such as how nomadic Bedouins bake bread or where to find the best cookies in France. *Cook's Illustrated* was founded in 1993 by editor Christopher Kimball and offers thoroughly tested recipes in a formal style without any print advertising. Stylized black-and-white illustrations and photos accompany the instructional content. Nongourmet publications include *Taste of Home*, founded in 1993, which features no-fuss recipes from home cooks that are vetted by culinary experts on the magazine's staff. *Cooking Light* was first launched in 1987 and focuses on health and nutrition, with lower-calorie fare and editorial content about healthy lifestyles. In 2013, website AllRecipes bucked the industry trend of shifting their content from print to digital and instead launched a print magazine inspired by the website with content like seasonal offerings, recipes, and menu planning.

Many food magazines have explored different avenues than traditional recipe- and entertainment-centric periodicals. *Lucky Peach* was founded in 2011 by Momofuku chef David Chang and journalists Chris Ying and Peter Meehan. The content was initially conceived as an iPad app but was transposed into a quarterly publication that became a critically acclaimed source of food writing. *Lucky Peach* blended academically minded editorial content with irreverent essays penned by food celebrities like critics Ruth Reichl and Todd Kliman, writers Anthony Bourdain and John T. Edge, and chef Wylie Dufresne. Ranging in content from sophisticated to profane, the illustration-laden magazine closed in 2017. Online-only publications include *First We Feast* (2012–), a digital magazine that explores food and culture, and *Eater* (2005–), a food and dining guide that covers news specific to a large number of American cities and the food and beverage industry in general. *Cuisine Noir* launched in 2007, which offers culinary editorial content that specifically pertains to African Americans, such as profiles of notable black chefs, and food-related passions of celebrities like Maya Angelou and jazz trumpeter Terence Blanchard. Other periodicals focus on a single food or beverage, like cheese-centric *Culture* and *Whisky* magazines. Several additional titles cater to specific demographics like *Cooking Wild*, which offers content for readers who prefer fishing, hunting, and foraging their own food.

DESSERT

Meatpaper ran from 2007 to 2013, labeling itself as a "journal of meat culture." The quarterly publication explored topics like meat's role in politics, religion, and pop culture, blurring the lines between high-end art mag and irreverent spoof. Sasha Wizansky and Amy Standen, the magazine's founders, were both former vegetarians who claim that bacon lured them into adding meat into their diet. In their first issue, they noted that the magazine's readership appealed to both readers who "assume it's some kind of vegan hate letter addressed to their salami sandwich" or think the magazine is "subsidized by the National Cattlemen's Beef Association," noting "that's how we know we're on to something" (Carlson 2008).

SUGGESTED PAIRINGS

See also: Chang, David; Culinary Awards, The Evolution of; Fiction, Food in; Nonfiction, Food in.

Entry best enjoyed while eating: A grilled hot dog topped with poutine (*Real Simple*, 2019); Tex-Mex deviled eggs (*Southern Living*, 1990s); radicchio and romaine salad with Pecorino cheese and figs (*Cook's Illustrated*, 2019); honey refrigerator cookies (*Gourmet*, 1942).

Further Reading

Carlson, Peter. 2008. "A Choice Quarterly That's Well Done, and Rare." *The Washington Post*, April 14, 2004.

Ember, Sydney, and Andrew Ross Sorkin. 2017. "Time Inc. Sells Itself to Meredith Corp., Backed by Koch Brothers." *The New York Times,* November 26, 2017.

Matsa, Katerina. 2014. "Time Inc. Spinoff Reflects a Troubled Magazine Business." Pew Research Center, June 5, 2014. https://www.pewresearch.org/fact-tank/2014/06/05/time-inc-spinoff-reflects-a-troubled-magazine-business/

Nielsen. 2016. "The Keys to Unlocking the Millennial Mindset." September 7, 2016. https://www.nielsen.com/us/en/insights/news/2016/keys-to-unlocking-the-millennial-mindset.html

Severson, Kim. 2009. "Closing the Book on *Gourmet*." *The New York Times*, October 6, 2009.

Maine Lobster Festival

STARTERS

The Maine Lobster Festival is a five-day festival held in Rockland, Maine, each year during the first weekend of August. It was founded in 1947, and like many food festivals, it was created to help revive lobster-fishing communities along Maine's midcoast region. The festivities consist of eating lobster dishes, beer and wine tastings, carnival rides, cooking contests, a grand parade down the city's

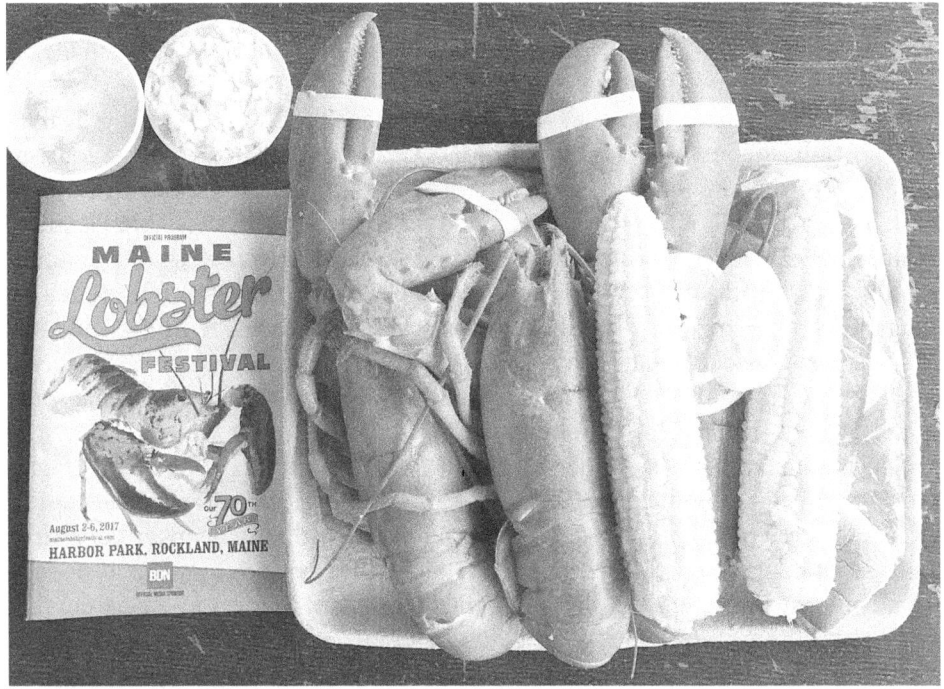

Lobster fishing is one of the oldest continuously operated industries in the country. In the 1600s, lobsters were so plentiful in the northeast that people caught them offshore by hand. By the mid-1800s, trapping became a popular method of catching lobster in the region that would later become the state of Maine. (Yuan Kai Yeo/Dreamstime.com)

main street, and a beauty pageant. Numerous local musical acts entertain the crowds, and more than 300 runners take to the streets for a 10K, 5K, and children's fun one-mile run. Proceeds from the event go toward the festival's funding, and the remaining proceeds are donated to local organizations. The festival operates as a 501(c)(4) nonprofit and has been run by a board of directors with volunteer help for its 73-year run.

ENTRÉE

The city of Rockland was established in 1854, although traders initially settled in the area in the late 1700s to take advantage of the areas lumber, farmlands, and fish. Between the American Revolution and the Civil War, the area was prized for its lime rock and granite. By the late 1800s, fishing and lobster companies were abundant in the area, and by the turn of the century, Rockland had become the nation's leading provider of lobster. Today, Rockland's lobster industry is booming. In 2018, Maine fishermen caught a reported 119 million pounds of lobster, valued at $484.5 million. Despite strong sales, industry leaders are concerned about the effects of trade wars between the United States and China, as well as warming ocean waters in the Gulf of Maine, an area that scientists note is warming faster than ocean waters elsewhere (Whittle 2019). Rockland boasts a humble population of 7,000, although its Lobster Festival attracts as many as 70,000 visitors every summer.

The Maine Lobster Festival, like countless other food festivals in the United States, originated just after World War II in an effort to revitalize summer tourism due to dropping numbers during and after the war. Lobster and lobster fishermen were a natural focal point for the event, and the first festival was held in Camden, Maine, in 1947 before moving to Rockland for the next 70-plus years. Community is at the heart of the event, both due to its celebration of its prize lobster and its celebration of the region's fishermen, military veterans, cooks, families, and tourists. Numerous aspects of the festival hearken back to its earliest years, such as a Grand Parade that includes floats, marching bands, and antique vehicles and some lobster recipes that go back generations.

Serving piping-hot Maine lobster to tens of thousands of patrons poses a significant challenge, but in 2008, the festival arranged for the creation of the world's largest lobster cooker. The festival's website explains that the cooker comprises eight separate cooking components, each of which can cook up to 200 pounds worth of lobsters. Volunteers shuttle the freshly cooked lobsters to the eating tent in insulated bags, serving between 20,000 and 26,000 pounds' worth of lobster over the course of each festival. Festivalgoers can order single-, double-, or triple-lobster dinner served with rolls and corn on the cob or in the form of dishes like lobster mac and cheese, lobster Caesar salads, or lobster rolls. Other traditional Maine foods like mussels, clams, shrimp, seafood chowders, blueberries (found in abundance at the festival's pancake breakfasts and in its homemade desserts), and strawberries are also served each year.

The annual seafood cooking contest pits amateur chefs against each other to prepare a dish that is creative, uses sustainably sourced seafood, and implements a recipe that is complemented by the seafood. Winners receive a cash prize (and bragging rights), and their dishes often illustrate a wide range of culinary influences. In 2019, for example, the winning creations went to lobster and scallop corn chowder (a recipe combining several New England staples); a Cajun-influenced lobster and crab etouffee; ceviche, a raw fish appetizer with Peruvian origins; and tacos de pescado (fish tacos), a dish that originated along the coastal regions of Mexico. Educational booths are set up to educate people about Maine's marine creatures, where people can see small sea life close-up and watch lobster trap demonstrations. Visitors also learn about Rockland's history as a major shipbuilding hub, meet local authors and illustrators, and peruse fine arts and crafts made by local artists.

Some of the most notable events at the festival include a lobster crate race, in which nimble-footed contestants try to run across 50 lobster crates that have been strung together and are floating in the harbor. Those brave enough to try the contest must juggle the ideal blend of speed and balance as enormous crowds watch them try (and typically fail) to avoid falling into the cold water. The Maine Sea Goddess Coronation invites women who are high school graduates and under the age of 21 to compete in a pageant that tests competitors' knowledge of the state's Midcoast region, as well as their volunteer experience and "elegance." Pageant contestants must raise $500 from community sponsors as well as meet strict decorum standards and commit to a significant list of responsibilities during and after the festival. Events for youth also include a children's cod race in which youth dress up in foul-weather fisherman gear and race through a seafaring-themed obstacle course holding a 12-pound cod; a children's lobster eating contest; and a "little lobster diaper derby," in which crawling infants are coaxed by their parents to race for a (short) finish line.

Small Plates

Crustacean Sensations

Lobsters are fascinating creatures. The following details illustrate just a few of these animals' amazing attributes:
- Lobsters are typically hermaphrodites (having both male and female sex organs).
- Fishermen in Maine have seen lobsters whose colors deviate from the standard dark red and brown to unusual varieties like bright blue, albino (white), and yellow and even highly unusual catches such as a lobster whose colors were different on each half of its body: brown on the left and orange on the right.
- Lobsters of all colors (save for the albinos) turn red when cooked.
- A one-pound female lobster can carry upward of 1,200 tiny eggs underneath her tail for a year, only about 10 percent of which are expected to survive past the larval state.
- Lobsters have two different types of claws. The larger one is called the "crusher," which has molar-like teeth on its exterior and is used to smash hard objects like clam shells (the crusher can exert an astonishing force of up to 100 pounds per square inch). The smaller claw has numerous names, including the "ripper" or "pincer." It has sharp serrated teeth that are used for ripping soft textures like fish meat.
- If a lobster's claw is severed, the animal can regenerate it within five years. For those unintimidated by that fact, consider that a hungry lobster facing food scarcity will eat another lobster.
- Lobsters molt (shed their shells) upward of 25 times within the first five years of their lives.
- Unlike crabs (whose outer shell size eventually inhibits their growth) and people (whose height is capped when their skeletons stop growing), lobsters continue to grow larger throughout their entire lives. It's difficult to know how large they *can* grow, but some of the largest on record weighed in at 40 pounds and measured four feet long.
- Scientists don't know how long lobsters could live without hazards like fishing, changes in ocean temperatures, and natural predators, but it's likely lobsters have the ability to live upward of 100 years.
- Bucking the norm for most life forms on Earth, lobsters seem undeterred by aging (and show no negative effects from doing so). Scientists have discovered that the animals show no signs of increased weakness, inhibited mobility, or slowing down as they age. Even more surprising, lobsters' fertility improves with age.

(Gaylord 2011; Waxman 2015)

ACCOMPANIED BY

America can thank restaurant owner Carl Simmons for the invention of the widely beloved lobster roll (lobster meat and melted butter served on a hot dog bun), which Simmons first sold at Rockland's Sim's Lunch in 1927. The lobster festival's beauty pageant has a long history as well. As journalist Lauren Abbate writes, the winning young women join the ranks "of the state's other 'Commodity Queens'—the Maine Wild Blueberry Queen, the Maine Dairy Princess and the Maine Potato Queen, to name a few—who represent their respective festivals and region at events throughout the state" (2018). Ruth Roberts was the first winner crowned "Miss Maine Seafood" in 1948. Since then, many young women in Maine have dreamed of being crowned the festival's Sea Goddess, flanked at festival appearances by locals portraying King Neptune and pirate Blackbeard.

One such young woman was 2018's Sea Goddess Taylor Hamlin, who was controversially decrowned within 24 hours after years-old photos surfaced on social media that showed Hamlin using a vape pen and smoking marijuana as a teen. Many members of the community expressed dismay at her dismissal, calling for contemporary updates to the pageant such as more lenient decorum rules and allowing youth of both sexes to apply. In 2020, the festival gave the title of Grand Marshall to a resident named Virginia Oliver, who was affectionately referred to by locals as "The Lobster Lady." Oliver, a Rockland native who turned 100 shortly after receiving the honor, had been lobstering in the community for 91 years when she received the festival's honor.

DESSERT

What, no Cheddar biscuits? Today, lobster is often deemed an expensive and somewhat elite food, but this wasn't always the case. "In the colonial era, only the poor, indentured servants, and prisoners ate lobsters because they were cheap, too plentiful, and considered 'tasteless,'" *Time* writer Olivia Waxman wrote. "After prisoners in one Massachusetts town got sick of eating them all the time, a new rule said they only had to eat them three times a week."

SUGGESTED PAIRINGS

See also: Florida Strawberry Festival; Gilroy Garlic Festival; Maple Syrup Festivals.

Entry best enjoyed while eating: Deep-fried lobster mac 'n' cheese bites; lobster-stuffed risotto balls; boiled lobster with butter and sweet corn on the cob; homemade blueberry Maine cobbler. (Don't forget your lobster bib and claw crackers!)

Further Reading

Abbate, Lauren. 2018. "Controversy Spurs Calls to Change the Maine Lobster Festival Sea Goddess Tradition." *Bangor Daily News,* September 26, 2018.

Gaylord, Chris. 2011. "How Large Can Lobsters Grow? Big! But No One Knows How Big." *Christian Science Monitor,* June 16, 2011.

Maine Lobster Festival Staff. 2020. https://www.mainelobsterfestival.com

Rockland Historical Society. 2018. "History of Rockland." https://rocklandmaine.gov/community/about-rockland/history/

Waxman, Olivia B. 2015. "11 Lobster Facts That Will Leave You Shell-Shocked." *Time*, July 8, 2015.

Whittle, Patrick. 2019. "Maine's Lobster Catch, Value Grew Last Year, Officials Say." Associated Press, March 1, 2019.

Maple Syrup Festivals

STARTERS

Each spring, numerous maple syrup festivals are held throughout the Northeastern, Great Lakes, and Mid-Atlantic regions of the United States, as well as Eastern Canadian provinces. Many maple festivals are held in March, and they celebrate the maple syrup industry, the food's long history in Canada and the United States, and the various local communities that maple syrup helps support. The festivals are timed in conjunction with sugaring season, during which farmers collect sap from various species of maple trees to make syrup. Maple trees convert starch into sugar, and this substance mixes with water absorbed by the roots. In the spring, warm temperatures cause this sugary water mixture to expand beyond the roots into the tree trunks.

On average, sugar season lasts roughly 30 days, typically beginning in February and ending by April. In recent years, some sugaring seasons have started in early January due to changes in climate conditions. For many farmers, producing and selling maple syrup supports their primary agricultural specialty, such as dairy farmers who benefit from the secondary source of income. For many outside of the agricultural industry, visiting sugarhouses at maple festivals helps them feel connected to their local communities and offers a peek into life throughout American history.

ENTRÉE

Maple syrup might seem like an unassuming breakfast condiment, but bottles of pure maple syrup are prized around the world. Due to the laborious, time-consuming, and climate-dependent process of making syrup, its price has increased 182 percent since 1980. In fact, the pancake and waffle topping is considerably more expensive than crude oil. Canadian maple syrup accounts for 71 percent of the world's supply, 90 percent of which is produced specifically in Quebec. As an export, its value is so significant that the country created a global strategic reserve of syrup that's divided between three secured facilities, mirroring international storage solutions for other valuable products, like the United States' Strategic Petroleum Reserve. In 2019, Canada produced 13.2 million gallons of syrup, compared to 4.24 million gallons in the United States (USDA 2019; Canadian Press; 2019).

Some of Canada's notable festivals include the Elmira Maple Syrup Festival in Elmira, Ontario. The inaugural event was launched in 1965 in hopes of attracting

Maple syrup is poured onto snow to create candy during the 2012 Winterlude Festival, an annual maple syrup festival held in Ottowa, Ontario, Canada. (Paul Mckinnon/Dreamstime.com)

2,500 people to enjoy pancakes. Much to the organizers' surprise, 10,000 people attended. Decades later, the Guinness Book of World Records deemed the event the "World's Largest Single Day Maple Syrup Festival" with 66,529 attendees in the year 2000. Quebec's Festival Beauceron de l'Erable and New Brunswick's Maple Capital of Atlantic Canada Festival are two additional notable festivals. They draw large crowds with their celebrations of the syrup's local heritage, including tours of historic sugar shacks and vintage meals like maple-cured ham, sugar pie, and snow taffy (hot maple syrup that is poured onto snow and served on a stick).

Within the United States, New England is most closely associated with maple syrup production and celebratory events. Vermont is the largest maple syrup provider, producing upward of 20 million pounds a year (Vanek Smith 2019). Some of the state's annual festivals include the Vermont Maple Festival, founded in 1966, and the state's Maple Open House Weekend, in which sugarhouses across the state welcome visitors to see the process of how the syrup is made. Many sugarhouses also open their doors to visitors each year in Maine on a Sunday dubbed Maine Maple Sunday and the state's small-town Skowhegan Maple Festival, as well as neighboring New Hampshire's Maple Weekend held in late March. In Connecticut, events like the Hebron Maple Festival offer small-town fun in the form of tractor parade, sugarhouse tours, and wares from local artisans.

Maple festivals draw many visitors in the Mid-Atlantic and Great Lakes regions as well. The Pennsylvania Maple Festival draws thousands of visitors to the borough of Meyersville each year to enjoy events like a 5K run and a Maple Queen beauty pageant. Virginia Highland County Maple Festival, legally deemed the state's "official maple festival," originated in 1956 and also includes a Maple Queen pageant. Within Minnesota, maple syrup celebrations are widespread across the state, entailing various demonstrations in the state parks that invite visitors to make their own syrup. Massachusetts follows suit, with an annual

> **Small Plates**
>
> **Deliciousness of Unknown Origins**
>
> According to research by the University of Vermont, the origin story of maple syrup is widely unknown. The earliest written accounts about sugaring in North America date back to 1557, and historians can only speculate about whether sugaring techniques were first attributed to French explorers, European settlers, or Native Americans. Eastern Woodlands Indian legend holds that syrup originally poured straight from the trees, and it made people so lazy that they just lay in the forest letting syrup pour straight into their mouths. A god had to use magical powers to add water to the trees' sap, thus making the syrup inedible on its own and forcing the people to return to their work.
>
> Settlers and Native Americans found ways to make syrup and sugar from maple tree sap using kettles in the eighteenth century, and around the time of the Civil War (1861–1865), the invention of tools like evaporator pans and tin cans fueled the introduction of the maple syrup industry in the United States. Yet another century later, Americans began constructing tubing systems and other tools like vacuum pumps, transporting the sap from trees into sugarhouses where they could be boiled.

weekend dedicated to sugaring celebrations across the state. Some notable events include the Ipswich Flapjack Fling and various hikes around maple syrup farmlands. According to figures from the Massachusetts Maple Producers Association, these events draw upward of 60,000 visitors annually and bring in more than $2 million. Numerous other festivals stretch from Iowa through Indiana, Illinois, and Ohio, which lays claim to the oldest maple-centric celebration in the nation—the Geauga County Maple Festival, founded in 1926.

DESSERT

- **But was it a Mickey pancake?** In the year 2000, the Elmira festival proudly served its 500,000th pancake.
- **Better with age:** Maple trees can't be tapped until they're at least 45 years old. Some trees will produce syrup for 55 years!
- **Double, double, toil and trouble:** The watery-looking sap from a maple tree has to be considerably boiled down in order to make a thick, sugary, concentrated syrup. It can take as many as 40 gallons of sap just to make 1 gallon of maple syrup!

SUGGESTED PAIRINGS

See also: Cake and Cupcake Trends; Holidays and Food; Trends, Food.

Entry best enjoyed while eating: Fluffy buttermilk pancakes slathered in pats of butter and 100 percent maple syrup; piping hot maple pork sausage links; bacon served with a maple-dijon glaze; maple-roasted chicken thighs with millet and pomegranate; maple syrup ice cream sundaes; and a maple bacon porter beer.

Further Reading

Canadian Press Staff. 2019. "Canada's Maple Syrup Production Reaches Record High While Honey Output Drops." *The Canadian Press*, December 11, 2019. https://www.ctvnews.ca/business/canada-s-maple-syrup-production-reaches-record-high-while-honey-output-drops-1.4725815

Dmitrieva, Katia, and Ilan Kolet. 2012. "Maple Syrup Value Sweeter Than Crude Oil, Gold." *Vancouver Sun*, December 21, 2012. http://www.vancouversun.com/technology/maple+syrup+value+sweeter+than+crude+gold/7734989/story.html

Elmira Maple Syrup. https://www.elmiramaplesyrup.com/history/

Massachusetts Maple Producers Association. n.d. "Facts and Figures." https://www.massmaple.org/about-maple-syrup/facts-and-figures/

Vanek Smith, Stacey. 2019. "How Quebec's Maple Syrup Stockpile Can Impact an Entire Global Industry." NPR, All Things Considered. April 17, 2019.

United States Department of Agriculture (USDA). 2019. "United States Maple Syrup Production." June 12, 2019. https://www.nass.usda.gov/Statistics_by_State/New_England_includes/Publications/Current_News_Release/2019/Maple%20Syrup%202019.pdf

University of Vermont Libraries. n.d. "History of Maple." https://researchguides.uvm.edu/maple

MasterChef (2010–)

STARTERS

MasterChef is a reality television show on the FOX network in which amateur cooks compete against each other in various timed challenges. The program is based on an eponymous British show that ran from 1990 through 2001 on BBC One and was revived under the name *MasterChef Goes Large* in 2005 (through present day) on BBC Two. The British program was so popular that it inspired dozens of international versions. The initial American version of the show was called *MasterChef USA* and aired on PBS from 2000 to 2001. Nine years later, the show was rebranded for the Fox network with a different name and a slightly different format.

Each episode features roughly two dozen contestants who must compete in four challenges, and a panel of judges weighs in on the dishes and techniques the chefs used, announcing eliminations and winners for each round. The winner takes home a cash prize of $250,000, in addition to a relative amount of fame and new opportunities within the industry from appearing on the show. In 2013, a youth-centric spin-off titled *Masterchef Junior* premiered on Fox, based on BBC's *Junior Masterchef* that first aired in 1994. This spin-off features aspiring chefs who are between the ages of 8 and 13 years old, and—aside from much gentler commentary from the judges—the show largely mirrors the adult version. *Masterchef* has run for 205 episodes over the duration of 10 seasons, never straying from its style of nail-biting competitions and dramatic portrayals of contestants' emotions. The show won a Primetime Emmy in 2013 for Outstanding Art Direction for a Multi-Camera Series and Directors Guild of America Awards for Outstanding Directorial Achievement in Reality Programs in 2013 and again in 2018.

ENTRÉE

Masterchef embodies many of the qualities that have made food competition shows so popular in the United States over the last decades. Audience members ranging from culinary professionals to those who have little to no interest in cuisine can all be sucked into the excitement of watching anywhere between 10 or more than 30 amateur chefs racing around a studio kitchen, attempting to wow judges with dishes they have been asked to cook on the spot. Mistakes, disasters, epiphanies, and celebrations all take place, with the added fun of rooting for "underdog" cast members who wow judges despite a lack of professional industry experience. Episodes consist of various challenges referred to as the "mystery box," "elimination test," "team challenge," and "pressure test." The mystery box is similar to tactics used on numerous other cooking reality shows, in which each contestant receives a box containing the same ingredients that they must use to create an improvised dish. The elimination and pressure tests grant immunity to winners and send losing chefs home, and team challenges allow chefs to stay on the show if they are included in a group that wins. At the end of each challenge, judges taste and assess each competitor's dish.

Masterchef's popularity over the years is likely due to its blend of gladiator-style competitions (similar to those seen in shows like *Iron Chef* and *Chopped*) and the mixture of spontaneous and contrived drama that occurs among contestants. Audience members are often swept up in the spectacle and challenge level of some competitions, such as a *Masterchef Junior* episode in which the young contestants had to recreate a dish that they had tasted while blindfolded. Many question how real the "reality" show is, and as with many similar shows, some have claimed that the behind-the-scenes experience for contestants is controversial. In a 2018 essay in *Salon* magazine, season three *Masterchef* competitor Jessie Glenn details the amount of time, anguish, and personal funds many competitors invested in an attempt to be cast on the show. In addition to noting the work on each person's television-sensationalized "back story," Glenn also describes a written personality test followed by invasive interviews with a psychiatrist and a detective, which she believes were in large part to collect fodder for the show's crew to write "plot twists" for contestants and pit people against other personality types guaranteed to cause friction and distress.

Her salacious essay (which she was able to publish due to having never signed a contract and nondisclosure statement for the show) notes a number of ways in which vulnerable people were exploited. These include a 15 percent management fee contestants must pay the production company (owned by prominent *Masterchef* judge Gordon Ramsay), and wranglers on set, she says, are tasked with increasing contestants' stress levels and setting people "off balance" to increase the show's drama. Another former contestant wrote online that contestants were privy to cooking lessons to improve upon specific skills they'd need in upcoming challenges, calling into question how "spontaneous" the show's challenges really were (Graham 2014).

Presenting an opposite viewpoint, noted pastry chef and *Masterchef* judge Christina Tosi defended the show for its fair judging to now-defunct *Lucky Peach* magazine, noting that contestants' performances are monitored by officials who ensure no one has an unfair advantage over another.

ACCOMPANIED BY

Over the years, *Masterchef*'s most frequent judges have included powerhouse industry figures like chef Gordon Ramsey, a British restaurateur, chef, and noted culinary television figure in the United Kingdom and United States alike. Ramsay's role on *Masterchef* is similar to his judge and host appearances on other reality cooking competitions: one of a stern, intense, and often intimidating culinary authority figure who is quick to point out errors and make harsh criticism of mistakes. In the earlier years of the show, restaurateur and vintner Joe Bastianich served as a judge on the American show before achieving significant celebrity status in Italy for his work on *Masterchef Italia*.

Aarón Sánchez is a fellow restaurateur and television persona, known for costarring on shows like *Chopped* and *Iron Chef America*. Sanchez is frequently joined by fellow judge and industry celebrity Christina Tosi, pastry chef and founder of the hip New York City bakery Milk Bar. In a 2016 interview with *Lucky Peach* magazine, Tosi summed up the determination of the show's contestants by saying "never when someone is lost do they not produce something—and sometimes the best thing comes out of that (. . .) that fight-or-flight sense turns into fight, and I'm often amazed by how many clever things come out of people getting lost in a challenge."

DESSERT

Cracking under pressure: On a particularly grueling episode of the enormously popular Australian *Masterchef*, chefs were tasked with creating *verjus in egg*, a dish that looks like an egg sitting on a nest of noodles. The "egg" consists of numerous fragile layers of chocolate surrounding panna cotta that has been designed to look like egg white and a runny "yolk" center. The dish requires roughly 100 steps to complete, many of which are very complex, and utilizes nearly an equal number of ingredients.

SUGGESTED PAIRINGS

See also: *Chopped*; *Iron Chef*; Ramsay, Gordon; Tosi, Christina.

Entry best enjoyed while eating: Papaya salad with crab and vegetables; sous vide pork belly bao with mushrooms and crispy kale; and coconut lime sorbet with ginger—the winning menu from Christine Ha, season three's champion chef and the first blind contestant on *Masterchef*.

Further Reading

Glenn, Jessie. 2018. "I Am a MasterChef Survivor." *Salon*, February 18, 2018. https://www.salon.com/2018/02/17/i-am-a-master-chef-survivor/

Graham, Caroline. 2014. "Gordon Ramsay's US MasterChef in Coaching Cheat Storm after Ex-contestant Reveals in Blog That Hopefuls Are Given Secret Cooking Classes." *Daily Mail*, February 15, 2014.

Lucky Peach Staff. 2016. "What Really Happens on TV Cooking Competitions." *Lucky Peach*, Spring 2016.

Mind of a Chef, The

STARTERS

The Mind of a Chef is a documentary-style nonfiction television series that aired on PBS. Created by celebrity chef David Chang and culinary television persona Anthony Bourdain, the show ran for 86 episodes over the course of six seasons. It premiered in 2012, backed by Zero Point Zero Production, the company that backed popular food travel series and documentaries *Decoding Ferran Adrian* (2005), *The Getaway* (2013), and Bourdain's *A Cook's Tour* (2000–2003), *No Reservations* (2004–2012), and *Parts Unknown* (2013–2018). The sixth season was released on Facebook Watch, a video-on-demand service, in 2017.

The Mind of a Chef featured one or more chefs per season, diving into each individual's philosophy and passion for food in addition to their lifestyle, interests, and the history and scientific components of the foods and techniques they discuss. Each half-hour episode features chefs doing things like interviewing their friends in the industry about topics related to each episode and often traveling to influential restaurants or locations where food is sourced and prepared. The program received an award for "Best Television Program on Location" in 2013 and 2014 from the James Beard Foundation and won a Daytime Emmy in 2014 for "Outstanding Culinary Program."

ENTRÉE

"It takes a certain kind of crazy to open a restaurant in New York City, where such ventures are almost guaranteed to fail. Yet Gabrielle Hamilton went ahead, and—defying all logic—opened the intensely personal Prune. And Prune, from the beginning, defied all conventional wisdom. The menu was autobiographical." So begins the first episode of *The Mind of a Chef*'s fourth season. Executive producer and narrator Anthony Bourdain's smooth, personable voice is cut over dissonant music and documentary footage of Hamilton going about her day: navigating the streets of the city, slicing meat with a mandolin, rinsing the long, drooping tentacles of an octopus in Prune's kitchen. Inspired by David Chang's literary-culinary mashup magazine *Lucky Peach*, Bourdain and Chang shopped the concept of *The Mind of a Chef* to numerous networks in a quest to find a home for an "intellectual biography" about chefs and the food that is central to their lives.

PBS is known best for instructional, cook-to-the-camera shows like *The French Chef*, *Mexico, One Plate at a Time*, and *Yan Can Cook*, and the network struck some as an unusual home for the "combined star power and unruly personas of Mr. Chang and Mr. Bourdain," as *New York Times* writer Mike Hale described them. Despite its somewhat edgy, experimental style, Chang said the docuseries was a strong fit for PBS's audience due to the show's twofold goal of being educational and showcasing restaurants and chefs' passion projects in a positive light.

Unlike many ventures on networks like Food Network and Cooking Channel, the inspiration behind this show was to create an "intellectual biography" as opposed to a tutorial backed by sponsorships and product placement (Hale 2012).

ACCOMPANIED BY

Each season of *The Mind of a Chef* explores the intellectual and physical daily life of one or more chefs. The first season follows cocreator David Chang (1977–), founder of the international Momofuku restaurant group, food writer, and television personality. Shortly after *The Mind of a Chef* ended, Chang served as the host and executive producer of a similar food-themed travel docuseries: Netflix's *Ugly Delicious* (2018–). In season two of *The Mind of a Chef*, viewers follow Chang through large and small moments alike. In one, he slurps noodles in a widely renowned ramen restaurant in a subway station, teasing his friend whose appetite for heaping bowls of noodles doesn't measure up to the locals'. In another, the Michelin-star-holding chef stands alone in one of his restaurants' kitchens, biting into a dehydrated brick of instant ramen noodles with seasoning powder dusted on top, musing about doing the same throughout his youth.

Season two features chefs Sean Brock (1978–) and April Bloomfield (1974–). Brock illuminates the intersection of food, history, and culture represented in Southern cooking from his restaurants McCradys and Husk, located in South Carolina and Tennessee. Brock is a cookbook author and historian of Southern food's culinary and cultural history. He was featured on Netflix's biographical culinary show *Chef's Table*, in which he revealed what it was like to balance his passion for cooking while living with a rare disease called myasthenia gravis. Bloomfield is a Michelin-starred, British-born chef known for her restaurant empire that includes the Spotted Pig and the Breslin Bar & Dining Room in New York City. On *The Mind of a Chef*, Bloomfield shows viewers where her career began in London and pulls back the arduous process of preparing for the grand opening of the revitalized Tosca Cafe in San Francisco, California. In the wake of the #MeToo movement, Bloomfield came under fire in 2017 by numerous women who said that Bloomfield did nothing to prevent them from being sexually harassed and verbally abused by Bloomfield's business partner, Ken Friedman (Moskin and Severson 2018).

Season three chronicles two chefs as well: Edward Lee (1972–) and Magnus Nilsson (1982–). Lee is a Korean American chef and writer who grew up in New York City but became enchanted by the world of Southern cuisine. Described as putting a modern twist on Southern cooking, Lee is the chef and owner of restaurants 610 Magnolia, MilkWood, and Whiskey Dry in Louisville, Kentucky. On *The Mind of a Chef*, Lee shares his philosophy that foods within the same latitude across the globe tend to pair well together. He also pushes back on the trendy term "fusion," offering his view that blending foods from different cultures helps erase borders. Nilsson is a Swedish-born Michelin-starred chef and sommelier whose 12-seat restaurant Fäviken Magasinet was ranked 19th in the World's Best 50 Restaurants List. Nilsson's episodes shed insight into what it's like to cook world-class food in Scandinavia, with consideration to how he uses the region's short, dark months and long days flooded with light to help orchestrate his ingredient pairings.

Season four highlights Gabrielle Hamilton (1966–) and David Kinch (1961–). Hamilton is known best for her New York City restaurant Prune, as well as her memoir, *Blood, Bones, and Butter*. Her episodes' topics cover a gamut of topics. In "Garbage," the second episode, she examines how much food was thrown away by the chefs and her views on what should have been salvaged. The fourth episode highlights Hamilton's loneliness as a child and her challenges in getting enough food to eat: experiences that she weaves into her menu at Prune. Kinch is another Michelin-starred and James Beard Award–winning chef. Known best for his Los Gatos, California, restaurant, Manresa, Kinch reflects on various challenges in the industry, ranging from the challenge of American patrons' dietary restrictions to a fire that devastated his restaurant (and a second one, years later, that ironically broke out on the anniversary of the first).

Season five features French American chef Ludovic "Ludo" Lefebvre (1971–), a classically trained chef whose mentors include renowned chefs Marc Meneau and Alain Passard, among others. The season documents Lefebvre's influence on (and influences from) the culinary scene in Los Angeles, where he is known for restaurants including L'Orangerie and Petit Trois and the trend he helped launch of temporary pop-up restaurants. *The Mind of a Chef* illustrates the classical master's unlikely passion: quintessentially American fried chicken.

The final season features Danny Bowien (1982–), the Korean American founder of renowned Mission Chinese Food restaurants in New York City, Brooklyn, and San Francisco. Bowien takes visitors through an autobiographical background of his experimental flavors, gleaning inspiration from his childhood in Oklahoma to culinary mentors in China and Korea. Bowien's penchant for experimental fashion, unusual dishes, and tattoos complements the edgy, colorful, and graphic-novel aesthetic of both the show and its predecessor *Lucky Peach*.

SUGGESTED PAIRINGS

See also: Bourdain, Anthony; Chang, David; Magazines, Food; Television, Food Channels on.

Entry best enjoyed while eating: Canned sardines on Triscuit crackers with Dijon mustard and cornichons (Hamilton, in a nod to preparing food with limited options while growing up); "A Winter Tidal Pool": pickled kelp, oyster gel, mushroom gel, abalone, tidal broth, foie gras, spinach, sea urchin (Kinch); Naples-style sourdough crust pizza with Sichuan *mapo doufu*, a spicy tofu stir fry, to dip it in (Bowien); *Kalvdans*: a Swedish dessert pudding made from cow's colostrum—the first milk it produces after birthing a calf (Nilsson).

Further Reading

Hale, Mike. 2012. "Behind the Dish, There's a Chef with a Story." *The New York Times*, November 2, 2012.

The Mind of a Chef, Season Four, Episode 1. 2015. PBS, air date September 4, 2015. https://www.pbs.org/video/mind-chef-season-4-episode-1-prune/

Moskin, Julia, and Kim Severson. 2018. "April Bloomfield Breaks Her Silence about Harassment at Her Restaurants." *The New York Times*, October 16, 2018.

Nonfiction, Food in

STARTERS

Nonfiction works about food and eating have gained significant popularity in American pop culture over the last 50 years, and contemporary works exhibit an enormous range of subjects and styles. Despite the abundance of recipes and cooking tutorials that can be found online, cookbooks see very strong sales worldwide. In a report from market research group NPD, cookbook sales in the United States rose 21 percent in the first half of 2018 with help from popular trends like the growing appeal of cooking at home, the use of appliances like instant pots, and interest in publications by high-profile celebrities. A reported 80 percent of meals were cooked and eaten at home in America in 2017 (NPD Group 2018).

Other nonfiction categories like the history of food, culinary memoirs and travelogues, historical and sociological food research, and philosophies, ethics, and science surrounding food have also proliferated in recent decades as Americans' appetites for new culinary subjects continue to grow. Contemporary Americans are hungry to learn about different cultural foodways and recipes, discover the history and sociological background of various foods, and celebrate cuisine in new and exciting ways.

ENTRÉE

The history of American cookbooks illuminates trends, people in the public eye, and needs of home cooks in various decades. A popular 1909 *Good Housekeeping* cookbook was written for housewives and contained meticulously tested recipes and blank spaces for home cooks to make their own notes. The 1922 edition also offered things like tips on preparing the home for the holidays (Milligan n.d.). In 1931, amateur cook Irma Rombauer penned a cookbook as a way of coping with her grief after her husband died from suicide. Writing from the viewpoint of a home cook's friend—not a flour company or magazine, the authorial viewpoint of many previous cookbooks—Rombauer's *The Joy of Cooking* went on to become the most popular cookbook in American history. To date, more than 18 million copies of numerous revised editions have been printed (Mendelson 2012; Severson 2006). Julia Child took on a similar tone in *Mastering the Art of French Cooking* (Volume 1, 1961; Volume 2, 1970). The cookbook had an enormous resurgence in sales in 2009 after the release of the film *Julie and Julia* (Clifford 2009), which follows the true story of blogger Julie Powell's attempt to make every recipe in Child's cookbook in a year. Powell also published an eponymous nonfiction memoir about her experience.

Many contemporary cookbooks reflect Americans' growing interests in a variety of racial and ethnic cultural cuisines. Two critically praised 2018 titles include *Feast: Food of the Islamic World* by Anissa Helou and *I Am a Filipino: And This Is How We Cook*, by Nicole Ponseca and Miguel Trinidad. Other notable culinary titles from the same year include *You and I Eat the Same: On the Countless Ways Food and Cooking Connect Us to One Another* (Chris Ying and Rene Redzepi), *Buttermilk Graffiti: A Chef's Journey to Discover America's New Melting-Pot Cuisine* (Edward Lee), and *Catfish Dream: Ed Scott's Fight for His Family Farm and Racial Justice in the Mississippi Delta* (Julian Rankin). These works explore cultural diversity and ways in which food has the potential to unite people of all races, ethnicities, political associations, and nationalities.

Many nonfiction titles explore the history of various foods and foodways, such as Michael Twitty's *The Cooking Gene* (2017), which blends Twitty's genealogical and historical research into a discussion of the racial "ownership" of Southern cuisine. Compelling stories about the ways in which immigrants have changed American food and culture have been explored in books like *The Fortune Cookie Chronicles: Adventures in the World of Chinese Food* (Jennifer 8. Lee, 2009), *Taco USA: How Mexican Food Conquered America* (Gustavo Arellano, 2013), and *97 Orchard: An Edible History of Five Immigrant Families in One New York Tenement* (Jane Ziegelman, 2011). Other works explore communities in crisis and the pragmatic and emotional importance of serving meals to those in need, such as José Andrés's *We Fed an Island: The True Story of Rebuilding Puerto Rico, One Meal at a Time* (2018).

Other food-themed books take deep dives into niche food subjects, such as Mark Kurlansky's books about the history of milk, frozen food, oysters in New York City, salt, and cod fish. Similarly, Bee Wilson's *Consider the Fork* (2013) focuses on the history of cooking utensils. Other niche historical culinary books range in subjects from the role and importance of food in Jane Austen's seminal novels to Dave Eggers' *The Monk of Mokha* (2018), which tells the story of a Yemeni American who helped create the global trend of expensive cups of high-end coffee.

Nonfiction titles by celebrity chefs and other "foodies" in the public eye frequently see significant sales. Television personality Joanna Gaines's *Magnolia Table* cookbook sold 676,000 copies in 2018, thanks in large part to her popular HGTV show *Fixer Upper* (NPD Group 2018). Chefs' food memoirs often weave stories about culinary training with memories from childhood and the authors' personal attachment to food and cultural explorations. Some popular chef-penned memoirs include Anthony Bourdain's *Kitchen Confidential* (2000), Marcus Samuelsson's *Yes, Chef* (2012), Amy Thielen's *Give a Girl a Knife* (2017), and Gabrielle Hamilton's *Blood, Bones, and Butter* (2011), just to name a few. Other reflective life works include food critic Ruth Reichl's *Tender at the Bone* (1998), food writer M. F. K. Fisher's *The Gastronomical Me* (1948), and Bill Buford's *Heat* (2006), which chronicles a journalist's attempts at finding a successful career in professional kitchens. Author Elizabeth Gilbert's travel memoir documents eating and meditating her way through a divorce and new romance in *Eat Pray Love* (2006), and *Vogue* food critic Jeffrey Steingarten documented his attempt at overcoming the bevy of foods he found off-putting in *The Man Who Ate Everything* (1998).

Americans are also very interested in ethical and philosophical considerations regarding food, eating, and cooking. Author Michael Pollan's popular titles like *The Botany of Desire* (2001) and *Omnivore's Dilemma* (2006) explore issues within agricultural practices and human health, and he makes pointed arguments for specific cooking practices and diets. Other nonfiction works examine food rituals from a sociological viewpoint. The practice of letting inmates choose their final meal before their execution is illustrated in Ty Treadwell and Michelle Vernon's *Last Suppers: Famous Final Meals from Death Row*, and author Melanie Dunea explores the idea of a final meal in a different philosophical context in her book *My Last Supper: 50 Great Chefs and Their Final Meals* (2007). Dunea's book blends personal portraits of each chef with details like the location, music, and companions that would accompany their preferred final meals on earth.

DESSERT

What was the most unusual meal ever ordered by an inmate on death row? A "lump of dirt," according to the authors of *Last Suppers*, ordered by inmate James Smith in 1990. The inmate was a Tarot card reader who was accused of murder, and he wanted the dirt as part of a voodoo ritual. Smith was denied his request, and he "settled for yogurt instead" (Treadwell and Vernon, 2011).

SUGGESTED PAIRINGS

See also: Asian American Cuisine; Child, Julia; *Cooked*; Fiction, Food in; Films, Food in; Latin American Cuisine.

Entry best enjoyed while eating: Anchovy cheese fingers (*H'ors Doeurve and Canapes*, James Beard); split-pea fritters with chutney (*Climbing the Mango Tree*, Madhur Jaffrey); Eleanor Roosevelt's "Shrimp Wiggle" on toast (*What She Ate: Six Remarkable Women and the Food That Tells Their Stories*, Laura Shapiro), and a cup of tea with a side helping of its influence on British foreign policy (*A History of the World in 6 Glasses*, Tom Standage).

Further Reading
Clifford, Stephanie. 2009. "After 48 Years, Julia Child Has a Big Best Seller, Butter and All." *The New York Times*, August 23, 2009.
Mendelson, Anne. 2012. "The History of the Joy of Cooking." http://www.thejoykitchen.com/all-about-joy/history-joy-cooking
Milligan, Ceara. n.d. "The Most Popular Cookbook from Every Decade." *Taste of Home*. https://www.tasteofhome.com/collection/popular-cookbook-from-every-decade/
NPD Group. 2018. "Cookbook Category Sales Roles 21 Percent Year over Year." https://www.npd.com/wps/portal/npd/us/news/press-releases/2018/cookbook-category-sales-rose-21-percent-year-over-year-the-npd-group-says/
Severson, Kim. 2006. "Does the World Need Another 'Joy'? Do You?" *The New York Times*, November 1, 2006.

Tepper Paley, Rachel. 2018. "The Ten Best Books about Food in 2018." *Smithsonian Magazine*, November 19, 2018.

Treadwell, Ty, and Michelle Vernon. 2011. *Last Suppers: Famous Final Meals from Death Row*. Self-published.

Novelty Dining Experiences

STARTERS

Novelty dining experiences exist in many forms and have been popular for decades. Spurred on by diners who were delighted to be presented with new ways of enjoying and observing their food, many restaurants around the world have identified themselves as specializing in food that is unusual or prepared and served in an unusual way. Numerous restaurants serve food in a way that invokes the senses, asking patrons to mindfully observe the scent, texture, sound, and visual appeal of each dish in addition to its taste.

Some use the physical space around diners as a key part of the meal, ranging from unusually decorated restaurant interiors to meals served in creative spaces outdoors. Some novel dining experiences even take a traveling theme, shuttling patients to and from secret locales or multiple stops along a "traveling feast." Oftentimes, novel dining experiences are associated with being highly expensive and catering only to wealthy patrons, eliciting reviews ranging from criticism regarding elitism to rave reviews and trend-setting ideas.

ENTRÉE

In the United States, novelty culinary experiences run the gamut from *haute cuisine*—high-end dining—to downright campy. One unifying factor is often a sense of fun or playfulness; another tends to be steep prices. In cities like Los Angeles, California, those wishing to have an unusual meal can choose from a full spectrum of experiences. Barton G's restaurant specializes in theatrical props accompanying the food: popcorn shrimp spilling out of a movie-theater-style popcorn machine; lobster pop tarts served in a cartoonish, oversized toaster; and a garden salad served in a toy-sized wheelbarrow that a server mixes with a trowel and sprinkles with seeds. Other diners might head to Vespertine, a high-concept restaurant by chef Jordan Kahn that's housed in a building whose steel and glass facade appears to ripple like waves.

Guests are ushered between floors to the sounds of a curated soundtrack by a staff dressed in custom wool uniforms reminiscent of a science fiction tale. A *GQ* magazine profile on the restaurant described Vespertine as borderline absurd, noting details like dissonant sounds played at the entrance designed to instill relief upon entering the restaurant and 20-plus courses consisting of dishes like "bastard halibut hidden underneath plums," advertised on the restaurant's social media in a photo resembling a charcoal puck on an unidentifiable background resembling an alien moonrock.

Theatrical experiences such as these are all the rage with a number of restaurants, such as Chicago-based Alinea, founded by Chef Grant Achatz in 2005. "Alinea is not a restaurant . . . at least, not in the conventional sense," its website introduction begins, and its 15-year history of theatrical presentations proves Achatz's dedication to performance. Similar to concept restaurants like Vespertine, Alinea's guests pay upward of $385 per person for a 15- to 30-course tasting menu that entails eating in numerous parts of the restaurant (including in the kitchen, for some, where they hand-crank their own cocktails using a rare cast-iron machine). Courses run the gamut from dishes like gelatinous balls of grape extract, lemongrass aroma pouring out of a shell fueled by dry ice, and edible green apple taffy balloons filled with helium and secured to monolithic tables by heavy metal pins.

The theater of tableside service is thought to go back at least as far as the late nineteenth century, inspired by individuals like chef Georges Escoffier, who invented spectacles like igniting a dessert called cherries jubilee in front of his astonished guests. *LA Times* writer Jennifer Swann notes that the tradition of tableside service boomed in the United States during the 1950s through the 1980s, exemplifying "the height of American fine dining—a welcome extravagance following the meat rationing of World War II." American culinary writer Julia Child wrote about her memory of being dazzled by the tableside preparation of chef Cesare Cardini's Caesar Salad—a meal that many Americans flocked to Tijuana, Mexico, to experience during the Prohibition era. Food as a spectacle, served with panache, goes back throughout human history. During the Renaissance, Italian courtiers attended banquets of 80 dishes or more, some presented in fanfare such as peacocks cooked with their feathers and appearing to "spew fire from their beaks" (Real 2015).

Food & Wine writer Gowri Chandra notes that the general decline of tableside service in the 1960s signified a cultural shift of not requiring servers to have significant culinary technical skills. In the 1950s and 1960s, patrons in the United States or France might watch a team of waiters carve an elaborate leg of lamb tableside, whereas in contemporary society, such actions are thought to be the chef's job, largely hidden in an unseen kitchen. "The most ubiquitous takeaway from tableside dining, however, could be the open kitchen concept: it shatters the fourth wall of the kitchen and allows the food to be theater, giving diners a view of the stage. Food is, and always will be, an act of spectacle," Chandra writes (2018).

The fad of flambéing foods, like Escoffier's flaming cherries jubilee and other popular desserts like Baked Alaska and bananas foster, fueled a decades-long tradition of lighting food on fire tableside to delight customers. The 1990s saw the rise of *molecular gastronomy*, a scientific discipline focused on the chemistry and physics of cooking. The term (and field) was invented by chemist Herve This (1955) and physicist Nicholas Kurti in the late 1980s. Catalan chef Ferran Adria is credited with creating the contemporary trend of culinary foam at his Spanish restaurant El Bulli in 1994. Described as a chef who "refused to be limited by the physical properties of food," Adria was soon copied by other chefs worldwide. They poured substances like bean puree into a whipped cream canister, added liquid nitrogen, and used the aerosol feature to produce a foam substance that

Molecular gastronomy frequently entails foods served in unusual forms, such as foams, gels, and sculptural constructions. This dessert showcases raspberry dessert served as "caviar" shapes, with strawberry foam and a brittle nest of hardened caramel. (Shawn Hempel/Dreamstime.com)

could be crafted into all manner of bubbly, colorful shapes. The fad began to wane in the early 2000s, though some restaurants continue experimenting with it (Mishan 2019).

Molecular gastronomy, also referred to as avant-garde cuisine (with subgenres like "techno emotional cuisine"), is closely associated with chefs such as Adria, who coined the "deconstructed" food trend that is still popular today. *Deconstruction* entails serving ingredients in new ways, separating ones that are typically served together. One contemporary chef known for both deconstruction and molecular gastronomy is Wylie Dufrene, whose former restaurant WD-50 in New York City served items like columns of poached egg served with cubes of deep-fried hollandaise sauce dusted with English muffin crumbs. Achatz's Alinea is another restaurant that specializes in molecular gastronomy, as is Atelier Crenn, the San Francisco restaurant of chef Dominique Crenn. Atelier Crenn exemplifies a contemporary trend in which customers are asked to interact with their food in thoughtful ways; instead of listing the foods that will be served, the menu is a poem, and each line evokes some of the themes diners will encounter with each course.

Other trends at restaurants such as these play to the senses in different ways. One crowd-pleasing trick is to incorporate the smell (and theatrical sight) of wood smoke into a meal by gathering hot wood chips or smoked food in a glass cloche and asking guests to remove the lid and take a whiff before tasting their food.

In Britain, at a restaurant called the Fat Duck, servers ask diners to put their ears up to conch shells holding hidden iPods that play sounds of waves before presenting small bites of sashimi plated on small glass boxes filled with sand. An emerging trend toys with the idea of virtual reality dining, such as an event held at the James Beard House in 2019, called Aerobanquets RMX. Guests wore headsets orchestrating floating objects that danced to narration and music, as they sampled each course from a "food vessel," guessing what they were eating while essentially blindfolded.

Certainly not all novelty dining experiences come with price tags above $200, although they tend to cost more than the average equivalent of the same type of meals. Some are intended to spark dialogue and deeper understandings, such as

---

Small Plates

Theme Restaurants

Theme restaurants create stylized, theatrical environments that portray different locations, time periods, or even alternate realities for diners. One of the first theme restaurants was Café du Bagne in Paris, which opened in 1885. The cafe looked like a penitentiary, and waiters playing "convicts" dragged balls and chains from their ankles. This inspired a new trend in the United States starting around the 1920s, particularly in Los Angeles, where struggling out-of-work set designers found a new niche designing over-the-top eateries that drew in groups ranging from families to Hollywood celebrities.

During this era, a combination of Prohibition and widespread menus that were homogenous and somewhat bland helped fuel customers' appetite for restaurant theatrics. One famous example was the Pirate's Den, a restaurant based in New York City with multiple locations across the country. Actors portraying pirates carried out shenanigans such as playfully kidnapping women from their tables and awarding them with "scream certificates" behind the scenes if they protested loudly. Likely inspired by Café du Bagne, L.A.'s Jail Café seated delighted guests to dine in prison cells and be served by "convicts" in striped prison uniforms. In 1926, two men carried out an actual robbery during dinner. Patrons thought the hold-up was a performance until the men took off with $500 worth of their valuables.

The exotic appeal of novelty restaurants also inspired racist themes, such as the Zulu Hut, a fried chicken establishment made from dirt floors and a thatched roof. African Americans and white servers in blackface acted like "savages," wearing grass skirts, throwing knives, and dancing. The restaurant was the scene of multiple violent crimes and two fires, one of which sent patrons racing for their lives before burning the establishment to the ground (Saperstein 2015).

Whimsical eateries aren't limited to the United States; they can be found worldwide. One hot spot for kitschy dining is Taipei, Taiwan. In past years, the city was home to a hospital-themed restaurant in which drinks were filled by IV drips, and A380 In-Flight Kitchen, a restaurant designed like an airplane's interior. Customers were assigned a seat on the "plane" and were served by waitstaff who dressed and spoke like flight attendants, pushing small carts of food up and down the aisles. Taipei's Modern Toilet Restaurant features nonfunctional commodes as chairs and food like swirled chocolate ice cream served in toilet-shaped dishes. Japan is another country that is known for unusual dining experiences, such as cafes where people can interact with cats or owls, and themed restaurants where diners can go fishing for their own fish or be entertained by dancing robots while they dine.

The Blind Cafe, a traveling "social impact experience" in which attendees eat a meal, interact with servers and other guests, and listen to music in a pitch-black room. And since the 1980s, a chain called Medieval Times Dinner and Tournament has offered Renaissance-style theatrical performances. Guests dine on a multi-course meal with a "queen" while they are entertained by actors in a gladiator-style ring posing as knights jousting on horseback and giving falconry demonstrations.

DESSERT

One contemporary pop culture scene that pokes fun at molecular gastronomy (and novelty dining experiences, in general) is from *Always Be My Maybe*, a 2019 romantic comedy starring Ali Wong and Randall Park. The film explores questions about creativity, authenticity, and absurdity of the high-end culinary world as Wong's character, Sasha, opens a high-end "transdenominational" Vietnamese fusion restaurant in food-chic San Francisco, California.

In one memorable scene, Sasha's friend Marcus (Park) tags along with his girlfriend (Vivian Bang) on a double date to meet Sasha's new boyfriend, actor Keanu Reeves (playing himself). The foursome meet up at a fictional high-end restaurant called Maximal, where the interior is shaped like a giant cube and the guests' attire is some form of futuristic grunge. "Do you have any dishes that play with time? The *concept* of time?" Reeves asks his server, who responds that the restaurant's "venison sous vide comes with headphones so you can hear the exact animal you are about to consume, illustrating nature's life-to-death cycle." When the dish arrives, Reeves is shown listening intently to the sound of the deer through his headphones, sobbing briefly and raising his eyes skyward to proclaim "I'm sorry!" before taking a swig of red wine and digging into his meal with gusto.

SUGGESTED PAIRINGS

See also: Culinary Awards, The Evolution of; Films, Food in; Trends, Food.
Entry best enjoyed while eating:

- **Endive with oil and vinegar foam, heated with a blowtorch and dusted with tomato powder:** Wylie Dufresne's "salad," an off-the-menu exception created for Velvet Underground lead singer Lou Reed, who always requested salad despite the restaurant's general refusal to make or serve anything resembling one (WD-50, New York, New York).
- *Plato de las especias* **(spice dish):** one of Ferran Adria's courses consisting of a dish of green apple jelly dotted with tiny sprinkles of various herbs and spices spaced far apart from each other (El Bulli, Catalonia, Spain).
- **"Sitting on top of the dune, feeling of beach sand under my toes":** a line of Dominique Crenn's menu-poem describing a course of sweetbreads, shellfish, and phytoplankton (Atelier Crenn, San Francisco, California).
- **"Flowers marinated with pollen":** a butterfly-shaped dish served in a glass case. It comprises edible elements like flower petals, bee pollen, gooseberries,

currants, and even crushed ants. One server noted that each takes up to 12 minutes to make and that they had the arduous task of making up to 120 of them each day (Noma, Copenhagen, Denmark).

Further Reading

Brinkley, Renee. 2020. https://www.cnbc.com/2020/03/21/virtual-reality-dining-explained.html

Bull, Marian. 2017. "Welcome to Chef Jordan Kahn's Anti-Locavore Fine-Dining Spaceship." *GQ*, June 17, 2017.

Chandra, Gowri. 2018. "Old-School Tableside Service Is Making a Comeback." *Food & Wine*, February 22, 2018.

Mallory, Mary, and Larry Harnish. 2015. "Hollywood Heights: The Zulu Hut—Studio City's First Programmatic Architecture." L.A. Daily Mirror. https://ladailymirror.com/2015/09/07/mary-mallory-hollywood-heights-the-zulu-hut-studio-citys-first-programmatic-architecture/

Mishan, Ligaya. 2019. "Once Declared Passé, Foam Returns to the Restaurant Table." *New York Times*, Style Magazine, August 21, 2019.

Platt, Adam. 2019. "Dinner with the Nomaheads." *New York Magazine*, Grub Street blog. June 27, 2019. https://www.grubstreet.com/2019/06/noma-plant-kingdom-menu-platt.html

Real, Nancy Delucia. 2015. "How to Eat Like a Renaissance Courtier." *The Iris*, blog from the Getty museum. https://blogs.getty.edu/iris/how-to-eat-like-a-renaissance-courtier/

Saperstein, Pat. 2015. "Inside the Wild World of L.A.'s Early Theme Restaurants." Eater, November 3, 2015. https://la.eater.com/2015/11/3/9457775/los-angeles-early-theme-restaurants-racist

Swann, Jennifer. 2017. "The Lost Art of Tableside Service." *LA Weekly*, August 3, 2017. https://www.laweekly.com/the-lost-art-of-tableside-service-survives-at-this-midcentury-l-a-restaurant/

Vettel, Phil. 2016. "Review: Alinea, Now as Much as $385 a Head, Puts on Quite a Show." *Chicago Tribune*, July 15, 2016.

Waters, Michael. 2017. "Old Hollywood's Best Theme Restaurants Specialized in Abductions and Dungeons." Atlas Obscura, June 7, 2017. https://www.atlasobscura.com/articles/los-angeles-theme-restaurants-jail-cafe-pirates-den

P

Pépin, Jacques (1935–)

STARTERS

Jacques Pépin is a French American television personality, food writer, cooking instructor, and artist. Well known for his appearances in the PBS series *Julia and Jacques Cooking at Home* (1999) alongside his friend and culinary peer Julia Child, Pépin was also the host of programs like *The Complete Pépin* (1997), *Jacques Pépin Fast Food My Way* (2004), and *Jacques Pépin Heart and Soul* (2015). PBS also featured the chef in a documentary series called *American Masters* (2017). Pépin has made guest appearances on a number of television shows, such as acting as a guest judge on Bravo's *Top Chef*, and countless appearances as a guest speaker and cook on other programs.

In addition to having written 27 cookbooks and a memoir, Pépin has also been a contributing writer and editor to *Food & Wine* magazine and a *The New York Times* food columnist. The chef has been honored with a number of accolades, both domestically and abroad. France bestowed Pépin with the titles of La Legion d'Honneur, the country's highest civilian award, and the Chevalier des Arts et Lettres, awarded for a significant contribution to the French culture. Over the course of his lifetime, his programs and cookbooks have received 24 James Beard Foundation Awards, and he was given the organization's highest honor, the Lifetime Achievement award (2005). In 2001, *Julia and Jacques Cooking at Home* received a Daytime Emmy Award.

ENTRÉE

"I don't want people to come away from my table feeling that they have had some 'culinary experience,' I just want them to say to themselves, 'That was really good,'" Pépin wrote in the introduction to his 2015 cookbook *Jacques Pépin Heart and Soul*. And for many who did walk away from Pépin's table—either having dined with him in person or having mimicked his techniques at home—blending culinary mastery with a simple joy of eating would likely be their takeaway. Pépin is known as a king of cooking techniques, particularly as the author of the 1976 instructional work *La Technique*, which was a seminal cooking work for many contemporary chefs and amateur cooks alike. The book was unlike many before it in that it took cooks step by step through the process of many different skills they'd need in the kitchen, using photographs as supporting educational tools. The chef and his longtime friend Julia Child have been described by many in the culinary industry as pioneers of a new way of cooking and enjoying food—teachers who helped "average" cooks find a deeper sense of accomplishment and joy in the kitchen.

Born in Bourg-en-Bresse, France, Pépin dropped out of school at the age of 13 and began an apprenticeship in a hotel kitchen. Pépin studied with a number of highly skilled chefs, working his way up to eventually become the personal chef for French heads of state (including Charles de Gaulle). Pépin moved to the United States in 1959, where he continued to hone his skills in fine restaurants. He gained a significant understanding of Americans' culinary preferences (and the industry at large), working for a decade as the director of research at a hotel and restaurant chain called Howard Johnson's. While immersing himself in American cuisine and culture, Pépin simultaneously studied at Columbia University, where he received both his bachelor's and earned a master's in eighteenth-century French literature.

In an event that was similar to one of his contemporary culinary peers, Graham Kerr of the humorous travel cooking program *The Galloping Gourmet*, Pépin was in a serious car accident in the early 1970s that prompted him to make a serious shift in his career. He decided to focus on writing and teaching about the craft of cooking. As a teacher, his commitment to showing students how to master techniques through meticulous practice sometimes clashed with the motivation some students felt to rush through the rudimentary steps in a quest to become a celebrity chef. This frustration was echoed by numerous other classically trained chefs in the 1990s and 2000s who saw a rise of students who were more impatient to skip early training than many of their predecessors had been. This cultural shift has widely been attributed to the rise of programming on Food Network and the concept of celebrity chefs and culinary television personalities who often achieve rock star status in popular culture.

Pépin did not achieve "chef rock star" status in his career, but his influence as a celebrity chef has played a role in the way many Americans celebrate food in their own lives. Pépin and Child both blended a strict scientific approach to cooking with their love of French cuisine, demonstrating simple techniques that anyone could learn to make high-quality food. In many ways, Pépin's career could be seen as a cultural equalizer—as an immigrant with a passion for American life, he demonstrated techniques that people of all ages, genders, sexes, ethnicities, races, and nationalities could try. Even those on a shoestring budget can learn to make a French omelet if they have three eggs, a knob of butter, pepper, and a stovetop; anyone can learn Pépin's outstanding knife skills if they have a bulb of garlic and a chef's knife. Writer Gustavo Arellano wrote in his nonfiction work *Taco USA* that one of the first steps toward accepting other cultures and people begins with "foreign" foods infiltrating mainstream culture. To this end, Pépin helped infiltrate Americans' kitchens and televisions as an immigrant welcomed through the tantalizing lure of delicious food.

ACCOMPANIED BY

Jacques was raised by Jeanne and Jean-Victor Pépin, who owned a restaurant called Le Pelican that helped launch Pépin's lifelong love of food. In his memoir, *The Apprentice*, Pépin wrote that he nearly died at birth, weighing only two and a half pounds. A midwife attending his birth wrapped him in blankets and placed

> **Small Plates**
>
> **Slippery Slope to Love**
>
> Gloria Pépin, Jacques Pépin's wife of 52 years, shared in a PBS *American Masters* documentary how the two met. According to Gloria, Jacques worked for the ski school, and unbeknown to him, she worked for the ski patrol. Gloria was attracted to Jacques, so she hired him for a private lesson despite her superior skill as a skier. Gloria recounts the lesson, remembering that Jacques would hit her legs repeatedly with a ski pole, finding lots of problems with her form. "So I never got to first base," Gloria shared. "I had to take a second lesson." Jacques and Gloria married in 1966, and the groom was nearly late to his own wedding because he couldn't tear himself away from prepping food for the event with his chef friends in the kitchen beforehand (*American Masters* 2017).

him in a shoebox that was surrounded by bricks that had been warmed in the stove. Pépin's memoir also describes childhood memories of running through the streets with his mother and two brothers to hide under a railroad underpass during a World War II air raid.

Jacques wed Gloria Pépin in 1966, and the two established a home in Madison, Connecticut. The couple has a daughter, Claudine, and a granddaughter, Shorey. Claudine and Jacques cofounded the Jacques Pépin Foundation in 2016, which "supports community kitchens that offer free life skills and culinary training to adults with high barriers to employment, including previous incarceration, homelessness, substance abuse issues, low skill and education attainment and lack of work history."

DESSERT

- **Eggs from on high:** Pépin was a friend and mentor to television personality Anthony Bourdain. In an interview with *Slate* magazine, staff writer Kathryn Shulz asked Bourdain, "So is there a dish no one should tell you how to make?" To which Bourdain replied, "I feel that if Jacques Pépin shows you how to make an omelet, the matter is pretty much settled. That's God talking."

- **Cooking from the heart:** In 2014, Pépin wrote a column for the website The Daily Meal in which he confronted the combative, demeaning tone of many reality shows like *Hell's Kitchen*.

  After making an argument that real kitchens can, do, and *should* embody peace, collaboration, and mentorship, the chef also noted the toll this behavior takes on food itself—removing the most critical component of any dish.

  Pépin wrote, "This approach is certainly not conducive to creating good-tasting dishes. I have asked friends many times, 'What are the best fundamental dishes of your life?' Invariably, their response goes back to food prepared by a mother, a grandmother, a father, an aunt, or some other relative or friend. A main ingredient of those preparations is the love with which they are prepared."

SUGGESTED PAIRINGS

See also: Art, Food in (Antiquity through the Renaissance); Art, Food in (Impressionism through Contemporary Art); Bourdain, Anthony; Child, Julia; *Galloping Gourmet, The*; *Top Chef.*

Entry best enjoyed while eating: Skillet-fried duck with red-oak-leaf lettuce salad; camembert cheese coated in local honey and chopped pistachios; Maman's apple tart (a rustic French dessert he learned to make from his mother); hot tea brewed from the apple skins that were saved when making the tart (Pépin is a proponent of not wasting any part of one's food).

Further Reading

American Masters. 2017. "Jacques Pepin: The Art of Craft." Directed by Peter L. Stein. Public Broadcasting Service, release date May 26, 2017.

Gordiner, Jeff. 2011. "There's the Wrong Way and Jacques Pepin's Way." *The New York Times*, October 18, 2011.

Jacques Pepin Foundation. https://jp.foundation/about/jacques-pepin

Pepin, Jacques. 2003. *The Apprentice: My Life in the Kitchen*. New York: Houghton Mifflin.

Pepin, Jacques. 2014. "How Reality TV Cooking Shows Get It Wrong." The Daily Meal, July 14, 2014. https://www.thedailymeal.com/how-reality-tv-cooking-shows-get-it-wrong

Pepin, Jacques. 2015. *Jacques Pepin Heart & Soul*. New York: Houghton Mifflin.

Shulz, Kathryn. 2010. "Eat Your Words: Anthony Bourdain on Being Wrong." Slate, May 31, 2010. https://slate.com/news-and-politics/2010/06/eat-your-words-anthony-bourdain-on-being-wrong.html

Photography, Food

STARTERS

Food photography takes many forms and can be found in advertising, journalism, museums, the sciences, and the art world alike. The art of capturing food traces back to the earliest era of photography, and with the ease and availability of capturing photos today, it's more popular than ever before. Committing food to a permanent form traces back to ancient Egyptian and Roman art, even as far back as cave paintings depicting animals that were hunted for food. Since the mid-1800s, people have continued capturing everything from single ingredients to perfectly plated meals on film and digital media alike.

Throughout the twentieth century, food served as a subject in photography to illustrate political issues, document cultural trends and histories, convince readers to buy glossy magazines, lure consumers into restaurants, and spark the imagination as fine art. Today, social media sites like Pinterest and Instagram have fueled

A photographer shoots Hanukkah donuts for a marketing campaign in Zefat, Israel, 2019. (Anastassiya Bornstein/Dreamstime.com)

people's proclivity to photograph their food and beverages more than ever before. These sites are widely credited with sparking an international trend of posting the mundane details of everyday life like plates of pancakes, pints of beer, or freshly roasted chickens for a public audience.

ENTRÉE

The oldest photograph with food is a still life of a bowl, goblet, and bread taken in 1832 by Joseph Nicéphore Niépce, who is credited with taking the first camera photographs. This image is similar to some of the earliest moving pictures that also entailed everyday scenes of meals, depicting simple scenes that captured food's central role in people's lives and elevated presence in what we find interesting. Documentary photography has also frequently used food and meals as a prime subject, such as striking images of African American students seated at lunch counters that only served white customers in the Civil Rights era. In numerous photos of sit-in demonstrations during the early 1960s, the absence or lack of food is the unspoken subject matter. In one photograph, two African American college students sit next to a single slice of cake on a display stand while waitresses sit apathetically, refusing to serve them. Another image depicts a young white man taking a large bite of a hot dog while seated at a diner counter, surrounded by standing African American men and women who are empty handed.

Government organizations and advertising firms alike have harnessed the power of food photos to sell products and ideas through propaganda and marketing efforts. Throughout history, various government factions have tried convincing its citizens to eat more of some things and less of others using photos of happy people joyfully harvesting and eating certain foods. As journalist Tove Danovich wrote, "During World War II, Nazi Germany papered its citizens with propaganda convincing them to be happy on a diet of poor-quality meat and potatoes" (2017). Cookbooks and food-centric magazines paved the way for food stylists: individuals who were charged with preparing food to be photographed. In the 1960s and 1970s, the rising availability of commercial and professional color film elevated the quality and allure of print ads for food.

Food also plays fascinating subjects in fine art photographs, such as Henri Cartier-Bresson's iconic 1954 photograph "Rue Mouffetard, Paris," which shows a young boy beaming as he carries two wine bottles. The photograph exudes the child's joy and suggests an imminent celebration at home, in stark contrast to the reality of French life Cartier-Bresson had witnessed just over a decade prior, in which he was captured by the Germans while serving in the photography division of the French army during World War II. Similarly, a black-and-white 1930 photograph by Edward Weston transposes an unadorned bell pepper into an evocative form similar to a nude still life.

In the 1990s and 2000s, magazines and social media created enormous viral trends in food photography. Food-centric magazines and websites often perpetuate a specific aesthetic in food photography consisting of white backgrounds, square-shaped overhead shots, and immaculately staged, brightly lit food. In a 2019 interview with photography website PetaPixel, professional food photographer Andrew Scrivani said that the industry seems heavily driven by fads such as the aesthetic perpetuated by these magazines and Instagram "influencers." He noted that photo shoots have been drifting away from "food-forward" photography and led professionals like himself to rebel with more artistic and edgier editorial photographs (Schneider 2019).

In 2011, marketing agency 360i published statistics that 25 percent of food photographs posted online were mundane food diaries that simply showed what each person was eating; followed by 22 percent of photos that served to showcase foods people had made themselves. Food art accounted for 12 percent of the posts, and 16 percent were attributed to the documentation of special occasions. Interestingly, only 10 percent of photos showed friends and family members, illustrating how important many people deem the food and beverages in their photographs. As of 2020, social media site Instagram shows no signs of waning interest in the gastronomy department; the hashtag #food was applied to nearly 374,000,000 posts, while #delicious was tagged in approximately 106,000,000 posts.

ACCOMPANIED BY

Many photographers created especially notable food photography, such as Irving Penn (1917–2009), a still life and fashion photographer whose arresting and highly artistic still lifes of food were described by *Vogue* magazine as ranging from witty to Vermeer-like. Hungarian-born Nickolas Muray (1892–1965) was an

> *Small Plates*
>
> **Don't Eat the Leftovers**
>
> Food stylists and photographers use many substitutes in lieu of real ingredients to make food easier and more appealing to photograph. The following are just some of the many tricks used to make food look runway ready.
>
> - Mashed potatoes masquerade as vanilla ice cream, which melts quickly under hot studio lights, and are used to fill out floppy foods like crepes or enchiladas (giving them the appearance of being more stuffed).
> - Shaving cream and glue often take the place of whipped cream or milk.
> - Aerosol hair spray or deodorant are sometimes applied to foods like diced tomatoes to make them glisten.
> - WD-40 and motor oil add sheen to items like chopped meat or pancake syrup.
> - Hamburgers and tacos are sometimes stuffed with small sponges to make them look bulkier.

Olympic fencer and professional photographer who invented the print equivalent of Technicolor. The food photographs he did for *McCall's* magazine ranged from wholesome to unnerving, impressing audiences with stunning saturated color from the mid-1930s through the 1950s.

Japanese inventor Yoshiro Nakamatsu (1928–) uses photography to obsessively catalog his food intake, photographing everything he eats and analyzing his blood samples afterward to see which types and quantities of foods might have the potential to extend his lifespan (Lidz 2012). Andrew Zimmern's (1961–) interest in photography inspired him to write a college thesis on the early form of daguerreotype photography and its effects on cultural nationalism. The chef told *Food & Wine* magazine that although he documents many of his meals, his "jaw hit the floor" when a server at a weeks-old restaurant described a menu offering to him in serious tones as their "most Instagrammed dish" (Lewis 2018).

SUGGESTED PAIRINGS

See also: *Bizarre Foods with Andrew Zimmern*; Films, Food in; Documentary Films, Food and Beverages in; Websites, Food.

Entry best enjoyed while eating (inspired by well-liked food posts on Instagram): grilled corn and market vegetable chowder (@dennistheprescott, 14,540 likes); crispy buffalo cauliflower "wings" with homemade sauce and ranch dressing (@feelgoodfoodie, 9,848 likes); red and white "XOXO"-shaped Valentine's Day churros (@rosannapansino, 55,815 likes).

Further Reading

Bright, Susan. 2017. *Feast for the Eyes: The Story of Food in Photography.* New York: Aperture.

Danovich, Tove. 2017. "The Big Picture: How Food Photos Have Told Our Story Over the Decades." National Public Radio, The Salt, June 6, 2017. https://www.npr.org

/sections/thesalt/2017/06/06/531615608/the-big-picture-how-food-photos-have-told-our-story-over-the-decades

Lewis, Hunter. 2018. "The Evolution of Food Photography." *Food & Wine*, February 15, 2018.

Lidz, Franz. 2012. "Dr. NakaMats, the Man with 3300 Patents to His Name." *Smithsonian Magazine*, December 2012.

Schneider, Jason. 2019. "Instagram Has Changed Professional Food Photography Forever." PetaPixel, October 29, 2019. https://petapixel.com/2019/10/29/instagram-has-changed-professional-food-photography-forever/

360i Staff. 2011. "Report: Online Food & Photo Sharing Trends." May 25, 2011. http://blog.360i.com/web-design/360i-report-online-food-photo-sharing-trends

Pioneer Woman, The (1969–)

STARTERS

The Pioneer Woman is the name of a blog, product line, and Food Network television show created by and starring Ree Drummond, a blogger, television personality, writer, and food-media mogul. Drummond is the author of numerous cookbooks, children's books about ranch life, and a memoir in the style of a Western-themed romance. Drummond's first cookbook, *The Pioneer Woman Cooks: Recipes from an Accidental Country Girl* (2009) reached the number one spot on *The New York Times* best seller list. She published five more popular cookbooks in the next decade that were met with similar success, including *The Pioneer Woman Cooks: Food from My Frontier* (2012), *The Pioneer Woman Cooks: Dinnertime* (2016), and *The Pioneer Woman Cooks: Come and Get It!* (2017).

Drummond's line of children's books began with the publication of *Charlie the Ranch Dog* (2011), inspired by the family's affinity for Basset Hounds. Staring in 2017, she also published a series called *Little Ree*, a fictional account of her childhood. Her romance-themed memoir, *Black Heels and Tractor Wheels: A Love Story*, quickly reached number two on the best seller lists of *The New York Times* and the *Wall Street Journal*, and Sony pictures purchased the film rights to the book in 2011. Following the title's success, Drummond penned a collection of stories titled *Frontier Follies: Adventures of Marriage and Motherhood in the Middle of Nowhere* (2020).

Drummond's career in television took flight in 2010 when she was featured in an episode of *Throwdown with Bobby Flay*. Flay, a decorated restaurateur and celebrity chef, joined Drummond on her ranch to compete in a rapid-fire contest to see who could make the best five-course Thanksgiving meal (Drummond was named the winner by a narrow margin). The following year, Food Network invited Drummond to star in her own cooking show set on the ranch, blending cooking tutorials with vignettes of Drummond's daily life with family and friends. *The Pioneer Woman* debuted in August of 2011 and went on to air 30-minute episodes every Saturday morning for the next decade, accumulating more than 230 episodes over 15 seasons. Drummond has made food television appearances on a number of other cooking and cooking competition shows as a judge and cohost.

The Pioneer Woman show won a Bronze and Silver Telly Award in 2018 and 2019, respectively, and Drummond has been the recipient of numerous Weblog Awards (the "Bloggies") for her writing, including the award for 2009 Weblog of the Year.

ENTRÉE

One morning in 2006, Ree Drummond watched her husband shuttle her four children, then between the ages of one and six years old, out the door to work on the family's cattle ranch. As a homeschooling mom and housewife, Drummond was delighted to find herself with some free time and decided on a whim to "start one of those blog things." Using a simple domain name and free software, Drummond launched a new site entitled *Confessions of a Pioneer Woman* and, little by little, taught herself how to blog. As she gained a knack for the art of self-publishing her own content, Drummond's posts evolved from short updates to more involved personal stories and photo essays about her life as a mother and cattle rancher's wife in Pawhuska, Oklahoma. Her blog's readership began to grow from immediate friends and family to readers who didn't know her but were drawn to her accounts of life on the ranch (Brunner 2019).

Drummond's blog, later shortened to *The Pioneer Woman*, included humorous stories about her children, photo essays about the livestock and pets on her ranch, tips on gardening and interior decorating, and romantic stories about her history with her husband Ladd (whom she refers to as Marlboro Man—a nod to the resemblance she thinks he bears to the cowboy mascot for Marlboro cigarettes). Drummond published her first recipe– a step-by-step tutorial for a four-ingredient ribeye steak—in 2007. The inclusion of recipes attracted more readers by the droves, many of whom were just as excited to read her clear and witty cooking instructions as they were to read about her personal life. By 2011, *Forbes* had named Drummond one of only three women in a list of the top 25 web celebrities in in the world, and her blog was drawing over 23 million page views per month.

Between 2007 and the early 2020s, Drummond's blog evolved into a veritable media empire. Recipes continued to be a mainstay of the site, and included her signature step-by-step photos of every part of the process, ranging from photographs of the raw ingredients through prepping, cooking, and finished "hero shots" of each dish. Drummond's recipes run a wide gamut, such as "How to Easily Peel Hard-Boiled Eggs" to dishes like Cap'n Crunch Chicken Strips, Killer Kale Salad, and Chicken Milanese. Each tutorial is infused with witty banter and anecdotes, making them fun to read and easy to follow. The format makes cooking approachable for beginners, and the wide range of recipe types and difficulty levels appeals to a variety of readers. The humor and positivity infused in the recipe blog posts also presents food preparation in a nonintimidating way. Drummond is encouraging and nonchalant in her approach. Her tutorials encourage readers with informal directions such as "Don't let the salmon cook to smithereens. . . add some lime zest if you're feeling dangerous" and "Don't be intimidated; it's one of the easiest things in the world to cook, and it'll make your soul sing" (Drummond 2007, 2016).

> **Small Plates**
>
> **Serving Beef in an Era of Tofurkey**
>
> *Pioneer Woman* Ree Drummund's work is not only unusual due to its nod to the Wild West; it also bucks the trend with a prevalence of beef-centered dishes. The Drummond family runs a cattle ranch that was ranked as the 17th-largest property in the United States by *Modern Farmer* in 2013, at 433,000 acres. The Drummond's cattle business entails commercial cow/calf and yearling operations and caring for wild mustangs as part of a deal with the Bureau of Land Management. It's also a large working farm with an emphasis on wheat crops. Coming from the cattle ranching industry, Drummond unsurprisingly focuses on beef recipes frequently, but the popularity of these dishes and her brand *are* somewhat surprising given America's turbulent relationship with red meat over the last two decades.
>
> A 2017 report by the National Resources Defense Council (NRDC), an environmental advocacy group, indicated that beef consumption dropped by 20 percent between 2005 and 2014. This trend is attributed to a number of factors: the rising cost of beef; the publication of various studies linking red meat to serious health risks (and its classification as a "possible carcinogen"); competition with other proteins (such as pork, chicken, and tofu); and concerns about the environmental impact of raising and consuming beef. The U.S. Department of Agriculture (USDA) cites beef's peak popularity in the 1970s, after which its popularity waned considerably in the face of changing diets and health concerns.

While many others in the food industry focus on cutting-edge presentations and trends, Drummond has revived retro themes. Her persona of a pioneer woman, descriptions of homemaking and family life, and Western-themed, romance-infused memoirs appeal to America's fondness for Westerns—a fad that hearkens back to the 1950s. The term "homemaker" has fallen out of vogue in more recent years, sometimes seen as associated with bygone eras in which women were expected to spend their days raising children, cooking meals, and tending to the house. Drummond's blog and television show help reimagine what a twenty-first century homemaker can look like. Her brand blends the image of a coiffed housewife kissing her beau while lifting a high-heeled shoe with a tech-savvy media entrepreneur who has used her skills to create a one-woman empire.

Noting the hugely successful blog following in its early days, Drummond channeled her knack for recipe instruction into what would become her first cookbook, *Pioneer Woman Cooks: Recipes from an Accidental Country Girl*. She continued posting daily snapshots of life and recipes on her blog, while simultaneously developing additional books in the cookbook series. After numerous website redesigns, Drummond added sections such as online cooking communities and pages devoted to her products. Ad revenue became substantial with the addition of sponsorships, product giveaways, and corporate links, and her previously simple, amateur blog transformed into a full-fledged business venture.

In recent years, Drummond has joined forces with corporations such as Walmart, Kraft Heinz, and Land O' Lakes butter to do corporate sponsorships, product partnerships, and national commercial spots. Additionally, the media mogul has paired up with major retailers to sell a dizzyingly long list of Pioneer

Woman brand products, including cookware, bakeware, clothing, dog treats, home décor, kitchen appliances, wallpaper, quilts, fabric, condiments, coffee, and much more. In 2016, the Drummonds opened a retail store called the Mercantile in Pawhuska, Oklahoma. The general store shop offers western-themed and Pioneer Woman–themed products for the home, in addition to a deli and bakery that serve some of Ree's signature dishes. *Tulsa World* reported that on the store's opening day, people traveled from all over the country to shop and dine on dishes such as biscuits and gravy.

Ree Drummond's retail business, the Pioneer Woman Mercantile, draws tourists from all over the world. In 2017, the shop saw 6,000–15,000 visitors a day—a staggering number considering the population of 3,500 in the Mercantile's location of rural Pawhuska, Oklahoma. (Susan Vineyard/Dreamstime.com)

ACCOMPANIED BY

Drummond is joined in her blog and in her show by her husband, Ladd, and four children—daughters Alex and Paige and sons Bryce and Todd—all of whom were referred to by pseudonyms in the blog's early years to protect their privacy. Ladd has occasionally written guest posts on the blog, answering readers' questions about daily life on the ranch and the care and handling of the cattle. Extended family members, friends, and ranch hands also frequently appear on the show and the blog, typically seen digging into the comfort food Ree has prepared. The Drummond's beloved Basset Hounds are often captured in humorous photo essays, alongside stories featuring the family's numerous other dogs and cats. The cattle on the ranch are highlighted in stories ranging from the birth of new calves to the family's efforts to administer vaccinations to a herd. Occasionally, Drummond delights viewers with photo essays about the wild mustangs that share the family's ranchlands.

DESSERT

In one of her more memorable blog posts, "All I Wanted was a Doughnut," Ree describes an ill-fated stop at a convenience store in which she purchased a cup of coffee and was lured to a glass donut display case showcasing an apple fritter.

Distracted, Ree tried to open the case by gently tugging at the knob of the case's sliding window, which caused the entire glass case to shatter.

In her shock and embarrassment, Ree describes a seemingly involuntary reaction: to still reach for the donut, which was now lying on the floor, encased in broken glass shards: "I instinctively began reaching for the apple fritter (. . .) I didn't logically believe I should get the apple fritter; I think it was a desperate attempt to just carry on and pretend the whole thing hadn't happened. Or maybe I really just wanted a doughnut."

SUGGESTED PAIRINGS

See also: Nonfiction, Food in; Television, Food Channels on; Trends, Food; Websites, Food.

Entry best enjoyed while eating: Ree Drummond's "Marlboro Man Sandwich" (a concoction of sautéed cube steak and onions, Worcestershire sauce, and Tabasco); a mason jar of homemade applesauce; and a slice of "The Best Chocolate Sheet Cake Ever," served with a cold glass of milk.

Further Reading

Borné, Eliza. 2011. "A City Girl Finds Her Home on the Range." Interview in *BookPage*. February, 2011. https://bookpage.com/interviews/8663-ree-drummond-biography-memoir#.YMkpfTZKhTY

Brash, Sam. 2013. "America's Top 100 Land Owners." *Modern Farmer*, October 16, 2013. https://modernfarmer.com/2013/10/americas-top-100-land-owners/

Brunner, Jeryl. 2019. "How Ree Drummond Turned Her Blog into an Empire." *Forbes*, November 29, 2019.

Casserly, Meghan. 2011. "Black Heels to Tractor Wheels: The Pioneer Woman's True Harlequin Romance." *Forbes*, February 15, 2011. https://www.forbes.com/sites/meghancasserly/2011/02/16/black-heels-to-tractor-wheels-the-pioneer-woman-love-web-celeb-ree-drummond/?sh=79a1b7945b7d

Drummond, Ree. 2007. "How to Cook a Steak." *The Pioneer Woman* (blog post), May 30, 2007. https://www.thepioneerwoman.com/food-cooking/recipes/a8382/how-to-cook-a-steak/

Drummond, Ree. 2016. "Honey Soy Salmon." *The Pioneer Woman* (blog post), May 2, 2016. https://www.thepioneerwoman.com/food-cooking/recipes/a86550/honey-soy-salmon/

Fortini, Amanda. 2011. "O Pioneer Woman! The Creation of a Domestic Idyll." *New Yorker,* May 9, 2011. http://fortune.com/2015/10/27/red-meat-consumption-decline/

Haspel, Tamar. 2015. "The Decline of the (Red) Meat Industry—In One Chart." *Fortune*, October 27, 2015.

Lynch, Rene. 2009. "The Pioneer Woman, an Internet and Publishing Sensation." *LA Times*, September 23, 2009.

Rodrigo, Jessica. 2016. "Pioneer Woman Mercantile Welcomes Visitor from Across the Country." *Tulsa World*, November 1, 2016.

Warehime, Les. 2009. "Drummond Ranch." *The Encyclopedia of Oklahoma History and Culture*. Oklahoma City: Oklahoma Historical Society. https://www.okhistory.org/publications/enc/entry.php?entry=DR007

Politicians' Food Gaffes

STARTERS

Food has played a notable role in politics since the birth of America's democracy. Many people harbor strong feelings regarding the cultural values and regional etiquette associated with the food that they incorporate in their daily lives. As such, people often project favorable or unfavorable views of politicians based on whether those individuals like the same type of food and if they appear to prepare or eat it "correctly." Politicians running for office sample fare from places like local mom-and-pop restaurants and state fair food vendors in order to connect with (or at least give the appearance of connecting with) locals and the culture those locals embrace. Many Americans exhibit a fascination with the daily habits of celebrities, and as such, food is often one of the details that surfaces in political media coverage and gossip alike. Food has become a significant part of the intersection between popular culture and politics largely because—like discussions about politician's choice in and treatment of their pets—it is seen as a vehicle to better understand a person's character.

ACCOMPANIED BY

Politicians running for office at the highest level go through a veritable theater of hand shaking, photo-taking, and baby kissing throughout their travels, but few things are dissected as critically as the meals and other food-tasting sessions that take place on the campaign trail. Few politicians get through their career without some form of food-focused press, ranging from interview questions about their favorite foods to suffering minor and even significant career consequences due to food-related gaffes. The first president was even tied to a food-related myth. George Washington never uttered the famous words "I cannot tell a lie" in relation to cutting down his father's cherry tree. According to historian Jay Richardson, the parable about honesty was—ironically—a lie concocted by one of Washington's early biographers to make the politician seem more virtuous.

In 1840, William Henry Harrison's political rival, Martin van Buren, attempted a smear campaign against Harrison to cast him as a country bumpkin who drank too much. Harrison's team cleverly successfully twisted the tale into a public relations campaign so that his fondness for hard cider made him relatable to common citizens. In 1909, president-elect William Taft dug into an 18-pound whole roast possum dinner at a banquet in Atlanta, and he was subsequently asked to endorse a stuffed animal trademarked "Billy Possum." The toy was designed to try to emulate the successful wave of teddy bears named for Theodore Roosevelt (Danner 2015). In 1981, President Ronald Reagan faced considerable backlash (and mockery) when, in the face of slashed funding for school lunch budgets, his administration proposed counting condiments such as pickle relish and tomato ketchup as a dietary serving of vegetables in students' lunches. Eleven years later, President George H. W. Bush faced critical media coverage for appearing incredulous during a demonstration of an electronic scanner used at grocery stores. Some critics used the press to paint Bush as being out of touch with daily American life and also used it to negatively illustrate his economic prowess. Two years earlier, Bush made headlines for publicly stating his distaste for broccoli, which outlets like the *New York Times* covered through the lens of a welcome reprieve to many Americans who were weary of 1980s' diet trends and echoed the president's penchant for junk food.

Vice President Dan Quayle made headlines in 1992 when, on the campaign trail to endorse a Bush-Quayle reelection, he attended an elementary school's mock spelling bee and added a letter "e" to 12-year-old William Figueroa's correct spelling of the word "potato," incorrectly modifying it to "potatoe." In his memoir entitled *Standing Firm*, Quayle noted that the school provided him with a flash card with the incorrect spelling and went on to describe the gaffe as "a 'defining moment' of the worst possible kind" (Fass 2004).

During his time in office (1993–2001), President Bill Clinton made news for stopping at McDonald's for fast food during his morning jogs, which became fodder for a satirical sketch on the show *Saturday Night Live*. In more recent years, President Barack Obama was accused by critics for being "out of touch" and elitist on more than one food-themed occasion, such as ordering a cheeseburger served only with Dijon mustard at a burger joint and asking a crowd in Iowa if they echoed his irritation at how much arugula cost at Whole Foods (the chain did not exist in the state at that time, and some consider arugula to be a food associated with wealth).

For presidential hopefuls, the stakes can be even higher in regard to food failures, as some can be arguably career ending. In 1976, Gerald Ford made a significant gaffe on the campaign trail dubbed the "Great Tamales Incident," in which he was served a tamale in San Antonio, Texas, and he bit into the outer corn husk that's meant to be removed. The mistake received a lot of press, and some have speculated that the gaffe may have been a significant factor in his loss of the presidential race. In 2003, Democrat John Kerry sent shock waves through Philadelphia when he ordered a Philly Cheesesteak with swiss cheese at iconic restaurant Pats—a far cry from the local tradition of Cheez Whiz, American cheese, or provolone traditionally served on the sandwiches.

Secretary of State Hillary Clinton received a fair share of press in 2016 for saying that she always had hot sauce in her purse and naming jalapenos as her favorite campaign trail food. Media publications like the *New York Post* commented that these claims, and a Univision appearance in which she said her favorite cuisine was Mexican food, could imply pandering for Hispanic votes. In response, outlets like *Time* rushed to print Secretary of State Clinton's documented love for chili peppers, stretching back to 1992. In 2016, Donald Trump was also scrutinized for "Hispandering," slang that emerged during this campaign meaning pandering to Hispanic voters, in which he tweeted a photo of himself eating a taco salad with the caption "Happy #CincoDeMayo! The best taco bowls are made in Trump Tower Grill. I love Hispanics!" (Trump 2016). Many critics weighed in, criticizing his tone for being at odds with his unfavorable statements and policies toward Mexicans and Mexican Americans. Others criticized his understanding of

Cinco De Mayo's history and culture and argued that taco bowls were an American bastardization of authentic Mexican food.

In 2015, *People* magazine interviewed each of the presidential candidates on their daily lives. Answering questions about their daily eating choices, the candidates' responses provided some insight into their personalities. Daily food choices ranged from "turkey jerky and almonds" (Jeb Bush) to "I very rarely eat breakfast, but when I do, it's usually Cracklin' Oat Bran" (Chris Christie) to a tangential 179-word response from Donald Trump about his lack of snacking and the size of the rallies his team had recently thrown. Mike Huckabee proclaimed favoring "chicken from Pizza Ranch," a Christian midwestern chain favored by many politicians on the campaign trail for schmoozing with locals (McAfee and Sobieraj Westfall 2015).

In a highly competitive 2020 race to become the presidential nominee, Minnesota Senator Amy Klobuchar's press swirled with rumors that she was an abusive boss to her current and former aides. In 2019, the allegations were further fueled by reports that while on the road, Klobuchar ate a salad with a comb from her purse instead of a fork and made the aide (who had forgotten to get a fork when fetching her lunch) clean her comb after the meal.

With every passing year, it seems that food—or at least ample press coverage of food—is gaining more interest and adding more weight to the public's votes.

DESSERT

During the 2000 presidential campaign, GOP hopeful Gary Bauer had an embarrassing snafu that may have helped end his campaign. Bauer participated in an event called the "Bisquick Pancake Presidential Primary Flip-Off," and he flung his pancake high in the air, toppling over backward as he tried to catch it. Bauer, who later said it took him five years before he could eat a pancake again, was reported as saying that as he fell backward into a curtain behind him, he realized that his political rival George W. Bush was standing there and heard him say, "Careful, here comes Bauer." The American public may as well have been whispering, "Careful, here comes a career-ending pancake."

SUGGESTED PAIRINGS

See also: Latin American Cuisine; Politics and Food; Roadside Food Attractions; Television, Food Channels on.

Entry best enjoyed while eating: Squirrel sliders (inspired by former GOP presidential candidate Mike Huckabee, who admitted to frying one of the rodents in a popcorn maker as a college student) Pumpkin spice latte (inspired by vice presidential hopeful Sarah Palin, who did a cheerful television interview with a Starbucks cup in hand while a scene unfolded behind her of a man cramming turkeys into a machine at a slaughterhouse) *Boba*, a Taiwanese tea with sugar, milk, and tapioca balls (inspired by numerous internet jokes after Secretary Clinton described her first sip of the treat as "chewy tea" on the campaign trail)

Further Reading

Danner, Chas. 2015. "History of Presidential Food Controversies." *New York*, Intelligencer. http://nymag.com/intelligencer/2015/07/history-of-presidential-food-con troversies.html

Fass, Mark. 2004. "Politics; How Do You Spell Regret? One Man's Take on It." *The New York Times*, August 29, 2004.

Flegenheimer, Matt, and Sydney Ember. 2019. "How Amy Klobuchar Treats Her Staff." *The New York Times*, February 22, 2019.

McAfee, Tierney, and Sandra Sobieraj Westfall. 2015. "Who's a 'Gifted Rap Artist,' Who Loves Jalapeños and Who Went to See Adele on Date Night: Democrats' and Republicans' Guilty Pleasures Revealed." *People*, December 9, 2015.

Memmott, Mark. 2007. "The Perils of Presidential Politics: Bauer Can't Forget Pancake 'Flip-Off' Fall." *USA Today*, October 10, 2007.

Richardson, Jay. n.d. "Cherry Tree Myth." George Washington's Mount Vernon. https://www.mountvernon.org/library/digitalhistory/digital-encyclopedia/article/cherry-tree-myth

Trump, Donald. 2016. Twitter Post, "Happy #CincoDeMayo…" May 5, 2016. https://twitter.com/realDonaldTrump/status/728297587418247168

Politics and Food

STARTERS

Food is a frequent subject matter in the political arena, ranging from broad topics that affect the agricultural and food service industries to small food-related details associated with specific politicians. Food plays a major role in Americans' lives and livelihoods, making it a natural topic for policy debate. The food people eat, the access they have to their food, and the amount of money they have to pay for it are subjects that people often cast a vote for on their ballots. Many trends within the agricultural and food and beverage industries have taken on political weight in recent decades.

These trends include organic and free-trade practices; debates over livestock and the environment; proposed tax hikes on sodas to discourage unhealthy eating; food deserts (areas with low or no access to affordable healthy food); and the gentrification of lower-income areas with the introduction of things like high-priced coffee shops, breweries, and specialty grocery stores. Culturally, food is also closely linked with values. The media and the public often seize on small details related to what and how politicians eat and frequently link these food-related details to judgments on those individuals' intelligence levels, character, health, and likeability.

ENTRÉE

Throughout history, many politicians, political organizations, and social activists have incorporated food into their missions. Food played a strong role in various aspects of the civil rights movement. One example is the Greensboro Four,

four African American college students who defied segregation at a Woolworth's lunch counter by sitting in the section reserved for white customers and ordering coffee. When they were denied service, they remained seated in a nonviolent act of protest. A restaurant called Paschal's in Atlanta, Georgia, served as an important place for civil rights protestors to gather. In Montgomery, Alabama, political activist Georgia Gilmore served food out of her home to upward of thousands of activists, and her home became an undercover location where civil rights leaders like Martin Luther King Jr. gathered (Bloudoff-Indelicato 2016). In the 1960s, activist Fannie Lou Hamer organized a farm-share program in the Mississippi Delta to help create self-sufficiency among African Americans.

One prominent food-related political group was the Black Panthers, who organized in 1966 to protest police brutality against African Americans. For many, the Black Panthers are closely associated with various acts of violence and other militant behavior. However, the organization also started several important social programs. One of the most notable of these was a free breakfast program for school-aged children, which provided a significant source of nutrition (and a motivating factor to go to school) for many youth living in poverty. This program helped pave the way for federally funded school breakfast and lunch programs that are still in place today.

The act of providing self-sustaining measures for the African American community was a central part of the Panthers' mission, which is not far removed from the role communal meals play within contemporary politics. During the Trump administration years, which have been marked by heated controversy across the nation, numerous stories have been aired in the media about diffusing political arguments through food. Many have been drawn to the idea of bringing people from diverse racial, ethnic, and political backgrounds together at a shared meal to help de-escalate sensitive conversations and humanize all parties. In a 2017 opinion piece for the *New York Times*, Julia Turshen wrote, "The most valuable tool in our kitchens (is) the table. Remember that Derek Black, whose father was a grand wizard of the Ku Klux Klan, began to rethink his white nationalist views after being invited to Shabbat dinner by a college classmate."

Today, many Americans are turning to the power of shared meals to create cultural bridges. One example is a dinner series entitled Blackness in America organized in 2016 by Tunde Wey, a Nigerian chef. Wey hosted a traveling dinner party that brought people from different backgrounds together to discuss difficult issues pertaining to African Americans. As part of the dinner experiences, which could be emotionally uncomfortable or painful given the focus of the discussions, Wey served Nigerian food. The chef didn't explain much about the food or how to eat it correctly, saying of the dinner conversations and cuisine, "What I'm trying to do is detach us from our reference points" (Judkis 2016).

Many contemporary political discussions focus on people's social connections (or lack thereof) and discord. Media pieces about cultivating connection and constructive dialogue over shared meals have been plentiful. Writer Sarah Gray started a viral trend with an online essay published by *Serious Eats* called "Friday Night Meatballs," in which she encouraged readers to follow her family's tradition of inviting friends and friends-of-friends to a no-fuss spaghetti dinner at their home each week. The ensuing popularity of the idea was one of many national conversations about meals providing a valuable stage for bringing diverse communities together and bridging political divides (Paynter 2017).

ACCOMPANIED BY

A number of politicians have made news for food-related habits and statements. One was Hillary Clinton when her husband Bill Clinton was vying for the Democratic presidential nomination in 1992. His opponent, California Governor Jerry Brown, alleged that Clinton had provided unethical assistance to the law firm where Hillary worked. Angered by the accusation, Hillary responded, "I suppose I could have stayed home, baked cookies and had teas," in regard to the fact that her career had taken an unfavorable spotlight since her husband entered public life. A number of homemakers took umbrage with the comment and reported feeling slighted by her attitude toward women who didn't work outside the home. *Family Circle* magazine took advantage of the situation by creating an annual cookie-baking contest between the candidates' spouses. Some consider the competition entertaining, while others feel that it casts modern women (since presidential candidates are still mostly men) in an outdated light, relegating their skills to things like baking cookies, as opposed to their husband's political skills.

The contest came full circle in 2016 when Hillary ran for president and her husband was the first man in the role of the "politician's spouse." Rather uncreatively, the Clintons resubmitted the same chocolate chip recipe for the contest that year that Hillary had used in 1992 and 1996 (the recipe won all three years). President Bill Clinton often made news for his habit of eating McDonald's fast food during or after his morning jogs during his time in office. In his post-presidency years, he made news again many times for adopting a vegan diet (and then adding back some meats), losing weight in the process, and proclaiming the health benefits of veganism.

For President Barack Obama, food scrutiny took place within the first two weeks of his time in office. Media outlets commented on the fact that the president personally offered a tray of freshly baked oatmeal-raisin cookies to members of Congress he had invited to the Oval Office for a Super Bowl party. A 2009 *New York Times* article analyzed the act of offering cookies in relation to how the president would "try to build relationships—and dispatch controversies—during his time in office" (Zeleny 2009). First Lady Michelle Obama also made food news frequently for her "Let's Move!" campaign, which was aimed at promoting healthy diets for youth and reducing childhood obesity. Political adversaries speculated that Michelle Obama's White House vegetable garden would be one of the things that Donald and Melania Trump might do away with to "remove everything related to Obama" from the grounds. The *Washington Post* reported on the political symbolism of the vegetable garden, noting that "the future of these vegetables has deep roots in agricultural and public-health issues that are fiercely contested and raise charges of elitism on one side and protecting big business at the expense of children's health on the other" (Day 2018).

SUGGESTED PAIRINGS

See also: Politicians' Food Gaffes; Super Bowl Sunday; Twitty, Michael.

Entry best enjoyed while eating: Non-GMO, Paleo bacon–wrapped shrimp, Georgia Gilmore's biscuits and gravy, a cup of free-trade coffee, and a bowl of granola (inspired by the free food delivered to the hungry, peace-proclaiming attendees at Woodstock in 1969). Serve at a communal table with a side of resistance and activism.

Further Reading

Bloudoff-Indelicato, Mollie. 2016. "Four Important Foods of America's Civil Rights Movement." *National Geographic,* The Plate, February 4, 2016. https://www.nationalgeographic.com/people-and-culture/food/the-plate/2016/02/04/4-important-foods-of-americas-civil-rights-movement/

Day, Anastasia. 2018. "How the White House Garden Became a Political Football." *The Washington Post*, April 3, 2018.

Judkis, Maura. 2016. "Discomfort Food: Using Dinners to Talk about Race, Violence and America." *The Washington Post*, August 23, 2016.

Paynter, Kevon. 2017. "The Power of a Communal Meal." Civil Eats, November 23, 2017. https://civileats.com/2017/11/23/the-power-of-a-communal-meal/

Shute, Nancy. 2012. "Cooking Up Change: How Food Helped Fuel the Civil Rights Movement." NPR, The Salt, January 16, 2012. https://www.npr.org/sections/thesalt/2012/01/16/145179885/cooking-up-change-how-food-helped-fuel-the-civil-rights-movement

Turshen, Julia. 2017. "The Resistance Is Hungry." *The New York Times*, October 5, 2017.

Zeleny, Jeff. 2009. "Obama Woos G.O.P. with Attention, and Cookies." *The New York Times*, February 4, 2009.

Puck, Wolfgang (1949–)

STARTERS

Wolfgang Puck is an Austrian-born American chef, restaurateur, television personality, cookbook author, and philanthropist. The Wolfgang Puck brand is a veritable empire, spanning a large number of restaurants worldwide, catering services, a frozen food line, and products ranging from cookware to appliances and wine. Puck's influence in American cuisine and pop culture began in the early 1980s with the launch of his first restaurant, Spago, in Los Angeles, California. Today, he is a household name in the United States. In addition to running his restaurant, catering, and product empire, he contributes syndicated columns, makes guest appearances doing cooking or guest judge spots on talk shows and reality competition shows, and is exec producing a documentary series for HBO Max network on the trials and tribulations of running his high-profile events.

Puck's decorated career has stretched over nearly four decades. He received seven James Beard Foundation Awards between 1991 and 2012. These honors included the organization's Lifetime Achievement Award; the Who's Who in Food and Beverage Award, which recognizes substantial influence in the culinary world; and the Humanitarian Award, which notes significant work in the culinary field to improve the lives of others. As of 2012, he was the first chef to have

Chef Wolfgang Puck serving high-end treats at the 2009 Academy Awards in Los Angeles, California. Puck is known as a frequent caterer to the stars in Hollywood. (Featureflash/Dreamstime.com)

received the James Beard Foundation's Outstanding Chef honor twice. In 2007, Puck's restaurant CUT—a steakhouse in the Beverly Wilshire hotel—received a Michelin star and was named "Restaurant of the Year" by *Esquire* magazine. In 2008 and 2009, his restaurant Spago Beverly Hills received two Michelin stars. Puck was also honored for his television career with a star on the Hollywood Walk of Fame in 2017, and he was only the second chef to have received one.

ENTRÉE

"America has undergone a total food and wine revolution. When you looked back thirty years ago, sun-dried tomatoes and goat cheese were a novelty . . . all these cooking shows have transformed our profession one-hundred percent. Thirty-five years ago, being a cook was the same as being a used-car salesman," Wolfgang Puck told *Esquire* magazine in 2012. Puck, a world-class chef who many consider to be one of the first celebrity chefs, was at the forefront of leading that food and wine revolution in the early 1980s. Born in Austria, he gained a passion for food from his mother, who was also a chef. He initially dreamed of pursuing a career as an architect, but settled on his second love: pastries.

At the age of 14, assisted by his mother, Puck quit school to immerse himself in culinary training. Puck's stepfather, a coal miner, responded with disdain. "You're good for nothing, cooking is for women," he told his stepson (Inc Editorial Staff 2009). Puck left anyway and started his career as an apprentice in a hotel kitchen. Within three weeks, Puck was fired by a hot-tempered chef who blamed the young man one evening (seemingly without cause) for a shortage of potatoes. Puck has acknowledged in interviews that this was the low point of his life, and the night he was fired, he stood on a riverbank contemplating suicide.

Instead, he returned to the hotel kitchen, intent on continuing to learn the trade. He covertly continued his work peeling vegetables until he was discovered and reassigned to a different restaurant. Puck began to master the trade, climbing the ranks and working for a number of high-end French restaurants before moving to the United States at the age of 24. He worked as a line cook for an upscale restaurant called La Tour in Indianapolis, Indiana, from 1973 through 1975 before handing in his apron to pursue a new life in California.

From the mid-1970s through the 1980s, Puck went on to become a culinary pop star who also launched the state of California to culinary stardom. After a brief stint as a chef at Ma Maison, a French restaurant in Los Angeles that was known to draw celebrities, Puck opened his first restaurant, Spago, as a solo venture in 1982. Located in West Hollywood, Spago was unusual in many ways. For one, it was an Italian-style trattoria, a departure for a classically trained Austrian chef with an emphasis in French cooking. Additionally, Spago intentionally bucked formal trends in the industry, such as introducing the concept of having an "open kitchen" visible to diners (a design that enabled the chef to keep an eye on everyone in the building at once) and being served by wait staff who wore button-down shirts with aprons instead of formal attire like ties. Puck also championed fresh ingredients that had been locally sourced, a "farm-to-table" concept that California would become renowned for in the coming decades.

Celebrities have played a significant role in elevating Puck's restaurants and brand to great heights. Spago became a celebrity magnate early on, and Puck's other restaurants have followed suit, drawing musicians, actors, politicians, and other well-known figures in pop culture. The restaurant's success inspired the launch of additional Spago locations domestically and internationally. In 1992, Spago opened at Caesars Palace in Las Vegas, Nevada, making Puck the first name-brand chef to draw visitors to the strip. The restaurateur also opened a number of other restaurants in cities around the world, including his renowned steakhouse CUT, Asian-fusion restaurant Chinois, pizzerias, and express versions of his upscale restaurants in international airports and Walt Disney Resort. Puck—an immigrant cast out of his home at a young age who had never even completed formal education—was rising to celebrity status from Detroit to Dubai.

In an era marked by "high cuisine" in the form of edible foams, tiny portions, and unrecognizable concoctions, Puck was making a name for himself with dishes like freshly picked produce, gourmet wood-fired pizza, and lamb sourced from a nearby farm. In a 2015 interview with journalist Kai Ryssdal of the radio show Marketplace, Puck said that he, Paul Prudhomme, and "Alice Waters were really the first chefs who controlled the destiny of the restaurant. We cooked whatever we felt like. Not what somebody told you." Puck's work ethic can be seen in his schedule of traveling at least 100 days a year, working 6 days a week. He runs more than 20 restaurants and a frozen foods line, writes syndicated newspaper columns, makes television appearances, and manages a catering business (Puck's catering line is the official caterer for the Academy Awards, among others). His enormous name-brand product line runs the gamut from coffees and fine wines to housewares.

Puck's story bears a strong resemblance to those of numerous other renowned contemporary chefs who immigrated to the United States or were first-generation children of immigrants and worked their way up the ranks, challenging the status quo in American cuisine and braiding flavors from numerous cuisines into modern dishes. The son of poor parents, Puck went on to command a food empire worth hundreds of millions, forging new culinary trends along the way.

ACCOMPANIED BY

Wolfgang Puck was raised by his mother, Maria Topfschnig, and stepfather, Josef Puck, a coal miner. Topfschnig raised Wolfgang and his three half-siblings in the small town where she worked, Sankt Veit an der Glan, which Puck described as being so small that "it wasn't even a village, it was like two farmers and five houses" (Denning 2018). Puck has been married three times: to Marie France in 1975, Barbara Lazaroff in 1983, and handbag designer Gelila Assefa in 2007. A 1984 *People* feature on the chef's relationships noted Lazaroff's significant role in Puck's restaurants, remodeling the restaurants in lavish decor and entertaining diners "in a sequined bodysuit, with streamers floating from her waist and a pet cockatiel perched on her head (. . .) Barbara maintains two separate wardrobes, one for each restaurant, with a combined total of some 400 exotic designer dresses" (Brawley 1984).

Lazaroff, who was described as having to share Puck's home with his first wife on occasion when France visited to do laundry, continues to be involved in Puck's businesses. Puck has four sons: Cameron, Byron, Oliver, and Alexander. In recent years, Puck has stated that his family is his greatest priority, and he weighs business ventures in terms of whether they would give him enough time with his youngest sons.

DESSERT

- **From an independent city-state to an independent Steak 'n' Shake:** In 1973, Wolfgang Puck boarded a Greyhound bus destined for Indianapolis, Indiana, full of hope and excitement about making the city his new home and culinary playground. Why Indianapolis? Puck assumed that because the city was renowned for its racetrack that it would be similar to life in Monaco. "'I thought it would be more like Monte Carlo because of the car race,' Puck recalls; the memory of preparing too many well-done steaks still gives him pause" (McDonald 2017). In the 1970s, Puck decided to make Indianapolis, Indiana, his new home and culinary stomping ground based on his assumption that the city would be similar to Monaco since both cities had famous race car circuits.
- **Je quitte!** Puck has a history of speaking his mind. In 1975, a French restaurant's manager wrote a menu and told Puck "cook it." The chef, who didn't care for his boss, replied, "*You* wrote it, *you* cook it" and left, never to return.
- **Order now and receive . . . #$@!** In more recent years, Puck has been known to let profanity slip on his Home Shopping Network product demonstrations, touting his own cupcakes, "You're going to say, oh s—, this is the best thing I ever ate!" and criticizing a competitor's sauté pan, "[This cost] six hundred and fifty dollars? I said, I have to f— try it out. How will it work?!"

- **When the stars are out:** Puck's secret for making everyone feel special? Making the rounds of every table at his restaurant, leaving celebrities for last. He says this makes the other guests feel special (*the chef stopped to ask how my salad was before talking to Tom Cruise!*) and grants celebrities privacy until they're about to leave.
- **Heeeere's dinner!** Wolfgang Puck had a conundrum. Talk-show host Johnny Carson loved coming to Spago and ordering multiple gourmet pizzas to take home, but when asked why he ordered so many, he confessed that he froze them to eat later. Puck was initially horrified but discovered that Carson was onto something—frozen pizza was quite tasty when cooked. Puck ran with the idea, which proved to be profitable: in 2012 alone, his frozen pizza sales were in the millions of dollars worldwide.

SUGGESTED PAIRINGS

See also: Flay, Bobby; Laurentiis, Giada De; Pépin, Jacques; Ramsay, Gordon.

Entry best enjoyed while eating: Corn and bacon soup with jalapeno crema; Spago pizza with smoked salmon and caviar; Kaiserschmarren (a Viennese dessert souffle) with strawberry sauce.

Further Reading

Brawley, Peggy. 1984. "Wolfgang Puck and Barbara Lazaroff Have Cooked Up a Marriage, Not to Mention Two Sizzling Restaurants." https://people.com/archive/wolfgang-puck-and-barbara-lazaroff-have-cooked-up-a-marriage-not-to-mention-two-sizzling-restaurants-vol-21-no-12/

Denning, Stephanie. 2018. "How Wolfgang Puck Became a Superstar Chef: His Seven Principles." *Forbes*, June 26, 2018. https://www.forbes.com/sites/stephaniedenning/2018/06/26/how-wolfgang-puck-became-a-superstar-chef-his-seven-principles/#4ef869c41a8f

Inc Editorial Staff. 2009. "How I Did It: Wolfgang Puck." *Inc*, October 1, 2009.

James Beard Foundation. 2012. Press Release. January 30, 2012. https://jbf-media.s3.amazonaws.com/archive/jbf-2013/pressreleases/2012_JBF_Awards_Lifetime_Award_FINAL.pdf

McDonald, Kathy A. 2017. "Wolfgang Puck Dishes on His Walk of Fame Honor." *Variety*, April 26, 2017.

Ryssdal, Kai. 2015. "Wolfgang Puck: Don't Call Him a Celebrity." Marketplace, National Public Radio. Aired December 17, 2015.

Vilas-Boas, Eric. 2012. https://www.esquire.com/food-drink/restaurants/interviews/a16987/wolfgang-puck-interview-14793198/

R

Radio and Podcasts, Food-Themed (1920s–1970s)

STARTERS

Food has been a central topic of discussion on America's airways for over 100 years. The Golden Era of radio began after World War I, when the use of the media to talk between two or more individuals evolved into creating nonfiction and fictional entertainment for specific audiences. In the 1920s through the 1950s, radio played a vital role in news and entertainment for people all over the country and was a considerable driving force in popular culture. The rise of television and the internet may have cast radio as an assumed antiquated form of entertainment, but market data shows that over the last decade, nearly 90 percent of Americans have consistently been listening to AM/FM radio in a given week (Pew Research Center 2019). During this era, cooking programs were the most common form of food-themed programming, helping to lend technical instruction in addition to a sense of companionship for many women navigating home cooking on their own. Food's changing role in pop culture was also seen through the evolution of radio commercials, ranging from sponsored ads in the earliest radio programs to commercials mirroring the sounds of music and cultural revolutions in the 1960s and 1970s.

ENTRÉE

Food programming has been part of public radio since the dawn of the medium. In 1924, a show called *Betty Crocker Cooking School of the Air* debuted, sharing cooking instructions from a fictional home cook named Betty Crocker. The first writer and host of the show was actually Marjorie Child Husted, although as the show quickly grew in popularity, different "Betties" sprung up at various radio stations. The show typically featured ways to cook using the sponsored product—Gold Medal Flour—and listeners could send in their cooking reports to be "graded," seeking validation for their cooking while simultaneously providing the station's parent company with tens of thousands of forms providing invaluable demographic data about their audience. NBC went on to pick up the show in its early years, a wise move, as the program garnered a million listeners in its 24-year history.

The show would go on to become one of the longest-running shows in radio history. Food-themed radio shows during the Consumer Era (1940s–1970s) held deep significance for its listeners, the majority of whom were housewives. Writer Nathalie Cooke notes that many of these women experienced feelings of isolation and loneliness while caring for their children and preparing meals at home, and these conversational radio shows served as both a companion and another source of pressure to "produce dishes of greater complexity in this economy of rising expectations." Ironically, characters like "Betty" who helped reinforce women's duties in the kitchen were voiced by women successfully working outside the home (Cooke 2015).

Radio food programs often reflect the times, as did the show *Mystery Chef*, which aired in the 1930s and 1940s. The man behind the mystery was John MacPherson, a Scottish-born cooking hobbyist who maintained his anonymity (perhaps because there were some stigmas against men who cooked for pleasure during this era). His program offered budget-friendly recipes, and his tutorials were infused with creative and artistic ideas: a welcome trio of topics for Depression-era housewives. In the late 1940s, influential chef James Beard used his penchant for theater and notable voice for short radio segments on cooking, which served as a bridge to his early television cooking spots. In 1957, satirist and radio actor Stan Freberg created a series of commercials called "Who Listens to Radio?" in an effort to convince advertisers to allocate more money to the medium. His most memorable campaign entailed a theatrical description of tens of thousands of onlookers cheering as they watched Lake Michigan being drained, filled with hot chocolate, and topped with hundreds of feet of whipped cream and watching the Canadian Royal Air Force lower a 10-ton maraschino cherry on top.

The next several decades saw a stark change in radio food programming. Sponsored commercials in the late 1940s and 1950s had often conjured up imagery of nuclear families and wholesome meals, such as this ad for Cream of Wheat that aired on Saturday mornings during the radio show *Let's Pretend*: "Yes we have it every day . . . and it makes us shout/Hooray!" (Ramsburg 2019). By the 1960s, the tone and mood of many radio programs and ads had dramatically changed, reflecting the moods of a country under duress from civil rights protests, the Vietnam War, and political assassinations. The younger generation was driving a counterculture, anti-establishment revolution.

Radio, particularly music, was deeply entwined in American culture during this era, and bands and solo artists alike were experimenting with new, psychedelic sounds that challenged traditional boundaries. These themes even permeated radio commercials. In the 1960s, some high-profile rock bands even provided the tracks, such as a Rice Krispies ad sung by British rock group The Rolling Stones. In harsh contrast to the more wholesome ads like "Cream of Wheat," these ads featured wailing harmonicas, electric guitars, and feverish drums under lyrics like "Wake up in the morning there's a snap around the place! Wake up in the morning there's a crackle in your face!" Similarly, an enormously successful radio campaign for the soda 7Up rebranded its image as a young person's drink and set it apart from its competitor, Coca-Cola, with radio and print ads branding it the "un-cola." Set to music along the stylings of Jefferson Airplane or the Mamas and the Papas, 7Up's radio ads were a nonsubtle nod to anti-establishment culture, a move that helped launch the beverage into popular favor.

By the 1970s, the popularity of FM radio (the quality of which was stronger than AM) was growing exponentially, as was the realization on broadcasters' part that children and teenagers were a valuable marketing demographic to target. Fast-food chains like McDonald's invested a significant amount of money into radio, print, and television advertising in this era, leading to somewhat of a golden era of marketing campaigns. Coca-Cola's highly successful "I'd Like to Buy the World a Coke" campaign was launched by members of the corporation's radio team. Other historic food campaigns were born in this decade as well, flooding television and radio airwaves with catchphrases like Burger King's "Have It Your Way" and McDonald's "You Deserve a Break Today." The mid-1970s saw the emergence of fast-food drive-throughs, making cars both a notable new way to listen to ads for food and a place in which to eat it.

SUGGESTED PAIRINGS

See also: Beard, James; Magazines, Food; Radio Shows and Podcasts, Food-Themed (1920s–1970s).

Entry best enjoyed while eating: Betty Crocker's 1956 "eggs ala goldenrod" (toast topped with chopped hard-boiled eggs and white gravy); McDonald's debut of the Happy

---

Small Plates

One Mystifying Fruit

In 1944, a fictional character called Miss Chiquita made her debut on major American radio shows. The self-proclaimed "First Lady of Fruit" was a marketing campaign aimed at educating consumers about how to determine the ripeness of bananas and offered recipe suggestions. The fruit had been hard to come by in the first half of the century, and virtually nonexistent during World War II, so Americans were relatively clueless as to how and when to eat them.

The Chiquita Banana jingle included helpful tips like "Bananas like the climate of the very tropical equator / so you should never put bananas in the refrigerator" and (surprisingly) advised putting them in a salad. Writer and vintage media enthusiast Laura Macfehin notes that in the first half of the twentieth century, bananas "apparently mystified Western cooks. There are whole books dedicated to 'how to serve bananas' and some of the solutions are enough to make the most ardent banana fan shudder" (2017). Macfehin shares various banana recipes printed in popular magazines and cookbooks in United States and abroad, including "banana jam" and "banana soup" (a concoction of fruit mixed with turnips, Worcestershire sauce, onions, tomatoes, and beef stock) in the 1930s; bananas with ham and Hollandaise sauce in the 1970s; and banana "sardine boats" with lettuce and lemon.

In an effort to bring the banana jingle into the twenty-first century, Chiquita rewrote the lyrics in 1999, with lines like "Underneath the crescent yellow, you'll find vitamins and great taste / with no fat, you just can't beat 'em / you'll feel better when you eat 'em." There was no mention of ways to use it like Chiquita's own 1947 recipe "Ham Banana Rolls with Cheese Sauce," which Vice writer Hilary Pollack recreated. Pollack wrote about the process, "You may ask yourself how you ended up seven years into a career as a food writer, standing over a pot of processed cheese that you are about to dump onto a pile of meat-wrapped, slightly unripe bananas and then consume out of self-hatred (. . . but) I made it. I made the Terrible Banana Thing" (Pollack 2018). Perhaps an ode to that particular triumph will be written for the *next* jingle revamp.

Meal in 1979: hamburger, small french fry, a chocolate sundae, and a toy stencil; and a cold glass of 7Up, served with anti-establishment ice cubes.

Further Reading

Chiquita Banana Staff. n.d. "The Chiquita Banana Jingle." http://dev.chiquita.com/Our-Company/The-Chiquita-Story/The-Chiquita-Jingle.aspx

Cooke, Nathalie. 2015. "Lessons from Generations Past: Timely and Timeless Communication Strategies of Some Canadian Cooks of Note." In *Food & Communication: Proceedings of the Oxford Symposium on Food 2015*, edited by Mark McWilliams. Prospect Books: London.

Macfehin, Laura. "Five Things our Grandmothers Did with Bananas (That We Don't Do Now!)." Eclectic Ladyland, blog post, April 9, 2017. https://eclecticladylandblog.wordpress.com/2017/04/09/5-things-our-grandmothers-did-with-bananas-that-we-dont-do-now/

McDonald, Amy. 2017. "Uncola: Seven-Up, Counterculture and the Making of an American Brand." Duke University Libraries, blog post. December 4, 2017. https://blogs.library.duke.edu/rubenstein/2017/12/04/uncola/

Pew Research Center. 2019. "Fact Sheet: Audio and Podcasting." https://www.journalism.org/fact-sheet/audio-and-podcasting/

Pollack, Hilary. 2018. "I Bought a Vintage Banana Cookbook and Accidentally Opened a Sarcophagus of Horrors." Vice, November 29, 2018. https://www.vice.com/en_us/article/vba3x3/i-bought-a-vintage-banana-cookbook-and-accidentally-opened-a-sarcophagus-of-horrors

Ramsburg, Jim. 2019. "Let's Pretend!" Jim Ramsburg's Gold Time Radio. http://www.jimramsburg.com/lets-pretend.html

Radio and Podcasts, Food-Themed (1980s–)

STARTERS

Since the 1980s, food-themed radio programming has seen a relatively radical transformation as radio itself has changed form and reached new audiences. Once the only form of radio programming, traditional terrestrial (AM/FM) radio was joined by satellite radio programming with the founding of XM radio in the late 1980s. The early 2000s also saw the invention of online radio and podcasts, which are audio programs available to download and/or stream digitally. Podcasting led to the largest number of food-themed audio programming to date and has seen enormous popularity as a format. As of 2019, there were an estimated 660,000 podcast shows in existence, reaching an audience of 62 million listeners (Sternbergh 2019).

Podcast productions vary in complexity, budget, and quality, making the medium one that amateurs and professionals alike can create and distribute. As a result, the combination of contemporary radio and podcast programming offers an impressively diverse catalog of food and culinary programs, ranging from small shows geared toward very limited audiences to award-winning journalists who command crowds of tens of thousands. As the first century of radio's history has shown, food-related entertainment on Americans' airways will not be in short supply any time soon.

ENTRÉE

Starting in the 1980s, American cultural shifts were reflected in significant changes to radio programming, food, and women's roles both inside and outside of the family. Talk radio segments rose from 200 to 850 between 1984 and 1994, reflecting listeners' growing appetite for dialogue and stories. Additionally, food-related radio programming specifically targeted toward housewives was falling out of favor because men and women were beginning to share more cooking and food preparation duties, and upward of 50 percent of mothers with young children were now members of the workforce (Guilder 1986). Food was a prevalent theme on many radio shows' humorous and dramatic discussions alike, such as frequent episodes of the National Public Radio (NPR) comedic talk show *Car Talk* (1977–2012). The show's hosts, brothers Tom and Ray Magliozzi, talked shop with live callers whose (real) car problems spanned the spectrum from broken clutches to determining the best van in which to transport Nigerian goats to various pool parties. Over the years, food and food service topics snuck into the show in unexpected ways. In one, a caller was advised to put oatmeal in a radiator to try sealing cracks in a cracked gasket; in another episode, a distraught caller admitted he'd left a fresh turkey in his car for a week and was dealing with the fallout.

The decades between 1980 and 2020 saw a significant and steady rise of serious food-themed radio content. Throughout each of these decades, Vertamae Smart-Grosvenor served as a food commentator on various NPR shows, including her own series called *Seasonings*. As a culinary anthropologist and food writer, some of her most personal pieces were about foodways of the Gullah people, descendants of West Africans in the Lowcountry region of South Carolina. Writer Allison Gibson wrote that in the 1990s "food radio met the public airwaves, ushering in a new era of coverage concentrating on the culture and politics of food as much as recipes" (Gibson 2017). One example she cites is a 2014 episode of *Good Food*, a long-running radio show hosted by chef Evan Kleiman. In her interview, Kleiman spoke with the writers of a vegan food blog and cookbook dubbed "Thug Kitchen," written in the persona of a fictitious "thug" who used heavy profanity. She asked if the persona was merely comedic or if it could be deemed a digital form of blackface since it was seen by some as a stereotypical portrayal of Black criminals.

Over the last three decades, many radio shows have addressed similar issues, covering topics like sustainability, health, agricultural practices, the history of food, and the intersections of food, culture, race, and ethnicity. American Public Radio's *Splendid Table* was launched in 1994 by food writer Lynne Rossetto Kasper, who was at the forefront of movements like introducing more organic and local foods into American households. In 2018, food writer Francis Lam took over the show, and he continues to take listener calls on air, infusing the show with stories and explorations of topics like multicultural cuisines. Radio storytelling experienced a significant resurgence around the same time. Some examples include Chicago Public Radio's *This American Life*, which launched in 1997 and currently reaches a listenership of 2.2 million on the radio and 2.5 million via podcast. Each of the show's hour-long episodes have a central theme, many of which have included food-themed tales ranging from the comedic qualities of artisanal toast to somber explorations of the role that food and meals play in the wake of events like family tragedies.

In 2009, the nonprofit Heritage Radio Network was founded in Brooklyn, New York, with the mission of airing entirely food- and beverage-themed shows. The organization's content is broadcast from two shipping containers behind a local pizza restaurant. The founders were inspired by the pirate radio work of Carlo Petrini, an Italian who started the Slow Food movement in the mid-1970s. Heritage Radio's audience has amassed over 1 million listeners across 200 countries, and their lineup of dozens of weekly shows range from cheese-centric *Cutting the Curd* to an interview series focusing on women in the culinary world called *Speaking Broadly*.

Today, there are nearly countless podcasts whose central or secondary focus is on food, beverage, the culinary arts, or food-related social or history topics. Coming full circle to the Great Depression era of radio cooking instruction, a 2020 podcast called *Home Cooking* featured chef Samin Nosrat and podcast producer Hrishikesh Hirway, who helped listeners cook meals using pantry staples. The duo also touched on themes like associating comfort and love with food and quelling anxieties and food conundrums from callers in the midst of the coronavirus pandemic of 2020. A large number of publications and television shows have podcast "spin-offs," such as *Proof*, a technical, philosophical, and historical exploration of food hosted by Bridget Lancaster of America's Test Kitchen. Some walk the line between comedy and drama, like *The Sporkful*, with themes ranging from the pitfalls of eating corn dogs on the political campaign trail to culturally insensitive terms used in contemporary menus.

DESSERT

Are you a fan or just hungry? Food writers and comedians Molly Wizenberg and Matthew Amster-Burton present food and eating through the lens of humor on their podcast *Spilled Milk*.

In an interview with *Seattle Weekly*, Wizenberg described a humorous conundrum she'd experienced as a result of the podcast. "I was at a Seattle Arts and Lectures thing the other evening, and a woman came up to me, introduced herself, and goes 'I was listening to ravioli on the way over here.' And in my mind I was like, *Did we record a ravioli episode recently? Is she talking about our podcast?* I don't even remember." Amster-Burton added, "[Maybe] she just had her ear up to a bag of frozen ravioli" (Sommerfeld 2018).

SUGGESTED PAIRINGS

See also: America's Test Kitchen; Nonfiction, Food in; Radio Shows and Podcasts, Food-Themed (1920s–1970s); Websites, Food.

Entry best enjoyed while eating: A banana, in order to test whether or not its peel can actually make someone slip and fall (Food 52 *Burnt Toast*, episode 64); pickled mushrooms for snacking and running water to muffle the sound of dissident discussions in a

KGB-bugged, Soviet-era kitchen (*Kitchen Sisters*, "Communal Kitchens"); a small, plastic cow on the table that moos to make guests laugh, thus improving their mood and making them think highly of their meal (NPR's Ted Radio Hour, "The Food We Eat"); a glass of wine created in a vineyard designed with ethical agricultural practices in mind (sommelier-hosted *I'll Drink to That*, episode 469).

Further Reading

Gibson, Allison. 2017. "Welcome to The Golden Age of Food Radio." Eater, July 15, 2017. https://www.eater.com/2015/7/15/8962823/food-radio-evan-kleiman-heritage-radio

Guilder, George. 1986. "Women in the Workforce." *The Atlantic*, September 1986.

Heritage Radio Network. 2020. Heritageradionetwork.org

Kleinman, Evan. 2014. "The Thug Kitchen Controversy." *Good Food*, October 25, 2014. KCRW.

Sommerfeld, Seth. 2018. "Laughing Over Spilled Milk." *Seattle Weekly*, April 18, 2018.

Sternbergh, Adam. 2019. "How Podcasts Learned to Speak." Vulture, March 18, 2019. https://www.vulture.com/2019/03/the-great-podcast-rush.html

Ramsay, Gordon (1966–)

STARTERS

Gordon Ramsay is a Scottish-born chef, television personality, author, and restaurateur who is best known in the United States for his reality television appearances. He owns a large number of restaurants across the world that span from Las Vegas, Nevada, to Versailles, France. He is internationally known for his frequent and long-term appearances on reality cooking television shows, including a number of programs that were originally aired in the United Kingdom and later produced for American audiences primarily by Fox Network. Some of his most popular shows include *MasterChef* (1990–2001, United Kingdom; 2010–, United States), *Hell's Kitchen* (2004–2009; 2005–), *Kitchen Nightmares* (2004–2014; 2007–2014), and *The F Word* (2005–2010; 2017).

Several of Ramsay's restaurants have earned Michelin stars, starting with London-based Aubergine in the mid-1990s. In 1998, Restaurant Gordon Ramsay received a coveted three Michelin stars, and he currently holds the record for maintaining three stars longer than any other London restaurant. In 2005, the chef received a British Academy of Film and Television Arts (BAFTA) award for *Ramsay's Kitchen Nightmares*, and in 2008 and 2009, he won an Australian television Astra award for "Favourite International Personality."

ENTRÉE

Much like his larger-than-life television persona, Gordon Ramsay's list of life adventures is anything but understated. In 2008, the chef had a harrowing near-death incident while filming a segment for his British television show *The F Word*. Ramsay was hunting for puffins on cliffs off the coast of Iceland when he slipped and fell 280 feet, landing in freezing water. He nearly drowned, unable to kick his heavy boots off while his lungs began to fill with water. In 2011, while filming a documentary in Costa Rica about the shark fin industry, he was held at gunpoint and doused in gasoline by Taiwanese fin smugglers who caught him sneaking onto rooftops and into boats to document their abusive animal practices. Ramsay stays fit as an MMA fighter, has a black belt in karate, and has had a spontaneous punch or two thrown at him in the kitchen.

Ramsay brand encompasses a wide array of businesses and media, including a large network of restaurants, decades' worth of television shows, consulting work, and an international production company. Ramsay embodies the contemporary "rockstar" celebrity chef status, complete with a fan club and various mansions in numerous cities around the world. Ramsay's childhood was vastly different. His family had so little money that food was relatively scarce at home, and he and his siblings often relied on vouchers for free dinners at school. He was raised in an unstable home environment and moved around Great Britain often. Ramsay's father pushed him to be a soccer player (referred to as a "footballer" in the United Kingdom), and at the age of 16, his family moved from England to Glasgow in order to position the teen to play for the Rangers, a professional club in Scotland. He made the team the following year, but was cut after sustaining a bad knee injury.

Gordon Ramsay has achieved "celebrity chef" status in the United Kingdom and United States alike, both for his restaurants and his television shows. (Hotshotsworldwide/Dreamstime.com)

On whim, Ramsay enrolled in a local college to pursue a career in catering. In his autobiography, he describes it as "a complete accident," noting that as he got more involved in restaurants, he became enthralled. One of his first jobs was a dishwasher at a curry restaurant, and he notes that he remembers feeling "enraptured" listening to the kitchen staff yelling at each other (2006, 62). By 1998, Ramsay was a noted up-and-coming chef, and he caught the attention of a documentary film crew who filmed him as the star of a British miniseries entitled *Boiling Point*. The docuseries followed Ramsay in the immediate aftermath of walking out of his role at Aubergine over a personnel dispute and pursuing the launch of his own restaurant. The show helped launch him to television fame, introducing audiences to his now-famous hot temper, harsh tongue, and penchant for rebellious behavior. Over the course of the show, Ramsay fired servers for making seemingly innocuous mistakes and was caught in a controversy after accepting money from a local association to promote a specific variety of apple, only to secretly feature a different type of apple in his dishes, claiming no one would notice.

Ramsay's critical reception has been similar to that of fellow British reality television star Simon Cowell. Much like Cowell, a judge on the NBC competition show *America's Got Talent* (2006–), Ramsay is described by some as a celebrity with whom people have a "love/hate relationship," likely due to some of his contradictory characteristics. On shows like *Hell's Kitchen* and *MasterChef*, he is known for his fiery temper, harsh criticism, and penchant for expletives. On *MasterChef Junior*, his vulgar outbursts are replaced with more restrained sternness and even heartwarming moments with children. He is praised in the media for his contributions to charities that support female victims of domestic abuse, but criticized for allegations of making crass and misogynistic statements about women in professional kitchens. He's starred on shows focused on rehabilitating failing businesses, but has been publicly chastised for doing so in the manner of a bully.

The chef has had a number of highly public feuds with people ranging from his former mentor (and fellow hot-tempered chef) Marco Pierre White to culinary figures Anthony Bourdain. In one famous incident, Ramsay threw critic AA Gill out of his restaurant along with Gill's dining companion, actress Joan Collins, in retaliation for Gill having described Ramsay as "a failed sportsman who acts like an eleven-year-old" (McCann 1998). He has been the subject of public ire from animal rights activists for hunting puffins and serving rare eels and bluefin in his restaurant, but he risked his life advocating for the brutal practice of shark finning to become illegal. In these ways, Ramsay is a strong example of a modern celebrity chef in popular culture. He has helped push reality cooking shows deeper into "entertainment" territory, moving away from educational shows of the past with shock value and formulaic reality show competitions. He is also a seemingly inexhaustible "jack of all trades," keeping up with fellow celebrity chefs' demanding pace in front of the camera, behind the scenes of their kitchens, and traveling the world in search of their next big adventure.

ACCOMPANIED BY

Gordon Ramsay was born in Johnstone, Scotland, and spent part of his youth in Stratford-upon-Avon, England. In his memoir *Roasting in Hell's Kitchen*, he describes his father's inability to keep a job for long. His father, Gordon Ramsay Sr., had been a star swimmer as a youth but had difficulty maintaining steady work as a swimming coach in his adult years. Gordon's mother, Helen Cosgrove, worked as a nanny and a nurse. She married him when she was only 17 and learned she was expecting the couple's first child, Diana, within a year of her wedding. Ramsay's other siblings include his sister Yvonne, half-sister Sharon, and brother Ronnie, the latter of whom has struggled with heroin addiction. Ramsay's family's experiences and his observations of drug addiction within the restaurant industry inspired him to make a documentary in which he tested his restaurants for traces of cocaine and met with his staff to confront the dangers of the drug.

Ramsay has written that his father, who passed away in 1997, was an alcoholic and didn't hold down any of his jobs long enough to allow the family to remain in any of their homes for a significant period of time. The Ramsay family was subjected to domestic violence as well. In an article Ramsay wrote for CNN, he described his father by saying "every time he got violent, any present that my brother, sisters, or I had given mum would be smashed, simply because he knew it belonged to her" (2007). On numerous occasions, the police arrested his father, and the Ramsay children temporarily stayed in children's homes while Helen recovered in the hospital. In 1996, the chef married Cayetana "Tana" Ramsay, nee Hutchenson (1974–), an educator, cookbook author, and television host. The two have five children together: Megan (1998–), twins Holly and Jack (2000–), Matilda (2001–), and Oscar (2019–).

DESSERT

Shame and Cheese on wheat: In a spoof about his own television programs on *The Late Late Show with James Cordon*, Ramsay jokingly held slices of bread over a chef's ears, yelling, "What are you?" prompting the dejected woman to sadly reply, "An idiot sandwich." The clip went viral as a meme in 2015, prompting humorous tweets such as "I am an idiot sandwich . . . these exams have helped me realize that."

SUGGESTED PAIRINGS

See also: Fieri, Guy; Flay, Bobby; *MasterChef*

Entry best enjoyed while eating: Beef Wellington, or his vegan *Beet* Wellington, with truffle and brie mashed potatoes and red wine jus; pork belly ramen (a more ethically sourced and delicious alternative to shark fin soup, which Ramsay reports is devoid of any taste aside from the broth); banana sticky toffee pudding; and a cocktail he serves with a name inspired by his own insult, a "Wake Up, You Donkey" cocktail of tequila, elderflower, and honey.

Further Reading
"About Gordon." n.d. https://www.gordonramsay.com/gr/about-gordon/
Guardian Staff. 1999. "Gordon Ramsay." *The Guardian*, June 10, 1999.
Krystina (@mmooseblood). 2015. "I Am an Idiot Sandwich n These Exams Have Helped Me Realise That." Twitter post, May 17, 2015, 4:21 p.m.
McCann, Paul. 1998. "Chef Serves Restaurant Critic a Taste of Rejection." *Independent*, October 14, 1998.
Platt, John. 2011. "Shark-finning Gangsters Assault Celebrity Chef Gordon Ramsay." *Scientific American*, blog post. January 10, 2011. https://blogs.scientificamerican.com/extinction-countdown/shark-finning-gangsters-assault-celebrity-chef-gordon-ramsay/
Ramsay, Gordon. 2006. *Roasting in Hell: Temper Tantrums, F Words, and the Pursuit of Perfection*.

Ramsay, Gordon. 2007. "Ramsay: No One Should Suffer Abuse Like My Mum." CNN, September 25, 2007. https://edition.cnn.com/2007/LIVING/personal/09/25/ramsay.commentary/

Ray, Rachael (1968–)

STARTERS

Rachael Ray is a celebrity cook, television personality, cookbook author, brand owner of a wide range of cooking and lifestyle products, corporate product spokesperson, and philanthropist. Her television career began with a recurring segment on the CBS news in Albany-Schenectady, New York, in which she taught viewers how to make meals in 30 minutes. The popularity of her news appearances led to the launch of a related cookbook and a show on the Food Network called *30-Minute Meals*, which ran for 11 seasons between 2001 and 2012. Ray was a frequent cooking contributor on various episodes of *The Oprah Winfrey Show*, which helped the cook to launch her own talk show. *Rachel Ray* (2006–) has run on CBS for more than 2,000 episodes and is produced in part by Winfrey's production company. In addition to hundreds of recurring spots on daytime and late-night television like *Good Morning America*, *The Tonight Show with Jay Leno*, and *The Chew*, Ray was also the star of the Food Network's *$40 a Day* (2002–2005) and *Rachael Ray's Tasty Travels* (2005–2011).

ENTRÉE

Looking into the cameras on the set of the Food Network's early years of *30-Minute Meals*, Rachael Ray began each show by introducing herself and promising viewers that by the end of the 30-minute episode, she would have shown them how to make a delicious and easy meal from start to finish. Over the years, Ray drew some criticism from critics and families who struggled to replicate her speed in the kitchen, but Ray's cooking demonstrations drew in home cooks, aspiring cooks, and cooking-averse audience members alike who wanted to revel in the cozy feeling of being in Ray's kitchen while aspiring to create the same ambiance at home. For a straightforward cooking show, Ray's *30-Minute Meals* also held entertainment value for audiences. Ray was a hurricane in the studio kitchen, filling her arms to the brim with as many ingredients as possible while talking a mile a minute about cooking, food, and personal anecdotes. Her speed, permissive attitude toward embracing imperfections in the kitchen, and steadfast enthusiasm and good-natured cheer proved to be an immensely popular combination for viewers.

Ray's interest in food and cooking began at a very young age. In high school, she came up with a food gift basket business that she dubbed "Delicious Liaisons." After graduating, she studied communications and literature for two years at Pace University before working at the candy counter of a Macy's Marketplace gourmet candy counter in New York City. Despite climbing the ranks quickly, the intensity of Ray's schedule and pressure to work in other retail roles threatened to pull her away from her passion for food. After a frightening experience in which she was mugged outside of her apartment in Queens, and then violently assaulted by the same assailant again within a week, Ray left the city for life in a rented cabin in New York's Adirondack mountains.

Away from "the city that never sleeps," Ray landed a job as a cook and buyer for a gourmet food store in Albany, New York. She noticed that shoppers were more drawn to prepackaged meals, so the cook started teaching classes in the art of whipping up dinner on a tight schedule. The popular demonstrations led to recurring news spots on a local news station and a cookbook touting her "thirty-minute meals." A producer from the *Today* show caught wind of the book and asked Ray to do a cooking segment on the morning show. Despite the fact that a serious snowstorm had moved into the area, Ray and her mother drove together for nine hours to get to the set on time. Her long commute paid off: one day later, the Food Network called and offered her a $360,000 starting salary to join their lineup of on-air cooking talent. Despite her immense success and wealth in the food entertainment industry, Ray has said that one of the most significant purchases in her life was buying a (humbly priced) cabin in the Adirondacks to transform the home she used to struggle to rent during her youth into her permanent home.

Celebrity cook Rachael Ray poses with a Daytime Emmy award she received in 2019 in the category of Outstanding Informative Talk Show. (Hutchinsphoto/Dreamstime.com)

Ray helped the Food Network broaden its appeal, charming audiences with her bubbly personality and taking the fear factor out of cooking for families strapped for time (or lacking enthusiasm) in their respective kitchens. In 2005, New York Times columnist Kim Severson described the cook with high praise, writing "(after) more than 4 million books in print and four shows on the Food Network, Ms. Ray has shown America the way back to the kitchen." Ray has described herself as a cook instead of a chef, citing the lack of innovation in her cooking. Instead of pushing the culinary envelope, she focuses on helping others learn basic and intermediate cooking skills. Much like her predecessors Julia Child and Graham Kerr, Ray adds levity to her shows and isn't finicky with her methods. For example, she teaches audiences to have a "garbage bowl" on the counter to save them from multiple trips to the trash can and demonstrates how to pour oil into a pan for a certain duration instead of measuring it. She also incorporates ingredients that busy home cooks are likely to turn to, such as using jarred sauce in a pasta dish in lieu of making pasta from scratch.

Between 2005 and 2020, Ray's brand grew to encompass an eponymous syndicated talk show with an enormous viewership (2006–) and a cooking and lifestyle magazine, *Rachael Ray's Every Day*, with a circulation of 1.7 million readers. She also wrote and published two dozen cookbooks and developed cookware products and an olive oil line. Ray became one of the most influential figures on the Food Network. The network's president, Courtney White, told the *Washington Post* that Ray was one of the first personalities on the network who boosted viewers' confidence in making a nice meal without professional culinary training. White described the star as having an "uncanny ability to engage viewers," noting her relatability to audiences as someone who felt both like a friend and someone who understood firsthand how busy the lives of her viewers were. When asked about why fans adored *30 Minute Meals*, Ray responded that food programming provides comfort, which helped audiences embrace cooking more comfortably. "It's like a hug. 'Cause food appeals to all your senses, and it's kind of magic. It's this big, raw pile of ingredients, then a few minutes later it's this whole other thing (. . .) it's like a little roller-coaster ride" (Krystal 2019).

ACCOMPANIED BY

Rachel and her two siblings, Maria and Emmanuel (Manny), were raised by their parents, Sicilian American Elsa Scuderi and James Ray. The children grew up in their parents' restaurants in Cape Cod, Massachusetts, and Lake George, New York. Ray told *People* magazine that her first memory was "grilling my thumb to the griddle in our restaurant on Cape Cod" (Hamm and Tauber 2007). Her parents divorced when she was 12, and her mother ran 9 restaurants on her own, putting the children to work prepping food and bussing tables. In 2005, Ray

---

Small Plates

Queen Bé and the Case of the Wrong Becky

In 2016, singer Beyoncé released an album titled *Lemonade*, in which she alluded to her husband, rapper Jay-Z, having an affair in lyrics such as "He better call Becky with the good hair." Beyoncé's notoriously loyal fan base went on a frenzied mission to sleuth out with whom the affair may have been, quickly zeroing in on American fashion designer Rachel Roy as the "Becky" in question. In an unfortunate twist of mistaken identities, a fleet of livid fans went after Rachael *Ray* online. "Oh I loved (your) hot chicken fajitas but I will never make them again after what you did to the Queen," one dismayed commenter posted on Ray's social media, using a common nickname for the singer (Mettler 2016). The mistaken identity was eventually cleared up. For those wishing to cling to the erroneous accusation, perhaps a case could be made that Beyoncé's 2005 song "Check In On It" was a secret message about Ray, instructing the cook to peek at how her "one-pan seafood bake" was doing in the oven.

married John Cusimano, an actor, producer, entertainment lawyer, and musician. Cusimano is the lead singer in a rock band called The Cringe and is passionate about cooking and mixology. In 2020, Cusimano and Ray found themselves having to film her shows from home as a result of the global coronavirus pandemic. In an interview with Buzzfeed News, Ray joked that she worked closely with her team of three: John as a cameraman, herself as the star, and their 15-year-old pit bull as the studio audience. In addition to continuing her shows from quarantine, the star donated $4 million to coronavirus relief efforts. "John and I don't have human children. We want to pay it forward to the next generation—and, of course, because of how I make my living, our avenue to do that is to offer our service through food and care for our neighbors in the best way possible," Ray said (Yandoli 2020).

DESSERT

- **Please excuse Rachael:** Ray's mother, Elsa Scuderi, told *People* magazine that her daughter has always had a big, outspoken personality. "I used to have these cards that said, 'Please excuse,' and then there was a line and you'd write 'Rachael,' (. . .) then it said, 'I'm sorry she did [fill in the blank],' and there was a list of things I would check off" (Hamm and Tauber 2007).
- **Ray-Ray's say-says:** Ray has used a number of signature catchphrases in her shows over the years, including calling Extra Virgin Olive Oil *E-V-O-O* (a trend that many viewers went on to adopt) and dubbing spoon/spatula hybrids *spoonulas*. Stew-like soups are *stoups*, and many of her dishes are *delish*—so it's no surprise that her line of healthy pet food is named *Nutrish*.

SUGGESTED PAIRINGS

See also: Fieri, Guy; Flay, Bobby; Garten, Ina; Radio and Podcasts, Food-Themed (1980s–).

Entry best enjoyed while eating: Salad with kale, Spanish chorizo, garbanzo beans, and leeks; tomato-fennel soup with parmesan-crusted grilled cheese "soldiers"; Pignoli cookies (almond and pine nut macaroons that originated in Sicily); and John Cusimano's spicy watermelon margarita garnished with watermelon cubes and cilantro.

Further Reading

Fuller, Melynda. 2019. "'Rachael Ray Every Day' to Become Newsstand-Only Quarterly." Publishers Daily, September 26, 2019. https://www.mediapost.com/publications/article/341238/rachael-ray-every-day-to-become-newsstand-only-q.html

Hamm, Liza, and Michelle Tauber. 2007. "All the Dish!" *People* cover story, May 14, 2007.

Krystal, Becky. 2019. "Rachael Ray's '30 Minute Meals' Changed How We Cook. Now She's Back to Teach a New Generation." *The Washington Post,* April 11, 2019.

Severson, Kim. 2005. "Being Rachael Ray: How Cool Is That?" *The New York Times*, October 19, 2005.

Yandoli, Krystie Lee. 2020. "Rachael Ray Donated $4 Million to Coronavirus Relief—And Shared How She's Doing in Quarantine." Buzzfeed News, April 7, 2020. https://www.buzzfeednews.com/article/krystieyandoli/rachael-ray-coronavirus-donation

Roadside Food Attractions

STARTERS

Roadside attractions are widely considered to be an American institution. Their popularity grew with the expansion of highways in the United States in the early twentieth century. As motorists began to venture further from home than ever before, small business owners set out to draw tourists off the highways to patronize their restaurants, storefronts, and farm stands. Throughout the first half of the twentieth century, new roadside attractions continued to emerge in large numbers, many of which were concrete statues of subjects that were touted as the "world's largest" of their type. Other popular attractions used novelty architecture styles to catch motorists' attention. Not all roadside attractions are food-themed (such as Nebraska's car-studded sculptural park called Carhenge or the "World's Largest Ball of Twine" advertised in a small town in Kansas), but many celebrate foods and culinary traditions that are important to their communities and nation at large.

ENTRÉE

Many iconic roadside attractions fall into a category referred to as *mimetic architecture*: structures that are constructed to look like the things that are sold or performed there (also known as "form following function"). Some examples of this style include Hollywood, California's Ben-Hur Delicious Drip Coffee shop, which delighted customers in 1930 with its coffeepot shape, and the Big Basket building, which was constructed in Newark, Ohio, in 1997 to mimic a giant maple wood picnic basket. Today, the Big Basket is still home to the basket-making Longaberger Company's operations. Similarly, The Big Duck in Long Island, New York, was built by a farmer in 1931 to drum up business for sales of his ducks and duck eggs. The Big Duck joins a number of other mimetic architecture sites that are now listed on the National Register of Historic Places, such as the Benewah Milk Bottle buildings. These Spokane, Washington, landmarks were built to advertise and house the Benewah Creamery Company's dairy operations in 1935. Dairy is a prevalent roadside attraction theme; across the country from Benewah, two milk bottle–shaped towers that flank the sides of a building in Richmond, Virginia, were once home to the Richmond Dairy Building. The dairy business closed in the 1970s and was repurposed in recent years as apartment buildings (a unique housing option for anyone wishing to wake up in a giant milk bottle every day).

Many roadside attractions are restaurants that hold quirky appeal, such as the Little A'le'Inn: a combination restaurant, bar, and motel near Area 51 in Rachel, Nevada (population 96). Set against a vast desert, the restaurant draws visitors off the deserted highway with its giant alien sculpture and UFO held aloft by a crane on the back of a truck. Los Angeles, California, became particularly entranced with oddly shaped restaurants in the early twentieth century. Some of its iconic eateries include a hot dog–shaped stand called Tail o' the Pup (1946), the whiskey barrel–shaped Idle Hour Bar (1941), the Bulldog Cafe (1928), shaped like a black-and-white dog smoking a pipe, a silver Zeppelin-shaped Zep Diner, and a series of buildings shaped like enormous bowls of chili. Californians looking for a sweet treat flocked to locations like the Hoot Owl Cafe (1926) for ice cream, which was housed in a giant owl with a head that could swivel and blinking eyes made from two Buick headlamps (Shatkin 2018). One restaurant that became an especially beloved icon is Randy's Donuts (1953), a small shack with a giant classic donut on its roof that nonprofit Los Angeles Conservancy described as representing "the postwar optimism and whimsy of the city in a way few other places can."

Americans' proclivity for pulling off the highway to see the "world's largest" (anything) can be traced back to the late 1800s, fueled by rapid automobile popularity and highway expansion into the Roaring Twenties. The Bottle, a six-story structure shaped like a glass soda bottle, was erected in Alabama in 1924 as an advertisement for Nehi soda. Claiming to be the world's largest of its kind, the "bottle" contained a grocery store, inn, and service station and attracted tourists and locals alike until reportedly burned down in 1936 (Thorson 2015; Wickman 2015). Similarly, the World's Largest Catsup Bottle was erected in Collinsville, Illinois, in 1949. Many roadside attractions claim to hold the same titles advertised elsewhere, such as numerous attractions that are called the World's Largest Frying Pan. One was created in Long Beach, Washington, and weighed 1,300 pounds, measuring nearly 10 feet in circumference and 20 feet from the edge of the pan to the tip of the handle. Commissioned for a clam festival in 1941, the functional pan cooked a fritter made with 200 pounds of clams, 20 pounds of flour, and 13 gallons of salad oil. In the early 1950s, the first publication of the *Guinness Book of Records* further propelled Americans to up the ante in the realm of large roadside objects.

A number of buildings shaped like milk bottles dot America's cities. One of the first was the 40-foot-tall Hood Milk Bottle restaurant in Boston, Massachusetts, constructed in 1930. (Ritu Jethani/Dreamstime.com)

Although the golden era of roadside attractions is nearly 100 years in the past, the tradition still lives on today. And for travelers who grow weary of stopping to see enormous concrete replicas of various foods, there are countless quirky restaurants, museums, and public artworks that warrant a roadside detour as well.

> ### Small Plates
>
> **Roadside Nuts**
>
> Reviewing the nation's history of roadside attractions, it becomes clear that Americans are smitten with oversized nuts. Every year, tourists flock to attractions like the World's Largest Pistachio, erected in 2008. The 30-foot nut lives in a pistachio orchard in New Mexico and draws in tourists who are charmed by the cheerful green and beige structure that towers over the desert. The plucky pistachio has even been featured in a number of television shows. Brunswick, Missouri, hosts the curiously specific World's Largest Twentieth-Century Pecan, a 12,000-pound concrete replica that used to accompany a roadside stand called the Nut Hut. Staff writers at the Roadside America website note that the Nut Hut is decorated with a cartoon of "a mad, murderous hammer with arms and legs, chasing a very sad giant pecan." The hammer (named "Wham") is a character from an eight-by-eight-foot book written and illustrated by the son of local pecan farmers.
>
> In the competitive realm of nut statue contests, a particularly strange roadside attraction is the Jimmy Carter Peanut: a faceless goober with an oversized, toothy smile that greets motorists passing by in Plains, Georgia. The nut was constructed in 1976 as a Democratic campaign move to improve Carter's favor with Georgian voters. Inspired by the former president's prior career as a peanut farmer, the installation is considered the second-largest peanut replica in the world. According to numerous sources, the World's (actual) Largest Peanut was erected in 1975 in Ashburn, Georgia. Roadside America writers describe other "world's largest peanut" runners-up in Floresville, Texas; Pelion, South Carolina; Dothan, Alabama; and Durant, Oklahoma diplomatically, writing about them in terms like "big civic peanuts" and "generously-scaled goobers." They also note the "most-stolen peanut of them all," a peanut statue made in the likeness of Elvis that now lives in the Dothan, Alabama, visitor's center to protect it from further peanut-nappings.

In Yermo, California, visitors pull off the highway at Peggy Sue's 1950s Diner and Diner-Saur Park to see dinosaur and King Kong sculptures before ordering milkshakes in a vintage diner filled with nostalgic kitsch. In Door County, Wisconsin, travelers stop for lingonberries and pancakes at Al Johnson's Swedish Restaurant, where goats graze on a grass-topped roof above their heads. In Lucas, Kansas, artist Erika Nelson runs The World's Largest Collection of the World's Smallest Versions of the World's Largest Things, a (sometimes traveling) museum showcasing miniature versions she has made of roadside attractions like the World's Largest Ball of Gum and the World's Largest Strawberry.

In Dublin, Ohio, artist Malcolm Cochran's public art installation Field of Corn (with Osage Orange Trees) draws onlookers to a former cornfield to admire 109 concrete corn statues placed upright, six feet apart. Inspired by grave markers at cemeteries like Arlington, Cochran created the piece in 1994 as a statement about the erasure of the town's agricultural heritage in light of rapid real estate development. Across the nation, and the globe at large, countless roadside attractions stem from small simple joys, such as the Dog's Roasted Sweet Potato Stand in Sapporo, Japan. Here, a tiny stand is run by a single employee: Ken-kun, a gentle Shiba Inu. Ken-kun is accompanied by a sign encouraging customers to pay on the honor system, clarifying, "Because I'm a dog, I can't make change" (Lukk 2019).

DESSERT

- **Who else wants to take a quack at one?** Inspired by The Big Duck, professionals in the architectural field often refer to all mimetic architectural styles as "ducks."
- **Stop for a fill-up, stay for pending impeachment:** The Teapot Dome, a gas station shaped like a kettle in Yakima, Washington, was built in 1922 as a play on words alluding to a political scandal. The prior year, President Warren G. Harding had transferred control of federally protected oil reserves in Teapot Dome, Wyoming, to a Secretary of the Interior who illegally leased the reserves to oil executives and raked in a personal fortune as a result.

The Jimmy Carter Peanut statue smiles blindly at passersby in Plains, Georgia. (Glenn Nagel/Dreamstime.com

- **This little piggy got . . . eccentric:** In 1984, several musicians who were drawn to an underground arts collective in the Richmond Dairy Building formed a punk metal band called Death Piggy. They made offbeat amateur movies together, fashioned outrageous costumes, and practiced music in the basement of the iconic milk bottles. The band, who couldn't even play their instruments properly upon the group's initial formation, quickly rose to fame as the "original shock-rock" group called GWAR. Carpenter Lenny Lancaster told the *Richmond Times-Dispatch* that the band's early practice sessions were so bad "I used to turn my saws on just to drown 'em out" (Holmberg 1990 [2014]).

SUGGESTED PAIRINGS

See also: Fiere, Guy; Food and Beverage Museums, U.S.; International Horseradish Festival; Politics and Food; Unusual Food Events, U.S. (Midwest, West, and Southwest Regions); Unusual Food Events, U.S. (Southeast and Northeast Regions)

Entry best enjoyed while eating: An alien burger with a side of homemade potato salad at the Little Ale'Inn; a nibble from the World's Largest Popcorn Ball, a 5,000-pound wonder in Sac City, Iowa; and two scoops of salted Oreo ice cream from Little Man Ice Cream, housed in a 28-foot tall metal milk can in Denver, Colorado.

Further Reading

Holmberg, Mark. (1990) 2014. "Richmond's Own GWAR Will Ruin You." *Richmond Times-Dispatch*, March 24, 2014. Reprinted from the archives. https://richmond.com/entertainment/music/richmonds-own-gwar-will-ruin-you/article_3b9d0046-b366-11e3-9369-001a4bcf6878.html

Los Angeles Conservancy. n.d. "Randy's Donuts." https://www.laconservancy.org/locations/randys-donuts

Lukk, Tiffany. 2019. "Meet the Dog That Runs a Sweet Potato Stand in Japan." *Lonely Planet*, October 4, 2019. https://www.lonelyplanet.com/articles/shiba-inu-sweet-potato-stand

Meyers, Donald. 2017. "It Happened Here: Political Scandal Inspires Gas Station. *Yakima Herald*, May 14, 2017, updated June 15, 2018.

Oesterheld, Frank. n.d. "The Benewah Milk Bottle." Spokane Historical. https://spokanehistorical.org/items/show/295

Roadside America Staff. n.d. "World's Largest 20th Century Pecan." https://www.roadsideamerica.com/story/2138

Shatkin, Elina. 2018. "L.A.'s Awesome History of Weird, Food-Shaped Restaurants." LAist, August 1, 2018. https://laist.com/2018/08/01/tail_o_the_pup_will_reopen_its_not_las_only_awesomely_weird-shaped_restaurant.php

Thorson, Katy. 2015. "Locals to Remember 'The Bottle' in Dedication." *The Auburn Villager*, April 23, 2015.

Wickman, Forrest. 2015. "A Mini History of Mega Tourist Traps." Slate, August 11, 2015. https://slate.com/human-interest/2015/08/worlds-biggest-roadside-attractions-a-history-of-worlds-largest-tourist-traps.html

S

Samuelsson, Marcus (1971–)

STARTERS

Marcus Samuelsson is an American chef, restaurateur, author, philanthropist, and television personality. The chef, named Kassahun Tsegie at birth, lived in Ethiopia until the loss of his mother in 1974, at which time he was adopted and moved to Gothenburg, Sweden. As a young man, he attended the Culinary Institute of Gothenburg and pursued apprenticeships in Switzerland and France. Samuelsson moved to New York City in 1994 and became the youngest chef to receive a three-star *New York Times* review the following year for his culinary talent at Aquavit restaurant. He launched his first restaurant, Riingo, in 2003 before venturing outside of Manhattan's midtown culinary scene to launch Red Rooster (2010), Ginny's Supper Club (2012), and Streetbird Rotisserie (2015) in New York's Harlem neighborhood.

In 2012, Samuelsson revisited his Swedish roots with the launch of Norda in his hometown of Gothenburg and Kitchen and Table in Stockholm. Over the next eight years, he opened nearly two dozen restaurants across Sweden, Norway, and Finland; Red Rooster outposts in London, England, and Miami, Florida; Marc Burger restaurants in Southern California and Chicago, Illinois; and a number of other brasseries, taquerias, and neighborhood pubs spanning from Bermuda to Canada. His published works include *Aquavit: And the New Scandinavian Cuisine* (2003); his 2013 memoir *Yes, Chef*; and a number of cookbooks inspired by his restaurants, collaborations with other chefs, and celebrations of the intersection between culture and cuisine.

Samuelsson became a recognizable figure on television as a competitor on popular food reality shows like *Top Chef Masters* and *The Next Iron Chef*, as well as judge roles on shows like *Chopped*, *Chopped Junior*, *Cooks vs. Cons*, *Tournament of Champions*, and *Worst Cooks in America*. He became a mainstay on food-centric Bravo and Food Network lineups, a guest on travel-themed food shows like *Anthony Bourdain: Parts Unknown*, and a frequent addition to culinary segments on morning news and lifestyle programs. In 2018, Samuelsson became executive producer of his own show, *No Passport Required*, on PBS. The chef has been honored with numerous James Beard Foundation Awards, including Rising Star Chef of the Year (1999), Best Chef, New York City (2003), International Cooking (2007), Writing (2013), and Who's Who of Food and Beverage in America (2016).

ENTRÉE

In 1995, Marcus Samuelsson received a remarkable offer: a promotion to become the executive chef at New York City's Aquavit restaurant. Samuelsson's talent was worthy of the honor, but he was only 24 at the time, was essentially unknown in the culinary industry, and had just recently moved to the United States and started working at the Scandinavian restaurant. And yet, here he was: a young immigrant who confidently donned an apron every day at the helm of an upscale restaurant, making a name for himself within a highly competitive culinary scene. The next 25 years of the chef's career denoted the same passion and ambition, including the launch of an international restaurant group, the publication of more than a dozen books, philanthropic ventures, and his participation in (and creation of) food festivals and television shows. Throughout his career, he has continued to eschew labels and defy stigmas as he seeks to braid food and communities together through his work.

Marcus Samuelsson was born in 1971 in a small village of Meki, Ethiopia. At the time of his birth, his country was in the throes of a tuberculosis pandemic, decade-old civil war, and widespread malnutrition. By the time he turned one, Marcus, his mother, and four-year-old sister Fantaye became infected with tuberculosis, joining roughly 800,000 other afflicted people in the country. His mother walked more than 75 miles to Addis Ababa, the closest hospital, with both children. Marcus and Fantaye recovered after months of care, but their mother passed away shortly after arriving in Addis Ababa. A nurse took the two children to live with her briefly until she was able to place them with an adoption agency that found a home for them in Sweden, where they were renamed Marcus and Linda.

Samuelsson's first culinary inspiration came from his family members, who fished, foraged, and cooked homemade food every day. He studied at the Culinary Institute of Gothenburg before widening his horizons to take an apprenticeship as a *commis* (basic chef) at the renowned Victoria Jungfrau resort hotel in Interlaken, Switzerland, when he was 18. From there, the young chef traveled through Europe, learning techniques that honed the narrative of the type of chef he wanted to become. "I wanted to find ways to incorporate the efficiencies of Switzerland, the soulfulness of Austria, the reverence for ingredients I found in France, but I wanted to do it with a Swedish accent," he wrote in his memoir (2013, 186).

Samuelsson followed his success at Aquavit by expanding his culinary style and locales, beginning his publishing and television careers simultaneously. In 2009, the chef was selected to cook for President Obama's first state dinner. Samuelsson's menu honored Indian Prime Minister Manmohan Singh and the Obama family with foods like cornbread and Indian chapati, curried shrimp, pumpkin tarts with garam masala spices, and salads made from the White House's garden (Davies 2012).

In 2010, Samuelsson opened Harlem-based Red Rooster, where the decor, food, and clientele braid Harlem's rich history with its colorful present. Its menu includes American comfort food like cornbread and fried chicken and international influences such as Scandinavian cured fish, Asian sauces, and African spices. Between 2008 and 2011, the chef also competed in (and often won) intensely high-pressure cooking competition shows like *Iron Chef America*, *The Next Iron Chef*, and *Top Chef Masters*. He frequently made guest appearances on shows like *Rachael Ray*, *Unique Eats*, and *Martha Stewart* in addition to experimenting with documentary formats like his first solo-hosted show, *Inner Chef* (2005), on the Discovery network.

In 2018, PBS premiered Samuelsson's nonfiction documentary series *No Passport Required* in partnership with Eater, a food-and-dining website network brand under Vox Media. The show explores and celebrates immigrant communities' culinary influences in American food. Part sociology program, part travelogue, the show celebrates people, art, and culture on equal footing with food. Samuelsson's upbeat and calm television persona serves in stark contrast to some of the environments in which he was trained. In interviews, he has shared that over the course of his career he's experienced having food thrown at him, witnessing violent outbursts, and seeing cruel reactions to kitchen workers' serious accidents. He said that the immense pressure from these working conditions caused him to experience panic attacks that made him vomit every day at work over the duration of three years, yet he still values the experiences for helping him learn the skills he needed (Davies 2012).

Adding to his stress as an up-and-coming chef, he was often one of the only Black members of the upper echelons of the kitchen. He has joked that many hiring managers looked surprised to see a Black man come in for a job after reading a Swedish name on his resume. Samuelsson said in an interview with CBS *Sunday Morning* that in the wake of the terrorist attacks on September 11, 2001, he reexamined his purpose and identity within the culinary world. The tragic attacks, which took place just one week after he had cooked in the World Trade Center's Windows on the World restaurant, helped him clarify his desire to focus more on cultivating communities. In recent years, he estimated that he employs roughly 700 people, and he has made efforts reach out to people who are often excluded from successful kitchens, such as women, people of color, and refugees. His philanthropic work includes co-chairing the Careers through Culinary Arts Program, which provides disadvantaged youth with culinary education and employment. He also co-produces HarlemEatUp!, an annual festival that promotes Harlem's culinary and arts scenes.

ACCOMPANIED BY

In his memoir, Samuelsson said that he has no clear memories of his birth mother, Ahnu, but sees cooking as a means of connecting with her. "I have taught myself the recipes of my mother's people because those foods are for me, as a chef, the easiest connection to the mysteries of who my mother was. Her identity remains stubbornly shrouded in the past, so I feed myself and the people I love the food that she made," he wrote in his memoir. As an adult, he and his sister Linda (whose Ahmaric birth name was Fantaye) reconnected with his Ethiopian past, including his birth father, Tsigie, and siblings. Samuelsson and his sister were adopted by his Swedish parents, Ann Marie and Lennert Samuelsson. He has described his blended and diverse family, including older sister Anna and his grandmother Helga, as cultivating his passion for fresh ingredients and homemade food. In 2009, Samuelsson married international model and philanthropist Gate Maya Haile in Addis Ababa, Ethiopia. He is the father of Zoe, a daughter from a past relationship he had in Austria, and Zion, born to Maya and Marcus in 2016.

DESSERT

- **Signed, sealed, delivered:** Chef Samuelsson has frequently turned to the power of writing letters to advance his career. When he was young, his mother helped him send letters to every Michelin-starred restaurant they could find in Sweden asking them to hire him. After roughly 30 rejections, he finally received one "yes." He also mailed letters to talk-show hosts Oprah Winfrey and David Letterman, among others, asking them to open a joint-venture restaurant with him in an attempt to move to the United States. He had never met the celebrities, nor are they associated with the restaurant industry, but Samuelsson told NPR "those are the Americans (he) knew" (Ocner and Frias 2019; Davies 2012).
- **Something borrowed, something blue:** Samuelsson sports unique clothing fashion that incorporates vibrant colors, chunky scarves, playful shoes, and mix-and-matched patterns. He has said that he tries to wear something every day that represents Sweden, Ethiopia, and Harlem.
- **Some of Chef Samuelsson's words to live by:**
  - "Stay invisible unless you're going to shine" (2013, 91).
  - "Meet expectations? No, no, no, no. 'Exceed.' None of this was built on meeting anything. *Exceed*!" (CBS News 2015).
  - "Work hard and be passionate. You will have an incredible journey. It's a delicious life" (PBS Staff 2013).

SUGGESTED PAIRINGS

See also: Bourdain, Anthony; *Iron Chef*; Lagasse, Emeril; *Top Chef*.

Entry best enjoyed while eating: Samuelsson's signature fried yardbird and chicken shake (fried chicken spicy seasonings); Helga's Swedish meatballs with braised cabbage, pickled cucumbers, and lingonberry preserves; seared mackerel with sour cream and chive mashed potatoes; a cup of Ethiopian *doro wett* (chicken stew) with *injera* (spongy bread); and a slice of black-bottom peanut pie.

Further Reading

CBS News. 2015. "Marcus Samuelsson: Living the Dream." CBS *Sunday Morning*, interview with Jane Pauley. November 22, 2015.

Davies, Dave. 2012. "Marcus Samuelsson: On Becoming a Top Chef." Fresh Air, National Public Radio interview. https://www.npr.org/transcripts/155909328#:~:text=He's%20written%20several%20cookbooks.,village%20you%20were%20born%20in

Icon Mann Staff. 2018. "Marcus Samuelsson." Icon Mann, May 2018. https://www.iconmann.com/home/2018/5/18/marcus-samuelsson

Ocner, Matias J., and Carlos Frias. 2019. "La Ventanita: Marcus Samuelsson Discusses the Adoptive Family That Shaped His Life." *Miami Herald*, January 29, 2019.

PBS Staff. 2013. "Kitchen Careers: Celebrity Chef Marcus Samuelsson." https://www.pbs.org/food/features/kitchen-careers-chef-marcus-samuelsson/

Samuelsson, Marcus. 2013. *Yes, Chef: A Memoir*. New York: Random House.

Sherman, Sean (1974–)

STARTERS

Sean Sherman is an American chef, author, culinary educator, caterer, and restaurateur. He is the CEO and founder of The Sioux Chef: a company that provides catering and education services showcasing Indigenous foods. Sherman, a member of the Oglala Lakota tribe, was born in South Dakota's Pine Ridge reservation in 1974. He is based in Minneapolis, Minnesota, where he ran a food truck, launched a nonprofit and catering company, and opened a restaurant called Indigenous Food Lab with his partner. In 2017, Sherman published a cookbook entitled *The Sioux Chef's Indigenous Kitchen*, which was met with widespread critical acclaim and won the James Beard Award for Best Cookbook in 2018. He has also been honored with a First Peoples Fund Fellowship (2015), a Bush Foundation Fellowship (2018), and a James Beard Leadership Award (2019).

ENTRÉE

Within the United States, the Bureau of Indian affairs has identified 574 federally recognized tribes. Despite the fact that these tribes stretch across the country, accounting for millions in the U.S. population, there are virtually no commonly known Native American chefs or widely embraced Native culinary staples within the mainstream culture. Contemporary chef Sean Sherman seeks to change that, and he has devoted his professional life to connecting people of all cultural and ethnic backgrounds with sustainable practices that ground them to the land, as well as the people they share it with.

In 2016, *Atlantic* writer Emily Deruy wrote about various nascent Native American restaurants and their struggles to flourish and expand. Citing research that showed American Indian cuisine has significant potential to become a new trend, Deruy noted that many potential restaurant investors and commercial landlords lack confidence that enough people will be informed about—or enthusiastic to try—a widely underappreciated and misunderstood cuisine. The vast number of diverse tribes in the country also makes definitions like "Native American cuisine" problematic, as indigenous peoples in the United States enjoy a multitude of different culinary staples and diets, ranging from foods like root vegetables that grow in semiarid prairielands to eels and clams caught in the Mid-Atlantic region.

> **Small Plates**
>
> **Frybread: A Simple Food with a Complicated Past**
>
> Within mainstream American culture, the only food commonly associated with indigenous people is *frybread*, a puffy deep-fried dough that bears some similarity to funnel cakes, sopapillas, and beignets. The bread—which consists of simple ingredients like flour, salt, processed sugar, and lard—was conceived from limited and non-nutritious ingredients that the government provided to people living on reservations. Sherman seeks to push American's understanding of Native foodways beyond frybread, which is a controversial food due to its painful past.
>
> Author and screenwriter Sherman Alexie has defended frybread as "the story of our survival," joining many who see it as a nostalgic and deeply meaningful symbol of their family's bonds and perseverance. For many, frybread also symbolizes a unifying element for people of different tribes and a way for people from different regions to bond. Native American musician Keith Secola has an upbeat song dedicated to the treat, and Alexie's screenplay for the indigenous film *Smoke Signals* features a character wearing a T-shirt with the humorous phrase "Frybread Power!"
>
> For others, however, the food's close association with Native foodways erases the rich culinary history shared by millions of indigenous people. The bread's history stems from the mid-1800s, when Native Americans who were forcibly removed from their ancestral homelands and relocated to arid locations that didn't support the agriculture they lived on, forcing them to survive off inadequate provisions (Miller 2008).

As a youth, Sherman was often responsible for preparing meals for himself and his siblings while his mother worked. He has written about the stark contrast of food stocked in his family's pantry—government-issued powdered milk, boxes of oats, potted meat—and the foods they foraged on the reservation like prairie turnips, chokecherries, and juniper berries. These early experiences and his growing awareness of the disproportionate number of Native American people who suffer from diet-related illnesses fueled his passion for educating communities on the benefits of fresh, foraged, local, and culturally meaningful foods. At the age of 13, Sherman began working at a steakhouse in Spearfish, South Dakota. He went on to study the medicinal and culinary properties of different plants while working for the United States Forest Service in college, and he became fascinated with precolonial culinary traditions while visiting Mexico. During his travels, he realized "how food weaves people together, connects families through generations, is a life force of identity and social structure" (Sherman and Dooley 2017).

Sherman brought his passion for precontact culinary traditions back to his career in Minneapolis, launching a catering busines called The Sioux Chef and starting a food truck in 2015. His goal with both ventures was largely to introduce and educate communities about authentic Indigenous cuisine. The chef and his wife, Dana Thompson, launched a nonprofit in 2018 called North American Traditional Indigenous Food Systems (NATIFS) based on years of their shared culinary and historic research into foodways of the Lakota and other tribes. In 2020, the pair opened Indigenous Food Lab, a nonprofit restaurant with a "decolonized menu." The nonprofit offers education about indigenous foods and increases accessibility to Native foods and culinary training opportunities.

Interest in and acceptance of diverse culinary traditions continues to grow nationwide, whetting many Americans' appetite for dishes they're less familiar with. Sherman's efforts may help launch a significant future indigenous foodways trend within popular culture. His goal is to bring the Indigenous Food Lab project to more communities, launching tribally operated kitchens around the United States in the process. The goal is to help communities embrace the fact that "Native American food" is synonymous with "American Food." Sherman hopes that in the next decade, people will be able to learn about the rich diversity of tribes by stopping at numerous locally run indigenous restaurants across the country.

Sherman's work through NATIFS to reimagine decolonized cuisine is not far from alone; "culinary activism" is gaining momentum in a number of cities. These activists include contemporary chefs Brit Reed and Hillel Echo-Hawk. Reed is a Choctaw chef who made headlines when she published an essay entitled "Food Sovereignty is Tribal Sovereignty," outlining ways in which many Native people had become physically and spiritually disconnected from their ancestors' hunting, foraging, and agricultural ways of life. Echo-Hawk is a Pawnee and Athabaskan chef and catering company founder who also promotes the use and protection of indigenous foodways. On the airways, Navajo radio producer Andi Murphy connects many of these issues in a podcast called Toasted Sister, drawing ancient practices into a remarkably modern conversation.

DESSERT

- **Fast food, but hold the fries:** When Sean Sherman retired his Minneapolis-based food truck, Tatanka (Lakota for "big beast"), it didn't go to waste. Instead, Tatanka became the new mobile food unit for the White Earth reservation in northwestern Minnesota. The Anishaabe (Ojibwe) people who live there have identified as much as 90 percent of the reservation as a food desert, meaning an area with inadequate access to fresh, high-quality, nutritious foods. Tatanka's second life entails deliveries of fresh fruits and vegetables to individuals across the widespread reservation's community (McLaughlin 2017).
- **Exceptions for donuts:** Sherman is passionate about eating culturally authentic and nutritious foods, but that doesn't stop him from enjoying an occasional treat either. When asked which local restaurants he and his son Phoenix recommend, Sherman noted their love for a local donut shop that has "like, a thousand donuts" (Pirnia 2019).

SUGGESTED PAIRINGS

See also: Deer River Wild Rice Festival; Holidays and Food; Latin American Cuisine; Radio and Podcasts, Food-Themed (1980s–).

Entry best enjoyed while eating: Roasted squash and *timpsula* (wild turnips) with toasted sunflower seeds and agave glaze; bison pot roast with hominy, dandelion greens, fresh sage, and white cedar; indigenous tacos assembled with corn cakes, ground bison, cedar-braised heirloom beans, wild rice, and *wojape*, a sauce made from chokecherries and maple syrup.

Further Reading

Deruy, Emily. 2016. "Why It's Hard for Successful American Restaurants to Expand." *The Atlantic*, June 30, 2016.

Halter, Nick. 2016. "Sioux Chef Founders Discuss the New Native American Food Movement." *Minneapolis/St. Paul Business Journal*, August 25, 2016.

McLaughlin, Shaymus. 2017. "The Sioux Chef's Tatanka Truck Is Going Away—But for a Good Cause." *Bring Me The News*, September 25, 2017. https://bringmethenews.com/news/the-sioux-chefs-tatanka-truck-is-going-away-but-for-a-good-cause

Miller, Jen. 2008. "Frybread." *Smithsonian*, July 2008.

Pirnia, Garin. 2019. "These Are the Best Places to Eat in Minneapolis, According to Chef Sean Sherman." *USA Today*, April 20, 2019.

Sherman, Sean. 2019. "Sean Sherman's Ten Essential Native American Recipes." *The New York Times*, Food section. November 4, 2019.

Sherman, Sean, and Beth Dooley. 2017. *The Sioux Chef's Indigenous Kitchen*. Minneapolis: University of Minnesota Press.

South Beach Wine & Food Festival

ENTRÉE

The South Beach Wine & Food Festival is a large-scale culinary event that takes place annually in Miami Beach, Florida. The five-day festival is held in February and draws celebrity chefs, vintners, and food enthusiasts from all across the country. The proceeds from the event, which has run every year since 1997, benefit the Florida International University Chaplin School of Hospitality & Tourism Management. In recent years, more than 65,000 visitors have gathered annually to take part in the festival, which includes attractions like cooking demonstrations, exclusive beach parties, live music, educational seminars, and hundreds of opportunities for wine and food tastings.

The high-end culinary beach party began in 1997 as a one-day festival on the Florida International University's campus. Originally dubbed the Florida Extravaganza, the focus was on celebrating fine wines from around the world. In recent years, the festival has grown to include more than 100 events, which span from its central location in South Florida up the coast as far as West Palm Beach to accommodate all of the activities and participants. The event's name has changed over the years, most recently rebranded with the lengthy title The Food Network & Cooking Channel South Beach Wine & Food Festival presented by Capital One (SOBEWFF).

Food Network and Capital One join a lengthy list of current and prior sponsors who have seized on the opportunity to market to high-end consumers, the likes of whom are willing to spend a significant amount of money at the festival. Each event is priced separately, with tickets ranging from roughly $35 for a pizza-making event to $500 to dine with chefs like Mauro Colagreco (whose Mirazur restaurant was named "best in the world" in the 2019 "World's 50 Best" list) and

American restaurateur and television personality Marcus Samuelsson. In recent years, festival organizers have created a special category of "under $100" family- and pet-friendly events and even developed a layaway plan for attendees who wished to buy tickets using multiple payments. In addition to numerous beach parties held at brunch or after dark, attendees also flock to the Grand Tasting Village, and long lines lead to countless samples of various wines, cocktails, and foods from over 100 restaurants and vineyards.

ACCOMPANIED BY

Five years after the festival's inception, Lee Brian Schrager rebranded the event, moving it to South Beach and modifying it to become a larger, more upscale festival. The event draws celebrities from the culinary sphere and Hollywood alike, many of whom host the event's parties, cooking competitions, and demonstrations. South Beach's celebrity chefs (and cooks) have included Guy Fieri, Rachael Ray, Giada De Laurentiis, Bobby Flay, Andrew Zimmern, Cat Cora, Martha Stewart, and Tricia Yearwood; music performances by Busta Rhymes and Rev Run; and competition judging and hosting by actor Neil Patrick Harris, fashion designer Zac Posen, and Bravo network host Andy Cohen, to name a few.

DESSERT

In 2017, the beach party "Burger Bash" featured more than 20 different burgers for attendees to choose from. The event required more than two tons (and nearly a dozen different types) of ground meat, more than 100 gallons of ketchup and mustard, and an estimated 300 pounds of bacon to feed the late-night revelers (Krader 2017).

SUGGESTED PAIRINGS

See also: Aspen Food and Wine Classic; Austin Food + Wine Festival; Florida Strawberry Festival; South Beach Wine & Food Festival.

Entry best enjoyed while eating: A smorgasbord of sponsored treats, including a "Miracle Berry" (available only to Capital One cardholders), which makes sour and bitter foods taste sweet; make-it-yourself pastelitos (Cuban pastries) and Havana Club daiquiris; and Green Giant veggie tots to get a little serving of vegetables in before noshing on Bloody Marys and soul food served by chef Pharoah Williams and his son, singer Pharell Williams.

Further Reading

Florida International University. "About the Festival." 2020. https://corporate.sobewff.org/about-the-festival/

Krader, Kate. 2017. "Top 5 Reasons I Want to Go to the South Beach Wine & Food Festival." https://www.foodandwine.com/travel/top-5-reasons-i-want-go-south-beach-wine-food-festival

Mayo, Michael. 2020. "South Beach Wine & Food Festival 2020: 3 Counties, 5 Days, 111 Events ... and a Gazillion Calories." *Sun Sentinel*, February 13, 2020.

Spam Jam Festival

STARTERS

Spam Jam is an annual street festival that celebrates a canned ham product made by Hormel Foods. The event originated in Austin, Minnesota, where Hormel Foods' factory and a Spam Museum are also located. In 2002, the festival was adopted by the residents of Waikiki, Oahu, in Hawaii, becoming an annual tradition that is celebrated during the last week in April. Waikiki's Spam Jam attracts close to 40,000 people each year for a single day of live music, food vendors, arts and crafts. The event is free, and the city's Kalakaua Avenue is closed down to host Spam-fried treats from local restaurants. The festival's mascots, "Sir Can-a-Lot" and "Spammy" mingle with the crowd, and attendees visit rows of tents selling Spam-themed clothes, toys, and accessories. One contest attracts skilled social media users to photograph Spam dishes with prizes ranging from T-shirts to free plane tickets. Attendees are encouraged to donate cans of Spam that volunteers deliver to the Hawaii Food Bank.

A vendor at the 2013 Spam Jam festival in Waikiki sports a shirt with a picture of a popular Hawaiian Japanese hybrid snack called musubi: a block of rice topped with nori and a slice of Spam. (Rico Leffanta/Dreamstime.com)

ENTRÉE

According to the lyrics of a vintage Hormel commercial, "you don't say ham, you say Spam! Spam is *real spiced ham*!" The product's marketing team also resorted to numerous puns to convince consumers to try the canned meat, with lines like "Spam in tacos? *Pork favor*" and "Spam: don't knock it 'till you've *fried* it." It is intriguing to some that this product– a salted square of canned pork shoulder that, until recent years, created a thin layer of gelatin that settled just under the can's lid– could elicit the enthusiasm of tens of thousands of event-goers. What some find even more interesting is Spam's unlikely longevity. The product was invented in 1937, but its meager beginnings would lead to the sale of more than 8 billion cans spread out over 44 countries globally. In the United States, Spam's popularity is highest in Hawaii, a state boasting just over 1.4 million people but where 7 million cans of the pork product are sold each year (DeJesus 2014; Spam Jam Staff 2021).

During WWII, many American and Allied troops would see Spam at meals up to three times a day. Due to the fact that it was both shelf stable and not on the list of rationed sources of protein, canned meat was in high demand. Hormel Foods would go on to send 100 million pounds of the product overseas over the course of the war (Mattison 2018). Growing tired of its appearance so often, some soldiers joked that the meat was ham that hadn't passed the Army's physical, or meatloaf that had failed to graduate from basic training. Those with darker senses of humor joked that *Spam* is what made the great war so terrible.

When the war ended, many families on the mainland grew weary of the tinned meat and relegated it to side dishes (served mixed with eggs, or by itself, studded with cloves). In an interesting twist, Spam's popularity boomed during the same years in the Hawaiian islands. The canned meat became prevalent in the Pacific islands. After being imported from GIs, the tropical-friendly, shelf-friendly meat was easy to find and purchase for Hawaiian residents. It was particularly important to those facing food insecurity after sanctions were placed on Hawaiians restricting them from fishing for their meals, in lieu of placing the state's large Japanese population in internment camps during the war (Lauden 1996). Today, Spam is still a major ingredient in many dishes dotting Hawaiian restaurants' menus. In the mainland United States, some regions never lost their appreciation for Spam, and in many other regions Spam has crept back into vogue on higher-end restaurant menus thanks to the trend of featuring "working class ingredients" in higher-end fare.

ACCOMPANIED BY

One modern chef known for helping to fuel the "highbrow/lowbrow" food movement is Roy Choi, a contemporary Korean-American chef whose hip menus have occasionally featured Spam in dishes like *budae jjigae*, referred to as "Army Stew" during the Korean War. Choi and his peers can thank Julius Zillgitt for the trend, the Hormel employee who's credited with inventing technology to vacuum-seal the meat, preventing it from sweating in its can. Hormel's second acting president, Jay Hormel, had tasked his employees with designing a consumer-friendly packaged product to compete with similar pork products he saw housewives ordering at deli counters (DeJesus 2014).

Waikiki's Spam Jam festival was founded by a local resident named Bitsy Kelley, whose original vision was to modify the Minnesotan event into a local affair that would treat her hotel and resort chain's housekeeping staff to breakfast. Today, Kelley's vision draws not only locals, but international guests. Two enthusiastic globe-trotting attendees include British couple Mark Benson and his wife Anne Mousley. Mark's passion for Spam runs so deep that in 2016 he legally changed his middle name to "I Love Spam," and the following year Mousley surprised Benson with a wedding she planned at the Spam Museum in Austin, Minnesota.

DESSERT

What's in a Name? There are many theories and urban legends citing the reason Spam is named as such, including Jay Hormel's claim that it was a combination of the words "spice" plus "ham," in spite of the odd fact that neither spices nor ham exist in the product. Other theories include its origins as an acronym of "Shoulder of Pork and Ham," or—from snarkier sources—Scientifically Processed Animal Matter.

SUGGESTED PAIRINGS

See also: Eating Competitions; Trends, Food; What the Fluff?

Entry best enjoyed while eating: Spam cheesecake cup with Oreo topping; Hawaiian loco moco (a hamburger with a beef patty, Spam, gravy, and fried egg); Spam *musubi* (a Japanese sushi / Hawaiian mashup of spam slices atop a bed of cooked rice on nori)

Further Reading

Compton, Natalie B. 2017. "I Went to the World's Largest Spam Festival." Vice, May 5, 2017. https://www.vice.com/en_us/article/jpymeb/i-went-to-the-worlds-biggest-spam-festival

DeJesus, Erin. 2014. "A Brief History of Spam, an American Meat Icon." Eater, July 9, 2014. https://www.eater.com/2014/7/9/6191681/a-brief-history-of-spam-an-american-meat-icon

Laudan, Rachel. 1996. *The Food of Paradise: Exploring Hawaii's Culinary Heritage*. Honolulu: University of Hawai'i Press.

Library of Congress. n.d. "Minnesota: Spam Festival." American Folklife Center. http://memory.loc.gov/diglib/legacies/loc.afc.afc-legacies.200003186/

Mattison, Lindsay. 2018. "Spam: The Wonder Food." Taste of Home, April 3, 2018. https://www.tasteofhome.com/article/spam/

Rudnansky, Ryan. 2014. "Hawaii Celebrates 12th Annual Spam Jam in Style." https://www.travelpulse.com/news/destinations/hawaii-celebrates-12th-annual-spam-jam-in-style.html

Spam Jam Staff. 2021. "About The Event." Spam Jam Hawaii. https://spamjamhawaii.com/about

Stremple, Claire. 2019. "Spam Jam Festival: Celebrating Musubi & More." Hormel Foods, April 19, 2019. https://www.hormelfoods.com/inspired/story/spam-jam-festival-celebrating-musubi-more/

Wyman, Carolyn. 1999. *Spam: A Biography*. San Diego: Harcourt Brace.

Stewart, Martha (1941–)

STARTERS

Martha Stewart is an American television personality, cook, author, entrepreneur, and brand spokesperson. She is the founder of Martha Stewart Living Omnimedia (MSLO), a media and merchandising company that encompasses a large number of publishing, merchandising, internet, and broadcast media product lines. Stewart was a significant leader in numerous "DIY" (do-it-yourself) entertainment and cooking trends in the 1990s and 2000s, and her shows, magazines, books, and merchandise sales catapulted her to fame. Her first book, *Entertaining*, was published in 1982 in response to the success of a small catering company she was running at the time.

Stewart is a best-selling author of more than 90 books, ranging from niche topics like wedding cakes, appetizers, and crockpot recipes to entertainment and craft tutorials. The entertainment mogul founded lifestyle and cooking magazine *Martha Stewart Living* in 1990, followed by an eponymous syndicated television series on CBS that ran from 1993 to 2004. In the late 1980s, she became a spokesperson for Kmart and launched her first merchandising line with the company in 1998, becoming one of the earliest celebrities to merge her merchandising line with her media endeavors. Stewart became a mainstay on American television as the host of *Martha Stewart Living* and her second syndicated show, *Martha* (2005–2010), in addition to hundreds of appearances as a host, judge, and interviewee on talk shows, cooking shows, and reality cooking competition programs. MSLO's television shows have received 18 Emmy awards, and Stewart has been honored with 7 James Beard Foundation Awards, including the organization's Who's Who in Food and Beverage (1995) and best in-studio television show for *Martha Stewart's Cooking School* (2013–2015). In 2007, Stewart opened the Martha Stewart Center for Living, a holistic care center for elderly adults, in conjunction with Mount Sinai Health System in New York City.

ENTRÉE

In front of the cameras, Martha Stewart has spent her career embodying a homemaker and dinner party hostess reminiscent of a more vintage era, yet behind the scenes she has been at the helm of a significant multimedia and merchandise empire for close to four decades. Since the early 1990s, Stewart has been a constant staple in popular culture and has remained closely associated with a thriving DIY cultural trend that has inspired fans to return to traditional hobbies such as cooking, baking, gardening, crafting, and making art. Stewart became the country's first female self-made billionaire as she fed Americans' inexhaustible appetite for making their homes, meals, and parties look picture perfect.

Martha Stewart (née Kostyra) was born in Jersey City in 1941 and grew up in Nutville, New Jersey. As a teenager, she began modeling in fashion editorials and fashion shows, as well as acting in television commercials. Some of the brands she modeled for in the 1960s included Clairol, Lifebuoy soap, Tareyton cigarettes, and Chanel. She continued her relatively lucrative modeling career throughout college as a way to supplement the partial scholarship she received from Barnard College in New York City. Stewart majored in history and architectural history in addition to studying literature, economics, and art.

In 1961, while still a student, she married Yale law student Andrew Stewart. After graduating, she worked as a Wall Street stockbroker at boutique firm Monness, Williams, and Sidel and gave birth to her daughter, Alexis. The Stewart family eventually left their Manhattan apartment for an old farmhouse in Westport, Connecticut, that they spent many years renovating and decorating. Their home, dubbed Turkey Hill, gave the couple ample space and opportunity to host frequent dinner parties, grow vegetable and flower gardens, and cook. Martha launched a highly successful catering business in 1973 from her home kitchen, which led to the publication of her first book at the age of 40. She has written that she began pursuing her dreams in earnest years later when her first magazine issue came out in 1990, noting that at the time she was 49, had a grown daughter, and was a divorcee. "I've been dubbed a 'late bloomer,' and I love the moniker," Stewart wrote about her career arc (2017).

In 1993, *Martha Stewart Living* was translated to a half-hour television show. Stewart's brand and popularity exploded during this decade, leading to recurring guest appearances on a long list of television shows, the launch of *Martha Stewart Weddings* magazine in 1995, and daily episodes of *Martha Stewart Living* in extended hour-long formats. She launched a major home product line at Kmart retailers in 1998 and celebrated MSLO going public on the New York Stock Exchange in 1999. During these years, Stewart became highly visible in popular culture. Fans ranging from novice to professional cooks and bakers found her shows and magazines inspirational, and her recipes could be found on dinner tables across the world.

Celebrity cook and television personality Martha Stewart became the first female self-made billionaire in the country from her culinary media career. (Shutterstock)

Her popularity led to a significant number of parodies as well. Stewart's notoriously serious demeanor, wholesome content, and seemingly *always* perfect dishes and projects became fodder for comedians and screenwriters across the country. Her most well-known catchphrase, "it's a good thing," has been widely used by journalists and comedians alike. On sketch comedy show *Saturday Night Live*, comedians such as Ana Gasteyer, Kristin Wiig, Kate McKinnon, and David Spade have donned prim blond wigs and turtleneck sweaters for decades to impersonate the homemaker. *Saturday Night Live*'s outrageous fictional scenes from *Martha Stewart Living* join countless other nods to (and often jabs at) the "doyenne of homemaking," including unflattering and crass spoofs in shows like the animated comedy *South Park* and even a parody in which she played herself in the animated sitcom *The Simpsons*.

Stewart has frequently been the target of harshly critical attention in popular culture, such as her relentlessly unflattering portrayal in *Martha, Inc.*, a 2003 made-for-television movie based on a book of the same name. Many fictional characters have also been based on the star, such as a conniving criminal named

Judy who receives preferential treatment in a women's correctional facility in *Orange Is the New Black*. In the early 2000s, Stewart shocked members of her fanbase and made headlines internationally when she was accused of illegal insider trading after receiving nonpublic information from her broker regarding the future value of her shares in ImClone, a biotechnology company. After allegedly receiving a tip that one of ImClone's featured cancer treatment products was on the brink of being rejected by the FDA, Stewart sold her shares. In 2004, after a six-week-long trial, a jury found her guilty on four counts of obstructing justice and lying to investigators about her actions, resulting in a five-month sentence in federal prison.

Stewart's company, personal image, and brand took a significant hit as a result of the controversial conviction. At its peak, MSLO was valued at over $1 billion, but rapidly depreciated after the criminal conviction. The company eventually sold for $353 million to Sequential Brands Group in 2015. However, Stewart's tarnished image and unrelenting negative press didn't end her career by any means. After serving her sentence, Stewart resumed growing and revitalizing her brand, launching new television shows, and publishing books and magazines. Her talk show *Martha* launched in 2005, as well as a reality game show called *The Apprentice: Martha Stewart* (a spin-off of Donald Trump's 2004 business-themed reality show).

In 2011, Stewart launched *Martha Bakes* on PBS before branching out with an unlikely partnership with rapper Snoop Dogg in VH1's *Martha & Snoop's Potluck Dinner Party* (2016–), cohosting cooking demonstrations and celebrity guests. As of 2020, her company reportedly had a reach of 100 million consumers across media platforms and types, with a stronghold of product sales at retailers like Macys, Amazon, Wayfair, Staples, and Michaels. In her late seventies, Stewart showed no sign of resting on her success. On any given day, fans can find her in avenues like late-night talk shows—where she has made increasingly informal and even highly risqué comedic appearances—and Instagram, where followers watch her pose with giant flowers in her garden, play with her grandchildren, bathe her trio of donkeys, and even incoherently scold someone's care and feeding of chickens after imbibing on too much wine. As Martha would say, "It's a good thing."

ACCOMPANIED BY

Martha has described her parents, Edward Kostyra (1912–1979) and Martha (Ruszkowski) Kostyra (1914–2007), as "avid do-it-yourselfers" who taught their children the art of cooking, decorating, home repair, and gardening. Her parents were both teachers, and Edward also made a living as a pharmaceutical salesman. Martha was the second born in a family of six children: Frank, Kathryn, Laura, Erik, and George. In 2014, Laura passed away from a brain aneurysm, and in 2017, George died of a suspected heart attack. The Stewart family came from Polish immigrants on both sides of the family, which Stewart explored in an episode of the genealogical PBS show *Finding Your Roots* in 2012.

At the age of 19, Martha—who had recently been dubbed as one of the "Best Dressed College Girls of 1961" by *Glamour* magazine—married Yale student Andrew "Andy" Stewart (1938–). Martha wore a dress that she and her mother had made together and carried a bouquet of daisies. In 1965, the Stewarts welcomed a daughter, Alexis, and Andy pursued work as a publishing executive in New York City. The couple ended the marriage in 1990, and since the divorce, Alexis has been vocal in the press about her criticism of (and emotional distance from) her father. She has also publicly cited a disharmonious relationship with her mother, though the two have worked closely together for many years.

In 2008, Alexis and her colleague Jennifer Koppelman Hutt cohosted a television show called *Whatever, Martha!* The comedy show, which aired on Fine Living Network, featured the two women mocking decades-old episodes of *Martha Stewart Living*. The pair also hosted a weekly two-hour radio show called "Whatever with Alexis and Jennifer" that aired on Martha's Sirius channel. Their radio show frequently entailed topics and language that were considered highly controversial for the brand's image. Alexis and her two children are frequently highlighted in Martha's personal and professional life updates.

DESSERT

- **What became of your lamb chop, Clarice?** Martha Stewart was once romantically involved with actor Anthony Hopkins, but reportedly broke off the relationship due to her inability to shake the actor's association with Hannibal Lecter, a sociopathic villain he played in psychological thriller *Silence of the Lambs*. Could this affair (and film) have inspired her numerous fava bean recipes over the past two decades? The world may never know.

- **Pet imitation is the sincerest flattery:** Stewart is frequently referenced in television and film dialogue to highlight characters' successes or failures in their pursuits of domestic bliss. One example is the comedy-drama *Gilmore Girls*, which made numerous joking nods to Stewart's culinary influence over its seven-season run. While some were blatant, others were subtle, including two precocious Chow dogs named Chin Chin and Paw Paw, who served as comic foils (while the show did not explicitly state this, Stewart owned two Chows by the same name).

- **A woman of many trades:** As a teenager, Stewart modeled for a Tareyton cigarette print ad. In the ad, she sports a sizable black eye and coquettishly holds up a cigarette under the text "Us Tareyton smokers would rather fight than quit!"

- **And a partridge in a Macramé pear tree:** Stewart loves animals and writes that she's owned "at least 20 cats, 25 dogs, 10 chinchillas, and scores of canaries and parakeets . . . two ponies, three donkeys, 10 horses, many sheep and goats, and hundreds of chickens, geese, turkeys, guinea fowl, quail, peacocks, and homing pigeons" (n.d.)

SUGGESTED PAIRINGS

See also: Magazines, Food; Ray, Rachael; Television, Food Channels on; Trends, Food.

Entry best enjoyed while eating: Fingerling potatoes served with goat cheese fondue; kale and shredded Brussels sprouts salad with kumquats; salt-baked Arctic char wrapped in leeks; ricotta gelato with fresh berries; and pink gin martinis poured from a bottle of gin frozen into a block of ice decorated with foraged wildflowers.

Further Reading

Hays, Constance L., and Leslie Eaton. 2004. "The Martha Stewart Verdict: The Overview; Stewart Found Guilty of Lying in Sale of Stock." *The New York Times*, March 6, 2004.

PBS. n.d. Martha Stewart. https://www.pbs.org/food/chefs/martha-stewart/

Shoulberg, Warren. 2019. "Martha Stewart Brand Finds a Buyer, but Even at Cheaper Price, There's No Guarantee Deal Pays Off." Forbes, April 16, 2019.

Stewart, Martha. n.d. "Martha's Ark: A Look Back at the Animals She's Raised." https://www.marthastewart.com/1533019/martha-stewart-on-her-pets-ghenghis-khan

Stewart, Martha. 2017. "The Martha Stewart Story: How I Became a Household Name." *Martha Stewart.* https://www.marthastewart.com/1510431/the-martha-stewart-story-how-became-household-name

Super Bowl Sunday

STARTERS

Super Bowl Sunday is an annual sporting event in the United States that marks the final championship game of the National Football League's (NFL) season. Held each year in January or February late in the day on a Sunday, two teams square off in front of as many as 114 million viewers in a game broadcast to more than 70 countries. The Super Bowl has proven to be one of the most significant sporting events in the country, as well as one of the most significant *eating* events for many Americans. Each year, a staggering amount of food is purchased, cooked, delivered, and consumed for the championship game, resulting in significant food and beverage sales.

In 2020, the National Retail Federation published survey data that American viewers spent an average of more than $88 each on food and beverages, resulting in an estimated $14 billion overall in sales (plus an additional $3.2 billion in apparel, televisions, decorations, and furniture for the event). Fans who watch the game in person can expect to shell out between $4,000 and $5,000 per ticket, not including the cost of concession prices in the stadium, which can run upward of $20 for an alcoholic beverage or $15 for a bucket of popcorn. Those traveling to the game might also spend money on "food tourism," seeking out popular foods, restaurants, breweries, or wineries the area is known for. Additionally, networks charge as much as $5 million or more per 30-second advertising spots, many of which seek to boost sales for the same types of alcoholic beverages, snack foods, and sodas viewers are consuming as they watch.

ENTRÉE

The Super Bowl dates back to 1967, when the Green Bay Packers played—and beat—the Kansas City Chiefs. Perhaps it was an omen when two cities closely related with food (cheese curds and barbecue, anyone?) were the first to face off against each other? Whether or not foreshadowing was at play, both the event and feasting *during* the event have become deeply embedded in American culture. Super Bowl Sunday is largely associated with unhealthy foods: pizza, Buffalo chicken wings, beer, cheese in nearly all forms, chips, soda, and sweets tend to top the list. Other popular choices include guacamole, chili, pigs in a blanket (miniature hot dogs wrapped in crescent rolls), and dips of nearly every type (primarily any type ensconced in cheese).

Every year, the buildup to the Super Bowl is accompanied by a virtual tsunami of publications about the snacks Americans can, should, or shouldn't eat during the game. News stories make claims that the event is the second-largest "eating event" in the United States after Thanksgiving and estimate that the average

---

Small Plates

Domestic Snacks with Global Impacts

Avocados weren't on most party menus in the early years of the Super Bowl, but that all changed in recent decades thanks to an astronomical increase in the fruit's popularity. In 1994, Mexico, Canada, and the United States enacted the North American Free Trade Agreement (NAFTA). The resulting increase in Mexico's agricultural exports helped fuel Americans' increased interest in (and love for) avocados. Californian growers provide a vast majority of avocados sold in the United States, but demand is so high that Mexico still provides upward of 1.7 billion pounds of Haas avocados to supplement the nation's supply. In recent years, an estimated 130–200 million avocados have been consumed on Super Bowl Sunday. Popular uses include guacamole (a savory dip), avocado-studded salsa, or toppings for fare like burritos and chili.

Game-day avocado sales have significantly contributed to skyrocketing sales in Mexico, which has attracted unwanted attention and extortion from drug cartels. In the Michoacan town of Tancitaro, avocado farm workers have risked bodily harm or even death if they failed to comply with gangs' demands for regular payments. In 2014, the town organized a large police force consisting of both professional law enforcement and civilians to stave off the violent threat, but funding for the farmworkers' protection depends in large part on the continuation of strong avocado sales (Kahn 2018).

Another Super Bowl trend that has caused an international ripple effect is the extreme popularity of chicken wings. Fifty years ago, Americans typically roasted or grilled whole chickens, but in the 1980s and 1990s, growing preferences for boneless or skinless meat inspired restaurants to sell smaller, more select chicken portions. Restaurants soon found smash success with Buffalo chicken wings coated in hot sauce: a dish created in Buffalo, New York in the mid-1960s. Restaurateurs found that the spicy sauce made patrons clamor for more beer, leading to improved beer sales as well. In 2015, the National Chicken Council estimated that Americans bought 1.25 billion chicken wings for the Super Bowl. Aside from these wing portions (and the breast and thigh meat that Americans tend to prefer), a considerable amount of waste is left over from the chickens. This chicken waste is exported to countries such as Russia, Indonesia, and China, which prize things like feet, leg quarters, and even feathers as ingredients for human and livestock food, respectively.

viewer will consume anywhere between 1,000 and 3,000 calories. The two teams on the field aren't the competitors facing off on Super Bowl Sunday, as the event sparks extreme competition between similar brands. In 2020, corporate pizza giants Dominos estimated selling roughly 2 million pizzas for the event, just ahead of rival Pizza Hut with 1.5 million.

Similarly, soda competitors squared off in exorbitantly expensive commercials, with Pepsi corporation going as far as to make an obvious (negative) reference to Coca-Cola. Ads also reflect Americans' changing tastes and current trends, such as a 2019 Anheuser-Busch beer commercial depicting an enormous barrel of corn syrup being delivered to Coors Lite and Miller Lite in medieval times, an inflammatory suggestion at a time when corn syrup was in the spotlight for its suggested health detriments. Four months after the spot ran, the beer giant landed in court regarding its use of the ingredient in its attack ads. Historically, food and beverage commercials often land among the most watched and re-watched Super Bowl commercials, including brands like Budweiser, Coca-Cola, McDonalds, and Doritos.

DESSERT

In popular culture, fun (and strange) facts about Super Bowl foods and games have dominated the news for years. In keeping with that tradition, here are some surprising nuggets to chew on:

- In 2019, Pizza Hut claimed that they served 10 million ounces of cheese and enough pizzas to cover more than 41,000 football fields (Genovese 2020).
- In 1967, NBC featured an interview with comedian Bob Hope during the game's halftime and failed to capture the halftime kickoff. As a result, the game came to a screeching halt, and the teams were forced to redo the kickoff. (Hope was the face of food in popular culture as well; he served as a spokesperson for Star Kist Tuna brand, which advertised Hope's love of their "macaroni tuna loaf.")
- Recent estimates show that Americans eat 14,500 tons of potato chips during the big game, as well as 2 million cases of various types of beer.
- Filed under "not a coincidence:" Considering the amount of food and alcohol is consumed during the Super Bowl, it may come as no surprise that analysts estimate that 17 million Americans call in sick the day after the Super Bowl. Convenience store chain 7-11 has reported that sales of antacid products also rise by as much as 20 percent every year on that Monday.

SUGGESTED PAIRINGS

See also: Barbecue; Eating Competitions; Holidays and Food; *Super Size Me*.

Entry best enjoyed while eating (inspired by popular Super Bowl snacks through the decades): 1970s | Pepsi and a scoop of Watergate salad, pistachio pudding, pecans, Cool Whip, pineapple juice, mini marshmallows; 1980s | A slice of delivery pepperoni pizza dipped in Ranch dressing (a dip created by Nebraska cowboy Kenneth Henson in the early 1950s and sold in major retailers in the early 1980s); 1990s | Ham and Cheese Hot Pockets, 3D Doritos, mozzarella cheese sticks; 2000–2020 | Guacamole and tortilla chips, hard seltzer, Italian sub sandwiches, Keto-diet-friendly cauliflower "popcorn."

Further Reading

Genovese, Daniella. 2020. "Pizza Hut, Domino's Expect Super Bowl Fans to Order Millions of Pies." *Fox Business*, January 23, 2020.

Gomez, Alan. 2020. "Super Bowl Concession Prices: Prices Are Steep for Beer, Food for 49ers vs. Chiefs." *USA Today*, February 2, 2020. https://www.usatoday.com/story/sports/nfl/super-bowl/2020/02/02/super-bowl-concession-prices-beer-food-chiefs-49-ers/4624889002/

Kahn, Carrie. 2018. "Blood Avocados No More: Mexican Farm Town Says It's Kicked Out Cartels." National Public Radio: Morning Edition, February 2, 2018.

McKenna, Maryn. 2015. "Wings for the Super Bowl, and What Happens to the Rest of the Bird." *National Geographic*, The Plate, January 30, 2015. https://www.nationalgeographic.com/culture/food/the-plate/2015/01/30/wings-for-the-super-bowl-and-what-happens-to-the-rest-of-the-bird/#close

National Chicken Council. 2017. "Chicken Wing History." https://www.nationalchickencouncil.org/chicken-wing-history

Super Size Me (2004)

STARTERS

Super Size Me is a documentary by filmmaker Morgan Spurlock that criticizes the McDonald's corporation and the fast-food industry at large, alleging that the chain's food contributes to health issues like the obesity epidemic in the United States. Created on a budget of $65,000, the film went on to gross $11.5 million, ranking it as the 28th highest-grossing documentary since 1982 (Box Office Mojo 2018a, 2018b). Spurlock's first feature film tracks the results of eating nothing but McDonald's food every day for a month to test his ideas about the harmful effects that fast food has on people's physical and mental health. *Super Size Me* was received enthusiastically at its 2004 premiere at the Sundance Film Festival, where it won the award for best directing. Acquired shortly thereafter by Roadside Attractions and Samuel Goldwyn Films, the film did well at the box office and received an Academy Award nomination in 2005.

ENTRÉE

Super Size Me was one of the earliest food-centric documentary films to gain widespread appeal. The film debuted two years after filmmaker Michael Moore's *Bowling for Columbine* (2002), a documentary that analyzed gun laws in the United States. Moore's early films used blunt personal narratives, sarcastic humor, and entertaining cinematic elements that weren't traditionally used in documentary films before. *Super Size Me* followed in the same tone, offering an irreverent take on the film's subject and a candid format that was similar to the style of popular reality television shows at the time. In the documentary, Spurlock used himself as a guinea pig to test the deleterious effects of a fast-food diet on an otherwise healthy body. He set rules for the experiment that included solely eating McDonald's food over the course of a month; eating breakfast, lunch, and dinner at the chain daily; and accepting any time a McDonald's employee asked if he'd like to "Super Size" his meal. (At the time of filming, the chain's "Super Size" option increased customers' orders to extra-large beverage and french fry portions.) Spurlock also required himself to try everything on the McDonald's menu at least once and limited his exercise regime to fewer than 5,000 steps a day.

Spurlock documented the entire experience, which included appointments with various physicians and interviews with people like his vegan and natural-food chef girlfriend about changes in his health. Over the course of the experiment, he gained nearly 25 pounds; developed severe liver problems; experienced extreme increased cholesterol levels; and reported lethargy, loss of libido, depression, and feeling addicted to fast food. Many were drawn to the film's entertainment value and enjoyed seeing an individual taking a bold stance against a powerful corporation. Some also took the film's message to heart, reevaluating their fast-food intake and overall nutrition and exercise goals.

Critics of the film took issue with the nature of the experiment, arguing that Spurlock was consuming an unnecessarily large number of calories each day (upward of 5,000, compared to the USDA's recommended intake of 2,400 calories for an adult male with a sedentary lifestyle). Other questions about the experiment's scientific soundness were raised, such as how much his health results were affected by the swift and extreme nature of his diet and exercise change. In February of 2006, the experiment was replicated at the University of Linkoping in Sweden. Inspired by the film, a physician and associate professor at the university put seven healthy medical students through a month of following the same type of diet and exercise. The students gained between 5 and 15 percent body fat and reported feeling lethargic and uncomfortable, but did not see the same severity of mood swings, cholesterol changes, or liver problems that Spurlock had (Blomkvist 2006).

The filmmaker says that he didn't intend to solely single out the multibillion-dollar corporation. "I wanted to ask the question, 'where does corporate responsibility end and personal responsibility start?' The film isn't an attack on McDonald's, it's an attack on the fast food culture that's taken over our lives, including our schools," Spurlock told the *New York Times* (Dominus 2004). The film was particularly criticized by attorney Samuel Hirsch, who filed a lawsuit against the filmmaker and distributor, citing defamation of character for being portrayed as pursuing a liability case against McDonald's solely for monetary gain.

ACCOMPANIED BY

Morgan Spurlock was born in 1970 in Parkersburg, West Virginia. After graduating with a BFA in film from New York University's Tisch School of the Arts in 1993, Spurlock started his career as a playwright before striking success with *Super Size Me*. Spurlock wed Alexandra Jamieson (1975–) in 2004, who appeared in the film as his then-vegan girlfriend who was concerned about the toll the fast food was taking on Spurlock's body. The couple had a son, Laken, in 2006.

Spurlock has worked on many documentary film, television, and web programs after *Super Size Me,* including a 2008 film called *Where in the World is Osama Bin Laden,* in which he traveled throughout the Middle East in search of the leader of Al-Qaeda. The film was met with criticism from many reviewers for lacking depth and presenting insubstantial information. He founded a production company called Warrior Poets and worked on titles such as *The Greatest Movie Ever Sold* (2011), *New Britannia* (2012), and *Morgan Spurlock Inside Man* (2013–2016). In 2011, Jamieson and Spurlock divorced, which Jamieson attributed to infidelity on his part. In 2013, Jamieson announced through her holistic nutrition website that she was adopting an omnivorous diet and faced backlash from many in the vegan community for doing so. Spurlock remarried in 2016 to film producer and executive Sara Bernstein, and the couple had a son, Kallen, later that year.

In 2017, the filmmaker debuted a sequel entitled *Super Size Me 2: Holy Chicken!* The film, which premiered at the Toronto International Film Festival, presents Spurlock's views on the fast-food industry's claims of providing "healthier" fare than they used to. Spurlock opens his own chicken sandwich franchise to demonstrate how easy it can be for a chain to pass its products off as healthier than they actually are. The film was slated for a theatrical release and streaming deal via YouTube Red. However, the project has been in limbo since December of 2017, when Spurlock published a tweet accepting responsibility for sexual misconduct and infidelity in light of the #MeToo movement. The film's stagnancy has come as a significant disappointment to nearly two dozen farmers who have filed lawsuits against the poultry industry, citing cruel practices by corporations such as Tyson that they claim force chicken farmers into debt and mistreat poultry. The farmers hoped that *Super Size Me 2* would draw enough public attention to help dismantle what they see as significant corruption within the industry.

DESSERT

Six weeks after the premiere of *Super Size Me,* the McDonald's corporation stopped offering their "Super Size" option in restaurants. Shortly thereafter, the restaurant chain also released a new campaign touting healthier options, such as premium salads, and even a short-lived Happy Meal for adults called "Get Active!" Happy Meals. For $5.99, grown-ups could purchase a colorful box containing a salad, a toy that helps calculate daily step counts, and a pamphlet containing exercise tips. A spokesperson for the corporation vehemently denied that the campaign, cancelation of the Super Size promotion, or other new healthier options had anything to do with the film.

SUGGESTED PAIRINGS

See also: *Cooked*; Documentary Films, Food and Beverages in; Websites, Food.

Entry best enjoyed while eating: Baked chicken nuggets made from free-range, organic chicken meat rolled in panko crumbs and served with homemade ketchup; baked heirloom carrot "fries" with olive oil, salt, and pepper; and a chocolate McDonald's milkshake. Conclude the meal with a brisk two-mile walk for good measure.

Further Reading

Blomkvist, Marten. 2006. "Only Another 5,500 Calories to Go…" *The Guardian*, September 7, 2006.

Box Office Mojo. 2018a. "Documentary." https://www.boxofficemojo.com/genres/chart/?id=documentary.htm

Box Office Mojo. 2018b. "Super Size Me." https://www.boxofficemojo.com/movies/?id=supersizeme.htm

Brooks, Jake. 2005. "Spurlock's Super Size Lawsuit; Which Critics Beat the Odds?" *Observer*, March 7, 2005.

CNN. 2004. "McDonald's Adult Happy Meal Arrives." *CNN Money*, May 11, 2004. https://money.cnn.com/2004/05/11/news/fortune500/mcdonalds_happymeal/

Dominus, Susan. 2004. "Film; You Want Liver Failure with That?" *The New York Times*, May 2, 2004.

Guerrasio, Jason. 2018. "Morgan Spurlock's #MeToo Confession Crippled 'Super Size Me 2,' and a Main Subject of the Movie Feels Abandoned." *Business Insider*, June 25, 2018.

Jamieson, Alexandra. n.d. "About Me." https://alexandrajamieson.com/aboutme/the-story/

Spurlock, Morgan. 2017. "I Am Part of the Problem." Twit Longer, December 14, 2017. http://www.twitlonger.com/show/n_1sqc244

"Super Size Me." n.d. IMDB. https://www.imdb.com/title/tt0390521

T

Taste of Chicago

STARTERS

The Taste of Chicago is an annual five-day event that's held in Chicago, Illinois. Touted as the world's largest food festival, the celebration welcomes close to a million visitors each year, down from 3.68 million visitors at its peak in 1988. The Taste of Chicago highlights a wide array of the city's diverse culinary offerings and talent, ranging from food trucks to upscale restaurants and famous chefs. Attendance is free, and tickets are sold for $10 in quantities of 14 that can be used to purchase sample-sized or full-sized offerings from nearly 100 restaurant vendors. In addition to feasting on local fare, attendees also enjoy cooking demonstrations, parades, arts and crafts, pairing sessions, and live dance performances. Live music performances from local and international solo artists, orchestras, and bands also contribute to the festival's enormous crowds and include headlining acts that span across genres, including bluegrass, rock, classical, and R&B. The festival attracts locals and tourists alike, maintaining a decades-old tradition of providing a fun and affordable homage to the city's culinary heritage.

An aerial view shows crowds gathering to celebrate at the Taste of Chicago in Chicago's Grant Park. (Kenneth Ilio/Dreamstime.com)

ENTRÉE

For some, simply hearing the word "Chicago" can cause a conditioned Pavlovian response, inviting a hint of drool and a sparkle in the subject's eye as they reminisce about the city's vast food offerings. Culinary historian Bruce Kraig wrote that the city's name itself is food related—after the Potawatomis' term "Chicagu" for a strongly scented wild onion that once grew in abundance in the region. "Chicago's existence and its wealth were founded on food," Kraig wrote in the *Chicago Tribune*. "From its incorporation, the city was the collection and shipment center for the Midwest's agricultural bounty. And Chicago grew to become the heart of America's new food processing industries" (1997). Today, the city's cuisine represents its rich history as a melting pot of immigrants, ranging from German to Polish, Irish, Italian, Greek, and many more. The flavors found at the Taste of Chicago also highlight the city's past, with nods to the region's history as a hub for hog butchers, African American–owned barbecue restaurants, and tamale crazes that swept urban areas in the early 1900s, just to name a few.

The Taste of Chicago not only includes unique contemporary offerings but also sheds a spotlight on the city's most iconic foods, such as Italian beef sandwiches, Chicago-style hot dogs, Polish kielbasa sausages, and deep-dish pizza. The Taste of Chicago was founded in 1980 by a group of restaurant owners who wanted to host a food-centric festival on the Fourth of July. Much to the city's surprise, an estimated 250,000 visitors attended the first event, setting the tone for decades of success that were to follow. After its inaugural year, the festival moved from Chicago's bustling Michigan Avenue to Grant Park in order to accommodate the immense crowds and provide a music pavilion for live shows.

By 1988, the festival expanded its schedule to a 10-day period, attracting more than three and a half million visitors as a result. In 2013, event organizers shortened the festival to five days as the result of financial losses in prior years. Attendance has continued to thrive, drawing crowds like the 1.6 million in attendance at the 2017 festival. In recent years, the event has included more than 3,000 restaurant employees and 600 artists and performers. Additionally, the Taste of Chicago boosts the city's economy by an estimated $106 million (Carrino 2017). According to surveys conducted at the festival, the event's visitors range from Chicago residents to international visitors, and more than 70 percent of visitors identify as Black, Hispanic, or Asian, mirroring the diversity of the event's culinary offerings as well (Greene and Bentle 2018). The festival's events range from celebrity chef cooking demonstrations to a daily March of the Puppets parade that features a drumline and people dressed in larger-than-life-sized puppet costumes.

DESSERT

- **Prank wars are now be-Heinz us:** You'll find many things on a Chicago-style hot dog, but one of them is not—by firm cultural rule—ketchup. The regional specialty consists of an all-beef hot dog, dill pickle, tomato, onion, yellow mustard, bright green relish, celery salt, and pickled sport peppers . . . and *no* exceptions, in the eyes of many die-hard fans. In 2015, Chicago-based

Heinz brand attempted to trick Chicagoans into accepting the brand's locally vilified ketchup on hot dogs through a promotional campaign that disguised ketchup under the moniker "Chicago-dog sauce." Upon learning they'd been had, taste-testers' responses largely ranged from chilly to hostile, cementing ketchup's efforts as a lost cause in the Windy City.

- **Supreme fighting words:** U.S. Supreme Court Justice Anthony Scalia was quoted by numerous sources over the years with his verdict on the nationwide battle of *New York Thin-Crust Pizza v. Chicago Deep Dish Pizza*. Scalia voiced his opinion that New York style was "the real" pizza and that the deep-dish style beloved by Midwesterners was more like "tomato pie." The verdict was out on how Justice Scalia's longtime colleague and friend, the honorable Justice Ruth Bader Ginsburg, prefers her a-pizza pies.

SUGGESTED PAIRINGS

See also: Austin Food + Wine Festival; Craft Brewing and Microbreweries; Deer River Wild Rice Festival; Food and Beverage Museums, U.S.; Maine Lobster Festival.

Entry best enjoyed while eating: A smattering of local samples, including Robinson's baby-back ribs; a hot dog and fries from Superdawg; fried chicken with mild sauce from Harold's Chicken Shack; a slide of bleu cheese praline pear pie from Justice of the Pies; and, to cleanse the palate, a stick of Wrigley's spearmint gum.

Further Reading

Carrino, Christine. 2017. "The 2017 Taste of Chicago Welcomed a Record 1.6 Million Visitors, Offering a Cultural Experience for All the Senses with Food, Music, Arts and Family Fun Over Five Days in Grant Park." Chicago Department of Cultural Affairs and Special Events, Press Release, July 9, 2017.

Greene, Morgan, and Kyle Bentle. 2018. "Who Goes to the Taste? We Looked at the Data." *Chicago Tribune*, July 12, 2018.

Kraig, Bruce. 1997. "Glazing through Chicago's Food History." *Chicago Tribune*, July 16, 1997.

Television, Food Channels on

STARTERS

Food-themed channels debuted in the early 1990s and continue to offer culinary content to television and internet audiences around the clock today. The most significant cable channel devoted to food and beverages is Food Network, founded in 1993, and Cooking Channel (both of which are owned by Discovery, Inc.), launched in 2010. While many channels offered some cooking shows on their lineup long before the early 1990s, cooking shows became more prevalent across many networks in response to the enormous popularity of long- and short-format culinary content that exploded on television during Food Network's rise. Today, cooking shows represent a significant portion of daytime and evening television across a number of networks, including PBS, the Travel Channel, Bravo, ABC, CBS, and FOX, among others.

ENTRÉE

The influence of Food Network has arguably changed the way Americans cook and eat. It also created the concept of celebrity chefs, a title largely unheard of before the early 1990s. Fans of shows found on Food Network and other stations have flocked by the thousands to restaurants owned or starring the creations of their favorite television stars, creating a mutually exclusive business between the television and restaurant industries. Food television traces back to the BBC's *Cookery* in 1946, starring a cook named Philip Harben, and James Beard's *I Love to Eat* on NBC the same year, a live 15-minute program that aired on Friday nights in the United States. One of the first "celebrity chefs" was Fanny Cradock, whose show *Kitchen Magic* aired on the BBC and ITV in Britain was fueled by her eccentric and sometimes sharp-tongued on-camera personality—a pioneer for the fiery-tempered chefs to follow on television.

Julia Child was a mainstay on television for many years on her show *The French Chef*, which aired on WGBH (Boston public television) and PBS between 1963 and 1973. Other breakout cooking hosts in the 1960s included Joyce Chen and Graham Kerr of *The Galloping Gourmet*, and 1980s hosts like Rick Bayless, Martha Stewart, Martin Yan, and Jeff Smith continued to increase Americans' interest in cooking programs. Until the early 1990s, however, food programming was considered to be educational television, not drama or comedy (or, as it's known in some business circles today, "edutainment").

Despite the fact that Food Network's cofounders had no interest in or experience with food, they banded together to form a cable network that offered something they identified as lacking in the current television lineup. When executive producer Pat O'Gorman heard the concept for the network, he recalls saying, "That's the stupidest thing I've ever heard. Who in God's name would watch food shows? I guess I was wrong." And wrong he was. The network began in New York City on a shoestring budget under the name Television Food Network due to a trademark conflict (the names "The Food Network" and "Cooking Channel" were already in use by other entities). The producers fielded tapes sent in by aspiring cooking hosts and started drafting and assigning early show content to hosts like television personality Donna Hanover. Early content ranged from news-like content discussing agricultural conditions that year to cooking tutorials.

One of the most difficult challenges chefs face when attempting to cross over from kitchen notoriety to on-camera hosting is the ability to be personable on camera, cook, and explain what they're doing simultaneously, and Food Network hosts were not immune to these challenges. Chefs were under pressure to perform well, amicably describe what they were doing as they did it, hold food where the cameras could easily film it, and wrap up segments in required time limits. This led to a series of issues, such as forgetting to explain what they were doing, missing key steps in their recipe tutorials, or frequently cutting themselves while working (Salkin 2013). The network began to gain mass appeal when they offered chef Emeril Lagasse his own show. *Essence of Emeril* premiered in 1994, and his familiar fare and welcoming personality was met with significant popularity, effectively putting Food Network on the map. Food critic Ruth Reichl also attributed the network's success to the fact that chefs were outstanding public speakers who were also well versed in subjects like the cuisine's history (Sugar 2017).

Shows like *Iron Chef America* (2005), the American spin on the Japanese smash success; *Good Eats* (1999) starring Alton Brown; and Ina Garten's *Barefoot Contessa* (2001) helped bring in additional traffic, and the network began seeing significant viewership upticks with each passing year. By 2019, the network had amassed an enormous number of food-related shows, ranging from traditional cooking instructional shows to reality television and travelogues, including *Diners, Drive-Ins and Dives, Cupcake Wars, The Pioneer Woman, Wolfgang Puck, Giada at Home*, and hundreds of others. The network even began making shows about its own ability to create all-star chefs, launching *Food Network Star, Food Network Star Kids, Food Network Challenge*, and more. Today, the network touts distribution to almost 100 million households in the United States and says its affiliated website attracts 46 million unique web users monthly (Food Network 2019).

Taking note of audiences' appetites for food-related entertainment, other networks scrambled to add culinary shows to their lineup as well. Bravo TV saw significant success with *Top Chef* (2006–), which went on to launch a number of chefs' high-profile careers as well. Other Bravo shows included *Around the World in 80 Plates, Best New Restaurant, Chef Roble & Co., Rocco's Dinner Party*, and several *Top Chef* spin-offs, among others. The Travel Channel also saw enormous success with Anthony Bourdain's culinary travel shows, including *No Reservations* and *The Layover*, as well as Andrew Zimmern's *Bizarre Foods* and *The Zimmern List*. Other popular programs included *Man vs. Food* and *Amazing Eats, Chowdown Countdown, Edge of America, Booze Traveler, Food Wars*, and *Food Paradise*.

Food programming on networks ABC, CBS, and FOX is typically limited to cooking demonstrations on news and lifestyle shows and reality competition cooking shows. ABC's *The Taste* (2013–2015), *Family Food Fight* (2019–), and *Jamie Oliver's Food Revolution* (2010–2011) vied for viewership against shows like CBS's *Rachael Ray* talk show (2006–), *American Baking Competition* (2013), and *Rehab* (2012–2015). On FOX, viewers tune in to a number of shows starring chef Gordon Ramsay, including *MasterChef* (2010–), *MasterChef Junior* (2013–), and *Hell's Kitchen* (2005–).

In 2018, the ABC network pulled two successful cooking shows off the air during the #MeToo movement, a nationwide movement protesting sexual harassment and assault in the workplace. Daytime cooking and lifestyle show *The Chew* (2011–2018) was canceled shortly after several women raised sexual misconduct allegations against chef Mario Batali. ABC fired Batali, a cohost of the show, and shortly thereafter canceled *The Chew*. In light of the allegations, Food Network put a freeze on six new episodes of *Molto Mario* that were set to air. ABC also temporarily canceled *The Great American Baking Show* in the wake of allegations against one of the show's stars, pastry chef Johnny Iuzzini. These changes came just weeks after PBS dropped chef John Besh from his shows *John Besh's New*

Orleans (2011–2018) and *Family Table* (2013–2018) for allegations of the same nature.

The PBS network was among the earliest in the nation to promote and broadcast food-related television, and it still hosts a number of popular shows today. Iconic programming includes *The French Chef* with Julia Child, *Yan Can Cook* with Martin Yan, *Simply Ming* with Ming Tsai, *Everyday Cooking* with Jacques Pépin, *Lidia's Kitchen* (2013–) with Lidia Bastianich, and Rick Bayless's shows like *Cooking Mexican* (1979) and *Mexico One Plate at a Time*. Additional shows like *America's Test Kitchen*, *Cook's Country*, *Martha Bakes*, and *Pati's Mexican Table* provide scientific experimentation and home-entertainment tips, whereas programs like *I'll Have What Phil's Having* and *Food Flirts* provide a more humorous take on dining and shared meals. Contemporary additions reflect some of American viewers' changing interest, like *A Chef's Life* (2013–2018), a documentary series that follows chef Vivian Howard as she works in her North Carolina restaurant, and *The Mind of a Chef* (2012–2017), which profiles one chef per show in a blend of travelogue, cooking documentary, and art.

ACCOMPANIED BY

One of Food Network's founding members is Reese Schonfeld, the network's managing director, who reportedly was so personally apathetic toward cooking that he did not even have a kitchen in his apartment when he launched the network. Additional cofounders include Providence Journal Company president Trygve Myhren, production VP Joe Langhan, and CEO Jack Clifford, among others (Salkin 2013). In Food Network's earliest years, executives and producers primarily worked with local chefs who were able to get their own transportation to the studios, tape their segments quickly, and return to their restaurants, such as budding talents like Bobby Flay, Marcus Samuelsson, Alton Brown, Rachael Ray, and Guy Fieri. Other early stars on the network included chefs Sarah Moulton, Jacques Pépin and Robin Leach. The network also helped broaden American appeal for international stars like British chef Nigella Lawson. The individuals who appeared on Food Network in the channel's early years often received low pay for their work and had exhausting schedules, sometimes taping upward of five to eight shows per day. However, many of them saw a significant return for their effort when the network helped launch them to national or even international fame.

PBS helped launch the careers of modern-day moguls like Martha Stewart, whose breakout show *Holiday Entertaining with Martha Stewart* in 1986 marked the beginning of her craft and food empire. The network was also instrumental in transforming Rick Bayless from an on-air chef into a contemporary media mogul. While many have attributed cooking educational and "edutainment" programming to the nation's growing interest in home cooking and broadening their culinary horizons, writers like Michael Pollan criticize viewers of Food Network for sitting on their couches watching others cook instead of making nutritious meals in their own homes.

DESSERT

- **Lights, camera, Fido:** In an effort to help television hosts warm up to the cameras during Food Network's early years, producers sometimes taped photos of the host's dog to the camera so the host had a familiar (furry) face to talk to while filming.
- **The color of whoops:** On his first taping of *Molto Mario*, chef Mario Batali cut himself badly while grating carrots. In an attempt to hide his injury, he plunged his hand into a can of tomatoes and continued his demonstration as if nothing happened. Unfortunately, "blood red is not tomato red, so you could see it," the celebrity chef said (Larry King Now 2017).
- **Switcherooni:** Sara Moulton recalls that in the early days of filming with Food Network, she didn't even have a working oven: "I would pretend that I was putting things into the oven by putting them under the counter, and then somebody at my feet would either hand me the piping-hot thing or there would be a swap-out under the counter that looked vaguely hot" (Sugar 2017).
- **And its Sequel, *Watching Paint Dry*:** Emeril Lagasse's first show on Food Network was called *How to Boil Water*. "It was terrible," Lagasse says (Sugar 2017).
- **Celebrity celebrities:** Ming Tsai wasn't very fond of the new "celebrity chef" label that emerged in this era of television, saying he hated the term because "Brad Pitt is not a 'celebrity actor' and Tom Brady's not a 'celebrity quarterback.' He's a quarterback! I'm a chef" (Sugar 2017).

SUGGESTED PAIRINGS

See also: Batali, Mario; Brown, Alton; *Cooked*; Fictional Television (1980s–), Food and; Flay, Bobby; Lagasse, Emeril; Ray, Rachael; Samuelsson, Marcus.

Entry best enjoyed while eating: Chinese eggplant grilled in chilis, ginger, garlic, soy sauce, and black vinegar (Martin Yan, *Yan Can Cook*, PBS); clam hash and sticky honey peanut cake (Vivian Howard, *A Chef's Life*, PBS); deep-fried lobster elote with corn and garlic aioli (*Food Paradise*, Travel Channel); and freshly boiled water (*How to Boil Water*, Food Network).

Further Reading

Cahn, Lauren. 2019. "The Most Popular Cooking Shows the Year You Were Born." Taste of Home, January 9, 2019. https://www.tasteofhome.com/collection/most-popular-cooking-shows/

Food Network. 2019. "About the Food Network." https://www.foodnetwork.com/site/about-foodnetwork-com

Larry King Now. 2017. "Interview with Mario Batali." http://www.ora.tv/larrykingnow/2017/4/10/mario-batali-cut-himself-his-first-day-on-television

Maynard, Micheline. 2018. "As ABC's 'The Chew' Goes Away, How Networks Have Been Burned by Celebrity Chefs." *Forbes*, June 17, 2018.

Migliori, Simone. 2018. "How The Food Network Went from Bust to Big Time." WGBH, July 23, 2018. https://www.wgbh.org/news/lifestyle/2018/07/23/how-the-food-network-went-from-bust-to-big-time

Salkin, Allen. 2013. *From Scratch: Inside the Food Network*. New York: G.P. Putnam's Sons.

Sugar, Rachel. 2017. "How Food Network Turned Big-city Chef Culture into Middle-America Pop Culture." *New York,* Grub Street, November 2017. http://www.grubstreet.com/2017/11/early-days-food-network-oral-history.html

Top Chef (2006–)

STARTERS

Top Chef is a popular American reality cooking competition show that first aired on Bravo network in 2006 and has run for 17 consecutive seasons. The reality cooking show pits professional chefs against each other in a series of varying cooking challenges, after which one or more chefs are eliminated until one chef is named the winner of the season at large. Chefs compete for top prizes, consisting of winnings ranging between $100,000 and $200,000, a lavish prize package, and guaranteed appearances in high-profile culinary magazines and events, such as the elite annual Aspen Food & Wine classic.

The show's 44-minute episodes are split into various challenges, as well as interviews with judges and competitors. Its success has spurred a number of spinoffs, including *Top Chef Masters*, *Top Chef: Just Desserts*, and *Top Chef Junior*. More than two dozen international versions of the show have also been produced, including adaptations specific to numerous countries all over the world. In 2008, *Top Chef* received a Primetime Creative Arts Emmy Award in the category of Outstanding Picture Editing for Reality Programming and a Primetime Emmy for Outstanding Competition Program in 2010.

ENTRÉE

In episode nine of *Top Chef*'s second season, judge Tom Colicchio stands in front of the episode's three lowest-scoring chefs and says: "You all had to choose one of the Seven Deadly Sins and create a dish you thought best represented that sin. Unfortunately, each one of you committed a *culinary* sin." Such is the world of *Top Chef*: reality television served with a slice of drama, a cornucopia of unusual challenges, and a scoop of shame or hubris every so often for good measure. In this episode, chefs had been tasked with creating a meal based on a specific color—a particularly daunting task for the cast's colorblind contestant—as well as cooking a seven-course meal reflecting the seven deadly sins. Contestants served dishes like ceviche and chile popcorn for "wrath" and hot soup in glass tubes for "slothfulness." For home audiences, this new genre of culinary reality entertainment was a far cry from the "cook to the camera" tutorials of past television shows.

Top Chef consists of an elimination format commonly seen in other competition shows. Contestants vie to impress the judges in a quick-fire challenge, followed by an elimination challenge. In somewhat of a "Martha Stewart meets *The Real World*" show mashup, producers require the castmates to live together during filming, and chefs have highly restricted contact with the outside world. After completing their high-stress, strictly time-enforced challenges, chefs sit in a small room adjacent to the kitchen dubbed the "Stew Room," where they wait for the judges' verdicts. For the chefs, the experience of filming the show is physically demanding, stressful, and strenuous and requires very quick thinking and long days of filming.

The combination of long days, sleep deprivation, sharing tight quarters with competitors, and missing loved ones often leads to the type of frayed nerves and short tempers that reality producers rely on to create viewer-approved dramatic scenes. As the show's producers learned in season two, *Top Chef* audiences wanted a different flavor of drama than many other reality shows offered. The show's second season received criticism for going too deep when various cast members resorted to bullying and physical assault. Over the course of the season, contestant Michael Vigneron was mocked, and at one point, he was physically assaulted by a group of his castmates, who forcefully restrained him and attempted to shave his head without his consent.

Over the last two decades, more than 200 chefs and an equal number of guest judges have appeared on *Top Chef* and its closely associated spinoffs. *Vox* writer Alex Abad-Santos deemed the show as " one of the best and most enduring competitive reality television shows in the history of the genre," noting its steady track record of hooking viewers despite the fact that they can't smell or taste the fare being judged, making the show's success highly surprising. Year after year, viewers continue to tune in to delight in culinary mishaps and crowning achievements, sitting on the edge of their seats wondering who Lakshmi will tell to "pack up their knives and go home" in the final round.

ACCOMPANIED BY

The show's long-term judges include Padma Lakshmi (1970–), Gail Simmons (1976–), and Tom Colicchio (1962–). Lakshmi has served as an executive producer and the show's host from the second season onward. Born in Delhi and raised primarily in the United States, the former model turned culinary professional is passionate about global cuisines and immigrants' influence on American food trends, and she has written books ranging from international cuisine cookbooks to a memoir. Colicchio serves as the head judge and chefs' mentor on the show, coming from a background as a successful restaurateur and author. Raised in New Jersey, the chef is best known by many for Craft, an upscale restaurant he opened in New York City in 2001. Named "Outstanding Chef" in 2010 by the James Beard Foundation, Colicchio is also a published author.

Longtime co-judge Gail Simmons is a respected food writer. Hailing from Toronto, Canada, her career includes events management for *Food & Wine* magazine and chef Daniel Boulud. She hosted the show's spin-off *Top Chef Just Desserts* in addition to judging *Top Chef Jr.* and a number of other cooking competition shows in Canada and the United States, and she has published several books of her own. *Top Chef's* talent has also included cookbook author and food critic Katie Lee (1981–), the host of the first season. Frequent guest judges included renowned food writers and television hosts Ted Allen (1965–) and Anthony Bourdain (1956–2019), and chefs Eric Ripert (1965–), Dan Barber (1969–), and Graham Elliot (1977–).

Some of the most successful and well-known contestants include fan favorite Carla Hall (1964–), who competed in two seasons before opening a successful Southern restaurant, publishing a best-selling cookbook, and cohosting ABC network's *The Chew*. Stephanie Izard (1976–) was the first woman to claim the *Top Chef* champion title and went on to earn a James Beard "Best Chef" award in 2013 from her widely renowned Chicago restaurant Girl & The Goat. The show's sixth season winner, Michael Voltaggio (1978–)—referred to by Colicchio as the most talented chef to have appeared on the show—later opened an acclaimed restaurant named ink in West Hollywood, California. His brother Bryan Voltaggio (1976–) was placed second to Michael on the same season of *Top Chef* and went on to co-own a number of restaurants with his sibling. In 2020, Mumbai-born chef Floyd Cardoz, a *Top Chef Master* winner, was mourned when he died from coronavirus complications. The same year, season five winner Hosea Rosenberg made headlines around the nation when he announced that his three-year-old daughter had been diagnosed with an extremely rare degenerative genetic disorder, galvanizing many in the food industry to help raise money for research and treatment.

DESSERT

- **Common workplace challenges:** Padma Lakshmi estimates that she consumes between 5,000 and 8,000 calories a day when filming, just from sampling each contestant's dish. Additionally, she faces the challenge of attempting to speak naturally while producers feed her legally approved language through an earpiece to ensure the host's descriptions about challenges don't land the network in legal trouble.
- **The man in the know**: A *Top Chef* camera operator referred to as T-Bone has the enviable job of filming the "beauty shots" of each finished dish. He's also one of the few on set who get to taste each dish. In some instances when the judges have reached an impasse trying to decide on a winner, T-Bone has been consulted to help tip the scales.
- **Smoke & mirrors:** Despite how it appears on television, contestants must make two versions of each dish: one for judging and one to be photographed. The judging process can last a very long time—up to eight hours!—such as one judge's table that didn't end until 4 a.m.
- **Unusual problems**: According to executive producer Andy Cohen, filming had to be paused during the first season's initial elimination due to an unusual thudding sound, which turned out to be host Katie Lee's heart pounding loudly enough for the microphone to detect it. In Season 3, the production crew also found themselves in an unusual situation when they began filming only to realize that the set wasn't tall enough for six-foot-eight contestant CJ Jacobson. Frantic painting and camera re-setting took place to extend the height of the set to accommodate the chef's height.

SUGGESTED PAIRINGS

See also: Aspen Food and Wine Classic; *Chopped*; *Cooks vs. Cons*; *Iron Chef*; *MasterChef*; Television, Food Channels on.

Entry best enjoyed while eating: *Lakshmi's favorite dish that told a story*: foie gras with bacon, pickled cherry, beets, and pumpernickel surrounding beet juice in the shape of a bloody handprint (Paul Qui, "fairy tale" challenge); *Simmons's all-time favorite dish on the show*: chilled sunchoke dashi soup with raw vegetable ribbons, croutons, and crispy prosciutto (Paul Qui); *Tom's favorite* Top Chef *dessert*: strawberry lime curd with toasted yogurt, milk crumble, and mint (Mei Lin).

Further Reading

Abad-Santos, Alex. 2016. "After Ten Years, Top Chef Is Still One of the Best Reality Television Shows Around." Vox, March 11, 2016. https://www.vox.com/2016/3/11/11201204/top-chef-10-year-anniversary

Feiner, Abby. 2020. "Fan Favorite Melissa King Shares Her Top Chef Winning Recipe." Bravo, June 23, 2020. https://www.bravotv.com/top-chef/style-living/winner-melissa-king-shares-winning-recipe

Martin, Brett. 2008. *Top Chef, The Cookbook*. Foreword by Tom Colicchio. San Francisco: Chronicle Books.

Ram, Archana. 2010. "Top Chef Secrets Revealed: From the Judges' Mouths to Your Ears." *Entertainment Weekly*, January 12, 2010.

Tosi, Christina (1981–)

STARTERS

Christina Tosi is an American pastry chef, television personality, cookbook author, and pastry teacher. She is the founder, owner, CEO, and driving creative force behind Milk Bar, a trendy Manhattan-based bakery that serves inventive, nostalgic-themed treats such as cereal milk soft serve, rainbow-sprinkle-speckled birthday cakes, and cornflake marshmallow cookies. Tosi opened the bakery under the name Momofuku Milk Bar in 2008 to accompany David Chang's Momofuku Ssam Bar, which has been named one of S. Pellegrino's "50 Best Restaurants."

She has written three cookbooks, *Momofuku Milk Bar* (2011), *Milk Bar Life*, and *Milk Bar Cakewalk* (slated for 2018), which share popular recipes from her bakery, as well as creative spins on salads, entrées, and appetizers. Her career was profiled in an episode of Netflix's *Chef's Table: Pastry* in 2018, and she was featured in Cooking Channel's *Unique Sweets* and several episodes of PBS's *The Mind of a Chef*. Tosi was a judge on Food Network's *Chopped*, as well as on Fox network's show *Masterchef* and its youth-centric spin-off, *MasterChef Junior*.

Tosi has expanded Milk Bar from a single bakery into a dozen locations in New York City, Washington, D.C., Las Vegas, and Toronto in addition to launching an exclusive series of cake mixes with the retail chain Target. Milk Bar has a large ecommerce line that ships signature desserts, baking mixes, and apparel around the world. Shortly after opening her first bakery, Tosi was honored with the first of her two James Beard awards. In 2011, she was the first pastry chef to receive the "Rising Star Chef" award, and in 2015, she received the "Outstanding Pastry

Chef" award. Additionally, she was listed on Crain's "40 under 40" list in 2016 and was named "one of the most innovative women in food and drink" by *Fortune* and *Food & Wine* magazines in 2014.

ENTRÉE

"Despite the fact that many of us are formally trained and have worked in great restaurants, we also crave and embrace food with a more down-home, lowbrow approach. We long for FLAVOR, not fuss," Tosi wrote in her second cookbook about the characteristics she shares with the Milk Bar staff. Tosi, who was born in Ohio and raised in Springfield, Virginia, is known for her joyful character, determined work ethic, shrewd business skills, and highly innovative take on her culinary inventions. Baking wasn't always at the forefront of her life, however. In her youth, she pursued electrical engineering at the University of Virginia, studied applied mathematics and Italian in Florence, and graduated from James Madison University, all in three years' time. After graduation, Tosi made the decision to change course and pursue her passion for baking. She attended the French Culinary Institute to learn the pastry arts before beginning her career as a restaurant hostess, caterer, and food stylist.

Tosi was hired at high-end restaurants Bouley and (the now shuttered) wd~50, where she worked an exhaustive schedule as a pastry chef. She began working at wd~50 at the age of 23, asking to work without pay to improve her odds of working at the exclusive restaurant. She went on to work side by side with its owner, Wylie Dufresne, fine-tuning successful components of dishes and seeking creative presentations and reimaginations of various desserts. Despite being in some of New York's leading-edge restaurant kitchens, Tosi felt out of place and unfulfilled by the work she was doing. She left Dufresne's restaurant to work for David Chang, who wanted to leverage her business operation skills to help him get in the Public Health Department's good graces. After learning about Tosi's pastry skills and work ethic, he convinced her to create dessert offerings for Momofuku, which did not serve desserts. Tosi told *First We Feast*, "I think Dave just got so sick of me bringing in baked goods and not working in the kitchen that one day he said, 'I'm not even going to talk to you, just go in the kitchen and bake something, I don't care what you make'" (Brickman 2012).

With only hours to prepare for her first Momofuku dessert creation, Tosi developed a sophisticated take on strawberry shortbread to complement Chang's menu, which stars fare such as pork buns and ramen. After winning over Chang's diners, Tosi worked on the development of a new dessert that was inspired by one she had made at wd~50, a cornbread ice cream made from cornbread steeped in milk. Seeking inspiration in a bodega (a small urban grocery store, usually Mexican-owned), Tosi found herself drawn to the cereal aisle, which evoked the flavors and memories of her childhood. Tosi brought a box of cornflakes back to her kitchen, which she toasted, steeped in milk, and used as a base for an inventive panna cotta. Chang's reaction to Tosi's invention was that people were about to "go crazy" for her concoction—a prediction that proved to be right.

Side Plates

Recipe for Milk That Tastes Like Cereal

One of Christina Tosi's most popular confectionary creations has been her cereal-flavored milk, which the pastry chef eventually trademarked. Despite being understandably protective of her intellectual property, Tosi is also very generous with her culinary creations and shares recipes for "cereal milk" and her other famous concoctions on the Milk Bar websites and her cookbooks.

The following recipe is an approximation of the treat she became famous for, and has been adapted from the recipe in Momofuku Milk Bar. It can be used as the base for other recipes; try your hand at cereal milk ice cream, shakes, or the Tosi dessert that started it all: panna cotta! It can also be enjoyed splashed in your morning coffee or simply served cold in a glass as a taste of childhood.

- 2 3/4 cups cereal (try corn flakes to replicate Milk Bar's famous flavor)
- 3 3/4 cups cold milk (cow's milk, almond, soy, etc.)
- 2 tbs light brown sugar, tightly packed
- 1/4 tsp kosher salt

1. Preheat your oven to 300 degrees Fahrenheit and cover a sheet pan with parchment paper.
2. Spread cereal evenly over the pan and bake until lightly toasted (if using corn flakes, roughly 15 minutes). The toasting process will enhance the cereal's delicious flavors.
3. Cool completely and transfer cereal to a large pitcher.
4. Pour the milk over the cereal, stir for 30 seconds. Let the mixture mingle at room temperature for 20 minutes.
5. Strain through a fine-mesh sieve, using a bowl below to collect the milk. Gently press the cereal against the sieve to get the remaining milk out.
6. Whisk salt and brown sugar in the milk until well-incorporated (adjust per your preference; to tone down the sweetness, add a small amount of milk and salt. To increase, add brown sugar).
7. Store refrigerated in a closed container for up to a week.

Serves four (or two very thirsty) people; yields 2½ cups

In 2008, a retail space adjacent to Momofuku Ssam became available, and Chang encouraged Tosi to open a bakery there that would serve as a sister eatery to Ssam. In the course of 45 days, then-27-year-old Tosi brought Momofuku Milk Bar to life. On opening day, the staff emerged from their pre-dawn baking shift to discover a line that wrapped around the corner, eagerly anticipating a first bite of the treats inside. In short order, Milk Bar opened a second location with an 11,000-square-foot kitchen of whirring activity and pastry experimentation. "Momofuku" was dropped from the name, and Milk Bar became a separate brand of its own. Tosi's low-fuss, high-fun attitude continued to direct the menu, which includes things like "bagel bombs," un-fussy wedding cakes, cereal milkshakes, and truffles inspired by snacks the staff used to make from leftover cake parts.

In the span of eight years, pasty chef Christina Tosi's line of cookies, cakes, and pies went from being sold in a single retail location to being shipped nationwide and sold in national retailers such as Whole Foods, Target, and numerous regional grocery stores. (Alexander Bernardo/Dreamstime.com)

In *Milk Bar Life*, Tosi wrote, "The most honest, loving people make the most honest, loving food," a far cry from the often fiercely competitive, cutting-edge mentality of the culinary industry. Tosi's innovative and sophisticated take on food could have been lost in the seemingly simple kitchiness of her creations, but Milk Bar has become a trendy pop culture phenomenon. Tosi has created a veritable empire from cups of soft serve, "compost cookies" made with various bits of potato chips, pretzels, chocolate, and coffee grounds, and sprinkle-filled cakes. The cakes are unfrosted on the sides, in part due to Tosi having felt burned out after striving to achieve frosting perfection in culinary school and in part because "we're not in pottery class," as she puts it (Whitney 2018).

ACCOMPANIED BY

Family

The women in Christina Tosi's family loved baking, creating a nostalgic attachment to the kitchen that would go on to shape Tosi's career. As a child, Tosi was a very picky eater, so her mother—a managing partner at an accountancy firm—would insist that she drink the milk from the cereal bowl to get some nutrients from the sugar-laden meal. Tosi's father worked for the U.S. Department of Agriculture (fittingly, in the dairy department) as an agricultural economist.

In 2016, Tosi married fellow chef Will Guidara, a co-owner of the Michelin-starred restaurant Eleven Madison Park. The couple were wed in a summer-camp-themed wedding while wearing ponchos and saying their vows in the pouring rain. During the reception, the couple and their guests dined on Momofuku's Bo Ssam and a seven-tiered wedding cake from Milk Bar: the bakery's largest to date.

DESSERT

- **Taste the rainbow:** Milk Bar's locations have used a combined 11 tons of sprinkles since the flagship bakery opened in 2008 (Whalen 2018).
- **Keeping up with demand:** As Milk Bar's popularity exploded, Tosi's kitchens were stocked with electric mixers as large as 140 quarts (roughly 35 gallons), and they have had to introduce machines that scoop cookie dough and package cookies.
- **The division of this and that:** Due to the wide range of duties she was asked to do in her Momofuku office job, Tosi's job title was called "et cetera." Today, she has an entire group of employees called "the et cetera team" that is simply tasked with helping to do miscellaneous jobs in the kitchen.
- **That's a flop:** The list of "Milk Bar inventions that didn't go over so well" includes gummy bear sorbet, cheesecake made with a saltine crust and green tomato sorbet, and barbecue-flavored ice cream.
- **Ripple effects:** After the release of her first cookbook, Tosi's cakes became so trendy that Amazon experienced a major run on acetate sheets (plastic that Tosi instructs bakers to use while assembling the layer cakes).
- **Thanks-ssants?** During the holiday season, Milk Bar makes more than 15,000 Thanksgiving croissants, which are made with celery salt in the dough and stuffed with turkey, cranberry sauce, and gravy.

SUGGESTED PAIRINGS

See also: Chang, David; *Chef's Table*; Ice Cream Trends; *MasterChef*; *Mind of a Chef, The*.

Entry best enjoyed while eating: A croissant with kimchi butter and blue cheese, a cereal milkshake, and a slice of "crack pie": toasted oat crust with a gooey butter filling.

Further Reading
Aspan, Maria. 2018. "How Milk Bar's Christina Tosi Went from Momofuku Employee to Bakery Chain CEO." *Inc.*, March/April 2018 issue.
Brickman, Sophie. 2012. "The 10 Dishes That Made My Career: Christina Tosi." *First We Feast*, October 8, 2012.
Calderone, Ana. 2016. "Chef Christina Tosi Is Married!" *People*, August 1, 2016.
"Cereal Milk." n.d. https://milkbarstore.com/recipes/cereal-milk/
"History of Milk Bar." n.d. https://milkbarstore.com/history-of-milk-bar/
Leve, Ariel. 2012. "Christina Tosi: 'My Diet Was Crazy for the First 27 Years of My Life.'" *The Guardian*, April 21, 2012.

Tosi, Christina. 2011. *Momofuku Milk Bar*. New York: Clarkson Potter, p. 10.

Tosi, Christina. 2015. *Milk Bar Life: Recipes and Stories*. New York: Clarkson Potter.

Whalen, Andrew. 2018. "How Milk Bar's Christina Tosi Invents Exhilarating New Desserts Like Crack Pie." *Newsweek*, April 13, 2018.

Whitney, Alyse. 2018. "The Best Scene from the New Season of 'Chef's Table.'" *Bon Appetit*, April 16, 2018.

Witchel, Alex. 2011. "Christina Tosi, a Border-Crossing Pastry Chef." *The New York Times*, May 3, 2011.

Trends, Food

STARTERS

Food trends date back to ancient times, when scarcity of an ingredient made it worth its weight in gold in some cultures. Explorers who sailed to distant lands returned home with foods that changed cultural diets on a global scale, starting countless trends perpetuated by royalty and others who were attracted to these chic, exotic pleasures. Christopher Columbus's exploration of the Americas in 1492 opened up a passageway for imports and exports between the Old World and the New World that brought agriculture and livestock to new corners of the world. In contemporary society, tools like television and the internet help fuel modern trends in pop culture, such as foods that see skyrocketing popularity after being endorsed by celebrities, or trends that have humble beginnings from street carts that grow to national notoriety.

ENTRÉE

Food trends throughout history teach us about what was (or still is) valuable, prized, novel, or simply humorous to any given culture in any given time. Food trends go back possibly to the earliest humans. Figures like Spain's Medici dynasty used lusted-after treats like jasmine-infused chocolate to showcase their power. Using thousands of delicate jasmine flowers, cacao sourced from the West Indies, and cutting-edge scientific processes, the Medicis flaunted time, money, and resources (Buchanan 2015). In the eighteenth century, Fourth Earl of Sandwich John Montagu (1718–1792) is credited with popularizing the habit of eating meat between two slices of bread—a sandwich trend that would sweep Europe and the rest of the globe and is still a favorite food in contemporary American culture.

Around the 2000s, pineapple motifs became a highly trendy clothing and home decor staple—a remnant from pineapple's popularity tracing all the way back to 1496, when Columbus returned from his second voyage to the Americas with pineapples (only one of which survived the trip). Inspired by King Ferdinand's love of the fruit, and delighted by the rare opportunity to taste sugar in this era, other monarchies across Europe began using the pineapple as a status symbol, even proclaiming that God had deemed the fruit "royal" because it appeared to have a crown on its head. Pineapples were grown in elaborate coal-heated greenhouses in Britain during the Georgian era (1713–1830) and were shared between homes and rented out for dinner parties to impress guests. Given the roughly $8,000 it cost to grow a single pineapple in Britain, the fruit was admired instead of eaten—an irony, considering how much Europeans prized their flavor. By the 1800s, pineapples could be delivered by steamships, and as such, their demand waned (Miralles 2018).

Wine pairing at dinner is a trend that's considered to go back to sixteenth-century Italy, and more than 400 years later, the trend gained appeal in the United States. *Wine Spectator* writer Harvey Steiman notes that baby boomer helped make wine fashionable in the 1970s and 1980s, helping to boost the popularity of Italian and Californian wines in addition to traditional French wines. Generation X and the millennial generation made emerging wine regions like the Pacific Northwest, Australia, South America, and New Zealand on trend. In the 1970s and early 1980s, another party food that was en vogue was quiche Lorraine, a pastry crust filled with baked eggs, cheese, bacon, and cream. Some have attributed this trend to recipes shared in this era by Julia Child and *The Joy of Cooking*, a somewhat chic update of the trendy casserole dishes of prior decades. In keeping with America's love of cheese, the Swiss invention of dipping bread into melted cheese using long forks called fondue also swept through the nation in the 1970s thanks to its appearance at the 1964 World's Fair in New York (Petreycik 2018). This era also saw the rise of Asian food trends like sushi, whose popularity in the United States began to rise exponentially in the mid-1960s, and Chinese food takeout. Today, these trends are still a mainstay of American diets, and Asian fusion cuisines are strongly on trend as well.

The 1970s and 1980s also saw the birth of America's relationship with fad diets and other types of diet trends. In 1975, a doctor named Sanford Siegal invented the Cookie Diet, which consisted of eating six of Siegal's mystery-ingredient cookies and a low-calorie dinner every day to lose weight. Since then, additional entrepreneurs have hopped aboard the cookie diet marketing train

---

Small Plates

Invention of the Chinese Takeout Container

The Chinese takeout box is one of the most enduring symbols of Americanized Chinese food. It was invented in 1894 by Chicagoan Frederick Weeks Wilcox, who filed a patent for his charming origami-style container that folds up and is held in place with a wire handle. The folded design prevents leaks (in theory, at least) and is thought to be an improved version of a wooden pail that used to be popular long ago for transporting raw oysters.

"Chinese food in the Chinese takeout box is as American as apple pie," New York's Museum of Food and Drink (MOFAD) executive director Peter Kim told CBS's *Sunday Morning*, adding that the box was designed to unfold completely and serve as a plate. The takeout box became very popular in the mid-twentieth century and was adorned by illustrations of red Chinese pagodas and cheerful text in the 1970s. Today, more than 300 million Chinese takeout boxes are created each year in the United States, and the container has been initiated as one of the featured artifacts at MOFAD, signifying its notable role in American culture (CBS News 2016; Greenbaum and Rubinstein, 2012).

(Schmall 2008). In the late 1970s, meal-replacement shakes like Slim-Fast became very popular and are still consumed today, joined by brands like Shakeology and Nutrisystem. In 1980, the Cabbage Soup Diet served as a precursor to the cleanse diets and detoxes that gained popularity in the 1990s and beyond, which consist of all-liquid diets such as lemon water with cayenne pepper, fruit juices, or vegetable juices. In 1988, television talk-show host Oprah Winfrey received strong criticism when she attributed a recent 67-pound weight loss to an all-liquid protein diet, which later she admitted was a form of starvation (Mcnamara 2005).

The 1980s also saw a resurgence in the popularity of the similarly calorie- and nutrient-deficient Grapefruit Diet that started in Hollywood in the 1930s, in which participants only eat grapefruits for one to two weeks. Carbohydrates were shunned or limited in many diets in the late 1990s and early 2000s, such as the South Beach and Atkins diets or a more contemporary variation called Keto. In the last decade, a return to past ways of eating has been popularized in things like the Raw Food Diet and the Paleo Diet, which is based on the premise of eating foods that humans might have eaten during the Paleolithic era, as long as 2.5 million years ago. Today, diets like the Whole30 stress the elimination of many food types, such as alcohol, grains, processed sugar, dairy, and soy.

Over the last two decades, Americans have gained an appetite for a variety of ancient foods and beverages. Kombucha, a fermented beverage made from a bacteria-yeast culture and tea, is thought to trace back to China's Tsin Dynasty in 220 BCE. The drink became trendy enough to hit grocery store shelves in the United States in the 1990s, and today, a number of kombucha followers even brew their own at home. In 2010, a number of ancient grains have been met with wild appeal due to their nutritional properties, relative novelty on the market, and (in some cases) gluten-free status. Trendy ancient grains include amaranth, buckwheat, chia, bulgur, and barley. A popular semolina-based grain product called couscous is thought to date back to the early 1400s in North Africa, and quinoa, produced primarily in the Andean region of South America, became so popular in the United States and United Kingdom that the price tripled between 2006 and 2013 (Cherfas 2016).

In addition to having ancient health-food appeal, many of these grains are also part of a widespread superfood trend. The term "superfood" applies to foods that are considered to have dense amounts of certain healthy compounds like antioxidants, healthy fats, and fiber. The term is a controversial one, as it is not always weighted in science; "superfood" is thought to have been derived from a World War I era marketing campaign to help sell bananas. According to market data group Mintel, the resurgence of this marketing tool is a highly effective one; foods labeled "superfood," "supergrain," or "superfruit" saw an astounding 202 percent increase between 2011 and 2015 (Mintel Press Team 2016). One beloved American "superfood" is avocado, whose trend ranges from eating the fruit raw to serving it via copious quantities of guacamole. In the 1990s, avocado toast (mashed avocado served on toasted bread with salt, pepper, and lemon juice) began popping up on menus around the world, a dish that went on to become somewhat of a craze in the United States after 2010. Fueled in part by celebrity promotions, the item became ubiquitous on many brunch menus. Both avocados and brunch are closely related with the millennial generation.

In the early 2000s, America's long-standing relationship with bacon flourished after the prior two decades, during which the breakfast staple had developed a widespread bad reputation for its fat and cholesterol content. The resurgence in its popularity yielded what was referred to by many as a cult following and even a bacon renaissance, spurring on products like artisan bacon, high-end restaurant dishes with bacon, and bacon-flavored novelties like toothpaste, soda, candy, mints, and vodka. The latter is likely to be featured in another 2000s trend, namely in the form of Bloody Marys during a Sunday brunch. The term "brunch" is a mashup of the words "breakfast" and "lunch" due to the fact that it is typically served mid-morning. The brunch trend began in the United States in the early twentieth century and reemerged as a fad in the late 1930s, 1960s, and 1990s. Farha Turnikar, author of *Brunch: A History*, noted that the fad began within the upper class and is more popular on the coasts than in the Midwest. Mixing alcohol with fruit juice started during the Prohibition era to mask the taste of poor-quality alcohol, and juice-blended cocktails went on to help embolden women and members of the middle class to drink during the day, since they received less criticism when the contents of their drink weren't easy to visually identify (Ferdman and Ingraham 2015).

One of the largest fads in recent history is the explosion of flavored coffee, which began its meteoric rise in the 1990s courtesy of coffee heavyweights Dunkin Donuts and Starbucks. A nationwide proliferation of pumpkin spice-themed products sprang from the popularity of Starbucks' pumpkin spice latte (abbreviated as "PSL" in pop culture). The fad began in the early 2000s and rose to exceptional prominence roughly a decade later as other food retailers attempted to cash in on the national craze. Pumpkin spice, a loose rendition of pumpkin pie seasoning, has since been featured in an enormous array of foods, including cookies, yogurt, protein bars, waffles, breakfast cereal, ice cream, coffee creamers, tea, table butter, alcohol, and even dog treats, just to name a few.

DESSERT

I avoca . . . do? In 2018, Americans' affinity for avocados seemed to reach a new level when photos began popping up on social media site Instagram that featured avocados being used in lieu of a wedding ring box during marriage proposals. The hashtag #avocadoproposal was used on a number of photos depicting people down on one knee, opening an avocado to reveal a diamond ring to their beloved. (The downside? Some of the proposers-to-be failed to consider how quickly avocado flesh turns brown and mottled when cut open.)

SUGGESTED PAIRINGS

See also: Asian American Cuisine; Cake and Cupcake Trends; California Avocado Festival; Celebrities and Food; Coffee Culture; Food Trucks; Latin American Cuisine.

Entry best enjoyed while eating: Ramen with braised pork belly, vegetables, and soft-boiled egg; kale chips with sea salt; a green tea matcha latte; and molten chocolate cake.

Further Reading

Buchanan, Ashley. 2015. "The Politics of Chocolate: Cosimo III's Secret Jasmine Chocolate Recipe." The Recipes Project. https://recipes.hypotheses.org/tag/medici

Cherfas, Jeremy. 2016. "Your Quinoa Habit Really Did Help Peru's Poor, but There's Trouble Ahead." NPR, The Salt, March 31 2016. https://www.npr.org/sections/the salt/2016/03/31/472453674/your-quinoa-habit-really-did-help-perus-poor-but-theres-trouble-ahead

Ferdman, Roberto, and Christopher Ingraham. 2015. "How Brunch Became the Most Delicious and Divisive Meal in America." *Washington Post*, April 10, 2015.

McNamara, Melissa. 2005. "Oprah's 'Fattest' Mistake." *CBS News*, November 16, 2005.

Mintel Press Team. 2016. "Super Growth for 'Super' Foods." May 5, 2016. https://www.mintel.com/press-centre/food-and-drink/super-growth-for-super-foods-new-product-development-shoots-up-202-globally-over-the-past-five-years

Miralles, Nina-Sophia. 2018. "The Strange History of the King Pine." The Paris Review, April 25, 2018. https://www.theparisreview.org/blog/2018/04/25/the-strange-history-of-the-king-pine/

Orenstein, Jayne. 2016. "How the Internet Became Ridiculously Obsessed with Avocado Toast." *The Washington Post*, May 6, 2016.

Petreycik, Caitlin. 2018. "The 40 Biggest Food Trends of the Past 40 Years." *Food&Wine*, August 14, 2018.

Real, Nancy Delucia. 2015. "How to Eat Like a Renaissance Courtier." The Iris: Behind the Scenes at the Getty. April 29, 2015. https://blogs.getty.edu/iris/how-to-eat-like-a-renaissance-courtier/

Schmall, Emily. 2008. "Bite Fight." *Forbes*, October 30, 2008.

Shen, Aviva. 2012. "Why Are We So Crazy for Bacon?" *Smithsonian*, January 17, 2012. https://www.smithsonianmag.com/arts-culture/why-are-we-so-crazy-for-bacon-20784529/

"Superfoods or Superhype?" n.d. Harvard T.H. Chan School of Public Health. https://www.hsph.harvard.edu/nutritionsource/superfoods/

Twitty, Michael (1977–)

STARTERS

Michael Twitty is a contemporary American food writer, culinary historian and anthropologist, independent scholar, and historical interpreter. He is the author of the blog Afroculinaria (2010–), which explores African and African Americans' influence throughout history on American foodways. In 2016, Afroculinaria won the *Saveur* Editors and Readers' Choice Blog Awards. Twitty is also the author of *Kosher Soul* (2021), which explores his Jewish and Black culinary and genealogical roots. He is best known for his first novel, *The Cooking Gene* (2017), for which he received a James Beard Award for Cookbook of the Year and a James Beard Award for Writing in 2018. Throughout his career, he has shared historical insights through presentations, lectures, and appearances on culinary documentary television shows. On social media, lectures such as his 2016 TED talk "Gastronomy and the Social Justice Reality of Food" have received tens of thousands of views in addition to selected blog posts that have gone viral.

ENTRÉE

In 1989, a professor of law named Kimberlé Crenshaw coined the term "intersectionality"—a lens through which to study discrimination and privilege through various aspects of one's social identities such as race, nationality, gender identity, or disability.

Topics about both intersectionality and food justice have become increasingly popular in the publishing, news, and documentary industries nationwide, particularly among younger people. The meaning of food, and foodways' cultural roots, is also becoming increasingly popular within American entertainment. The concept of intersecting identities and interest in food's meaning is the focus of much of Michael Twitty's writing and cooking. Self-described as "four time blessed (large of body, gay, African American, and Jewish)," Twitty has explored the layers of his physical and spiritual identity through the history of food and culinary traditions (Weissman 2016).

In his writing and interviews, Twitty often speaks about humans' culinary memories and genetic ties to the food that defined their ancestors for generations. He doesn't shy away from heated social topics, often lecturing and writing about systemic racism, myths about the roots of soul food, cultural appropriation (taking ownership of and benefiting from other cultures' cuisines), or racially insensitive behavior. Twitty penned open letters in 2013 and 2016 to celebrity chefs Paula Deen and Sean Brock, both of whom had been in the news for controversial issues regarding race and racial heritage. In the letters, Twitty asked the chefs to engage in a dialogue with him regarding the origins and ownership of Southern cooking, as well as the importance of elevating Black cooks and chefs whose authentic contributions were overshadowed by their white peers.

Twitty was raised in Silver Spring, Maryland, where he learned the arts of cooking and storytelling from his maternal grandmother, who was a domestic worker for a Jewish family, and his mother. Despite being raised in the Christian faith, he was drawn to Judaism at the age of seven and formally converted in his twenties. He has said that he "became Jewish through food" and selected a Sephardi Mizrahi synagogue in part because of its culinary traditions as well as its more inclusive atmosphere regarding racial diversity. After the publication of his first book, Twitty embarked on a scholarly journey through the South that he called the Southern Discomfort Tour. The tour blended lectures, research into his own genealogical and cultural ancestry, cooking demonstrations, and conversations over shared meals about complex issues regarding race, history, and foodways.

Throughout his career, Twitty has acted as a historical interpreter, dressing in period clothes and demonstrating the firsthand experience of enslaved people in the South at historic sites. Using "food (as a) vehicle for interpretation," Twitty has harvested, prepared, and cooked food in the conditions his ancestors had, lecturing for groups in the process. In 2016, the living history city Colonial Williamsburg named Twitty their first Revolutionary in Residence to help bring more

Chef Michael Twitty demonstrates what cooking used to be like for enslaved African Americans in locations like this colonial-era kitchen in Williamsburg, Virginia. (Mvogel/Dreamstime.com)

"civil, interesting and innovative discourse" to the city's educational offerings (Twitty 2019; Komp 2017).

Far from simply posing as an actor or "reenactor," Twitty's work as an interpreter has entailed working 16-hour days picking cotton and preparing food for enormous crowds using nineteenth-century cooking tools, ingredients, and utensils. In 2010, he launched a collection of heirloom seeds with D. Landreth Seed Company: the result of significant research on Twitty's part to determine historical culinary staples used by African Americans, originally sourced in West Africa and the Caribbean. When not writing, the author still travels and lectures widely, residing in Maryland with his partner Taylor Keith.

DESSERT

Twitty showed a strong penchant for reading and writing at an early age; at the age of three, he loved reading from the family's dictionary. His love of words and ideas matches his love of self and others, as seen in his offers to cook while talking through differences with peers. In 2020, he told *Hadassah Magazine* about spiritual connections with shared meals: "Negative situations that I have incurred cannot and will never outweigh my positive experiences. When we are at our best, we look out for each other. You don't want any Jew to be alone. To not have a place at the seder table, a place to break the fast. In Judaism, being together is more than just community building, it is human sustaining. You are part of a family" (Sussman 2020).

SUGGESTED PAIRINGS

See also: Barbecue; Deen, Paula; Latin American Cuisine; Nonfiction, Food in.

Entry best enjoyed while eating: Black-eyed pea hummus; sweet potato biscuits baked in a cast iron skillet; West African brisket served with herbs and hot sauce; Gullah Geechee winter greens and rice; Twitty's mother's heirloom apple crisp: "the streusel topping screams Germany, but the taste screams Soul."

Further Reading

Dolsten, Josefin. 2017. "How This African-American Jew Uses Cooking to Fuse His Identities." *The Times of Israel*, June 3, 2017.

Komp, Catherine. 2017. "At Colonial Williamsburg, Culinary Historian Michael Twitty Elevates Stories of Creativity and Courage." Virginia Public Media, February 23, 2017. https://vpm.org/news/articles/2600/at-colonial-williamsburg-culinary-historian-michael-twitty-elevates-stories-of

Sussman, Adeena. 2020. "Michael Twitty's Kosher Soul." *Hadassah Magazine*, September 2020.

Twitty, Michael. 2017. *The Cooking Gene: A Journey through African American Culinary History in the Old South*. New York: Harper Collins.

Twitty, Michael. 2019. "Dear Disgruntled White Plantation Visitors, Sit Down." Afroculinaria Blog Post, August 9, 2012. https://afroculinaria.com/2019/08/09/dear-disgruntled-white-plantation-visitors-sit-down/

Weissman, Michaele. 2016. "His Paula Deen Takedown Went Viral. But This Food Scholar Isn't Done Yet." *Washington Post*, February 16, 2016.

Two Fat Ladies (1996–1999)

STARTERS

Two Fat Ladies is a documentary food show that originally aired on the BBC2 network in Britain in 1996 and ran for four seasons. The program debuted in the United States starting in 1997 via Food Network, Cooking Channel, and PBS. Its co-stars included Clarissa Dickson Wright (1947–2014) and Jennifer Paterson (1928–1999), an irreverent and humorous pair who spent each episode traversing the countryside of England in a Triumph motorcycle and sidecar, cooking and eating along the way. The show was embraced by diverse audiences across the United Kingdom, Australia, and the United States, inspiring the release of cookbooks entitled *Two Fat Ladies* (1996), *Two Fat Ladies: Gastronomic Adventures (with Motorbike and Sidecar)* and *The Two Fat Ladies Ride Again* (1998), and *Two Fat Ladies Obsessions* and *Two Fat Ladies: Full Throttle* (1999).

ENTRÉE

To understand the appeal of *Two Fat Ladies*, one must first understand the appeal of the two ladies in question: hosts Jennifer Paterson and Clarissa Dickson Wright. The latter—whose full name is Clarissa Theresa Philomena Aileen Mary Josephine Agnes Elsie Trilby Louise Esmerelda Dickson Wright—spends part of each show driving around the countryside with Patterson in a Triumph

Thunderbird motorcycle with an attached sidecar. (This may give new audiences all they need to know to understand what type of program they are dealing with.) Each 30-minute episode blends the women's comfortable banter with guests in various locations, laissez-faire cooking, copious tasting and eating, and small snippets of travelogue in the form of footage through the English, Irish, or (on one occasion) Jamaican countryside.

The show joined the growing ranks of documentary and reality competition food television shows in the mid- and late-1990s, such as *Martha Stewart Living*, *Good Eats*, *Julia and Jacques Cooking at Home*, and *Emeril Live*. During this time period, the newly formed Food Network was rapidly expanding its programming for American audiences who were developing an appetite for a wide variety of culinary themed shows. *Two Fat Ladies* offered a comedic avenue for people who enjoyed their cooking with plenty of politically incorrect and off-the-cuff dialogue. The hosts didn't shy away from their unfiltered opinions or copious amounts of carbohydrates, lard, and other cooking fats. These elements were welcome additions to some viewers who were weary of the diet-heavy, saturated-fat-adverse 1980s or leery of the picture-perfect contemporary recipes on shows like those of craft and baking doyenne Martha Stewart. In an interview, Dickson Wright shared her opinion that their show told Americans "that it's O.K. to eat red meat and cook with butter . . . I don't know why they feel they need permission."

Two Fat Ladies was conceived by British video producer Patricia Llewellyn (1967–2017), who also kick-started the television careers of British chefs Gordon Ramsay and Jamie Oliver. Llewellyn met Paterson at a party and introduced the motorcycle-driving guest to Dickson Wright, who had worked on a previous show with the producer. In an interview, Dickson Wright said the show's creators likely thought the pair would fight, "but we got on like a house on fire, and I think the sheer anarchy of that was why the series was so successful." Llewellyn's gift for casting paid off: *Two Fat Ladies* rapidly became the most popular culinary show, attracting 3.5 million viewers each week in the United Kingdom and 70 million a week internationally (Handley Macmath 2013).

Remarkably, neither Dickson Wright nor Paterson had any formal cooking experience. As a youth, Wright read recipes to help the family's illiterate cook, which helped her learn the techniques. She was the youngest barrister in the country at the age of 21. After a lengthy struggle with alcoholism, she stopped drinking and left her legal career at the age of 40. Turning toward her passion for food, she started a catering company, ran a culinary-themed bookstore, served as a cricket umpire, and became the second woman after the Queen Mother to become a Guild Butcher within London. Paterson was diagnosed with lung cancer while filming the fourth season of the show and passed away from the disease shortly thereafter. Her bawdy sense of humor and penchant for driving her motorcycle matched her spirited character in her youth: she was expelled from school at the age of 15 for being "disruptive," and she spent much of her free time "bothering (the family) cook and making horrible little pies" (Owen 1999).

In 1998, *New York Times* reviewer Suzanne Hamlin described the show as akin to watching someone's "dotty aunts" and criticized the cookbooks for producing recipes that were disastrous when Hamlin attempted to create them at home. In a cultural pushback to the prim and proper decorum of housewives of the previous generation, *Two Fat Ladies*' popularity was likely *due* to this haphazard style of cooking. Its ratings nodded to viewers' delight in watching an eccentric and unconventional duo who "delighted in skewering the pretensions of haute cuisine" and dotted their chicken carcasses in butter with wild, life-is-short abandon (Nemy 1999).

DESSERT

- **About as PC as an Apple computer:** Throughout her lifetime, Clarissa Dickson Wright was no stranger to controversy. She admitted as an adult to having researched poisonous mushrooms in her childhood as a fantasy to seek vengeance on her abusive alcoholic father. In 2007, she pled guilty to having attended an illegal dog racing event called hare coursing. She argued that she thought the event was legal, but joked to a reporter that after being caught she was "quite looking forward to going to jail in Yorkshire and writing the prison cookbook. It would have been a rest." Animal rights activists were also not thrilled with the *Two Fat Ladies*' frequent jokes about vegetarians (they "looked sallow and miserable and wore yellow shorts and sandals with socks"), penchant for driving their motorcycle with a dead animal precariously perched on their laps, or Dickson Wright's defense of eating badger meat as a snack (*The Telegraph* Staff 2014; Yardly 2014).
- **Get well soon, XOXO HRH:** When word of Jennifer Paterson's illness became public, Prince Charles sent the cook a get-well present fit for royalty: organic homemade tomato soup and vanilla ice cream. The prince had received many lunches from Paterson over the years in her roles as a cook; she once even served him ceviche with a rather unceremonious announcement of "*raw fish*, your Majesty." Her former boss from *Spectator* magazine, for whom she worked when serving the prince, told the *Los Angeles Times* that he remembered Paterson as "drunk, disorderly, quite a good cook really. I fired her once. I can't remember for what. She had this fantastic trick of not leaving. She just stayed" (Green 1999).

SUGGESTED PAIRINGS

See also: *Great British Bakeoff, The*; Pioneer Woman, The; Ramsay, Gordon.

Entry best enjoyed while eating: Bubble and squeak (fried breakfast potatoes with onions and cabbage); Scottish gigot of monkfish-tail romarin with anchovies and tomato vinaigrette; adult chocolate cake (a decadent flourless dessert made with five eggs and two sticks of butter).

Further Reading
Green, Emily. 1999. "Drunk, Disorderly, Quite a Good Cook." *Los Angeles Times*, August 18, 1999.

Handley Macmath, Terence. 2013. "Interview: Clarissa Dickson Wright Barrister, Cook, Television Presenter, Actress, Author, and Campaigner." *Church Times*, June 7, 2013.

Nemy, Enid. 1999. "Jennifer Paterson, 71, Dies; TV Cook from '*Fat Ladies*.'" *The New York Times*, August 11, 1999.

Owen, Emma. 1999. "Jennifer Paterson." *The Guardian*, Obituaries, August 11, 1999.

The Telegraph Staff. 2014. "Clarissa Dickson—Obituary." *The Telegraph*, March 17, 2014.

Yardley, William. 2014. "Clarissa Dickson Wright, Rebel TV Chef in 'Two Fat Ladies,' Dies at 66." *The New York Times*, March 18, 2014.

Unusual Food Events, International

STARTERS

When Americans think of food festivals in other countries around the world, it's likely that several major events will spring to their minds. One of which is Germany's Oktoberfest, an enormous annual celebration in Munich that draws thousands of tourists to its beer halls and German food. Another is likely Italy's PizzaFest, a yearly festival in Naples (the birthplace of the globally celebrated food) that draws top *pizzaioli* (pizza makers) from all over the globe. With a global rise in food tourism, also referred to as culinary tourism, international food festivals are becoming increasingly popular for American tourists. While many of these food festivals and other food-related events are considered somewhat serious and sophisticated in nature, many rival a number of American festivals in the categories of quirkiness and lack of decorum. Despite their lighthearted nature, many (if not most) of these unusual international food festivals have deep roots in ancient history and tap into stories, values, and traditions that are deeply woven into each region's culture.

ENTRÉE

Europe is no stranger to food celebrations, many of which date back to ancient times. Each year, many food tourists flock to Italy with serious intentions to sample or study its centuries-old cuisine and wine, but events like Ivrea's Battle of the Oranges invite visitors to have a bit more fun in the culinary country's landscape. The festival, which has run for more than 200 years, reenacts a twelfth-century battle that is presumed to have been the result of an uprising against a violent marquis and the Napoleonic army. Participants wielding oranges clash on foot and in carts for a whopping three days, sometimes sustaining injuries despite wearing protective gear (onlookers wear bright red hats in an attempt to signify that they are not to be pelted). Germany, another country known for drawing visitors with food-related travel ambitions, is home to a number of whimsical events as well. One notable example is Filderkraut Fest, a boisterous celebration in Leinfelden-Echterdingen honoring pointy-topped cabbages. Filderkraut are a regional specialty there and are enjoyed in all forms, particularly *sauerkraut*, a fermented condiment closely related to German fare that originated in China (rumored to have been brought to Europe by Gengis Kahn).

Not to be outdone, France enlists various brotherhoods and orders of knights to carry out centuries-old food-related traditions. One popular festival is the Féria du

Participants hurl oranges at each other in the Battle of the Oranges, a centuries-old tradition at the annual Ivrea Carnival in Italy. (Francesco Zanon/Dreamstime.com)

Melon in the city of Cavaillon, which pays homage to a small melon in the cantaloupe family called Charentais. The melon has helped define the region as far back as the fourteenth century. In celebration of the Charentais (which even has its own Brotherhood of Knights to judge each melon and verify its authenticity), this summer festival concludes each year with a dramatic running of 100 Camargue horses through the city (Peppler 2019). At Easter, the French town of Bessiers is flooded with thousands of onlookers who watch as the Brotherhood of the Knights of the Giant Omelette cook a 15,000-egg omelette. The production is staged outdoors over a fire, using an enormous pan that is 13 feet wide and decorated with a "handle" made from a telephone pole. Numerous cooks stand around the pan pushing the egg yolks with giant wooden "spoons" that look more like giant pizza peels. The event celebrates local lore that a local innkeeper made an omelette that Napoleon Bonaparte found so delicious he ordered the town to recreate a giant-sized version for his troops.

Spain is another country with an affinity for giant food, as witnessed in its Giant Paella festivals. Paella is a quintessential Spanish dish consisting of rice, saffron, vegetables, and meats and seafood (especially chicken, clams, snails, rabbit, and shrimp) that are cooked in a large pan over an open flame. Many historians believe the dish originated in Valencia, where the celebration is held. Valencia is known for making larger-than-life quantities of paella using an enormous pan supported over a fire for crowds who will wait up to hours for their serving. The event became so popular that giant-paella festivals now take place around the country.

If Spaniards love anything as much as paella, according to their unusual festivals, it seems to be food fights. Every year on December 28th, residents of the town of Ibi reenact a mock coup called Els Enfarinats (Valencian for "the floured ones"). The centuries-old performance has roots to the New Testament, specifically the story in which King Herod called for a massacre of all infant boys in an attempt to kill the baby Jesus. In modern times, the festival has a lighter tone. People dressed in military garb (els enfarinats) take over the town, appointing a faux mayor and coming up with absurd laws that citizens must pay real fines for if the laws are violated. A battle breaks out between the floured ones and "the opposition," and everyone is pelted in clouds of flour and showers of raw egg yolks. Onlookers often become covered in the goopy batter as well, making the festival (like many others) an "attend at your own risk" event.

For tourists whose appetite for airborne food hasn't yet been satiated, additional festivals across the country offer countless additional food fight opportunities. The island of Mallorca welcomes guests to a two-week celebration every September called Festa des Vermar, which highlights the winemaking tradition that dates back thousands of years in the region. The festival includes a harvest dinner and wine-themed parade featuring giant puppets, but the primary draw for many is a competitive grape-stomping contest and a large-scale grape battle in which hundreds of people sling the fruit at each other. In the northwest Rioja region of the country, the town of Haro hosts thousands each June for its Batalla del Vino en Haro, or Haro Wine Battle.

The battle is thought to be rooted in numerous traditions. One dates back to the sixth century, in which an annual pilgrimage began to honor the patron saint of Haro in the nearby Cliffs of Bilibio. The next was a territory dispute that began between Haro and a neighboring community in the twelfth century that asked residents to plant purple flags along its territory lines each year. In the early 1700s, the procession marking the territory reportedly began flinging red wine at each other in jest. Today, revelers wearing white shirts and red bandanas hike four miles behind Haro's mayor (who leads the procession on horseback) and gather for mass along the highest point of the cliffs. Mass concludes with a massive beverage battle, thanks to the help of trucks carrying 20,000 gallons of red wine and a crowd wielding everything from buckets to squirt guns.

In the east of Spain, the 9,000-person Valencian town of Buñol hosts La Tomatina every year in late August. The tomato celebration drew upward of 50,000 visitors annually until 2013, when a ticketing system was put in place to restrict visitors to 20,000. As local lore has it, the food fight (deemed by some to be the largest in the world) stems from an event in the mid-1940s in which a fight broke out between onlookers and participants in a parade, resulting in a spontaneous food fight from a nearby vegetable stand. In the early 1950s, the event was canceled under General Francisco Franco's dictatorship due to a lack of religious significance. The townspeople of Buñol protested in 1957 by holding a faux funeral, carrying a large tomato in a coffin to signify their desire to resurrect the event (Barr 2019).

Today, the event is all in good fun and is even family friendly (a children's "mini-tomatina" is held a few hours before the adult version). The festival's rules are shaky: theoretically, the event doesn't begin until someone is brave enough to scale a tall, greased pole in the center of town, claiming a ham hanging from the top as their prize. As the event's website notes, the process may take a long time and the prize may go unclaimed, so water cannons fire to signify the official start. In the course of an hour, festivalgoers (dressed in everything from tomato-drenched clothes to swimsuits, goggles, snorkels, or just their underwear) sling 120 tons of tomatoes at each other. A firework signifies what is supposed to be the end of tomato throwing (although as any schoolteacher can attest, holding 20,000 individuals to this rule is likely challenging), and fire trucks blast the street with hoses using water from a Roman aqueduct.

Whereas many of France, Spain, and Italy's festivals entail giant portions or food fights, offbeat food festivals in the United Kingdom often focus on individual winners in humorous contests. Scotland hosts the Golden Spurtle World Porridge Making Championship, which draws people from around the world to the highland village of Carrbridge in order to compete in two categories: traditional and specialty. Traditional competitors can only use untreated oatmeal, water, and salt and are judged on the "consistency, taste and color of the porridge and on the competitor's hygiene in the cooking process." The traditional porridge is a requirement for the base of specialty dishes, which are judged on the "blending and harmony" of the porridge with any other ingredients of the cook's choosing. A junior division invites youth to compete as well. Competitors vie for the title of world champion, in addition to an award shaped like a golden *spurtle* (a wooden rod used to stir porridge). Tradition dictates that porridge-makers stir their spurtle in a clockwise motion in a superstitious effort to "keep out the devil" (Golden Spurtle 2020).

In England, foods of all shapes and sizes are thrown, tossed, rolled, and shot through straws. Many of these whimsical contests have real (or at least legendary) roots in medieval history. One example is Witcham's World Pea Shooting Championship, in which contestants shoot dried maple peas through a pea shooter toward a target 12 feet away. The peas are supplied by the event, but the pea shooters can be provided and modified by participants. The official rules state that the shooters must be fired by blowing with the mouth and "may be made of any material but must not exceed 12 inches in length and may include sighting devices (. . .) laser pointers or similar laser assisted pea shooters are not allowed in the children's competition." Funds raised from the event go toward fixing the village hall.

Another English tradition is the annual celebration of Pancake Day, held on Shrove Tuesday, the day before Lent begins. The Olney Pancake Race is thought to be the epicenter of the tradition, marking what many believe is an age-old anniversary. The tale goes that in 1445, a woman was making a pancake on Shrove Tuesday and, suddenly realizing she was late to church, raced to the service with the frying pan still in hand. A race commemorating the event is thought to go back for centuries, even taking place in the midst of England's War of the Roses (1455–1485). As with many festivals around the world, World War II put a temporary stop to the fun, but the event resumed and is still held every year. Contestants must be women and are held to requirements of racing in a skirt and head scarf,

> *Small Plates*
>
> **Slapping-Good Pancakes**
>
> England isn't the only country to celebrate Pancake Day. Shrove Tuesday, the day before Lent, is also thought of as "Pancake Day" by people in many different regions. Pope St. Gregory (540–604 CE) forbid the consumption of any animal products during Lent, which inspired many Christians to use up ingredients like butter, eggs, and milk the previous day (this is where the tradition of eating treats like king cakes on Mardi Gras comes from as well). In Russia, a widely celebrated festival called *Maslenitsa* translates loosely to Pancake Week and entails seven themed days of celebrating the ancient Slavic customs and pagan rituals to cast out winter and embrace spring. Here, Russian-style pancakes called blinis are thought to symbolize the round, warm presence of the sun.
>
> Each day of Maslenitsa has a specific theme with traditional activities. The festival has a number of unusual traditions, including:
>
> - Dancing bears
> - Organized fist-fighting and slapping contests
> - Burning a scarecrow wearing women's clothes and holding a pancake in effigy
> - Wearing braids with pancakes woven into them (thought to ward off evil spirits, this tradition was largely abandoned in the mid-1800s)
> - Creating, and then besieging, a giant ice castle
> - Riding a horse clockwise around the village
> - For sons-in-law: visiting their mothers-in-law on Wednesday (and eating pancakes)
> - For mothers-in-law: visiting their sons-in-law on Friday (and eating pancakes)

holding a frying pan and flipping a pancake at the start and finish. Winners typically flip their way to the pancake championship down the 415-yard course in just under a minute. In 1950, members of the chamber of commerce in Liberal, Kansas, learned about the event and challenged Olney to a pancake race duel, which went on to become an annual tradition as well.

The World Nettle Eating Championships in Dorset challenge contestants to gobble as much of the noxious weed as they can stand to within an hour's time limit. Tiny spikes along the plant deliver a burning sensation that can cause people's skin to turn black and their tongues to swell, but contestants can only relieve the pain by drinking water or beer. In an amusing twist of irony, the record holder is named Philip Thorne, a local who has beat his own records multiple times, devouring as much as 104 feet of stinging nettles in under an hour. This isn't the only English festival in which participants put their physical well-being on the line in competitions. Every spring, locals and visitors convene near Gloucestershire, England, for the Cooper's Hill Cheese-Rolling Competition. Despite its tame-sounding name, the race entails chasing a nine-pound wheel of cheese down a 200-yard hill that is so steep participants have to sit instead of stand at the start line.

Once the cheese is released to roll to the finish line, participants run, roll, somersault, and otherwise fling themselves down the incredibly steep hill in the quest to "catch" it (an unlikely outcome, since the cheese reaches up to 70 miles per hour).

The rolling Double Gloucester was replaced with a foam replica due to the fact that even the *cheese* risked harming spectators. The first individual who reaches the finish line, and presumably doesn't need emergency first aid upon reaching it, claims the championship title and the wheel of cheese.

Some international festivals focus on turning food into art, including Noche de Rabanos (Night of the Radishes) in Oaxaca, Mexico, and Rabechilbi (Turnip Party) in Richterswil, Switzerland. Night of the Radishes takes place on December 23 and dates back over a century to when vegetable merchants would carve whimsical sculptures out of their vegetables to attract shoppers on their way to or from church services in town. Today, hundreds line up to see artists' carvings of giant radishes that depict everything from Day of the Dead scenes to recreations

---

Small Plates

The English Art of Throwing

The following is just a sample of some of the off-the-wall food festivals in England that involve throwing food:

- The Egg-Throwing World Championship in Swaton is the most seriously organized silly food event in the country. Run by the World Egg Throwing Federation, which has worked hard (and been denied) to officially regulate the sport, the contest draws competitors who train for the event and travel from locales like New Zealand and Japan.
- The contest dates back to a fourteenth-century abbot who tossed free eggs to church parishioners. Today, two-person teams toss eggs and step further apart every time they successfully catch one without breaking it. Other events include an egg toss for youth, a static relay down a line of participants, long-distance egg launches from (participant-constructed) trebuchets, throwing eggs at a human target, and a Russian-egg-roulette, in which participants have six eggs to smash on their heads and must guess at which five are hard boiled and which one is raw.
- The World Custard Pie Throwing Championships in Coxheath look like something out of an old slapstick film. Teams of four square off against each other to throw custard pies at each other, gaining various point values depending on where their pies land on their opponents' bodies (a direct hit to the face earns the maximum points possible: six). Upward of 2,000 pies are launched in this annual summer event, all of which must be thrown with the left hand per event rules.
- The Black Pudding Throwing Championship takes place in the town of Ramsbottom and is thought to commemorate an ancient battle in 1445, the same year that the Olney Pancake Race was thought to begin. As the story goes, soldiers ran out of ammunition during a War of the Roses battle, so they resorted to throwing food from their respective regions: black pudding (made from blood sausage) and Yorkshire pudding (a baked pudding).
- As travel writer Tony Dunnell noted, "You'd think their daggers, which most bowmen carried, would have been more effective than black pudding. Or rocks. Or branches. Or pretty much anything other than blood sausage and batter."
- Today's competition consists of hurling pucks of black pudding at a tall scaffold of Yorkshire pudding. The individual who knocks down the most Yorkshire puddings is deemed the champion.

of famous works of art. The Swiss Rabechilbi entails carving of turnips similar to the American tradition of carving Jack-O-Lantern pumpkins at Halloween. The turnips are used as miniature lanterns, signifying warmth and comfort in the cold month of November. People all over town place glowing turnips in the windows of their storefronts and homes, and crowds flood the streets to see beautiful floats decorated with the flickering light of hundreds of turnips.

Asia is also no stranger to fascinating food festivals. In some countries, festivals attempt to cultivate a better understanding of cultural rituals that are at risk of extinction. One example is the Jinshan Sulphuric Fire Fishing Festival in Taiwan, which was founded in 2013 to spread awareness of and interest in the century-old tradition of fire fishing. This method, which has largely been abandoned by younger generations, entails fishing at night for sardines. The fishermen use sulfuric rocks (which are plentiful in the region) to set off a small explosion from a bamboo torch that extends away from the boat. The sardines are attracted to the light and leap from the water in frenzied droves by the thousands. Illuminated by fireballs and the outstretched arms of eager fishermen, the scene is quite a dramatic spectacle. In 2014, the Taiwanese government filed the fire fishing technique for consideration to be designated as a cultural asset.

In Lombok, Indonesia, a folk festival called Bau Nyale ("to catch sea worms") recounts the legend of Princess Mandalika, who flung her body into the sea out of despair when frenzied scores of suitors battled for her hand in marriage. As the story goes, her people rushed into the ocean to save her, but only found scores of sea worms. Today, ancient echoes of this legend lives on in the festival's parades, horse races, and reenactments of traditional combat, in tandem with modern additions like a Princess Mandalika beauty pageant, beach volleyball, and selfie competitions.

Not all food festivals are geared toward food for human consumption, such as the Monkey Buffet Festival in Lopburi, Thailand. Here, giant buffets of fresh fruits, cans of soda, eggs, and other treats are unveiled for the hundreds of long-tailed macaques that roam freely and are deemed holy by the town. Feeding the monkeys is thought to bring good fortune, and—in the case of the festival itself, which was founded in the late 1980s to draw more tourists to the area—that has literally come true. In Kushihara, Japan, unusual animals are both the cause for celebration and the food in question: black wasps, celebrated in a November festival called Hebo Matsuri. Wasps and even a species of aggressive hornet are grilled, deep-fried, chocolate-coated, and more in this celebration of a food source that is dwindling in Japan. Hunting and harvesting was important to some members of the older generations, and the festival honors this culture. The event features a competition in which people bring wasps nests they've found (the heaviest is deemed the winner), and wasp nests are sold to those interested in taking one home and cooking it.

DESSERT

- French writer Alexandre Dumas, known best for his works *The Three Musketeers* and *The Count of Monte Cristo*, was so enchanted by the Charentais melons that when the Cavaillon Library asked him to donate some of his works in 1864, he agreed to swap several hundred copies of his works for 12 Charentais melons for the rest of his life. Before his death in 1870, he had received 72 melons from the city.

- Chinchilla, Australia, hosts a melon festival that includes, among other events, watermelon skiing, in which contestants push their feet into hollowed-out melons and are pulled by a rope through a course; a foot race in which contestants must carry a watermelon as they run; and a chariot race consisting of chariots the contestants must assemble from melon packing boxes and event-supplied axles.

SUGGESTED PAIRINGS

See also: Chocolate Events and Destinations; Food and Beverage Museums, International; Unusual Food Events, U.S. (Midwest, West, and Southwest Regions); Unusual Food Events, U.S. (Southeast and Northeast Regions).

Entry best enjoyed while eating: A 2013 entry in the Golden Spurtle World Porridge Making Championship by contestant John Boa:

"Foraged Fruits of the Forest Porridge"
Ingredients:
Freshly made SCOTTISH oatmeal porridge
2 handfuls of assorted SCOTTISH Fruits of the Forest
1 tub of SCOTTISH Double Cream
1 large knob of SCOTTISH butter
A SCOTTISH amount of sugar (Boa 2013).

Further Reading

Atlas Obscura. n.d. "Food Festivals." https://www.atlasobscura.com/unique-food-drink #festivals

Barr, Sabrina. 2019. "What Is La Tomatina, How Did It Begin and Where Does It Take Place?" https://www.independent.co.uk/life-style/food-and-drink/la-tomatina-festival-spain-food-tomatoes-what-when-where-begin-history-a9080226.html

Boa, John. 2013. "Recipe: Foraged Foraged Fruits of the Forest Porridge." https://goldenspurtle.com/recipes/foraged-fruits-forest-porridge/

Chan, Melissa. 2016. "France Cooks Up a 15,000-Egg Omelette for Easter." *Time*, March 28, 2016.

Dunnell, Tony. n.d. "Black Pudding Throwing Championships." Atlas Obscura, March 29, 2020. https://www.atlasobscura.com/foods/world-black-pudding-throwing-championship

Godoy, Maria. 2013. "It's Russian Mardi Gras: Time for Pancakes, Butter and Fistfights." NPR, The Salt, March 24, 2013. https://www.npr.org/sections/thesalt/2013/03/14/174097702/its-russian-mardi-gras-bring-on-the-pancakes-and-butter

Golden Spurtle. 2020. https://goldenspurtle.com/

La Tomatina Tours. n.d. "History of Buñol, Valencia Province, Spain." https://www.latomatinatours.com/history-of-bunol.asp

Lipich, Olga. 2013. "Maslenitsa: Russians Start Celebrating Pagan Spring Festival." *Russia Beyond*, March 11, 2013. https://www.rbth.com/arts/2013/03/11/maslenitsa_russians_start_celebrating_pagan_spring_festival_23631.html

Peppler, Rebekah. 2019. "This French Melon Is Everything Cantaloupe Wishes It Could Be." *Saveur*, August 17, 2019.

Siu, Tyrone. 2016. "Keepers of the Flame: Taiwan Keeps the Art of Fire Fishing Alive." Reuters, June 27, 2016.

Unusual Food Events, U.S. (Midwest, West, and Southwest Regions)

STARTERS

Food tourism, or travel that takes place with food as a central focus, is popular from coast to coast within the United States, and around the world at large. A number of whimsical, humorous, and otherwise unusual food events draw large crowds in the Midwest, West, and Southwest regions, helping to bring tourists from afar (even abroad) to large cities and small towns alike. One notable type of food tourism found in these regions is culinary *agrotourism*, food tourism at events rooted in agricultural practices and traditions. Many of these celebrations incorporate cultural ties to each region, such as paying homage to specific foods and farms that helped shape the community and adding local flavor in the form of unusual customs, outlandish games, and the often joyful spirit of tight-knit communities.

ENTRÉE

How do you celebrate one of the largest fungi—and one of the largest single living organisms—in the world? For the citizens of Crystal Falls, Michigan, the answer is to throw a yearly bash called the Humongous Fungus Fest. Despite a dispute regarding whether a larger one has been identified in Oregon, festival organizers still tout their local "honey mushroom" as the longest continuous mushroom in the world. Experts estimate that the organism weighs in at 200,000 pounds and might be upward of 9,000 years old. The August festival entails sporting events, mushroom foraging demonstrations, tubing in a river, mushroom cook-offs, and a 100-square-foot pizza topped with—what else—mushrooms.

Michigan residents celebrate not only what goes underground, like the humongous fungus, but also what can sail over the ground. From 1974 until 2019, Eau Claire was home to the International Cherry Pit-Spitting Championship, a nod to the fact that in recent years Michigan has supplied 72 percent of domestic tart cherries. The art of cherry pit spitting contests is surprisingly detailed: contestants' height determines where their foul line will be drawn, and each individual is prohibited from having any foreign objects in their mouth or using their hands to aid with their pit spitting. Each participant receives three cherries that have been chilled to 55–60 degrees. Participants are allowed to take one minute to pop a cherry in their mouth, chew the fruit, and spit the pit as far as they can. The world record is considered to be just shy of 41 feet and 9 inches.

Another local tradition steeped in agricultural pride is Barnesville's, Minnesota, Potato Days, which celebrates the noble spud in a two-day fete. Festivalgoers compete in events like mashed potato eating contests, mashed potato sculpture-making contests (in which embellishments and thickening agents are allowed, but paint is not), a race to stack ten 100-pound bags of potatoes, and a contest to peel as many potatoes as possible in three minutes. One of the main draws is mashed potato wrestling, in which two wrestlers face off in a tarp-covered pool filled with hundreds of pounds of potato flakes and water. The event website reassures visitors that no food goes to waste in this over-the-top event due to the fact that the pool is filled with potato scraps from factory floors and expired products.

Sweets are popular in Western states, such as the Baker's Dozen Half Marathon and Relay in Hurricane, Utah. Runners compete by doing four laps of a 3.25 mile loop, passing a "sugar shack" treat station with each loop. Participants can only earn a medal if they complete the course and eat a (verified) minimum of three sugar-laden treats along the route, selecting from items like donuts, Twinkies, and cupcakes. Grand champion title of "Sugar Slayer" goes to the individual who eats the most goods. One runner (and crowned Sugar Slayer) named Rebecca wrote this experience of what it felt like trying to complete her twenty-seventh dessert and third lap: "The sugar was warping my brain and while I was searching for a descriptor like 'dizzy' or 'vertigo,' all I could come up with was 'Gepetto.' I'm clearly not doing well" (50 Half Marathons in 50 States 2013). In the neighboring state of Colorado, the residents of Manitou Springs host The Great Fruitcake Toss as a humorous wink regarding the routinely maligned Christmas holiday food. "How do you get rid of fruitcake? Just throw it as far as you can. That's what we do," the city's web page states. Participants can bring their own fruitcakes to toss (after receiving an official inspection from the Fruitcake Tech Inspect team) or "rent" a cake from the event for $1.

DESSERT

Colorado and Utah's neighbor to the south, Arizona, seems to have missed out on the sweet tooth memo, as the city of Yuma began hosting an annual Lettuce Days festival in 1998. Like a duty-bound older sister resigned to offer a healthy entertainment option, Yuma's event lineup featured "kale gating" to pump crowds up before visiting a large salad bar, enjoying live music and celebrity chef demonstrations, and learning from machinery displays and fertilizer management presentations. Somewhere along the way, Lettuce Days became rebranded as the BBQ & Brew Festival, although the city still stays true to its leafy roots with a New Year's Eve "iceberg lettuce drop" downtown at midnight.

SUGGESTED PAIRINGS

See also: Gilroy Garlic Festival; Unusual Food Events, International; Unusual Food Events, U.S. (Southeast and Northeast Regions).

Entry best enjoyed while eating: Alligator-stuffed pierogi, celebrated with a high-five from a festival character named Miss Paczki—pronounced "poonch-key"—a woman dressed like a jelly donut (Pierogi Fest, IN); Rocky Mountain oysters—deep-fried bull testicles—dunked in ranch dressing (Testy Festy, MT).

Further Reading

"Baker's Dozen Half-Marathon: Race Recap." 2013. Blog post, December 16, 2013. http://50halfmarathonsin50states.blogspot.com/2013/12/bakers-dozen-half-marathon-race-recap.html

Iron Mountain Daily News Staff. 2019. https://www.ironmountaindailynews.com/news/local-news/2019/08/humongous-fungus-fest-starts-friday/

National Agricultural Statistics Service. 2019. "Press Release." June 11, 2019. https://www.nass.usda.gov/Statistics_by_State/Idaho/Publications/Crops_Press_Releases/2019/CH06_01.pdf

Potato Days. n.d. http://www.potatodays.com

Unusual Food Events, U.S. (Southeast and Northeast Regions)

STARTERS

Food tourism, or travel that takes place with food as a central focus, is popular from coast to coast within the United States and around the world at large. A number of food events in the Southeast and Northeast regions make a name for themselves by selecting unusual, creative, and sometimes controversial foods to celebrate. Within the South, many festivals draw on deep cultural ties to the complex and fascinating history of Southern cuisines, ranging from unassuming dishes like grits, which are used to hilarious ends in South Carolina's World Grits Festival, to frog legs—a food rarely consumed outside of the Southeast and Northeast regions.

ENTRÉE

A number of wonderfully colorful and unusual food events in the United States can be found in the South. One is the World Grits Festival in Saint George, South Carolina. In 1985, the manager of a local grocery chain called Piggly Wiggly learned from numerous vendors that his small town (population of roughly 2,000) ordered a disproportionately large amount of grits. This Southern breakfast staple is a type of coarsely ground hominy, a food product made from removing the hull from dried dent corn. The three-day festival attracts an estimated 45,000 attendees. The biggest attraction is a contest called "Rolling in the Grits" in which participants are weighed, and then they lower themselves into an inflatable pool filled with 3,000 pounds' worth of grits, attempt to sop up as much as possible, and are weighed again to see how many grits they were able to absorb. In 2015, the winning contestant accumulated 66 pounds' worth of grits with her winning choice of attire: extra-large pants held up by suspenders.

In Raleigh, North Carolina, the Museum of Science hosts a free celebration of insects every year, called BugFest, where participants can dine at Cafe Insecta, which serves chef-prepared food featuring insects. Those serving fare like "antchiladas" (enchiladas topped with ants) and cricket bruschetta help educate visitors about the sustainability and health benefits of diets that incorporate insects. Two additional festivals that make many feel squeamish include Florida's Fellsmere Frog Leg Festival and West Virginia's Autumn Harvest Festival and Roadkill Cook-Off. The Frog Leg Festival was conceived in 1990 as a way to raise funds for local youth recreation. Organizers intentionally tried choosing an unusual focal point to create interest, but they did not imagine that 30 years later they would be serving 7,000 pounds of frog legs and 2,000 pounds of gator meat over a four-day festival to an estimated 80,000 participants. Popularity has been so high for the novelty fried fare that the festival has won two Guinness World Records: one for being the "Largest Frog Leg Festival in the World" and one for the "Most Frog Legs Served in the Course of One Business Day."

The Roadkill Cook-Off and Festival started just a year after Florida's frog leg festival kicked off, in 1991. "The whole thing is tongue and cheek," Ed Blackford told the BBC news in 2016. "It's a stab at what other Americans think of us West Virginians. They call us rednecks, but that can be a compliment down here. This is about having fun. It's about economic rejuvenation." Blackford resides in Marlinton, a town just shy of 1,000 people where the festival is held. The Roadkill Cook-Off draws up to an estimated 12,000 visitors each year, racking up a significant income for the town (Northcott 2016).

According to the festival's official rules, all entries must consist of at least 25 percent wild game and "must have, as their featured ingredient, any animal commonly found dead on the side of the road." West Virginia is one of about 20 states in which harvesting roadkill to eat is legal. These laws have spurred debates ranging from potential health and sustainability benefits of eating ethically sourced food to concerns about highway safety and the potential hazards of preparing and safely preparing the salvaged food. Each state's laws vary regarding whether permits and reporting the salvaged meat are required.

Another festival that requires sourcing one's own meat is the Arkansas World Champion Squirrel Cook-Off in the city of Bentonville. Every year since 2012, teams have competed for a $1000 prize for best dish featuring a minimum of 80 percent squirrel meat. Cooks' methods range from grilling, sauteing, emulsifying, deep frying, and more, whimsically referring to their meals with titles like "chickens of the tree." Festival organizer Joe Wilson was quoted saying, "To keep us somewhat grounded, I wanted to show the public that . . . we also still have the ability to cook squirrel that the festival" in response to the trending style of "high Southern cuisine" selling for higher price points in the city (Giaimo n.d.).

In a nod to the state's French heritage, Louisiana hosts an annual event called the Giant Omelette Celebration, a sister event to the Easter festival in Bessiers, France, called the Brotherhood of the Knights of the Giant Omelette. Hosted by the Confrerie D' Abbeville (a brotherhood in the city of Abbeville), participants cook a 5,000-egg Creole-style "omelette of friendship." The feast honors a legend in which Napoleon Bonaparte helped feed a poor village by ordering a local innkeeper to whip up a particularly large serving of a delicious omelet he'd served the general.

Washington, D.C., is home to one of the nation's most gut-testing athletic events: the D.C. Half and Half Marathon. The annual event takes place in November, with a course that starts at a restaurant called Ben's Chili Bowl in Arlington, Virginia. Runners loop back to Ben's and must stop halfway through their 13.1 mile race to eat potato chips and a regional meal called the "half-smoke" (half pork, half beef sausage) with chili, mustard, and onions. Once the meal is complete, runners hit the street again to complete the second leg of their race. Despite a brutally timed steep hill shortly before the finish line, a 2017 *Runner's World* article noted that "in the five-year history of the race, no one has barfed, organizers say" (Shilton).

Members of Albany, Ohio, pay homage to a fruit unknown by many in its Pawpaw Festival, which celebrates the pawpaw, a fruit grown on trees in the eastern region of the United States. The fruit has a short shelf life, making it a poor candidate for nation-wide production and sales, but is a beloved staple for many in the region. The festival hosts pawpaw-eating contests, prizes for the best pawpaw grown that season, and even a contest for pawpaw-related art. In the neighboring state of Pennsylvania, Pittsburgh's annual Picklesburgh pays tribute to the humble pickle. Pittsburgh is home to the food company Kraft Heinz. In 2019, the corporation commemorated its 150th anniversary in the city by giving out golden pickle pins reminiscent of a collector's item pin Heinz distributed during the 1893 Chicago World's Fair. Contestants flock to compete for the "Mayor of Picklesburgh," a title awarded to the individual who can drink the most pickle juice.

For those who prefer their celebrations to be of a more diminutive scale, Baltimore hosts an annual Small Foods Party. The event began in 2006 as a gathering between artist friends whose bite-sized hors d'oeuvres led to a humorous competition to see who could provide the smallest food. Today, the event is hosted by the American Visionary Art Museum, and prizes are awarded for the tiniest recreated food, most miniature meal, and most delicious tiny entry. A giant can of (miniature) corn is awarded to winners, whose prior entries have entailed dishes like dime-sized pulled pork sandwiches on tiny homemade biscuits, miniscule sub sandwiches, and "Crappy Meals," described by the festival's website as "assembly line-type performative entry in which apron-clad 'employees' distributed tiny red and yellow printed boxes filled with French fries, burgers, along with a soda cup, complete with straw and lid" (Small Foods 2020).

DESSERT

- **Beauty pageants are in the eye of the beholder:** "Do I really want my daughter to be Miss Roadkill?" Stephanie Blankenship remembers asking herself. The mother of nine-year-old Baylee Blankenship was featured in a *Washington Post* article outlining the unusual title awarded to Baylee, who competed in a 2011 beauty pageant as part of West Virginia's Roadkill Cook-Off. "In the end, (Stephanie) did," reporter John Kelly wrote, and Baylee went on to don "a blue-and-white sash embroidered with 'Little Miss Roadkill 2011,' put on a silvery tiara and took her place among a court that also included Miss Roadkill, Miss Teen Roadkill, Miss Pre-Teen Roadkill and Tiny Miss Roadkill."

- **Don't get squirreled away:** In an interview with Get Out in the Ozarks, a website dedicated to outdoor recreation in the Ozarks, World Champion Squirrel Cook-Off founder Joe Wilson admits that the idea for the annual event came from a faux pas. "I lied to some people and told them we threw a world champion squirrel cook-off, and we really didn't," Wilson was quoted as saying. "And you know what we've got now? A world champion squirrel cook-off" (Reyes 2019).

SUGGESTED PAIRINGS

See also: Bizarre Foods with Andrew Zimmern; Roadside Food Attractions; Unusual Food Events, International; Unusual Food Events, U.S. (Midwest, West, and Southwest Regions); What the Fluff?

Entry best enjoyed while eating: Fried dragonfly and sauteed mushrooms with Dijon and soy butter (Cafe Insecta, North Carolina); an RC cola with a chocolate, marshmallow, and graham cracker cookie called a Moon Pie (RC-Moonpie Festival, Bell Buckle, Tennessee); pickle-back whiskey and dill-pickle flavored gourmet fudge (Picklesburgh, Pennsylvania).

Further Reading

Frog Leg Festival Staff. n.d. "History." https://www.froglegfestival.com/history

Giaimo, Cara. n.d. "World Champion Squirrel Cook-Off." Atlas Obscura. https://www.atlasobscura.com/foods/world-champion-squirrel-cookoff

Green, Richard. 2015. "Bizarre Competition Attracts Big Crowds to the World Grits Festival." *Spectrum News*, April 17, 2015.

Kelly, John. 2011. "W.Va. Roadkill Festival: It's Very Tongue-in-Cheek." *Washington Post*, September 26, 2011.

Northcott, Charlie. 2016. "Eating Roadkill in West Virginia." *BBC News*, October 3, 2016. https://www.bbc.com/news/world-us-canada-37501036

Pittsburgh Downtown Partnership Staff. n.d. "About Picklesburgh." https://www.picklesburgh.com/about-picklesburgh/

Pocahontas County Chamber of Commerce. 2019. "Roadkill Cook-Off Registration Form." https://pccocwv.com/wp-content/uploads/Raodkill-entryandrules-2019.pdf

Reyes, Tony. 2019. "Crowd Goes Nuts Over World Championship Squirrel Cook-Off." Get Out in the Ozarks, October 3, 2019. https://www.getoutintheozarks.com/2019/10/03/video-photos-crowd-goes-nuts-over-world-championship-squirrel-cook-off/

Schilton, A.C. 2017. "Race to These Afterparties." Runner's World, https://www.runnersworld.com/races-places/g20851658/race-to-these-after-parties/?slide=9

Small Foods. 2020. "Our Story." https://www.smallfoodsparty.com/our-story

Unusual Foods

STARTERS

For many countries and cultures, foods that are deemed novel, exotic, and unusual have long provided a source of fascination, an occasional advertisement of socioeconomic status, and a source of pride. One's estimation of how "unusual" a food is may denote their lack of familiarity or comfort with a food deemed common in another culture, but some foods are globally considered oddities. Within contemporary American culture, foods and means of serving foods that are considered unusual have become increasingly popular in recent decades.

ENTRÉE

Food traditions and preferences vary significantly from country to country, making the term "unusual food" highly subjective to one's own country and culture of origin. Many American preferences for unusual, inventive, or flat-out *odd* foods can be found in the realm of specialty products, as seen in the annual Winter Fancy Food Show that showcases upward of 80,000 products from thousands of vendors. In 2020, the food show's offerings included products like milked oats, functional teas (whose makers claim will alleviate symptoms of depression), and upcycled ingredients such as brownie mix that incorporates pulp waste from tofu and soy plants. Other contemporary trends include nonfoods, such as edible ash. The tradition of using burnt material to add flavor dates back hundreds of years, but was popularized in a new light by Spanish chef Ferran Adria when he created hot jellied vegetables topped with charcoal oil. Inspired by the trend, other chefs began using things like charred leek tops, burnt hay, charred eggplant, and ash from dehydrated citrus peels (Fredrich 2012).

Other takes on nonfoods include edible gold, small servings of the precious metal in the form of thin leaves or powder as a garnish or coating. Twenty-four-karat gold leaf is often used (unsurprisingly) in haute cuisine and other high-end restaurant settings as a decoration on dishes like chocolate desserts and sushi. Gold-topped or infused dishes often run staggering price tabs, such as $40 strips of chocolate- and gold-coated bacon, and Exousia Luxury, Italian spring water infused with 24-karat gold sold in glass bottles. Touting anti-aging, cell-regenerative, and anti-anxiety properties, the water sets patrons back $24,000 for its self-purported fountain of (gold) youth.

In keeping with the theme of earthen objects, famous haute cuisine restaurants like Copenhagen, Denmark's Noma often delight high-paying customers with some form of edible dirt, often made from ground, dehydrated, or burnt ingredients such as nuts, mushrooms, barley malt, legumes, or olives. The faux dirt is often sprinkled on top of entrées or used to "plant" part of the meal in, ranging from quail eggs to radishes, in an effort toward "reminding people where food actually comes from" (Kaufman 2010). Many of these unusual foods are the creations of chefs like Adria who helped popularize *molecular gastronomy* in the 1990s and beyond, a study of the science behind food, and use those findings to improve and re-imagine creative ways in which food is sourced, cooked, and presented. This trend spurred an international craze with culinary foams made from all manner of pureed foods (typically dispensed with whipping siphons filled with nitrous oxide) or unusual ingredient combinations such as savory cheese-flavored ice cream or guacamole and sea urchin tacos.

In recent years, interest in insects as a food source has become considerably popular, particularly among environmentalists seeking alternatives to agricultural practices that harm the earth as well as livestock. The practice of eating insects ranging from ants to cockroaches, silkworms, and weevils is common all over the world, particularly across Asia and Africa. Seen as unusual in the United States, eating insects caught on in popular culture thanks in part to reality competition shows like *Fear Factor* (2001–2006) that dared competitors to down all manner of bugs. Today, insect farming is a rapidly growing domestic industry, and recipes featuring ingredients like cricket flour are becoming more common than ever. Similarly, other sources of protein rarely used in contemporary American cuisines have gained popularity in recent years, such as reindeer, rattlesnake, goat, alligator, octopus, and ostrich meats. In somewhat of a socioeconomic reversal, these dishes used to be more commonly associated with foods working and lower social classes resorted to cooking due to limited means. Today, many of these proteins come with high price tags and are sold everywhere from food trucks to chic restaurants.

An ice cream cone is topped with edible gold leaf in Japan. The country is a hot spot for unusual ice cream toppings, including small gold flakes dusted on top of milkshakes or soft serve wrapped in large leafs of edible silver. (Dpselvaggi/Dreamstime.com)

Although many "unusual" foods have become popular in the last few decades, strange food trends go back throughout American history. No-cheese cheese and partial-cheese cheese first became part of American diets when James Kraft patented the original "American cheese," still created today in the form of various cheese scraps melded together with ingredients such as salt, emulsifying agents, and artificial colors. Spray cheese, such as Cheez-Whiz brand, joins products like "sandwich slices" on the spectrum of containing minimal to no cheese ingredients. Americans took interest in the unusual texture and sculptural possibilities for gelled and congealed salads starting in the 1930s, which often entailed a strange mixture of ingredients like Jell-O, cheese, spices, and mayonnaise into gelatin molds. This helped pave the way for Americans' preference for food baked in the form of loaves and casseroles, often containing a multitude of processed and

> *Small Plates*
>
> **The 30-Million-Dollar Sandwich**
>
> Corned beef sandwiches may not be deemed an unusual food in the United States, but one certainly earned the honor of "most unusual food smuggled into space via an astronaut's pocket." In 1961, astronaut John Young (1930–2018) tucked a corned beef sandwich into his space suit right before takeoff for the Gemini 3 mission, the first two-person spacecraft mission in the United States. His copilot was Virgin "Gus" Grissom (1926–2967). The mission's dialogue was recorded via official transcript:
>
> > Grissom: What is it?
> > Young: Corn beef sandwich.
> > Grissom: Where did that come from?
> > Young: I brought it with me. Let's see how it tastes. Smells, doesn't it?
> > Grissom: Yes, it's breaking up. I'm going to stick it in my pocket.
> > Young: . . . It was a thought, anyways.
> > Grissom: Yep.
> > Young: Not a very good one.
> > Grissom: Pretty good, though, if it would just hold together.
> > Young: Want some chicken leg?
> > Grissom: No, you can handle that.
>
> The lunch-turned-prank drew the ire of the U.S. House of Representatives' Committee on Appropriation, which launched a review upon Young's return due to safety concerns. The proceedings—in which a member of Congress described the corned beef sandwich as a now $30-million sandwich (given the amount of political time and labor devoted to its discussion)—resulted in NASA's associated administrator for manned space flight promising, "We have taken steps . . . to prevent recurrence of corned-beef sandwiches in future flights." In his memoir, Young went on to lament that the sandwich didn't even have mustard or pickle. Today, a (different) corned beef sandwich encased in resin sits on display in Mitchell, Indiana's Grissom Memorial Museum, to educate the museum's visitors about the fateful launch's lunch. It was one small step for man, but one giant leap for . . . corned beef (Spacelog Gemini 3 1965; Howell 2018).

artificial ingredients. In the 1980s, trends like "astronaut food" (freeze-dried ice cream and Tang drinks) tricked the nation's youth into thinking that astronauts were eating the ice cream, which actually wasn't favored by astronauts and posed a safety threat due to its crumbly texture. From the 1980s through the 2000s, a trend of deep-fried foods found at summer fair grounds plunged into highly unusual food territory with treats such as deep-fried butter, deep-fried Oreo cookies, and deep-fried Coca-Cola.

SUGGESTED PAIRINGS

See also: *Bizarre Foods with Andrew Zimmern*; Trends, Food; Unusual Food Events, U.S. (Midwest, West, and Southwest Regions); Unusual Food Events, U.S. (Southeast and Northeast Regions).

Entry best enjoyed while eating: "Diamond and gold lasagna" made with white diamond truffles, Kobe beef, iberico ham, Buffalo mozzarella, foie gras, and edible gold leaf

(Mirage Hotel and Casino, Las Vegas, Nevada; $100 per slice); deep-fried peanut butter, jelly, and banana sandwich (2015 Texas State Fair winner).

Further Reading

Fredrich, Lori. 2012. "Burn, Baby, Burn: Edible Ash Rounds Out Restaurant Flavors." *On Milwaukee*, September 19, 2012. https://onmilwaukee.com/articles/edibleash

Howell, Elizabeth. 2018. "How John Young Smuggled a Corned-Beef Sandwich into Space." https://www.space.com/39341-john-young-smuggled-corned-beef-space.html

Kaufman, David. "Will Edible Dirt Make You Clean Your Plate?" http://content.time.com/time/magazine/article/0,9171,2019612,00.html

Spacelog Gemini 3. 1965. "Phase 3: Gemini Orbit." Transcript, April 1965. http://gemini3.spacelog.org/original/46/

Strassberg, Rebecca. 2013. "The History of Deep-Frying Foods at Fairs." Thrillist, June 17, 2013. https://www.thrillist.com/eat/nation/the-history-of-deep-frying-food-at-fairs

Websites, Food

STARTERS

Websites devoted to food, beverages, cooking, and the culinary industry at large date back to the earliest websites, as we now know them as, in 1991. Over the nearly three decades that followed, countless websites have been built in the form of recipe sites, cooking and restaurant forums, food-specific personal blogs, and journalism and features sites similar to (or as supplements to) print forms of magazines and newspapers. Culinary websites have helped cement food's place in pop culture, spreading topics like food-related trends, gossip, and new recipes in live time around the world. Today, renowned institutions like the James Beard Foundation and the International Association of Culinary Professionals have award categories for things like best food blogs, best digital media, and best writing in both print and digital arenas.

Most celebrity chefs, culinary institutes, and other culinary people in the public eye have professional or personal web pages of their own, in addition to actively maintaining social media accounts on Twitter, Instagram, YouTube, and Facebook. Web apps, tech companies, and websites have also proliferated to meet consumer demand for grocery and meal delivery services, food reviews, and food-centric social media outlets. Additionally, video-sharing site YouTube has an entire section of cooking channels, ranging from those professionally produced by Food Network to amateur cooks who film low-budget tutorials out of their own homes. Some YouTube cooking stars have reached enough notoriety to rival their television celebrity counterparts.

ENTRÉE

Food websites—or at least food *on* websites—trace back to the earliest pages on the web, making a strong case for the argument that food is one of the most universal themes in pop culture. ACME Laboratories started offering free online software in 1991, including a link to a "chocolate registry" detailing the specific location and chocolate preferences of each individual who has filled out the form. In 1991, the first webcam was devoted to one of America's most ubiquitous beverages: office coffee. The University of Cambridge set up a live webcam aimed at the coffeepot to help employees time their trek to the often-used pot when it wasn't empty. In 1998, the then-infamous Trojan Room coffeepot webcam surpassed 2 million views. By 2001 the webcam—which was referred to as a "historical item" by some—received front-page press by both the *London Times* and

Washington Post in anticipation of temporarily being turned off to facilitate a computer lab move.

In another story conjoined by Americans' love of caffeine, the nation's first *IoT* device (which monitors physical devices via internet) was a Coke machine on the Carnegie Mellon University campus. In the 1980s, several computer science students installed computer components that let them gauge if the machine was well stocked and whether the bottles would be cold enough for their liking. In 1994, another computer programmer named Dan Bornstein registered the domain milk.com, inspired by a nickname he received due to his affinity for milk drinks. Today, the domain name's estimated value is roughly $10 million thanks to the number of dairy companies that would like to use it for their own marketing purposes (McFadden 2017). Bornstein's page isn't specific to the dairy industry; instead, it houses his miscellaneous photos, recipes he likes for dishes like potato kugel, and a FAQ page in which every question is answered with the word "moo."

One of the earliest food websites is known today as Epicurious, launched in 1995 by Condé Nast to provide internet content for the web's early users. Today, the content is merged with other Condé Nast brands such as *Bon Appetit* magazine, offering more than 300,000 recipes as well as articles and instructional videos. Another early website was Chowhound, founded in 1997 as a forum where users swapped information about places to find good food. The site was later purchased by CNET and CBS and merged with a print magazine called *Chow*. It continues to host regional cuisine forums, as well as menu planning, coupons, recipes, tutorials, and food news.

Similar popular online communities include Food52, which originated in 2009 with the theme of offering recipes for all 52 weeks of the year. The site hosts a large number of recipes that readers contribute to and a "hotline" section where readers can ask for help on subjects ranging from recipe substitutions to kitchen storage. Serious Eats was founded in 2006 by Ed Levine, a food author and *New York Times* food contributor. The venture grew from a food blog into a broad website offering research-backed instructional techniques, recipes, and equipment reviews. Many contemporary food websites are targeted toward millennials, such as Genius Kitchen, founded in 1999 and rebranded in recent years to target the site's food videos and hundreds of thousands of recipes toward younger viewers (Spangler 2017).

A large number of print and radio news and magazine outlets have also developed websites to supplement or duplicate their food-related print offerings. National Public Radio's website features a blog called The Salt, which publishes features and news stories ranging from the history of food to culinary pop culture news. The *New York Times* Cooking site is a subscription page that's described as a "digital cookbook and cooking guide alike." Popular food and beverage magazines like *Bon Appetit* and *Food & Wine* offer substantial websites with articles, essays, videos, and recipes. Subscription packages offer print magazine and digital access to keep up with the numerous ways in which today's cooks consume media. Culinary education is also widely available online. Degrees and certificates are available through avenues like Le Cordon Bleu's online Culinary

Management bachelor of arts degree or the International Sommelier Guild's sommelier certification. Classes for aspiring professionals and hobby enthusiasts are offered through a large number of websites, such as online video courses taught by celebrity chefs Gordon Ramsay, Rick Bayless, and Curtis Stone via "EduTech" companies MasterClass and Bluprint.

ACCOMPANIED BY

Blogs

The term "blog" comes from "web log," a phrase attributed to Jorn Barger. The early blog pioneer self-published his own writing on the internet starting in 1995 and referred to his practice as logging the things he found on the web. In 1999, web designer Peter Merholz was attributed with the abbreviated term "blog," and the same year, food blogs began gaining traction on the internet. Writers like David Leibowitz took to the web to share recipes and food anecdotes, and food forums like eGullet (started by food writers Steven Shaw and Jason Perlow) and Chowhound (started in 1997 by Jim Leff and Bob Okumura) served as places for food enthusiasts to trade notes and share restaurant suggestions. In 2002, food writers like Regina Schrambling of Gastropoda and Julie Powell of the Julie/Julia Project joined the ranks of early food writers on the web. Powell's blog documented a self-imposed challenge of making Julia Child's 536 recipes from *Mastering the Art of French Cooking* in a year. The effort attracted significant media attention and inspired a book that was later adapted for a film called *Julie & Julia* (2009), directed by Nora Ephron.

In 2002 and 2003, do-it-yourself blogging software Blogger and Wordpress came on the market, which made blogging widely available for amateur and professional writers alike. These platforms were used by writers like Elise Bauer, who founded the blog Simply Recipes in 2003 as a way to track the recipes she was learning to cook. Over the next 10 years, Bauer's site received millions of monthly page views, and in 2016, it was acquired by Fexy Media corporation.

Over the next decade and a half, food blogs exploded in popularity. Writers attracted readership using a wide range of styles and cuisines. Bloggers like Kristin Porter of Iowa Girl Eats appeals to home cooks seeking easy family meals and step-by-step tutorials, and Deb Perelman has attracted millions of readers through her chic website Smitten Kitchen, where lighthearted daily life is captured in a chic format reminiscent of upscale cookbooks. Some blogs serve as modern alternatives to once-popular Zagat guides. One example is kevinEats by blogger Kevin Hsu, who writes straightforward restaurant reviews including a photo, description, and price of every dish. Niche pop culture food websites also abound, such as Film and Food, which offers recipes and cinematic commentary inspired by various films, as well as essays on sites like Refinery29, entitled "I Logged Everything Rory & Lorelai Ever Ate On *Gilmore Girls*," in which writer Olivia Harrison logged every instance of food documented in the television show's seven seasons.

DESSERT

One deliciously simple food shown on the internet is a YouTube cooking series called "Cooking with Dog" that launched in 2007. The show features an unnamed Japanese female host who simply goes by "Chef," and her loyal companion Francis, a toy poodle. Chef's step-by-step instructions are narrated in English by a male who pretends to lend the voice of Francis, complete with a French accent. In 2016, Francis passed away just shy of his 15th birthday, prompting many of the show's 1.25 million followers to share an outpouring of affection for the canine cook on social media.

SUGGESTED PAIRINGS

See also: America's Test Kitchen; Culinary Awards, The Evolution of; Magazines, Food; Pioneer Woman, The.

Entry best enjoyed while eating: Seriously seared steak cooked with a patent-pending blowtorch "Searzall" created by food science blogger Dave Arnold (Cooking Issues); Persian herb frittata *kuku subzi*, blogged about by chef and food writer Ruth Reichl; *Aam Ki Dal*, Toor Dal with raw mango (YouTube's Manjula's Kitchen); and pecan pie, which Delish reports was the number-one most Googled recipe of 2018.

Further Reading

McFadden, Christopher. 2017. https://interestingengineering.com/top-12-oldest-websites-from-the-80s-and-90s-still-online-today

Spangler, Todd. 2017. "Scripps Networks Launches 'Genius Kitchen' Online Food Network, Folding Food.com Recipes into the Mix." https://variety.com/2017/digital/news/scripps-networks-genius-kitchen-food-com-1202563297/

Stafford-Fraser, Quentin. n.d. "The Story of the Trojan Room Coffee Pot: A Timeline." https://www.cl.cam.ac.uk/coffee/qsf/timeline.html

Suthivarakom, Ganda. 2011. "A Brief History of Food Blogs." Saveur, May 8, 2011. https://www.saveur.com/article/Kitchen/A-Brief-Food-Blog-Timeline#page-11

Teicher, Jordan. 2018. "The Little-Known Story of the First IoT Device." IBM, February 7, 2018. https://www.ibm.com/blogs/industries/little-known-story-first-iot-device/

Weigl, Andrea. 2013. "Loss Leads Author to Share." *Times Union*, May 1, 2013. https://www.timesunion.com/living/article/Loss-leads-author-to-share-4479845.php

What the Fluff?

STARTERS

What the Fluff is an annual festival in Somerville, Massachusetts, that celebrates Fluff, a marshmallow condiment spread made by Lynn, Massachusetts' company Durkee-Mower, Inc. Proceeds from the day-long celebration benefit economic development and historical preservation within the Union Square neighborhood in which it's held. The free festival advertises its commitment toward inclusivity toward people of all ages and demographics and "salutes the spirit of innovation" in the community. What the Fluff embodies a spirit of fun through costumes, humorous contests, music, demonstrations, craft stations, food, merchandise, games, art, and more. An estimated 20,000 people from the Greater Boston area and beyond visit the Fluff festival every year, aided by the work of more than 100 volunteers.

ENTRÉE

Marshmallow Fluff is over 100 years old, and Fluffernutter sandwiches (marshmallow spread and peanut butter typically sandwiched between two slices of Wonderbread) have been a familiar word in the American lexicon since the 1960s, thanks to a Fluff public relation campaign. Although the sweet condiment is sold nationwide, Fluff is particularly embraced along the East coast: 50 percent of all sales take place in upstate New York and New England. In 2017, 23 people were employed at the Durkee-Mower manufacturer, generating an estimated 7 million pounds of Fluff that are sold each year (Cusachs 2017).

Each September since 2006, crowds have descended upon the Somerville Union Station neighborhood to celebrate this wholesome, nostalgic, classic American food. The festival, much like the food itself, is whimsical in nature. Over the years, it has grown from a more modest affair to the current setup of four event stages and 75 vendors. Attendees can choose from a lengthy list of activity options, including Fluff Jousting, in which two people dip foam pool noodles (long floatation devices made of foam) in Fluff and face off on a balance beam, whacking each other in an attempt to knock their opponent over. In the Fluff Lick-Off, contestants gobble piles of Fluff off large plexiglass squares, and Blind Man's Fluff entails attempting to feed Fluffernutter sandwiches to a partner while blindfolded. Another humorous (and messy) affair is the Fluff Hair-Do Contest, in which participants and a partner style their hair (including beards) in outrageous sticky styles.

Fluff cook-offs ask competitors to flex their creative skills, pairing the marshmallow creme with unusual ingredients to make dishes like Fluff baklava and Fluff pierogis. After judges taste each entry, the Somerville mayor crowns the winners. Some vendors and visitors dress up in character, such as frequent appearances of characters from *The Ghostbusters*, based on a 1984 film's iconic scene in which a giant paranormal Stay Puft Marshmallow character explodes, spraying marshmallow goop all over Times Square in New York City. Eater writer Whitney Filloon notes that in pop culture, fluffernutter sandwiches have occasionally been written into television scripts as a character development tool to indicate childlike facets of adults. For an empty-calorie snack consisting of merely corn syrup, sugar, dried egg white, and vanilla—the process of how they're combined is a mystery—Fluff continues to inspire wholesome fun for all generations.

ACCOMPANIED BY

Joseph Archibald Query is credited by many with inventing Fluff. Query was an Irish immigrant who had to establish citizenship in Canada and change his surname before gaining entry to the United States. Query was Somerset door-to-door salesman who sold his homemade Fluff in 1917, but lost business due to supply shortages during World War I. He sold his formula for $500 to H. Allen Durkee and Fred L. Mower, owners of a local fledgling candy factory that would become the Fluff supplier for the nation. Durkee-Mower sponsored a music and comedy radio show called the Flufferettes, which went on to help launch a number of careers in the entertainment industry.

For fans of sweets, early 1900s-era Massachusetts was the time and the place to be. A few years before Query sold his formula, great-great-great-grandchildren of Paul Revere and brother-and-sister duo Emma and Amory Curtis of Melrose, Massachusetts, were marketing a product called Snowflake Marshmallow Creme. Like Fluff, Marshmallow Creme was wildly popular throughout New England. During World War I, Emma published a recipe for a treat called the "Liberty Sandwich," considered to be the first fluffernutter sandwich. In modern times, Query is impersonated at the festival each year by enthusiastic Fluff superfan Michael Katz, a local resident and theater professor. The festival exists thanks to Mimi Graney, who founded the event in 2006 and wrote a nonfiction history work entitled *Fluff: The Sticky Sweet Story of an American Icon* (2017) celebrating the confection's 100th anniversary.

DESSERT

- **Got milk?** In 2006, upon discovering the fact that his son was being served Fluffernutter sandwiches at school, Massachusetts Senator Jarret T. Barrios announced his intention to file an amendment that would restrict how many of the sandwiches could be served each week. Barrios underestimated the state's love of Fluff, as legislators responded with an attempt to name Fluffernutter the official state sandwich. Barrios retracted his proposal.
- **Star power:** Fluff is so beloved by some that it has even been packed away as essential food items for multiple astronauts aboard the International Space Station. Astronaut and Massachusetts native Richard Linehan enjoyed Fluffernutter on the Endeavor mission in 2008, and in 2012, astronaut Sunita Williams requested that a jar of Fluff be on board as a special treat that reminded her of her childhood.
- **Parlay vew Frahn says?** Durkee and Mower initially considered giving their sweet treat a French pun for a name, but "Toot Sweet" failed to launch. The product has actual French roots: the original marshmallow creme was invented by French pharmacists to be used as—curiously enough—a sore throat remedy (blech).

SUGGESTED PAIRINGS

See also: Cake and Cupcake Trends; Ice Cream Trends; International Horseradish Festival; Unusual Food Events, U.S. (Midwest, West, and Southwest Regions); Unusual Food Events, U.S. (Southeast and Northeast Regions).

Entry best enjoyed while eating: An empanada made with guava, chorizo sausage, and Fluff; Rice Krispy Treats (rice crisp cereal baked into bars with butter and marshmallow Fluff); a Fluff margarita in a glass lined with Fluff in lieu of salt; and a cup of warm water, which is one's best defense in removing Fluff from unwanted surfaces.

Further Reading

Cusachs, Cathleen. 2017. "Here's Lookin' at You, Fluff." *Boston Globe*, September 15 2017.

Filloon, Whitney. 2017. "The Sweet, Gooey History of Marshmallow Fluff." Eater, February 9, 2017. https://www.eater.com/2017/2/9/14551084/marshmallow-fluff-history

Melrose Mirror Staff. n.d. "The Revolutionary Roots of the Fluffernutter Sandwich." The New England Historical Society, originally published in the *Melrose Mirror*. https://www.newenglandhistoricalsociety.com/revolutionary-roots-fluffernutter-sandwich/

Slane, Kevin. 2019. "What the Fluff?: Your Guide to This Weekend's Sweet and Sticky Somerville Fluff Festival." Boston, September 20, 2019. https://www.boston.com/culture/food/2019/09/20/what-the-fluff-your-guide-to-this-weekends-sweet-and-sticky-somerville-fluff-festival

Wine and Spirits

STARTERS

Wine and spirits have been a significant part of countless cultures around the globe dating back to ancient times. Liquor fads through the decades indicate significant clues about what was happening in various societies, such as the community's level of prosperity (or lack thereof), the status of new international trade deals or embargos, diet and health trends, and people's reactions to traumatic and celebratory events, alike. In the twentieth and twenty-first centuries, wine and liquor trends have been reflected in—and often driven *by*—popular films and radio and television shows. Many alcoholic beverage trends that evolved from the scarcity of high-quality (and legal) ingredients in the 1920s and 1930s have come into vogue again 100 years later, illustrating the cyclic nature of fads and crazes.

ENTRÉE

The earliest known form of wine goes back at least 8,000 years, based on the discovery of Neolithic earthen jars that contained traces of wine compounds in the European city of Tbilisi, Georgia. Tales about wine can be found in ancient Persian mythology and in the mythologies of ancient Greece and Rome. Numerous biblical passages warned against heavy drinking and intoxication, such as a description in the Book of Genesis about Noah planting a vineyard as his first post-flood order of business and subsequently getting intoxicated upon his first sampling. Wine and its related pitfalls and virtues were central to the ancient mythologies of the Greek, Roman, and Italian gods of wine: Dionysus, Bacchus, and Liber. These figures, and the debaucherous festivals devoted to them, were widely heralded in their communities.

Wine was also highly valued by the ancient Egyptians. Archaeologists found sealed jars of wine in Egyptian tombs, including Tutankhamun's (c.1341–1324 BCE), that had labels similar to those used on wine bottles today. The labels included the region, style, and year in which the wine was produced, as well as its quality. Before Mount Vesuvius erupted and destroyed Pompeii in 79 CE, the

Old-fashioned cocktails—made from a mixture of whiskey, bitters, sugar, and citrus—are enjoying a skyrocketing resurgence of popularity in the 2000s, despite having been available in American bars for close to 200 years. (Bhofack2/Dreamstime.com)

ancient Roman city served as the empire's wine port. Archaeologists have determined from the well-preserved ruins that wealthy families in the region seemed to cultivate private vineyards as a status symbol, much as people do today, and 120 different sites have been excavated that are believed to have been Pompeiian bars (Clarke 2015).

Fast-forward a couple of thousand years, and wine is still deeply prized around the world, central to countless religious ceremonies and cultural rites of passage. In contrast to these ancient roots, America's broad public appreciation for liquor was largely fueled by an unlikely event: Prohibition. This era began with the ratification of the Eighteenth Amendment, which outlawed the "manufacture, sale, or transportation of intoxicating liquors" and the passing of the Volstead Act in 1919. Between 1920 and the ratification of the Twenty-First Amendment in 1933, which nullified the restrictions, significant shifts took place within the American alcohol industry and drinking culture. Historian Daniel Okrent has written about profound changes that occurred during Prohibition, such as the galvanization of political activism, significant improvements in social relationships between men and women, and political party realignments (2010).

Driven primarily by religious groups and women, Prohibition extolled the virtues of sobriety. Many of its supporters sought to end the abusive behavior of men who drank heavily at saloons spanning from the Western frontier to the city streets of New York. The implementation of Prohibition caused new societal ills, most notably the rise of organized crime. Across the nations, *speakeasies* (illicit, underground establishments that served alcohol) provided places to secretly drink alcohol, listen to live music, and mingle. Those responsible for making and selling cheap, illegal alcohol—referred to as *bootleggers*—financially benefited from a widespread, corrupt network of low-quality alcohol production. Americans' insatiable appetite for both alcohol and rule-bending led to a different type of violence, such as the ruthless rule of mob boss Al Capone (1899–1947).

Prior to 1919, distilled spirits only accounted for 40 percent of the alcohol consumed in America, but by the end of Prohibition, spirits accounted for 75 percent or more of alcohol sales (Miller 2020). Bootleg alcohol in this era, often referred to as *moonshine* or *bathtub gin*, was of as nauseatingly low quality as one could imagine. These spirits were often made from industrialized alcohol that was used for commercial products like ink and perfume. Because this alcohol wasn't intended for human consumption, it had to be *denatured* (treated with toxic chemicals) and then modified again with some semblance of flavor to make it ingestible. Bootleggers attempted to recreate the unusual and complex flavors of bourbon, gin, and other spirits by adding gruesome ingredients such as dead rats and creosote. Many of these ghastly concoctions were also masked with flavors from fruit juice and syrups, which is how mixed drinks called *cocktails* were first invented.

With this history in mind, there is no shortage of irony that 100 years later, cocktail culture is heralded in the United States as chic, hip, and often glamorous. Entirely legal "speakeasies" dot a large number of American cities, many of which sport Art Deco interior decor, dim lighting, theatrically designed "secret entrances," and word-of-mouth advertising to give the establishments the allure of faux secrecy. In a far cry from the 1920s' cheap drinks made from ingredients like altered campfire fuel, today's cocktails often boast adjectives like "organic," "sustainable," and "foraged" and can cost as much as diners' entrées at upscale restaurants.

The entertainment industry has also played an enormous role in spirits' booming popularity. The AMC period drama *Mad Men* (2007–2015) centered around the martini-swilling, brandy-snifter-obsessed Manhattan ad agency culture of the 1960s and 1970s. The show inspired many fans to dress in period attire and served vintage drinks at viewing parties. Throughout the 2000s, Americans' romanticized views of the 1960s and the Roaring Twenties brought classic cocktails like old-fashioneds (whiskey, bitters, sugar, citrus) and perfect martinis (gin, equal parts sweet and dry vermouth, and lemon peel or olive garnish) back into staggering vogue.

Fads from the 1950s are also still prevalent today, such as the frozen "tiki" drinks invented by Hawaii bartender Harry Yee, garnished with maraschino cherries and miniature umbrellas. Vintage-era brunch cocktails like Bloody Marys, Bellinis, and mimosas have also seen tremendous popularity in the 2000s. These drinks originated in Paris in the 1920s and caught on in the United States in the years following Prohibition. By the 1970s, these brightly colored brunch beverages helped sway public opinion that drinking during the day was not a hedonistic practice. In recent years, Bloody Mary drinks (a blend of vodka, tomato juice, horseradish, lemon, and any number of outrageous garnishes) have even inspired scores of Bloody Mary festivals and contests nationwide.

Over the last century, wine and spirits have gained the reputation of almost being recurring characters in and of themselves in various radio programs, television shows, and films. In 1934, the film adaptation of Dashiell Hammett's novel *Thin Man* provided a martini-soaked film noir in which the characters, played by Myrna Loy and William Powell, "drink cocktails day and night and solve crimes at their leisure." In addition to murder mystery mayhem, the story also served as a way for viewers to thumb their noses at the Volstead Act during Prohibition, and the drinking scenes artfully shed light on "some of the social issues of the time—including the country's class hierarchy and the women's lib movement" (Archibald 2019).

In the 1980s, bartenders began infusing more craft into their trade, helping to usher in a decade of audiences' affection for bartender and pub patron protagonists. Kitschy "tropical drinks" also saw a boom in this decade, thanks in part to episodes of *Miami Vice* (1984–1990) and Rupert Holmes' chart-topping song "Escape" (commonly referred to as the Piña Colada Song) in 1979. Episodes of *Cheers* (1982–1993), a wildly popular sitcom on NBC, were primarily based within the confines of a neighborhood bar. The 1988 film *Cocktail*—which starred Tom Cruise as a bartender who theatrically juggled bottles, shakers, and glasses as he served—achieved a cult following despite being largely excoriated by critics.

Shows in the 1990s and early aughts also made major waves in the bar industry, particularly the HBO series *Sex and The City* (1998–2004), which elevated the bright pink retro cosmopolitan cocktail to global heights. *Observer* writer Sage Lazzaro noted "the *Sex and the City* induced Cosmo craze is perhaps the greatest example of pop culture's influence on cocktails to date." In the 2000s, Chardonnay was featured in the romantic comedy *Bridget Jones* (2001), in which actress Renee Zellweger drank her single-woman blues away straight from the bottle. Wine critic Oz Clarke blamed a dramatic drop in British sales of Chardonnay in 2008 on the film, saying the uncool character Bridget Jones made consumers turn away from a wine that had previously been considered "sexy." (Others have refuted Clarke's claim, citing the steep drop in sales on changing palates and droughts in Australia's wine country.) Wine and spirits also played a central theme in HBO's long-running series *The Sopranos* (1999–2007), delighting wine aficionados who weighed in on internet forums, debating the labels and symbolic significance of various bottles of red wine they spotted throughout each episode.

In current popular culture, domestic distilleries are gaining significant popularity, and classic cocktails still dominate the most popular liquor drinks, nodding to Americans' affection for cocktail culture of bygone eras. Many celebrity actors and musicians have contributed to America's ever-growing adoration of spirits by venturing into the liquor business as a side or full-time career. Some examples include actors Matthew McConaughey, creative director of Wild Turkey Longbranch, a bourbon company; Dan Aykroyd, cofounder of Crystal Head Vodka (filtered over crystals and bottled in glass shaped like skulls); and Ryan Reynolds, owner of Aviation Gin company. In 2017, actor George Clooney sold the tequila company for a billion dollars. Numerous musicians and athletes have also found prosperous partnerships in the spirits industry.

In the spirits industry, gimmicky trends are also gaining popularity, such as elaborate drinking cups in the form of snowglobes, oversized and sculptural ice

> **Small Plates**
>
> **The Sounds of Spirits**
>
> Songs about Americans' love of wine and spirits have permeated the radio for nearly a century. Many of them have boosted sales for various types of alcohol, and in recent decades, song lyrics about specific brands have served as product placements for brands. In the 1990s, hip-hop musicians from the Wu-Tang Clan group as well as Jay-Z (Shawn Carter), The Notorious B.I.G. (Christopher Wallace) and P. Diddy (Sean Combs) thrust Cristal champagne into the spotlight. The expensive brand was portrayed as part of a lavish rapper lifestyle, which many fans wanted to emulate. Shortly after endorsing the $300-a-bottle product, Jay-Z withdrew his endorsement, citing a Cristal executive's comments that the hip-hop industry's interest in the drink was "unwelcome," which the rapper described as racist.
>
> Many other artists have been closely associated with the drinks mentioned in their songs, such as singer/songwriter Rupert Holmes, who penned the 1979 pop song "Escape (The Piña Colada Song)." Holmes—who had never tried a Piña Colada before and swapped out a line about "Humphrey Bogart" with the infamous Piña Colada lyric mere *moments* before recording the song—would see the song top the Billboard chart as the number one song in 1979 and 1980. Many songs in the Country genre have also been wildly popular, such as Jimmy Buffett's 1977 "Margaritaville" and Garth Brooks' 1990 whiskey- and champagne-themed "Friends in Low Places."
>
> Rapper Snoop Dogg's song "Gin and Juice" reached Billboard 100's number eight spot in 1994 and has been covered by numerous artists worldwide. Not to be left out, wine-themed songs have also topped the charts over the years, such as UB40's "Red Red Wine" (1983), Carrie Underwood's "Wine after Whiskey" (2012), Billy Idol's "Scenes from an Italian Restaurant" (1977), and Deana Carter's "Strawberry Wine" (1996).

cubes, and fruit-flavored alcoholic seltzer. Highbrow trends like highly expensive drinks with foraged, handmade ingredients are met with equally lowbrow trends, like a Taco Bell limited release of a red wine in Canada dubbed Jalapeño Noir. While cocktail culture has waxed and waned over the years, America's 50-plus-year love affair with wine culture has remained a cultural staple. As *Wine Spectator* Harvey Steiman notes, baby boomers "came of age along with wine (culture) in the U.S.," Generation X sought out emerging international regions, and millennials will help shape future changes in how we buy, market, and sell wine.

DESSERT

- **Trying her signature drink:** Actress Sarah Jessica Parker has gained a decades-old association with Cosmopolitan cocktails due to her character's affinity for drinking a veritable gallon of them over the course of many episodes in *Sex and the City*. In 2014, 10 years after the show had gone off the air, Parker admitted to *Vanity Fair* magazine that she'd only recently ordered her first one in real life. "I'm not a drinker, so I don't know what else to order," she told the magazine, "but it was delicious" (Marcus 2014).

- **This is Brooklyn:** At Aska, an upscale Scandinavian restaurant in Brooklyn, New York's hipster-teeming Williamsburg neighborhood, the foraged cocktail trend has been taken to new heights. One of the restaurant's managers described their process for making an in-house drink Decanter Bitters to *First We Feast*, saying, "We took a little gathering trip and found a great collection of birch saplings (. . .). After our giant Swedish cook Sebastian pulverized them with a sledgehammer, we infused it into whiskey—this *is* Brooklyn—and softened it with molasses."

SUGGESTED PAIRINGS

See also: Child, Julia; Coffee Culture; Craft Brewing and Microbreweries; *Galloping Gourmet, The*; Novelty Dining Experiences.

Entry best enjoyed while drinking: Vault Bar "Tapache Shakur" (Fayetteville, Arkansas): cognac, Jägermeister; house-made *tepache* (fermented beverage made from cinnamon-seasoned pineapple rind): barrel-aged carrot and citrus juices, orgeat, and egg, topped with carrot ash; a Moscow Mule: vodka, ginger beer, and lime over ice, served in a copper mug; a Bloody Mary served with a full-sized club sandwich on top as a "garnish"; and a Baby Yodaiq: a frozen daiquiri decorated to look like the *Star Wars* character Yoda using lime-wedge ears, cherry eyes, and a cocktail napkin wrapped around the stem of the glass for a makeshift futuristic robe.

Further Reading

Akkam, Alia. 2013. "10 Cocktail Trends You Need to Know." *First We Feast*, February 25, 2013. https://firstwefeast.com/drink/2013/02/10-cocktail-trends-you-need-to-know/

Archibald, Annie. 2019. "Martinis & Wit: The Thin Man's Enduring Effect on Cocktail Culture." *Daily Beast*, July 30, 2019. https://www.thedailybeast.com/dashiell-hammetts-the-thin-man-had-an-enduring-effect-on-cocktail-culture

BBC Staff. 2017. "World's Oldest Wine Found in 8,000-Year-Old Jars in Georgia." BBC News, November 13, 2017.

Clarke, Oz. 2015. *The History of Wine in 100 Bottles: From Bacchus to Bordeaux and Beyond*. New York: Sterling Epicure.

Lazarro, Sage. 2014. "Through the Decades: A Brief History of Iconic Cocktails." *Observer*, November 27, 2014.

Marcus, Bennett. 2014. "Sarah Jessica Parker Launches Fashion Line." *Vanity Fair*, February 26, 2014.

Miller, Jeffrey. 2020. "The Modern Craft Cocktail Movement Got Its Start during Prohibition." *Smithsonian*, January 15, 2019.

Okrent, Daniel. 2010. *Last Call: The Rise and Fall of Prohibition*. New York: Scribner.

Shaw, Lucy. 2008. "Bridget Jones Effect Blamed on Slump in Chardonnay Sales." *Decanter*, May 28, 2008.

Steiman, Harvey. 2016. "The Future of Wine." *Wine Spectator*, 40th Anniversary Issue. November 15, 2016.

Ternikar, Farha. *Brunch: A History.* Lanham: Rowman & Littlefield.

Worst Cooks in America (2010–)

STARTERS

Worst Cooks in America is a reality cooking television show on Food Network that has run for 20 seasons since its debut in 2010. The premise centers around a dozen or more contestants who lack cooking experience and skill. In each episode, contestants participate in an elimination-style competition modeled as an intensive introduction to culinary basics taught by renowned chefs. The cooks compete to be dubbed the "best of the worst": the most accomplished at cooking by the end of their training. Winners receive a $25,000 cash prize and the ability to cook for renowned culinary critics.

The show's popularity has led to the creation of two spin-offs: *Worst Cooks in America: Celebrity Edition*, starring television and film actors, and *Worst Bakers in America* (2016–), a competition between average Americans with dismal baking skills. Over the course of nearly 160 hour-long episodes, the hybrid reality program and game show has gained a loyal and enthusiastic audience following. The season premiere in June of 2020 was ranked as the third most popular cable program among 25- to 54-year-olds, reaching more than 3.3 million viewers nationwide (Newsbreak 2020).

ENTRÉE

Amid a landscape of television shows featuring professional chef competitions, picture-perfect meal tutorials, and celebrity cooks working out of glamorous kitchens, *Worst Cooks in America* offers viewers something else: culinary disasters. The meals created on the show span from heinous to mediocre, at best, many of which are the inventions of self-proclaimed terrible cooks. In an interview with *People* magazine, cohost Anne Burrell shared her opinion that the show's popularity is largely due to its relatability. Contestants' mistakes make for humorous television, but viewers end up rooting for the amateur cooks' successes as they work hard to improve over the course of each episode.

In addition to its humor, *Worst Cooks* also appeals to viewers for its straightforward cooking tips contestants learn in their culinary "boot camps." For many, attempting to recreate dishes like picture-perfect pies, elaborately brined turkeys, or salads with foraged ingredients on other popular cooking shows may feel too challenging, expensive, or time-consuming. For these viewers, *Worst Cooks in America* lowers the pressure audiences may feel to achieve culinary perfection by featuring contestants who are probably even worse at cooking than home viewers. In the process, they get to enjoy the slapstick of people haphazardly wreaking havoc in the kitchen as they also learn from the experts how to chop, sauté, deglaze, broil, julienne, and much more.

ACCOMPANIED BY

The show's primary judge is chef Anne Burrell (1969–), a frequent host and competitor in a number of Food Network shows. Burrell's history includes serving as the sous chef for Mario Batali and Lidia Bastianich and executive chef and owner of a number of other restaurants. Other recurring judges include television hosts and Food Network personalities Beau MacMillan (1971–), executive chef of Arizona's Sanctuary on Camelback; Alex Guarnaschelli (1972–), executive chef/owner of popular New York City restaurants Butter and The Darby; and Tyler Florence (1971–) of New York restaurant Cafeteria and California's Tyler Florence Rotisserie and Wine, among others. Celebrity chef Bobby Flay (1964–) and cooks Rachael Ray (1968–) and Alton Brown (1962–) have also held recurring roles. The show's contestants have included Domaine Javier, a California-based nurse who made history as the network's first openly transgender contestant. Celebrity-edition episodes have featured a wide range of current and former pop culture stars, including former Olympic figure skater Tonya Harding (1970–), MTV reality star Jenni "JWoww" Farley (1986–), and actors Vivica A. Fox (1964–) and Dave Coulier (1959–).

SUGGESTED PAIRINGS

See also: *Chopped*; Food Failures; Ray, Rachael; Television, Food Channels on.

Entry best enjoyed while eating: (*Safety note: The following entail hazardous methods of cooking and should not be tried at home!*) A lump of dense meatloaf baked into the rough likeness of a teddy bear, served on an asymmetrical oval of inconsistently mashed potatoes; avocado that has been arduously thinly sliced without first removing the pit; and cheesy toast, made by turning a toaster on its side and inserting cheese-topped bread in its slots.

Further Reading

Newsbreak Staff. 2020. "Worst Cooks in America Premiere Nets Double-Digit Ratings Gains." Multichannel Online, June 26, 2020. https://www.newsbreak.com/new-york/new-york/news/1590936065511/worst-cooks-in-america-premiere-nets-double-digit-ratings-gains

Slater, Georgia. 2019. "Anne Burrell Says the New Season of Worst Cooks in America Is Full of 'Lovable Losers.'" *People*, January 4, 2019.

Bibliography of Recommended Resources

Adleman, Andrea. 2012. "The Psychology of Cupcakes." *Washington Post*, February 7, 2012.

Allen, Ted. 2012. *Esquire's Eat Like a Man*. Edited by Ryan D'Agostino. San Francisco: Chronicle Books.

Anderson, Brett, Sara Camp Arnold, and John T. Edge, eds. 2012. *Cornbread Nation: The Best of Southern Food Writing*. 6th ed. Published in association with the Southern Foodways Alliance. Athens: University of Georgia Press.

Arellano, Gustavo. 2012. *Taco USA: How Mexican Food Conquered America*. New York: Scribner.

Armitage, Lynn. 2016. "Sioux Chef Has a Plan: Introduce Traditional Native Cuisine One Region at a Time." *Indian Country Today*, September 1, 2016. https://indiancountrytoday.com/archive/sioux-chef-has-a-plan-introduce-traditional-native-cuisine-one-region-at-a-time-kRHj785-ME6ysGSetsISjQ

Bourdain, Anthony. 2000. *Kitchen Confidential: Adventures in the Culinary Underbelly*. New York: Bloomsbury.

Bramen, Lisa. 2009. "Woodstock—How to Feed 400,000 Hungry Hippies." *Smithsonian Magazine*, August 14, 2009.

Bright, Susan. 2017. *Feast for the Eyes: The Story of Food in Photography*. New York: Aperture.

Brillat-Savarin, Jean Anthelme. (1825) 2011. *The Physiology of Taste: Or Meditations on Transcendental Gastronomy (Vintage Classics)*. Translated by M. F. K. Fisher. New York: Random House.

Byrn, Anne. 2016. *American Cake: From Colonial Gingerbread to Classic Layer, the Stories and Recipes Behind More Than 125 of Our Best-Loved Cakes: A Baking Book*. Rodale: New York.

Chang, David. 2020. *Eat a Peach: A Memoir*. New York: Clarkson Potter.

Clark, Robert. 1993. *James Beard: A Biography*. New York: HarperCollins.

Collins, Kathleen. 2009. *Watching What We Eat: The Evolution of Television Cooking Shows*. London: Bloomsbury.

Daniels, Serena Maria. 2019. "The Paleta War." Eater, October 22, 2019. https://www.eater.com/2019/10/22/20908347/la-michoacana-paleta-legal-battle

De Laurentiis, Giada. 2018. *Giada's Italy: My Recipes for La Dolce Vita.* New York: Clarkson Potter.

Dunea, Melanie. 2007. *My Last Supper: 50 Great Chefs and Their Final Meals. Portraits, Interviews, and Recipes.* Introduction by Anthony Bourdain. New York: Bloomsbury.

Farris, Valerio. 2019. "The Oldest Cake Recipe from the Oldest House in New York." Food52, December 28, 2019. https://food52.com/blog/24895-lott-house

Ferdman, Roberto A., and Christopher Ingraham. 2015. "How Brunch Became the Most Delicious—and Divisive—Meal in America." *Washington Post*, April 10, 2015.

Fuji Television. 2001. *Iron Chef: The Official Book.* Translated by Kaoru Hoketsu. New York: Berkley Publishing Group.

Fussell, Betty. 2016. *Eat, Live, Love, Die: Selected Essays.* Berkeley: Counterpoint Press.

Gabaccia, Donna. 2000. *We Are What We Eat: Ethnic Food and the Making of Americans.* Cambridge: Harvard University Press

Giorgis, Hannah. 2020. "Foodie Culture as We Know It Is Over." *The Atlantic*, May 5, 2020.

Glatter, Hayley. 2018. "The Timeless Bliss of Eating Hometown Food." *The Atlantic*, December 29, 2018.

Godoy, Maria, and Scott Simon. 2017. "Why The Story Of Southern Food Is As Much about People As Dishes." NPR, *The Salt*. https://www.npr.org/sections/thesalt/2017/06/11/532086897/grappling-with-race-class-and-southern-foods-great-debt-of-pleasure

Goldfarb, Aaron. 2017. "An Illustrated History of Craft Beer in America." First We Feast, March 6, 2017. https://firstwefeast.com/features/illustrated-history-of-craft-beer-in-america

Heritage Radio Network. 2009. https://heritageradionetwork.org/

Inamine, Elyse. 2013. "The Most Iconic Food Photographs of All Time." *First We Feast*, June 11, 2013. https://firstwefeast.com/eat/2013/06/the-most-iconic-food-photographs-of-all-time/

Jones, Evan. (1975) 2007. *American Food—The Gastronomic Story.* New York: Abrams. Reprint.

Judkis, Maura. 2019. "In Ali Wong's New Netflix Rom-com, Food Is the Butt of Jokes—And Her True Love." *Washington Post*, May 31, 2019.

Lakshmi, Padma. 2016. *Love, Loss, and What We Ate.* New York: Harper Collins.

Lam, Francis, and John T. Edge, eds. 2014. *Cornbread Nation: The Best of Southern Food Writing.* 7th ed. Published in association with the Southern Foodways Alliance. Athens: University of Georgia Press.

Lawson, Nigella. 2020. *Cook, Eat, Repeat.* London: Chatto & Windus.

Leonard, William. 2002. "Food for Thought." *Scientific American*, December 2002.

Li, Shirley. 2020. "In 1950, Americans Had Aspic. Now We Have Dalgona Coffee." *The Atlantic,* April 29, 2020.

Long, Lucy. 2009. *Regional American Food Culture.* Santa Barbara: Greenwood.

Martyris, Nina. 2018. "The Strange Pathos of the Turkey in *Madame Bovary.*" *The Atlantic,* November 22, 2018.

Mason, Michela Cesarina, and Adriano Paggiaro. 2009. "Celebrating Local Products: The Role of Food Events." *Journal of Foodservice Business Research* 12, no. 4: 364–383. https://doi.org/10.1080/15378020903344323

McCarron, Meghan. 2019. "Toward a Theory of American Festival Cuisine." Eater, August 21, 2019. https://www.eater.com/2019/8/21/20826647/iowa-state-fair-food-corn-dog-peppermint-square-cheese-curds

Miller, Adiran. 2013. *Soul Food: The Surprising Story of an American Cuisine, One Plate at a Time.* Chapel Hill: The University of North Carolina Press.

Morton, Mark. 1997. *Cupboard Love: A Dictionary of Culinary Curiosities.* Toronto, ON: Insomniac Press.

Muhlke, Christine. 2019. *Signature Dishes That Matter.* New York: Phaidon.

National Museum of American History, Behring Center. 2016. "Capturing the 1970s Food Movement in Design: David Lance Goines and Alice Waters's '30 Recipes Suitable for Framing.'" October 27, 2016. https://americanhistory.si.edu/blog/1970s-food-design

Nosrat, Samin. 2017. *Salt, Fat, Acid, Heat: Mastering the Elements of Good Cooking.* New York: Simon and Schuster.

O'Nan, Stewart. 2008. *Last Night at the Lobster.* New York: Penguin.

Onwuachi, Kwame. 2019. *Notes from A Young Black Chef.* New York: Knopf.

Organ, Kate, Nicole Koenig-Lewis, Adrian Palmer, and Jane Probert. 2015. "Festivals as Agents for Behaviour Change: A Study of Food Festival Engagement and Subsequent Food Choices." *Tourism Management* 58 (June): 84–99. https://doi.org/10.1016/j.tourman.2014.10.021

Pashman, Dan. 2020. The Sporkful (podcast). http://www.sporkful.com/

Powers, Rebecca. 2019. "Cornmeal Is Baked into the History of the Americas, and It's Time to Dust Off Those Roots." *Washington Post,* March 7, 2019.

Regan, Iliana. 2019. *Burn the Place: A Memoir.* Chicago: Midway Books.

Rhodes, Jesse. 2011. "The Birth of Brunch: Where Did This Meal Come from Anyway?" *Smithsonian Magazine,* May 6, 2011.

Rosner, Helen. 2017. "Christ in the Garden of Endless Breadsticks." Eater, October 3, 2017. https://www.eater.com/2017/10/3/16395312/olive-garden-review

Samuelsson, Marcus. 2013. *Yes, Chef: A Memoir.* New York: Random House.

Shapiro, Laura. *What She Ate: Six Remarkable Women and the Food That Tells Their Stories.* New York: Penguin.

Shute, Nancy. 2012. "Cooking Up Change: How Food Helped Fuel the Civil Rights Movement." NPR, *The Salt,* January 16, 2012. https://www.npr.org/sections/thesalt/2012/01/16/145179885/cooking-up-change-how-food-helped-fuel-the-civil-rights-movement

Smith, Andrew F., ed. 2007. *The Oxford Companion to American Food and Drink.* New York: Oxford University Press.

Smith, Reginald. 2019. *Vinegar, the Eternal Condiment*. Southport: Spikehorn Press.
Stein, Peter, dir. 2017. *Jacques Pepin: The Art of Craft*. PBS American Masters documentary film. Premier May 26. 2017.
Straub, Emma. 2020. *All Adults Here*. New York: Riverhead Books.
Strong, Jeremy. 2011. *Educated Tastes: Food, Drink, and Connoisseur Culture*. Lincoln: University of Nebraska Press.
Stuckey, Charles, and Wyatt Allgeier. 2017. "Art and Food." Interview with Mary Ann Caws. *Gagosian*, Winter 2017.
Sugar, Rachel. 2017. "How Food Network Turned Big-city Chef Culture into Middle-America Pop Culture." *Grub Street*, New York Beginnings. November 30, 2017. https://www.grubstreet.com/2017/11/early-days-food-network-oral-history.html#_ga=2.100585757.2096644730.1602860505-110100257.1602535211
Ternikar, Farha. 2014. *Brunch: A History*. Lanham: Rowman & Littlefield.
This American Life. 1998. "You Gonna Eat That?" Radio Show. *This American Life*, WBEZ Chicago. Episode 117, originally aired December 11, 1998.
Tobias, Ruth. 2020. "Is There Such a Thing as 'American' Food?" Tasting Table, May 14, 2020. https://www.tastingtable.com/culture/national/defining-american-food-cuisine
Tosi, Christina. 2015. *Milk Bar Life: Recipes & Stories*. New York: Clarkson Potter.
Turshen, Julia. 2017. "Food Photography, Over the Years." *The New York Times*, May 18, 2017.
Twitty, Michael. 2010. "Afroculinaria: Exploring Culinary Traditions of Africa, African America and the African Diaspora (Blog)." https://afroculinaria.com/
Vigneron, Peter. 2017. "The Curious Case of the Disappearing Nuts." *Outside Magazine*, June, 2017.
What's Cooking America. n.d. "Legends and Myths of Ices and Ice Cream History." https://whatscookingamerica.net/History/IceCream/IceCreamHistory.htm
Whitehead, Nadia. 2015. "Cheetos, Canned Foods, Deli Meat: How the U.S. Army Shapes Our Diet." The Salt, National Public Radio, July 31, 2015. https://www.npr.org/sections/thesalt/2015/07/31/427854425/cheetos-canned-foods-deli-meat-how-the-u-s-army-shapes-our-diet
Wyman, Carolyn. 1999. *SPAM: A Biography*. San Diego: Harvest.

Index

Page numbers in **bold** indicate main entries

Achatz, Grant, 95, 266
   Alinea, 138, 266, 267
Activism and social change
   alcohol, 122, 387
   anti-war, 289
   breastmilk and formula, 33–34
   decolonization, 318–319
   fast food industry, 63, 288–289, 332–334
   food festivals, xvi
   #MeToo movement, xxiii, 48, 72, 260, 340
   self-sufficiency, 2, 287
   slow food movement, xxii, 299
African cuisine and culture, 25, 28, 70, 105, 110, 195, 298, 314, 353, 355–358, 377
   Egypt, 8, 81, 148, 274, 386
   Ethiopia, xvi, 115, 184, 313–316
   Morocco, 71, 117
   Nigeria, 287
All-Star Chef Classic, **1–3**
America's Test Kitchen, **4–7**, 299, 341
Andrés, José, 3, 65, 263
Ansari, Aziz, 81, 93
Appropriation (cultural), 27, 53, 238, 356, 378
Art, food in (antiquity through the renaissance) **7–10**
   ancient art, 5, 7–10, 81, 274
   art history, xiv, 5, 7–14, 64, 325
   medieval. *See* Medieval era
Art, food in (impressionism through contemporary art), **10–14**, 19, 53, 95–97
   contemporary artists and artworks, xiv, xxii, 34, 53, 103, 118, 174, 177, 205, 246, 274, 276, 310, 315, 341
   festivals and fairs, xxii, 84, 191, 367, 368, 374, 384

   Japanese art, 19, 91–93
   pop art, 12, 13, 79
Asian American cuisine, **15–20**
   Bangladesh, 17, 198
   Cambodia, 15
   China (traditional), xix, 15–18, 81, 127, 216, 261, 330, 353, 362
   Chinese food (Americanized), xvi, 15–18, 155, 212, 261, 263, 352
   India, 15–17, 42, 60, 117, 121, 166, 236, 238, 314
   Indonesia, 228, 330, 368
   Japan, xxii, 15–19, 25, 74, 75, 91, 92, 96, 138, 165, 169, 174, 219, 220, 226, 227–231, 238, 268, 310, 322–324, 367, 368, 377, 383
   Korea (North and South), xvi, 5, 15–17, 42, 60, 93, 94, 96, 136, 174, 183, 238, 260, 261, 323
   Malaysia, 15, 72
   Mongolia, 16
   Pakistan, 15, 17
   Philippines (Filipino cuisine), 16, 203, 263
   Russia. *See* Russian cuisine
   Singapore, 48, 66, 71
   Taiwan, 17, 18, 175, 268, 285, 301, 368
   Thailand, 15, 71, 227, 368
   Vietnam, xxi, 15–17, 63, 69–72, 84, 116, 228, 238, 269
Aspen Food and Wine Classic, **20–22**, 343
Astronauts and space travel, xxii, 100, 108, 153, 235, 239, 378, 385
Austin Food + Wine Festival, **23–26**, 62
Ayden Collard Festival, **27–30**

Baby boomer generation, 350, 390
Baby food, **31–36**, 108, 251

Bacon, 29, 40, 85, 87, 116, 120, 131, 132, 158, 161, 219, 222, 235, 248, 255, 289, 293, 321, 346, 352, 354, 376
Bar Rescue, **36–41**
Barbecue, xvi, 5, 17, 24, 26, 29, 30, **41–45**, 50, 51, 60, 65, 75, 93, 126, 160, 168, 177, 178, 203, 214, 236, 238, 239, 330, 337, 350
Barefoot Contessa. *See* Garten, Ina
Bastianich, Joe, 47, 49, 258
Bastianich, Lidia, 49, 205, 341, 393
Batali, Mario, 22, 42, **45–50**, 230, 242, 340, 342, 393
Bayless, Rick, 22, **50–56**, 339, 341, 382
Beard, James, 39, **56–59**, 264, 268, 295, 339
  James Beard Foundation Awards. *See* Culinary awards, the evolution of
Beer. *See* Craft brewing and microbreweries
Best Thing I Ever Ate, The, **59–61**, 159, 241
Bizarre Foods with Andrew Zimmern, 26, **61–66**, 340
Black Panthers, 287
Boulud, Daniel, 22, 93, 126, 344
Bourdain, Anthony, xi, xiii, xxiii, 44, 49, **66–73**, 157, 273, 302
  television shows, 91, 235, 259, 313, 340, 345
  writing, 93, 94, 235, 247, 263
Bowien, Danny, 18, 261
Brown, Alton, 22, 57, 60, **73–78**, 112, 230, 340, 341, 393
Bush, George H. W., 209, 210, 283, 284
Bush, George W., 99, 240, 285
Bush, Jeb, 285
Bush, Laura, 18

Caesar, Julius, 209
Caesar salad, 103, 250, 266
Cakes and cupcake trends, xi, 3, 19, 34, 63, 76, **79–83**, 97, 104, 110, 144, 161, 171, 172, 175, 178, 211, 214, 219, 233, 282, 292, 318, 324, 325, 342, 346, 348–350, 355, 360, 371
  books, 148–150
  historical, xxiii, 79–83, 148, 178, 212, 275, 371
  television, 3, 60, 155–156, 196–198, 340
  websites, 81, 82, 179–180
California Avocado Festival, **83–86**
Carter, Jimmy, 240, 310, 311
Catholicism. *See* Religion
Celebrities and food, 18, 22, 44, 49, 60, 74, **87–90**, 105, 131, 157, 195, 222, 247, 262, 268, 279, 283, 291, 293, 316, 321, 325, 342, 351
Chang, David, 18, 22, **91–94**, 157, 247, 259–261, 346–348
Cheers, 156, 389
Chef's Table, **94–98**, 260, 346
The Chew, 47, 48, 119, 187, 304, 340, 345
Child, Julia, ix, xi, xvii, 21, 22, 46, 50, 54, 57, 58, 74, 97, **98–104**, 188, 204, 205, 207, 242, 352
  Mastering the Art of French Cooking, xxi, 98, 102, 104, 262, 266, 271, 305, 382
  television, xv, xxi, 98, 102, 118, 158, 185, 232, 339, 341
Chinese food. *See* Asian American cuisine
Chocolate events and destinations, **104–109**, 176, 223, 380
Choi, Roy, xvi, 18, 157, 183, 238, 323
Chopped, xxiii, **109–112**, 119, 257, 258, 313, 346
Christianity. *See* Religion
Civil War, 43, 115, 130, 182, 221, 249, 255
Claiborne, Craig, 52, 58, 205
Clinton, Bill, 10, 240, 284, 285, 288
Clinton, Hillary, 99, 284, 285, 288
Coffee culture, xiv, xxi, 89, 105–107, **113–116**, 154, 155, 157, 159, 167, 175, 182, 219, 223, 263, 286–289, 298, 308, 348, 349, 354, 380
Colicchio, Tom, 22, 65, 92, 94, 343–345
Cooked, **116–118**
Cookies, 5, 65, 119, 149, 158, 171, 190, 196, 212, 218–220, 247, 248, 288, 307, 346, 349, 350, 352, 354, 375, 378
  fortune cookies, 18, 19, 263
  madeleines, xiii, 149
Cooks vs. Cons, **119–120**, 313
Coolidge, Calvin, 210–211
Coolidge, Laura, 210–211
Cora, Cat, 60, 230, 321
Craft brewing and microbreweries, 23, 84, 89, **121–123**, 138, 153, 194, 214, 286, 329
Crenn, Dominique, 96, 97, 267, 269
Culinary awards, the evolution of, **124–127**
  Julia Child Foundation and awards, 50, 99, 204
  James Beard Foundation Awards, 18, 24–26, 44, 46, 50, 56, 58, 60, 61, 67, 73, 91, 110, 124–126, 168, 169, 204, 232, 259, 261, 271, 289, 290, 313, 317, 325, 344, 345, 346, 355, 380

Michelin Guide awards, 18, 48, 52, 71, 91, 96, 124–127, 137, 138, 260, 261, 290, 300, 316, 350

Death and grief, xx, xxiii, 13, 58, 67, 76, 96, 128, 149, 158, 198, 205, 262, 264, 269, 300, 313, 330, 369
Deen, Paula, **128–132**, 356
Deer River Wild Rice Festival, **132–135**, 320
Dickens, Charles, 148, 149
Diets, fad, 35, 58, 87, 89–90, 136, 137, 153, 211, 248, 264, 280, 283–284, 288, 332–334, 351, 352–353, 359, 373, 377, 386
Diners, Drive-Ins, and Dives, 159, 161, 340
DiSpirito, Rocco, 112, 340
Documentary films, food and beverages in, xvi, 18, 43, 75, 93, 95, 116–118, **135–138**, 259, 271, 273, 275, 289, 301, 303, 315, 332–335, 341, 355–356, 358–359
Dogs, 14, 29, 64, 110, 129, 244, 278, 281, 308, 310, 354, 360, 383
Dufresne, Wylie, 3, 94, 247, 269, 347

Eating competitions, 27, 29 35, 83, 84, 106, **140–144**, 165, 170, 172, 174, 251, 366, 371, 374, 384, 388
Egypt, ancient, 8, 81, 148, 274, 386
Enslaved peoples. *See* Slavery

Farmers markets, 27, 146
Farmhouse Rules, **145–147**
Farm-to-table, 46, 57, 63, 118, 136, 145, 146, 291
Fashion, xxiii, 79, 106, 235, 244, 276, 306, 311, 316, 321, 325
Feminism and female trailblazers, xxiii, 13, 18, 97, 98–104, 153, 230, 243, 278, 325, 326
Fiction, food in, xiv, xx, 66, 69, **147–150**, 294, 296
Fictional television (1950s–1970s), food and, **150–154**, 155
Fictional television (1980s–), food and, **154–159**, 284, 326, 328, 382
Fieri, Guy, **159–161**, 180, 234, 321
Films, food in, **162–167**, 389
Flay, Bobby, 22, 57, 75, **167–170**, 229–230, 241, 278, 321, 341, 393
Florida Strawberry Festival, xiv, **170–173**

Food and beverage museums, international, 88, 105, 107, **173–175**
Food and beverage museums, U.S., 44, 54, 99, **176–178**, 179, 309, 310, 322, 323, 352, 372, 374, 378
Food failures, xi, 100, **178–180**, 240, 284, 328, 350, 354, 385
Food fights, 157, 166, 340, 364–365, 367
Food Network, xxii, xxiii, 2, 3, 17, 18, 21, 43, 45, 47, 59, 60, 69, 73–75, 80–81, 89, 109–112, 119–120, 128–131, 145–146, 159–160, 168–169, 183, 187–189, 227–228, 232–236, 241–244, 260, 272, 278, 304–306, 313, 320, 338–342, 346, 358, 359, 380, 392–393
Food trucks, 2, 18, 84, 90, 158, **181–184**, 201, 203, 238, 317–319, 336, 377
Ford, Gerald, 240, 284
Frozen dinners. *See* TV dinners

Galloping Gourmet, The, **185–187**, 232, 272, 274, 339
Garten, Ina, 60, **187–191**, 340
Gentrification, 27, 114, 286
Ghosts and spirits, 89, 208, 366, 384
Gilroy Garlic Festival, **191–194**
Goldman, Duff, 3, 60, 81
Great British Bake-off, The, 79, 189, **194–200**
Grilled cheese festivals, xiv, **201–203**
Greece, ancient, 8, 9, 81, 195, 228, 386
Greene, Gael, 56, 168
Guarnaschelli, Alex, 112, 119, 120, 393

Hall, Carla, 22, 345
Handwerker, Nathan, 141, 143
Harding, Warren G., 311
Hazan, Marcella, 21, 22, **204–207**
Hell's Kitchen, 273, 300, 302, 340
Holidays and food, 107, **208–215**, 262
  Christmas, 71, 107, 165, 208–215, 371
  Cinco de Mayo, 284, 285
  Easter, 107, 208–215, 363, 373
  Hanukkah, 208–215, 275
  Thanksgiving, xxi, 27, 153, 155, 208–215, 244, 278, 330, 350

Ice cream trends, xix, 61, 65, 84, 87, 106, 108, 111, 147, 152, 158, 177, 183, 194, 199, 214, **216–221**, 225, 226, 229, 268, 277, 309, 311, 347, 348, 350, 354, 360, 376–378
Imagery found in foods, 11, **222–224**
Indian cuisine, 15–19, 42, 60, 117, 166, 236, 314

International Horseradish Festival, **224–226**
Intersectionality, 11, 114, 213, 260, 283, 298, 313, 356
Iron Chef, xxii, 17, 19, 26, 47, 60, 75, 110, 112, 119, 168, 169, 191, **227–231**, 233, 234, 241, 257, 258, 313, 315, 340
Iuzzini, Johnny, 48, 340
Izard, Stephanie, 22, 345

Jell-O, 167, 176, 377
Jelly beans, xxii, 223
Johnson, Claudia "Lady Bird," 240
Johnson, Lyndon B., 240
Jones, Judith, 58, 207
Judaism. *See* Religion

Kale, 27, 28, 33, 60, 184, 210, 212, 236, 258, 279, 307, 329, 355, 371
Kerr, Graham. *See Galloping Gourmet, The*
Kombucha, 63, 153, 353
Korea. *See* Asian American cuisine
Korean War, 155, 323

Lagasse, Emeril, 22, 60, 119, **232–235**, 339, 342
Lakshmi, Padma, 158, 344–346
Latin American cuisine, xvi, 201, 212, **236–241**
  Argentina, 42, 96, 175
  Brazil, 90, 175, 236, 238
  Costa Rica, 107, 301
  Cuba, 25, 130, 236–240, 321
  Ecuador, 70
  Mexico, xx, 42, 50–54, 85, 96, 185, 236–241, 250, 266, 310, 318, 330, 341, 367
  Peru, 107, 117, 175, 238, 250
  Puerto Rico, 239, 263
Laurentiis, Giada De, 22, 60, 75, **241–244**, 321, 340
Leach, Robin, 169, 341
Lee, Jennifer 8., 18, 93
Legal issues
  lawsuits, 5, 38, 89, 106, 120, 128–130, 333
  lawyers, 146, 169, 230, 307
  trials, xxiiii, 136, 223, 327
LGBTQIA+ communities, x, 58, 59, 111, 172, 356, 393

Madison, James, 220
Magazines, food, 4, 5, 57, 91, 111, 114, 198, 210, **246–248**, 274, 276, 296, 324–327, 343, 347, 380, 381
Maine Lobster Festival, **248–252**
Maple syrup festivals, **253–255**
MasterChef, 26, 91, **256–259**, 300–302, 340, 346
Medieval era, 8–10, 13, 107, 225, 269, 331, 365
Mexico. *See* Latin American cuisine
Michelin stars. *See* Culinary awards, the evolution of
Middle Eastern cuisine and culture, 2, 3, 25, 61, 70, 71, 115, 158, 216
  Iran (and Persia), 70, 383, 386
  Israel, 3, 70, 227, 275
  Yemen, 263
Millennial generation, xxiii, 114, 146, 177, 246, 352, 354, 381, 390
Mind of a Chef, The, 18, 66, 91–94, **259–261**, 341, 346
Morimoto, Masaharu, 26, 169, 229, 230
Moulton, Sarah, 341, 342
Mythology, Greek. *See* Greece, ancient

Native American cuisine, xv, xvi, 41, 132–135, 237, 255, 317–320
Nixon, Richard, 190, 223
Nonfiction, food in, xiv, **262–264**, 272, 385
Norse mythology, 141–142
Novelty dining experiences, **265–270**, 308
Novelty foods, 213, 219, 290, 353, 373

Obama, Barack, 44, 46, 48, 52, 54, 209, 240, 284, 288, 314
Obama, Michelle, 28, 46, 52, 54, 288, 314
Oliver, Jamie, 340, 359

Pageants, beauty, 27, 170, 172, 191, 193, 225, 249, 252, 254, 368, 374
Passard, Alain, 3, 96, 261
Pépin, Jacques, 24, 98, **271–274**
Photography, food, xi, 5, 12, 34, 77, 180, 246, 271, **274–277**, 279, 322, 345
Pickles, 142, 225, 226, 239, 283, 337, 374–375, 378
Pioneer Woman, The, 89, 145, **278–282**, 340

Pizza, 10, 48, 60, 91, 93, 126, 142, 144, 155, 157, 171, 177, 222, 237, 261, 285, 291, 293, 299, 320, 330–332, 337–338, 362–363, 370
Politicians' food gaffes, **283–286**
Politics and food, xxii, 10, 18, 28, 44, 46, 48, 52, 54, 99, 190, 209, 210, 211, 220–223, 240, 283, 284, 285, 288, 283–286, **286–289**, 291, 310, 311, 314
Pollan, Michael, 116–118, 264, 341
Prison, food and
  celebrities and, 327, 360
  criminal behavior, 10, 28, 70
  final meals (death row), 264
  portrayals in film, 163
  portrayals in television, 157, 158, 326
  theme restaurants, 264, 268
Prohibition era, xix, 103, 121, 138, 266, 268, 354, 387–389
Proust, Marcel, xiii, 149, 166, 190
Prudhomme, Paul, 291
Public Broadcast Service (PBS), 17, 18, 43, 50–53, 137, 189, 194, 232, 256, 259, 271, 273, 313, 315, 327, 338–342, 346, 358
Puck, Wolfgang, 21, 22, 242, **289–293**, 340

Queer Eye for the Straight Guy, 111
Query, Joseph Archibald, 384–385
Queso, 25, 239, 240
Quinoa, 33, 90, 353

Radio and podcasts, food-themed (1920s–1970s), **294–297**
Radio and podcasts, food-themed (1980s–), **297–300**
Ramsay, Gordon, 37, 126, 198, 257–258, **300–303**, 340, 359, 382
Ray, Rachael, 47, 157, 159, 232, 247, **304–307**, 315, 321, 340, 341, 393
Reagan, Ronald, xxii, 221, 283
Reichl, Ruth, 93, 247, 263, 339, 383
Religion, xxiii, 7, 8, 11, 13, 15, 63, 92, 148, 197, 248, 364, 387
  Buddhism, 15, 96, 148
  Catholicism, 9, 13, 148, 212, 222, 223, 351, 366
  Christianity, 77, 148, 171, 186, 212, 213, 222, 285, 351, 356, 364, 366
  Hinduism, 15, 148
  Islam, 148
  Judaism, 9, 63
  religious iconography and imagery, 222–224
  religious studies, 92
  Taoism, 148
Ripert, Eric, 71, 94, 96, 345
Roadside food attractions, 44, 126, 165, 177, 218, **308–311**, 332
Rome, ancient, 9, 28, 81, 209, 220, 274, 365, 386–387
Roosevelt, Eleanor, 264
Roosevelt, Franklin, 122
Roosevelt, Theodore, 283
Russian cuisine, 97, 167, 175, 330, 366–367

Samuelsson, Marcus, xvi, 22, 26, 65, 112, 120, 263, **313–316**, 321, 341
Scandinavian cuisine, 155, 260, 261, 313–316, 391
  Denmark, 162, 174–175, 270, 376
  Norway, 115, 195, 313
  Sweden, xvi, 175, 260, 261, 310, 313–316, 333, 391
Shakespeare, William, 148
Sherman, Sean, xvi, **317–319**
Silverton, Nancy, 2, 97, 112
Simmons, Gail, 22, 344, 346
Simpsons, The, 156, 158, 326
Slavery and enslaved people, xv, 28, 43, 130, 210, 214, 220, 355–358
Social media, 35, 39, 48, 73, 77, 79, 130, 179–180, 183, 197, 199, 202, 246, 252, 265, 274, 276, 306, 322, 354, 355, 380–383
Soul food, xvi, 27, 137, 210
South Beach Wine & Food Festival, **320–321**
Southern cuisine, xvi, 2, 3, 23, 27–29, 74, 128–131, 177, 248, 260, 263, 345, 356, 372–373
Spam Jam Festival, **322–324**
Stewart, Martha, xxiii, 112, 180, 210, **324–328**, 339, 341, 343, 359
Super Bowl Sunday, 288, **329–332**
Superfoods, 2, 353
Super Size Me, 136, **332–335**
Sushi, 14–19, 24, 69, 95, 136, 137, 160, 226, 324, 352, 376

Tacos, xv, 5, 23, 24–25, 51–52, 142, 183, 236–240, 250, 263, 272, 277, 320
  Americanized, xv, xx, 24–25, 51, 183, 222, 239, 272, 284
  Taco Bell, xxii, 181, 239–240, 390
  variations, 25, 171, 183, 320, 322, 376
Tamales, xix, 52, 168, 178, 212, 237–240, 284, 337
Taste of Chicago, **336–338**
Technology, xvii, 57, 102, 137, 323, 327
Television, food channels on, xv, **338–342**, 380
Top Chef, 3, 22, 25, 50, 52, 66, 92, 111, 158, 232, 234, 271, 313, 315, 340, **343–346**
Tosi, Christina, 25, 26, 92, 97, 112, 215, 257–258, **346–350**
Treme, 72, 94, 234
Trends, food, **351–355**
Trump, Donald, 284–285, 287, 327
Trump, Melania, 288
Tsai, Ming, 18, 22, 25–26, 242, 341–342
TV dinners, xxi, 153
Twitty, Michael, xvi, 263, **355–358**
Two Fat Ladies, **358–360**

Unusual food events, international, xvi, **362–369**
Unusual food events, U.S. (Midwest, West, and Southwest regions), xvi, **370–372**
Unusual food events, U.S. (Southeast and Northeast regions), xvi, **372–375**
Unusual Foods, 61, 71, 119, **375–379**

Vegan cuisine and veganism, 24, 70, 82, 96, 131, 138, 183, 212, 248, 288, 298, 303, 333–334
Vegetarian cuisine and vegetarianism, 94, 96, 156, 248, 360
Vietnam War, xxi, 16, 186, 295
Voltaggio, Bryan, 3, 345
Voltaggio, Michael, 3, 345

Waters, Alice, xxii, 157, 291
Waxman, Jonathan, 94, 168
Websites, food, xvii, 4, 19, 21, 34, 35, 37, 41, 47, 48, 60, 81, 88, 125, 160, 161, 179–180, 192, 210, 213, 222, 234, 237, 273, 276, 279, 280, 315, 340, 375, **380–383**
Wells, Pete, 161, 179, 181, 243
What the Fluff?, xiv, **383–386**
Wine and spirits, **386–391**
  cocktails, 5, 14, 23, 24, 39, 57, 61, 122, 156, 167, 177, 225, 226, 256, 303, 321, 354, 387–391
  distilleries, 388, 389
  sommeliers, 20, 23, 24, 26, 136, 138, 260, 300, 382
  spirits and liquor, xix, 61, 73, 89, 104, 122, 124, 147, 156, 167, 169, 170, 175, 219, 225, 260, 308, 354, 375, 386–391
  wine, 1, 9, 20–22, 23–26, 45, 48, 62, 101, 102, 105, 111, 114, 122, 124, 126, 134, 136, 138, 148, 157, 161, 162, 164, 175, 183, 185, 194, 202, 204, 206, 214, 236, 246–248, 266, 269, 276, 289–291, 300, 303, 320–321, 327, 329, 343, 347, 352, 362, 364, 381, 386–391, 393
Winfrey, Oprah, xxiii, 89, 304, 316, 353
World War I, xix, 115, 141, 203, 294, 353, 385
  food trends, 115, 141, 203, 353, 385
  rationing, xix, 385
World War II, ix, xiv, 16, 46, 68, 82, 170, 186, 193, 197, 273, 276
  art, 276
  food trends, xxi, 16, 32, 46, 178, 201, 203, 208, 211, 250, 266, 296, 365
  international foods, 16, 46, 68, 101, 296
  propaganda, 276
  rationing, xxi, 82, 197, 201, 208, 211, 266, 276
  service in, 58, 100–101, 276
Worst Cooks in America, **392–393**

X, Generation, 352, 390
Xoco (restaurant), 52

Yan, Martin, 17, 18, 259, 339, 341, 342

Zagat (guidebook), 125, 382
Zimmern, Andrew, xvii, 22, 26, 61–66, 230, 277, 321, 340

About the Author

Jane K. Glenn is a course developer in the field of online graduate education and a development editor in the field of academic publishing. Her career has entailed writing, producing, directing, and editing content for documentary and educational media, primarily in the arts, history, and social studies. Outside of work, Jane's interests include volunteering with underserved youth, playing the cello, enjoying time in nature, and filmmaking (particularly documentaries and indigenous films). A lifelong devotee of studying the stories that make us human, she majored in comparative literature at Hamilton College and studied documentary filmmaking at the Maine Media Workshops. She lives with her husband, Tom, and children, Milo and Lucia, along the front range of Colorado.

www.ingramcontent.com/pod-product-compliance
Lightning Source LLC
Chambersburg PA
CBHW082022300426

44117CB00015B/2317